Islanders in the Stream

Islanders in the Stream

A History of the Bahamian People

VOLUME TWO

From the Ending of Slavery to the Twenty-First Century

MICHAEL CRATON AND

GAIL SAUNDERS

The University of Georgia Press

Athens and London

University of Georgia Press paperback edition, 2000

Athens, Georgia 30602
www.ugapress.org

Designed by Sandra Strother Hudson
Set in Palatino by G&S Typsetters

Most University of Georgia Press titles are
available from popular e-book vendors.

Printed digitally

The Library of Congress has cataloged the cloth edition
of this book as follows:
Craton, Michael.
Islanders in the stream : a history of the Bahamian people /
Michael Craton and Gail Saunders.
2 v. : ill., maps ; 25 cm.
Includes bibliographical references and index.
Contents: v. 2. From the ending of slavery to 21st century.
ISBN 0-8203-1926-0 (alk. paper) (v. 2)
1. Bahamas--History. 2. National characteristics, Bahamian.
I. Saunders, Gail. II. Title
F1656 .C72 19920002
972.96—dc20 91021737
ISBN: 0-8203-2284-9 (pbk. : alk. paper)
ISBN-13: 978-0-8203-2284-1

British Library Cataloging-in-Publication Data available

Contents

PART THREE

On the Eve of the Twenty-First Century: The Present and Future of the Bahamian Past, 1973–1999

Maps, Figures, and Illustrations

Maps

Figures

Illustrations

Tables

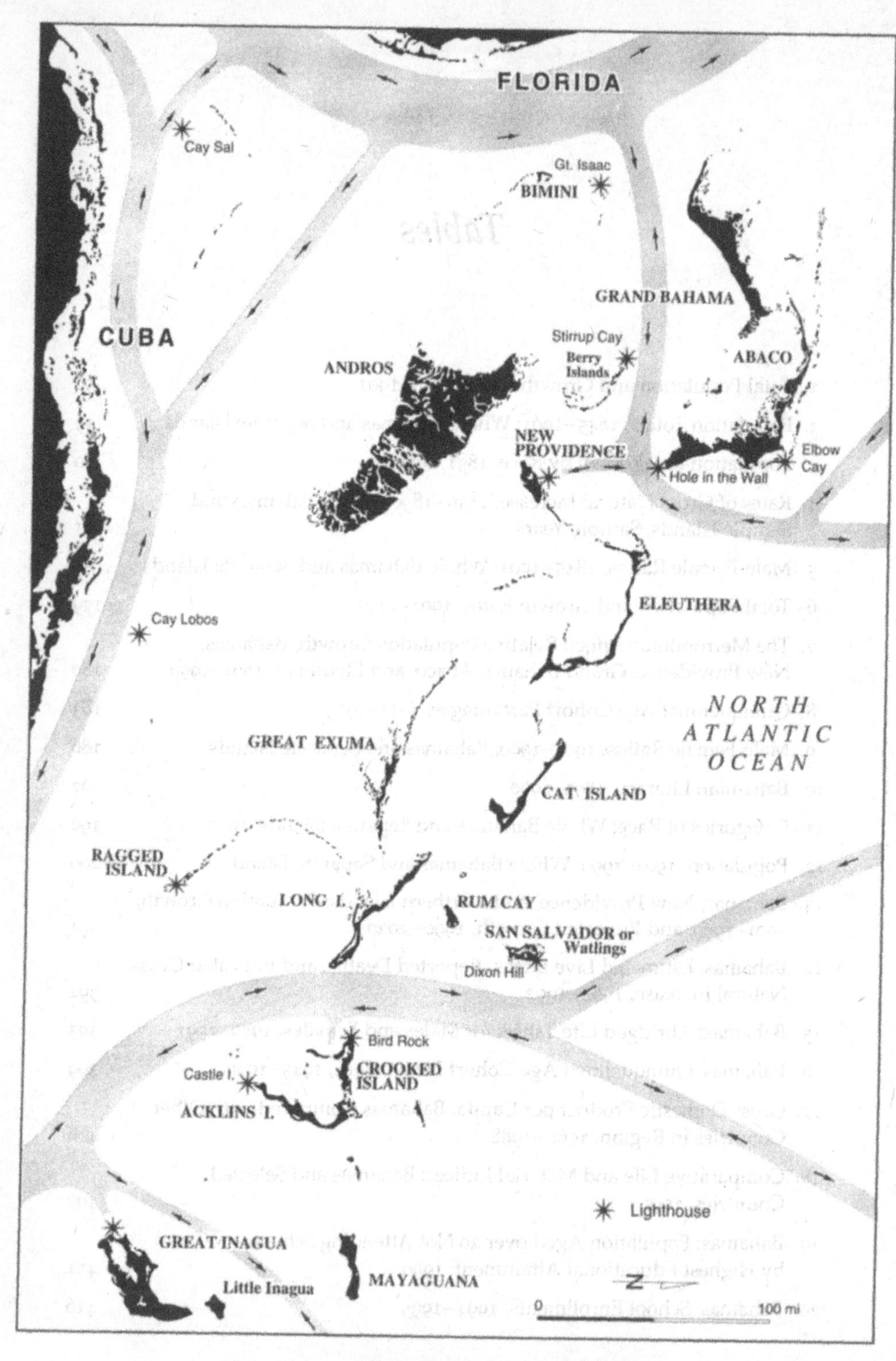

Map 1. Bahamas: Nineteenth-Century Steamer Routes

Preface

This second and concluding volume of the story of the people of the Bahamas and their achievement of nationhood begins with the ending of formal slavery between 1834 and 1838 and ends with the imminent approach of the twenty-first century. Like Volume 1 it consists of three main parts. Broadly, the first deals with the great adjustments that had to be made by former slaves and slave owners as slavery gave way to free wage labor and a fishing and farming subsistence economy in a colony more than ever marginal in the British imperial scheme. The second covers the greatly delayed and gradual accession of the Bahamian people into a modernizing Western world. The third and final part concerns the optimistic but problem-ridden attainment of self-government and independence in the last third of the twentieth century.

Though this is essentially a social history, strongly influenced by the cross-disciplinary and cliometric approaches that have transformed the writing of peoples' history over the last half-century, it is also a national history. Events and political developments that had important social effects are woven into a narrative of the development of a unique archipelagic nation. The method remains largely chronological, but in each of the three parts convenience of presentation sometimes results in overlapping of the strict chronological sequence of chapters and even backtracking when necessary. For example, although the volume ostensibly begins with the ending of formal slavery in the 1830s, its first part necessarily reaches back some years to consider more fully than was fitting in the third part of Volume 1 those Africans liberated from foreign slave traders who contributed so much to the evolving Bahamian identity and who first arrived as early as 1811. Similarly, such topics as the development of the police, of education, and of Freeport-Lucaya are treated unitarily rather than split between chapters. Likewise, toward the end of the volume, coverage of the Bahamian Haitians is wholly located in the chapter concentrating on the period 1973–95, when their presence became critical, though necessarily backtracking to look at the origins of Haitian migration to the Bahamas and its development before 1973.

A few further notes about the methods employed are perhaps necessary, especially for those who look for a strictly academic treatise or for adventures at the trendy forward edge of postmodernism. This is intended to be a popular history in the sense that it is of the Bahamian people, *for* them, and to the greatest degree possible, *by* them too. It is a comprehensive narrative aimed to be the definitive national history of the Bahamas: a text in the traditional meaning of the word, rather than in the negatively limiting sense used by deconstructionists. It is, though, essentially a "thick narrative" as defined by Clifford Geertz, an artfully fashioned and soundly supported story, not a formal thesis or set of theses, analytically driven. Above all, it attempts to avoid the stiff academic style of proceeding only from previous scholarly authorities and established models. Instead, it relies almost exclusively on primary sources, honestly chosen and simply deployed, along channels they themselves suggest and determine.

Besides official documents, semiofficial letters and memoranda, and newspaper reports, our sources include informal written and oral memoirs, derived as far as possible from Bahamians and long-term residents of the Bahamas. Despite the unfortunate bias toward male (or, more strictly, upper-class, middle-aged, white male) informants and viewpoints in the traditional sources, we have striven, particularly in the use of oral testimonies, to make this a fairly balanced study in respect to gender, as well as in regard to the divisions and nuances of class, color, and age. Above all, we have sought to enliven and illuminate the narrative with what might be called emblematic testimonies, that is, substantial sections of description or comment that seemed to us to provide authentic viewpoints that go beyond mere subjectivity and shed light where statistics are unavailable, irrelevant, or inadequate. Carefully selected to illustrate particular sets of ethnic and social realities according to time and place and firmly placed in context, they are yet intended to be contemporary voices that speak largely for themselves. Likewise, we hope we have been sufficiently objective to leave all readers room to make conclusions of their own, particularly in the later sections dealing with the era of living memories, the immediate present, and speculations about the future.

As professional scholars we have striven to be fair, but as seasoned historians we recognize the futility of claiming absolute neutrality or of absolute authority or even absolute accuracy. If there is a teleological theme for this volume and the book as a whole we willingly admit it to be that encapsulated in the title originally chosen for the work, the Afro-Bahamian proverb, *Time Longer Dan Rope*. This title was intended to convey the authors' belief that though the Bahamian past has been largely the story of material hardship and socioeconomic conflict and the present remains problem-strewn, the history of the Bahamian people has been distinguished by endurance, adaptability, and a latent sense of a shared identity that in due course will be universally acknowledged. Islanders in a larger world stream Bahamians may always have been, but they stand proudly athwart the current nonetheless.

As well as including a rationale for the entire work, Volume 1 listed most of the institutions and individuals to whom the authors have been indebted since the project got under way in 1983. More than a decade has passed, but the work's plan and ideal have not greatly changed. To a heartening degree, though, there has been a recent surge of popular interest in Bahamian history and of writing on the Bahamas, especially in the modern period. Though this has magnified the task of research and enlarged the second volume beyond the already substantial dimensions of the first, we have benefited greatly from this resurgence, not least through the generous way in which scholarly specialists have shared their work, institutions their resources, and ordinary Bahamians their personal testimonies.

To a blanket reiteration of our gratitude we therefore add thanks to those who have specially helped us since Volume 1 was written. Most unstinting and invaluable has been the assistance of the staff of the Department of Archives in Nassau, though gratitude must also be expressed to the staffs of the Nassau Public Library, the Bahamas National Trust, the Bahamas Historical Society, the Pompey, Junkanoo, Wyannie Malone, and Albert Lowe Museum, the Ministry of Education, Departments of Lands and Surveys and Statistics, and other Bahamian government departments.

Distinguished help has come in visible ways from Brent Malone and other Bahamian artists and from Barry Levely of the University of Waterloo Cartographic Centre, and inspiration from Bahamian literary practitioners, including Winston Saunders, Ian Strachan, Jeanne Thompson, Susan Wallace, Mizpah Tertullian, Eric Minns, Robert Elliot Johnson, Patrick Rahming, Rupert Missick, Telcine Turner, and Obediah Michael Smith. Certain scholars—John Holm, Alison Shilling, Colin Hughes, Peter Barratt, Steve Dodge, Neil Sealey, Susan Love Brown, Dean Collinwood, Tracey Thompson, Anthony Dahl, Nicolette Bethel, Roseanne Adderley, and above all Howard Johnson—have become virtual collaborators in sections of this volume. Nonscholarly firsthand accounts, multiplying the closer one reaches to the present, have been gratefully tapped, making vital—if not exactly voluntary—contributors of Louis Diston Powles, George Northcroft, Mary Moseley, Amelia Defries, Rosita Forbes, Sir Etienne Dupuch, Cleveland Eneas, Sir Randol Fawkes, Evans Cottman, Haziel Albury, Jack Ford, Ruth Rodriguez, Sir Henry Taylor, and Sir Sidney Poitier, among others. But we should express equal gratitude to those contemporaries who so fruitfully provided direct oral testimony, especially Cecil Bethel Sr., Keva Bethel, Howland Bottomley, Sir Alvin Braynen, Holly Brown, Edwina Burrows, Bert Cambridge, Jenny Cancino, Treffor Davies, Rt. Rev. Michael Eldon, Rowena Eldon, Ileana Esfakis, Leila Greene, Alphonso Blake Higgs, Sir Kendal and Lady Patricia Isaacs, Hon. Geoffrey Johnstone, Hon. Sean McWeeney, Fr. Irwin McSweeney, Cecil Marche, Anthony Morley, Mgr. Preston Moss, Archibald Nairn, Basil North, Terry North, Keith Parker, Barbara Pierre, Eliezer Regnier, Antonius Roberts, Oris Russell, Winston Saunders, Jeanne Thompson, Sir Maxwell Thompson, and Penny Turtle.

In addition to those named above, we would like to thank the two anonymous reviewers selected by the University of Georgia Press for their encouragement and constructive criticism. As with Volume 1, Gail Heideman of Waterloo transformed much of the huge manuscript into type with uncomplaining efficiency. Unfortunately, the process was so protracted that her well-earned retirement supervened. By a neat instance of generational baton-changing, though, during the last stages of preparation invaluable advice and help with the computer (essential for authors barely literate in the medium) were willingly provided by the older author's youngest child, Darius Craton—born in the year the project began. Beyond this specific assistance, in more general terms, we acknowledge once more the indispensable support and continuing faith of our nearest colleagues and dearest relatives.

I

From Slavery to Unfreedom, 1834–1900

Mother and six children in an Over the Hill shanty yard, around 1890.
Jacob Coonley photograph, Michael Craton Collection.

1

Transition Not Transformation: Apprentices, Liberated Africans, and the Reconstructed Oligarchy, 1834–1860

Introductory Overview

The period of formal apprenticeship (1834–38), during which the former slaves throughout the British West Indies were constrained to work for their previous owners, passed more quietly in the Bahamas than in almost any other colony. There were several reasons for this relative calm. As was described in Volume 1, during the last phase of slavery in the Bahamas one-sixth of the slaves obtained their formal freedom through manumission, and during the early 1830s civil liberties had been extended to all coloreds already freed—thanks as much to the demands of such free colored leaders as Stephen Dillet as to the desire of the white regime to detach them from the black majority. Even for those still technically enslaved, such a favorable combination of work and living conditions had been achieved that most were already more like free laborers and peasants than slaves.[1] Moreover, the terms of apprenticeship were rarely enforced harshly, and some features of the system—particularly the substitution of stipendiary magistrates for local justices of the peace (JPs) and the provision of written labor contracts—seemed to be actually beneficial to the former slaves.

Perhaps the most potent reason why the transition of 1834–38 was made so easily, however, was because an experimental system of apprenticeship had already been tried and proven since 1811. This system applied to the Africans liberated from foreign slavers and landed in the Bahamas after the abolition of the British slave trade in 1808, who totaled about 1,400 before 1826, a further 4,150 before 1838, and perhaps 6,500 in all.[2] Despite the opposition of the black freedmen, who feared for their jobs, and the doubts about the wisdom of importing new native Africans expressed by whites without pressing labor needs, the first wave of these liberated Africans was more or less successfully assimilated into the Bahamian socioeconomic system between 1811 and 1828. Grateful to be saved from total slavery, the liberated Africans willingly filled the temporary shortage of unskilled labor caused by the export of slaves to the sugar islands and the rising tide of manumissions. The much larger second wave between 1831 and 1838 presented graver problems. But from the point of view of the ruling class at least, this new

Celebration or letting off political steam? Emancipation Day parade, Harbour Island, late nineteenth century. From Charles L. Edwards, *Bahama Songs and Stories* (Cincinnati, 1892), courtesy of Bahamas Archives.

influx of liberated Africans was potentially both an ethnic counterweight to the black Creoles and a topping up of the reservoir of cheap "free" labor against whom the former slaves would be forced to compete.

The immediate transition out of chattel slavery was thus smooth, and the apprenticeship system was ended two years early, on August 1, 1838. The period from 1838 to the onset of the worldwide slump around 1846 can even be considered a time of hope and optimism for the nearly freed in the Bahamas, as in the British West Indies in general.[3] Over the longer run, however, the ending of formal slavery aroused only qualified enthusiasm because the change proved more legal than real—if not an outright illusion. The loss of their former owners' protective responsibility was accompanied by a steady worsening of the conditions of work, land tenure, and material welfare, without a compensatory expansion of political and legal rights. With local variations, the pattern throughout the British West Indies—indeed, throughout plantation America—was that the ending of slavery saw not only the creation of a wage slave proletariat but the gradual deterioration in the status of would-be peasants, as the white former slave owners and their brown middle-class allies tightened their control over both the political system and the mercantile economy.[4] The annual celebrations on Emancipation Day, observed with increasing fervor as the memory of formal slavery faded, were therefore (for the liberated Africans and their descendants as well as for former slaves and theirs) as much a popular demonstration against continuing oppression and deprivation and an expression of future hopes as a memorial of what actually happened on August 1, 1834, or August 1, 1838.

The Liberated Africans, 1811–1838

The first 450 liberated Africans settled in the Bahamas were from three foreign slave-trading vessels adjudicated in the Nassau Vice-Admiralty Court in 1811. By the Abolition Act of 1807, such "condemned" recaptives were declared the responsibility of the Crown and placed in the charge of the local collector of customs. Those who could not be repatriated were to be voluntarily recruited into army or naval service or apprenticed to suitable employers for up to fourteen years. An order-in-council of March 1808 stipulated that the collector should bind such apprentices to "prudent and humane masters or mistresses to learn such Trade and Handicrafts or Employments as they seem from their bodily and other Qualities most likely to be fit for and to gain their livelihood most comfortably by after their Terms of Apprenticeship or Servitude shall expire."[5] The freed captives of 1811—two-thirds of whom were males and almost all under thirty years of age—were initially housed in hutments in the grounds of Fort Charlotte and provided with medical treatment and clothing. Repatriation was said to be out of the question, and the collector distributed those who did not succumb to disease as best he could. A fifth were recruited into the Second West India Regiment, the local detachment of the Royal Artillery, and the naval flotilla on station, while the remainder were apprenticed as laborers for seven years (renewable for a further seven) or as domestic servants for fourteen years. Apprentices whose time had expired and all children under the age of twelve were to be treated like any other black freedmen, and the employment of women in hard laboring tasks was prohibited. Of those indentured in the first two years, about a quarter were employed by the Crown, almost three-quarters were settled in Nassau, and little more than one hundred were taken up by Out Island employers.[6]

The arrival of cargoes of unassimilated Africans at the very time Bahamian slave owners (who had ceased importing slaves long before the official ending of the British slave trade) were exporting their surplus slaves naturally caused perturbation in Nassau. The first arrivals provoked a complaint in the *Bahama Gazette* about the further depreciation of the value of "negro property" and a petition from the Council and Assembly disingenuously claiming that the established free coloreds would suffer "because there will be the same work, but many more to do it." Although the unacclimatized newcomers suffered most severely from infections such as yellow fever caught after arrival and were bound to be suffering from sexual deprivation because of the preponderance of males, other locals complained of the dangers of imported African diseases, or, with equal injustice, of the moral effects of the Africans' "too prevalent practice of Indiscriminate Intercourse with the sexes."[7]

Though some of the Crown's apprentices were underemployed, most of the liberated Africans proved at least as industrious as slaves, quickly picked up useful crafts, or developed and passed on skills learned in Africa. They seemed to derive from a wide swath of West Africa, and though the "Congos" from the equatorial forests had the fewest transferable skills, the Iboes and Yoruba from the area of modern Nigeria proved particularly ingenious craftsmen, traders, and organizers, and a few from northern savanna areas (including "Mangoes" or Malinke) were even literate in Arabic.[8] Local whites still claimed that all liberated Africans were ignorant and troublesome and signed petitions against fresh importations whenever a slave ship and its cargo appeared before the Vice-Admiralty Court. For example, when a Spanish slaver was wrecked at Green Turtle Cay, Abaco, in 1816, and a proposal was made to free the three hundred Africans it was carrying in New Providence, certain "People of Nassau" petitioned Governor Charles Cameron. They claimed that the liberated Africans already in New Providence were the most "worthless and troublesome class of black people in the Town of Nassau where unluckily they are nearly all centred." The liberated Africans did not associate with the other Negroes because of their unique status as neither slave nor free; they misbehaved at work and leisure because they knew that they would eventually be fully free; and they had no desire or need to work properly for their masters and behaved in a superior manner because they felt they were protected by the Crown and had no loyalty to the colony. Finally, and inconsistently, the petitioners asserted that the introduction of more liberated Africans would further depress the labor market because the newcomers would be working almost for nothing and would displace more Creole laborers.[9]

Opposition to the acceptance of more liberated Africans and denigration of their qualities and customs by some whites did not prevent others from exploiting the newcomers whenever possible. Collector of Customs Alexander Murray (Lord Dunmore's son) complained in 1816 that too many of those applying to get such indentured servants were "poor illiterate people residing upon the Out Islands," and he feared that females would be employed as salt-rakers and in other laborious and unhealthy tasks despite the protective provision of the order-in-council. He also reported that some applicants for domestic servants in Nassau intended to ship them to the Out Islands as laborers.[10] Such outcomes were naturally resisted by Africans and colonial officials alike.

By 1825, when the indentures of the first African apprentices were expiring, Murray's successor as collector, Charles Poitier, though claiming that he and many other white Nassauvians were happy to employ liberated Africans and "thereby best fulfil" their "duty in preventing their becoming burdensome to the community,"[11] was sufficiently concerned that the Africans might be exploited or underemployed that he initiated a new policy to take care of the surplus of liberated Africans, both time-expired and newly arrived. In May 1825, with the consent of Acting Governor Vesey Munnings, Poitier purchased four hundred acres of Crown land some seven miles southwest of Nassau to form a self-sufficient African settlement. This settlement was called Headquarters, later renamed Carmichael in honor of Governor James Carmichael Smyth, who was responsible for its development between 1830 and 1834. The initial settlement consisted of a double row of forty strips of ten acres, each considered sufficient for a family's subsistence. These units were allocated to family heads, who nominally owed the government $10, payable in installments at their convenience. Though each allotment was joined by a path to a road through the center of the settlement, there was no serviceable road through the three and a half miles of bush between Headquarters-Carmichael and the public road running due south from Nassau until the settlers built one in 1831.[12]

When Governor Smyth first visited Headquarters in March 1830, he reported that many of the settlers were "tolerably industrious" and lived "in comparative comfort" but that the absence of moral instruction, useful training, and an arm of the law meant that some of the Africans were idle, profligate, or turning to petty crime. Despite its complaints about the Africans' behavior, the Assembly refused any funding, but Smyth on his own authority appointed a superintendent at Headquarters who was to combine the functions of preacher, teacher, and protector of the Africans' interests and asked for a police constable to be permanently stationed at the settlement. Besides setting up the African Hospital at Fort Charlotte for new arrivals, Smyth also arranged for the army's local doctor to provide medical attention for the Africans in the inland settlement.[13]

Governor Smyth hoped to create a sanitary enclave in which the Africans would be acclimatized and trained to be useful and untroublesome members of society but kept apart from the rest of the blacks (and from predatory whites) as long as was necessary or possible. This plan was frustrated, however, not only because Headquarters—as a settlement of authentic Africans who were essentially free—became the refuge for runaway slaves and apprentices and was often scoured by angry masters but because its more ambitious inhabitants preferred to move closer to the Nassau market and opportunities for wage employment. The mix of the newly arrived with Africans who had already served a term of apprenticeship was also uncomfortable, especially when the arrival of more and more cargoes of liberated Africans during the 1830s threatened to turn the settlement into a human dumping ground and slum with far too many people trying to wrest a livelihood from its indifferent soils.

Thomas Rigby, the first superintendent, was overwhelmed by the problems of management. He was unable to find the right balance between force and conciliation to satisfy the local whites, the African settlers, and a governor whom the Africans regarded as their friend. At its peak around 1832, Headquarters-Carmichael contained more than five hundred Africans, many of them independently farming land well outside the bounds of Poitier's original four hundred acres. Neighboring whites complained both of illegal squatters and of Africans raiding their farms, yet when a white master named Johnson arrived at the settlement ostensibly to pay a social call on Rigby but actually to recover a runaway slave woman, he was met by a group of Africans armed with sticks who demanded a paper of authority from the governor.[14] Similarly, when a consignment of 150 Africans released from the Portuguese schooner *Rosa* by HMS *Pickle* was settled at Headquarters and Rigby ordered them flogged to make them work, a delegation of seven walked all the way to Nassau to complain to Governor Smyth. Not surprisingly, Thomas Rigby found it difficult to get the Africans to come to his Anglican church services or to send their children to his school. In defending himself after his sacking, the superintendent blamed the former on the subversive activities of the black Baptists and the latter on the Africans' preference that their children help in the growing and marketing of produce.[15]

Governor Smyth's short-term answer was to replace Rigby with a more able administrator, John Minnis, and to give him much wider powers and the title protector of liberated Africans. Shortly afterward, an African board of officials and liberal local inhabitants was appointed to look after the welfare and interests of the liberated Africans, particularly those not yet, or no longer, under apprenticeship. The general and long-term concern of Smyth and his immediate successors, however, was to facilitate the assimilation of those Africans who were ready to enter the socioeconomic mainstream while continuing to separate those who were not in ever more distant African settlements.

John Minnis reformed the administration of Carmichael. A chapel and new schoolhouse were constructed at the heart of the settlement and an infant class and a "Female School of Industry" added to the original school, with a resident female teacher. Visits from an Anglican minister and an army doctor became more frequent, and resolute attempts were made to keep out unwelcome white visitors. Charles R. Nesbitt, the energetic liberal colonial secretary appointed by Governor Smyth, issued the following minatory notice in 1836: "All Persons are hereby warned from trespassing upon the premises at Roslyn, Carmichael, the African Hospital, or any other settlement occupied by the liberated Africans. No person will be admitted without permission in writing from two members of the African Board, and any person or persons who seduce, entice, or carry away, harbour or conceal any liberated African, will be subject to a penalty of twenty pounds, which penalty will be immediately inflicted upon the offender."[16]

To relieve overcrowding at Carmichael, several other settlements had been established to house newly arriving Africans, or at least those who could not immediately be recruited into the army or indentured as laborers or domestics elsewhere. Two were in New Providence—at Adelaide, five miles beyond Carmichael on the swampy southwestern coast, and at Gambier, nine miles from Nassau on the West Bay road. These two settlements, both started in 1831 on virgin or "ruinate" Crown land tracts, were even more isolated than Carmichael and less supervised, thus even more African in style. The first settlers were simply provided with clothing, tools, and seeds and instructed to build their own houses and set up provision grounds as they wished. Consequently, the original plan for separate family smallholding units was soon modified so that both settlements consisted of a cluster or double row of small house plots, surrounded by much larger tracts of farmland, some in private ownership, others casually worked in common.[17] The formal center of both villages, however, became the school (doubling as an Anglican chapel), where, by the mid-1830s, dedicated white teachers, usually unmarried young women, strove to instill the rudiments of English reading and writing, some Christian instruction of an Anglican slant, and at least a modicum of useful skills. In November 1835, for instance, the *Bahama Argus* reported: "The Infant School at Adelaide, under the care of Miss Scott, is improving; the number of children attending is about 20. Some of them have learned the Alphabet, and are spelling words of 3 letters, are spending part of the day in reading, and attending to the various lessons that are taught; and part in learning to sew. When it is remembered that these children of African parents were growing up in ignorance of all that is useful and good, and to whom the English language was almost unknown, the [Adelaide Committee of the African Board] cannot but regard the establishment of a School among them as one of the most valuable favors which they have received from the British nation."[18]

The first attempt to settle a sudden influx of liberated Africans on an undeveloped Out Island was far less cause for self-congratulation. In July 1832, the HMS *Nimble* captured the Portuguese slaver *Hebe* with 401 "Angolan" slaves on board. Like most such cargoes, so many were suffering from disease, malnutrition, and physical abuse incurred on the Middle Passage that the Army Medical Board decided that they had no chance of surviving a return passage and were of negligible immediate use as indentured workers. The board therefore recommended that they should be kept by the government until they were fit to be distributed as apprentices in the Bahamas or shipped to the African resettlement colony of Sierra Leone.[19] The facilities at Fort Charlotte were overtaxed and the New Providence settlements thought to be overcrowded so the collector of customs advised that the Africans be placed on Highburn (later Highborne) Cay, a deserted island two miles long in the northern Exumas. The Africans were divided into squads under their own leaders and issued clothing, corn, seed, and tools, shipped the thirty miles south to Highburn Cay, and left more or less on their own, though John Minnis was instructed to establish a school and ensure that they were not sexually promiscuous.[20]

A year later, Acting Governor Blayney Balfour was forced to report that the Highburn Cay colony was "in total disarray." Far from cooperating with each other, the so-called Angolans came from so many different tribes that they could not communicate among themselves. The cay lacked sufficient fresh water, timber, or even thatch, and the crops had failed because of a drought so that the settlers were suffering as cruelly as they had on the Middle Passage from exposure, dehydration, or starvation. Balfour ordered that the colony be abandoned and the survivors brought back to Nassau. There, many of the men were recruited into the Second West India Regiment, and the remainder of the adults were apprenticed for seven years, either in New Providence or the Out Islands.[21]

The Highburn Cay fiasco, however, did not end the government's attempts to colonize the less developed Out Islands with groups of liberated Africans. Mostly in the 1830s, smaller official settlements were established, with varying success, at Williams Town and Victoria on Stirrup's Cay in the Berry Islands, Bennet's Harbour on Cat Island, the Bight and Great Harbour on Long Island, and on Rum Cay and Ragged Island. Besides these, groups of time-expired liberated African apprentices formed distinctive settlements in many undeveloped Out Island areas, with or without government assistance, at Gold Rock, West Head, South Point, High Rock and the Bight on Grand Bahama, at Cedar Harbour, Abaco, on Little Abaco and parts of Great Exuma, in several places on Andros, and on Raccoon Cay, Grand Cay, and Salt Cay in the Turks and Caicos Islands.[22] In all, perhaps half of the sixty-five hundred liberated Africans and their Bahama-born children ended up in the Out Islands, bringing African-style peasant farming to many previously untouched or deserted cays and tracts of larger islands and helping to reverse the decline in Out Island population (and the resulting increase in the proportion living in New Providence), which had begun with the transportation of surplus slaves in the first two decades of the nineteenth century.[23]

Despite the great surge in the numbers of new liberated Africans after 1831, the fears of the Bahamian elite about the problems of socioeconomic absorption proved excessive, if not completely misplaced. A demand continued for the cheap and relatively reliable labor of indentured Africans, as well as for army recruits,

Main Street, Grant's Town, late nineteenth century. John Fondas Collection, Courtesy of Bahamas Archives.

and the surplus immigrants, if not treated generously or always wisely, were at least looked after by the imperial government at little or no expense to the colonial exchequer. Even more important, the Africans proved remarkably adaptable in compensating for the deficiencies of government sponsorship, in making a life of their own once their indentures expired, and in melding African folkways and institutions to the new environment and established culture.

The symbol of this adaptability and independence was the development of the Nassau suburb christened Grant's Town in 1825. Even before 1820, the area between the traditional slave and free colored quarters just Over the Hill and the inland Blue Hill ridge was the favorite location for African apprentices working in town. There they found adequate soils and plentiful well water close to the surface and built houses of daubed wattles and thatch with "enclosures" or yards, adjacent to their tribal fellows or "shipmates." In 1825, the smaller area between Blue (or Baillou) Hill Road and East Street as far south as what is now Wulff Road was surveyed and subdivided into quarter-acre lots by Surveyor General J. J. Burnside, at the behest of Governor Lewis Grant. These 474 lots were to be sold on a long leasehold at 10 shillings each, or £2 for an acre block.[24]

The original inhabitants of Grant's Town were soon augmented by time-expired apprentices and, in due course, by refugees from Carmichael and the other distant settlements, tired of their isolation and the difficulties of carrying produce so far to market. These Grant's Town Africans continued to sell their labor and skills in town and to cut firewood, grow provisions and fruits, and raise hogs and fowls for the Nassau market. But they also developed a vigorous internal social life and economy, with their own churches, meetinghouses, informal crossroads markets, and shops. Within ten years—that is, on the eve of apprenticeship for slaves—more than five hundred persons lived in Grant's Town, nearly all of them liberated Africans.[25] More than half of Burnside's original lots were occupied, but the form of tenure was so uncertain, so many boundaries indistinct, and so many lots already subdivided that Governor William Colebrooke, anticipating a flood of former slaves, authorized the freehold sale of lots in Grant's Town at auction. By the end of 1835, nearly all of the township had been snapped up, at prices varying from 13 to 17 shillings a quarter-acre, and the most enterprising of the liberated Africans were well on the way to becoming a minor landlord class.

Governor Colebrooke also sponsored an Anglican chapel and school, built on the site of the present St. Agnes parish church, for the established Grant's Town settlers and the newcomers, and to a certain extent to counter the proselytizing efforts of the black Baptists. By the end of 1835, the chapel was said to be drawing a small, faithful congregation, and the infants' school, thanks to the efforts of the Misses Walker, Wylly, and Deward, to be ministering to "upwards of 100 children."[26] Missionary efforts by the "white" Baptists and the Methodists (for whom the governor granted a site for a chapel in 1838) began at much the same time, and within a generation Grant's Town had gained a reputation for being the most thoroughly Christianized black settlement in the Bahamas with church observances ranging from the relative decorum of the Anglicans to the uninhibited fervor of the "native" Baptists.[27]

The most distinctive Afro-Bahamian institution that originated in Grant's Town, however, was the friendly society. The original Grant's Town Friendly Society was formed by liberated Africans and former slave apprentices some time before October 1835 as a self-help organization, designed to promote African solidarity and to provide benefits for the sick, aged, widows, and orphans and, above all, a fitting and stylish burial for each of its members. In October 1835, a petition signed by 152 men who described themselves as "natives of Africa" who were "friends of all Englishmen," begged the governor for continuing support for the Grant's Town Friendly Society and for all such "Christian African organisations." Governor Colebrooke responded by arranging for the incorporation of the society under the law of 5 William IV, c. 39, with twelve directors, separate funds for benefits and expenses, properly audited accounts, and all monies kept in the newly established Nassau Savings Bank.[28] Thus regulated and endorsed, the Grant's Town society became the model for a proliferation of similar societies and "lodges," whose activities became one of the most important, as well as the most colorful, features of Afro-Bahamian life. Some of these organizations, including Yoruba and "Egbar" societies, with a hall in Bain Town, an Eboe Society, the two Congo societies of Fox Hill and Grant's Town, and the Knights of King George (formerly the Hausa Society) long retained strong subethnic affiliations.[29]

The indentures of all liberated Africans were canceled in 1838 shortly after the former slave apprentices were made "fully free."[30] But the nonslave Africans had already achieved formal acceptance two years earlier when, in response to a decision of the local attorney general that all Africans must be residents for seven years in the Bahamas before they were eligible for service in the militia, the Colonial Office decreed that African origins alone could not debar any free inhabitant from all the rights others enjoyed. "If they can meet the requirements imposed on all colonists," the order stated, "they are entitled to whatever privileges all others have."[31] This edict was no real blow to the ruling elite, however, for even before 1834 the liberated Africans had not only demonstrated the value of apprenticeship over formal slavery but shown that, paradoxically, even an expansion of the black majority and an apparent move toward greater freedom could serve the cause of white hegemony. Not only had the liberated Africans filled a labor shortage in certain unpopular employments and contributed to the development of backward islands, they had also provided a willing (and far from wholly unskilled) addition to the general labor force, which would help to drive down wages. Moreover, whether or not they were integrated, the sixty-five hundred liberated Africans were bound to aid the white elite by their very distinctiveness. Either they would facilitate white rule by the differences and divisions between themselves and the black Creoles, or, by reinforcing and reinvigorating the African elements in Afro-Bahamian society, they would further open up the socioracial divisions in Bahamian society as a whole.

Apprentices and Stipendiary Magistrates, 1834–1838

Despite the advantage of having a distinct and competitive element within the laboring class (at first, only instinctively felt by the ruling class), many members of the regime were understandably nervous in the summer of 1834 as the first stage of slave emancipation approached. Acting Governor Blayney Balfour, in complaining that the three stipendiary magistrates appointed to protect the interests of apprentices and owner-employers alike had not yet arrived, reported that the slaves of Eleuthera and Exuma were announcing that they would stop work immediately on August 1. Apparently, the belief was prevalent that the masters were attempting to trick the laborers into remaining slaves—probably a misapprehension of Balfour's recent proclamation that domestics and sailors (that is, "Non-Praedials") would be free within four years, whereas "Praedial" laborers would have to wait six.[32]

Balfour sent out the two armed naval schooners stationed in the Bahamas to the Out Island hot spots with detachments of troops, while using the New Providence clergy and a touring group of officials led by Lieutenant Graham Egerton to explain the nature of apprenticeship and the former slaves' duties and rights. Meanwhile, the *Royal Gazette* piously hoped that the "labouring population" would use the apprenticeship system as a "school of instruction . . . in which to learn how to conduct themselves as industrious and useful, worthy members of society, when they became entirely free," though because few former slaves in Nassau and fewer still in the Out Islands would have read the establishment newspaper, this was a sermon preached to the wrong audience, or it was the wrong sermon.[33]

The relief of the masters at the generally peaceful transition to apprenticeship before either Governor Smyth's successor or the stipendiary magistrates had arrived was expressed by the president of the Council, the same Joseph Hunter whose slaves had rebelled only three years earlier. "The peaceable demeanour of the Apprenticed Labourers in the more distant islets where they are under no kind of surveillance cannot fail to be a matter of heartfelt gratification," he wrote to Lord

Aberdeen in February 1835. He attributed this situation to the generally satisfactory conditions and the good sense of both masters and former slaves, as well as to Balfour's mixture of tact and force.[34] Yet, while the first reports of the new governor, William Colebrooke, and of the stipendiary magistrates after their first circuits of the Out Islands confirmed the impression of general quiescence, they added qualifying details that suggested a far more patchy and tenuous state of affairs. The former slaves were quiescent only where they were left to their own devices, had a mutually satisfactory understanding with the masters, or were overawed, cowed, and socialized by the forces and agents of law, order, and "civilization."

Governor and stipendiary magistrates alike were thus faced with the problems of patching and smoothing, while guaranteeing the underlying strength of the social edifice. One of Governor Colebrooke's first actions was to send Stipendiary Magistrates Thomas Winder and Hector Munro on a tour of Exuma and southern Eleuthera, where there had been some instances of unrest, with a letter of instructions that was cannily published in the *Royal Gazette.* Acting on reports of "uprisings" among the apprentices, especially those on Mrs. Ferguson's estate, Colebrooke authorized the magistrates to "select such persons as from Conduct and Character, are most fit to be appointed Special Constables," in a ratio of one to each ten families, "according to local circumstances." The specials would have no power to act unless called on by a JP "to assist in the suppression of tumults and disorders," though they would at all times be "competent to advise the Apprentices to preserve order" and could advise the magistrates of trouble before it got out of hand. Ideally, wrote Colebrooke, they would therefore be drawn from the "Heads of families who are thought well of by their employers, and who are possessed of some influence with the Apprentices."[35] This system, initiated so quietly and emerging so smoothly out of the method of appointing "confidential" drivers during the slavery era, was to remain a permanent feature of Out Island life.

To maintain socioeconomic relations between masters and workers, Colebrooke also built on the system developed in the late slavery period by recommending the extension of the custom already found in some islands that the apprentices be allowed to work for three full days "cultivating their own grounds" (that is, grounds allocated for their use by their masters) to provide for their own subsistence at no cost to their employers.[36] More generally, though, William Colebrooke seemed dedicated to the principle that the former slaves would remain informally tied to their old owners by making it difficult for former slaves to purchase land of their own. In August 1835, in response to an appeal from manumitted apprentices of Pitman's Cove, Eleuthera (later called Gregory Town), the governor did release tracts of Crown land, but for sale at auction, so that they were sold at £5 an acre, even though most of the surrounding land had been preempted by the former slave owners at two shillings an acre. This policy of making land relatively dear, though painted as a concession to the newly freed and justified by the need to discourage speculation, was more likely motivated by the principles later attributed to Edward Gibbon Wakefield of keeping the ownership of land mainly in the hands of those most able to develop it and retaining a pool of landless laborers or land-tied smallholders, while also increasing government revenue.[37]

At the same time, however, Governor Colebrooke also warmly encouraged the former slaves to emulate the liberated Africans and become involved in self-help friendly societies, savings schemes, and the building and support of schools. This aspect of policy was exemplified by the officially sponsored first celebration of emancipation held on August 1, 1835, and reported enthusiastically in the *Royal Gazette*. In the morning, the Bahamas Friendly Society (formed about the same time as the Grant's Town society but with membership predominantly of former slaves) assembled in town to march to church, each member decorated with an emblazoned blue scarf. At 7 P.M. the group reconvened for a "handsome dinner" at the schoolhouse, where two hundred persons ("several white guests included") toasted the governor and listened to a speech by the philanthropic Judge Robert Sandilands "encouraging the negroes to work hard, be loyal, and grateful for their boon."[38]

The actions of the stipendiary magistrates were a similarly subtle mixture of coercion and encouragement under the pretense of evenhandedness. On their first circuit of Exuma and Eleuthera, Magistrates Winder and Munro found the Rolle apprentices at Steventon peacefully going about their own work and eager to discuss the project of setting up a school to train their young in useful skills. They managed to settle the recurrent trouble between Mrs. Ferguson and her Negroes without having to set up a court, though on Ann Hunt's estate on Hog Cay they found "that despite good treatment the negroes were poorly behaved" and deserved exemplary punishments. In most of Exuma and in parts of Eleuthera they found relations between masters and apprentices "in good order." But on returning to Nassau after visiting Rock Sound and Tarpum Bay, Eleuthera, where resident owners monopolized the best arable land, they felt bound to make the following summary remarks in reporting to the governor and Colonial Office: "We only regret that there appears to be very little disposition on the part of some owners to promote the industry and well-being of manumitted slaves, or acknowledge the new state and relations of society in which the law has placed them, but rather attempts to exact from them the requirements of slavery. We rejoice, however, that these remarks are not generally applicable, and that there are to be found . . . many highly honourable exceptions."[39]

After representations to London, the number of stipendiary magistrates was raised from three to six, and Governor Colebrooke also withdrew the commissions of eighteen of the most notoriously biased JPs. Perhaps as a result, it was not found necessary to repeat the criticism of some former slave owners in the report printed in the *Royal Gazette* of a much more extensive circuit of the islands made by the stipendiary magistrates at the end of 1835. In nearly every settlement, amicable and mutually beneficial arrangements between apprentices and their masters were reported, though the magistrates were equally ready to adjudicate disputes, to punish recalcitrant individuals, and to make suggestions for the more orderly relocation and reorganization of those newly freed—coupling in many cases a recommendation for the building of a jail with one for a school. As part of their mandate, the magistrates also made suggestions as to where in the Out Islands liberated Africans might be settled to social and economic advantage.

In this last respect, particular attention was paid to the salt-producing islands because work at the salt pans was known to be unpopular with the former slaves, and liberated Africans were considered suitable replacements. On the Ragged Islands, for example, the magistrates consulted with all the apprentices as well as their masters and found few complaints on either side. Where there were small disputes over work arrangements, the magistrates negotiated compromises "equitable to both sides," including wages in lieu of provision grounds and extra pay for raking salt on Saturdays. Some liberated Africans, though, were sent to Duncan Town, where they were apprenticed to local salt producers. Similarly, at Rum Cay, they recommended that the area around the only anchorage (Port Nelson) be developed into a town, with liberated African as well as former slave apprentice inhabitants. The magistrates listed as favorable features the availability of Crown land and the proximity of the great salina, "where labour is always in request." But they also mentioned that many of the apprentices, while expressing a desire to purchase house lots, were already farming Crown land without title in preference to working at the salina. Four hundred miles to the north, on Green Turtle Cay, the magistrates were happy to report "that great improvement has been made in the appearance of the settlement since the inhabitants have been permitted to purchase their lots; the streets have been properly laid out, and cleansed, which much very greatly contribute to the health and comfort of the people." They added, though, that it might be a good idea to use the money received for the town lots to send twenty liberated Africans to the cay, "with a responsible person to overlook them," to fill and drain the adjacent swamps, "because the locals would not do it."[40]

Significantly, at Ragged Island, Rum Cay, and Green Turtle Cay (as well as at other settlements), the building of a school and a jail were regarded as priorities. The purpose of the former was said to be the inculcation of "habits of industry" and "good Christian behaviour"; that of the latter to be a visible sign of the magistrates' authority, as well as for the exemplary punishment in their native settlements of the few troublesome individuals. One typical such person was the Eleutheran apprentice Sam, against whom his master, William Durham, brought a case before Stipendiary Magistrate Thomas Winder on June 6, 1835. Sam had absented himself for ten months, ignoring orders to return issued by Justice George Smith (a planter JP). During this time, Sam had squatted on and worked a piece of Crown land in company with his lover, another runaway apprentice called Tulip. Despite a plea of guilty and a request for mercy, Sam was sentenced to thirty lashes, a month at hard labor, and the extension of his term of apprenticeship by the ten months of his absence.[41]

Such cases, however, were comparatively rare, and the condition of many Out Island settlements during the second year of apprenticeship was reported in glowing terms. The stipendiary magistrates' showplace was Millar's, in southern Eleuthera, where the behavior of the owner was clearly one of the "highly honourable exceptions" mentioned by Winder and Munro in August 1835. In June 1836, it was reported that Millar had manumitted fifty-six of his apprentices for fixed sums, payable over twelve months, and freed fourteen others without payment on the sole stipulation that they, not Millar, be responsible for looking after their aged parents. Millar's former apprentices were allowed to keep their houses and grounds and were provided with enough wage labor to allow the industrious to fulfill their obligations and still live comfortably. The magistrates thought Millar an extremely humane master, reporting that the only two cases of punishment on the estate were for child neglect. Overall, the only complaints recorded on the magistrates' second circuit were the lack of ministers licensed to perform marriages and the difficulties experienced in getting crops to market in Nassau.[42]

In their annual report to the Colonial Office at the end of 1836, the stipendiary magistrates claimed that the apprentices were "peaceful and orderly" throughout the islands, that relationships between employers and workers were "generally good," and that the willingness to work had increased since the adoption of "voluntary engagements." Complaints and punishments had steadily decreased, and the abolition of the whip at work in particular had "raised the level of civilisation." Much good had come from the formation of friendly societies in the capital, and schools and churches were gradually spreading from Nassau to the Out Islands, though there remained a need for a "School of Industry." The recent law compelling parents to support their illegitimate offspring had immediately cut down the custom of concubinage and greatly encouraged formal marriage. On one circuit alone, the magistrates had received no less than 150 applications for marriage licences.[43]

The most negative remark by the stipendiary magistrates in 1836 was, on the surface, relatively mild: that only in Nassau, where the wages for laborers were as high as three shillings a day, did the apprentices often earn "real money"—payments commonly being commuted into sharecropping arrangements, payments in kind, or the system of manumission on credit adopted by Millar in Eleuthera. Apprentices, indeed, were "generally desirous to purchase their remaining term." At least 1,000 manumissions were said to have occurred within the first two years of apprenticeship, rising to an official total of 1,387 by January 31, 1838. By that time, the total number of apprentices had fallen to 8,813 from 10,200 on August 1, 1834.[44]

All in all, with the former slaves optimistic that freer access to land and wages would afford them greater practical freedom and the owners both eager to shed their financial responsibilities to the former slaves and confident that (with indirect help from the liberated Africans) they could control the terms of employment, it is not surprising that proposals were put forward to end the apprenticeship system early—with the form of the proposals inevitably demonstrating chiefly the interest of the proposers and their class. The most cogent and ingenious scheme was that put forward in the *Royal Gazette* "for the more speedy emancipation of the apprenticed labourers in this colony, in the hope of combining the mutual advantage of employer and apprentice, with the general welfare," by a writer calling himself "Spero," on December 27, 1836.

Spero praised the system of apprenticeship for having rendered the transition out of slavery peaceful and having "made all parties thoroughly acquainted with their relative condition." But he clearly regarded the unexpired period of apprenticeship as a profitless and demoralizing limbo, with the former slaves simply marking time until they were completely free, rather than being constrained toward "industrious habits." Adapting Adam Smith's argument of enlightened self-interest by claiming that "the rewards of industry are generally sufficient incentive in free countries with most men, where they themselves reap them; but not so when others enjoy them," he proposed that the apprentices be nominally freed forthwith but effectively bound by chains of debt through the colonial legislature and the recently created Savings Bank.[45]

Apprenticeship did end two years early, though without the benefit of Spero's inventive capitalist scheme. The initiative came from the Colonial Office, which had been under great pressure from the antislavery lobby in England over the manifest inefficiency and injustices of the system in the sugar colonies—particularly the scandalous operation of the workhouses.[46] Despite the constant vigilance of British philanthropists, such strictures could not be applied to the Bahamas, where the Colonial Office's face-saving claim that apprenticeship was ended early because its purpose had been served had considerable plausibility. In the Bahamas, both former slave owners and slaves (and liberated Africans) indeed felt themselves ready for "full freedom" on August 1, 1838. For the latter, though, such optimism was unfounded. Events would soon prove that the master class had simply reshuffled the same cards, and the black laborers and peasants were deluded in their hopes of either lastingly better times or true socioeconomic freedom.

Legerdemain: The Oligarchy Reshuffles the Deck

The more blatant attempts of the Bahamian oligarchy to sustain its power were scotched by the Colonial Office under the influence of James Stephen. Laws denying the franchise and jury service to former slaves were vetoed, and in September 1838 a circular from Lord Glenelg, the colonial secretary, proposed almost a new code of laws for postslavery society in the British West Indies concerning master-servant relations, the reorganization of the magistracy, militia, and police, the control of crime, vagrancy, and squatting, the protection of the poor, and the promotion of religion and education.[47] Even where fully implemented (and in self-legislating colonies such as the Bahamas they could not easily be enforced), such laws were far from radical, being no more than a somewhat liberalized (and Whiggish) form of social control such as was being developed in the metropole itself.

In general, moreover, imperial policy increasingly inclined toward the liberal principles of laissez-faire, eschewing protection and letting market forces follow natural lines, not interfering in colonial affairs more than was strictly necessary, and expecting even the poorest colonies to be self-supporting. In the Bahamas (as in Bermuda and Barbados) the imperial government was pleased to find a society able to sustain at least the semblance of a local elected Assembly rather than giving the trouble and expense of direct Crown colony rule. This meant in effect that, with minimal interference from Westminster, by making constant pleas of poverty and retrenchment, and even under the guise of alleged reforms, the Bahamian ruling class was easily able to continue, reshape, and even reinforce its local hegemony. Thus in due course was created the white Bahamian agrocommercial oligarchy labeled "Bay Street," which in many respects paralleled—though in others demonstrated intermediate characteristics between—the white Front Street commercial oligarchy of Bermuda and the postemancipation white plantocracy of Barbados.

All former slaves nominally gained full access to the courts, and the impartiality of the judiciary was aided by the continuance of the system of stipendiary magistrates after apprenticeship ended and the gradual phasing out of unpaid local JPs—though this was more because of the shortage of suitable and willing candidates than a theoretical objection to the principle of having members of the local gentry on the bench. The bias of the law itself against the laboring and peasant classes was not so easily rectified, though, and the involvement of the black majority in the judicial process through jury service was long delayed by high property qualifications. In the first jury list drawn up after emancipation, for example, when eligibility for petty juries was limited to those owning property worth £100 and for service on the Grand Jury to those worth £1,000, only 225 persons in New Providence qualified for jury service of any kind, of whom a mere 61 were eligible for Grand Juries.[48]

Though the Bahamian electoral system never degenerated to the farcical levels found in some West Indian islands (47 electors in St. Kitts in 1855 choosing 22 members to represent a population of 22,000), it did remain strongly slanted toward the property-owning whites through comparatively high property qualifications, the inequitable distribution of seats, and outright bribery and corruption. (Women, of course, did not vote, or, for that matter, sit on juries, until the twentieth century.) On the surface, the Bahamian electoral roll attained respectable dimensions, with 5,949 registered voters in 1864 out of a population of 35,287 (or 16.9 percent). This represented an average of 214 voters out of a population of 1,267 for each of the 28 seats. The actual distribution, though, was far less balanced, with more than half the voters being found in New Providence, which contained only eight constituencies.[49] In New Providence there was a comparatively healthy spread of classes and colors to be found on the rolls, some alignment on socioeconomic issues, and often the semblance of genuine electioneering. Colored, even black, representatives were elected even before the end of slavery—the first being the prosperous and distinguished Haitian-born free colored Stephen Dillet in 1833.[50] But these men were inevitably drawn from the most respectable and conservative elements in their class (if anything, promoting the interests of their own marginal micro-class) and never numbered more than a fifth of the members of the House of Assembly (MHA) before the mid-twentieth century.

The foundation of the long-lasting dominance in the legislature of the white oligarchy was firmly laid in the Out Island constituencies. Not only were those constituencies increasingly overrepresented (60 percent of the population was represented by 72 percent of the MHAs by 1900), but the constituencies with large or sizable white populations were much better represented than those where nearly all the people were black. In Harbour Island, for example, where half the population was white, 22 percent of the two thousand inhabitants voted for three MHAs in an open list (with each elector having three votes). In Eleuthera, another three-member constituency where less than a quarter of the population were whites, only 9 percent of the five thousand people voted, while in all other islands save Abaco and Long Island, both the representation and the proportion of voters were lower. Additionally, in a system that did not pay MHAs salaries until 1967, the cost of elections and taking time off for legislative business and the difficulties both of attending the House and making a living from an Out Island base determined that virtually all Out Island representatives were nonresident and comparatively wealthy whites, that is, members of the Bay Street oligarchy. A final compounding factor was the undoubted corruption of a system in which open balloting (ironically said to be a safeguard against underhanded practices) was not abolished in New Providence until 1949 and 1959 in the Out Islands. Particularly where the people had no hope of true representation in the legislature, habits of dependency and financial opportunism died hard, and votes were regarded as a commodity to be exchanged for direct payment at elections and intermittent patronage in between. This was not a custom peculiar to the blacks or entirely a by-product of the slavery system, for poor white voters notoriously took advantage of contested elections when all the candidates were white. Yet the way the system of bribery and patronage skewed the elections toward those who had most to start with and thus could deliver most further reinforced the dominance of the white Nassau oligarchy over the black majority, binding them in far tighter bonds than ever suffered by the poorest and most ignorant whites, the so-called Conchy Joes.

Though most factors determining social relations and the quality of life—such as the perennial shortage of money in circulation, the limited opportunities for wage labor and the development of a true proletariat, and the even greater poverty of the Out Islands compared with Nassau—were beyond the reach of legislation, a study of the laws passed by the Bahamas Assembly during the late nineteenth century predictably discloses a far greater concern for the interests of the propertied classes and for social management and control than for social welfare and only a token or disingenuous acceptance of liberalizing directives from the imperial authorities.

On the legal fiction that all persons were now equally free, no laws were enacted to protect the rights of blacks or former slaves as such. Likewise, no law specifically protected the interests of employees. All such matters were regarded as the province of the stipendiary magistrates—temporarily imported officials rarely welcomed and often obstructed by the local whites. Few stipendiaries, however, had any natural sympathy for the blacks or willingly courted ostracism by their own kind; and in any case they were bound to administer the provisions of Masters and Servants Laws that throughout the nineteenth century invariably favored the interests of employers. In the Bahamas, as in the rest of the British West Indies, it was far more difficult for an employee to prosecute a case against his employer than vice versa, even over the terms of a written contract. Far from expecting protection over work conditions, wages, holidays, and sickness benefits, a worker could actually be sued by his master for the amount of wages due (or, in lieu, expect a prison term at hard labor) if he or she chose to desert from work already undertaken.

All members of the laboring classes, moreover, were subject to Vagrancy Acts that decreed in effect that it was a misdemeanor not to be gainfully employed. By the Workhouse Act of 1812, all "indigent and idle persons refusing to work for customary wages" were "to be deemed rogues and vagabonds," who could be rounded up by the constables and sent to the workhouses by the magistrates. In 1821, itinerant unlicensed preachers were classed as vagabonds, and on the eve of emancipation the classification was further broadened to include all "people of idle, drunken or disorderly habits, not exercising any trade or visible means of livelihood," or who could not "satisfy the Magistracy of the correctness of their lives."[51] Similar subsequent enactments, threatening all "idle vagabonds," "suspicious loiterers," and persons "without visible means of support," continued in force for another century. Even to be poor was more than a mere misfortune. In line with metropolitan Poor Laws, the indigent unemployed could be consigned to the colonial workhouses, which were run on the precepts candidly expressed by Sir George Shaw-Lefevre in 1839: "That the relief afforded to the destitute, at the expense of the community, should be afforded in such a manner as to render the condition of those who receive it less desirable than that of the independent labourer, or those who, by their previous industry, or the aid of their friends, have the means of self-support."[52] The only local modifications of these principles were the result of the general poverty and backwardness of the Bahamas. Because there were normally far more laborers seeking wage employment than were needed for the available jobs, the employers rarely needed to place the laborers under legal constraint, and because there was always less public money available than was needed for an effective Poor Law system, the "idle" and poor were generally neglected in Nassau and almost totally ignored in the Out Islands.

The Bahamian Police Force, 1789–1893

Though officials and local whites often castigated the blacks as lazy and torpid, this did not prevent them from feeling the need for a more efficient system of police, especially in Nassau, to enforce the laws and keep the peace without having to resort to either the garrison or the militia. The original police force, on the English model, was parochially based, with churchwardens and vestries appointing honorary constables, who from 1789 came under the overall authority of a colonial provost marshal. Under the social pressures of the Loyalist influx and the Napoleonic Wars, the system was expanded and centralized. In 1802, the office of provost marshal was regularized and given more status and the holder placed under a bond of £1,000. Under the authority of the provost marshal were sixteen constables, appointed each year by a panel of JPs and largely honorific. There was also a separate night guard of seven paid watchmen, whose duties were to ring the curfew bell at sunset and sunrise, to patrol the town throughout the night, and to attempt to "prevent all mischief arising from fire, and all murders, burglaries, robberies, breaches of the King's peace, riots and all other outrages and disorders, and all tumultuous assemblies of free people of colour or slaves." On Sundays and other holidays when slaves and nonslave workers were free to roam, this tiny force was augmented by a company of the colored militia, set to patrol the streets throughout the day, with similar grand instructions.[53]

The cumbersome triple system survived the coming of peace, and the involvement of the militia was reduced and the number in the night guard increased to fifteen in 1821.[54] A salaried police magistrate was appointed in 1829, but as the end of slavery approached, the police system was thought to be too complex, haphazard, and ineffectual. A writer in the *Bahamas Argus* in June 1832, for example, claimed that

> the deplorable state into which our police has fallen is the everyday conversation of almost every inhabitant of the town. . . . Rarely does a day pass, but may be seen from many of the houses of the bay, persons of all ages and of all colours, not only bathing, but positively parading the wharves, as naked as they were born. . . . The spaces around [the Vendue House] are now daily occupied by men and boys playing at different games—gambling, swearing, and fighting. Every seat in the inside of the building is

commonly filled by basket women, as they are called; attendant on whom are a number of idle vagabonds, whose conduct and conversation are a most intolerable nuisance to the respectable Inhabitants who reside in its neighborhood [along with] a certain class of notorious females, who, at all hours of the day, parade the most public part of the town, and outrage all decency.[55]

Not coincidentally, in November 1833 one act set up a formal constabulary for the first time by authorizing the police magistrate to appoint six "able bodied men" as salaried policemen for New Providence and the Out Island JPs up to a further dozen for the other islands, while the new Vagrancy Act declared as unlawful "all assemblages of persons in or near the Vendue House, Market House or elsewhere in or near the streets for any lewd, vicious, idle or disorderly purpose" and also outlawed "all loitering, carousing or the like in or about any shop where liquor is sold by retail; all loud wrangling, scolding, quarrelling, shouting, singing or whistling."[56] The separate night guard was abolished in 1839, when the Nassau force was made responsible for twenty-four-hour policing, provided with uniforms to be worn when on duty, and placed under the command of an inspector general. At the same time, five extra constables were appointed to serve the new black suburbs Over the Hill; a separate police station was built in the middle of Grant's Town a few years later. The far more isolated Out Island policemen were given a great deal of independent authority by another act passed in 1839, being made responsible for jails along with their other duties. In Nassau, though, the new central prison built during this period had its own separate small establishment.[57]

By 1845, the police force consisted of the inspector general, two sergeants, two corporals, and twenty-six constables, but its quality and standards were not impressive. Governor George Mathew described the inspector general as "a gentleman whose age and habits of life render him obviously unfit for the service" and the constables as "broken down domestic servants or artisans."[58] More seriously, there were complaints of police brutality, though attitudes toward such charges were predictably contradictory. In August 1849, after a magistrate had fined two policemen for "exceeding their authority" in arresting a drunk, a writer to the *Bahama Herald* expressed surprise that complaints of ill-usage by policemen were not more frequent. "I myself have been witness to several acts of cruelty from the use of the cords and staves which they carry," he wrote, "and with which they seem to delight not only in terrifying, but tormenting their victims. The use of them is cruel in the extreme, for, when the tourniquets as I shall call them, are applied to the wrist, and screwed up as I have seen them, they must cause the most excruciating anguish. . . . I have even seen women and little boys spoken to by a constable for looking at him!"[59] In contrast, in November 1854, after two violent criminals had held warders and policemen at bay with a stick and hatchet and made their escape from the prison, leaders complained in both the *Gazette* and *Herald* of the laxity and pusillanimity of the police.[60] These newspapers clearly expressed the views of the ruling whites, but a more telling critique of police behavior and prison conditions was the following letter, inserted in the *Herald* by the Bahamas Friendly Society just before Christmas 1858:

Sir—As we so seldom trouble you, allow us a corner in your paper while we make a suggestion on this subject. Has the law any favourites? Is it partial to any one? Does it

> treat all men alike that fall within its reach? Is such the case in our day? Are all men punished alike according to their crimes? No, Sir, as it stands now, it bears heavily upon the coloured and black man; if they are detected in a fault and cast into prison, before the week is ended, you see them chained hand and foot, and driven about the town like savage beasts. Are they more likely to run away now, that they should be bound in fetters as in the days of old? Are they more ferocious now than ever, or whether in British or Foreign dominions, are the sons of Africa to bear the yoke of oppression and cruelty? We do not mean to say that the guilty ought not to be punished: far from it, but punish every transgressor alike. If the British laws are partial to one Class of men more so than to another when they both commit the same crime, then we are content. But, Sir, we ask, where is the white man when he does a crime? Is he chained? No. They are seldom seen, unless by chance you may have occasion to go into the den where they are kept. He that knoweth his Master's will and doeth it not shall, or should, be beaten with many stripes.[61]

Minor reforms were introduced in the police force during the 1850s, including the award of insignia for each year's good conduct, with a crown for seven years' faithful service—which could be forfeited for "any misconduct, neglect of duty, disobedience of orders, or other offence . . . in addition to any form of penalty which may be inflicted by any court."[62] Medical and moral conditions at the main prison were also improved with the institution of regular visits by a doctor, weekly services by a chaplain, and the supply of "a library of Religious useful and moral books." Male and female prisoners were firmly segregated for the first time and not allowed "to hold intercourse with each other."[63] More substantial reforms, however, were long delayed on the pleas of expense and the satisfactorily low levels of crime and disorder. Between 1847 and 1849, for example, only sixty-four criminal cases were brought to trial in Nassau (with a conviction rate of 80 percent): forty-two for larceny, nine for assault, five for sundry misdemeanors, and only one each for murder, felony, burglary, prison-breaking, conspiracy, forgery, embezzlement, and sodomy.[64]

The 1860s, however, saw a marked increase in crime and unrest, which accelerated during the American Civil War, when blockade runners and easy money flooded into Nassau. In 1863, for example, Governor Rawson W. Rawson reported that in 1851 the average number of prisoners in jail was thirteen but now was over a hundred.[65] As a consequence, demands arose both to enlarge and further professionalize the police force. A related concern was the decreased effectiveness of the militia as a subsidiary arm of the police. After emancipation the prestige of the militia had declined steadily because almost all males became eligible to serve in it. Unlike the members of the free colored militia in the last phase of slavery, blacks in the militia were increasingly reluctant to police their fellows, and whites became reluctant to serve at all. By an act of 1857, the Bahamian militia (like those of all other slave colonies) was virtually disbanded, the governor retaining the right to reactivate it in times of external threat.[66]

Three years later, an act was passed "To Consolidate the Stipendiary Police Force of the Colony." The force was now to consist of an inspector, two corporals, twenty-eight first-class constables, six second-class constables, and thirty-three of the third class, distributed among Nassau, its suburbs, and the Out Islands. In 1863, another act increased all police salaries from the inspector downward and placed police officers "on the same footing as other Public Servants," specifically providing that the inspector should hold no other office and be ineligible for election to the House of Assembly. In the following year, an even more comprehensive Police Act detailed duties, rules, and fees and more precisely distributed the force, adding a second subsidiary station in Nassau's Eastern District. Though clauses in the act specified penalties for constables guilty of misdemeanors, at least equal weight was given to restrictions on the prosecution of the police and penalties for assaulting them in the course of their duties. A further act in 1865 added new police stations at Spanish Wells and Gregory Town, Eleuthera.[67]

The reorganization of 1860–65 lasted for a quarter-century, not because the police force advanced spectacularly in either efficiency or rigor but because financial stringency and relative social quiescence returned after the end of the blockade-running era. During this period the militia faded altogether, and some members of the white regime began to wonder whether even the police force could be trusted in cases of serious social disturbance because of their "local sympathies and connections."[68] The garrison troops of the West India Regiment remained in Nassau, however, as a backup for the forces of law and order—rarely used and often mistrusted by the whites as being blacks themselves but in fact more than willing to act against local disturbances.[69] A crisis loomed only once it became clear in the early 1880s that there were plans for the removal of the garrison.

In 1881, a royal commission recommended that the scattered detachments of the West India Regiment stationed in the Bahamas, British Honduras, Barbados, Trinidad, and British Guiana be more strategically and economically concentrated in Jamaica and St. Lucia.[70] This suggestion was vigorously opposed by Governor Charles Lees in December 1882. "The population of the Bahamas is docile and law-abiding," he wrote to the colonial secretary, Lord Kimberley, "but your Lordship is aware that it is almost entirely composed of a race easily excited, and when under the influence of passion, capable of but little self control."[71] When the decision to withdraw the garrison was announced in 1885, the House of Assembly sent a memorial to Governor Henry Blake asking for a reconsideration. "Such a step as this we cannot but regard as one that will be absolutely fatal to the future progress of the Colony," they proclaimed; "its good government will be placed in jeopardy, and insecurity to life and property will, under these circumstances universally prevail." Blake agreed that there was a danger but attributed it less to the volatility of the blacks than to the social discord between blacks and whites. "While I cannot speak too highly of the general conduct of the population," he wrote in August 1885, "the fact remains that there is a strong feeling on the part of the black and coloured peoples against the white population of Nassau. I have heard this from too many sources to have any doubt on the subject." The governor's feelings were apparently underlined by the wave of antagonism against whites expressed by black Nassauvians when a black policeman was shot to death by a deranged white man named Sands in 1886.[72]

In 1888, the colonial secretary recommended that the removal of the troops be offset by a substantial increase in the size and strength of the local police force. Governor Ambrose Shea replied that he thought the public security might be weakened rather than strengthened by such a measure. He had no reason to complain of the general comportment of black Bahamians but feared for their conduct

In place of a local constabulary backed up by the garrison troops of the British West India Regiment, the Bahamian police were reorganized as a quasi-military force, recruited mainly from Barbados just before the troops were transferred in 1891. From *Stark's History and Guide to the Bahama Islands* (New York, 1891), courtesy of Bahamas Archives.

if their racial prejudices were excited. Worse, that these were the people from whom the present police force was recruited raised the specter that a larger and more efficient local police force might come down on the popular side in such an emergency. The colonial under secretary Edward Wingfield responded caustically that the chief trouble was that local social conditions ensured greater antipathy between the black majority and white minority than "in any other Colony" but that should not compel the imperial government to maintain a garrison of troops in Nassau simply to preserve internal order.[73]

Ultimately, a canny and lasting solution was found to the problem along lines followed in many other parts of the empire. The formulation was largely the work of the colonial secretary of the Bahamas, Captain H. M. Jackson, who had previously served in Sierra Leone and the Gold Coast, where the police were drawn from foreign parts and combined civil with quasi-military functions. Jackson's plan was to double the Bahamian police force by creating a separate unit, recruited from outside the Bahamas, trained almost like soldiers, and housed in barracks rather than living at home. In due course, the new paramilitary police would supplant the original force through natural attrition. Governor Shea's inclination was to recruit policemen from the "warlike tribes" of India, particularly the Sikhs of the Punjab, who had proved their loyalty to the British Crown since the time of the Indian Mutiny and were already employed as police elsewhere. Such distant recruiting proved impractical, and in any case Captain Jackson preferred Barbadian blacks, who had impressed him by their reliability as soldiers in the West India regiments during the Ashanti War and were already serving as police replacements for the troops withdrawn from British Honduras.[74]

The Police Act of July 1891 stipulated that the additional police unit was to consist of a commandant, inspector, subinspector, sergeant, two corporals, and forty constables (later to be increased to seventy-five). The pay for the new police constables (PCs) was set at £36 a year, compared with the £52 paid the existing PCs.[75] The new pay scale was considered more than sufficient to attract recruits from overcrowded Barbados but not enough to draw Jamaicans or other West Indians. It would also discourage local recruitment and hasten the reduction of the Bahamian component in the police—which in any case was soon demoralized by being treated as an inferior arm. The new police force, consisting almost entirely of Barbadians, was in being well before the last soldiers of the West India Regiment left Nassau at the end of 1891, though it was months before it was trusted out of barracks and years before it provided the majority of police patrolling the streets. Even then, the "foreign" accents and style and supposed officiousness and superior attitudes of the new policemen often provoked resentment and resistance, such as the riot that erupted in Grant's Town in April 1893.[76] By 1900, however, the system was entrenched, and the Bahamian police consisted of a majority of black West Indian constables under white European officers—an effective adjunct of the machinery of social control that survived until emergent black nationalism enforced the progressive re-Bahamianization of the Bahamas police in the 1960s and 1970s.

Nineteenth-Century Bahamian Education

The weak Bahamian educational system reflected and cemented class and racial division in the Bahamas and widened the dichotomy between Nassau and the Out Islands. Education suffered much more from lack of government funding than the police force. Money was in short supply, but its disbursement for schooling was curtailed because the ruling class was broadly divided between comparative moderates who believed that the ordinary blacks were incapable of profiting from more than the most rudimentary learning and that expenditure on education was therefore a waste and more pragmatic supremacists who opposed an efficient, democratic, and free system of education so as to perpetuate the existing socioeconomic pattern.

As throughout the British West Indies, with the possible exception of Barbados, the best, or most prestigious, education was reserved for those whose parents could afford to send them abroad, thus retarding the development of an indigenous culture. Yet even the best local education (including virtually all secondary education) was not only based on foreign models but was private, charged a fee, and was almost completely segregated on racial lines. Because the Board of Education was chronically underfunded, a majority of Bahamian schooling was left in the hands of the churches, with the Anglican church predominant throughout the nineteenth century despite its formal disestablishment in 1869. All church schools were dedicated to the notion, congenial to the ruling regime, that an educational system firmly based on "sound Christian principles" would generate an industrious and peaceable populace that would know and keep its place in the social order. Yet the perennial conflict and competition between the Anglican and other churches and the larger ideological tension and rivalry between proponents of secular and sectarian education—fanned by metropolitan controversies that increased in the second half of the nineteenth century—complicated and even enriched the Bahamian educational system, resulting in a higher level of general literacy and slightly better chances of upward mobility through education for colored and black youngsters than might otherwise have occurred.

The Sunday schools attached to the churches in the last period of slavery provided the first vestiges of education for the black majority of Bahamians. The established Anglican church entered the field only to sustain its primacy under competitive pressure from the nonconformist chapels. For example, though there had been a public school attached to Christchurch for a hundred years, with free places for the children of the poor since at least 1825, monitoring by rector, vestry, and JPs had restricted it to whites and a few free coloreds. A Sunday school aimed at a wider social spectrum was not founded until 1830. By July 1831 this school had five male and thirteen female voluntary teachers in charge of sixty-three male and thirty-one female pupils, nearly all free coloreds and blacks but including some slaves. In 1832, Governor James Carmichael Smyth set up full-time schools in the liberated African townships of Carmichael and Adelaide and attempted to reform the Christchurch day school on more liberal lines. Rechristened the King's School, it was to admit one hundred children without fees, on a first-come basis, regardless of color or sex, taking boys up to the age of fourteen and girls up to twelve. The school was to be open each weekday except holidays from nine to two, to follow the teaching system used by the National Society in England, and to have compulsory prayers taken from the Anglican Prayer Book.[77]

The King's School was bitterly opposed by the governor's many enemies; the old school's trustees objected to the liberal admissions policy and others to the continuing affiliation with the established Church.[78] The new school reverted to its previous form in 1835, soon after Carmichael Smyth was posted to British Guiana, not just because its chief supporter had gone but because its purpose was ostensibly to be fulfilled by the newly created Bahamian Board of Education. This body was set up chiefly to administer the minuscule allocation to the Bahamas from the Colonial Education Grant, which was specifically designed to provide a minimal level of schooling for the former slaves' children. The board thus came under some pressure to liberalize from the Colonial Office, though it could never be (and never wished to be) entirely free of dependence upon the contribution to education of the churches and their missionary societies, and its overriding aim was the promotion of a system of schooling regarded as socially "sound."

The Board of Education, indeed, became the focus of intrigue between the churches and between the advocates of secular and religion-based education, or, more accurately, between those politicians who believed that the purposes of education were better served by a government board than by churches potentially influenced by egalitarian principles and those who believed that churches were themselves a potent socializing force. In 1839, membership of the board was made interdenominational, but since this increased acrimony rather than the reverse, all clergymen were removed from the board in 1841. Three years later, however, Archdeacon John Trew insinuated himself onto the board and provoked a crisis through his zeal for the established church which was resolved only by the permanent laicization of the board in 1847.[79]

This change, though, occurred under the pressure of an even more fundamental crisis. In 1846, the Colonial Education Grant was revoked on the unspoken principle that colonial governments should be responsible for their own expenditures but with the hypocritical and misleading official explanation that the "civilizing" of former slaves for which it had been instituted had been accomplished.[80] Far from encouraging the development of an effective indigenous system of education, the removal of the subsidy not only slowed the rate of expansion and retarded the implementation of secular and popular education but placed educational policy more firmly in the hands of the local regime. This control was signaled by the creation of an Educational Committee of the Executive Council in 1847 and by the reconstitution of the Board of Education to consist solely of the governor and five members of the legislature in 1864.[81]

In 1847, an act with the grandiose aim of establishing "a system of Popular Education and Training in the Bahama Islands" entrusted the tasks of "superintending and regulating the existing scholastic Establishment" to the Educational Committee, with the assistance of a full-time secretary and an inspector of schools, who was to double as a normal schoolmaster to train local teachers.[82] Within two years, twenty-one board schools were set up or redesignated, of which six were in New Providence. The most notable of these was the Boy's Central School in Nassau Court, founded in 1847 with a curriculum consisting of "Arithmetic, Geography, Writing, Spelling, Grammar, Handicrafts (including shoe-making), Vocal Music and Prayers." By 1851, this school was something of a showpiece. Governor John Gregory described an open house crowded with "visitors of all ranks," claimed that the school was "becoming the main source of teachers in the colony," and proudly reported that all nine of its "monitors" were either black or colored. To a more critical eye, the situation was far less impressive. The monitors, for example, were simply the more capable pupils from the senior classes delegated to pass on their imperfect skills to the younger children. In the same year, moreover, Gregory had to report that because of "lack of support from the Assembly" five of the twenty-six schools in full operation in 1850 had been forced to close.[83]

Conditions in the outlying parts of New Providence were bad enough, but those in most Out Islands were primitive. The difficulties faced even in one of the nearer islands were shown by the report of a teacher called Wildgoos, sent to open a new school at Rock Sound, Eleuthera, in September 1847. Literacy in the settlement was no higher than 5 percent. A building twenty-one feet by eighteen feet was rented from the Wesleyan Mission, in which eighty-five children were taught—about half those in need of instruction. Wildgoos voluntarily held evening classes for adults, but his request for a larger building was turned down by the Board of Education for lack of funds.[84] In general, the board schools were able to accommodate only about half the children who went to school, or less than a quarter of those requiring education. Education not only continued to depend heavily on the church schools, but the more zealous churchmen were able to carry on their campaign against the alleged evils of secular education or even those of every denominational school but their own.

The chief of these zealots was the Anglican Rev. W. J. Woodcock, curate of St. Agnes church in Grant's Town (consecrated by the bishop of Jamaica in 1848). A consumptive who had come to the Bahamas for his health, Woodcock burned himself out in a brief but brilliant campaign to provide Anglican-based education for the underprivileged blacks of Over the Hill Nassau. "He has built in the heart of the settlement, at his own expense, a fine school house," reported the *Bahama Herald* in July 1849, "on land purchased by himself for that purpose, and provided moreover on his own resources a Master and Mistress for the school, and built for their accommodation a house adjoining."[85] Funds were raised by such functions as a "Rural Fete" on Woodcock's birthday in July and a "Grand Bazaar" in October (later an annual event), which in 1849 was attended by Governor Gregory and his family as well as thirteen hundred others and made almost £100 profit. The original schoolhouse was soon extended, a second school established in Bain Town at the end of 1849, and a third school built at the western edge of St. Agnes parish by a memorial fund shortly after Woodcock's death in December 1851.[86] By 1853, more than three hundred children were attending the Woodcock schools each day, and many adults attended literacy classes in the evenings. The syllabus of the day schools was scholastic rather than vocational, with a strong emphasis on religious education and a bias toward the Church of England. The subjects taught were listed in the following order: "The Word of God, Reading, Writing, Arithmetic, Geography, Natural History, Grammar, History, Algebra, Vocal Music."[87]

Only a month before he died, Woodcock published a hard-hitting pamphlet outlining the deficiencies of the Bahamian education system, suggesting his own solution, and bitterly attacking the Board of Education. The supply of education, he claimed, fell well short of the demand for it among the working classes. The education offered was not only greatly inferior to that in England but bore no relation to the special needs of the colony. Of the 4,000 eligible children in the colony, 2,215 were either being taught only at Sunday schools or not at all. Even the governor admitted that the government's education grant was insufficient to provide for a proper education and that much of what children learned at home or were taught in their nonconformist Sunday schools merely kept them in ignorance. The Board of Education was not only weak and inconsistent in its policies but was "unworthy of a Christian and Protestant Country." In a colony where the Church of England was established, not only did it fail in its duty to insist that its teachers be Anglicans, but it made religious instruction in schools a permitted activity rather than an enforced requirement. "Should the impending tempests of infidelity, republicanism or Popery strew these islands with the wrecks of order," wrote Woodcock in concluding his final testament, "forget not then at least that an observer of the social horizon foretold the danger, and suggested the defence."[88]

Woodcock's apocalyptic warnings were not fulfilled, though his pleas for a reform of the Board of Education, a much larger allocation to education in the colonial budget, and a great increase in the authority of the Church of England fell on deaf ears. In fact, the Woodcock schools flourished, and church-based schools (nonconformist and, later, Catholic, as well as Anglican) continued to teach more than half the children, as the Board of Education took advantage of what it was unwilling to change. The general tone of official reports on education was remarkably complacent. In 1857, Governor Charles Bayley (incidentally, one of the most blatantly racist of Bahamian governors) not only bragged that the Bahamas spent proportionately more on education than many richer colonies but that without the efforts of "the Government and church schools the poor would be left to grow up amidst the ignorance, idleness and prejudice of their own barbarous and uneducated parents."[89] More specifically, the inspector of schools in his 1853 report claimed that "for many years past the annals of crime in the town of Nassau have not contained the name of any person who has regularly passed through any of the public schools. Another pleasing proof of the influence and success of the system may be witnessed any Sunday in every place of worship in this Island New Providence. In some where formerly only a solitary Bible, prayer or hymn book here and there was to be seen, at the present time the large majority use books. Being able to read is now the rule."[90]

The actual statistics were in contrast to the official euphoria. In 1859, there were twenty-six board schools in the Bahamas but a total of only thirty-nine paid teachers. In 1864, the number of children in the board schools totaled only 1,570 out of a population of 36,000 and the entire bill for teachers' salaries was £1,920. Reliance on the monitorial system, which had been abandoned in England in the 1840s as merely perpetuating ignorance, was an inevitable concomitant of the lack of teachers, surviving in the more backward islands until the 1960s.[91]

Some small educational advances were made in the last quarter of the nineteenth century, signaled perhaps by the appointment of George Cole, a relatively liberal local white, first as headmaster of the Boy's Central School in 1871 and then as inspector of schools in 1881. Under Cole, the Boy's Central School was multiracial; poor whites were educated alongside the sons of the more prosperous coloreds and blacks. Because junior clerks and pupil teachers were enlisted at the age of fourteen, the school became the chief recruiting ground for the local civil service as well as the teaching profession. Though the best jobs and the surest promotions went to whites, this system did offer some chances for upward mobility to the most outstanding, and amenable, nonwhites.

In 1878, eight years after a similar move in England, compulsory education was introduced into the Bahamas for children of both sexes up to the age of twelve. It applied, however, only to Nassau until 1889 and was almost certainly motivated less from a concern over educational deprivation than the perennial problem of truancy, which was held to be the cause of an increase in crime and irresponsible behavior. Even in 1883, a Special Commission on Education reported that of ten thousand children of school age, only six thousand attended school, two thousand having no school to go to and two thousand having a school they did not attend. Fees were still collected for public school education until 1892, and the age at which one could leave school was not raised to fourteen until 1897. Corporal punishment was a feature of Bahamian educational practice for a further sixty years.[92]

In general, Bahamian education was designed to provide minimal literacy and sound moral training rather than social mobility or even useful skills. Though an English spinster named Fletcher, a teacher at St. Agnes Woodcock School, started a class in a room opposite the Royal Victoria Hotel on Tuesday afternoons to train young girls in "needlework and industrial habits" in 1871, the best the government could do to build on this foundation was to employ Fletcher to establish the Industrial Reformatory School in 1874.[93] With the exception of Boy's Central School, the board schools resolutely concentrated on the "three Rs" (or four, if religious knowledge is included), with only the skimpiest treatment of history, geography, and natural history and no science or manual training. There was no government secondary education whatsoever until the foundation of Government High School in 1925.

The failure to promote popular education beyond the primary level, indeed, was the worst indictment against the Bahamian regime. The only local secondary education was patchily provided by the churches, with a lamentable bias against those who could not pay fees and against girls as well as all nonwhites. A high school affiliated with King's College, London, was founded by the Anglican church in 1836 "to give proper English education to the young men of the Bahamas," but it was dissolved by an Act of Assembly in 1849 as a result of the sectarian conflict between Governor George Mathew and Archdeacon Trew.[94] A similar Anglican establishment called Nassau Grammar School was formed by Nassau's second bishop, Addington Venables, in 1864, though a parallel grammar school for girls, St. Hilda's, had to wait until 1886. Both lasted until the 1920s but never flourished, being unable to attract enough fee-paying pupils to pay for adequate full-time teachers and too dependent on the part-time teaching of overworked, sometimes underqualified, persons. More successful was Queen's College, formed by a consortium of Wesleyans and Presbyterians in 1890 out of the Wesleyan Nassau Collegiate School started in 1871. Queen's College accepted both girls and boys, but its admission policy was even more racially restrictive than that of its Anglican rivals. A sprinkling of middle-class coloreds gained a secondary education from the Anglicans, but no nonwhites attended Queen's College before 1900—and precious few before 1950. Even after Government High School was established in 1925, taking over the premises of the recently closed Boy's Central School and opening its doors competitively to children of all classes and both sexes, it was held back because of the continuing favor shown to Queen's College by most members of the government, competition from new Catholic high schools, and its ability to attract only the sons of the poorest whites and virtually no white girls.[95]

As a result of the combined efforts of board and private primary schools, the figures for bare literacy rose to levels seemingly respectable by Caribbean standards by the beginning of the twentieth century. In 1901 the Bahamian census reported that 19,975 people, or 37.1 percent of the population of 53,735, could read and write, and a further 6,220 or 11.6 percent could read but not write (those who could write but not read being, of course, a negligible number). Though the percentage of those able to read had risen only from 46.9 to 48.7 in the previous decade, those claiming both to read and write had increased 7 percent from 30.1 percent in 1891 and by 13 percent from no more than 24.4 percent in 1871. Despite this overall advance, though, there was a marked disparity between the figures for Nassau and the Out Islands, between those for whites and nonwhites, and for males compared with females.[96]

Even more significant and damaging, however, was the gross disparity in numbers between those with bare literacy—even those able to read a newspaper, write a simple letter, and keep rudimentary accounts—and those with a postprimary education. Into the mid-twentieth century, the ratio between Bahamians with only a primary school education and those who went to secondary schools—sixty-seven to one in 1957—was the highest in the region, Haiti not excluded, and only a tiny elite went on to higher education outside the Bahamas.[97] Here the figures for whites (females as well as males), though not impressive, were hugely superior to those for nonwhites for whom the racial, social, and economic filtering system excluded all but a handful from the educational qualifications needed for professional, clerical, and government employment.

2

Hegemonic Imperatives: The Economy, Land Tenure, Demography, and Settlement Patterns, 1838–1900

Banking and the Control of Capital

Bahamian society was divided on racial and ethnic grounds, but the divisions were enforced, or reinforced, not so much by legal enactments, police action, or educational opportunity as by economics: the economic leverage Nassau and its white elite always exerted over the Out Islands and the black majority and the peripheral effects on the Bahamas of the capitalist intensification of the world economy. The Nassau-based oligarchy, the small number of substantial landowners in the nearer islands, and the developers of salt pans in some of the more distant ones sustained their dominance, with or without legislative help, through competition in the wage labor force, sharecropping arrangements, and systems of payment by "truck" that were not far short of debt peonage. The majority of the Bahamian population was saved from complete socioeconomic subjugation by the very marginality of the Bahamas in the world economy, the large areas of land suitable for peasant subsistence but not commercial exploitation, and the sheer doggedness and ingenuity of the people themselves.

In the harsh economic climate of the later nineteenth century, the poor whites of the northern islands, while consciously separating themselves from the descendants of slaves, also suffered from social and economic deprivation. Like the black Out Islanders, they were largely driven back on their own resources and their tightly knit family and community groups. The twentieth century, though, was to show that this separation of the Conchy Joes from the white mainstream was far from irreversible. The white Out Islanders, moreover, did not share in the conflict between official and customary systems of land tenure that helped distinguish and sustain the Afro-Bahamian community. However poor, all whites proved to be culturally (and in the long run, advantageously) tied to concepts of land tenure that originated in Europe and stressed real property, individual title and possession, and lineal transfer, in contrast to looser concepts of community land, commonage, and "generational property" that probably had their roots in Africa and characterized the landholding and land-use customs of many, if not most, Afro-Bahamians.

The failure of plantations and the burden of mortgages and other debts meant that capital was chronically short in the Bahamas, and this problem was compounded by the perennial shortage of money in circulation. During the age of free trade, such an unpromising colony did not attract British capital, and despite repeated assistance from the Bahamas government, a local banking system never really succeeded in the century after slavery ended. By the Currency Act of November 1838, British sterling was declared the official money of account, and British coins became legal tender, but currency remained in such short supply that foreign gold and silver coins were allowed in circulation.[1] All sections of Bahamian society were affected by these conditions, though predictably—almost definitively—the ruling class was most able to adapt and adjust to them.

The first Bahamian bank was the Savings Bank created by an act in 1835, which opened for business in 1836. It became the Public Bank of the Bahamas in 1837 once it had developed full banking functions, including loans, discounting, and the issue of currency notes, as well as the operation of deposit and current accounts. The scale of its operations can be judged, though, by the fact that the entire currency in circulation in the Bahamas in 1844 was only £21,000. The weakness of the Public Bank's loan policy and its lack of liquidity were also evident in that when it failed in 1885 it had a cash balance of only £466, though the sum standing to the credit of depositors was £86,000.[2]

The Bahamas government raised £35,000 by a loan in London at a high interest rate for those days (5 percent) through a special act to settle the affairs of the collapsed bank, while at the same time authorizing, regulating, and guaranteeing a Post Office Savings Bank as an alternative. In 1888, though, it supported the incorporation of the Bank of Nassau by ten local businessmen with capital of £10,000 (later raised to £25,000), which began operations in June 1889. This bank lasted for twenty-eight years, but even though it was backed by the government (its banknotes in denominations as small as five shillings were personally signed by the colonial treasurer) it never flourished. The passage of a modern banking act in 1909, with strict regulations such as requiring payment of dividends only out of profits and publication of annual accounts in the colonial *Gazette*, placed it under such extra pressure that it was unable to compete with the neoimperialist capital represented by the arrival of the Royal Bank of Canada in Nassau in 1908. Though as late as 1913, the Bank of Nassau nominally had as much money on deposit as the local branch of the Royal Bank of Canada, it suddenly failed in December 1916. The Bank of Nassau's issued notes were redeemed under the government's guarantee, but its assets were taken over by the Royal Bank of Canada, which paid off the depositors in full yet by the end of 1917 had as much money on local deposit as both banks had held in 1913.[3]

Quite apart from the way they alone were able to control and take advantage of what local banking there was throughout the nineteenth century by their dominance in the House of Assembly, the group Howard Johnson has called "the agro-commercial bourgeoisie" was always more able to cope with the shortage of capital and cash than were the ordinary Bahamian people. This acuity was demonstrated even before emancipation by the ingenious ways slave owners exploited the capital value of their slaves and in later years by the former slave owners' use of their chief remaining capital asset, their land.

When slaves no longer produced direct profits for their owners and, indeed, were a net liability because of the legal requirements to feed and clothe them and to maintain the young, old, and sick, Bahamian owners devised numerous schemes to reverse the trend. Urban and craftsmen slaves had long been allowed to engage in outside work for wages, which they shared with their owners. Slaves were thus provided with an incentive to work hard at a time when the owners' powers of formal coercion were on the wane. The owners of rural slaves (as seen, for example, in the case of Wylly, Rolle, and Millar) were also willing to allow them an ever-increasing share of land and working time so they could become self-supporting. They built up in the process a lasting spectrum of customary practices such as the traditions that major plantation crops such as cotton belonged to the master, ground provisions to the worker, and corn, peas, and small stock animals were shared.

In a more direct transaction, the manumission of slaves by their owners as emancipation approached, either for cash or credit provided by the slaves themselves, was less an intentional way of easing the inevitable transition than a clever way of raising money on a declining commodity while simultaneously saving the cost of upkeep. It was also popular with many slaves because it required that they be permitted to make what money they could, ostensibly for themselves. Presumably, the terms negotiated balanced the value the slaves placed on the extra years of freedom against their decreasing market value—or rather, the hypothetical amount owners would receive from the anticipated slave compensation payments. This alone would explain the acceleration of manumissions as emancipation grew closer, at least up to the point when the expected compensation exceeded what the slaves could be expected to pay. Similar calculations were entered into by employers who volunteered to take on liberated Africans as apprentices as early as 1811, balancing the possible returns from hiring out the apprentices against the minimum legal cost of their upkeep and selling back to them the unexpired period of their indentures for the maximum price they would, or could, pay.

After 1838, the urban and maritime former slaves and liberated Africans were mostly thrown into the difficult arena of the "free" wage labor market. But for many rural and Out Island former slaves the transition was less abrupt because the basis was already laid for a sharecropping system. Particularly in the nearer islands (above all Eleuthera), a shortage of free or cheap land was combined with the possibility of raising provisions for Nassau or an export crop such as pineapples for more distant markets. Thus the self-interest of the former slaves who had no land of their own and little chance of raising the money needed to buy any synchronized with the self-interest of those owners, usually absentees unwilling or unable to pay wages, who had preempted lands that were of little worth without a resident labor force. The advantage of the sharecropping system, though, was just as heavily weighted in favor of the landowner as was the system of wage labor toward the employer. "What a revenue, without risk, might the judicious landholder thus derive!" quotes Howard Johnson from an editorial in the *Bahamas Argus* in June 1835, before going on to demonstrate how the Bahamian sharecropping system could allow absentee landlords to retain and even extend their landholdings at minimal labor cost, while at the same time (in contrast to some of the islands of the Lesser Antilles) retarding the development of an independent freehold peasantry.[4]

The earliest, and ultimately the most oppressive, examples of true sharecropping occurred in the pineapple areas of Eleuthera, which had begun a profitable export trade to the United States as early as 1832. In 1835 it was claimed that good pineapple land could return £100 to £150 per acre per year after expenses.[5] Most of this land was already in private hands, with some magnates holding hundreds of acres and needing only a guaranteed continuing source of dependent labor. Although some areas of Crown land around Gregory Town were sold to manumitted apprentices for £5 per acre in 1835, this was exceptional. For the majority of former slaves the chances of owning any land, let alone land suitable for pineapple growing, were minimal. Consequently, there was never a shortage of laborers ready to work pineapple lands on shares and willing to pay back at least half the produce as rent.

By mid-century, Bahamian sharecropping was institutionalized wherever conditions were right, with a wide spectrum of arrangements depending on land ownership, soil fertility, the existence of markets, and the availability of sufficient suitable and willing workers. As an official report stated in 1847, "On some Estates of New Land one half, if old one third of the produce; and on others from two to three days labour are given for the privilege of working the land."[6] At the benign end of the spectrum, sharecroppers developed a wide range of customary privileges, made verbal rather than written contracts, and were not interfered with in either their husbandry or tenure as long as they delivered the agreed share of their produce. For example, in 1847, the colonial secretary noted as established customs some of the privileges for which Pompey and his followers had rebelled in 1830. By custom it had become a rule to give six months' notice to the tenant to quit possession. A tenant who paid rent in kind or gave two days' labor in lieu of rent had become entitled to remain until he had reaped all the growing crops planted with the landlord's permission. And in 1882, Governor Blake inadvertently recorded another carryover from slavery days when he observed that cultivators considered that the corn crops alone ought to be shared with the landowner because all ground provisions were properly the property of the cultivator.[7]

In the more productive islands, particularly where a landless population pressed against finite resources of fertile land, and as a peripheral effect of the worldwide intensification of the capitalist economy, absentee landlords were able to exact progressively harsher terms from their sharecropping tenants. Even in San Salvador, where in 1840 it was stated that the working class was not willing to work on shares because they could farm for themselves as squatters, at least one "improving" landlord in the 1860s was able to enforce written contracts on sharecropping tenants. This was Alexander Forsyth, who took over the Farquharson Estate at a time when raising stock animals for the Nassau market was unprofitable because of competition from Cuba and some of the best lands in the island were being encroached upon by squatters and ruined by improvident slash-and-burn farming methods.[8]

The only chance of a profit from the estate was a more efficient form of agriculture, which Forsyth sought to achieve by appointing under contract a resident manager named Jacob Deveaux Sr. and having each of the tenants sign a binding sharecropping contract outlining his duties and rights. By this agreement, enforced by penalties of £2 for nonobservance on either side and renewable each year "by mutual consent of both parties," the tenant was to deliver to the management at appropriate times in the year one-third of all products of the soil without exception, including "corn, sugar cane, plantains, yams, cassava, beans, peas, pumpkins, melons and groundnuts." In a clause remarkably echoing that imposed by

The Bahamian pineapple industry, as illustrated in *Frank Leslie's Illustrated Newspaper*, 1879. *Above*, white owners and manager survey a field adjacent to Lake Killarney, New Providence. *Below*, Bahamian workers canning fruit for export to the United States or England. From *Frank Leslie's Illustrated Newspaper*, June 21, 1879, courtesy of Bahamas Archives.

William Wylly on his slaves half a century before, the tenants signed an addendum allowing them to keep just one sow and its offspring. Those wishing to keep a larger number of hogs were bound to deliver one pig from each litter to the landowner in lieu of rent. Each tenant also promised to be "honest, faithful and careful" of the landowner's interest by not burning standing woods prematurely or abandoning fields to weeds before their soil was exhausted and by obeying all lawful orders given them by Jacob Deveaux, the resident manager, as to where they could and could not farm. Deveaux's own contract stipulated that in return for "directing and controlling the tenants" he would be allowed to keep a quarter of the crops collected and have "the use for cultivation free of all Shares and Rent Three Acres or twelve tasks" of the land he managed.[9]

Alexander Forsyth's system was parasitical in that he obtained an agricultural income from land otherwise worthless to him without having to pay wages. But it was a comparatively mild form of exploitation because it was more or less voluntary and had some reciprocal benefits. At least it gave the sharecroppers legal access to some of the most fertile tracts of the island at the price of a third of their labor. A far more oppressive form of sharecropping was found in Eleuthera once the intensification of the pineapple industry toward monoculture enriched and entrenched the absentee merchant-landlord class. The best pineapple lands were consolidated into tighter and more impersonal ownership (including partnerships and limited companies), while the main commodity (as in the sugar islands) was grown to the exclusion of less profitable provision crops. The sharecroppers were increasingly dependent on the purchase of provisions through the sale of pineapples in a retail and export market controlled, as far as they were concerned, by their own merchant-landlords. Quite apart from the cost of shipping the fruit, the risks of spoilage and fluctuating foreign markets, and the delays in final payments (burdens all passed down to the growers), there was an eighteen-month delay between the planting and harvesting of the crop. As a cumulative result, the sharecroppers increasingly had to rely on advances cannily offered by their merchant-landlords. These were sometimes in cash at high rates of interest but more often in the form of provisions, clothing, tools, fertilizer, or seedlings at inflated prices, on highly disadvantageous credit terms. The least fortunate sharecroppers fell into a descending spiral of debt and dependency approaching destitution.[10]

Sharecroppers sought to escape their bondage whenever they could by shipping and selling their produce independently, seeking extra income at sea by fishing and wrecking, looking for alternative employment during bonanza periods such as the early 1860s, signing up as laborers outside the colony, or migrating with their families. Migration within the Bahamas, though, either from the Out Islands to Nassau or from one island to another, was rarely a permanent solution, for the system of advances, credit, and payment with truck goods rather than true wages permeated almost all forms of Bahamian employment and involved all sections of the laboring population. Like sharecropping, this method of ensuring an impoverished and therefore dependent labor force had its roots in slavery days, was exacerbated by labor competition, economic slumps, and the shortage of cash in circulation after emancipation, and reached its nadir as the most exploitative elements in the local capitalist class tightened their grip in the last quarter of the nineteenth century.

The Truck System: Origins and Development

Governor James Carmichael Smyth noticed that embryonic forms of the truck system were well established by 1832. "It has long been the custom in this Colony," he wrote to the Colonial Office in August 1832, "to permit the more intelligent of the Slaves, and more particularly Artificers, to find employment for themselves & to pay to their owners either the whole or such a proportion of what they may gain as may be agreed between the Parties. Almost any slave is anxious to enjoy this Species of Liberty and will readily promise and undertake to pay more than, at times, he may be able to acquire. Many of them have a sort of Account Current with their Owners, and in hopes of better times get deeper into debt every month."[11] Howard Johnson suggests that this system originated, or at least was made more oppressive, by the methods used for paying the apprenticed liberated Africans who arrived in the Bahamas as early as 1811. Not only was the imperial government so eager to find local employment for these displaced persons that controls against exploitation were very weak, but the very presence of the liberated Africans represented a competitive superfluity in the wage labor force that was extremely advantageous to local employers.

Howard Johnson cogently describes the three main methods of employing liberated Africans used by their licensed employers—all of them militating against the receipt or retention of cash wages by the apprentices, substituting food and clothing costed on the masters' terms. First were apprentices who were hired out by their employers to other persons. The wages received went to the employers, who provided the apprentices with the same clothing and provisions prescribed by law for slaves, plus a maximum cash payment of two shillings (currency) per week. Second were apprentices allowed to hire themselves out, who were obliged to pay their primary employers a specified sum each month and to pay for their own food and clothing as well. Finally, apprentices employed directly by their primary employer usually received no more clothes and provisions than slaves similarly employed and often no cash wages in addition.[12]

The oppressiveness of this system was illustrated by the example of three liberated Africans employed by the Lightbourne family, cited by the scrupulous Governor Lewis Grant in 1827. Two of the African apprentices had first been employed in agriculture and the third in raking salt in the Turks Islands, but all three had been transferred to cutting hardwoods for ships' timbers and quarrying stone, the most arduous of Bahamian laboring tasks. The Lightbournes received $2.50 a week for the hire of each apprentice but in return provided them with no more than eight quarts of corn a week, two suits of osnaburghs a year, and a weekly cash payment of twenty-five cents apiece. The average weekly cost to the Lightbournes was probably one day's earnings.[13] Neither Governor Grant's revelations nor the operations of the African Board (whose duties to protect the interests of the liberated Africans were overridden by the need to find them employment) managed to mitigate the liberated Africans' terms of employment. In June 1837, for example, it was at last decreed that at least part of their wages had to be paid in cash, but only a month later this order was rescinded in the case of Out Island apprentices in response to representations from employers.[14] The liberated Africans therefore entered the era of "full freedom" in 1838 tied, just like the former slave apprentices, to a system that was not only one of free labor competition but traditionally geared to the payment of wages in truck, not cash.

That they could expect no other conditions should have been obvious from the similar hold the Nassau merchant class had over the poor whites of the northern islands. Governor Carmichael Smyth wrote as early as 1832 that few of the white Abaconian fishermen could read and write and they scraped a meager living from turtling and wrecking. Of necessity, they exchanged their turtles and wreck goods in Nassau on credit for flour, other essential supplies, and "the few comforts which they possess." Consequently, they were entirely dependent and "under the influence and guidance" of the "shopkeepers and vendue masters" in the colonial capital.[15] From this economic dependency directly sprang political power. Four years later, in writing of the general election of 1834, the last before emancipation, Governor William Colebrooke described how the Nassau merchants took advantage of the fact that they alone could afford the time and money to stand for the Assembly. Some of them bought their way into seats for "thinly populated districts where but few Electors could attend" the elections, despite being virtually unknown to their constituents. "In closer communities, a commercial interest had grown up by the dependence of the poor classes on the Merchants for their necessary supplies, and the debts they had thus generally contracted."[16]

After emancipation, such a system of bribery-patronage and dependency was easily adapted to a widened electorate, with the only modification being that the poor white voters became more obviously the political, if not true class, allies of the agrocommercial bourgeoisie. Though instances of exploitative wage labor and dependence on advances lingered on in the poor white communities to the end of the nineteenth century—in shipbuilding, wrecking, and fishing—the poorest whites always found it easier to obtain minor government employment, to borrow money, to be self-employed, and to avoid wage labor than did the black majority.[17] Their consequent (if scarcely conscious) status as a petty bourgeoisie, as much as their growing sense of racial superiority, thus gave them an identification with the interests of the ruling class.

In contrast, the black wage laborers in the salt, sponge, sisal, and pineapple industries must have felt themselves in an ever-tightening socioeconomic vice. Of these industries, salt production had been the longest established and had a reputation for labor conditions that were relatively harsh and exploitative even in slavery days. For this reason, some commentators feared that the wages the leaseholders of salt pans would have to pay to attract free laborers after slavery ended would wipe out all profits from salt production.[18] Yet in fact the employers were brilliantly able to manipulate the transition out of slavery and apprenticeship and the mechanics of the truck system to avoid actually having to pay cash wages. In 1840, after a tour of the chief salt islands, Governor Francis Cockburn reported how both shares and truck were imposed on laborers who were nearly all liberated Africans, providing them with a level of subsistence only marginally higher than in slavery days. Some of them paid rent for land in the form of labor to the landowner almost like medieval serfs, while the remainder were meagerly recompensed for their labor with eight quarts of Indian corn, two pounds of salt fish or meat, and two cups of molasses or sugar a week, two dollars a month as wages, three suits of rough clothing a year, and rudimentary medical care when sick.[19] Reports later in the

1840s described how such major employers as Wade Stubbs (formerly one of the largest slave owners) allowed his laborers a share of the salt they produced but then, being the only shipper and a retail merchant too, bought it back from them, not for cash but for "articles of the lowest quality . . . charged at the highest prices." Virtually every leaseholder was said to be a "shopkeeper" and every laborer to have to pay "weekly 100 per Cent. on the prime cost in the US of America for the necessaries of life."[20]

Some of the most notorious examples of exploitation in the salt industry ceased to concern the Bahamian authorities when the Turks and Caicos Islands were separated from the Bahamas and placed under the control of Jamaica in 1848. But as long as salt remained a profitable commodity, Bahamian merchants were eager to develop substitute salt islands of their own, sustained by the most exploitative conditions of employment possible. The island of Inagua, with an ideal hot dry climate, ten times the size of Grand Turk yet without a resident farming population, indeed, had even greater potential than the older salt islands. In March 1849, Timothy Darling and five other prominent Nassauvians formed the Heneagua Salt Pond Company with capital of £10,000 sterling. In 1865 it was reconstituted as the Inagua Tramway and Salt Company, proud possessor of the colony's first (and only nineteenth-century) railroad. Black migrant workers and merchants alike settled in the new township named after Governor Mathew, particularly after Inagua became a stopping point for steamers to pick up stevedores before entering the Windward Passage. By 1880, Mathew Town, with a population of more than a thousand and at least a dozen shopkeepers calling themselves steamship agents, commission merchants, importers, and retail dealers, could claim to be the second township in the Bahamas.[21]

The combination of a large transient laboring population who lacked the option of subsistence farming and a mercantile section that consisted of employment agents if not actual employers, however, meant that Mathew Town was an artificial and brittle community that experienced the Bahamian truck system in almost its extreme form. This situation was revealed by a former government employee, Louis N. Duty, in two letters to the *Nassau Guardian* in 1889. "During the period of my official life there the Truck System was in full sway and I have a lively remembrance of the *modus operandi,* having been personally present on numerous occasions on pay day in the office of the greatest Salt Rakers and Merchants," he wrote, "and the only kind of payment I ever saw made to the large number of labourers, male and female, employed in that establishment was by paper orders stamped with the employer's name, and which orders could only be exchanged at his stores for the necessaries of life, spiritous liquors and tobacco. I have heard stalwart men on more than one occasion plead in the most earnest and abject terms for only one shilling in cash from the week's labour, and in some instances the plea was granted, not as a right but as a great favour." According to Duty, the Inagua saltraker-merchants marked up the lowest-quality goods to the price of the best in Nassau and pressed their employees to take goods on credit as an advance on wages. By such means they were always able to demand the employees' labor on their own terms, a system that was "but a modified form of slavery."[22]

Louis Duty's attack on the operation of the truck system in the salt industry was overshadowed by an indictment of similar practices that dominated the sponge fishing industry made by a former magistrate, Louis Diston Powles, in a book called *Land of the Pink Pearl,* published in 1888.[23] Sponges from the Great Bahama Bank had first been processed and exported in 1841 and were soon seen not only to be comparable to the best from the Mediterranean but so plentiful as to command a new mass market. In the late 1850s, the average annual export was a quarter million pounds, but with the opening of the Little Bahama Bank, the shallows southwest of Eleuthera, and Acklins Bight, exports rose to 625,000 pounds a year by 1870 and a million pounds by 1900, worth £100,000. At its peak in 1901, the industry was said to employ 5,967 men and boys fishing from 265 schooners, 322 sloops, and 2,808 open boats.[24]

The intensification of the industry was fueled both by a world demand for cheaper sponges and by local conditions. From the beginning, the outfitting of boats, employment of fishermen, and purchasing, processing, and export of sponges were all controlled by Nassau merchants. Not only did these men become progressively more efficient and ruthless, but they were aided and augmented after the 1870s by the arrival of expert spongers from the Greek Aegean Islands. Though they had been mainly poor fishermen in their native islands, they found such a reservoir of impoverished black mariners that they quickly took advantage of their color, their expertise, and their family connections in outside markets to graduate into the role of middlemen: overseers at the sorting, clipping, and baling sheds, auctioneers and valuers, wholesale buyers, and consignment agents. In contrast to the Greeks' upward mobility, the black fishermen suffered not only from racial prejudice and their own lack of education but also from the increasing competition among themselves which resulted from the decline of the wrecking industry—itself the result of the increase of steam navigation and the setting up of lighthouses and beacons by the Imperial Lighthouse Service after 1860.[25]

Since a sponging voyage normally took from six to eight weeks, the fishermen were willing candidates for advances from their employers, paid more often in truck goods than in cash and credited against the proceeds of the voyage. Even had the returns been sufficient to free the mariners from an almost permanent cycle of debt, the payment of advances mainly in flour and other foodstuffs tempted the improvident to neglect farming while ashore and thus increased their dependence on the sponging trade. The most obnoxious feature of the fishermen's exploitation in the early 1880s, though, was the final payment for the delivered sponges, which was not only rigged but secret. "After the sale of the cargo," wrote Governor Blake, "the total amount of which was not made known to the men, they were paid off in the merchant's office each man receiving generally but a few shillings, which, he was informed represented the balance due to him after the payment of the vessels outfit, the amount of which he did not know, and of his private debt, of the items of which he knew nothing."[26]

The fishermen's only recourse was to sell their sponges directly to the foreign buyers whose agents frequented the sponging grounds, despite prohibitions by the outfitters to whom they were indebted. The Assembly moved to stamp out this practice in an 1886 act ostensibly aimed at protecting all those involved in the sponging industry. The payment of the crews' shares in truck goods was forbidden, and some limits were placed on cash advances. The amount an outfitter could retain from a fisherman's final share was officially limited, and a fisherman could request a copy of the accounts of sponges sold and of the division of the proceeds. The chief provision of the act, however, was the requirement that sponges gathered

A glamorized view of human exploitation. The Bahamian sponge industry, as pictured in *Frank Leslie's Illustrated Newspaper*, 1878. From *Frank Leslie's Illustrated Newspaper*, June 20, 1878, courtesy of Bahamas Archives.

by crews outfitted by Nassau merchants could be sold only through the Nassau Sponge Exchange. The disposal of sponges otherwise could be treated as larceny.[27]

As Powles pointed out, the 1886 act did no more than concentrate the trade and entrench the power of the Nassau merchant cartel. Far from the system of advances being outlawed, the limits on cash advances actually aided the outfitters, who continued to provide truck goods of indifferent quality at inflated prices. Even if the most illiterate fishermen could understand the accounts provided, excessive charges for outfitting vessels and the fixing of the prices paid for delivered sponges continued. Moreover, quite apart from the inability of legislation to prevent the fishermen from running up debts not directly covered by each voyager's contract, even the limit on what the outfitter could retain from the fisherman's share at the end of the voyage was removed.[28]

The plight of the Bahamian sponge (and turtle) fishermen memorably described by Powles in 1888 continued well into the twentieth century. "Let us follow the career of one of these unfortunates from its commencement," he wrote.

> He applies to the owner of a craft engaged in the sponge or turtle fisheries, generally in the two combined, to go on a fishing voyage. He is not to be paid by wages, but to receive a share of the profits of the take, thus being theoretically in partnership with his owner. At once comes into play the infernal machine, which grinds him down and keeps him a slave for years and years—often for life. His employer invariably keeps, or is in private partnership with someone who keeps, a store, which exists principally for the purpose of robbing employés, and is stocked with the offscourings of the American market—rubbish unsaleable anywhere else. As soon as a man engages he has to sign seaman's articles, which render him liable to be sent on board his vessel at any time by order of a magistrate. He is then invited, and practically forced, to take an advance upon his anticipated share of the profits. . . . These advances, I need hardly say, are generally made in kind, consisting of flour, sugar, tobacco, articles of clothing, or some other portion of the rubbish that constitutes the employer's stock-in-trade. Probably the fisherman does not want the goods, or, at any rate, he wants money more to leave with his family; and in order to get it he sells the goods at about half the price at which they are charged to him.[29]

One unfortunate sponge fisherman, Sam Gowan, told Powles of a voyage on which he and his shipmates fished, cleaned, and dried 900 strings of nine sponges, 8,100 in total, which altogether realized only £11 at the Nassau Sponge Exchange, an average of about a half-penny each for sponges that could command from sixpence to five shillings apiece in London. The short-lived radical newspaper the *Freeman* estimated in 1889 that the sixty or so Bahamian sponge "outfitters" averaged profits of £400 a year, while the return for each of the fishermen was no more than £9.[30]

The oppressions of the Bahamian sponge industry exemplified the ways the capitalist few (and, to a certain extent, metropolitan consumers) benefited at the expense of the proletarian many in the colonies during the heyday of laissez-faire imperialism. Another equally skewed enterprise (giving rise to even greater hypocrisy) was the Bahamian sisal industry, which was briefly in vogue between 1890 and 1920.

The sisal plant (*agave rigida sisilana*), which seemed suited to the climate and sparse soils of the Bahamas, was introduced by the colonial secretary C. R. Nesbitt in 1845. But it was not until the governorship of the "progressive" Sir Ambrose Shea (1887–94) that sisal and hemp production was strongly promoted to take advantage of seemingly ever-rising world demand. Shea and others argued that as long as processing and export were efficiently organized, sisal might well be a new peasant crop, returning impoverished Bahamian mariners to the land, and for this reason, Crown land ought to be made cheaply available to willing small farmers. In fact, it was obvious to the promoters that sisal could be profitably grown only by substantial capitalists controlling their own factories as well as large areas of land and that the chief advantage of encouraging black Out Islanders to grow their own small crops of sisal was to tie them to the land as semipeasant wage earners. Sisal grown by smallholders, moreover, could be processed only in factories owned by their wage employers and sold either to the factories or, after the deduction of processing charges, to Nassau exporters. The proposal was thus merely a variant of the exploitative cane-farming system prevalent in all sugar islands once central factories had become established.[31]

At Governor Shea's urging, Crown lands were offered to "poor settlers" in ten-acre lots at five shillings an acre; the land would become freehold property if it was developed in sisal within ten years. In contrast, huge acreages were leased on extremely generous terms to companies and individual investors, including the secretary of state for the colonies, Joseph Chamberlain, whose son Neville, the future prime minister, managed the twenty-thousand-acre family estate in Andros for several years.[32]

As Neville Chamberlain's experiences in Andros showed, sisal became a losing prospect for large as well as small producers, though, as always, the worker suffered more than the owner. The disruption of production in Cuba and the Philippines as a result of the Spanish-American War and short-term demands down to the end of the Boer War led to a profitable spurt in the world price of hemp. But the American takeover and revitalization of the Cuban and Philippine industries led to a slump, followed by a steady slide ever farther below profitable levels. At the best of times, most sisal workers relied almost completely on wage employment, and very few chanced growing sisal for themselves. Even then, wages were commonly paid in credit tokens, redeemable at company stores, rather than in cash. And when the market declined, levels of payment were cut back, more and more workers became indebted to their employers, and it was no longer worthwhile for even the most industrious small producer to grow sisal. Virtually no sisal workers became small freeholders under the terms of Governor Shea's allotment scheme, and the miserable conditions under which those who could not escape were forced to live matched those of the sponge fishermen described by Powles.

An even neater and more melancholy example of the ways in which the worldwide capitalist intensification at the turn of the twentieth century (led by the United States) squeezed the colonial proletarian ever tighter occurred in the Bahamian pineapple industry. The capitalist monopoly of land, distribution, and finance led from the share system to ever more oppressive systems of advances, credit, and truck. This process was speeded as competition from American producers enforced economies of scale following the acquisition and development of Hawaii and the passage of the protectionist McKinley Tariff of 1897, almost throttling the export of fresh Bahamian pineapples.

The Bahamian pineapple magnates had one remaining card to play, the seemingly progressive move of setting up factories to process, preserve, and can the fruit for a wider and longer-term market. The pioneer in this field was J. S. Johnson, MHA, who formed a company and set up a canning factory in Nassau in 1876. By 1900, the factory and its branch plants in Eleuthera were processing as many as seventy-five thousand cases of canned pineapples in a season.[33] Significantly, however, the most important factory development in the Bahamas up to that time also saw the most extreme example of exploitation of workers. At the Johnson factory at Governor's Harbour, all wages were paid in the form of tokens, which could be exchanged for goods, initially at all local stores but eventually only at the company store during the canning season. "For the last few years the Factory checks and cheques on the Nassau Bank [were] the only money [that] could be seen in circulation," wrote "Eye Witness" in a letter to the *Nassau Guardian* in 1906. "In fact the Factory Tin Checks were used all the year round until this year when the Proprietors sent around to all the stores a notice stating that they would not redeem them and forbidding any store to take them. This caused quite a disturbance when it was found out that the Pineapple Factory had built a large store and had imported a very large stock, and forced the labourers to spend their tin checks as they refused to settle with them until the Factory closed."[34]

Salt laborers, sponge fishermen, sisal farmers, and pineapple workers all suffered from various forms of exploitation. But as Howard Johnson shows, even those who sought employment outside the Bahamas did not easily escape similar impositions. The earliest steamships calling at Long Cay and Inagua to pick up stevedores paid their employees entirely in cash. But some time after 1880, once the supply of eager laborers exceeded the demand and local agents and merchants had begun to shape the system to their own advantage, payment in truck goods became the rule. "A great deal of discontent has prevailed owing to the 'truck' system," reported the resident magistrate at Long Cay in 1897, "the labourers asserting that the balances due to them on the termination of their voyages are not paid them in cash, and that they are compelled to wait for long periods before obtaining a settlement."[35]

At Inagua, even the laborers signing on with American and German companies as stevedores at the Haitian and Cuban ports and as short-term mahogany and plantation workers in Central America, iron miners in Cuba, and railroad and canal diggers in Panama and Mexico were entrapped by the local merchants and agents. Ostensibly, the agent received only a dollar in commission for each recruit, from which he had to pay all the local expenses of recruitment. His real profit came from the store he owned and through the operation of the credit and truck system. The standard practice was for laborers to be paid one-half of their wages in cash in the country where they were employed and the other half in Inagua on their return. The local merchant-agent had at least three ways of taking the lion's share of the laborer's wages. Laborers were signed up long before the arrival of their transportation and encouraged to take advances of food and drink while they waited. While they were away, the merchants provided for their families with provisions on credit at extortionate rates, charging extra if food and goods had to be sent to families on other islands. Finally, the agents often delayed settling laborers' accounts so that they ran up further debts. In one case, a laborer's debt with a Mathew Town merchant reached £40—considerably more than he could expect to earn by a year's hard labor overseas.[36]

White Law and Black Custom: Bahamian Land Tenures

Commentators on the transition out of formal slavery in the Caribbean, most notably Nigel Bolland in a powerful series of articles beginning in 1981, have argued that the control of land resources by the former slave owners drove the former slaves and later black immigrants into a peasant-proletarian form of subordination. As Howard Johnson has pointed out in contrast, however, the Bahamian case is more complex, if not completely different.[37] The official system of land tenure and transmission, which allowed the agrocommercial bourgeoisie to preempt and monopolize the best lands and resources, clearly gave that class a great advantage. Yet a complete monopoly was not necessary to create an impoverished and dependent wage labor force sufficient for the limited and fitful needs of Bahamian capitalist enterprises. This could be achieved quite satisfactorily by dominance in all branches of trade, in boatbuilding and boat ownership, and, above all, by the ability to exploit the great disparity between the ordinary Bahamian's need for wages and the shortage of cash in circulation.

The customary system of land tenure and transmission that emerged out of slavery greatly modified the picture of unmitigated exploitation. Although it may be argued that the occupation and usage of lands without commercial potential by black Bahamians who were surplus to the labor needs of the capitalist economy was advantageous to the capitalists, it seems more plausible that the customary systems of squatters' tenure, commonage, and "generation" property provided the black majority of Bahamians with a basic, supplementary, and alternative lifestyle, saving them from complete dominance by the Bay Street whites.

To a degree, the ordinary people were also helped by the theory and practice that all land initially and basically belonged to the Crown, could not easily be converted into absolute freehold, and was certainly not to be monopolized by bourgeois individualists. These principles emerged from the Middle Ages, when absolute and permanent ownership of land was invested in a monarchy, a hereditary line of kings, whose power was originally established through conquest or "surrender and regrant," recognized by a renewable act of personal submission (later commuted into nominal rent), and delimited by the effective radius of their legal writ. The reciprocal advantages of this "feudal contract"—particularly the practices that allowed faithful "tenants-in-chief" to become hereditary landowners and their younger sons to acquire land under similar terms outside traditional boundaries—led to the creation of ever-larger states and, eventually, overseas empires. The Crown long retained the tradition of absolute sovereignty, maintaining that all land was essentially Crown land as long as it could, remaining through its monopoly of the legal system the ultimate authority for all tenures and rarely and reluctantly alienating land altogether.

Against this basic system, however, as centuries of relative stability led to commercial expansion and the emergence of a bourgeois class (planters as well as merchants), a demand for freehold property developed and extended into the ownership of land as part of the crucial growth of "possessive individualism" of which C. B. McPherson writes.[38] The dissemination of freehold tenures, strictly speaking, was an invasion of the royal prerogative, though at the same time part of that partnership between bourgeois individualism and royal authority that made modern states and empires possible. It also required a complex, evolving structure of conveyance, inheritance, survey, and registration. It was no coincidence that the profession of lawyer changed from being part of the royal bureaucracy to one of the most bourgeois (and thus acquisitive) of avocations.

Such trends and tensions were clearly delineated in the development of the Bahamas up to the nineteenth century. Almost more than any other British colony, the Bahamas began with a quasi-feudal system of tenures. The archipelago was claimed by King Charles I by right of conquest or first effective Christian settlement.[39] The abortive grant to Sir Robert Heath in 1629 specified that the islands were to be held after the manner of the County Palatine of Durham "in free and common socage," while the marginally more effective charter given to six of the eight proprietors of the Carolinas in 1670 specified that lands be held in the form of socage customary "in our manor of East Greenwich in the County of Kent."[40] This meant in effect that the proprietors, as tenants in chief of the king, could grant acreages as large as they wished to any individuals, provided that the holders paid an annual quitrent—usually less than a penny an acre. The land could be escheated (that is, returned to the Crown) if not developed or if the quitrents were not paid. But if developed, it would be regarded as virtually freehold property and could be transmitted to family heirs, bequeathed to others, or even sold as long as the annual quitrents continued to be paid.[41]

From the beginning, the Bahamian system was not so simple. The very first settlers came during the republican interregnum, drawn partly by promises of unencumbered freehold land that combined the shareholder concessions found in Bermuda and the "headright" grants common throughout the mainland colonies.[42] Thus even before the Bahamas were granted to the proprietors in 1670 there were settlers who regarded themselves as having absolute property not just in their house lots in the settlements (an analogue of the "burgage" tenures in New England towns) but over the farming land needed for their households for subsistence as well. Since the Articles of the Eleutherian Adventurers specified that farmland be worked in common for the first three years or more, there may also have been the germ of the idea that all adjacent farmland was for common use, which for the Harbour Islanders at least became a legal reality between 1783 and 1842.[43] The proprietors attempted to augment their revenue by asserting their rights to quitrents from established settlers and by attracting new settlers with generous grants of quitrent land. These moves, however, were doomed to failure by the immigration of the pirates, who condemned New Providence to anarchy, isolated the settlements of northern Eleuthera, and made the rest of the Bahamas extremely insecure for potential settlers.

Order, if not prosperity, was restored when the Crown assumed political control in 1718, though by a curious compromise the proprietors retained the right to collect quitrents until 1787.[44] Significantly, one of the first acts passed after the creation of the Assembly in 1729 was aimed at settling claims on land, especially (in what may have been the majority of cases) where "never laid out, since deserted, never surveyed or titles and patents lost." In the absence of a valid counterclaim, those who could prove possession for a mere three years, with improvements made, were promised clear title, "confirmed to them and their heirs for ever, any law, usage or custom to the contrary notwithstanding," subject only to the payment of an annual quitrent of three shillings to the lord proprietor.[45] An even more vital enactment was the Registry Act of 1764, which required that deeds or conveyances of all "lands, tenements or hereditaments, negroes, vessels, goods or effects" be registered to prevent the confusion and frauds that had followed a rapid turnover of lands and mortgages and "many evil minded persons" taking advantage of "bad and insufficient titles and securities."[46]

The condition of tenures and titles, though, remained confused until the coming of the Loyalists. The purchase of land by the Crown between 1784 and 1786, the final buying out of the proprietors in 1787, and the passing of another act to establish the validity of land claims in 1789[47] were necessary parts of the process whereby the British government compensated the Loyalists with grants of land—up to one hundred thousand acres in all. These land grants were free of initial charges and of quitrents for the first ten years, but the Crown had no intention of giving up the principle that these were conditional tenures, dependent on the development of the land. A comprehensive Quit Rent Act was passed in 1802, calling for the surrender and regranting of all lands allocated by the Crown since 1787, subjecting them to the payment of annual quitrents of five shillings for each town lot and two shillings for every one hundred acres of developed land.[48] Theoretically at least, lands were to be escheated either for nonpayment or for nondevelopment. Even more important, a new Registration Act in 1805 decreed that not only were all deeds and conveyances to be registered, but registered documents had priority over all others, even those of an earlier date.[49] The only other significant changes in official tenure policy before emancipation were the evolution of different forms of lease for salina, farming, and building land and the distinction between public land, leased by the Crown to the local government for public purposes, and true Crown land.[50]

The process of emancipation, when the black majority of the Bahamian population instantly changed from being property to owning it, though, was a crucial watershed in Bahamian landholding for the imperial government as well as the former masters and slaves. The basic principles finally established between 1787 and 1805—that all unalienated land belonged to the Crown, that Crown grants were not easily to be converted into absolute freehold, and that no land tenures, including freeholds, were secure without duly registered title—came under pressure from at least three groups, whose interests were different and in many respects conflicting. Liberal elements in the imperial government felt at least an intermittent concern that the property rights of the newly freed be protected, even that the former slaves and the liberated Africans be encouraged to become peasant smallholders. Such intentions, however, were weakened by the spread of laissez-faire principles and threatened by the influential ideas of Edward Gibbon Wakefield that Crown land should be disposed of only at a price sufficient to attract those with capital, leaving those without capital as a reservoir of landless agricultural labor.[51] The Bahamian agrocommercial bourgeoisie argued for an even cruder allocation of land in their favor, largely because they were relatively short of other forms of capital and unable or unwilling to pay wages to a large labor force. The black majority wished to have the free use of all undeveloped lands, following customary systems of tenure and transmission along family and communal lines, without much concern for formal title.

The resettlement schemes promoted for certain newly arrived and time-expired apprentice liberated Africans after 1825 (considered in detail in Chapter 1) might have been a useful model for the Bahamas government after 1838. Faced by the socioeconomic uncertainties of slave emancipation, however, the Bahamian ruling class opposed similar generosity toward the ten thousand former slaves and the few liberated Africans not yet freed from their indentures or already settled. The Colonial Office gave permission to sell Crown land for as little as £1 an acre in 1836, but in the Bahamas tracts were generally only released for sale by auction (with £1 thus the "upset" or minimum price), and in 1839 the minimum size of lots was restricted to forty acres. Although the size and price of lots were later reduced to twenty acres at twelve shillings an acre, even this was beyond the means of most former slaves or liberated Africans, especially in the Out Islands.[52]

A typical situation was revealed in a dispatch from Watling's Island sent by Stipendiary Magistrate William Heild to Acting Governor Charles Nesbitt in June 1842. Heild reported that some fourteen half-acre house lots in Cockburn Town had been sold three years earlier ostensibly for £5 each. Not only had this money remained unpaid, but the ninety-two inhabitants of Cockburn Town had encroached on the two hundred acres of Crown land adjacent, which they worked in common. Despite their lack of title, they tended to refer to the other islanders who still worked for white proprietors as "slaves." Heild recognized that the half-acre lots were insufficient to support the families living on them and that without access to more land the people would be forced to "trespass, steal or starve," but he gave his opinion that if the squatters were not evicted, the remaining "peasantry" would be encouraged to leave their employment or sharecropping tenures to settle unclaimed lands on Watling's or other islands.[53]

In reporting to London the following month, Acting Governor Nesbitt complained of the problems of resettling the former slaves and liberated Africans and disposing of Crown lands. He pointed out that much of the land in the settled islands was privately owned but that the proprietors cultivated very little of it and never offered continuous employment for money wages. In many islands even the best private holdings were of such limited fertility that sharecroppers could barely make a living. Nesbitt argued that the blacks could best survive if allowed to form their own small communities and given enough land to support themselves by peasant farming. Nearly all former slaves and liberated Africans seemed to desire land and such a lifestyle, but the method of land allocation and sale was not to their advantage. Nesbitt therefore recommended that Crown land be made more readily available, paid for in installments with long-term credit. Failure to help in this way would lead to an increase in "depredation, vagrancy and even mass emigration."[54]

Nesbitt's advice went unheeded. Even the Commutation Act of 1846, which ended the quitrent system—the most significant change in official tenure policy between emancipation and the twentieth century—was "liberal" only in serving as an economy move, benefiting the large landowners far more than the newly emancipated and the Crown most of all. The collection of quitrents had fallen hopelessly in arrears, and the cost of administering the system had long exceeded the income from it. The 1846 act allowed for the conversion of quitrent tenures for house lots and lands into absolute freehold on the payment of arrears dating back up to sixteen years. This undoubtedly increased the number of freeholds, especially in New Providence and the other older settlements. Yet since the act required payment within three months and the production of valid documentation, the net effect was a very large increase in official Crown land through default in all the most recently settled islands and the weakening of tenure wherever ownership had been, or become, obscure.[55]

The only formal scheme to settle former slaves (as well as liberated Africans) was a semiphilanthropic private venture at Fox Hill, New Providence, three miles east of Nassau. There in 1840, Judge Sandilands subdivided his estate into one hundred lots of one to ten acres for sale at modest prices, forming a village that was named after him in 1849.[56] The great majority of former slaves were left to fend for themselves, and those who spurned peasant subsistence farming and wished to live close to Nassau had particular difficulties. Some of them joined with liberated Africans (mainly Yoruba) in a settlement called Bain Town after its black developer, G. H. Bain.[57] But a far greater number crowded into Grant's Town, which for a century after 1850 was to contain more than half of Nassau's population. The price of house lots multiplied regularly; most were divided and divided again. A common pattern was for the original owners to become landlords, with tenants even moving their wooden houses from lot to lot.

Yet the gradual emergence of classes (or subclasses) did not Europeanize even the nearest of Nassau's black suburbs before the twentieth century. Many white visitors commented on the African appearance of Grant's Town, Bain Town, and the outlying villages and on the persistence of African customs. And beneath the exotic surface was a community structure that continued to owe more to African notions of family, kinship, property ownership, and inheritance than to the master culture and official legal system. These characteristics resulted not only from the presence of many native Africans who had never been enslaved but from the arrival of former slave migrants from the Out Islands, who from the mid-nineteenth century formed transplanted mini-communities owing more to island and family connections than to the new urban environment.

The conditions in New Providence applied with even greater force in the Out Islands, where the former slaves were proportionately even more cut off from the cultural and legal as well as socioeconomic influences of the colonial metropolis. Following the Commutation Act of 1846 and the greater attention paid to the surveying and registering of lands and deeds based on Wakefield's theories, there was a progressive increase in the number of officially registered titles and somewhat greater precision in the delimitation of private, public, and officially unalienated Crown lands. But though the value of legal title for at least a house lot became more apparent, this did not fix the method of conveyance in the European mold or determine that ordinary farmers would restrict themselves to areas over which they had strictly legal tenure.

Commonages, Generation Property, Squatting, and Sharecropping

One institution that emerged out of slavery, with roots chiefly in Africa (though owing something to medieval English practice), was the Bahamian system of common land. Even where former slave owners continued to hold legal title to the land—even still live on it—the former slave residents often developed a communal sense of attachment, belonging, that was quasi-proprietorial. This feeling was signified by the voluntary adoption by many former slaves of their previous owners' names and by the retention of the names of former estates (not infrequently named after the former owners) as the names of the subsequent settlements of free black peasant farmers. Once the former master's family left, or through generations of miscegenation folded into the majority (as seems to have happened in parts of mainland Eleuthera and Long Island), the land was regarded as belonging to the former community and its descendants, in custom if not in law. The title might have lapsed or been long forgotten or claimed by a colored descendant of the original owner, but it was almost invariably challenged by all family heads still living in the settlement.

The senses of community reinforced by actual or fictive kinship, of an attachment to a particular location amounting to a communal quasi-proprietorship, and of being what Sidney Mintz has termed proto-peasants rather than praedial slaves occurred even earlier, and with greater intensity, on the increasingly large number of Out Island plantations owned by absentees. Under the management of a poor white or even free colored overseer, these operations were initially concerned with extracting whatever profit could be made from cotton or salt. They therefore lacked the manorial ambience of, for example, Farquharson's Estate (described in Volume 1)[58] and were characterized by tensions between managers and slaves. The slaves' sense of community, though, was aided by their isolation, a common ethnicity, and ever-tightening kinship ties. Moreover, as the prospects of plantation profits faded, the slaves, though constrained to live within a regulated settlement and limited in their mobility by the boundaries of their owners' estate, were increasingly left on their own and encouraged to subsist for themselves by slash-and-burn agriculture and raising small stock. The result was the closest replication possible in the new environment of an African-style village-based peasantry.

The most outstanding and best-known case was that of the Rolle estates on the island of Great Exuma—the result of a combination of an exceptionally vigorous population and an accommodating (if not exactly liberal) absentee owner. Left almost on their own by 1834, Lord John Rolle's former slaves served a nominal apprenticeship, and when they were declared fully free on August 1, 1838, they took over Rolle's five tracts of Exuma and set up a well-regulated system of commonage based on the villages of Rolleville, Steventon, Mount Thompson, Ramsey's, and Rolletown, even though they had no formal deed of conveyance from their former owner.[59] More as a statement of community and a form of identity than as an expression of gratitude (let alone the result of massive miscegenation), they all took the surname Rolle. Thenceforward, in an absolute converse of the system of primogeniture upon which aristocratic European tenures depended, any person with the surname Rolle—by the twentieth century more than four thousand persons—or anyone who could prove descent from a Rolle on either male or female side—a veritable host—could theoretically claim house plot and subsistence allotment on the five thousand acres of Exumian common land.

Though less well studied, similar processes occurred in other Out Islands, with a range of results. Nearly everywhere, the former slaves tended to form villages based on the old plantation slave communities and to allocate farmland among themselves according to each family's needs. Such common-land practices were extremely informal in islands (such as Andros, Crooked Island, Acklins, Mayaguana, and Inagua) where the available land greatly exceeded the needs of the inhabitants and very little land was in private ownership. But there was a tendency toward more strictly regulated commonages either where a former owner (such as

Rolle) encouraged the practice or where (as at Cockburn Town, Watling's Island) the unappropriated land around an emergent village was hemmed in by estates still privately owned and managed. Such was most notably the case in Long Island, Eleuthera, and mainland Abaco, where private ownership remained the rule but sizable tracts of land regarded as for common use and regulated by the users were found adjacent to most former slave villages.

In Eleuthera, the development of the commonages around the mainland settlements of the Bluff, Savanna Sound, Tarpum Bay, and Rock Sound after emancipation were doubtless aided by the existence of common farming land on northern Eleuthera since the very first English settlements, though this original Bahamian commonage owed its origins to an entirely different legal tradition. Legend asserts that this two-thousand-acre tract was awarded to the inhabitants of Harbour Island for their assistance in the "recapture" of Nassau from the Spaniards by Andrew Deveaux in 1783, though in fact it had been worked by the "Brilanders" for a century or more and was not formally deeded until 1842.[60] Both the legal recognition of the Harbour Island commonage and its less formal usage since the days of the early settlers clearly stemmed from English rather than African origins: the common rights held by ordinary tenants in medieval manors over certain areas of woodland and grazing land, extended and entrenched by customary usage and protected through the accumulation of cases and precedents in the (coincidentally entitled) common law. This legal tradition eventually led to the general recognition and regulation of Bahamian commonages by the Commonage Act of 1896, which listed all authentic commonages whether established by law or customary usage, made general rules as to who was entitled to occupy and use the common land, and set up a machinery of management by the commoners' elected representatives.[61] The pragmatic origins of most of the Bahamian commonages in the needs of the village group, their empiric use by family units, and the leaders chosen to make local regulations, allocate lands, and arbitrate disputes, however, argue for their essential derivation from African roots.

Such a provenance, however, was by no means restricted to the limited areas of formal commonage. The predominant Out Island economy had become a shifting form of peasant farming that depended heavily on the family unit. But the interdependence of all family members—females as much as males—the need for a shifting and seemingly casual form of farming, the prevailing vagueness about other persons' titles and boundaries, and the general availability of unused land reinforced the African traditions that all land was for common use according to need, that land belonged equally to the user group, and that this informal tenure existed within the family from generation to generation. This was the genesis of the concept of generation property, which held that even where official title resided in a single family member, he or she held it in trust for the family at large, any member of which might be the actual user, and that even though wills might give priority to one descendant over another, all descendants retained a fundamental claim. Some wills and deeds actually specified this method of transmission, naming the immediate tenant but reserving the rights in the land to all descendants, even, in some cases, ones who were technically illegitimate.[62]

Generational land was often found in areas first developed and then deserted by Loyalist planters. Yet the loosest and most general of all generational customs were found, naturally, in those islands least developed before slavery ended. One such was Andros, scarcely touched by the Loyalists and, for the most part, first settled in the mid-nineteenth century by former slaves from nearby islands that had less free and unexhausted land, such as Exuma and Long Island. At Long Bay Cays in central Andros a century later Keith Otterbein found and analyzed the extreme form of generational tenure and transmission that could allow on one tract of land "not only the descendants of the ancestor, but also some of his sister's descendants, a niece of his son-in-law, and his grandson's mother-in-law." Otterbein termed this system "bilateral with unrestricted land-holding descent," in contrast to the more strictly "ambilineal" Jamaican system of family land described by Edith Clarke, or the more formal and self-regulating Barbadian system described by Sidney Greenfield. Otterbein attributed the difference mainly to the comparative abundance of land in Andros, the fact that many of the ancestors' direct descendants were off in Nassau or elsewhere and thus not eager to exercise their rights, and the greater sophistication of the Barbadians in adapting the English legal concept of entail.[63]

As in Jamaica and other West Indian colonies with large areas of vacant land, many former slaves and liberated Africans in the Bahamas became squatters. This trend was anticipated at least as early as 1834, when an act empowered JPs to order the summary ejection of unauthorized persons from private land on the plea of the titleholder, though at the same time an important principle was established by making an exception for squatters who had enjoyed uninterrupted possession for twenty years.[64] In 1839, just after the granting of "full freedom," the law was tightened to allow stipendiary magistrates to order the ejection of untitled settlers from any land, including Crown land, and to imprison at hard labor those who resisted the order. Again, though, the law was mitigated to except from immediate dispossession those who had enjoyed "quiet possession" for at least five years—that is, since before the first Emancipation Act of 1834.[65]

Forcible ejection of squatters, however, proved impracticable, especially from Crown lands, and the savage eviction process enacted in 1839 was amended within a year to except those who had enjoyed quiet possession for at least twelve months.[66] The Crown simply insured itself against "unlawful alienation" by decreeing that unauthorized settlers could gain title by "squatters' right" after sixty years of unchallenged occupation, rather than the twenty years for private land.[67] In practice, then, the former slaves and liberated Africans found it relatively easy to gather wood, run sheep or goats, farm, or even live on lands belonging to the Crown but never easy to gain title by squatters' right. Their access to free land by informal custom, moreover, was curtailed wherever landowners were able to enforce leasehold or sharecropping tenures or during periods when the government was willing, or able, to encourage development by foreign investors.

In sum, black Bahamian peasants operated most independently through a process of benign neglect. The system of loose and shifting tenures which the black peasants preferred, or found necessary, was feasible, however, only where there was an abundance of land not considered suitable for development by either government or the local agrocommercial bourgeoisie or where it was socially, politically, or economically convenient for the ruling class to allow such tenures or marginal lands as a subsistence buffer for a population only intermittently needed for labor on the more profitable tracts of land or in the few nonagricultural enterprises. Such conditions predominated in most islands for the first century after emancipation, and their remnants have lingered to the present day.

Throughout the 150 years since emancipation, however, Afro-Bahamian customary tenures, including commonage, have increasingly come under pressure or threat from at least three directions. Along with all territories in the region, an increasing population has pressed on finite and declining resources, while modernizing tendencies have both called for more efficient development of the land and inclined the black majority away from a rural life of mere subsistence.

The practices of rotational slash-and-burn agriculture and the overcropping of the meager surface vegetation by cattle, sheep, and goats hastened the process whereby the land became insufficient even for a steady population. The inefficient and undercapitalized subsistence farmers filled up or exhausted all vacant lands on their native islands, and the surplus population migrated to less exploited islands until they in turn were overfilled and (because of the simple and inefficient farming methods) overworked. Even without the resumption of lands by their titular owners or government campaigns against illegal squatters, the plight of subsistence farmers could become desperate, especially in the less fertile islands in times of drought or hurricane.

Competitive tension between agrocommercial entrepreneurs and peasants made the advantages of freehold over leasehold or loose customary tenures ever more apparent. But the chief benefit inevitably lay with those with the necessary capital and legal expertise to purchase and register freehold land, entrenched in the colonial capital, and possessing the means to adopt more efficient and larger-scale farming techniques against peasants who were virtually outside the money economy, often illiterate and ignorant of legal processes, almost immobilized on distant islands, and, above all, saddled to a form of agriculture that required them to roam rotationally over a large area for their subsistence.

Thus the majority of black Out Island farmers were committed to the practice of squatting and had almost no chance to convert their customary tenure into freehold, either by purchase or through squatter's right. In most islands they remained undisturbed until at least the third decade of the twentieth century, when sales to foreign investors and would-be settlers spurted and speculation in land revived. Even when customary tenants came under pressure, they were often saved from eviction by a complex and conflicting web of squatting and generational and commonage claims. The general trend, however—through the Commutation Act of 1846 and the reforms in the systems of registration and surveying in the late nineteenth century, down to the Quieting of Titles Act of 1959[68]—was inexorably in favor of formal tenures and was greatly accelerated once the black Out Islanders began to prefer the greater security and precision of registered freehold title, individual possession, and orderly inheritance over looser customary tenures.

Ironically, this final trend occurred not simply because developers and speculators were encroaching on the black Out Islanders' customary lands but because the rapidly expanding Out Island population was moving out of subsistence farming and wanted to develop or sell their patrimonial lands. Under the ambivalent pressure of such modernization, squatting satisfied neither the small farmer nor the large-scale developer, and generational tenures were seen as an impediment by both landholders and would-be buyers. Even the Bahamian commonages—the proudest achievement of the Afro-Bahamians after emancipation—came to seem a hindrance to progress rather than a hedge against exploitation. Not only were the commonage areas no longer adequate to support the increased population of commoners in the style they had come to expect from the modern world, but any chance of communal benefit through sale or lease to foreign investors was prohibited by the terms of the Commonage Act. The full realization of this dilemma was delayed until the mid-twentieth century, but by 1900 visitors to Exuma were reporting that the descendants of Pompey still living on the Rolle commonages were little if any better off than the sponge fishermen and small sisal farmers of Andros, the pineapple-growing sharecroppers of Eleuthera, or even the Crown land squatters of Grand Bahama, Inagua, and Mayaguana.[69]

Nineteenth-Century Censuses and Demographic Trends

The fading of the metropolitan philanthropic impulse after slave emancipation, the onset of the era of laissez-faire and "free trade imperialism," and the Bahamian oligarchy's ability to entrench its hegemony more or less without impediment resulted in a general lack of concern for the ordinary Bahamian people. As an index of this indifference, the period also saw a decline in the quantity and quality of demographic statistics. Yet though the available data lack the detail and consistency of both the Slave Registration Returns of 1822–34 and the official census reports published in the twentieth century, it is possible to illustrate the changing demographic patterns of the postemancipation years by carefully collating what remains: the colonial censuses normally taken every ten years on the metropolitan model, the annual *Blue Book* reports, occasional information found in the governors' correspondence, and even more fragmentary material from the records left by lesser colonial officials.

The Bahamian censuses taken in 1838, 1845, 1851, and every tenth year thereafter generally provided only population totals by sex and islands of residence. Adults and children (along with aliens and absent residents) were distinguished only in 1845, and no breakdown of "Whites" and "Coloureds" was made after 1851 because the Executive Council wished "not to offend any portion of the population." Governors were instructed to compile statistical accounts of the colony each year, though the resulting *Blue Books* concentrated on matters of trade, revenue, and expenditure, and those of such a backwater colony as the Bahamas doubtless moldered on some Colonial Office shelf. Between the decennial censuses, the *Blue Books* repeated the same population totals each year, though they did add the annual returns of births, deaths, and marriages when these were available. The *Blue Books* and the governors' correspondence also occasionally provided details of immigration, emigration, and medical statistics, including causes of death.

From these somewhat patchy materials it is therefore possible not only to trace the general morphology of the Bahamian population in the decades after slavery ended but to discern patterns of growth, decline, and diffusion within and between the islands and to make at least rough comparisons with the preceding age in respect to fertility, mortality, age profiles, life expectancy, and general health. The

Table 1. Total Population and Growth Rates, 1838–1901

Intercensal period	*Number of years in interval*	*Total population at end of interval*	*Total growth*	*Average annual growth rate (%)*
1838–45	7	23,410	4,316	2.96
1845–51	6	27,519	4,109	2.72
1851–61	10	35,487	7,968	2.57
1861–71	10	39,162	3,675	0.99
1871–81	10	43,521	4,359	1.06
1881–91	10	47,565	4,044	0.89
1891–1901	10	53,735	6,170	1.23

Source: Adapted from Norma Abdulah, *The Bahamas and Its People: A Demographic Analysis* (St. Augustine, Trinidad: CARICOM and ISER, 1987), 15. Abdulah's rates for the first two intervals were in error because she failed to deduct the totals for the Turks and Caicos Islands, which were administered by the Bahamas only until 1848.

fortunate survival of a detailed map of Exuma dating from just after 1900 (made to illustrate the annual report of an unusually zealous resident justice), showing the number of houses and persons in each settlement in relation to land ownership, also allows us to correlate the demographic patterns and movements suggested by the statistics to the types and patterns of settlement and to draw conclusions about the reconstruction of Out Island society after slavery which apply not only for the single island of Exuma but for a wide section of the central Bahamas and for all similar islands.

All in all, these findings bear out the conclusions from the literary evidence that the ending of formal slavery, far from leading to permanently better conditions for ordinary Bahamians, was succeeded, after a brief interval of optimism and achievement, by an era of struggle and depression both demographically and socioeconomically (Table 1 and Figure 1).

The general population trend was ever upward, but at a rate of natural increase that until the mid-twentieth century was never higher than during the late slave period and declined markedly between 1860 and 1890 (see Table 1 and Figure 1). To a certain extent, this critical underlying trend can be seen in the overall population totals, but its full implications can be unraveled only after the effects of emigration, immigration, and epidemics and the differences between whites and nonwhites and between New Providence and the other islands are taken into account.

The total Bahamian population rose by 33 percent in the thirty years after 1810, though the rate of natural increase during the 1830s (for whites together with slaves) was around 3.0 percent per year. The percentage increases in the total population for each decennium between 1840 and 1900 were, successively, approximately 31, 29, 12.5, 11, 10, and 12.5, suggesting an overall rate of natural increase that was sustained at the previous level for the first decade and fell only slightly in the second but plunged suddenly in the 1860s, declined even further in the following two decades, and recovered only to the level of the 1860s in the 1890s. More detailed analysis, however, discloses subtly different levels of effect and cause: for example, the effects of the declining ratio of whites to nonwhites and of the de-

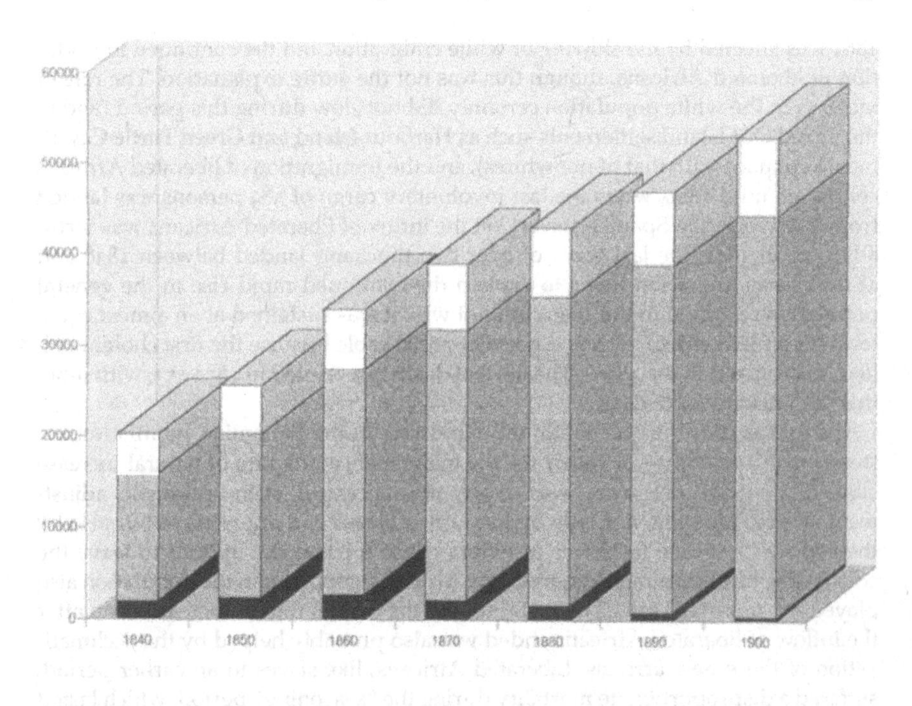

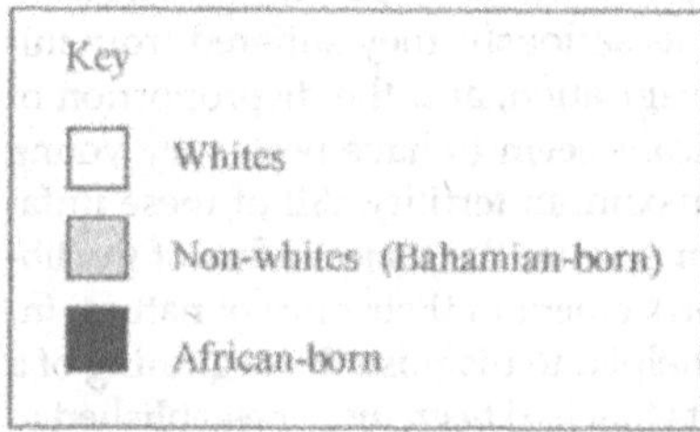

Figure 1. Bahamas, Total Population, 1840–1900

clining proportion of the population living in New Providence. These, in turn, reflected differences in the rates of natural increase, caused, among other things, by different lifestyles and the prevalence and spread of epidemic disease.

During the late slave period, remarkable levels of fertility in conjunction with declining mortality rates led to a rate of natural increase among slaves that rose to about 3.2 percent in the period 1831–34. The rates among Creole whites and free coloreds and blacks were also healthy, if, in combination, slightly lower than among the most fortunately circumstanced slaves. The record of the late slave period was confused, however, by the wholesale transportation of slaves down to 1825, by the crescendo of slave manumissions, and by the continued emigration of disappointed planters and their families.

Likewise, the continuing surge in the Bahamian population between 1838 and

1861 was affected by the slowing of white emigration and the continued importation of liberated Africans, though this was not the entire explanation. The rate of increase in the white population certainly did not slow during this period (and in the mixed Out Island settlements such as Harbour Island and Green Turtle Cay almost kept pace with that of nonwhites), and the immigration of liberated Africans continued until 1860, when the last involuntary cargo of 389 persons was landed from the wreck of a Spanish slaver. Yet the influx of liberated Africans was virtually over in 1841; the last wave of over two thousand landed between 1838 and 1842. This in-migration helps to explain the continued rapid rise in the general population recorded in the 1840s but not why it was sustained at an almost equal level for a further decade. It is especially remarkable because the first cholera epidemics occurred in the 1850s. The normal death rate tripled in 1852–53, with more than a thousand extra deaths.

The explanation for the continued rapid rise in the Bahamian population between 1838 and 1861—or rather for the maintenance of a rate of natural increase close to 3 percent per year—was clearly the successful, even optimistic, adjustment to emancipation, not only by the former slaves and apprentices but also by their former masters, far fewer of whom chose (or had the option) to leave the colony. The hitherto almost ignored new African component in the population also played an important role. The sustaining of the overall rate of increase even after the inflow of liberated Africans ended was also probably helped by the acclimatization of these new arrivals. Liberated Africans, like slaves in an earlier period, suffered a disproportionate mortality during the "seasoning" period, which lasted at least three years and probably longer. Just as seriously, they suffered from initially low fertility rates because of disease, dislocation, and the disproportion of the sexes. Finally, many of the liberated Africans seem to have been very young when they arrived—well below the age of maximum fertility. All of these unfavorable factors were adjusted in the decade or so after the major influx of the liberated Africans ended, and the resulting improvement in their rates of natural increase (which may well have been dramatic) helped to disguise the beginning of a slide in the rates of natural increase of elements that had been longer established in the Bahamas.

The serious downturn and further slide in the rate of natural increase between 1860 and 1890 was initiated by recurrent epidemics, which, ironically, peaked during the short-lived boom period of the American Civil War. But the decline was entrenched by the steady deterioration of work and living conditions that followed that boom. The downward trend was exaggerated by voluntary migration by both blacks and whites to Central America, Cuba, and the United States, although this was not a critical factor because the slight upturn in the general population curve during the 1890s occurred when emigration, though still minimal, was greater than in the preceding decades.

These general trends are elucidated and refined by a closer examination of the differences between the white and nonwhite segments of the population and between those living in New Providence and the other islands. Between 1810 and 1851, the total population of the Bahamas (less the Turks and Caicos Islands) increased from 14,829 to 27,519, or by 85.6 percent. The white population increased from 3,660 to 5,499, or by 50.2 percent, whereas the population of nonwhites ex-

Table 2. Population Totals, 1845–1901: Whole Bahamas and Separate Islands

	1845	1851	1861	1871	1881	1891	1901
Bahamas	23,410	27,519	35,487	39,162	43,521	47,565	53,735
New Providence	8,385	8,159	11,503	11,410	11,653	10,914	12,534
Harbour Island	1,745	1,840	1,994	2,172	1,970	1,472	1,232
Eleuthera	3,445	4,610	5,209	6,058	7,010	7,358	8,733
Spanish Wells	267		331	395	440	414	534
Grand Bahama	812	922	1,299	743	890	1,780	1,269
Abaco	1,890	2,011	2,362	3,025	3,610	3,686	3,314
Bimini		150	210	746	663	566	545
Berry Islands	161	336	202	250	185	215	382
Andros	759	1,030	1,366	2,138	3,434	4,589	6,347
Exuma	1,682	2,027	2,289	1,984	2,090	2,915	3,086
Cat Island	674	1,828	2,370	3,100	4,226	5,244	4,658
Long Island	1,286	1,477	2,571	2,226	2,573	3,174	3,562
Ragged Island	313	347	272	321	271	348	365
Rum Cay	560	858	654	681	367	402	529
San Salvador	315	384	489	634	675	772	667
Crooked Island			636	791	1,057	1,244	1,597
Long Cay	935	1,092	470	381	446	498	499
Acklins			503	698	611	1,192	1,565
Mayaguana	9			180	246	265	335
Inagua	172	530	994	1,120	1,083	998	1,453
Cay Sal and Cay Lobos	—	—	—	9	21	30	18

Sources: Bahamas Censuses, 1845–1901. Spanish Wells included with Eleuthera, 1851; Bimini included with Abaco, 1845; Acklins and Long Cay included with Crooked Island, 1845; Mayaguna included with Inagua, 1851, 1861; Cay Sal and Cay Lobos added separately, 1871–1901.

panded from 11,169 to 22,020, or by 97.2 percent. This difference, which led to a decrease in the percentage of whites in the total population from 24.7 to 20.0 was, however, skewed by a surplus of perhaps 3,000 in the number of liberated Africans settled over the number of slaves transported and by the emigration of hundreds of whites. Similar conditions prevailed nearly everywhere, but a close analysis over the same period of those islands (such as Harbour Island and Eleuthera) where immigration and emigration were not major factors suggests that the differential between white and nonwhite rates of natural increase was in the order of 25 rather than 50 percent. Projected forward, this would have led to a decline from 20 to 16.5 percent in the proportion of whites in the total population between 1850 and 1900 (close to figures estimated from other sources), with a further decline to the actual figure of 12.5 percent found by the census of 1943, which was the only census since 1851 to provide a racial breakdown (Tables 2 and 3).

The slow but steady decline in the proportion of whites in the Bahamian population, coupled with the traditionally slightly greater fecundity of nonwhites, makes the actual decline in the overall rate of natural increase between 1860 and 1890 all the more notable (Table 4). The reasons, surely, are to be found in compar-

Table 3. Population Breakdown by Race, 1851 Census

Area	*Whites*	*Percent*	*"Coloured Population"*	*Percent*
All Bahamas	5,499	19.98	22,020	80.02
New Providence	1,534	18.80	6,625	81.20
Eleuthera (and Spanish Wells)	1,211	26.27	3,399	73.73
Harbour Island	953	51.79	887	48.21
Abaco and Cays	1,178	58.58	833	41.42
Bimini	103	62.80	61	37.20
Long Island	194	13.13	1,283	86.87
Ragged Island	16	4.61	331	95.39
Inagua and Mayaguana	61	11.51	469	88.49
Grand Bahama	1	0.01	921	99.99
Exuma	144	7.10	1,883	92.90
Cat Island	30	1.64	1,798	98.35
Watling's Island	13	3.39	371	96.61
Rum Cay	37	4.31	821	95.69
Crooked Island, Long Cay, and Acklins	12	1.10	1,080	98.90
Andros	1	0.01	1,029	99.99

Source: Bahamas Census, 1851.

ing the changing populations and suggested differences in rates of natural increase of different islands over the period, including comparisons between those with large white populations and those with hardly any whites (Tables 2, 3, and 4).

In some respects, the changing pattern of New Providence's population presents the most remarkable picture of all. Between 1845 and 1901, despite the extension of Nassau and its suburbs, the population of New Providence grew only from 8,390 to 12,530, or by 49.3 percent, compared with an increase of 129.5 percent in the overall Bahamian population. Though almost a third of Bahamians lived in New Providence a decade after slavery ended, less than a quarter did in 1900. The reasons for this trend can be traced in the birth and death statistics as well as in the general history of the colony and its capital during the period. Despite a far greater superfluity of females over males than in any other Bahamian island (peaking twice at 126:100 in 1845 and 1881, with a low point of 106:100 in 1861; see Table 5), the gross birth rate in New Providence was never higher than the Bahamas average, though never substantially lower either. The death rate was consistently far above the Bahamian average, in some years of epidemic such as 1866, indeed, producing a net natural decrease in the capital island's population (Table 5).

Of eight years between 1856 and 1890 analyzed, in only one did the natural increase in New Providence match that of the colony as a whole. For the remaining seven years the average was 0.43 percent, compared with 1.90 for the whole Bahamas. Had there been the same proportion of females in New Providence as in the rest of the colony and a proportional decrease in the gross birth rate, it is almost certain that New Providence would have been no more capable of sustaining itself

Table 4. Rates of Gross Natural Increase, 1856–1890: Whole Bahamas and Sample Islands, Sample Years[a]

Area		1856		1861		1866		1870		1876		1879		1890		Average % Increase, 1865–90
		Total	%	Total	%	Total	%	Total	%	Total	%	Total	%	Total	%	
Bahamas	births	1,276	4.12	1,267	3.62	1,373	3.61	1,483	3.71	1,549	3.60	1,617	3.76	1,871	3.98	
	deaths	480	1.55	687	1.96	948	2.49	775	1.94	724	1.68	847	1.97	889	1.89	
	increase		2.54		1.66		1.12		1.77		1.92		1.79		2.09	1.84
New Providence	births	389	3.89	339	2.95	381	3.31	395	3.46	377	3.30	373	3.27	292	2.68	
	deaths	197	1.97	289	2.51	402	3.49	347	3.04	282	2.47	340	2.98	249	2.28	
	increase		1.92		0.44		−0.21		0.42		0.83		0.29		0.40	0.58
Harbour Island	births	105	5.71	107	5.37	91	4.56	123	5.66	127	5.85	125	5.76	57	3.87	
	deaths	40	2.17	71	3.56	44	2.21	33	1.52	43	1.98	58	2.67	29	1.97	
	increase		3.54		1.81		2.35		4.14		3.87		3.09		1.90	2.95
Eleuthera	births	193	4.19	201	3.86	225	4.32	212	3.50	319	5.27	333	5.50	340	4.62	
	deaths	83	1.80	87	1.67	130	2.50	86	1.42	136	2.24	154	2.54	162	2.20	
	increase		2.39		2.19		1.82		2.08		3.03		2.96		2.42	2.41
Abaco	births	102	5.07	102	4.32	133	5.64	120	3.84	143	4.58	114	3.65	156	4.23	
	deaths	35	1.74	37	1.56	54	2.29	40	1.28	33	1.06	41	1.31	58	1.57	
	increase		3.33		2.76		3.35		2.56		3.52		2.34		2.66	2.48
Andros	births	50	4.85	57	4.17	61	4.47	98	4.61	89	4.16	91	4.26	200	4.36	
	deaths	8	0.78	20	1.46	38	2.78	31	1.45	15	0.70	23	1.08	59	1.29	
	increase		4.07		2.71		1.69		3.16		3.46		3.18		3.07	3.05
Cat Island	births	107	5.85	98	4.14	98	4.14	117	3.77	151	4.87	147	4.74	271	5.17	
	deaths	27	1.48	48	2.03	51	2.15	66	2.13	63	2.03	63	2.03	140	2.67	
	increase		4.37		2.11		1.99		1.64		2.84		2.71		2.50	2.60

Table 4. (continued)

Area		1856		1861		1866		1870		1876		1879		1890		Average % Increase, 1865–90
		Total	%	Total	%	Total	%	Total	%	Total	%	Total	%	Total	%	
Exuma	births	78	3.85	82	3.58	80	3.49	77	3.88	93	4.69	86	4.33	97	3.33	
	deaths	18	0.89	25	1.09	45	1.97	23	1.16	30	1.51	37	1.86	32	1.10	
	increase		2.96		2.49		1.97		2.72		3.18		2.47		2.23	2.51
Long Island	births	55	3.72	86	3.35	70	2.72	75	3.37	46	2.07	73	3.28	151	4.76	
	deaths	16	1.08	23	0.89	38	1.48	30	1.35	15	0.67	23	1.03	39	1.23	
	increase		2.64		2.46		1.24		2.02		1.40		2.25		3.53	2.22
Crooked Island	births	38	3.48	44	6.92	28	4.40	31	3.92	45	5.69	36	4.55	61	4.90	
	deaths	11	1.01	20	3.15	5	0.79	6	0.76	5	0.63	11	1.39	10	0.80	
	increase		2.47		3.77		3.61		3.16		5.16		3.16		4.10	3.63
Inagua	births	23	4.34	-	-	36	3.62	56	5.00	33	2.95	33	2.95	28	2.81	
	deaths	8	1.51	13	1.31	25	2.52	30	2.68	17	1.52	27	2.41	20	2.00	
	increase		2.83				1.10		2.32		1.43		0.54		0.81	1.51

Sources: Bahamas Annual Reports, 1856–1890.

[a] Years with best data selected at roughly five-year intervals.

Table 5. Male-Female Ratios, 1845–1901 (males per 100 females): Whole Bahamas and Separate Islands

	1845	*1851*	*1861*	*1871*	*1881*	*1891*	*1901*
All Bahamas	98.8	99.8	98.0	97.7	90.7	90.2	87.0
New Providence	79.4	87.9	94.5	90.2	79.6	76.1	78.0
Harbour Island	103.4	103.3	96.1	99.8	96.8	84.7	86.9
Eleuthera	103.0		96.2	99.9	98.8	88.8	90.9
		101.3					
Spanish Wells	115.3		114.9	112.4	91.3	80.8	103.0
Abaco	99.4	98.5	103.3	103.8	97.4	100.1	89.8
Grand Bahama	126.8	114.4	194.6	90.0	95.6	99.8	95.4
Bimini	—	120.6	125.8	198.4	111.1	92.5	93.3
Andros	112.0	102.0	103.9	105.0	103.0	101.5	101.2
Exuma	111.8	103.7	101.0	92.6	85.3	95.6	80.2
Cat Island	106.7	100.2	94.3	94.6	86.7	94.2	81.4
Long Island	105.1	102.9	94.9	100.0	98.1	95.0	82.5
San Salvador	111.4	100.0	104.6	95.1	90.1	82.9	78.3
Rum Cay	114.6	104.3	90.1	95.1	86.3	92.3	79.9
Ragged Island	112.9	111.6	94.3	87.7	84.4	98.9	111.0
Crooked Island (incl. Long Cay)			105.8	103.9	93.9	100.3	84.4
	106.9	103.0					
Acklins Island			103.5	102.3	88.0	93.8	81.8
Inagua							106.1
	90.5	235.4	114.2	102.2	102.8	109.7	
Mayaguana							92.5

Sources: Bahamas Censuses, 1845–1901.

demographically during the second half of the nineteenth century than were the sugar colonies at the height of slavery.

One effect of New Providence's low rate of natural increase—or rather, an effect that also became a reinforcing cause—was the island's relatively aging population. The 1845 statistics showed that only 35.9 percent of the New Providence population was under fourteen years of age, compared with 40.9 percent in the other islands and 39.0 percent for the Bahamas overall. This disparity, which certainly deepened as the century wore on, was only marginally a result of the preponderance of young adults among the migrants to Nassau, for these persons were in the most reproductive years, and such migrations also left the elderly as well as young children behind. The comparative aging of the New Providence population was related to its "wasting," that is, the effects of crowding, unsanitary conditions, and family dislocation in reducing the number of children born and raising the number of persons who died prematurely. It was also related, somewhat paradoxically, to the fact that those adults who did survive lived longer—the gradual disappearance of the phenomenon that however healthily an Afro-Bahamian slave family reproduced itself, remarkably few of its members passed the age of sixty. For even the proportions of 39:61 for those under and over the age of fourteen in the overall Bahamian population in 1845 contrasted with those at the end of the slavery period, when 40 percent of all slaves were under the age of thirteen and probably 44 percent were under the age of fourteen.

As the intermittent statistics for causes of death, along with the reports on the periodic visitations of cholera, yellow fever, and other epidemics, indicate, New Providence suffered even more in the nineteenth century from its normal vulnerability to diseases imported by foreign visitors and incubated in crowded, unsanitary conditions. Like London and other large cities in metropolitan countries down to the time of the health reforms of the mid-nineteenth century, Nassau constantly drew on its hinterland for recruits, many of whom were too easily subject to fatal disease. But the capital also served as a local source of epidemic contagion, which radiated to the outer islands as a malign index of the relative efficiency of the communication system.

These effects were all amply illustrated by the cholera epidemic of 1852–53, which, being the first, was both the most severe and most terrible in its psychological effects. Governor Gregory reported in October 1852 that the disease first reached Nassau from New York in early September, in a Bahamian boat ironically called the *Reform.* Once landed, the cholera spread rapidly among the "humbler classes," particularly affecting the southern black settlements of Grant's Town and Bain Town and the poor white settlements in the swampy area called the White Ground (later, the Pond) in the eastern suburbs. Perhaps a tenth of the New Providence population was afflicted, of whom a quarter died. At the height of the epidemic, there were seventy deaths a week, and some of the dead remained aboveground in their coffins for want of gravediggers. The life of downtown Nassau came to a standstill, as the wealthy inhabitants stayed in their houses and the farmers from the outlying districts declined to bring their produce into the market.

From Nassau, the epidemic quickly spread to the nearby and better-served Out Islands, to Andros, Harbour Island, and the chief settlements of Eleuthera and Abaco. That the disease was carried by passengers in the boats was quickly recognized, and a serious riot occurred at Governor's Harbour in November when the local inhabitants refused to let Stipendiary Magistrate P. A. Carleton and his servants land for fear of infection from their persons or their baggage, repelling them with sticks and stones. Carleton returned to Nassau, and the governor sent him back under the protection of a detachment of troops, his visit being all the more execrated as the epidemic spread.[70]

By December, the cholera had spread to nearly all Bahamian islands (it was particularly severe in Ragged Island, where forty persons died), but it was waning. Far fewer people were affected and died in the most isolated islands than in the capital, where the death toll had fallen below a dozen a week before Christmas. Finally, on February 17, 1853, Governor Gregory declared a public holiday and day of prayer and thanksgiving for the passing of the scourge. Altogether, though, more than 1,000 people died during the five-month epidemic, including 696 in Nassau, 178 in Harbour Island, perhaps 200 in the rest of Eleuthera, and 108 in the Abaco settlements. Sieges of cholera recurred several times during the 1850s and 1860s. Their diminishing severity was offset by the cyclical epidemics of yellow fever for which Nassau became notorious during the blockade-running era of the American Civil War.[71]

Though Harbour Island, as the "second city" of the Bahamas (with a population density almost as great as that of Nassau), suffered some of Nassau's demographic problems, it was in general a far healthier place than the colonial capital. Its rate of natural increase was as high as in most Out Islands, and its population was kept stable (or actually declining by 1900) by the migration of some of the most ambitious and restless inhabitants to the Eleutheran mainland, Abaco, Nassau, or out of the Bahamas altogether. The Abaco settlements, which enjoyed rates of natural increase similar to Harbour Island's, increased steadily despite the migration from mid-century to Key West in southern Florida of many Abaconian "Conchs."

The chief reservoirs of the expanding Bahamian population were the other Out Islands, particularly those that were underdeveloped by the end of slavery. Except for Inagua and Long Cay, where the population growth was artificial because of the opportunities opened up by the steamer traffic through the Crooked Island and Windward Passages, the islands that grew most in population during the late nineteenth century were Cat Island and Andros. The former, from which many of the slaves were withdrawn before emancipation, expanded in population from 674 in 1845 to a peak of 5,244 in 1891, or by 778 percent in forty-six years, compared with the overall Bahamian figure of 203 percent. The population of the huge and almost untouched island of Andros expanded even more remarkably, increasing from 759 in 1845 to 4,589 in 1891, or by 605 percent, but then surpassing Cat Island (where there was a slight decline) to reach a peak of 7,545 in 1911—an increase of 994 percent over sixty-six years, compared with 239 percent for the Bahamas overall. Such increases, of course, were not achieved by natural demographic growth alone but chiefly through migration from Out Islands with less free fertile land. The rates of natural increase in Cat Island and Andros, though healthy compared with New Providence and generally greater than in Harbour Island and Abaco, declined after 1850 as the new lands filled up and would not have accounted for more than a tripling of the population of either island over the entire period.

Many of the Andros immigrants, if not those of Cat Island too, came from Exuma, where the natural increase almost matched that of Andros and Cat Island but the population rose from 1,682 in 1845 to 3,086 in 1901, or by 184 percent. The reasons for this differential were the comparative overpopulation and underpopulation of the source and destination islands as well as the very different patterns of land ownership, settlement, and use in the six decades after slavery ended.

Hardly any of the land in Andros and little of that in Cat Island had ever been alienated from the Crown, and most of the private estates in Cat Island had also reverted to the Crown because of nondevelopment and the nonpayment of quitrents. Both islands were therefore ideal for settlement by small farmers holding their land on squatting tenures. Andros had the additional real or imagined advantages of greater proximity to Nassau markets for the sale of produce and opportunities for wage employment or cash returns from the turtling and sponging grounds of the Great Bahama Bank. The typical settlements in both islands were therefore tenuous "ribbon" developments along the most fertile and accessible stretches of coast (Map 2). Family units were dispersed at intervals along a single coastal road on narrow but contiguous holdings—the classical forms being the six-mile stretches of the "settlements" of Mangrove Cay, Andros, and Old and New Bight, Cat Island. Similar conditions applied, in different degrees according to the fertility of the soil, the climate, and the proximity to Nassau, in other underdeveloped islands with much Crown land. These included Crooked Island and Acklins, the Abaco mainland, and Grand Bahama, in the last of which was probably the most attenuated of all Out Island ribbon settlements, the fittingly named Eight Mile Rock (Map 2).

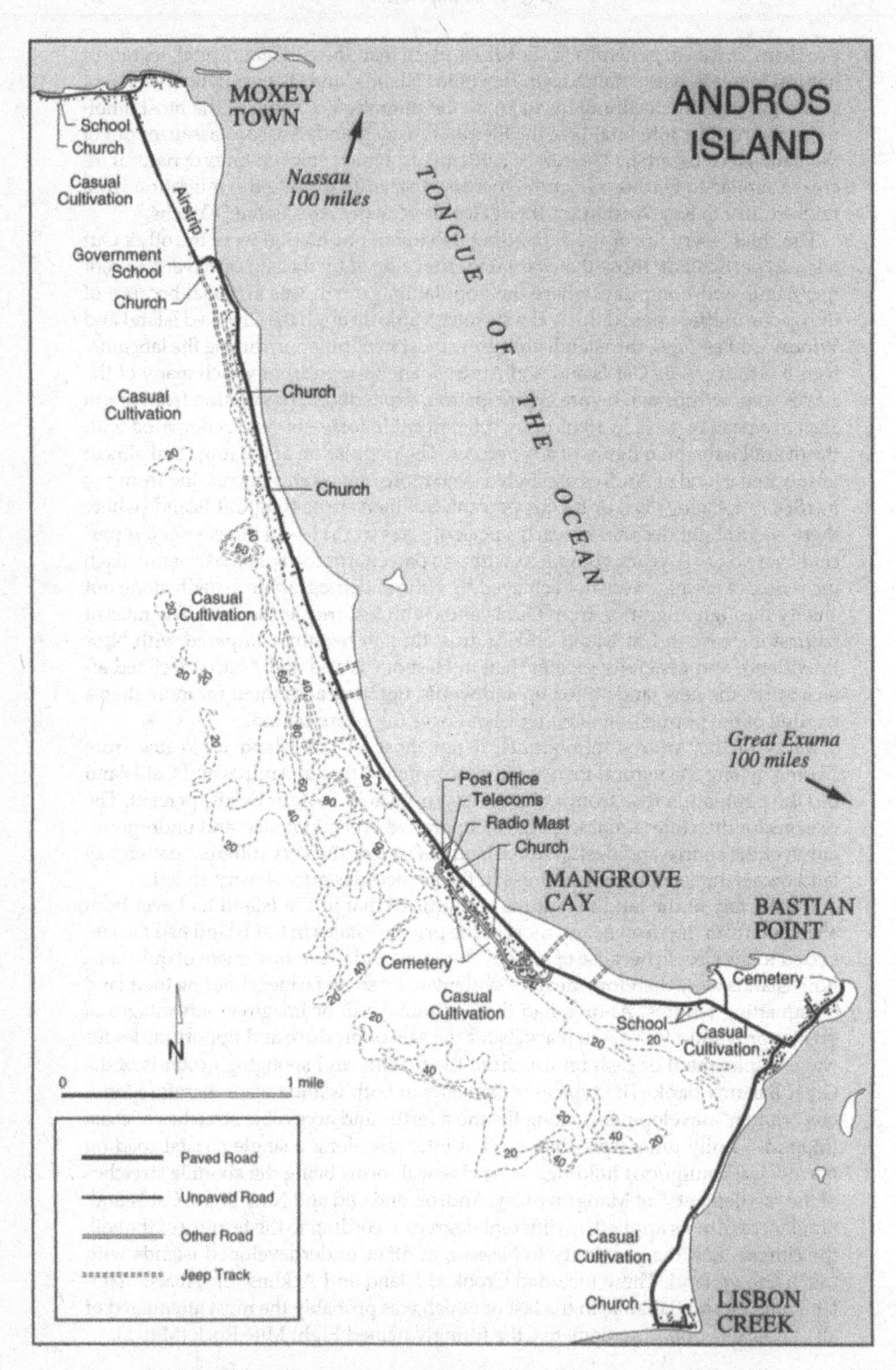

Map 2. Typical Ribbon Settlements: Mangrove Cay, Andros, Twentieth Century

The case of Exuma was very different, though typical of all islands still largely in the hands of their former owners or their successors and with little Crown land, including Long Island, Watling's Island, and Eleuthera. Here the characteristic settlements were formal townships (at least one in each island, serving as the chief port of entry and export and the seat of the resident magistrate) and nucleated villages or hamlets—though even these might be strung out like beads on a necklace along a single coastal road, as in Long Island.

The original land survey map of Great and Little Exuma, drawn up by Josiah Tatnall, the surveyor general in 1792, showed the two islands almost completely taken up by Loyalist planters. In all, there were 115 plots delimited and allocated, officially totaling 29,150 acres, for an average of 253 acres, though varying from 27 to 1,200 acres in extent. These 115 plots were owned by 88 different planters, of whom 64 owned 100 acres of more, 15 more than 500 acres, and 6 more than 1,000 acres. The grandest of the major landholders were Philip Moore, with six strategically scattered plots totaling 2,470 acres, William Telfair, with 2,300 acres in four plots, and Denys Rolle and Roger Kelsall, with 1,975 and 1,490 acres respectively, in three plots each. At the other end of the scale of land ownership, only the 12 persons with 40 acres or less (out of 24 with less than 100 acres) were really smallholders rather than true planters. Altogether, there were no more than nine plots of unallocated Crown land, totaling perhaps 2,000 acres and consisting mainly of lakes, marshes, or otherwise unproductive land, as well as the great salina on Little Exuma and its margins (Map 3). By a special act later in 1792, the Crown snipped off from the 225 acres owned by Jacob Winfree the 25 acres fronting Elizabeth Harbour to form the township of George Town, where before the end of slavery were built (not necessarily in this order) the church and parsonage, the courthouse-cum-jail, the government dock and market square, a warehouse or two, and a few "town houses" for the meager local gentry.

Some of the original landholdings were speculative, and many were shuffled between owners, but even after cotton failed and perhaps a third of Exumian estates became deserted, very few were surrendered altogether. Some holdings were consolidated, such as the Rolle estate, which increased to 5,000 acres with the acquisition of two more tracts before 1800. A very few holdings were subdivided and sold off to accommodate freed coloreds and blacks, who numbered 53 out of Exuma's total population of 1,412 in 1810, and perhaps three times as many by the end of slavery, though none of these persons seem to have become more than poor subsistence farmers, fishermen, craftsmen, or small traders in town. Of the Exumian slaves, who numbered 1,266 in 1810, a few lived in single-family laboring units alongside their poor white or nonwhite freedmen owners, and perhaps 100 were domestics serving the households of the 93 whites, 60 of whom were males and perhaps 40 resident owners or overseers of estates. But the great majority of Exuma's slaves were concentrated in the slave quarters on the twenty-five to thirty larger estates, living more like a village-based peasantry than true plantation slaves.

When emancipation came, the rapidly expanding former slave population had little or no chance to raise its socioeconomic status in Exuma. Land was not readily available for sale even if the former slaves had the money to purchase it. The local whites became more settled, taking advantage of cheap labor and the willingness of former slaves to enter into sharecropping arrangements. The number of whites in Exuma increased from 93 to 144 between 1810 and 1845, divided almost

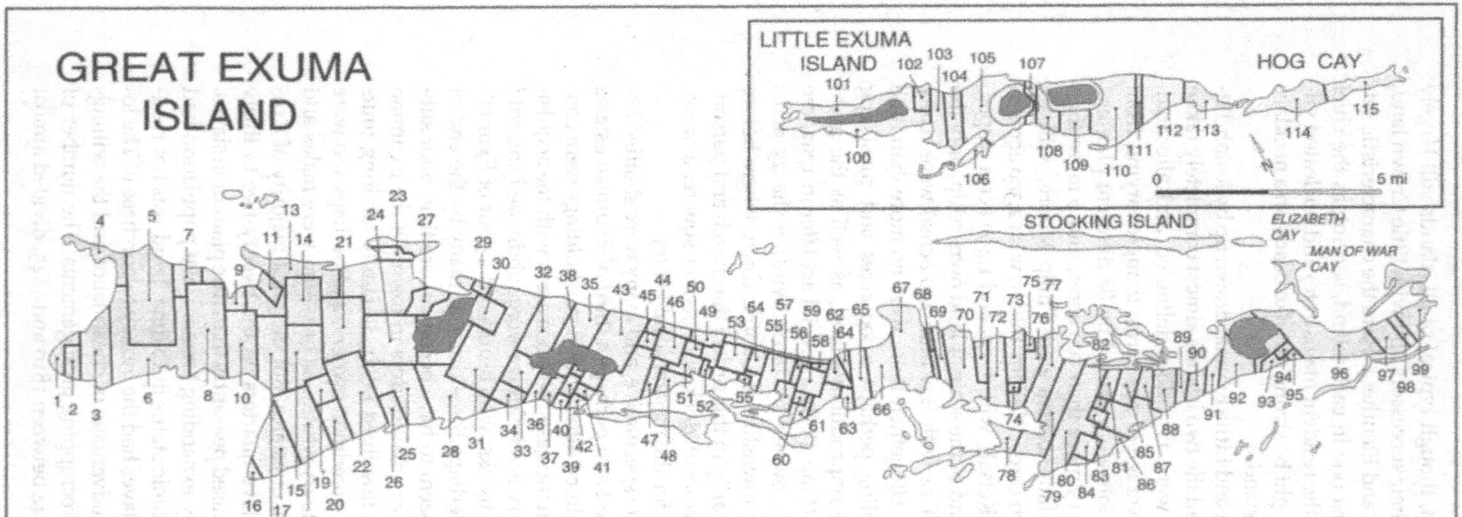

GREAT EXUMA ISLAND

LITTLE EXUMA ISLAND

HOG CAY

STOCKING ISLAND

ELIZABETH CAY

MAN OF WAR CAY

Lakes

0 5 mi

	Proprietors	Acres
1	I. W. Williams	40
2	I. W. Williams	220
3	W. Alexander	500
4	Denys Rolle	200
5	Denys Rolle	1000
6	John Stewart	900
7	John Cunningham	140
8	A. McKay	750
9	John Cruden	120
10	John McDonald	500
11	T. Johnson	140
12	Robert Wilson	500
13	Robert Wilson	700
14	Henry Yonge	400
15	William Telfair	500
16	Rose McLeod	27
17	William Wells	440
18	William Telfair	600
19	C. Dames	140
20	C. Dames	214
21	I. Cunningham	600
22	P. Moore	750
23	I. Roker	120
24	N. M. Almgreen	600
25	Andrew Deveaux	540
26	Philip Moore	140
27	Gilbert Grant	200
28	William Telfair	520
29	E. Barrow	60
30	Philip Ballard	205
31	Alexander Murray	1200
32	Nathaniel Hall	300
33	Nathaniel Hall	303
34	William Newman	100
35	William Bell	350
36	Martin McCartey	100
37	Gerrard Rush	100
38	Judith Conolly	40
39	Edward Barton	80
40	Honer Conolly	40
41	Samuel Freemantle	40
42	John French	40
43	Alexander Graham	500
44	Alexander Graham	110
45	Edward Morley	60
46	Joseph McKenzie	200
47	James Murphy	100
48	William Morley	100
49	Peter Carts	60
50	Edward Morley	60
51	William Scott	120
52	James Yonge	40
53	Nathaniel Morley	200
54	B. Morley	100
55	Nathaniel Morley	30
55	The Borrows	220
56	Nathaniel Borrows	33
57	Alex McKay	100
58	Daniel McKay	60
59	Ann McKay	205
60	Malcom McKay	40
61	Mary Robinson	80
62	James Braynen	120
63	Solomen Glass	46
64	Solomen Glass	54
65	Philip Bullard	235
66	Amelia Smith	325
67	N.M. Almgreen	575
68	Mary Robinson	60
69	Martin Jolfie	158
70	John Winnett	493
71	Mary Cruden	120
72	Walter Brown	320
73	Jacob Winfree	225
74	William Walker	30
75	Charles Dames	26
76	James Mattheason	240
77	John Mowbray	310
78	John McKay	400
79	Philip Moore	500
80	William Telfair	700
81	Roger Kelsall	135
82	Roger Kelsall	120
83	John Shirley	60
84	Roger Kelsall	130
85	Roger Kelsall	120
86	Fred Frasback	140
87	Alex McKay	520
88	John Allen	160
89	Ann McKay	100
90	James Moss	140
91	Rebecca Cuthbert	100
92	George Davis	200
93	Denys Rolle	65
94	E. Stevens	40
95	Jot Taylor	40
96	Denys Rolle	710
97	William Moss	140
98	Thomas Forbes	70
99	John Moultrie	160
	LITTLE EXUMA	
100	William Panton	500
101	Thomas Forbes	200
102	Samuel Walkins	86
103	William Clark	220
104	Jacob Winfree	198
105	Philip Moore	600
106	Ansel Ferguson	40
107	George Robinson	60
108	Charles Dames	180
109	Ann Wilking	160
110	Roger Kelsall	600
111	Roger Kelsall	68
112	Roger Kelsall	340
113	Philip Moore	480
	HOG CAY	
114	George Welch	430
115	Philip Moore	520

Map 3. Exuma: Loyalist Land Grants, 1792

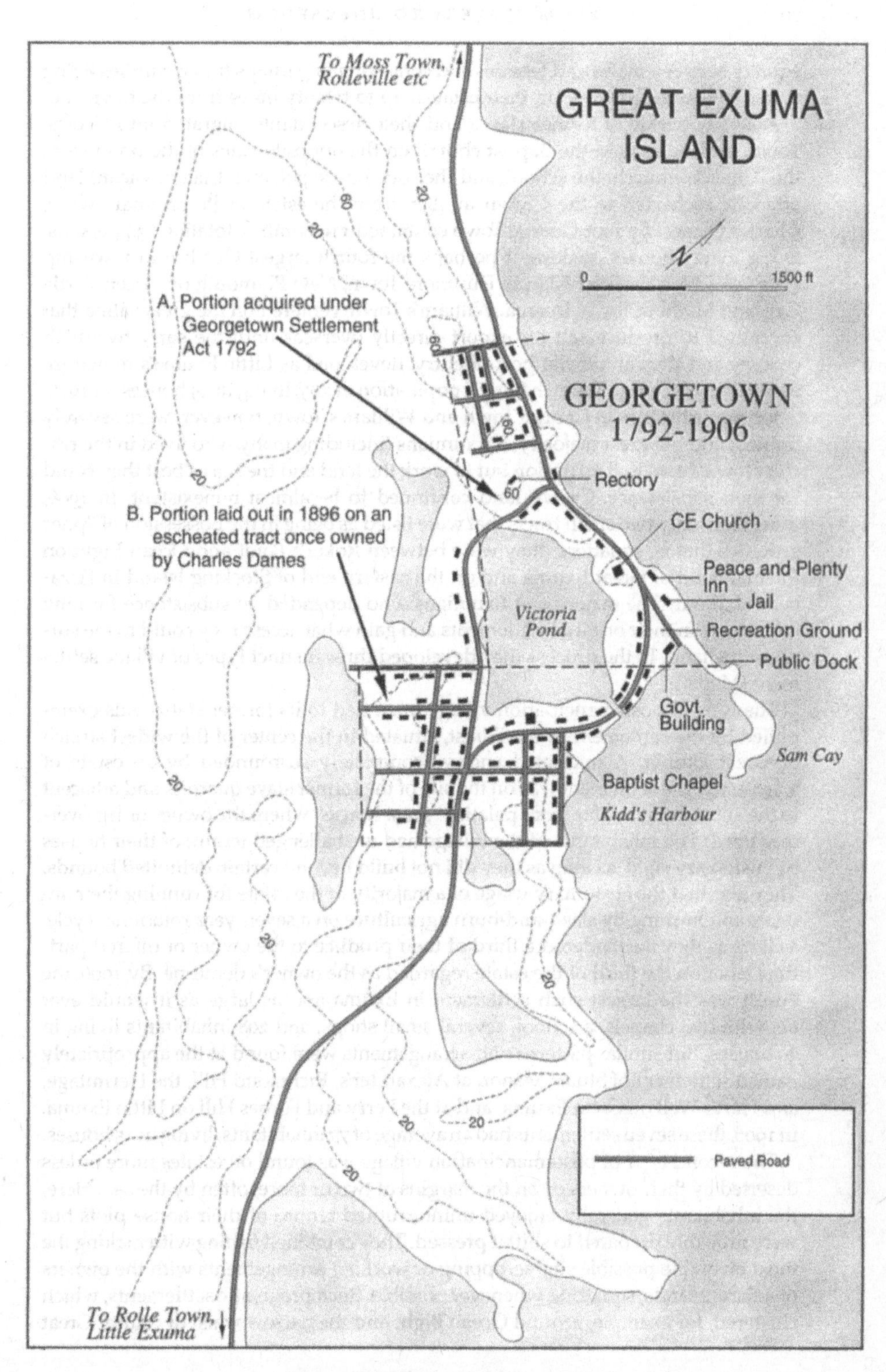

To Moss Town, Rolleville etc
GREAT EXUMA ISLAND
0
1500 ft
A. Portion acquired under Georgetown Settlement Act 1792
GEORGETOWN 1792-1906
Rectory
B. Portion laid out in 1896 on an escheated tract once owned by Charles Dames
CE Church
Peace and Plenty Inn
Jail
Victoria Pond
Recreation Ground
Public Dock
Govt. Building
Sam Cay
Baptist Chapel
Kidd's Harbour
Paved Road
To Rolle Town, Little Exuma

Map 4. Georgetown, Exuma, 1792–1906

equally between males and females and consisting of perhaps thirty families living either in George Town or on their estates, up to twenty miles from the township.

A steady trickle of former slaves and their descendants migrated into George Town, settling around the Baptist church on the opposite sides of the pond from the Anglican church, the school, and the courthouse-jail, on a tract of vacant land officially escheated to the Crown in 1896 from the estate of its original owner, Charles Dames. By 1906 George Town contained 119 families, totaling 534 persons, living in 125 houses, making it perhaps the fourth largest Out Island township (Map 4)—after Harbour Island's Dunmore Town, New Plymouth on Green Turtle Cay, and Mathew Town, Inagua. William's Town, centered on the great salina that continued to produce salt for export directly overseas until the early twentieth century and thus an official port of entry, developed as Little Exuma's miniature equivalent of George Town, having a population of 185, living in 35 houses, in 1906.

Job opportunities in George Town and William's Town, however, were severely limited, and the great majority of Exumians (including many who lived in the two chief townships) had no option but to work the land and the sea as best they could for their subsistence. Crown land continued to be almost nonexistent. In 1906, there were only two small tracts that were listed as being in the possession of "poor settlers," that is, squatters; they were between Roker's Point and Ocean Bight on the mainland of Great Exuma and on the eastern end of Stocking Island in Elizabeth Harbour. The majority of Exumians who depended on subsistence farming had to stay in their original settlements and gain what access they could to the surrounding land. In the process they developed three distinct types of village settlement (Map 5).

The type of postemancipation village most tied to its former status was exemplified by the settlement of the Forest, situated in the center of the widest stretch of Great Exuma. A nucleated enclave completely surrounded by an estate of 3,356 acres, the settlement was on the site of the former slave quarters and adjacent to the substantial but far from palatial "great house" where the owner or his overseer lived. The inhabitants of the village had unchallenged tenure of their houses by customary right, as long as they did not build beyond certain delimited bounds. They also had the customary usage of a majority of the estate for running their animals and farming by slash-and-burn agriculture on a seven-year rotational cycle, as long as they surrendered a third of their produce to the owner or offered part-time labor on the third of the estate regarded as the owner's demesne. By 1906, the Forest was the largest such settlement in Exuma and as large as it would ever be, with two chapels, a school, several small shops, and 208 inhabitants living in 40 houses. But similar patterns and arrangements were found at the appropriately named settlement of Stuart Manor, at Alexander's, Richmond Hill, the Hermitage, and Hart's Well on Great Exuma, and at the Ferry and Forbes Hill on Little Exuma. In 1906, these seven settlements had an average of 77 inhabitants, living in 15 houses.

The second type of postemancipation village was found on estates more or less deserted by their owners or on the margins of two or more, often by the sea. Here, the inhabitants generally enjoyed uninterrupted tenure of their house plots but were probably prepared to shift if pressed. They combined fishing with making the most favorable possible sharecropping or working arrangements with the owners of adjacent lands, squatting whenever possible. Such pragmatic settlements, which clustered, for example, around Ocean Bight and the narrow waist of central Great

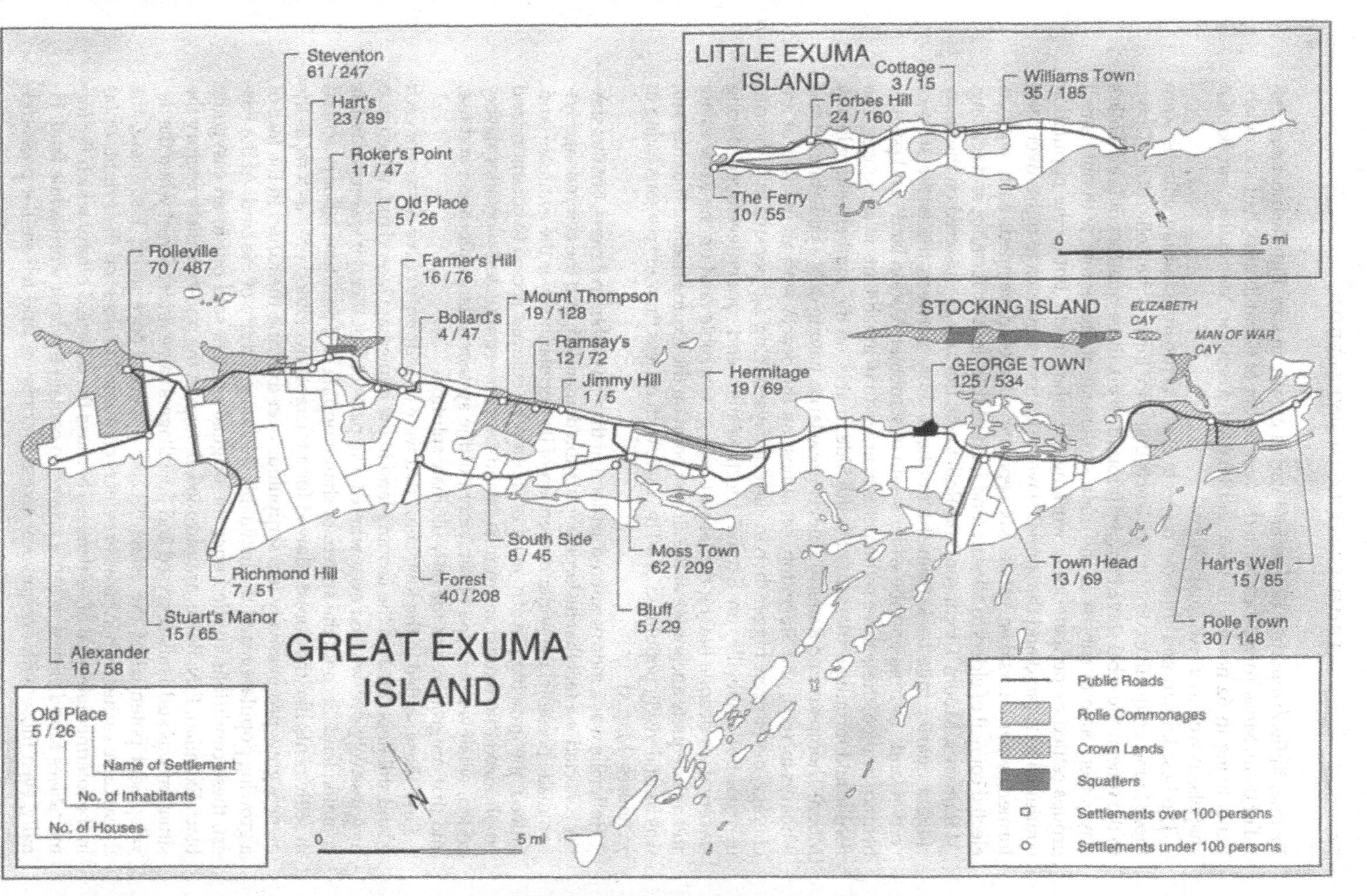
LITTLE EXUMA ISLAND
Cottage 3 / 15
Williams Town 35 / 185
Forbes Hill 24 / 160
The Ferry 10 / 55
0
5 mi
Steventon 61 / 247
Hart's 23 / 89
Roker's Point 11 / 47
Old Place 5 / 26
Rolleville 70 / 487
Farmer's Hill 16 / 76
Mount Thompson 19 / 128
Bollard's 4 / 47
Ramsay's 12 / 72
Jimmy Hill 1 / 5
Hermitage 19 / 69
STOCKING ISLAND
ELIZABETH CAY
MAN OF WAR CAY
GEORGE TOWN 125 / 534
South Side 8 / 45
Moss Town 62 / 209
Richmond Hill 7 / 51
Forest 40 / 208
Town Head 13 / 69
Hart's Well 15 / 85
Stuart's Manor 15 / 65
Bluff 5 / 29
Rolle Town 30 / 148
Alexander 16 / 58
GREAT EXUMA ISLAND
Old Place 5 / 26
Name of Settlement
No. of Inhabitants
No. of Houses
N
0
5 mi
Public Roads
Rolle Commonages
Crown Lands
Squatters
Settlements over 100 persons
Settlements under 100 persons

Map 5. Exuma: Settlements and Landholdings, 1906

Exuma, shifted from time to time and varied greatly in size. But the most successful of them, Moss Town, located in the very center of Great Exuma, had 209 inhabitants living in 62 houses in 1906 and boasted Anglican, Methodist, and Baptist chapels, as well as a few small shops.

The best known and in some respects most fortunate Exumian villages were those found on the five commonage tracts that once formed the Rolle estate. Down to the time of the rebel slave Pompey (around 1830), three-quarters of Lord Rolle's slaves were able to subsist in the main settlement of Steventon, with only small groups settled or peripatetically working the other tracts. But as the population continued to expand and the former slaves assumed commonage rights over their former owner's forsaken estate, six separate villages developed, each with its elected council of elders to allocate land for building houses, farming, and grazing. At Ramsay's, Mount Thompson, and Rolletown, the village clustered on the stony ridge a quarter mile back from the northern shore between the fertile strip of "onion land" in front and the wider swath of scrubbier "cotton land" and pasture behind. In 1906, these three settlements averaged 116 inhabitants in 20 houses. The fishing and farming settlement of South Side (that is, on the southern shore below Mount Thompson and Ramsay's) never grew large, having only 45 inhabitants and 8 houses in 1906, and Steventon, set almost on the beach, with an indifferent anchorage, never grew bigger than in slavery days, having 247 persons in 61 houses in 1906. But Rolleville, on Exuma's northwestern end, underdeveloped during slavery days despite having the largest tract of workable land on the Rolle estate and an adequate anchorage at the closest point on the Exuma mainland to Nassau, was most densely populated of all by 1906, with no less than 487 persons living in 70 houses (Map 5).

Rolleville was a more scattered settlement than any other in Exuma, but this simply reflected the fact that its large population demanded, and the commonage system made possible, the wider dispersion of its population over the available land. Indeed, the growing poverty even of those who enjoyed access to common land emphasized that Exuma and similar islands were overpopulated soon after slavery ended, whatever the type of settlement or the system of land allocation and use, and that emigration was the only ultimate solution.

First, those settled in the townships that were the administrative centers of each island still depended on the farming land in the immediate hinterland, which was progressively overworked even where (as in parts of Eleuthera) it was regarded as common land. Second, the system of sharecropping and part-time labor practiced in settlements like the Forest allowed for a tolerable livelihood only as long as the owners grew progressively less scrupulous over exacting their dues in the face of a growing population and the inevitably declining fertility of the land. At the Forest, these conditions applied once the original owners sold out to an easygoing black Exumian, F. N. Bowe, around 1890, though in the mid-twentieth century the situation was suddenly reversed and the villagers came under threat when the development potential of the estate became apparent once more. Elsewhere, the threat came earlier, either because owners continued to insist on their rights or (as in the intermediate type of settlement) because the deserted estates which the former slaves found easiest to settle proved to contain the least worthwhile land. Finally, even those with unequivocal access to common land felt similar pressures, and the inevitable overworking of the land was accelerated by the population growth stimulated by the initial development of a healthy peasant lifestyle.[72]

That these conclusions are far from fanciful and that Exuma and similar islands were bound to export their surplus people or perish is borne out by a comparison of the population densities indicated by the 1906 report. In 1906 Exuma attempted to support a population twice as large as in slavery days from a sorely depleted resource base, in housing that was considerably more cramped. In 1906, Exuma's 3,303 people lived in 658 houses (mostly thatched wattle-and-daub and no more than twelve feet square), an average of 5.02 persons per house, which was almost certainly higher than in slavery days. The density in George Town was a comparatively modest 4.27 persons per house, but in the rural settlements such as Moss Town and the Forest it was 4.72, and for the 1,164 persons crammed into an area Lord Rolle had complained in 1830 was insufficient to support his 350 slaves, the figure was 5.62.

3

Capital of a Backwater Colony: Nassau and Its Society, 1838–1900

Communications During the Transition from Sail to Steam

After the ending of slavery, the transition in maritime transportation from sail to steam was potentially the most influential change in nineteenth-century Bahamian social history. The sea passages through the Bahamas were more navigable for steamships than for sailing vessels and soon became a network of shipping lanes between Europe and North America and the Caribbean and Central America. Nassau, with its central location, became much more accessible to the outside world, and several Out Island settlements became occasional stopping places for passing steamers. Yet the transition to steam for the Bahamas was much more gradual than the technology warranted, for faster and more reliable vessels tended first to open up more distant destinations, and it was often neither necessary nor profitable to make intermediate stops. Moreover, though steamships gradually changed the quality and pace of life in the Bahamian capital between 1840 and 1900, the majority of the Out Islands remained fixed in the age of sail well into the twentieth century. This difference intensified the traditional division to the point that Nassau, "a sleepy Rip Van Winkle sort of place" to outside visitors, appeared a virtual dynamo compared with Out Island settlements sunk in a timeless torpor.

Sailing ships with auxiliary engines had crossed the Atlantic long before slavery ended; one, indeed, sailed and puffed its way toward India, by way of St. Thomas, Brazil, and the Cape, as early as 1829. Yet the earliest marine engines were so inefficient and dangerous that they required more coal than the ship could carry in cargo, frequently burst their boilers, or destroyed the vessel through fires started by the cinders spewed from their stacks. The full conquest of sail by steam took almost a century. Even auxiliary engines, however, could overcome doldrum stretches or adverse winds and currents and give captains greater assurance in navigating narrow and dangerous passages. By the 1840s, optimistic entrepreneurs were offering steamship services wherever speed and regularity were called for, freights were light and valuable, and passengers and mail helped pay the way. As early as February 1841 Governor Cockburn persuaded the Bahamian Assembly to pass an act "to Promote and encourage Steam Navigation between this Colony and Great Britain for the Conveyance of Mails and Passengers." He was probably responding to news of the plans of James McQueen of the Royal Mail Steam Packet

Company of London (founded in 1829), for only three months later McQueen announced plans to use Nassau as the distribution point for a regional steamship service and successfully petitioned the Assembly to allow his ships to avoid the normal customs delays. McQueen's intention was to organize a twice-monthly exchange of mails and passengers at Nassau between steamers plying the Atlantic and others steaming between Nassau and other regional ports.[1]

Cuba, fast becoming the world's richest plantation colony, was an obvious onward destination, and on February 17, 1842, Governor Cockburn announced the arrival from Havana of the first Royal West India Mail Steam Packet Company vessel carrying mail from England. McQueen's plans for Nassau, though, did not flourish. Nassau remained a stopping place to and from Havana but proved an inferior entrepôt for the rest of the West Indies. Royal Mail steamers found it simpler and cheaper simply to call at Long Cay (the General Post Office for the Bahamas since 1812) or Grand Turk on their voyage to and from the Windward Island Passage. The Danish island of St. Thomas became the essential coaling station and transshipment center for the entire Caribbean.[2]

The destiny of Nassau and the Bahamas was to be increasingly—if at first tenuously—tied to the North American mainland, with inevitable cultural consequences. In 1851, the Bahamian government signed a contract with a New York steamship company, but the enterprise proved ill-starred. The very first vessel on the run, the SS *Jewess*, arrived at Nassau in May 1851 burned almost to the waterline, and the spread of cholera epidemics from port to port during the early 1850s made more traffic than was strictly necessary unpopular with passengers and Nassauvians alike. Renewed efforts were made toward the end of the decade, with an act in 1857 to encourage steamship connections with North America and the purchase by the government of the site for a hotel in the very center of Nassau from Bay Street merchant Timothy Darling. In 1859 a contract was made with the Canadian-born transatlantic steamship pioneer Samuel Cunard to include Nassau on a regular monthly voyage between New York and Havana, carrying passengers and mails at the cost of an annual subsidy of £1,000.[3]

Samuel Cunard's service (and the long, if intermittent, association of the Cunard Line with Bahamian tourism) began with the arrival of the SS *Corsica* in November 1859, which encouraged the legislature to float a loan and begin the construction of the elegant Royal Victoria Hotel in the summer of 1860. Stone-built, four stories high, with ninety bedrooms, and on a scarcely less commanding site than Government House, it was easily the largest building in Nassau. To some it seemed itself like a magnificent stranded side-wheel steamer, with a central portico like a giant paddle housing, a cupola like a smokestack, and three superimposed piazzas like promenade decks. "As its site at the head of Parliament Street is ninety feet above tide water," enthused the first guidebook, "the views from these piazzas—like the air that fans them—are exceptionally fine. Here, for the benefit of those invalids who cannot journey about, is a promenade of one thousand feet."[4]

Completed before the end of the 1860–61 winter season, the Royal Victoria Hotel was intended to attract invalids and other refugees from the chilly North. Cunard's steamers promised a voyage of as little as three days from New York, compared with at least a week by sailing ship. But the round-trip fare of $95, as much as the threats of Bahamian reefs and Nassau's reputation for cholera and yellow

Rare proof copy of first Bahamian adhesive postage stamp, engraved and recess printed by Messrs. Perkins, Bacon of London and first issued June 10, 1859. The portrait of the young Queen Victoria by Edward Chalon, R.A. has relegated the Bahamian symbols of pineapple and conch to the lower margins. From the stamp collection of Michael Craton.

fever, guaranteed at first only a limited clientele. For the Bahamas as a whole, the Cunard connection was chiefly notable for greatly speeding communication—news and mail now traveling between Nassau and England in a fortnight or less. This improvement was accompanied by significant changes in the postal services, symbolized by the introduction of the first Bahamian adhesive postage stamps in 1859.

Before 1840, postal services were unreliable, slow, and expensive. Letters, whether sent or received by the official packet boat calling at Pitt Town, Long Cay, or by the ordinary "Ship's Letter" system, might take many weeks each way and cost a shilling a page, payable by the recipient. The bewildering variety of early Bahamian postal markings, although a delight for postal historians, indicates the difficulties and uncertainties of communications during slavery days. With Rowland Hill's advocacy of economies of scale, the innovations of prepaid postage, adhesive stamps and envelopes, and, above all, the introduction of steamship services in the 1840s, conditions immediately improved. During 1846, distinctive hand stamps for prepaid postage were issued from Britain, with the legend "Paid at Nassau" surmounted by a crown. Along with innumerable other locations, foreign as well as colonial, the Nassau Post Office was authorized to use British adhesive postage stamps in the 1850s, canceled in Nassau's case with a local "A05" overstamp. This temporary measure was succeeded by the importation of special Bahamian stamps for "interinsular" use in June 1859, which were cleared for overseas mail in April 1860.[5]

The original design for a Bahamian postage stamp featured a pineapple in the center, but loyalty or convention decreed that an image of the young Queen Victoria be substituted. The version chosen was an engraving of the beautiful portrait by Edward Chalon, R.A., which was superscribed "BAHAMAS, Interinsular Postage," with a pineapple, along with a conch, relegated to the lower corners. As in England, the very first stamps (now great rarities) were in the single denomination of one penny, though the 4d., 6d., and one shilling values more suitable for overseas mail were added in 1861 and 1865. The first stamps, like those in England down to 1853, were printed by Messrs. Perkins, Bacon by recess engraving, but this was superseded by the cheaper (and less aesthetic) typographic process once the printing was taken over by Messrs. De la Rue in 1863. The "Chalon Head" of Queen Victoria, though, was retained until 1884, when a version of the 1840 Heath portrait used on all English stamps was adopted. This was used until the queen died in 1901 so that Victoria's Bahamian subjects unrealistically retained an image of their sovereign that was up to sixty years out of date.[6]

All "classic" (that is, pre-1900) Bahamian postage stamps are now relatively rare and costly. But the 1884–98 printings, with denominations of 1½d., 5 shillings, and £1 added, were much more numerous than their forerunners, providing an index both to the great improvement in speed and efficiency of the Bahamian postal service and to the efficacy of Rowland Hill's principle that a huge increase in postal usage would follow and justify a drastic lowering of the unit cost. The cost of sending a letter anywhere within the Bahamas was fixed at a penny for a century after 1859, though the ideal of a universal imperial penny post was never achieved—letters to England cost 4d. until 1884, and 2½d. thereafter. Yet by the end of the nineteenth century mail was being carried between Nassau and England three times as fast as in 1800, at a tenth of the cost and at least as proportionate an increase in volume.[7]

The number of tourist visitors increased steadily in step with improvements in steamship services during the last four decades of the nineteenth century, reaching a peak of around 750 each winter season. This modest influx was dwarfed and distorted, however, by the illusory four-year surge of steamship traffic and nontourist visitors during the American Civil War (1861–65). As the Union blockade tightened its grip on the Confederate States, the price of cotton and the value of imported European goods escalated, and the ostensibly neutral Bahamas became the natural haven and base for sleek steam-powered blockade runners, most of them custom-built in England. As the earliest of Bahamian photographs show, Nassau was transformed by 1862 from a sleepy colonial port, in which a steamship was a rarity, to one of the busiest ports in the Americas, its docks crammed with more than 20 tall-stacked side-paddled steamers at a time. In all, 428 steamers (and 160 sailing vessels) left Nassau for Savannah, Charleston, or Wilmington between 1861 and 1865, and 287 steamships (and 109 sail) returned. The value of Nassau's trade, which totaled less than £400,000 in 1860, soared to more than £10,000,000 in 1864.[8]

The short-term effects on Nassau were dramatic. The wharves were piled with transshipped bales and boxes and the streets crowded with blockade runners, from captains to cabin boys, seemingly eager to spend their inflated wages. The new hotel was jammed, and Governor Bayley wrote of the need for another because newcomers had to scour the town to find a place to lay their heads. For Bahamians of all classes there were profits to be made. The 1862 *Blue Book* reported that local businessmen who invested in the blockade trade were making profits of 100 percent. The demand for labor was such that wages were sky high, and so many men were flocking to Nassau from the Out Islands that normal activities, such as wrecking, had almost halted, and farming was neglected. Storekeepers were making windfall profits, lawyers were in demand in maritime cases, and clerks, domestics, and "guides" were well paid. The ordinary seamen on the blockade runners provided a flourishing trade for bars and dance halls Over the Hill, and as the governor laconically reported, gifts of finery were bestowed on "several

Cotton from the Confederate States being unloaded at Nassau, 1864. From *Illustrated London News*, April 18, 1864, courtesy of Bahamas Archives.

of the better looking of the younger women of the middle and lower classes . . . by the generosity of their devoted, tho' transitory admirers."[9]

After two and a half years of prosperity, the editor of the *Nassau Guardian* optimistically compared the city with the Nassau of the early 1840s:

> When we first arrived in this colony—upwards of twenty years ago—there were, we believe, but two Bonded Warehouses; we have now about thirty, containing goods valued at $2,000,000. Bay Street was neither lighted nor paved. There were no quays along the strand; and instead of vessels lying, as they now do along the shore loaded and unloaded by a steam crane, they were approached only from the middle of the harbour by lighters. . . .
>
> Labourers who in former times were satisfied with 1s.6d. and 2s. per day, now ask and receive 10s.; and if they lie out during the night on bales of cotton or tobacco (with a sailcloth covering) they receive 12s.6d. Sterling. Until lately we had no boats for hire. The number of licenses now granted for these amounts to about 100. . . .
>
> We hope soon to see our streets better and more substantially paved, especially those trending towards the harbour at right angles. We trust that those unsightly relics of slavery—high walls—which still enclose so many residences, and generate so much reflected heat, may soon be supplanted by neat iron railings.[10]

In another year the bubble had burst. When first Savannah, then Charleston and Wilmington fell to Union forces, the blockade running slowed, then stopped. Wharves, warehouses, hotels, and boardinghouses emptied, the "dancing saloons in Grants Town" closed, employment and extravagant expenditure ended, and government projects were canceled before completion. So demoralizing was the sudden cutback to merchants, professionals, and workers alike and so great the fears among the ruling class of crime and popular discontent that many expressed the wish that the bonanza had never happened. The new governor, the splendidly reiterative Sir Rawson Rawson, reported at the end of 1865 that the windfall profits of blockade running had left an indelible mark on Nassau because ordinary profits were no longer enough and hard work no longer the norm. This pronouncement was echoed by a middle-class black writing in the *Nassau Guardian* in 1868, under the nom-de-plume Africus: "In our present state it can be truly said that labourers are plenteous, but there is very little field and scarcely any harvest. . . . There is not a glance of any more brighter days, or a prospect of pecuniary prosperity here. Previous to the late American War we were better off, I may say, in many things."[11]

As an index of depressed social conditions in 1868, the same newspaper reported the setting up of a soup kitchen by certain "philanthropic gentlemen" at Mrs. Cruikshank's hotel on George Street, Nassau, where many "indigent and deserving persons" received a "pint of good soup gratis" at 2 P.M. on Wednesdays and Saturdays. Nonetheless, the *Guardian* reported only a few days later a spate of burglaries involving only food and drink, including the theft of ham and a leg of mutton from the superintendent of the asylum and of vegetables from the pantry of the Hon. J. J. Burnside.[12]

Despite the feelings of such progressives as Governor Rawson that picking a living from wrecks was demeaning and that the prevalence of wrecks themselves was a reproach to modern technology, many Bahamian mariners went back to a trade in which 302 licensed wreckers had employed 2,679 men in 1858. In an average prewar year, some twenty-five vessels went aground in Bahamian waters, officially netting about £10,000 in salvage and an unknown additional amount that did not go through official channels. The devastating hurricane of 1866, which added to Nassau's economic woes by destroying or damaging hundreds of buildings, brought rich pickings for the wreckers—no less than sixty-three ships were destroyed and thirty-one seriously damaged during the year. Thereafter, though, wrecking profits declined sharply because shipping victims became fewer as the result of improvements in navigation and the extension of the Imperial Lighthouse Service (ILS) based in Nassau.

The first Bahamian lighthouse, the familiar white landmark at the entrance to Nassau Harbor, had been erected in 1817 at the behest of the Assembly. Four low-power lights, set up by the Admiralty on the orders of the British Parliament at Hole-in-the-Wall, Abaco, and on Gun Cay, Cay Sal, and Grand Turk, followed in the 1830s and 1840s. From 1857, however, an expanding network of powerful modern lighthouses was built, manned, and regularly serviced by the externally funded ILS on Great Isaac Rock (1859), Cay Lobos (1860), Stirrup's Cay (1863), Elbow Cay, Abaco (1863), Inagua (1868), Castle Island, Bird Rock, and Sombrero Cay (1876), and Dixon Hill, San Salvador (1887). With the addition of more than thirty automatic acetylene lights, by the end of the century not only were the chief shipping lanes guarded by major beacons, but there was scarcely a stretch of regularly navigated waters in the vast archipelago out of range of at least one guiding light.[13] In addition, cumulative reports and surveys by the British Admiralty, U.S. Navy, and ILS led to steadily improved navigational charts, though a few major cartographic changes were made after 1880, and as late as the 1960s aerial and satellite surveys led to the relocation of several Bahamian coastlines and an official increase in the total land area of the Bahamas from 4,400 to 5,500 square miles.[14]

Though some ships were still lost every year (and many more in hurricane years), shipping services continued to improve and tourism slowly to expand, in tune with improvements in navigation. By 1872, the Cunard mail contract had been taken over by the Atlantic Mail Steamship Company, but the loss to fire of its flagship the SS *Missouri* off Abaco in October 1872 was an immediate blow, especially since among the eighty-four out of ninety-five crew and passengers who perished was the dynamic manager of the Royal Victoria Hotel, Lewis, the brother of the future U.S. president Grover Cleveland.[15] The company collapsed, and the contract was given to Murray, Ferris of New York to provide at least two steamers a month throughout the year, alternately direct from New York and by way of Savannah, with an increase to three a month during the winter season. This venture also got into difficulties when the SS *Zodiac* was destroyed by fire—this time without loss of life—in September 1875.[16] Yet another mail steamer, the SS *Leo*, burned and sank in 1877, but in 1879 the mail contract between New York, Nassau, and Cuba was given to James E. Ward, who ran it successfully and without losing a vessel until 1917. During the winter season from December to May, the Ward Line employed two steamers on a fortnightly service, making the run between New York and Nassau in three and a half days. Passengers who took a round-trip ticket to Cuba could stay in Nassau or Havana for up to six months and also enjoy the two-week itinerary between three Cuban ports, using the ship as a comfortable hotel.[17]

By the 1890s, the Ward Line, consisting of a dozen vessels, was making a weekly run to Nassau throughout the year. But the Havana run from New York was now direct, and the Nassau boats instead connected with Santiago, Guantanamo, and Cienfuegos. The Ward Line, moreover, though luxurious, was regarded as expensive, and the extension of railways through the southern states led to increasing competition from Florida ports. One favored route around 1880 was by sea between New York and Savannah on one of the four fast steamships built for the Georgia Central Railroad Company in 1878–79, connecting by train (or steamer on the intracoastal waterway) to a weekly steamship service that ran between Jacksonville and Nassau—advertised as taking thirty-six hours but more often fifty-two. Charles Ives, author of an early travel book, in 1880 spent nearly ten days on this route from New York and was dreadfully ill on the long diagonal crossing of the Gulf Stream from Jacksonville on the venerable former blockade-running side-paddle steamer *Secret*. Once the railway was completed down the length of Florida to Miami and Key West in the 1880s, this route was made far easier than steamships plying between Miami, Nassau, and Key West and the overnight voyage from Miami to Nassau taking less than twelve hours.[18]

The pioneer of the Florida tourist route to the Bahamas (as of the Florida Railroad and the city of Miami) was the visionary Henry M. Flagler. Already the owner of a chain of hotels along the Atlantic coast of Florida ("the finest to be found at any winter or summer resort in the world"), at which well-heeled travelers were urged to break the tedium of their journey, Flagler negotiated the fourth and so far most ambitious Hotel and Steamship Act with the Bahamas government in 1898. Having already acquired the aging Royal Victoria Hotel, Flagler now purchased the old Fort Nassau site for a far larger establishment and signed a ten-year contract to

Above, SS *Corsica*, the first Cunard passenger and mail steamship from New York to Nassau, 1859. *Below*, SS *Miami*, the first passenger steamship from Miami to Nassau, 1890s. Photographs from (above) Bahamas Archives, (below) John Fondas Collection, Bahamas Archives.

provide frequent overnight steamship connections with Miami. The barracks recently vacated by the West India Regiment were torn down, foundations laid in 1899, and the huge and inelegant Hotel Colonial opened for business on the site of Woodes Rogers's old fort just as the century ended, auguring—if somewhat prematurely—a new era of Bahamian tourism.[19]

Nassau's summer and winter visitors were still counted in tens and hundreds in 1900, and a sense of the resort's isolation outweighed its antique charm; for the Out Islands the age of the tourist steamship was delayed by nearly a century. Louis D. Powles in 1886 found a tantalizing contrast between the luxury of the Ward Line's steamers and the shabby thirty-eight-ton sailing schooner *Eastern Queen* in which he and a seven-man crew (two Cuban whites as captain and cook, two "very light coloured men," and three "full-blooded Africans") embarked on the magistrate's circuit of the Berry Islands, Bimini, Grand Bahama, and Abaco. "Seen from England, my circuit had seemed the most agreeable part of my official life," he wrote in *Land of the Pink Pearl* (1888).

> A series of pleasant sails from one island to another a few miles off, in a nicely-appointed government boat, gliding gently over summer seas, and constantly stopping at pretty little towns! This was the fancy picture. It was now already clear that I was to travel in a wretched cargo boat, with a cabin void of furniture, comforts, or even decencies. . . .
>
> As we beat out of the harbour we had to pass close to the *Santiago* which had that afternoon come in from Cuba, and was waiting to continue her voyage to New York. As I gazed at her brilliantly illuminated hull, and heard the whirr of her engines, which were slowly getting up steam for a start, how I envied the occupants of those luxurious staterooms, about to sail to a land brimfull of modern civilization, and from thence, some of them perhaps, to the dear home across the Atlantic.[20]

In 1889, Governor Ambrose Shea obtained legislation for "interinsular steam communication" and even the promise of a subsidy from an imperial fund. But his plans did not materialize. The mail service for the Out Islands continued to be by sailing schooner until the 1920s, with a schedule that remained only as regular, reliable, and fast as the winds, currents, and weather allowed. Correspondents in Nassau could hope for a response from New York in less than ten days and England within three weeks, but the little mail that passed to and from the Out Islands traveled scarcely faster than in Loyalist days. Even for Nassau, the arrival of the mail steamers remained important events. Three ingenuous female tourists, the Misses Dickinson and Dowd, wrote in March 1886 how impatiently they watched for the flag signals from the forts or awaited the signal gun from Fort Fincastle that announced the arrival of the New York mail:

> Steamers are supposed to arrive at this port on alternate Mondays. . . . It is some time after one is sighted before we can know whether she is from Cuba or New York. We always wish the latter to come first, so that we can answer any important letters. Upon the third arrival we were awakened by the gun which signified that the steamer had anchored, but usually there is a period of more or less uncertainty, and the town actually seems to have a little life. People walk to and from the Post Office as if existence were not entirely a burden. Even women sometimes venture to post or receive their precious letters, while for a few hours the devoted postmaster needs the hands of Briareus, the patience of Job, the wisdom of Solomon, and the meekness of Moses, as he and his assistants attack the great bags of mail, and answer all sorts of unanswerable and ridiculous questions.[21]

Nassau and the First Tourists

For most late nineteenth-century tourists, Nassau was an idyllic, almost soporific retreat, providing much the same simple diversions as had been enjoyed by the first holidaying visitors in the 1820s. As a destination Nassau was still sufficiently exotic to inspire many travel books. Such visitors as Charles Ives, Lady Brassey, William Drysdale, Dickinson and Dowd in the 1880s, and George Lester and George J. H. Northcroft in the 1890s provided predictably picturesque and glamorized accounts, though some discordant notes could be seen between their lines once they penetrated the social surface or moved beyond Nassau's chief commercial thoroughfare and residential central ridge (Map 6). Then they were much more in line with the realistic picture that emerges from a careful reading of Nassau's newspapers or the harsh strictures of the one severe contemporary critic of Bahamian society, Louis Diston Powles, the disenchanted Irishman who resided in the Bahamas from 1885 to 1887.

Nassau's residential streets, with their brilliant white walls and gaudy flowers, made a quiet contrast to the bustle, clamor, and pungent aromas of market and dock. The even tenor of daily life was punctuated by the weekly parades at church, the arrival of boats with mail and tourists, and (as since slavery days) the annual celebrations of the monarch's birthday, Guy Fawkes Day (celebrating at a great remove the preservation of James I from the Gunpowder Plot of 1605), the official opening of Parliament, and the Christmas and New Year's Junkanoo. Since 1834 had been added to these the commemoration of Emancipation Day on August 1, including downtown parades by the friendly societies, a service and sermon in Christchurch (raised to the status of cathedral in 1864), loyal addresses in front of the public buildings, and a fete and children's party. For some years, the colony also celebrated the anniversary of the visit of Prince Alfred, son of Queen Victoria.[22]

To the excursions and picnics of the 1820s (described in Volume 1) were added carriage trips to view J. S. Johnson's pineapple farm and factory on the Western Road or the phosphorescent lake at Waterloo on the Eastern Road, or outings by glass-bottom boat to explore the wonders of the Sea Gardens east of Fort Montagu. By the end of the century, moreover, excursions by bicycle were not unknown, though Nassau boasted few such machines and the unpaved flattened-coral roads were hard on tires and riders.[23]

Public amenities remained few, though a fine new "library and literary institute" had been opened in the former jail in 1873. Visits by companies of actors and circus troupes (the latter usually from Cuba) were more common during the winter season now that communications were more frequent and reliable. But most entertainment was still homegrown, such as amateur dramatics, concerts, and the weekly whist parties held at Government House in the 1880s. Dances for the tourists and upper classes remained strictly formal, though dance halls for the ordinary blacks and more raffish white visitors existed Over the Hill, and Powles reported in 1886 that the Cuban "marengo" (alias *meringue*) was almost a craze among all classes—the clear forerunner of the predominant modern Bahamian style of dancing, popularly called (no doubt from a boating analogy) "sculling."[24]

Sports were much more common spectacles than in former times. Those that first involved blacks as participants rather than mere spectators were, predictably, involved with the sea. An annual regatta for working sailboats and rowboats was initiated as early as 1831, with a silver cup for first-class sailing vessels of fifteen to

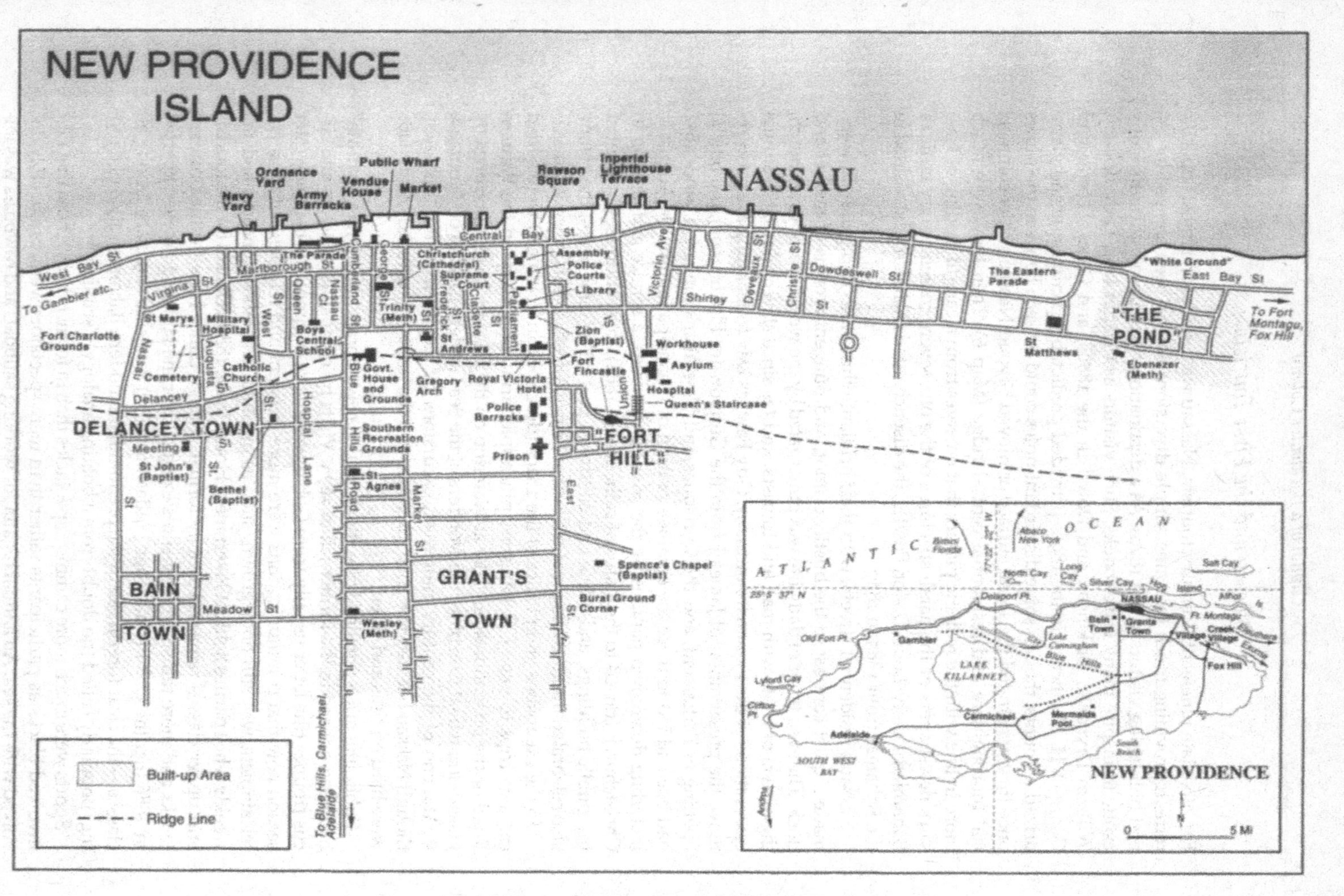

Map 6. Nassau: Downtown and Over the Hill, 1891

forty tons presented by Governor Carmichael Smyth,[25] and more frequent races were organized by the Yachting Club by the 1880s. Charles Ives reported vigorous games of rugby football and polo played by white residents and army officers, drawing many spectators on Tuesday and Friday afternoons, though the ordinary black soldiers of the garrison preferred flying paper kites and the "lowly and quiet game of marbles." Ives, however, seems to have missed many sporting activities, in some of which at least the colored middle class participated.[26]

Cricket apparently was played informally in Nassau in late slavery days, for an 1833 act legislated against "all playing of Cricket or other like Game or Games" on the Parade or public streets. The first formal cricket match reported in the Bahamas was a low-scoring two-inning game between the garrison and a team of civilians played at Fort Charlotte on Saturday, January 27, 1855, which the soldiers won by fourteen runs, though the newspaper accounts indicate that it was not the first game played in the colony.[27] The first contests were played by whites mainly to white spectators. At a match between the garrison and HMS *Galatea* in February 1863, for example, it was reported that "a number of the fair and beautiful were on the ground, who appeared to take a lively interest in the match if we might judge from their many laughs and sparkling eyes; and the fine Band of the 2nd. W.I. Regiment added a charm to everything."[28] In January 1873, however, the newly formed Nassau Cricket Club opened a custom-built cricket ground on East Shirley Street, and from then on, Saturday games were played between mixed teams to large gatherings of black spectators. The social value of cricket (so admirably illustrated in the modern history of Barbados) was, moreover, underlined by the speech of the white Bahamian J. H. Webb in opening the ground on Saturday, January 25, 1873: "Use your ground well . . . and learn scientific cricket as a manly outdoor amusement, for the development of pluck and muscle."[29] By 1899, Northcroft reported to his mainly American readers that "Cricket, not Baseball, is *the* game of the Bahamian young men. There is a host of Cricket Clubs in Nassau, but I know of no Baseball Club, though—I believe—an occasional game is played on the Eastern Parade under the leadership of certain eager spirits who acquired the art in America. But cricketing interests—as is natural in a British Colony—form a social cement of some adhesiveness; and a cricket match of any importance is generally well patronised by spectators."[30]

The newfangled game of lawn tennis had early adherents in Nassau. The first tournament of the all-white Nassau Lawn Tennis Club was held on July 11, 1881, and a rival club for the colored middle class came into existence some time before 1893. Very few blacks, however, had access to the game before the mid-twentieth century. The same held true for golf; a nine-hole course was opened for the use of tourists and local whites in the late 1890s.[31] A more significant augury for the future of Bahamian sports had been the first reported athletics match, held on Monday, February 21, 1870. It was organized by the officers mainly for the members of the garrison, with separate events for officers, noncommissioned officers and men, and "all-comers." Along with genuine athletic contests, it included such curiosities as bucket, sack, and wheelbarrow races, and a "catching and greased pig" competition, won by a Sergeant Fairclough (presumably white), who kept the pig as a prize. This pioneer occasion was said to have drawn together "at least 2000 of the inhabitants of all classes."[32]

Accounts of Nassau by seasonal visitors, aimed mainly at potential tourists, gave generally superficial, reassuringly bland descriptions of the society. James Stark's best-selling guidebook (1891), quoting Charles Ives (1880) to the brink of plagiarism, stressed Nassau's quiet and orderliness. Strangers, both claimed, were "much impressed by the absence of scenes of violence, drunken brawls and profane, abusive and irritating language in the public streets and places of popular resort." This was not, they reckoned, solely a benign result of the climate. "The criminal code, the swift and sure administration of justice by the courts, the police department with its efficient and fine looking black patrolmen—all are material factors in accomplishing so desirable a result," wrote Ives. Even the fact that convicts were made to work on the downtown roads in their white prison uniforms was regarded as an interesting and salutary rather than a degraded and degrading spectacle.[33]

Charles Ives also recognized the beneficial social effects of the "peaceful and conservative operation of a very efficient Church." He lumped together "the humble Methodists with their untiring zeal and spiritual sledge-hammers, up, through the more pretentious cathedral, to the loftiest kind of high church, with its choir of colored urchins in holy vestments." In contrast to the neighboring island of Cuba, with its Sunday theaters and bullfights, in Nassau "the first day of the week is marked by solemn stillness, entire absence from all secular employments, a display of neat and tasty costumes, and by a general attendance upon the devotional services of the churches as strongly as it is in any of the country towns of New England."[34]

Charles Ives, though, was either ignorant of, or disingenuously ignored, the inner tensions and turmoils that lay beneath the surface of Bahamian religion and the bubbling social pot of which the smart Barbadian policemen directing the road gangs of black Bahamian convicts formed the lid. His simple description picked up no echo of the bitter verbal conflicts and actual riots that accompanied the extension of burial ground privileges to nonconformist churches in the 1840s and the disestablishment of the Anglican church in the 1850s.[35] His treatment of the popular black churches was limited to descriptions of "shouter" services Over the Hill as primitive spectacles, and his praise of the respectable Methodists neglected to mention their rigid apartheid policy. Likewise, his differentiation of low and high church Anglicanism ignored the fact that the cathedral was the bastion of the establishment, shunned by most of the blacks for its segregation of the races, while the "ritualistic" churches—which resulted from the missionary extension of the English Oxford Movement during the 1860s—were preferred by ordinary blacks as much for their hardworking populist priests and their egalitarianism in the face of God as for their candles, incense, and colorful vestments.[36]

Like many nineteenth-century visitors, Charles Ives gave a vivid description of the throng of black and colored Bahamians who came forward to entertain or importune the tourists in the colonnaded entrance of the Royal Victoria Hotel—though he deplored the demoralizing effects of the visitors' obvious wealth, favored the lash for beggars, and even bewailed the economic decay and general indolence which, he considered, had resulted from the ending of slavery.[37]

Among those who crowded the Royal Victoria Hotel forecourt were the colored captains Sampson, Johnson, and Mitchell, offering "marine exploring parties," and the owners of the numerous carriages for hire. "This court is also a great bazaar," wrote Ives, "to which the colored people of all ages and both sexes who have anything to sell, resort in large number to dispose of their wares. . . . Many kinds of fruits, flowers and other vegetable products, corals in great variety, sugar cane and candies, sponges of all sizes and qualities, shells exquisitely shaped and beautifully colored, shell-work of unsurpassed excellence, canes of the orange, lignum vitae, ebony, satin and other woods, and many other articles made up their stock in trade." Just as local boys skillfully dived for small coins thrown from the decks of tourist steamers, "here also the colored boys came to scramble, in the most laughable manner, for pennies, thrown to them for that purpose upon the hard pavements of lime-stone and brick. When down, and struggling for the prize, in a wild tangle of arms and legs, they seemed a hideous, writhing mass of black and ragged reptiles of the most lively kind. When up, with faces beaming with fun and frolic, their eager calls for 'massa' to 'trow a penny dis way' soon dispelled the delusion. In these contests, as well as on other occasions, their good nature and amiability are pre-eminently exemplified."[38]

Other entertainment was provided by "native" singing and dancing. "The voices of women were soft and musical," wrote Ives,

> and they sang the religious songs which they had learned in "the shouting meetings," with perfect abandon, and with a fervour and zeal that glorified their dusky faces, swayed their bodies, and extended down their arms to the tips of their fingers. A *sacred* waltz was sometimes performed by "Sankey" and his female cousin [nicknamed, of course, "Moody"], two little dots of children, in the most cunning and comical manner imaginable, while they sang to the rhythm of the dance, "O it will be joyful" &c. When the miniature boy and girl near the close, alternately approached each other and withdrew, ogling, twisting, bowing and coquetting, while they continued to sing with many repetitions—"Meet to part no more; meet to part no more," the gravity of the audience was sure to give way in laughter and applause.[39]

Ignoring the way the eagerness of the impoverished Bahamians to entertain the tourists both demeaned themselves and degraded their culture, including religion, Ives merely stressed the way "novelty speedily degenerated into nuisance" for the visitors. For the blacks, he thought,

> the crowds of winter visitors are like the sugar hogsheads to northern summer flies. The "rich Northerners" constitute a great living tide, with deep, broad currents of unfailing wealth, and all are most eager to catch some of the drops of the golden spray. Not all of them who have a love of money are endowed with the gift of song, and as the choirs are not selected, and most of the black urchins believe that the louder they scream the better they sing, the extent of the annoyance may be in some small degree comprehended. This, together with an inveterate habit of begging at all times and on all occasions for money—a vicious practice constantly encouraged and fostered by the well-meant liberality of the guests—occasionally causes some of the old habitués of the hotel, when the salutary influence of the lash is not brought into requisition, to hire them to go away.[40]

An even greater contrast in views was provided between the glamorized accounts of Nassau's market and waterfront given by the *Illustrated London News* in 1856 and the far more realistic and heartfelt complaints by local whites and middle-class coloreds made in the *Bahama Herald* the same year. "The kind and gentle spirit of the aborigines of those beautiful islands still seems to linger here," rhapsodized the visiting London journalist,

> for the present inhabitants exercise an unostentatious but warm-hearted hospitality. There is an air of vitality as well as cheerfulness, about the clean, neat, quiet little town of Nassau, with its well-chosen library and literary institute. After the miseries of a long sea voyage, with what delight does the eye rest upon the green tints of New Providence: Nassau, and its long, lake-like harbour, dotted with swift-sailing schooners, presents, indeed, a very pretty aspect. In the distance is seen the tall, slender spire of a church, like that of an English village, rising from a rounded clump of trees. . . .
>
> Here, the population presents a lively scene. Gay groups of chattering negresses, in their many-coloured turban-tied kerchiefs, with abundance of bandanna, solicit the attention of passers-by: "Hi massa—my sweet massa!" Here and there lounges along some pale lemon-coloured creole, with broad Panama hat and never-ceasing cigar, some would say tainting the balmy breath of the cool fresh morning; then come grinning gigantic negroes; whilst on all sides lie neglected heaps of conch-shells. . . .
>
> Here is a quaint group of characters, one of the evilest-looking of genii, big and black enough to have tumbled out of the Arabian night. . . . Beside him stands a tall, graceful girl, like a bronze statue of the Queen of Sheba—a plenteous-lipped daughter of Ethiop, with great eyes, calm and placid as the Sphynx . . . curt, curled-like lip, delicate, but firmly-rounded oval chin, glorious front, and eyes so deeply set beneath they could not squint, nay, nor look furtively aside without turning the whole lordly head.
>
> But what is this to the athletic African as he sits sullenly, machete in hand, haggling with that fat old lady about the price of a bundle of grass he has brought from the interior?—the ferocity of his face strangely reminding one of the sons of the Sadites described in the Book of Chronicles "as men fit for battle, whose faces were like the faces of lions". . . . The family likeness is also perceptible in that black-satin boy beside him (with an aldermanic exaggeration of stomach), almost unencumbered by any clothing. Mere market-girls, bearing burdens on their heads, slow and stately in their every motion, they look as if they could not possibly be surprised into any angularity or sharpness of action—queenly! Yet . . . strange to say of one bearing the burden of a slave!—who shall say labour is undignified?[41]

Yet an editorial under the heading "Public Nuisance" in the *Bahama Herald* just six months later complained of "the congregating of cake-women, &c. on a Saturday night on the road-side with lighted torches, candles &c. for the purpose of, as we suppose, selling cakes and fruit, but which is to the quiet passers-by, a perfect nuisance. Every Saturday evening as we are wending our way homewards, we have to pick our steps through a crowd of disorderly persons, assembled round a grog-shop and are jostled to an fro ere we can pass the mob. Why is this allowed?" The article also deprecated "the practice of boys, good big ones too—bathing in the sea on Sundays in a state of nudity, exposing their persons to the neighbours and others."[42] Such concerns seem to have been perennial among "respectable" Nassauvians, as was indicated by a letter "On Obscene Language and Liquor" in the *Nassau Times* in September 1880. "Anyone walking down Bay-Street may count dozens of lewd characters of both sexes lurking especially in the vicinity of the Vendue House," wrote the anonymous complainant, "using most obscene language and very much to the annoyance of those who have to pass along the road to their respective callings; while perchance may be seen a policeman listlessly walking by, apparently heedless of what is happening; or should he be attracted to the noise by some offended individual . . . the nuisance is only stopped by a 'get out of the way', 'move on', 'don't let it happen again' or some such warning." While advocating far stiffer penalties in court cases, the writer placed much of the blame on the evils of drink because most offenders were gathered around the plentiful

Nassau Market. From *Stark's History and Guide to the Bahama Islands* (New York, 1891), courtesy of Bahamas Archives.

rum shops. "It is a fact to be seriously taken into consideration," he piously concluded, "that the majority of the lower classes of our citizens will not be improved morally until the vendors of the abominable 'fire-water' which tends more or less to steal the brains, and ruin the souls of all who take it, abandon the traffic, and enter into a more honest and less demoralising trade. In the space of not more than two hundred feet in Bay-Street may be counted, not less than six liquor shops, to say nothing of the 'milder' and what are called 'malt' liquors that are sold by scores of the more respectable dealers in the trade."[43]

Residential and Class Divisions and Their Determinants

Only L. D. Powles among nineteenth-century writers came close to providing an accurate explanation for the less fortunate aspects of Nassau's social life, which made such a contrast to the complacent Victorian ideals of prosperity and propriety, law and order. Though Powles borrowed some of his descriptions from an American writer, William Drysdale, author of *In Sunny Lands,*[44] his perceptive social analysis was based on his personal experience and observations as a stipendiary circuit magistrate, as well as being animated by the virulent antipathy generated between himself and the Bahamian white oligarchy by his comparatively liberal demeanor on the bench.[45]

Powles memorably described how the society of the Bahamian mini-metropolis revolved around Government Hill: "Nassau Society may be divided into the 'Upper

Upper ten,' eligible for invitation to Government House on all occasions, the 'lower Upper ten', only invited on state occasions; the 'respectable middle class,' including everyone who does not go to Government House, but is acknowledged as white, and the 'lower classes,' including everybody who is admittedly coloured. Some of the last are occasionally invited to Government House, but the Conchs [i.e., white Bahamians] include them along 'the lower classes' all the same."[46]

Powles ignored the poorest white Conchy Joes because they made comparatively little impact on Nassau at this time, but he made a devastating critique of the American journalist who had claimed in the *Century* in 1887 that there was an "utter absence of race prejudices" in Nassau. This writer, a Mr. Church, had cited "a high official, a full-blooded African, who is received everywhere," a reference either to Thomas William Dillet, London-educated son of Haitian-born Stephen Dillet and acting attorney general, or to his darker half-brother Stephen Albert Dillet, MHA, though neither were strictly "full-blooded Africans." Powles pointed out that this distinguished official's acceptance was strictly conditional: "As long as he is content to confine his acquaintance with the white ladies to a salute when he happens to meet them in the street, and a very occasional morning call; as long as he is content to go to Government House on state occasions and hang about the anteroom and piazza, without presuming to attempt to dance, the white Conch gentlemen are willing to use his pleasant piazza as a sort of club, and the Conch ladies are willing to say with a patronising air, 'Oh, yes, Mr——is certainly a gentleman; he knows his place so well.'"[47] In contrast, a colored gentleman who did not "know his place" scandalized Nassau's polite society and was personally ostracized for asking the governor's sister for a dance at a Government House ball. "Yet," claimed Powles, "he is intellectually, morally, and in point of education the superior of any white Conch I ever met, to say nothing that he is the legitimate son of an Englishman, and three parts white."[48]

Powles found it easy to ridicule the pretensions and style of Nassau's "upper crust," the absurd rituals of leaving calling cards and signing the governor's book (the latter on the monarch's birthday and on leaving and returning to the colony), the formality of their clothing in the hottest weather, their stuffy afternoon dinners, and the combination of a love of gossip with an uncertainty of how to make, or take, a joke. Only at dances did they relax, though Powles found their dancing manic and clumsy, as well as producing offensive odors on hot evenings. He was particularly dismissive of the pretentious debates in the House of Assembly and of the way that the Executive Council was regarded—by the councillors at least—as a miniature House of Lords. Despite their inferior imitations of English high society, however, Powles found the Conchs' accents and expressions distastefully American, including such mild deviations as the use of "fix" and "guess," "two weeks" for "a fortnight," "pappa" for "papa," and a drawl on the penultimate syllable, as in "piarzer" for "piazza."[49]

Two of the ironies of Nassau's rigid socioracial structure were that some locally acknowledged whites were of mixed descent—realities that southern Americans or West Indians often detected immediately[50]—and that many of the white elite were far from rich. Especially after the failure of the bank in 1885, no whites looked down on their fellows just for being poor, "neither are the ladies the least ashamed of acknowledging that they make their own dresses, assist in their households, or try to earn their own living."[51] Far less engaging and more insidious were the

Early American tourists walk the grounds of the Royal Victoria Hotel or set out by carriage for a guided tour of Nassau. From *Frank Leslie's Illustrated Newspaper,* May 25, 1878, courtesy of Bahamas News Bureau.

inflexible forms of discrimination practiced against the colored middle classes, a certain sexual hypocrisy left over from slavery days, the stereotypical contempt exhibited by all white Conchs (and even by many colored Bahamians) for "negro traits," and the ways the economic, educational, and legal systems callously kept the mass of the ordinary blacks impoverished, ignorant, and oppressed.

The Bahamian social system more closely resembled the harsh separation between whites and all nonwhites found in the United States than the more flexible West Indian mode with its important middling class and spectrum of relationships. From emancipation onward, the nonwhite middle class in the Bahamas gradually grew in numbers and influence, drawing the small white elite ever more toward the form of a "family compact," but it was never a homogenous faction and was rendered politically impotent by the prejudices against all things African ingrained even in those of partial African ancestry. The comparative lack of social tensions (at least on the surface) was the result partly of the physical separation of different classes and races, especially outside Nassau, but also of the almost universal, almost instinctual, recognition—natural in such a small population—of one's proper place in the complex social order and of the accompanying social conventions. Such subtleties were perhaps encapsulated in the ironic inversion reported by Northcroft in the ways the black servants announcing a visitor to their white employer differentiated between "a white woman," "a colored person," and "a black lady."[52]

As the corollary of an extreme color consciousness, all Bahamian nonwhites suffered from segregation in housing, education, work, and ordinary social intercourse, and "crossovers" were extremely limited. It was backed up when necessary by a decidedly (if unofficially) color-conscious legal system. In the Bahamas as a whole, the majority of the unequivocally black lived an almost entirely separate existence, as did the isolated communities of poor whites in Eleuthera and Abaco. Even in New Providence, Nassau's ridge—or rather, the city's limits a few hundred yards to its south—represented the northern boundary of all-black settlements. But the city itself was a complex meeting ground, whose residential population was numerically almost evenly divided between the dominant whites, "middle-class" browns, and a tenacious fringe of black laborers, mariners, domestics, craftsmen, and ambitious small entrepreneurs.

A residential map of Nassau in the 1890s distinguishing races and classes (if such precision were possible) would show the prime central sites still monopolized by white officials, professionals, and commercial oligarchs in a pattern of relatively low-density housing and a very few incursions by the wealthiest and lightest-complexioned of those not acknowledged as whites. Whites seeking to escape the increasingly cramped (and unhealthy) bounds of downtown Nassau by building on the eastern extension of the ridge, however, were more likely to have nonwhite neighbors. The majority of the "high yellow" and "brown" middle class lived either in the near suburbs to the east or in the swath of streets to the west and north of the old barracks (and New Colonial Hotel), particularly the area west of Government House grounds and south of Fort Charlotte called Delancey Town. Here, a few of the most successful and enterprising blacks had made inroads similar to those made by coloreds in central Nassau. The working-class blacks who did not live in Grant's Town or points further Over the Hill lived either in the crowded area south of Fort Fincastle or in slummy pockets of swampy land on Nassau's eastern margins, sometimes (as in the area known as the Pond) in uncomfortable proximity to tight-knit groups of poor white Conchy Joes (Map 6).

These patterns of residential separation paralleled and reinforced other forms of customary segregation. The Presbyterian kirk, St. Andrew's, in the center of town, was favored by the commercial elite, not so much for any Scottish family connections or even for the alleged compatibility between commerce and the Calvinist ethic as because its congregation was exclusively white.[53] In 1889, one Methodist missionary wrote that half of the kirk's congregation consisted of former members of nearby Trinity Methodist Church, who had become alienated not on theological but on social grounds because Trinity was attended by a poorer class of whites and had even admitted a few respectable light-skinned coloreds.[54] Most colored Methodists, however, worshiped at Ebenezer Chapel on East Shirley Street, and Wesley Chapel in Grant's Town catered almost exclusively to a black congregation.[55]

Similar differentiation was found among the larger number of adherents to the formerly established Anglican church. Christchurch (which was elevated to the status of cathedral on the creation of the Diocese of the Bahamas in 1861, raising Nassau to the dignity of a city) undoubtedly remained the government, official, and high society church, resolutely retaining low church "Prayer Book" observances even during the tenure of successive Anglo-Catholic bishops, Addington Venables (1863–75), Francis Cramer-Roberts (1875–85), and Edward Churton (1885–1900).[56] Eight hundred of Christchurch's twelve hundred seats were subject to pew rent, which ensured that the white elite commanded the center of the church, the coloreds were consigned to the side aisles, and the blacks took up the four hundred free seats at the back or went elsewhere.[57] A similar allocation by class and color applied at St. Matthew's in the eastern suburbs, where the congregation was far more mixed and the observances began to veer from the austerities of the Edwardian Prayer Book toward high church ritual after the death of the conservative Parson Richardson Saunders in the 1890s. Very different were St. Mary's in the western suburbs (formerly chapel-at-ease to Christchurch) and St. Agnes in Grant's Town, where the rituals included high mass, confession, and veneration of the Virgin Mary and Blessed Sacrament and consequently were said by one Methodist missionary to have "out-Romed Rome."[58] Very few whites ever worshiped at these two churches, the congregation of the former being predominantly drawn from the colored middle class and that of the latter almost exclusively black.

Among the attractions of the Anglican high churches for nonwhites were the opportunities they provided for their participation. Nonwhites became church officials and served on vestries (now shorn of their nonecclesiastical functions) and other church committees. Men and boys sang in the choirs and served at the altar; women were active in Sunday schools and guilds. A "native" ministry was also encouraged to a limited extent by the Anglo-Catholics. By 1894 it was reported that Nassau had already supplied over twenty candidates for holy orders, nearly all colored or black because "those belonging to the class most fitted to influence others, do not offer themselves." Nonwhite priests were trained abroad and sent to serve in foreign dioceses, the one exception being Rev. Marshall Cooper, who was placed in charge of all-black Andros in 1887. Priests in charge of Anglican churches in Nassau were exclusively white well into the twentieth century and seemingly preferred even by nonwhite parishioners.[59]

The Roman Catholic church was surprisingly late in entering the Bahamian field, though once begun it emulated and capitalized on the methods used by high church Anglican missionaries. The Bahamas had been theoretically attached to the Catholic see of South Carolina since 1858, but a resident priest was not sent to Nassau until 1885, when Father George O'Keefe laid the foundations of St. Francis Xavier's Church (later cathedral) on West Hill Street. The dedication of the first church to one of Roman Catholicism's most valiant missionary saints signified the church's attitude toward the Bahamas. But the Catholic mission effort became an American enterprise dominated by Benedictine monks as the result of the arrival in 1891 (and decision to stay until his death in 1928) of a dynamic American priest of German extraction, Father Chrysostom Schreiner, OSB, sent by his abbot from St. John's Abbey, Collegeville, Minnesota, to recover from tuberculosis. Schreiner, who divided his time between Nassau and impoverished San Salvador (where Columbus celebrated the first Christian service in the New World on October 13, 1492), set the pattern and tone of the expansion of Catholicism in the Bahamas. Theologically conservative if not simplistic and paternalistic if not authoritarian (like Schreiner himself), the Roman Catholic priests, even more than the Anglo-Catholic missionaries, offered their converts attractive churches, agreeable rituals, the salutary absence of segregation within the churches, and ample opportunities for participation. They were also aided from the beginning by nuns from several different orders, who, though meekly bound to be subordinate to the all-male priesthood, represented a more institutionalized feminine dimension than was provided by rival churches. In due course (if not before the twentieth century) non-white Bahamian females as well as males were attracted into Catholic orders.

For Nassau, the chief attractions of the Roman Catholic church were social as much as spiritual. The first local converts were ambitious and respectable non-whites who joined the small initial congregations of foreign white residents (such as Cubans) with a Catholic background. In the Out Islands, however, the Catholics made rapid progress in areas neglected by the Anglicans for lack of funds and personnel, the priests and nuns providing social, medical, and even mechanical and agricultural services more properly the duty of government in addition to spiritual comfort. Everywhere, but especially in Nassau, the Roman Catholics were prominent in education, introducing a system that was not only a powerful agent of proselytization but, like the schools provided by the other denominations, accurately reflected the social composition and philosophy of its congregations. In 1889, four Sisters of Charity founded St. Francis Academy for girls on West Hill Street, and by 1892, when a second school was established for boys, 280 children were enrolled though the total official Catholic population at that time was only 77.[60]

Once the Bahamas had become a separate Catholic (missionary) diocese, the original priory became a full-fledged monastery, and the islands were served by six orders of nuns, the Catholics became pioneers of secondary as well as primary education that did not discriminate on grounds of class, color, sex, or even church affiliation, and by the 1960s they had over five thousand children enrolled in more than a dozen schools.

Well into the twentieth century, though, Bahamian education was both backward and socially skewed. Many black Bahamians remained illiterate, and only the exceptional few whose parents could spare them and afford the fees aspired to any form of secondary education. A higher proportion of colored boys (though very few in total numbers) received secondary training at the Boy's Central School or the Anglican Nassau Grammar School, where they sat alongside some of the poorer whites. This limited phase of almost equal opportunity, though, did not last through the pupils' lifetimes. Very few colored secondary school graduates could afford the necessary excursion outside the colony to obtain higher education or professional training, and most became Board School teachers or entered—and stayed in—the lower ranks of the minuscule local civil service or the relatively non-color-conscious Imperial Lighthouse Service. Their white fellow pupils almost invariably did better, through preferential access to white-owned businesses and more rapid promotion in the public service, even if not sent away for further education. The wealthier whites, of course, bypassed the local educational system, paying for private tuition and sending their children to England, Canada, or, increasingly, the United States, for school, university, or legal training.

As to be expected from such a conservative social milieu, the postprimary education of girls lagged even further behind that of boys. Not only were there the archaic prejudices against preparing girls for anything but domestic roles and against coeducational schools beyond the primary level, but the idea of adolescent girls of different classes and races mixing indiscriminately was unthinkable to "respectable" colored as well as white parents. The Anglican church was the pioneer of girls' secondary education in the Bahamas with the creation of St. Hilda's in 1886, which struggled on, with some colored as well as white pupils after 1900, until 1924. The problems of secondary education for both sexes perceived by the white elite were more permanently solved, however, by the creation of Queen's College in 1889, under the aegis of the Methodist church, but through the initiative of the members of the Presbyterian kirk as well as Trinity Methodist Chapel, with the original trustees split eleven to twenty-two between the two churches. Virtually coeducational from the beginning (with separate divisions on adjacent sites in central Nassau), Queen's College never had a written color code but was virtually all-white—as well as the premier secondary school in the colony—until the 1950s.[61]

Between Upper Crust and Underclass: Nassau's Nonwhite Petty Bourgeoisie

If not as bleak as the prospects for ordinary blacks, job opportunities for the majority of coloreds were even less than for those few with a secondary education. Many of them were apprenticed to a trade, and a few of the most energetic, enterprising, and lucky even made limited economic—if slower social—advances. Although the lot of most blacks was to be unskilled laborers earning two shillings a day, coloreds aspired to be craftsmen making three to five shillings, or even to become masters, employing their own journeymen and apprentices. Certain trades were especially favored by coloreds. Boatbuilding and carpentry were shared by blacks and poor whites, but the more refined types of masonry (which included the architectural design and building supervision of such edifices as the Masonic Temple on Bay Street, raised in 1885), cabinetmaking, shoemaking, and tailoring were more or less monopolized by coloreds. The *Nassau Almanack* in 1901 listed fifteen master tailors with their own premises, all of them colored men.[62] Another trade, though originally dominated by whites, that attracted coloreds because of its chances for self-expression and upward mobility, was printing. The most notable example was Leon Dupuch, whose family claimed noble French antecedents but had arrived in Nassau as penniless colored refugees from the French Antilles. He was to go on to edit the opposition *Watchman* and found his own newspaper, the *Tribune,* in 1903, but had left school at nine and been apprenticed to the white owner of the *Guardian,* Alfred E. Moseley, at a shilling a week. James C. Smith had launched the *Freeman* in March 1887, outspokenly advocating the cause of his fellow coloreds until forced into liquidation by white opposition and lack of government advertising two years later.[63]

By 1900, a fair number of coloreds and even a few blacks had beaten the odds and become respectable citizens and men of modest substance, having found a niche on the socioeconomic margins of Nassau society. Most were craftsmen, minor civil servants, or teachers; but a few (as the *Nassau Directory* and the advertising pages of Northcroft's *Sketches of Summerland* show) owned their own small businesses. These included owners and operators of boats and carriages, a livery stable, and restaurants, importers of Out Island produce, and at least one sponge broker. Before white Bay Street had established a nearly absolute grip on the import and retail trades, there were a few non-white-owned groceries and dry goods and liquor stores, mainly in the less central sections of Nassau, though that owned by the remarkable W. P. Adderley at the corner of George and King streets enjoyed the grand title the "Big Store."

The cream of this nonwhite elite were the handful who managed to obtain election to the House of Assembly. In 1837 there were four, but this number scarcely increased for another century.[64] In 1889, there were six: Dupuch, Smith, Adderley, a civil servant, a resident justice, and a Cat Island farmer. Had they been more radical and united in their political aims, they would still have been powerless against the combined front of the remaining eighteen MHAs. Yet they were further weakened by the compromises they had been forced to make to ensure election, if not by a genuine conversion to the norms of the dominant social group. For a start, elections involved considerable expenditure, and parliamentary sittings, though rarely protracted, took members away from their normal livelihood. Not surprisingly, the chief concern of most nonwhite members (perhaps of all MHAs) was the dignity of their position and the personal advantage their office brought. The interest of their section of the community or constituency was a secondary consideration and the general welfare of the black majority scarcely a concern at all.

The wisdom of bitter experience had shown that "not knowing one's place" was to risk any social or economic advantages that had been painfully gained. The richest and most prominent nonwhite officeholders were forced to accept the prevailing (even intensifying) segregation practices. In addition to the subtle protocols at official functions and the informal separation in churches and schools, many restaurants, most clubs, and all hotels, as befitted institutions aimed to serve local whites and a North American clientele, were exclusively for the enjoyment of whites and had blacks or coloreds on the premises solely as servants. Even the mail schooners to the Out Islands—most notoriously the *Dart*, which served Harbour Island—were strictly segregated, only whites being allowed in the cabins, while coloreds as well as blacks were confined to the deck.[65]

In a system in which justices and grand and petty juries were all recruited exclusively from the white or most respectable colored classes, it was inevitable that the courts both served and reflected the dominant elements in society and their view of the world. For one critical outsider at least, a special brand of justice seemed to exist for the whites. Louis D. Powles may have exaggerated slightly when he said that "even-handed justice between black and white is all but unknown in the Bahamas." Yet when he sentenced a Methodist white, James Lightbourne, to a month's imprisonment without the option of a fine for assaulting a black girl, he provoked an uproar. There was a common saying in Nassau at the time that "no white man can go to prison in Nassau." Powles, a Roman Catholic, especially upset the white Nassau Methodists, who included several prominent MHAs. Accused by Governor Blake of stirring up racism, he was forced to resign, and the Assembly refused to pay the return passage to England for him and his wife. Almost inevitably, the Bahamian chief justice reversed Powles's decision in the Lightbourne case.[66]

The affair did not go unnoticed by the colored and black population. Led by Alexander Bain, the black developer of Bain Town, the poorest section of Over the Hill, they petitioned the secretary of state for Powles's return, arguing that he had "fearlessly and impartially discharged his magisterial duties." They believed that Powles had left because of "a persecution organized against him by persons who do not wish to see justice equally administered towards all classes of the community." Among the petitioners was George A. Bosfield, an educated colored man who worked as a master tailor. When he had been summoned before Magistrate Powles in 1887 for violating an act that compelled houses within the city limit to be built in a certain way and had filed information against seventeen of the leading whites for similar offenses, the House of Assembly immediately repealed the act.[67]

Regarded as even more serious by the ruling whites were Powles's fulminations against the truck and sharecropping systems—his attacks rising to a climax in the book he wrote after his dismissal and departure. In modern terms. Powles argued that the Bahamian legal and legislative systems sustained the economic and social hegemony of the white oligarchy. Yet the courts were also, in a more subtle way, the instruments of traditional social morality, with all its hypocrisies and double standards. Sexual morality and the relationship of racial miscegenation to the delicate social fabric were among the most sacred and unspoken taboos. Yet even these were occasionally revealed in court cases, the most scandalous of which surfaced in 1893, five years after Powles had left the Bahamas. The impregnability of white supremacy depended on the proposition that the marriage of an admittedly colored person to a white was out of the question, but the matter of interracial sexual relations was a fuzzier area. As throughout the West Indies, the notion of a white woman having a nonwhite lover was unthinkable. Yet it was by no means uncommon for men of the Bahamian white elite to have black or colored mistresses, termed "sweethearts," by whom children might be born. These offspring, naturally, would not be recognized by white society; being mulattoes, they would automatically belong to the colored or lower class.

At the other end of society, the blacks were not only open for sexual exploitation by those above them on the social scale but were, by the customary hegemonic inversion, regarded by them as naturally promiscuous. Certainly, as to all classes in which property, inheritance, and the canons of respectability had limited practical meaning, blacks (though tightly bound by kinship ties and affective bonds) were less concerned than were the "respectable classes" with the rules of formal marriage or technical illegitimacy.

The intervening classes, like middle classes everywhere, were most bound and oppressed by the rule of respectable morality, being able to enjoy neither the confident double standards of the whites nor the easygoing indifference of the lower-class blacks. Though the ideal of colored men and women alike to "marry up" to produce offspring of a lighter complexion than themselves posed certain genetic contradictions, the "good marriage" was almost sacred to the Bahamian middle class. Some colored men, emulating their white "betters," did carry on illicit liaisons with black women, but these were guilty secrets almost as much deplored as were sexual adventures by unmarried colored women—especially with men of a darker hue or lower class than themselves. If a girl from a respectable colored family got pregnant out of wedlock, she was either sent away to have the baby and give it up for adoption or, if she gave birth at home, suffered lifelong ostracism by her peers.[68]

Early in 1893, Stephen A. Dillet, respectable dark-colored first mate in the Lighthouse Service (and son and namesake of a more distinguished father)[69] discovered that his twenty-five-year-old unmarried daughter, Elizabeth, was pregnant by James C. Smith, then the most prominent of all Bahamian coloreds, a light-skinned man who was postmaster (in succession to Stephen Dillet's father) as well as an MHA for Nassau's Western District. Stephen Dillet insisted that an investigation be made and—because of Smith's official status—this was duly held before the governor and the Executive Council. The love letters discovered proved that Smith was indeed the father, but he obviously had no intention of marrying Miss Dillet. He had hoped, by all accounts, to keep her as his mistress and had been willing to settle £50 a year on her. He had also arranged for her to go to New York to have the baby.[70]

Smith clearly intended to conduct and settle the affair like a Bahamian gentleman. Far from planning to make an honest wife of the darker Miss Dillet, he was courting a white woman from Yorkshire who was visiting Nassau when the scandal broke and married her later the same year. On the other side, there were feelings that Miss Dillet had been jilted, and Smith was charged by Stephen Dillet with seduction and abduction. In response to questioning by the Council, Smith counterattacked by trying to prove that Elizabeth Dillet was virtually a prostitute. He brought as a witness a cigar-maker of Cuban extraction called Lorenzo Gomez—vulgarly nicknamed "Snapper Backbone"—who swore on oath that he had enjoyed Elizabeth Dillet's sexual favors while she was still a schoolgirl.[71]

The case did not go beyond the Council because no criminal charges were laid or any formal resolution made. But Smith's career and social standing, as well as Elizabeth Dillet's reputation, were permanently damaged. The Council—many of whose members had long resented Smith's political stance as unofficial spokesman and champion of blacks as well as coloreds—suspended him from his position as postmaster and rejected his subsequent petition for reinstatement. Though he continued as MHA until the end of his term in 1896, Smith had no chance of reelection, instead taking up an appointment in exile as assistant postmaster in Sierra Leone. Elizabeth Dillet was taken from New York, where her father found her in a "House of Refuge," to London, where she was placed in a special home. She vowed never to return to Nassau because "she refused to face the shame," in due course happily married a man called Colton, and lived in England until her death in 1951.[72]

In Nassau's rigid if informal caste system, the middling colored stratum suffered perhaps the worst frustrations. Disliked and distrusted, if not hated, by blacks, whom they in turn despised, they aspired to white social norms but faced insurmountable social barriers. Neglected when not actively oppressed, the black majority had at least the dubious advantage of being regarded as unequivocal social outsiders. Paradoxically, this allowed the exceptional few blacks who made sufficient money to find significant niches in the margins and interstices of Nassau's society, in competition with the lighter nonwhites—positions that required generations of acceptance and humiliation yet fewer cultural compromises and, in the long run, less ethnic ambivalence or psychological damage.

Among such exceptional black families were at least a majority of the descendants of the remarkable Stephen Dillet Sr. Another founding father was David Patton, a "full-blooded African" farmer whom James C. Smith took L. D. Powles to see to show him what "a lazy nigger could do with a bit of coral rock." Only a few years later, Patton (still living in Grant's Town) was the prosperous and respected owner of a livery stable and coach hiring house.[73] Even more outstanding was the dynasty founded by Alliday Adderley, a Yoruba enslaved by the Portuguese and

Nassau's blacks offer their wares and talents to winter visitors in the piazza of the Royal Victoria Hotel, 1878. The boy and girl in the left foreground might almost have been "Sankey" Toote and his partner "Moody." From *Frank Leslie's Illustrated Newspaper*, May 25, 1878, courtesy of Bahamas Historical Society.

released in the Bahamas, who, by "industrious habits," became the first liberated African man of substance in the 1860s. By the time of his death in 1885, two sons had been elected to the House of Assembly, and a grandson, the aptly named William Parliament Adderley, was fast on his way to becoming the wealthiest and most influential black Bahamian. Graduating from the family business of farming, trading in produce, and small-scale contracting to owning the modest shop grandly styled the Big Store in downtown Nassau, W. P. Adderley sat as MHA for the all-black constituency of Andros. His son Augustus Frederick Adderley (1883–1953), circumventing Nassau's racial bias, was educated in England at boarding school, Oxford, and the Inns of Court, returning to a distinguished legal and legislative career. A. F. Adderley's son Paul, also educated abroad and trained as a lawyer, was to hold major ministerial posts after the black Progressive Liberal Party (PLP) government came to power and the Bahamas became independent. Among the Adderleys who took flight to a more comfortable life in the northern United States in the early twentieth century were the famous jazz musicians Nat and Julian "Cannonball" Adderley.[74]

Perhaps most interesting of all for the social history of the Bahamas, however, was the destiny of the diminutive black entertainer nicknamed "Sankey" described by Charles Ives and other visiting writers in the 1880s.[75] As L. D. Powles discovered, Sankey's impressive real name was Thaddeus de Warsaw Toote. Besides having a singing, dancing, and miming talent that Powles reckoned would bring certain success in London's West End, Sankey Toote possessed much the character of Charles Dickens's Artful Dodger. By 1886 he had almost given up the entertainment business and was engaged in odd jobs ("good or bad is all the same to Sankey," said Powles) for anyone who would employ him. Powles's opinion was that "in a civilized country he would probably rise to a good position, or go for a long term of penal servitude. In earlier times he might have concluded a short, but brilliant, career upon the gallows!"[76] In fact, as an adult, T. W. Toote became a successful businessman and was elected MHA for San Salvador and Rum Cay in 1928. More significantly, he was the father both of Thaddeus Augustus Toote, MHA, councillor, and, along with A. F. Adderley, one of Nassau's two chief black lawyers and spokesmen for nonwhite causes, and Frederick Augustus Toote, who, migrating to the very different sociopolitical climate of Harlem, New York, became in the 1920s one of the most important lieutenants of the great radical black activist, the Jamaican-born Marcus Mossiah Garvey.[77]

4

Over the Hill and Far Away: The Life and Culture of Bahamian Blacks After Slavery

Settlements over the Hill

The ridge that separated respectable "white" Nassau from the exclusively black settlements adjacent to the south and in the rest of New Providence was as marked a social divide as that formed by the sea between Nassau and the Out Islands. There was, of course, a more than symbiotic relationship between the two sections of New Providence and some interpenetration. Some of the symbols and forces of the dominant culture, law, and order—for example, churches, schools, and police—were found beyond the ridge. Persons from the black suburbs and outlying settlements were also seen in Nassau every day at work or in the market and in more organized groups on special occasions such as the August and Christmas celebrations. Yet despite geographical proximity, the life and culture of Grant's Town, Bain Town, Fox Hill, Carmichael, Gambier, and Adelaide were so distinct that nineteenth-century writers regarded the settlements as exotic "native quarters," and modern social historians can study contemporary accounts to arrive at a sound understanding of what Afro-Bahamian culture was truly like in that crucial interim period between the ending of involuntary African migration and the onset of the blanketing influences, affecting blacks as well as whites, of North American modernization.

To a certain extent, distance lent enchantment to Nassau's outlying black settlements for outside viewers. For even as they began to be crowded together, the small houses were screened by the luxuriant foliage of bushes, fruit-bearing trees, and palms. From Nassau's ridge until modern times, Grant's Town, in contrast to the city's white cluster of buildings, appeared more like a green tropical garden than the overcrowded and unsanitary slum it was in reality. Even in 1900, most houses were surrounded by gardenlike yards, some an acre in extent, in which the more fortunate and industrious families grew potatoes, eddoes and yams, okras, pumpkins, beans and corn, bananas, coconuts, and a wide range of tropical tree fruits, including papaya, mango, guava, sapodilla, and citrus, as well as keeping a few hogs and fowls. Brilliant and sweet-scented flowers grew almost like weeds, and at least one enterprising black farmer grew roses for sale, in 1887 even sending weekly consignments to Jacksonville on ice.[1]

A rapidly increasing majority of yards were too small or infertile for a family's subsistence so that racially biased writers such as Charles Ives were torn between admiration for the achievements of families such as David Patton's, amazement at what could be coaxed out of honeycombed rock with pick, hoe, and sweat, and contempt for the majority of indolent, unhealthy, and seemingly lazy "natives" whom they saw. The disparity between families that could largely feed themselves and those that could not was indicated by the prevalence of petty praedial larceny (by far the most common local crime), which caused every substantial householder to keep a pack of fierce, or at least noisy, "potcake" mongrel dogs. Grant's Town, like the other black settlements, was low-lying, even swampy, and the early morning fogs that enveloped them—which some outsiders found picturesque—were decidedly unhealthy to a population without well-insulated houses or adequate clothing. Even more dangerous was the water supply, drawn either (for preference) from rainwater barrels and cisterns or from wells that tapped a water table increasingly polluted from the simple earth privies. These last inevitably provided one of the settlements' less favorable and lasting (though rarely remarked) characteristics: a nighttime aroma that was a sickly amalgam of "night soil" and night-scented jasmine. In settlements without public lighting in which people tended to rise and retire with the sun, clamping their doors and shutters against nocturnal vapors, the weekday nights were eerily free of human activities and noises, though the night air was riven by waves of sound from barking and howling dogs (rising to a climax at the full moon) and punctuated by the even sharper cacophony of crowing cocks in early morning.[2]

Four parallel north-south streets, quickly deteriorating into country lanes once they crossed the Hill, served Nassau's black outlying settlements. Grant's Town filled and overflowed a grid of even narrower lanes on either side of East and Market Streets, and Bain Town, south of both Delancey and Grant's Towns, followed a less orderly pattern between Blue Hill Road and Nassau Street. Signifying the importance of the intersection between side streets and the main roads, many of the former were "corners" rather than streets, lanes, or alleys. Most of the streets of Grant's Town's original grid were named, like Grant's Town itself, after important white officials (such as Governors Cockburn, Lewis, or Cameron). Others, developed later, acquired by popular usage the names of prominent residents or landmarks. The former covered most of the range of black Bahamian surnames, including the African-sounding Quackoo; the latter included such obvious labels as Jail Alley, Burial Ground Corner, Tinshop Corner, or Toote Shop Corner. More obscure were Lily-of-the-Valley Corner (named after a bar), Old Boat Alley, Sunlight Cottage, Lifebuoy Street, or, most curious of all, Eneas Jumper Corner, named for the location of the African Methodist Episcopal church presided over by Bishop William Venables Eneas, the son of a Yoruba liberated African who lived (appropriately on Eneas Street) in the center of Bain Town from 1860 to 1890.

Grant's Town in 1900 had about three thousand permanent residents, plus a fair number of transients, and Bain Town was home to perhaps fifteen hundred. The sprawling settlement popularly called Fox Hill, four miles southeast of Nassau's center, had perhaps twelve hundred inhabitants. Originally named after one of its earliest settlers, a free colored farmer called Fox,[3] it was officially renamed in 1849 after Judge Sandilands, who laid out its central area in two-acre plots and gave it a miniature "village square" around an ancient, and doubtless sacred, silk cotton tree. The Fox Hill Village area, however, extended a mile in each direction. It included the hamlet of the Creek, long established on Nassau harbor around the Anglican chapel (1740) that became St. Anne's Church and school in the 1850s to the north, and four popularly named and vaguely bounded "towns": Congo, Nango, and Joshua Towns settled by liberated Africans and Burnside Town (named for a white surveyor general), founded by Bahamian-born former slaves. Though by the late nineteenth century almost the whole of the Fox Hill area had been formally patented and roughly surveyed, most holdings were peasant-sized, and there were still undeveloped parcels and some vacant land on which peasant farmers could encroach and squat.[4]

Gambier, Carmichael, and Adelaide, respectively nine, ten, and sixteen miles due west, south-south west, and southwest of Nassau, together contained no more people than Fox Hill. They were settled almost entirely by liberated Africans, and their poverty, isolation, and steady emigration kept them small. But they retained their ethnic identity and sense of community almost intact, and their livelihood was guaranteed by the ample stretches of unpatented land on which their people could squat and farm and by the nearby fishing grounds. Carmichael Village was augmented, if somewhat poignantly, by the establishment there of the government leper colony, with up to 150 residents in the 1880s, in families as well as groups of single persons.[5]

The first stone building in most black settlements, built in a central location, was the police station and lockup. Even churches, church and friendly society halls, and schools were modest, single-story structures, and the few shops and bars were scarcely larger or more substantial than the dwelling houses. Of these homes, a few, like David Patton's, though small, stood out for their neat appearance, with a front veranda, glass windows, painted woodwork, and whitewashed plaster. Inside, under a white-painted ceiling, wrote Powles, "There is always as much furniture as he can cram in, and the most showy coloured prints and ornaments he can get hold of are hanging on the wall or dispersed about the room. If you are admitted to view the bedroom, you will be struck at once with the snowy whiteness of the bed-linen, and the remarkable stiffness of the starched pillow-cases, bordered all round with lace."[6] The majority of houses, though, were no more than huts, and many were "little better than collections of boards knocked together and thatched with palmetto straw, with just a bed, table and chair, and a few cooking utensils, by way of furniture."[7] Most were two- or three-roomed boxes of unpainted wood, either flat on the ground or raised on limestone rocks at each corner, though others had walls of plastered limestone rubble, wattle and daub, or even (in cases of poverty even greater than Powles noticed) thatched palmetto on flimsy wooden frames. Besides palmetto thatch (the making of which was a distinctively African skill), some houses were roofed with native cedar shingles. Nearly all had simple plank doors in front and back and top-hinged plank shutters over rough wooden frames. In-built fireplaces and chimneys were completely unknown, despite winter temperatures that could fall below 10° C. Though privies cut in the rock were screened by rough outhouses, separate kitchen shacks were uncommon. Cooking was normally performed in the open yard, as were common ablutions, with little fires "made of dead wood gathered in the forests and thickets . . . transported in little bundles upon the heads of women and children."[8] Collecting water from public wells (for piped water awaited the twentieth century) was a constant chore for those without wells or large rainwater tanks of their own.

To a large extent, the quality of housing was an index both of respectability and family organization and of poverty. The proportion of tightly knit nuclear families and strong kinship affiliations that, as was shown in Volume 1, distinguished

Three types of nineteenth-century Afro-Bahamian cottage, all roofed with palmetto thatch. *Above,* roughly cemented free stone. *Middle,* a pine-planking box raised on stilts. *Below,* wattle and "tabby" mortar. Stone foundations and shingle roofs were marks of comparative affluence. From (above) Bahamas Archives, (middle) John Fondas Collection, Bahamas Archives, (below) *Stark's History and Guide to the Bahama Islands* (New York, 1891).

social organization in slavery days and immediately after was only partially sustained by the efforts of the "respectable" churches to encourage formal marriage. Kinship groups grew weaker, the proportion of nuclear households steadily decreased, and the numbers of single female-headed households increased along with the decline of chances of maintaining a peasant lifestyle, overcrowding, and the migration of men in search of work. Yet the family unit remained predominant even in the most crowded settlements. Whole streets and small neighborhoods resembled extended families, and the level of technical illegitimacy was far short of that in the West Indies or even in the late twentieth-century Bahamas. Of the sixty-five hundred persons over eighteen years of age out of a total New Providence population of eleven thousand in 1891 (three-quarters of them black), 51 percent were married. The figures for the five thousand residents of Grant's Town and Bain Town were probably somewhat lower but did not approach the Jamaican level of 30 percent. The proportion of technically illegitimate to legitimate children baptized in Anglican churches in New Providence in 1893, however, was four to seven, compared to one to three elsewhere in the Bahamas.[9]

Although almost everyone in the black settlements had a decent set of clothes for Sunday church or other special occasions—especially the women, as Powles described—day-by-day clothing was shabby, threadbare, or ragged. Charles Ives expressed surprise not to see the "nearly naked negroes" of whom some had written, but he noticed that most blacks normally went barefoot and the rest wore such "poor apologies for shoes" that it was "impossible for them to walk except with a noisy, shuffling gait, which equally grates upon the ear and offends the eye of people from the States."[10]

Unemployment and low wages meant that cash was short for food not grown at home, as well as for clothing and other imported goods. The balance of trade was heavily in favor of the importing wholesaler over the retailer and the retailer over the small producer. In the more distant settlements there was much peasantlike sharing and barter, but the nearer to Nassau a small producer lived the more necessary it was to enter the cash and market economies. As in Africa, marketing played a large part in the lives of all black New Providence "villagers," and most of the vendors were women. Some sold vegetables and fruits from door to door, others from small stalls outside their yards, at the end of their lanes, or in Grant's Town's small formal market. This market, petitioned for in 1840, was authorized and regulated by an act in 1850 that transferred the island's second formal market from Nassau's eastern suburbs and established the monopoly of selling fish and fresh meat in Grant's Town. The original building, blown down in the 1866 hurricane, was rebuilt in 1873, but the Grant's Town Market never flourished and disappeared soon after 1900. It failed partly because local vendors were unwilling to pay rent for stalls in the formal market and were not constrained to do so but mainly because downtown Nassau remained the predominant island mart, preferred by sellers and buyers from Grant's Town as well as from the more distant settlements.[11]

The majority of vendors went to downtown Nassau to sell in the streets or market goods for which there was insufficient demand, or no sale at all, in the settlements. These included shellwork, hats and baskets made from plaited palmetto straw, or the African delicacy *accara*, made from cornmeal, as well as market garden produce. Many of the female vendors also purchased small items such as

Traditional outdoor baking oven, late nineteenth century.
John Fondas Collection, Bahamas Archives.

candies, peanuts, candles, matches, needles, mirrors, and combs at downtown prices and sold them for tiny profits Over the Hill. The daily passage of market women up and down Market Street under the stone arch named after Governor Gregory, completed in 1852, was one of the picturesque Nassau sights. Some vendors walked great distances, their goods expertly balanced in flat wooden trays on their heads. The Fox Hill women usually walked all the way to town, ambling along with a swinging but stately gait, calling out their wares as they walked. In marketing, Bahamian women, like their Caribbean counterparts, exchanged news, ideas, and gossip. Such activities were vital forms of socializing and created communication networks. Produce from the much more distant settlements of Adelaide and Gambier was usually brought up to Nassau Market on a donkey cart once or twice a week. If no carts were available, the vendor would walk—a roundtrip of up to thirty-two miles for wares sold at both ends of the journey for scarcely a pound in all.[12]

Those fortunate "natives" of the settlements who could afford to supplement their own produce by purchasing food imported into Nassau ate well, and they and their families stayed healthy. The majority, though, were less fortunate, and even producers often had to sell for cash food they needed for themselves. At worst, their diet was totally inadequate, at best, nutritionally poorly balanced. L. D. Powles, typically, went so far as to claim that it was worse than in slavery days, attributing the poor health and physique of most Bahamian blacks in the 1880s to this cause. "The food given to the slaves was no doubt coarse in quality," he wrote, "but they had as much as they could eat, and got it regularly, and no one can compare the darkies born in slavery, or even those born shortly after that time, with the present race, without seeing at once that the latter are physically inferior in every respect." Generally, said Powles, the people had fruits and plantains in plenty and ate much fish if they lived close to the sea and had the time, means, and will to go fishing. But meat, eggs, and milk were rarities because the few cows in New Providence served the richer whites and ordinary people could not afford to eat either the fowls they kept or the eggs the fowls laid. If they ever ate meat it was usually pork from the scrawny native hogs, said to be "a kind of cross between a small wild boar and a tapir, hairy, long-snouted, and seedy-looking."[13] Much of the corn and beans grown went to market, and it was difficult to grow sufficient root provisions in the rocky soil so most people depended heavily on the cheapest imported starch foods, the coarsest type of white hominy grits. Rice, butter, cheese, and sugar, even the cheapest grades, were too expensive for regular consumption, and the people had to purchase common necessities such as cooking fats and salt, as well as matches and candles. Coffee and tea were only occasional luxuries, though most of the men and some of the older women found the means to purchase the coarsest Cuban plug tobacco, sold in "ropes," which they either chewed or smoked in short clay pipes.

Powles noticed the large number of grog shops in Grant's Town, both licensed and unlicensed, that sold bottled English ale as well as fiery brands of Cuban and British West Indian rum. To a lesser extent than in the West Indies proper (where rum, of course, was exceedingly cheap) these were the informal meeting places of those black males who could afford to indulge or stood to be treated. But the bars' limited and irregular clientele and the remarkable lack of public drunkenness among the "lower crust," even at Christmas, which Powles noticed, was less owing to a climate of respectability (as Powles suggested) than to a shortage of means to indulge in a colony where the price of drink was kept relatively high by import duties and the profits culled by the Bay Street liquor importers. It was significant, however—though not noted by Powles—that the incidence of drunkenness and drink-related rowdiness was far greater away from the settlements and households, around Bay Street itself, especially near the market and wharves, where the liquor importers generally kept bars next to their warehouses and where the laborers and fishermen received their wages and the market and fish vendors their payments.

The View from Morley's Fox Hill Shop

A modern reader can similarly delve beneath the surface of the description of the socioeconomic world centered on a typical "village" shop called Morley's, probably in Fox Hill, which constituted the most colorful—and seemingly authentic—sections of the accounts given by William Drysdale and L. D. Powles. Morley's shop, one of a dozen similar scattered through Grant's Town and the other inland settlements, was externally unprepossessing—a wooden one-story shanty no more than twelve feet square. Inside, though, it was described as a regular cornucopia. "Here are hams hanging from the ceiling, and strips of bacon," wrote Drysdale,

> and here are barrels of salt pork, and tubs of lard and barrels of sugar and caddies of tea and tins full of coffee, and rows of bottles of Bass's ale, and more rows of bottles of sarsaparilla and ginger beer, and bundles of cigars stood up on end; and here is a plateful

of home-made cocoanut candy; and there stands part of a cheese protected by a wire box, and near by a barrel of crackers. And there are loaves of bread, and tins of canned goods, and an open barrel of flour, another of grits, and a great heap of bags of rice, and part of a tub of butter; and there are tins of ginger snaps and a big basket of guinea corn. All these things are before the counter and behind it as if all the customers were honest as saints, and would never touch anything they hadn't bought. And on the counter are a heap of stalks of sugar-cane ready to be chewed into white fibre by the first youngster who comes along with a small copper.[14]

In Drysdale's artfully artless description, he and another white male visitor stood in the shadows of Morley's modest emporium throughout a warm autumn evening in 1886, observing and noting a representative sample of customers and kibitzers. Some, in their distinctive ways, were calling at the shop to purchase small luxuries. A barefoot young black boy bought a sugarcane stalk for a farthing (quarter-penny) and was only half-jocularly called an "ourang-outrang" by Morley when he stared and grinned at the visitors. The black driver of a "Fox Hill barouche" (that is, a donkey cart) stamped proudly in, ignored the whites, made himself at home by running the grits in the barrel through his fingers, brusquely ordered "a check tobacco" (that is, one and one-half pence or three cents' worth, enough to last all day), before walking out into the dark and away. A party of four "young gentlemen of colour," who politely said, "Good evenin' boss," to Drysdale and his friend, ordered and drank a glass of ale each at the expense of one of their number. And (an almost salacious touch), a "pretty young yellow girl" of about fifteen, "who would pass for over eighteen years old in America," finding that Morley did not keep lace handkerchiefs in stock, shyly purchased a tiny bottle of scent for two shillings, no doubt, thought Drysdale, "to captivate some Nassau beau on Sunday."[15]

Two customers of Morley's shop, described at the beginning of Drysdale's account, stood for the normal unpicturesque run of poor purchasers of necessities for whom the shop was a vital part of their lives. The first was "a bare-headed and bare-footed girl, with a skin rather more than dusky, and an air evidently designed to tell us all she didn't care a continental for anybody or anything," who went straight up to the counter, took a penny and a halfpenny out of her mouth, slapped them down on the counter with a bang, and peremptorily called out, "Check lard." Scarcely breaking his conversation with his white visitors, Morley tore off a piece from a large sheet of brown paper, scooped a small handful of lard from the tub, and handed it to the girl in exchange for her two copper coins, which clinked into his drawer.

The second routine customer was a mature black woman, a street vendor with a rolled bandanna "cutter" and wooden tray on her head, who was more than ready to haggle for a half peck (four quarts, or a gallon) of Morley's grits. After putting down her tray and engaging in polite preliminaries about the weather, respective states of health, the wholesale and retail prices of grits in Nassau Market, and the quality of Morley's stock, Morley insisted on five cents a quart but agreed to sell a half peck for "two bits" (properly twenty-five cents, but eighteen cents or ninepence in local usage) because the woman was an old and regular customer. After a pantomime of searches through her pocket, tray, and bandanna, the woman came up with only seventeen cents. But when the patient shopkeeper made to take back a quart and give two cents change (that is, selling three quarts for fifteen cents) she suddenly extracted the missing "small copper" (halfpenny or "cent") from her mouth. "Oh yes, here it is," she was quoted by Drysdale. "I know'd I must have put it somewhere." "I thought you'd find it," replied Morley with a smile, indicating to his visitors that this was a performance hallowed by custom.[16]

A small party of young boys armed with tambourines and mouth organs went by the shop but, not seeing Morley's visitors or nervous about their possible reception from the proprietor, did not stop. But as "American millionaires" (the usual term for all white tourists), Drysdale and his friend could not expect to go all night unnoticed and unsolicited. An aged Congo woman, "black as coal, with some scars on her face," carrying a bundle and basket and "a tray on her head, piled up more than a foot high with bundles and bottles and cans," caught sight of them, curtsied, greeted them politely, and immediately begged for money, pleading, "Times is so hard." Morley intervened to suggest that if she really expected anything, "Aunty" should dance for the visiting gentlemen, to which she readily agreed. "There is something surprising about seeing a woman of her age drawing her scant skirts together in preparation for a dance," wrote Drysdale, "but she is as erect as a girl of twenty and strong as a man, and almost before we know what is going on, she is dancing in the small open space in the middle of the floor—dancing to a strange tune which she hums herself, of which the short words come out in jerks. She throws herself about wildly, giving us one of the half-graceful, half-awkward Congo dances we have often seen before. When it is done, and she is not a bit tired from the exertion, she looks at us in a way that says plainly enough 'There now, what are you going to give me for that?'" Drysdale gave the old Congolese twenty-five cents, for which "she thanks us many times . . . invokes blessings upon our heads, invests a 'check' of it in tobacco, resumes her tray, her bundle and her pail, and goes on her way." Drysdale and his friend escaped into the dark soon after, jokingly suggesting that if such an old crone would perform so readily and well they might not be able to withstand the temptation should "some of the younger and prettier girls come along and want to dance for us."[17]

With his predilection for the picturesque, his liberal sentimentality, and his professional journalist's preference for situations and a cast of characters neater than life, William Drysale underrepresented the humdrum majority to whom Morley's shop was vital and who presented Morley with his livelihood and profit, while at the same time misrepresenting the mainsprings of their actions and behavior. Yet the subtext is discernible: the pride, the politesse, the aspirations toward modest gentility of those with some cash, however little; the scrimping and subterfuges of the majority living on the margins of subsistence—highlighted by the purchase of single items at the critical point of need, in minimal quantities; the desperation of those without any cash at all that led to the begging, the offers of entertainment, even prostitution—which were at least one remove from the shame and danger of outright theft.

Curiously, the key figure in the colored-lantern-like show of "An Evening at Morley's," Morley himself, is the character least described. Yet the shadowy presence is clear: a genial but ambitious man, even ruthless, deferential and ingratiating to the whites and endlessly patient in weighing out small measures and haggling with genuine purchasers, but advancing little or no credit, discouraging beggars, chasing away potential thieves and troublemakers, and capable of making racist slurs against indigent black people darker than himself. Though clearly

Bahamian cottage industry. Basket making in a Grant's Town house, as pictured in Stark's *Guide.* This is the only known depiction of the interior of a nineteenth-century Bahamian cottage. From *Stark's History and Guide to the Bahamas* (New York, 1891), courtesy of Bahamas Archives.

regarded by Drysdale and Powles as the best type of industrious and enterprising Bahamian black (like David Patton, even Sankey Toote), Morley could be seen as a classic West Indian petty bourgeois, the largely unwitting intermediary of an exploiting overclass.

The visiting journalist writing for a New York audience and even the disgruntled sacked magistrate could not recognize the deepest and widest effects of a rotten socioeconomic system, but their writings provide ample clues. Powles ended his chapter "The Lower Crust of Nassau Society" with a telling anecdote and a final quotation from Drysdale which were wiser than either man knew. "Drysdale is right when he said that a check's worth of tobacco is of value to a Nassau man," wrote Powles, "but apparently he does not realize its full value. There is an ex-policeman in Nassau who has saved a considerable sum of money by care and economy, and has now commenced a successful career as a money-lender. One of his pet economies was to chew his tobacco thoroughly, till he had exhausted all the juice and prevented his appetite rising to too expensive a pitch, and then dry the *debris* of his chewings in the sun and smoke them as a luxury."[18]

Despite the obvious poverty and unhealthiness of what they called the "Nassau darky," his truculence toward his native employers and reluctance to work hard for pitiful wages, and his tendency to beg almost as a reflex action, Powles heartily endorsed Drysdale's conclusion that the ordinary inhabitant of New Providence was courteous to those he trusted, naturally cheerful and optimistic, and movingly resilient. "Outside of busy Bay Street," Drysdale significantly noted,

> I soon found, every negro speaks to every white person he meets, touching his hat and expecting a nod in return. A nod or a smile really seems to make the Nassau darky happy, and they are so cheap I don't see how anybody could refuse them; but in the country the colored people generally ask you for a penny. But I have noticed that if you give them a smile and no penny they are better pleased than if you give them a penny and treat them unkindly. They are as good-natured and good hearted as any people in the world. When they have only a penny, and buy a meal of sugar-cane with it, they will give you half the sugar-cane if you ask them for it.[19]

Afro-Bahamian Churches and Friendly Societies

What gave the Bahamian blacks their innate love of their fellows and fellow spirits, their propensity to share in adversity, and their remarkable resilience was the continuing, ever-growing strength of their Afro-Bahamian cultural life.

This proved to be true even for the diminishing minority of those to whom Africa remained an increasingly idealized homeland and possible refuge from the harsh conditions of Bahamian life. Probably the last generation of such dreamers was the remarkable group of liberated Africans "born in the Congo-land by the great river and have families still there," who, hearing of the king of the Belgians' annexation of the region, applied to him for repatriation in 1888.[20] According to their petition, they had been brought as slaves to the West Indies by the Spaniards but had been freed "by the naval Power of England" before reaching their destination, landed in the Bahamas, been treated kindly, given land, become British subjects and Christians, learned English, and given their children "some education." They were masons and carpenters as well as farmers, and some had been employed "laying the railways for salt transportation in the island of Inagua." But wage opportunities had almost disappeared, the lands they had been given or purchased were exhausted, and it was their hearts' desire "to return with our little ones, to our own land where the soil yields a return for labour." Provided only that they be allowed to form a settlement under their own Baptist minister, they would "engage to be loyal and devoted" to the Belgian king and his laws.[21]

Given the scandalous human exploitation that accompanied King Leopold's colonization of the ironically named Congo Free State, it was just as well that nothing came of the repatriation scheme. Somewhat suspiciously, the first response of the Belgian authorities was to inquire who would pay for the returnees' transportation and whether they would not expect to bind themselves as contract laborers to repay the cost of settlement and to pay rent for leasehold land. The Baptist superintendent in Nassau who was the Congoes' intermediary had to report obstructionism among the local whites and widespread skepticism and that the younger generation by no means shared their elders' enthusiasm. The African-born Congoes were prepared to sell all they had, but market conditions were poor and it was unlikely that the proceeds of the sale of their few possessions would be enough to keep them out of another species of debt peonage. In the event, negotiations were stalled on the pretext that until the railway line between Matadi and Leopoldville was begun there would be no opportunities for wage labor. But the reason the scheme did not resurface may well have been the complete silence of the Belgians on the matter that was vital to the applicants and their intermediary alike: the establishment of a Baptist community among a people overwhelmingly pagan in a colony run by ostensible Catholics.[22]

As all writers noted, the black people Over the Hill had become as observant Christians as any to be found in the West Indies. But it is a moot point to what degree they had been genuinely won over by a new religion, saw Christianity as a salve for miserable social conditions, or had merely found Christianity malleable to their traditional ways of thought, belief, and worship. Clearly, the different churches offered varied attractions, some of them seemingly contradictory: respectability, participation, spirituality, escape. Undoubtedly, too, the general effect of Christianity was to mitigate social discord and distract, if not provide an opiate for, the unfortunate majority. But religion was by no means imposed, and the different churches would not have succeeded had they not, on a weekly if not a daily basis, satisfied the people's choices, needs, and aspirations.

In 1900, the Anglican church and the missionary nonconformists, with their white expatriate priests and ministers, still commanded the allegiance of a majority of the people Over the Hill. The Anglican churches of St. Agnes in Grant's Town and St. Anne's at Fox Hill—significantly, on the edges rather than in the center of the settlements—continued to attract large congregations. But this was mainly because of their deviation from, rather than adherence to, the practices of the old established church. As the Misses Dickinson and Dowd presciently noted in 1888, St. Agnes was a pretty stone church surrounded by flowering trees and bushes and attractively decorated inside with banners, ornaments, and vivid lithographs of the Stations of the Cross (a celebration of Christ's tribulations that would strike a chord among the Bahamian poor). An inscription above the door read "Enter Mortal, Praise and Pray"—a message that would scarcely have been found at Nassau's Christchurch—and the 450 seats were customarily filled by a well-dressed congregation, almost exclusively black, without any visible sign of precedence. The two white female visitors chose to take an inconspicuous seat at the back of the church behind the font, which was a more vital item of theological furniture in this ritualist church than it had ever been in Christchurch or St. Matthew's.[23]

Nonetheless, with its informal dress code, its emphasis on formal wedding ceremonies and such family-oriented services as infant baptisms, and its venerable English priest (for nearly thirty years the hardworking Father James Fisher) that accorded great deference in the community, St. Agnes was an eminently respectable, even hierarchical, institution. To be baptized, buried, and, especially, married according to the rites of the formerly established church also retained residual social kudos. The priest's sermons were commonly social homilies, the church school, as well as its Sunday school classes, strongly promoted "Christian principles," and the regular social functions almost invariably included speeches by members of the white establishment or respectable colored class, stressing dutiful behavior, industrious habits, and clean living. All the same, church outings, picnics, fêtes, and organized sports were agreeable punctuations of a humdrum or uncongenial daily round and drew participants from all sections of the black community, not just regular Anglican churchgoers.

The respectable nonconformist churches—those presided over by ministers appointed and regulated by the Methodist and Baptist missionary societies in England and also mostly situated on the outer fringes of Nassau rather than deep in the settlements—offered similar attractions, if with a less flamboyant liturgy. All offered opportunities for their ordinary black congregations to "praise and pray," as well as to parade in their finery on Sundays and special church-sponsored occasions. They never supplanted or even rivaled in popularity those "Native Baptist" churches such as St. John's, which combined the attractions of a native black ministry, black management and participation at every level, a fervent spirituality centering on the custom of adult baptism in the open sea, and a location in the decent environs of Delancey Town.[24]

Despite the predominance of men as priests and pastors, all churches provided opportunities for women to participate, to enhance their respectability, and even to lead. In the Anglican and Methodist churches alike, women outnumbered men as Sunday school teachers, and they were invaluable in organizing annual bazaars, fêtes, and other fund-raising functions. More important still in a socializing role, they were increasingly active in the Anglican women's guilds and Mothers' Union and in the Methodist Women's League, and they formed the backbone of the church-based Temperance Leagues. Though generally less formally organized, women played an even more important part in the Baptist churches, as choristers, Bible and prayer class leaders, and, well in advance of the Anglicans and Methodists, as deaconesses.[25]

One result of the popularity of participatory forms of black Baptist church observance, with its focus on charismatic preachers, was the tendency to break up into splinter sects when groups differed on minor doctrinal points or cohered around rival personalities, and ambitious pastors carried their adherents with them to form new churches. By 1900, there were no less than six doctrinal factions and several other independent churches; they were loosely rejoined in the National Baptist Convention only in the 1970s. The followers of the separatist sects tended to come from the blackest and poorest sections of the community, and their churches consequently tended to be established in the heart of the settlements. Poverty and African ethnicity, indeed, became equal indexes of the "primitive" fervor and escapism of such runaway churches. By the same token, just as their pastors and elders were less demanding in standards of dress, social behavior, and forms of "respectable" family life than others, so the pastors themselves were almost akin to African patriarchs, enjoying great local authority, taking a modest financial tribute from their followers, and virtually practicing traditional polygyny by accepting the sexual favors of nubile female members of their congregations. In such respects they were paralleling the combination of worldly success and subscription to traditional canons of "reputation" (including sexual prowess) enjoyed and practiced by exceptional blacks who achieved leadership and eminence in the settlements by secular means.

The lineal descendants of the black Baptists of the Loyalist era had become relatively established, staid, even respectable, by the 1890s. But a new wave of popular black religion came to the Bahamas from the United States in the last decades of the nineteenth century that struck a chord and fulfilled a need among the poorest and most downtrodden blacks. The first and most famous of the Over the Hill churches to which white visitors flocked to wonder and scoff in the 1880s was the U.S.-originated African Methodist Episcopal or "Shouter" church—forerunner of

Outside the "Shouter" church before Sunday service, Over the Hill, Nassau, late nineteenth century. Mary Moseley Collection, courtesy of Anglican Church in the Bahamas.

many later Holiness, Pentecostal, or "Jumper" churches, especially the Churches of God and Prophecy, which proliferated in the twentieth century—adding with their electronically amplified rituals a third distinctive component, along with barking dogs and crowing cocks, to Nassau's nighttime aural tapestry.

Such churches stressed the importance of the third element of the Holy Trinity, the Holy Ghost, which was best approached not through a careful theology or fixed formal ritual but by techniques that facilitated direct access to the Spirit itself, as on the biblical Day of Pentecost: abandoned singing, incantatory repetition in call and response of significant verses (especially from the Book of Revelation), and intense concentration. Eventually the congregation began to "speak in tongues" and exhibit symptoms of mass hypnosis and hysteria—a stunning experience that served as a general and individual catharsis. As Stanley Johannesen has argued, these practices (which spread from black to poor white and immigrant communities and were in vogue for at least seventy-five years in the United States) were peculiarly attractive to people who were poor, oppressed, unlearned, displaced, and alienated because the Holy Ghost was the member of the Trinity least located in space and dissociated from the mundane and hierarchical implications of Father and Son. "Pentecostal" practices also, of course, struck a special resonance with traditional animist African religion, with its concentration on communion with the spirit world.[26]

Situated in the "black" heart of Grant's Town, the AME Shouter Church was a small stone building with a thatched roof and without glass windows. Dickinson and Dowd gave a mildly malicious but revealing vignette of a typical service in *A Winter Picnic* (1888). They were politely met and escorted inside by a portly bare-footed elder with rings in his ears ("the only fat negro we have observed") who was rehearsing a small Sunday school of "eight small darkies" in what sounded to the white visitors as a parody of the Anglican catechism. When the ragged congregation of some twenty-five was assembled, the service began with hymns, in which each verse was read before it was sung, and a long extempore "scriptural prayer" by the barefoot elder, which the visitors found almost incoherent. The preacher, a "tall, grave man, dressed in decent black," then gave "a very disjointed talk based on the text 'I was in the spirit on the Lord's day,'" which lauded the Book of Revelation, stressed the importance of "getting the spirit," and bewailed the absence of "fire in the island." But the climax of the service came when an elder called on "a brother" to make the "closing prayer." This man knelt down only about four feet from where the visitors were seated but began in such a low tone that they could not understand a word. He then gradually warmed up,

> freed no doubt by the responses, "Do, do!" "Oh, my!" "Yes, yes," or anything else that came handy. The peculiar intonation of the prayer was inimitable. The first thing audible . . . was something about Paul and Silas, earthquakes, wrath and thunder. The man was off his knees by that time, and swinging himself wildly about, sometimes stretching on tiptoe, sometimes leaning his long form far out over the railing. The fat brother behind us was shaking as if in an ague fit; a young woman was indulging in a fit of hysterical laughter; some were groaning as if in deadly agony, and right in all this hubbub came the high voice of the suppliant mentioning the "wite ladies," but we were so mixed in with "de wials of wraf," "de dead a-coming forf," "terrers o' de las' judgmint," "Gawd no respecter o' persons, black or wite," that [the ladies] . . . hadn't the least idea whether we were delivered over to deserved punishment, or recommended to mercy. For one dreadful moment I thought that they had all gone mad together, but suddenly "Silence like a poultice came, To heal the blows of sound."[27]

The beliefs, behavior, and language exhibited in the black churches were an integral part of the general Afro-Bahamian culture, just as there were secular equivalents of the black churches and their pastors in the community at large. The most important secular institutions in the settlements were the friendly or sharing societies or lodges, which were attuned both to African roots and to the sociopolitical cravings of the poor blacks and gradually changed their character under changed conditions and new influences, particularly from the United States. The original friendly societies emerged within the black community with subethnic affiliations but were tolerated, even encouraged, by the regime because they seemed salutary and calming influences on a potentially volatile section of society but were amenable to official control. Societies were immensely popular because they filled a need for belonging and a lost sense of kinship and ethnic association, as well as providing opportunities for active participation, an internal hierarchy, and a chance for leadership. Thus though shorn of direct political importance, they were undoubtedly proto-political organizations. Predictably, the grandiloquently styled officers of the Afro-Bahamian societies carried great prestige in the black settlements—indeed, were often chosen for qualities already acknowledged—and were consequently regarded as leaders and spokesmen by the dominant regime.

Though some friendly societies and lodges were male preserves, women played important roles in others, replicating their role in the family and their increasing importance in society at large. As a commission report stated in 1911, "A remarkable fact is the number of women who are members and take an active part in the work and management of many of these societies. Some of the largest—such as the Victoria Royal Union in New Providence with a membership of one hundred and seventy five—are composed almost entirely of women, and in no particular have we found such inferior to those consisting of men only."[28]

The societies, whether predominantly male or female or mixed, had vital practical purposes. The prime function of most was to bury their members in an appropriate style, giving them a send-off that was a contrasting climax to an often miserable life. With this end in view, society members were prepared to afford a relatively high proportion of their income in subscriptions and contributions and fervently participate in the ceremonies for each deceased member—and in so doing to replicate a hallowed African tradition. The second original function of the societies was to act as simple banks or insurance companies, collecting contributions and distributing them in eventual share-outs or cases of special need such as sickness, funerals, or weddings. Sharing societies also made loans, charging rates of between 2 and 3 percent per month.

In both their main functions, the black societies gradually changed over the course of the late nineteenth century. Originally they were responsible for all aspects of funerals, "laying out" the body and making the coffin, as well as special rituals at the religious service, a parade, the interment, and an elaborate wake. But gradually the preliminary functions of preparing the body and coffin became the responsibility of specialist undertakers—members of a lucrative new occupation that provided opportunities for a few fortunate blacks, as in black communities in the United States—to achieve a modest degree of wealth and professional respect (though perhaps without a proportionate degree of social status).

The financial roles of the early black societies met growing opposition from organized capital in the forms of the Bay Street and government-oriented bank and Post Office Savings system. After a long period during which the newspapers and government seized on any evidence of mismanagement or malfeasance to discredit the black societies, their financial operations were almost completely curtailed by law. This, however, did not end but merely drove underground the popular forms of financial organization within the black settlements, which had ramifications and a sophistication beyond the understanding of Bahamian whites. The basic system of saving and sharing, with African roots and an African name, was *asu*—known as "partner," or "meet and turn," or *susu* in the British West Indies. Largely participated in by women and often organized by them, this system involved regular contributions by individuals—small in size but often representing a large proportion of weekly earnings—which were paid out in largish lump sums in strict rotation.

Asu had the advantage of being a lottery with a guaranteed, if sometimes greatly delayed, return. Like poor people everywhere, the Bahamian blacks were also attracted to more outright games of chance, though the attraction seems to have increased with time. By the early twentieth century certainly, black Bahamians were enthusiastic participants in the Cuban national lottery as well as innumerable local "numbers" syndicates, the illegal operators of which earned considerable wealth as well as notoriety. A considerably less salutary effect of the appropriation of formal banking by the white regime was the proliferation of moneylending in the settlements. This provided chances for enterprising and forceful blacks (sometimes acting as commissioned agents of white or colored moneylenders) to make small fortunes, though with interest rates commonly far above the legal annual maximum of 25 percent and overdue debts often collected with brutal force, this system exacerbated the general exploitation of the lowest class.

A gradual change in the form if not the functions of the secular societies in the black settlements which paralleled developments in the black churches followed from the emulation of black societies and lodges in the United States and a growing number of affiliations with them. By the end of the nineteenth century, the original Bahamian societies had become more sophisticated, associated with or augmented by black Freemasonry lodges and such fraternal organizations as the black versions of Elks, Buffaloes, and Odd Fellows. Many blacks belonged to several organizations, but each had its subtly different character and membership, as well as complex, usually secret, rules, rituals, and regalias. White commentators tended to ridicule the imitative pretensions of the black societies, especially of their leaders—just as they scorned black Haitian rulers and their entourages—failing to recognize that in enthusiastically taking part in these organizations, with their arcane mysteries and mimic hierarchies, the blacks were psychologically displacing the alienation and deprivation imposed by the dominant social order. Few whites, moreover, acknowledged the degree to which membership in the societies and the performance of ritualized mysteries provided an institutional link to the kinship and community rituals and ceremonies of aboriginal Africa. Membership in the secular black organizations, as much as church participation, helped to facilitate and shape black political activity in the twentieth century, beginning, perhaps, with the ardent association of many Bahamian blacks with the quasi-religious and lodge-oriented Universal Negro Improvement Association of Marcus Garvey in the 1920s. Garvey, of course, was also to appeal, above all, to black Americans' African roots.

For the time being, the closest and most obvious link between the Bahamian friendly societies and African roots was the picturesque annual ceremony of the Crowning of the Eboe Queen. A report in the *Nassau Guardian* in February 1885 described how crowds, including curious American visitors, began to assemble at the hall of the Grant's Town Friendly Society as early as 10 A.M. Shortly after noon, Mrs. Caroline Rahming, chosen as queen by the Eboe Society, arrived in a carriage, to be escorted to a throne on the platform, surrounded by a bevy of comely black attendants. The coronation, which lasted half an hour and was followed by dancing, was presided over by the august president of the Eboe Society, dressed in an imposing uniform and carrying a drawn, if somewhat stagy, sword.[29]

African Legacies: Bush Medicine, Obeah, and Bahamian Creole

Despite faithful church membership, the great majority of black Bahamians also continued to believe in African sorcery medicine, obeah, the persistence of which fascinated, frightened, and confused the whites in equal measure.[30] Obeah, like its Haitian equivalent, voodoo, was regarded by the whites, at best, as mere superstition, at worst, as dangerous "black magic." Its practice was banned by legislation because it was thought to have evil purposes, often directed against whites. But in fact obeah was based on the fundamental belief that all good as well as all evil—everything good or bad that happened to individuals—emanated from and was controlled by the spirit world and could be conjured, changed, or cured by the intervention of sorcery medicine or magic formulas. Potions were therefore administered and spells cast to achieve wanted results or to ward off the unwanted: to ensure a fortunate outcome in affairs of the heart, good health, or flourishing crops, to harm an enemy or to counteract a spell cast by one, to shield possessions against theft, or to provide an antidote for a sickness—itself invariably regarded as the result of unfavorable medicine. It was a complex science, which required the secret skills of special practitioners, obeahmen (or women), if possible native Africans, who consequently commanded great prestige and power in the community.

At its most extreme, the administration of obeah could lead to death, though whether this was through poison, auto-suggestion, or real magic remained open to debate among the most educated persons. To an Anglican priest writing in 1896, obeah was simply mumbo-jumbo, and his Baptist rivals were "semi-heathen people . . . very slightly acquainted either with the creed or the Ten Commandments: living under obedience to their native elders, mixed with a superstitious dread of obeah and witchcraft."[31] Governor Blake reported in 1886 that the reason for the large mortality in the public hospital was that people rarely applied for admission until they had "exhausted the means of cure known to the 'Bush' doctors or obeah men." Many were almost dead when they arrived at the hospital—some of them doubtless consigned there in extremis by the obeahmen so that the white doctors and not themselves might be assigned responsibility for death. No whites in the Bahamas, it seems, shared the wisdom and rationality of Dr. Albert Schweitzer, who referred to the "witchdoctors" of Lambaréné as his "native colleagues" and posited three levels of African medicine. For attacks of fever that the native doctors knew from experience to be nonmortal and transient, they would utter some meaningless words, administer some harmless substances, and prescribe rest and patience—then take full credit for the inevitable recovery. For other afflictions they had medicines that were rarely harmful and often had genuine—even amazing—therapeutic value. Only in the most extreme and incurable cases would they have to resort to extreme measures, to ascribe irreversible decline and death to a medicine more powerful than their own or to hand over their patient to their rival white doctors for "civilized" medicine—including radical surgery.[32]

From slavery days, Bahamians, and not only blacks, certainly used "bush medicine" for nearly every ill. "For generations, people living in remote Bahamian settlements have looked to nature's own apothecary to succour their ills," wrote Mrs. Leslie Higgs, the chief white authority on Bahamian bush medicine in 1974.[33] The use of bush remedies was most prevalent in Out Island settlements that rarely, if ever, were visited by a physician. But most black Nassauvians also sought cures or palliatives from medicinal plants, developing an indigenous pharmacopeia. In the early 1900s, blacks pointed out to an inquiring Anglican priest the plants that would "cure consumption in tree [*sic*] weeks" and others that would "make de rheumatics go away out ob you legs."[34] Nearly every native plant—the majority of course not known in Africa—was ascribed a medicinal value, and many were used "with great faith." In Bain Town at the turn of the century, the breadfruit tree leaf, for example, boiled into a tea, was used for the symptoms of "high blood" or "swinging in the head."[35] Such usage—in this case of a tree native neither to Africa nor America but Polynesia—illustrates both a generic belief in the efficacy of natural remedies and an impressive tendency toward empirical experimentation—if not also a degree of wish fulfillment—in face of deprivation.

Bush medicine and obeah were intertwined. Cleveland Eneas, son of AME Bishop Eneas and social historian of his birthplace, remembered that "Bain Town people, on the whole, were superstitious people, and were true believers in obeah, 'fixing,' etcetera." He explained that people "fixed" their trees against thieves in a serious and expert manner. Apparently, obeah experts from Fox Hill were employed to make the "fix," and once completed it was "not to be messed with under any circumstances." The most common sign that a tree had been "fixed" was a conspicuous green bottle stuffed with wet moss, leaves, twigs, and sand hanging from a branch. If the fruit was stolen from such a tree and eaten, the miscreant would "swell up and die."[36] A similar situation was explained to the gullible Misses Dickinson and Dowd by their plausible colored servant Lemuel in 1888. A black cook working in Nassau was heard scolding her child "outrageously" for meddling with some corn found placed in a pattern on the kitchen doorstep. Lemuel said, "Somebody put *foo-foo* on her, mum, an' you hos to do some trick to take it off'n her. If de chile 'sturb de corn, she hos to pay de cunjur-woman to do some other trick, an' it make her ongry, mum."[37]

Essentially African traditions were not only present in the belief systems and religious practices of the Bahamian blacks but also in their recreational activities. Indeed, all three were melded, with common features shared with the black cultures of the United States and the West Indies more because of common origins than direct later influences. Music, derived from African measures and modes, the ancient slave songs of North America, and the sacred songs in the early Wesleyan and Baptist hymnals, was very important in the lives of ordinary blacks, not only at church but at work and play and in the traditional celebrations of the rites of passage—above all, at funerals and wakes. Involvement in the passage out of life was so important, indeed, that sometimes a preliminary or intercessionary wake was held when a community member was thought to be at death's door. Charles Edwards, in his path-breaking *Bahama Songs and Stories* (1895), described such ceremonies as "the strangest of all their customs . . . held on the night when some friend is supposed to be dying. . . . The singers, men and women, and children of all ages, sit about on the floor of the larger room of the hut and stand outside at the doors and windows while the invalid lies upon the floor in the smaller room. Long into the night they sing their most mournful hymns and 'anthems,' and only in the light of dawn do those who are left as chief mourners silently disperse."[38]

If necessary, the "mourners" returned each night to keep watch over the patient until he or she either succumbed or recovered. Death was usually followed by a formal nighttime wake, in which gender roles were firmly delineated. As late as the 1950s, Samuel Charters described a traditional wake in Andros, the island where old customs lingered longest: "The women sing early, and the men stay outside drinking until about midnight, when they slip into the room and begin singing the loud 'rhymed' spirituals. The women sing the slower hymns, often leading the songs from a hymnal. An older woman will sit in a reading chair, singing from her tattered book, reading by the light of the lantern."[39] At the far more elaborate and ritualistic funerals, held until modern times the day following death, everyone turned out for a parade, with music provided by the brass bands attached to each burial society and lodge. On the way to the cemetery the pace would be slow and the music of the mournful type found at wakes. An abrupt switch to a faster tempo and jollier tunes would happen once the interment had been made, a custom that was commonly observed in black communities in the United States.

Blacks also gathered at sunset on special occasions such as the eve of Emancipation Day or Christmas Eve to sing all night. In contrast to wake and funeral measures, the music was predominantly merry and was called "setting up." Before it began there was much joking and laughing. Gaily dressed people gathered in a largish building, such as a lodge hall, filled with chairs: "One man, better dressed than the others and probably better educated, 'lines off,' in a sonorous voice, the words of some good old hymn. Around the center table with him are the principal singers, and standing back of these, with a shining 'beaver' on his head as a badge of office, is the leader. He lifts his hands, his face shines with pride, his rich barytone [*sic*] voice pours forth the line, and the hymn begins. Then all voices joining together every shade of tone send out into the beautiful night the rapturous, voluptuous music . . . the hymn swells . . . and the wave of sound rolls on."[40] After midnight, refreshments of coffee and bread were served. After this came the less formal "anthems," or religious folk songs that had not been learned from a book but passed down from one generation to another.

L. D. Powles found it difficult to distinguish between Bahamian hymns and anthems, except that in the latter a refrain was repeated after every line. But that he never saw them written down or could get any person to quote the words without singing them indicates that they were an authentic oral folk tradition. Though lacking the exquisite poetry of the finest Negro spirituals of the United States (for example, those from the Gullah people of South Carolina), they had a metrical vigor, showed fluid invention, and eloquently expressed the philosophy and poignant longing of a poor and oppressed people to whom Christianity offered more than mere solace: the hope of final redemption. Powles quoted one favorite of the black mate of the schooner *Eastern Queen,* Theophilus Rolle—properly a hymn rather than an anthem—of which he could remember only the first of twenty-five verses:

When I go down to the wood for to pray,
Ole Satan, he say to me,
You Jesus dead, and de Lord, he gone away,
And he no hear you pray!
Oh, Lord, remember me!
Oh, Lord, remember me!
Remember me as de year roll round!
Oh, Lord, remember me![41]

In general, as in the Caribbean at large (and in most societies), the role of Bahamian women in the musical tradition differed from that of the men. Men and women often sang different parts in harmony, but a more common mode was antiphonal, with women leading the songs and men providing the choruses (occasionally vice versa). Both sexes took equal parts in dances, though with reciprocal roles, but women were seldom seen playing musical instruments in public.[42]

L. D. Powles had less difficulty understanding and transliterating the vernacular language of Bahamian blacks than did more casual visitors, but he still encountered problems. The lineaments of a standard Bahamian Creole language or dialect were established by the 1880s, spoken by long-established blacks, coloreds, and whites alike. But there were still hundreds of persons born in Africa who spoke one of a half-dozen African languages and an even greater number conversing in a form of English closer to pidgin than a true Creole, and this infusion both gave Bahamian English a continuing vitality and postponed its relative homogenization into the twentieth century.[43]

Dickinson and Dowd, writing in 1887, spoke of the many native Africans who distinctly remembered the land of their birth and spoke "their own language for the most part, and understand us but little better than we understand them." Of the several African ethnicities the *Bahamas Almanack* listed in the Bahamas, the American visitors encountered examples of only two, Egbar and Nango. Egbar women, by their account, tended to be smaller than average, some of them looked "wonderfully old," and many displayed teeth filed to a point and tribal markings on their faces. One Egbar market woman was called a queen, but the visitors reckoned that "if she merits a title, it should be Queen of Rags." Generally soft-spoken, she became a verbal tornado when excited but was difficult to understand at the best of times. In a style probably characteristic of former liberated Africans, she combined an equally fierce independency and piety, a guileful simulation of interest in the foreign visitors, and a tendency to beg. "I free to mon," she was quoted as saying. "I not free to God. By Goddes power you go. He say *'Come,'* by Goddes Powah you come bock."[44]

The American visitors also interviewed "a benevolent-looking old Nango man in the market who was much pleased to talk with us." They asked about the man's early life and quoted him as nearly as they could remember his words: "'Paniard 'teal me from t'ibe; two ships; one T'under; man-wah take we from 'Paniard. Lan' we come first, Jamaica; den take we Inagua; Inagua—we here." As best they could make out, the man had been shipped from the port of "Aboukuti"—probably Abeokuta on the Bight of Benin. He told them many Nango words, such as "*ahbaddo*, corn; *ahketta*, hat; *choketo*, handkerchief; *ahbahod*, spoon; *ahgeddi*, banana," which they were able to add to their small acquired vocabulary of Egbar words: "*masohbou*, banana; *umgazi*, spoon; *ahesscoo*, chicken; *ahka*, finger." Dickinson asked her colored servant Lemuel (probably descended from Loyalists, white and black) whether he understood the native Africans. "'No, missus,'" he replied; "'*nobody* cahn't unerstan' 'em but just they own selves. They's *Africans'*—with a look of such disdain on his face that I strongly suspect that boy of pride of birth."[45]

Yet Bahamian blacks not only shared with Africans and Afro–West Indians the habit of proverbial speech (for proverbs were, as Chinua Achebe says, "the palm oil of conversation") but some of the same proverbs. Many were so familiar and habitual as to become clichés, but others arose spontaneously out of a bottomless well of invention. A full anthology—now impossible—would serve not just as a treasury of "native wit and wisdom" but provide a compendium of folk philosophy, obliquely and succinctly commenting on everyday life, society, and social relations and the human condition in general, using homely and familiar analogies and metaphors.

Unfortunately, the Bahamian proverbs that have survived provide only an outline and suggestive hints. Not only did they constitute an essentially spoken rather than written medium, but only those whites heard, understood, remembered, and selected were likely to be recorded for posterity. Whites rarely heard and always ignored any proverbs unfavorable to themselves. Moreover, as proverbs themselves explain, a wise and gentle discretion was one of the essential characteristics of black conversation: "No ebry ting you yerry [hear] good fe talk"; "Shoe know if stocking hab hole"; "Trouble nebber blow shell"; "Stranger no know when de deep water." For discretion's sake, many proverbs distinguished human types and classes in the personified forms of animals with at least mythical similar characteristics: hogs, fowls, cockroaches, lizards, "John Crows" (turkey buzzards), spiders, and flies.

A fair proportion of surviving Bahamian proverbs deal with social life and human nature in general: "Hog run for him life; dog run for him character"; "John Crow nebber make house till rain come"; "When man say him no mind, den he mind"; "You shake man hand, you no shake him heart"; "When hand full, him hab plenty company"; "Cuss cuss [calling names] no bore hole in skin." A few, however, get closer to the harsh realities of the Bahamian class and race system and competition for socioeconomic status, though they lack the asperity and comparative specificity of some Jamaican Negro proverbs: "If you see fippence [three pence] you know how dollar made"; "Lizard no plant corn but him hab plenty"; "Parson christen him own pickaninny first"; "John Crow tink him pickaninny white"; "Goat say him hab wool; sheep say him hab har [hair]"; "When cockroach gib dance him no ax [ask] fowl"; "Spider and fly no make bargain." The most poignant black Bahamian proverbs, though, deal with the nature of poverty and the tactics of survival, including (the last one here) the proud comment on the value of patience and endurance that was the original choice for the title of this social history: "Seven year no 'nough for washy speckle off guinea hen back"; "No trow away dirty water before you hab clean"; "Follow fashion break monkey neck"; "When man no done grow him nebber should cuss long man"; "Sleep hab no massa"; "Cunning better dan strong"; "Time longer dan rope."[46]

Closely related to the propensity for proverbial conversation was the love for telling and listening to traditional folktales and other stories. In every settlement or neighborhood the chief storytellers (or "talkers") were important figures, sometimes in competition with each other. A few notable "talkers" were elderly women; the great majority were men. Almost equivalent to the griots of West Africa and possessing (in Peter J. Wilson's terms) more reputation than respectability, they were admired and regarded with affection though they rarely held much social status or even a steady job. Often poor and sometimes overfond of rum, they were highly observant, intelligent, at times caustic and salacious, exhibiting both the verbal felicity and fantasy of the person Roger Abrahams has characterized as the Caribbean "Man of Words" and the histrionic and emotive techniques of the popular revivalist preacher. "It is difficult to discuss old-stories in any but theatrical terms," wrote Daniel J. Crowley, and "it would seem that the Bahamian old-story talker is at once playwright, director, and cast, and that he calls upon his tradition for theme, theatrical conventions, and a modicum of characterization."[47]

Bahamian "old stories" were told around campfires when families were out farming in the distant bush, on weekend evenings at home, or after singing sessions on special occasions. The clustered auditors of all ages were attentive and active participants, riveted on the talkers' subtle variations on familiar themes and clever changes of pace and tone. Stories were often interspersed (like some of Shakespeare's plays) with sung interludes (called "sings"), and the narrative itself was dramatically punctuated by rhetorical questions or the curious interjection "Bunday!" The audience was expected to react much as congregations respond to calls in revivalist churches, by answering the questions posed, repeating "Bunday!" or responding, "Eh!" "Yeah!" or "Alright!" As was customary in friendly greetings, laughter was an important part of interchanges in old story sessions, to a degree that sometimes appeared excessive to outsiders. As Crowley expressed it, "When a joke or humorous happening occurred in the course of the story, laughter on the part of the audience was intense and of long duration. Tears of laughter came to many eyes, and there was much slapping of knees, clapping of hands, and agonized rolling on the floor in helpless merriment. This form of expression is socially approved, and I believe often exceeds the actual amusement felt."[48]

As Crowley affirmed, the primary function of Bahamian old stories was entertainment, but they also educated by providing vicarious experiences for the hearers, sharpening their wits, and informing them on a good variety of subjects. These uses and the way they melded local and everyday themes and modes with those from Europe and America as well as Africa gave the stories vitality as well as making them distinctly Bahamian in their syncretism. Sometimes stories and "sings," like West Indian calypsos, referred to recent events and familiar persons. Some were woven out of or shaped by Bahamian material, involving ships, voyages and wrecks, treasure and fabulous hauls of fish, or such historic misfortunes as the visitations of cholera in the 1850s and the hurricane of 1866. Specific Bahamian animals such as the iguana, turtle, or legendary chickcharnie owl were often featured, though just as frequently stories contained material clearly derived from or influenced by European fairy tales such as those with an outsider-hero called Jack or a cast of kings, queens, princesses, giants, and ogres.

But the most common and popular tales were those originating in Africa that were variants of those found throughout Afro-America, reaching the Bahamas either directly or by way of the United States and West Indies, with subtle changes on the way. Nearly all involved animals, given human characteristics and at least initially placed in everyday situations so that the audience could relate to and draw a moral from their subsequent adventures, however fantastical. The favorite characters were familiar types, mostly given a prefix akin to the "Brer" (short for "Brother") of the tales popularized in the United States by Joel Chandler Harris. These were the much loved stooge B'Booky (his name derived from the Wolof word for hyena), whose very mention drew laughter; the sagacious B'Short-Tusk (warthog); the noble B'Long-Tusk (elephant); B'Devil, the embodiment of evil; the ingenious hero B'Rabby (or Brother Rabbit, though the rabbit is an animal known neither in Africa nor the Bahamas); and the ultimate trickster B'Nansi (or Anansi), the Spider (the name derived from the Twi or Ewe word for spider), common to West Africa and the Americas.

That the central characters B'Rabby and Anansi were both trickster figures and that most of their stories involved the discomfiture or defeat of their enemies may reflect the aspirations of ordinary blacks to ridicule, thwart, pay back, or even destroy those above them in the socioeconomic system. Daniel Crowley analyzed such wish motivation also in the stories from Andros in the 1950s that relied on stock characters more clearly derived from European fairy tales. In these, the hero, Jack, was "described and referred to as a 'boy' and his youth, poverty, dirtiness and his Negro race all serve to intensify the degree to which he is the underdog. Sometimes he wins out by charitable actions that result in magic gifts. But more often he is a trickster; in many stories he is interchangeable with Rabby, Anansi or B'Short-tusk." Royal characters were similarly ambiguous. "The King's tragi-comic plight is a popular situation in old stories," wrote Crowley, "and his inefficient, inelegant actions are entirely consciously conceived by the narrators. High position is respected, but is also open to ridicule. Formal manners are second nature to Bahamians since so many of them have been house servants, so that the ready availability of the King or *lèse majesté* of saying 'Hush your mouth, Master King,' are actually a convention to make the story go smoothly." In many of these Androsian stories, the heroine is the king's daughter, called Greenleaf and described as "the prettiest goil in the woild." As Crowley commented, "She might be termed the Bahamian Helen, but unlike Helen she can be a figure of [salacious] fun. Her classic remark, 'Oh, but you got to wait awhile,' spoken in a lisping drawl, is certainly playing up the humor of the situation."[49]

The pantomime quality of old stories and their power to enliven and lighten a drab and oppressive existence are obvious. Their richness and adaptability to local conditions and events made them an essentially Bahamian art form. Like all fairy tales they provided an alternative world of fantasy, an ideal promised land of material success, social reversal, and ethnic equality. Yet at the same time Bahamian old stories fulfilled a nostalgic longing for an idealized African past, as was encapsulated in the invariable formula with which they began: "Once upon a time, an' a very good time."[50]

Afro-Bahamian Music, Dance, and Junkanoo

Minor popular diversions deriving from Africa included the posing of riddles and the ingenious board-and-bead game called *worri*. The latter, played either on a portable board fashioned from hardwood or one etched in the horizontal plaster or masonry of a building (an ancient example of which Northcroft noted at Winton Fort in 1899), rivaled dice, cards, and dominoes into the twentieth century.[51] The most popular form of entertainment, though, was always music and dancing. Clement Bethel has demonstrated that although religious music in the Bahamas was heavily influenced by Africa, it came almost exclusively from the United States, whereas secular music, with its emphasis on drumming and dancing, emanated more directly from Africa. Bain Town was the most famous center for the African-based ring dances in New Providence, but they were frequently also performed in Fox Hill, Gambier, and Adelaide. Most white missionaries and ministers saw that form of dancing as sinful, not just because it was so obviously enjoyed but because of the sexual overtones of the vigorous hip movements and coupling of the sexes and the general air of abandonment it engendered. An Anglican minister wrote in the mid-1890s, "The black population find their chief delight in dancing of a disreputable character, taking particular pleasure in a dance called the 'Gumbai' or jumping dance . . . a species of an African war dance."[52] Despite moves by the Christian churches to suppress such dances, wherever there was a strong African element in the population, ring dances to the accompaniment of goatskin "goombay" drums and perhaps a concertina and two pieces of iron remained extremely popular.[53]

Clement Bethel distinguished three distinct types of Afro-Bahamian ring dance: the fire dance, the jumping dance, and the ring play.[54] The basic requirement was a circle of participants and a rhythmic accompaniment, consisting of singing, chanting, clapping, drum rhythms, or a combination of these. The essence of each dance was rotational involvement, singly or in pairs, with an element of exhibition and competition and a rising climax. Sometimes the competitive excitement between the participants heightened to the point of frenzy and exhaustion, not much different from the hysterical climaxes of services at the Shouter and Jumper churches. Magistrate Powles was witness to a fire dance in Grant's Town in 1887 which was specially arranged for him and a Russian visitor staying at the Royal Victoria Hotel by the sergeant of police. "The people formed a circle and a fire was lighted in their midst," Powles recounted.

> The music consisted of two drums that would not work until frequently warmed at the fire. The company clapped their hands without ceasing all through the dance, chanting all the while in a sort of monotone, "Oh kindoiah! kindoiah! Many come along!" When the dance was about half through the refrain was suddenly changed to "Come down, come down," repeated over and over again in the same dreary monotone. Every now and then a man or woman, or a couple together would rush into the centre of the circle and dance wildly about. There appeared to be no step or idea of figure about the performance, the aim and object of the dancers, as far as we could make out, being to execute as many extravagant capers in and over, and around, and about the fire as they could without burning themselves. It was, in short, a savage African dance in European dress.[55]

Informal dances were held whenever possible, even put on for the benefit of white visitors, and small dances were to be found almost any weekend. But large, even formal, dances were a general feature of special annual occasions: the emancipation celebrations (August 1), Guy Fawkes night (November 5), Christmas night (December 25), and New Year's morning (January 1). The first of these, gradually growing in popularity, had from the beginning been more or less appropriated by the regime, on the principle that it celebrated the granting of freedom by a benevolent king, rather than an outcome achieved by the slaves (and liberated African apprentices) themselves. For the settlements immediately Over the Hill, the centerpiece of Emancipation Day celebrations was an orderly, if colorful, parade of society and lodge members and schoolchildren behind brass bands, from Grant's Town to downtown Nassau and back, pausing at the Government House grounds. These occasions traditionally included the presentation of petitions of current grievances to the governor, who seems to have regarded the event as the opportunity to give a speech combining benevolent platitudes, reminders of the generosity of king and Parliament in 1833, and exhortations to maintain law-abiding and industrious habits. Emancipation Day also included church services, at which similar sermons would be preached.[56]

For the outlying black settlements in New Providence—especially Fox Hill—however, the emancipation celebrations signified a deeper sense of liberation and a continuing, even increasing, rejection of any form of social bondage or restraint. By the 1880s, the celebrations at Fox Hill—perhaps significantly held not on August 1 but a week later—had become the most fervent expression of popular liberation and achievement. According to Cleveland Eneas, Bain Town people, who made preparations well in advance, moved to Fox Hill to stay with relatives up to a week before the great day. Women did most of the preparations and participated prominently in the church and Sunday school programs, including recitations, music, and some drama. They also played a vital role in the festivities, which included the plaiting of a maypole, ring play, and singing.[57] Stalls with all types of food, but especially African delicacies, did a lively trade, selling *accara*, *moi-moi*, *agidi*, and *foo-foo*, as well as fare more familiar in a later age—coconut cakes, peas and rice, stewed fish, and native fruit. Liquor was also dispensed to men from temporary bars.[58] Fox Hill Day was a spectacle as well as a celebration, drawing whites and nonwhites out of Nassau as well as blacks from settlements Over the Hill. In 1886, for example, the *Nassau Guardian* described how the steamer *Nassau* was chartered for the day, making trips down the harbor to Fox Hill Creek at 9 A.M. and 2 P.M., its decks crowded and the music of the band of the Bahama Friendly Society blaring forth, while many other persons made their way eastward in carriages, carts, or small boats or on foot.[59]

Guy Fawkes Day was enthusiastically, if less formally, celebrated as an excuse for letting off steam, with the added attraction of activities consonant with African traditions: troupes of mummers in masks, dancing around bonfires, and the burning of effigies. The original significance and purpose of the event—an annual celebration and reminder of a failure of radical revolutionaries to blow up the king and Parliament in 1605—was totally ignored by the Bahamian populace. Guy Fawkes, indeed, may have been confused in the popular mind with the original founder of Fox Hill and thus the progenitor also of Fox Hill Day.

The Bahamian celebration that unequivocally came out of slavery and African traditions and was, despite some involvement by whites, essentially a black "festival of the oppressed," was the Junkanoo. This event was held originally only at Christmas but by the twentieth century on New Year's morning as well. The Junkanoo, alias John Canoe or Jonkannu, found also in Jamaica, other British West Indian islands, and even North Carolina, was the institutionalized development of the "legitimate catharsis" of the slaves' Christmas celebrations—a tradition that had its parallel in the Carnival festivities before the beginning of Lent in slave colonies where Catholic influences were dominant. In the Bahamas, as in other British West Indian colonies, the slaves had three days free from work over Christmas, during which they celebrated "in their own way," which included dressing up in costumes and parodying their white masters behind the anonymous safety of masks. Such role-reversing masquerades were tolerated by the whites, even patronized, on the principle that a certain licensed letting off steam (and overeating) put the slaves in a better state of mind and body for the forthcoming crop season and the tacit assumption that only behavior that stopped short of open insolence and riot would be rewarded by largesse. The regime was also reassured by the knowledge that the forces of law and order were kept discreetly on the alert during the Christmas season and by the expectation that the drunkenness that invariably accompanied the festivities would render the celebrating slaves supine.

All such elements survived into the postslavery Junkanoo celebrations. Little formal work was done between Christmas and New Year's, and blacks delighted to form bands of masked revelers, which roamed Nassau's residential and commercial streets to the deafening music of drum, conch shell, bugle, and beaten pieces of iron, calling for contributions of money, food, or liquor. The pure spirit of

Classic Junkanoo group, clad in tattered papier-maché, masked, and shaking cowbells, 1960s. From the gleam in the trees it is almost sunrise and the masquerade revelry almost over. Courtesy of Bahamas News Bureau.

competition—or more likely, real competition for the available handouts—led to the increased size and sophistication of the bands, the elaboration of the costumes, and the development of themes. The bands most popular with white spectators and patrons were naturally those with patriotic, inspirational, or neutral themes of which the most common had maritime motifs, such as the "Neptune and Amphitrite" mentioned in 1857.[60] Equally predictably, bands that parodied whites or followed themes that commented unfavorably on current affairs were far less common, though generally there was a good deal of at least superficially humorous tolerance. Another factor that vitiated official white opposition was that at least some of the younger and more irresponsible whites "exhibited a taste for the same amusement" and formed their own bands—though this custom (in contrast to the increasingly multiracial Trinidad Carnival described by Bridget Brereton and others) had more or less died by 1900.[61]

Junkanoo bands varied from the large, formal, and staid processions organized by the friendly societies and led by their brass bands, to the small, ragged, and often rowdy "scrap gangs," with their improvised (and far more exciting) music—which were often deprecated, even feared, by the white regime. Even the moderately radical *Bahama Herald,* while praising the general sobriety of the populace during the "burning" (Guy Fawkes) and festive season (Christmas) of 1854, wrote, "We cannot look with any degree of approbation upon such silly affairs as 'John Canoes' &c. Such harlequinade cannot fail to attract crowds of the idle and profligate, and disorder, vice, and intemperance inevitably follow. . . . Money acquired by these means is sure to be spent in intemperate pleasures and low debauchery." Instead, the paper suggested the adoption in the Bahamas of "some good old customs observed in the Mother Country and the United States," such as family reunions, the reconciliation of animosities, and voluntary "thank offerings" to the poor.[62]

But the popular festival would not be denied. The Junkanoo phenomenon was not ordered into a formal regulated parade until the tourism era of the twentieth century, but it had risen to an almost frenzied crescendo by the 1880s. The *Nassau Guardian* gave a memorable description of the festivities in December 1886. Bay Street was brightly decorated and lit, and the shops remained open until 10 P.M. on Christmas Eve:

> People were in the streets all night. At midnight brass bands were heard in several directions, while concertinas, banjos, drums, whistles and human voices heralded in the "joyful morn." There were less noisy crackers than usual, while it seemed to us that more blue lights, rockets and other fireworks took their place. At 3 A.M. the Market was "all alive oh"! while at six it was difficult to get along Bay Street in front of the Market in comfort. All Nassau seemed to have turned out! Morris-dancers or some cousins of theirs held revel for an hour or two and then got either too tired with their carnival or too full of spirits from the "vasty deep" or elsewhere, to prosecute their gyrations. One grotesque figure took a snooze in a doorway for a time and then went at it again like a teetotum. The majority of these dancers are graceful in their movements and picturesque in their dress, but others are vulgar and dirty. A shower of rain about nine o'clock sent the revellers and more sober people to their houses where we hope they had a good Christmas breakfast.[63]

The sociopolitical threat posed by such volatile behavior periodically alarmed Bay Street and Government Hill, just as the respectable churches frequently deplored the deleterious effects of the festivities on what was to them a holy and sacred season. An Anglican priest bemoaning the poor attendance at Christmas services in 1889 wrote: "The coloured people have their own ways of holiday-making which certainly do not conduce to the religious observance of the festival. On Christmas Eve and throughout the succeeding night, there is an incessant letting off of crackers, beating of drums and blowing of penny whistles and trumpets, crowds are parading the streets, and many wearing masks and dressing themselves up in fantastic costumes."[64] And the very next year, the conservative *Nassau Guardian* anticipated that the usual festivities would be injected with dangerous political content by plans among certain young unemployed "mechanics and cigar makers" to divert the march of their "masked army" to Government House, where they intended to petition the governor for "advice as to whether they shall go to Cuba or wait here for employment."[65]

Pressure from the churches and commercial sections led to legislative measures to control and regulate Junkanoo, climaxing in the Street Nuisances Prohibition Act of 1899, which permanently fixed the timing if not the location and nature of the Junkanoo festivities. The act forbade the firing of crackers and blowing of horns on public streets but waived the regulations from 6 to 10 P.M. on Christmas

Eve and from 4 to 9 A.M. on New Year's morning, thus effectively leaving Christmas Day itself free for religious observances, while transferring the main celebration of Junkanoo from Christmas Day to the dawn of New Year's Day.

The development of Junkanoo toward the end of the nineteenth century pointed up the great social, economic, and political divide between Bay Street and Over the Hill—a division made all the more glaring by the continuing poverty and growing political awareness of the blacks, the natural healing of the rift between "old" Bahamian blacks and those who came as liberated Africans, and the almost paranoid fears among the whites stemming from their general ignorance of what life was really like on the other side of Nassau's ridge. That these white fears were not entirely groundless and that conditions in the black settlements were volatile to the point of combustion seemed to be illustrated by the small explosion that occurred in April 1893.

On April 15, 1893, a group of blacks stoned and almost wrecked the Grant's Town police station, guarded by three of the constabulary, and rescued a prisoner whom they considered wrongfully detained. The rioters then smashed the few public lamps in the vicinity and assaulted the inspector of police when he came to remonstrate with them. A small detachment of police reinforcements was sent to Grant's Town the following day, but they were forced to retreat by the violence of the "mob." Several tense days followed. When the police commandant's orderly returned to barracks seriously injured and a rumor circulated that policemen on solitary beats had been murdered, a large contingent of policemen broke barracks and, armed with rifles and bayonets, rushed at the rioters. Grant's Town was said to be "ablaze," and there was much scuffling and stone-throwing, but fortunately the constabulary were ordered back to barracks before anyone was seriously hurt. The retreating police, however, were followed by an angry and taunting crowd, apparently led by a man named Francis Bain, who accused the police of having handled him brutally and taken the cutlass he needed for his farming work.

The government acted quickly and decisively. Taking advantage of the telegraph cable laid down to Jupiter, Florida, and places beyond in the previous year, the governor immediately called on the gunboat HMS *Partridge*, though by the time it arrived the trouble had subsided. After six weeks offshore, the gunboat departed, leaving the government to set up a commission of inquiry into the recent events.[66] F. C. Halkett, the police commandant, made light of the incidents, claiming that they were incited and led by "a small minority," of whom only seven men were arrested. Although there was no evidence that the rioting crowd was drunk, the trouble was said to have originated in the Grant's Town rum shops, particularly that owned by the same Louis Duty, who was a vocal critic of Bay Street and the truck system at the time of L. D. Powles. Duty, who had recently written a letter to the *Nassau Times* highly critical of the police force, was accordingly labeled "the chief foment of the disturbance" by Governor Sir Ambrose Shea. It was determined, though, that the sparking cause of the conflagration was the presence and demeanor of the Barbadian policemen brought in as part of the reorganization of the Bahamas constabulary after the withdrawal of the troops in 1891. Several persons testified that the Barbadian policemen performed their duties roughly and insensitively, and a Rev. Willerup claimed that this was exacerbated by the way the police took advantage of the seedier aspects of Grant's Town life. He admitted that Grant's Town could be a difficult place to police, especially on Saturday nights, but said he had observed policemen in uniform in the "house of a loose woman drinking and playing cards."[67]

The government acted with great discretion in resolving the trouble. The final verdict of the committee of inquiry was that the riot was not premeditated and that the police were far from blameless. Of the seven men arrested, only two were convicted, and Francis Bain, originally sentenced to six months' imprisonment, had his sentence reduced on appeal to a fine of £1 for assaulting two constables. Louis Duty was not formally charged. Moreover, on the recommendation of the investigating committee it was decreed that the police force would be reorganized into two divisions. One, consisting mainly of Barbadians, would police the city district, while the other, consisting entirely of Bahamians, would be responsible for patrolling the eastern district, Grant's Town, the rest of New Providence, and the Out Islands on the principle that native policemen would best control those areas where it was most likely for "collisions to occur."[68]

The astute deflection of blame away from the true sources of Bahamian authority on to their non-Bahamian agents, the Barbadian policemen (taking advantage of the xenophobia that was the darker side of a growing sense of national identity), and the clever tactic of having the black settlements policed by black fellow Bahamians doused the 1893 outbreak so effectively that it was not repeated for many years. The twentieth century, though, was to show that these were not permanent solutions to the basic problems of the rift between Bahamian "haves" and "have-nots," whites and blacks, represented not only by the boundary between downtown Nassau and Over the Hill but also by those between Nassau and the Out Islands and within the Out Islands themselves.

5

The Margins of a Marginal Colony: The Bahamian Out Islands, 1838–1900

Introductory Overview

Nassau on New Providence Island dominated its hinterland as much as any colonial capital in the British Empire. It was also relatively well known and connected to the outside world by 1900, whereas the rest of the Bahamas was almost terra incognita and cut off. Yet the two dozen inhabited Bahamian Out Islands, scattered over 150,000 square miles of sea, represented 95 percent of the colony's meager land and in 1900 were still home for 75 percent of the total population. These forty thousand Bahamian Out Islanders, though suffering isolation and poverty in common and of necessity sharing many of the limited occupational options available, exhibited variations in lifestyle and socioeconomic divisions even greater (if sometimes less obvious) than those found in New Providence. Some of these differences stemmed from the varying distances from the colonial capital and greater propinquity to other territories or shipping lanes, from minor climatic and ecological variations, or from the differences in historical development and degrees of socioeconomic exploitation considered in earlier chapters. But the most significant causes of differences and divisions among Bahamian Out Islanders were ethnic and racial.

The Bahamas Out Islands displayed a much wider spectrum of ethnic communities than Nassau and New Providence. The commonest way they have been studied is the easiest: by concentrating on the extremes, the all-white and the all-black settlements. But this provides a distorted picture by ignoring the greater number and complex range in between. At one end of the spectrum were the six insular settlements of Spanish Wells and the Current in northern Eleuthera and Hopetown, Man-o-War Cay, Great Guana Cay, and Cherokee Sound in Abaco, which had determinedly, and at considerable social expense, remained genetically pure white. At the other end were the many communities, notably in the central and southern islands, that remained all black, less by the will of their inhabitants than through lack of interest in them by whites. In between these extremes were many variations. At least four of the most important Out Island townships, Dunmore Town on Harbour Island off northern Eleuthera, Governor's Harbour in central Eleuthera, Marsh Harbour on Abaco's central mainland, and New Plymouth on Green Turtle Cay off northern Abaco, were bifurcated or bipolar settlements, practicing a geographical and social apartheid that (having virtually no middle colored section) was more extreme than the situation in New Providence. Some communities, chiefly in the long-established island of Eleuthera but also in the Long Island–Ragged Island district, had a less rigid separation of ethnicities because the majority of the inhabitants—or at least of the families—were already of mixed race. Even among exclusively black settlements there were distinctions between those that had been founded pragmatically by families of former slaves and those established more formally by the government to settle either former slaves or liberated Africans. Some black villages based on commonages or nucleated villages around old slave quarters were complete and well-integrated communities, if far from flourishing. Others, settled by poor black migrant farmers or serving as dormitories for nearby sponge fishing grounds had a ramshackle, incomplete, and temporary character and appearance. Finally, there was at least one distant settlement, Mathew Town, Inagua (to which Rock Sound and Tarpum Bay, Eleuthera, and Alice Town, Bimini, might be added), where a black or colored majority was dominated by a small number of whites drawn by commercial opportunities who constructed a miniature replica of Nassau's socioeconomic system based on race, differential wealth, and economic power.

The All-White Settlements

White communities dominated the northwestern quadrant of the Bahamian archipelago, including Abaco and northern Eleuthera, though one should not ignore the adjacent or nearby black communities that provided some vital services even for the most proudly exclusive white settlements. Harbour Island, Spanish Wells, and perhaps the Current date from pre-Loyalist times, but the determination of white families to isolate themselves as far as possible from their Afro-Bahamian countrymen was reinforced by the Loyalist influx. At one level, it can be seen as the acceptance of continuing and theoretically avoidable poverty and isolation as the price of retaining vestiges of the prerevolutionary lifestyle they had left behind on the American mainland in which miscegenation was covert if not rare and open cohabitation unthinkable. At another level, it can be seen as a development very similar to that in certain sections of the American South once economic factors no longer bound the two races together in a plantation economy. In this outcome, both communities became competitively poor, racial tensions intensified, and residential and occupational separation widened.

Other factors influenced the development of the all-white and racially polarized communities in the Out Islands. The whites' lifestyle was intimately bound up with the sea, in fishing, shipbuilding, and maritime trade; that of the blacks was devoted more to the land and to farming. This difference determined that the whites—enjoying greater access to the land-patenting process—tended to seek the most favorable maritime sites for their settlements. These were the small offshore islands of Harbour Island and St. George's Cay adjacent to Eleuthera; Elbow, Man-of-War, Great Guana, and Green Turtle Cays off Abaco; and the mainland locations with excellent harbors of Marsh Harbour at the easternmost point of Great Abaco, Governor's Harbour in the very center of Eleuthera, and the Current on a peninsula commanding the narrow waterway between north and south Eleuthera. Besides finding the best maritime sites preempted, the blacks gravitated toward mainland sites with their relatively greater agricultural potential and stands of timber. There they lived as subsistence farmers or small independent producers but often supplied foodstuffs and timber to the white settlements on the offshore cays (as at the Bluff, Eleuthera) or worked as laborers on the lands still owned by the offshore whites, just as their slave forerunners had done.

The steady increase of both white and black populations led to migrations and new settlements by the whites from Harbour Island to Spanish Wells (and from St. George's Cay to adjacent Russell Island) and from the original offshore settlements in Abaco on Elbow and Green Turtle Cays to the smaller islands of Man-of-War and Great Guana Cays and by the blacks from the original nuclei to the scattering of settlements over the entire anvil-shaped territory of north Eleuthera (a hundred square miles in extent) or the bow-shaped three hundred square miles of mainland Abaco. Besides, the ethnic inconvenience or social discomfort felt by white families when it became clear that the slaves and free blacks who accompanied them from the American mainland were socioeconomic competitors rather than mere bondsmen was exacerbated once the nonwhites outstripped them demographically and created an intolerable pressure after slave emancipation. Harbour Island and Green Turtle Cay became bifocal settlements with internal ethnic boundaries. Spanish Wells was not just an overspill from Harbour Island but seems to have become an exclusively white settlement, with a mile-wide water boundary, only in the last days of slavery or even after emancipation. No blacks were allowed to reside on the island, and any nonwhite visitors or domestic servants were expected to depart by nightfall each day. This precedent has allowed the modern inhabitants of Spanish Wells to justify their tradition of racial segregation by perpetuating the myth that it originated from an abhorrence of the slavery system which equated race with class, conveniently ignoring the fact that at least some early white inhabitants of St. George's Cay were slaveholders who kept their slave bondsmen on the nearby mainland.[1]

A final reason given for the settlement of the offshore cays was their relative healthfulness. Conditions on Harbour Island were certainly more conducive to health than the crowded international port of Nassau, and it was known as the "health resort" or "Montpellier" of the Bahamas. Also, as late as 1834 one of the reasons why whites deserted Marsh Harbour for the breezy and drier offshore Abaco cays in certain seasons, if not permanently, was the persistence of malaria from the mosquitoes breeding in the mainland marshes.[2] But the argument that the all-white settlements were the result of white separatism if not outright racism, rather than any other reason, seems borne out by the existence and persistence of the most isolated all-white settlement of all, Cherokee Sound, Abaco. This small village was not set on a relatively high offshore cay but on a dead, flat segment of land barely separated from the Abaco mainland. It was cut off from black mainland settlements by creeks and marshland but did not enjoy either much agricultural land or, despite a thriving boatbuilding industry, an adequate harbor. Visitors, like L. D. Powles in the 1880s, sometimes had to wade or be carried to the settlement over half a mile of shallows, and reports of near starvation when crops failed or the mail boat was delayed were not uncommon.[3] That such an ill-favored settlement not only survived but gained a reputation for being the neatest, most orderly white village in Abaco, producing some of the best boats and some of the cleverest children from its tiny school, if not wholly vindicating the principle of white racial superiority when backed up by a system of apartheid, does seem to bear out the Toynbeean notion that communities flourish only when they are sufficiently well integrated and faced by a sufficient environmental challenge.

Though racial endogamy was the result of ethnic choice, the poverty and inertia of most of the all-white settlements resulted from inescapable conditions. The communal decision not to miscegenate led to excessive inbreeding with some unfortunate genetic consequences but was the result of fecundity coupled with lack of opportunities for acquiring "fresh blood" of an acceptable "color," rather than from the practice of racial endogamy in itself. Though the Out Island whites theoretically enjoyed relatively greater mobility and economic choices because of the inhabitants' boatbuilding skills, these advantages were severely limited in a marginal colony in which whatever wealth existed gravitated toward and was monopolized by the colonial capital.

Predictably, the all-white settlements showed an almost obsessive interest in genealogy, and this has enabled scholars to analyze both the degree of intermarriage and its consequences. The most thorough, and notorious, analysis was that made of the inhabitants of Hopetown, Abaco, in 1903 by Clement Penrose of the Baltimore Geographical Society (with the help of a local clergyman and one of the settlement elders). The population consisted of almost a thousand whites and a mere dozen or so nonwhites, crammed into a jumble of one- or two-story residences with an average of more than seven persons apiece.[4] The investigators drew up a huge genealogical chart that showed a complete absence of both illegitimacy and miscegenation and demonstrated that the entire white population was descended from one white Loyalist widow, Wyannie Malone, who had come to Elbow Cay with her four children in 1785.[5] One of the widow's daughters ran away with a Nantucket whaler and was never heard of again, another daughter was married to a fellow Loyalist refugee, and the two sons wed native whites from Harbour Island. Within a generation, the founding genetic input was closed with the arrival of "Old John" Albury from Harbour Island and Nathanial Key from St. Augustine, Florida. Virtually all subsequent generations for more than a century were the offspring of the complex intermarriage of Malones, Alburys, and Keys.

The smaller settlement of Spanish Wells, with fewer than five hundred inhabitants and no nonwhites, was even more involuted. A rare American visitor accompanying the Methodist minister on his circuit in 1875 described the township as the antithesis of "Philadelphia uniformity and precision . . . such an assemblage of houses as you ought to expect to see on Hog Island [Nassau] after a hurricane with the wind from the South." Because very few of the inhabitants married out of the settlement there was a drastic shortage of surnames, and this had an almost comic result. "One of the party who was here for the first time, found it convenient to address all he met by the name of Pinder," recounted the visitor, "and he discovered that in a great majority of the cases he was right, and it was rather amusing to see how astonished some seemed to be that a stranger who had never seen them before should . . . be able to call their name."[6]

Fears of accidental incest discouraged casual sex, encouraged formal marriage, and stimulated the interest in accurate genealogy. Yet marriages between first cousins were so common that it was jokingly said that second cousins were regarded as "distant family."[7] Houses tended to be small and households of the simple nuclear type, with daughters living with their parents only until they were married and sons building their own houses before they entered matrimony. The prevalence of formal marriage ties and the virtual ban on premarital sex, in combination with economic conditions that made it difficult for young men to find time, money, and land to build their own homes, meant that girls were usually married in their early teens (or even earlier) to men approaching thirty (or even older). The distaste for illicit unions, above all with nonwhites, and the early age of marriage for females made for large families, just as the necessity for the men, even after marriage, to roam the archipelago in search of a living made for a continuation of the white Bahamian tradition of capable and strong-willed female marriage partners. The general fecundity as well as poverty of the population and the tradition of creating neolocal households close by or adjacent to both parents' houses contributed to the cluttered and crowded appearance of some all-white settlements toward the end of the nineteenth century. This overcrowding, along with inadequate medical services, also contributed to distressingly high infant and child mortality rates, which inured white Out Island women to bearing large families but seeing no more than two-thirds of their children reach maturity.

Health conditions in the all-white settlements were less than ideal, though the effects of inbreeding were almost certainly not as dire as Clement Penrose and his Baltimore colleagues claimed in 1902. The social advisability of a larger and more widely dispersed population of whites in the Out Islands had occurred to Governor Mathew—the first governor to make a regular annual circuit of some of the Out Islands—as early as 1848. In response to an inquiry from the colonial secretary, Lord Grey, about the suitability of the Bahamas for the settlement of English agricultural laborers, Mathew had written that the white populations of Eleuthera, Harbour Island, and Abaco could usefully be augmented and the underdeveloped island of Grand Bahama was perhaps most suitable, though, given the problems faced with the Loyalists some sixty years earlier, the costs and other difficulties of settling white immigrants with sufficient land, tools, and provisions might prove insuperable.[8] The flood of British emigrants during the second half of the nineteenth century passed the Bahamas by and went to more suitable and attractive areas, not least the United States; by the 1880s American commentators were using the all-white Bahamian settlements as exemplary proof of neo-Darwinian ideas of natural selection and the deleterious effects of unfavorable environments.

In a pioneer study of the whites of Green Turtle Cay, T. Wesley Mills wrote in the *American Naturalist* in 1887: "Among a white population that does not travel, that does not receive accessions, and numbering only about 300 the play of 'sexual selection' must be of the most restrictive kind, and with corresponding results." He described most of the whites as having "the stamp of weakness and anaemia," in contrast to the blacks, who, though "not equal to the same race in the Northern States," were "scarcely inferior to negroes as found in some communities in the South."[9] Mills's assessment was mild compared with that of Penrose, who seems to have regarded the Baltimore Geographical Society expedition to the Bahamas in 1902 as a venture into the backward fringes of American civilization and described Hopetown and Spanish Wells as "an experiment conducted by nature" to prove neo-Darwinian theories. His genealogical table of Hopetown seems to be accurate enough, but it does not prove the "shocking condition of degeneracy" he claimed. Out of several hundred closely related persons (forming an incredibly tight-knit network of inbreeding) there were fifteen cases of idiocy which Penrose claimed were congenital, culminating in five idiots out of eight children in one fifth-generation

As yet unmodernized, the all-white Loyalist township of Hopetown on Elbow Cay, Abaco, in the 1950s. The candy-striped lighthouse, raised by the Imperial Lighthouse Service in 1863, was to guide vessels in transit past Abaco's dangerous eastern extremity. Courtesy of Bahamas News Bureau.

family. In addition, five cases of blindness, four of deformations, and three of deaf-mutism were also said to have been congenital. But Penrose (surely backward in his knowledge of genetics even for 1902) also attributed ten cases of leprosy, others of locomotor ataxia, and even one of cholera to genetic causes rather than to contagion. Some genuine ill-effects of recessive genes through inbreeding may have been adduced, but Penrose's own evidence suggests that overcrowding, ignorance, and poor hygiene were more serious health factors leading to infections of leprosy and syphilis, as well as tuberculosis. Even the cases of idiocy claimed to have been congenital (about which many cruel jokes have been perpetuated over the years) may well have resulted, like the locomotor ataxia symptoms, from the spirochetes of syphilis, transmitted by infection from parents to children rather than through genetic inheritance.[10]

The more sweeping observation by Penrose and his fellow scientists that the "mental acumen" of many of the inhabitants of Spanish Wells was "rather low" may have had some empirical validity but surely also had an environmental rather than purely genetic explanation. The cultural world of the all-white settlements was certainly narrow. Dismal educational facilities and a concern for practical rather than intellectual knowledge combined with a lack of communication with the outside world reduced the common fund of general knowledge and even discouraged normal cerebration. Such intellectual impoverishment was certainly regressive but was clearly the result of cumulative environmental factors and isolation, not genetic inheritance.

In sum, it is not surprising that such nineteenth-century Yankee progressives as Wesley Mills (who denigrated all Negroes but believed that those living in Yankeeland were superior to the rest) and Clement Penrose were predisposed to find the white inhabitants of Hopetown and Spanish Wells "degenerate." Yet their own researches might be turned on their head to show that given the social and environmental conditions in the all-white settlements studied, the Eleutheran and Abaconian Conchy Joes were remarkably healthy despite inbreeding. Certainly, investigators who were less culturally biased (and who examined more closely the more successful mixed as well as the all-white settlements) would have given more credit to the industry, endurance, ingenuity, and skills necessary for survival which the Out Island whites demonstrated, in especially their agricultural and domestic husbandry, their self-sufficient crafts and, above all, their woodworking, boatbuilding, and navigational expertise.

Boatbuilding and Wrecking

Absolutely central to the lifestyle, well-being, and even existence of the all-white settlements was the ability to build, maintain, and repair their own boats. In an age of sail (which for the Bahamas Out Islands lasted well into the twentieth century) boatbuilding skills were widely diffused. Many blacks as well as whites were boatbuilders, and those of Sandy Point, Abaco, Mangrove Cay, Andros, Long Island, and Exuma were especially noted. But the most numerous, expert, and productive boatbuilders were found in the mixed and all-white settlements of northern Eleuthera and Abaco.[11] In the mixed settlements, as well as Nassau and all-white communities that had socioeconomic relationships with nearby blacks, labor was divided along class lines between those who built the boats and those who extracted and worked the timber, between those who owned the boats and those who sailed them, or between those engaged in maritime activities and those who worked the land. But in the most isolated all-white settlements, the ability of virtually all males to combine boatbuilding with forestry, farming, fishing, trading, and sailing skills was the necessary corollary of their classless independence, as well as their ability to stay rooted in a single location over generations. Thus shipbuilding skill alone seems to have kept Cherokee Sound alive in the worst of times, and Hopetown owed its greater dependence on the boatbuilding industry over the mixed settlements of Green Turtle Cay and Harbour Island in the late nineteenth century mainly to its relative poverty of agricultural, trading, and human resources. Even though similarly undifferentiated by class, few all-black settlements (which were isolated by circumstances, not by choice) could match the flexibility of the all-white settlements, and those without a boatbuilding capability were specially subject to exploitation, as well as to endemic poverty, and periodic spells of destitution that could lead to enforced migration and the abandonment of settlements altogether.

Of all the central and northern islands, Abaco had the widest range and largest supply of boatbuilding timbers: the tall and straight, relatively hard, resinous, rot-resistant Caribbean pine for masts and planking and the naturally crooked

Traditional Bahamian sailing craft. Essential for lifelines and livelihood for nearly three centuries, by the 1990s they were fast becoming museum curiosities, the essential handicraft skills needed in their construction kept alive only by the interest of wealthy wooden boat enthusiasts and regatta competitors. From William Johnson Jr., *Bahamian Sailing Craft* (Nassau, 1977), used with permission.

hardwoods—horseflesh, dogwood, corkwood, mahogany, and lignum vitae—ideal for ribs and other curved timbers, keels, stem and stern posts, rudders, dowel pegs (trunnels), and tackle blocks. In the mixed settlements and in expansive times, blacks were employed to cut and saw timber, but boatbuilders preferred to oversee their own woodcutting and in the smallest settlements (and in all-white settlements in difficult times) the boatbuilders had no option but to send their own men off in lumbering parties and employ them in the tediously hard and hot work of sawing planks. In the hurricane season—June to October—when long-distance sailing ventures were too dangerous, those not directly involved in boatbuilding or farming would be sent to the nearby mainland for two or three days each week, carrying provisions and sleeping on the boat. Paths to the nearest stands of suitable timber were slashed with machetes and the trees cut and trimmed with axes, all but the mast pieces sawed into manageable lengths, and the logs carried or dragged to the shore. Back at the settlement, the hardwoods were seasoned and temporarily softened in seawater and the plankwood left for a few weeks before being sawed in rough timber pits with two-handed saws. Power tools and hauling equipment were unknown in the boatbuilding islands before the twentieth century, though a few steam engines had been introduced in Nassau before 1900.

Though native boatbuilding dated from the earliest settlements (discussed in the second part of Volume 1), it reached its peak after the Loyalists arrived. As Steve Dodge has argued, the first white Abaconians aimed to make their island an entrepôt to rival and supersede the independent mainland Americans now excluded from British West Indian trade. Bahamian sloops, schooners, and scows of up to two hundred tons—many built in Abaco—were engaged in trade between North America and the West Indies and even across the Atlantic in the late 1780s. But with the ending of the embargo on United States ships, the general decline of the Bahamian economy, and the remigration of many Loyalists, the colony's boatbuilding industry adjusted to serve the more modest needs of subsistence farming and fishing and limited interinsular trade, expanding only temporarily during the heydays of the pineapple, sponging, and timber exporting businesses.

Three basic boat types were produced by Out Island builders during the nineteenth century: the Abaco dinghy, the smack boat (a kind of sloop), and the sponge schooner. As Steve Dodge has written, the first of these was

> the Bahamian Model T. They ranged in size from 9 to 20 feet long and were used for fishing, sponging, conching, and general inter-island transportation. They had a round bilge with a great deal of deadrise and had a long, straight keel with deadwood aft. The rudder was outboard, hung in the sternpost and the transom. The sheer had a beautiful curve. Dinghies had a single mast with a single sail of the leg-of-mutton type. The sail was bent to the mast with lacing line, but was loose footed. The boom was quite long, with about one-fourth of its length overhanging the transom. A notch in the upper port side of the transom made it possible to scull the boat when there was no wind. The long keel provided the directional stability necessary for effective sculling. Dinghies intended for fishermen were equipped with live wells through which sea water flowed, making it possible to carry live fish home or to make the market.[12]

Smack boats were similar in lines to dinghies but twice as large—eighteen to forty feet long on the keel and somewhat longer overall. Their beam was broad, about one-third their length, and for obvious reasons they were shoal drafted. Like dinghies, they had a single mast but carried two sails, a leg-of-mutton mainsail, and a jib bent to a bowsprit. As Dodge wrote, "Smacks were generally built for fishing and had live wells. There was no cockpit; the entire hull was decked over and a hatch provided access to a cargo hold located forward. There was usually a small trunk cabin aft, but the crew of seven to ten men on a smack boat cooked, ate, and slept on the open deck rather than below."[13] Smack boats were often termed sloops, that is, single-masted vessels with more than one sail, but few were built in the post-Loyalist Bahamas in the classic Bermudian style with a complex of jib and topsails and the sleek lines and deep draft suitable for ocean voyages.

Sponge schooners were the largest of the three basic types of Bahamian workboat, typically from 35 to 38 feet on the keel and 50 to 55 feet overall, 16 feet wide, and drawing about 5 feet of water. Most displaced between 50 and 70 tons. Like most schooners, they were two-masted vessels, carrying a good deal of sail, "usually gaff-rigged with topmasts and topsails. They carried a foretopmast staysail and a jib bent to a long bowsprit and a jib boom." Sponge schooners carried as many as twenty crewmen and served as mother ships for small fleets of eight to ten two-man sponging dinghies. Even larger schooners were built for carrying freight on long voyages, such as the 80- to 100-foot pineapple schooners made in the 1880s, and just after the turn of the century, the largest of all Bahamian-built vessels, three-masted schooners up to 150 feet long, were constructed at Harbour Island and Hopetown to carry lumber from Abaco and Grand Bahama to the United States, Cuba, and the British West Indies.[14]

Such large-scale enterprises represented forays (of limited and short-lived success) into the larger realms of capitalism and the world market economy. As boats became larger and more numerous so as to widen the ambit of Bahamian trade, the custom already common in Nassau and Harbour Island of merchants owning a boat or gaining a controlling share in it by financing its construction spread more widely. For the less fortunate would-be builders—most of them black—this degenerated into yet another facet of the pervasive truck system. Particularly for constructing vessels over fifty tons, merchants advanced builders boatbuilding materials, truck provisions, or both. When the boat was finished, the builder either had to give up a share of its operation or hand it over to the merchant to operate until the debt was repaid. In some cases the debt was so great that the merchants took over the boat altogether.[15]

For the more independent and fortunate boatbuilding settlements, however, the normal business of boatbuilding was an egalitarian, almost non- (or pre-) capitalist operation during most of the nineteenth century. There was certainly a hierarchy consisting of young apprentices, laboring journeymen, and master builders, but considerable skill and hard physical labor were required of each member of the boatbuilding gang, and each person had a voice in managerial decisions. The supervisory authority of the master builder, like that of a captain at sea, was based on respect for superior expertise rather than age or wealth, let alone sole ownership of yard or finished boat. Though individual ownership was not unknown and became more common over time as modern capitalism widened and tightened its grip, boatbuilding was traditionally a sharing partnership, much like voyages once the boat was complete, and formal wages were almost unknown. Each member of the gang and his family contributed food and materials as well as services in return for a carefully calculated share of the finished product. Though most boats were made for the settlement's own use, if they were made for commercial sale, payment was commonly made in kind—in groceries and supplies if sold in Nassau or in agricultural produce or labor services if traded with black settlements that lacked boatbuilders—each member of the building gang receiving a proportionate return.

To a degree almost incomprehensible to the modern world, components for the building of Bahamian sailboats (as well as the timbers) were locally obtained, and the highly sophisticated and accurate—even elegant—results were obtained with simple tools and what the Abaconian whites termed "mother wit." No nineteenth-century boatbuilders drew or worked from plans, but master craftsmen had a wonderful eye and well-tried simple techniques to select and shape woods to produce vessels of a previsualized size and form. The highest skills were called for in the shaping of the ribs of the middle (or "rising") frame from natural crook logs before the frame was fitted to the laid-down keel and endposts and the "spiling" of the sideplanks (which had to be chamfered at their edges and shaved concave on the outside and varied in width with great exactitude from end to end). But each stage down to the fitting of decks, cabin, masts, boom, rigging, and rudder and the finishing touches of caulking, sanding, staining, and painting required its special expertise. These results were achieved with the simplest tools: handsaws, axes and adzes, wooden planes, augers and clamps, locally made mallets, and caulking tools made from an old-fashioned penny on a stick, with a lead plumb line, a pair of dividers, and some handmade lead shaping battens the only pretense of precision instruments.[16] Working in the open air under the shade of large trees from sunup to sundown (or "from can to can't," as Abaconians said), several men needed many weeks to make even a single dinghy, a rate of return on labor (not to mention skill) that bore no relation to established wage rates, even in such a poor economy as the Bahamas. As late as the 1930s, a ten-foot Abaco dinghy could command no more than £5 (or $25) in Nassau, often paid in flour, grits, other provisions, or even supplies needed for future boatbuilding.

Besides all the wood needed for Bahamian boats, cotton wool for caulking could be obtained from ancient cotton bushes or a silk cotton tree, and rope was locally produced from the sisal plant. This was laborious work. The leaves had to be cut, stripped, soaked for several weeks, beaten, and washed to produce the clean fiber, which was then spun into yarn on a wooden spinning wheel and plaited into rope by a three-person team. The secret of cotton spinning for the making of nets and sailcloth seems to have died by the mid-nineteenth century, but sisal yarn was used to make the coarser nets for catching turtles. Wrecking was a far easier and more popular source of rope, as well as for sails and all ships' stores not produced locally.

Though ships' cargoes were the chief magnet for most Bahamian wreckers and provided occasional easy fortunes for the first comers, boatbuilding Out Islanders visited wrecks and often took great chances in search of more fundamental plunder: rope, sails, nets, and netting yarn, boatbuilding tools and wares, timbers, including cargo lumber, and any metal that could be reworked into nails, tools, or boat fittings. As well as having its experts in resplicing old rope, making and remaking sails, and making and mending nets, each boatbuilding community had its smiths to work salvaged iron, copper, brass, and bronze. A correspondent in a Nassau newspaper in 1864 listed the chief occupations of the people of Hopetown as "farming, boatbuilding, copper nail making, the manufacture of turtle and fishing nets, and turtling." The same writer also significantly noted, "Everyone is his own servant and therefore domestic economy is carried out to the full without the anxieties experienced in the Metropolis of this colony."[17]

Though almost half of all adult able-bodied Bahamian males held wrecking licenses in the 1860s, few, and progressively fewer, made a permanent living from the produce of wrecks. The possession of a license was for most merely the necessary ticket to one of nature's lotteries. Wrecks made a fortuitous contribution to the islands' economy but were hardly a mainstay at the best (or worst) of times. Abaconians and Harbour Islanders told the story of the minister who tricked his flock in the race to a wreck by leaving them deep in prayer—a legend found also in North Cornwall in England and probably on every other "wrecker's coast." But they vehemently rejected as calumnies the tales—recounted by Governor Bayley in 1859—that Conchy Joe wreckers placed false lights to lure ships to their doom and ignored the fate of passengers in order to plunder rich cargoes.[18] Abaconians rightly point out that since lights are placed to indicate danger, extra lights would drive away rather than lure passing ships. Extinguishing lights might have had more purpose (and there is some evidence that this was occasionally done), but most Out Island mariners found the lights so vital to their own safe navigation that putting them out was counterproductive. On the contrary, Abaconians proudly quote the many occasions when their menfolk risked their lives in appalling conditions to rescue strangers. One such case was that of Captain Robert Sands of the wrecking schooner *Oracle*, who was awarded the silver medal of the Royal National Lifeboat Institution for saving many lives from the immigrant ship *William and Mary*, wrecked on the Great Isaac Rock in May 1853.[19]

Morality may also have prevented many Out Island wreckers from the practice attributed to Nassau merchants of arranging to insure cargoes before running them aground—a precursor to the common twentieth-century form of commercial arson nicknamed "Bay Street Lightning"—though cynics might point out that Out Islanders lacked the means to carry out such a complex subterfuge. However much they welcomed windfalls of provisions, stores, and adornments for their homes and cannibalized wrecks for their own boatbuilding industry, the white northeasterners lacked the desperate unscrupulousness of mariners who aimed to live solely off the proceeds of wrecking. The most notorious of these were the inhabitants of Bimini, on the ragged eastern edge of the narrowest, fastest-flowing, and roughest stretch of the Florida Channel. Bimini had been uninhabited before 1847, when Alice Town was laid out and settled in the hope of cultivating pineapples and citrus for the American market. Instead, the settlement became the resort of professional wreckers, who often outnumbered the 250 permanent inhabitants. In August 1851, Justice W. R. Inglis reported that petty crime and violence were common, necessitating the construction of a jail, and in March 1865 another circuit magistrate printed the following fairly damning report:

> The occupation of the inhabitants is principally that of wrecking, and the harbour and roadstead are frequently the rendezvous of numerous wrecking vessels, at which time the licentiousness of the people is painfully manifested. It is questionably the most immoral place in the district, being without the necessary officers and institutions for the repression of vice and the promotion of virtue. A church was erected about three years ago in connection with the establishment, but the incumbency has been vacant for some time, and I do not believe that a clergyman of any denomination has officiated here for more than two years past. . . . The wrecking system every day develops its sad depravity, and indicates the urgent necessity of more prompt and effective measures; if not for prevention of enormous plunder, for at least the recovery of some portion of the articles stolen.[20]

Similarly unfavorable remarks were made the following year by Governor Rawson Rawson about the inhabitants of Rock (formerly Wreck) Sound, Eleuthera, traditional center for wrecking in the central Bahamas. According to Rawson, who typically tinged his moral censure with racist prejudice, the inhabitants, though originally white, were "becoming very degenerate from constant intermarriage, and the poverty of their food." They were "very poor, and primitive, very ignorant and indifferent to improvement."[21]

Wrecking caused civil disturbances both when wreckers disputed the spoils among themselves and when they conflicted with officials about what constituted proper salvage and what share belonged to the government. For example, in 1877 there was a riot at Long Cay when the Court of Admiralty in Nassau decreed that a vessel with a valuable cargo that had gone aground there was not legally salvage because the wreck had been "wilfully occasioned" by its captain and the local wreckers had made no serious effort to save the ship. A local man named Collie gave the critical evidence on which the decision was based. While he was in Nassau his house was burned down, his boat destroyed, and his store ransacked, and when he returned to the settlement, he was met by a riotous crowd that threatened his life. An even more serious incident occurred at Port Howe, Cat Island, over the proceeds of the wreck of the German schooner *Catherine Leeds* in May 1882. The resident magistrate, J. B. Dorsett, was brutally clubbed with an oar when he attempted to arrest a local wrecker called Bowleg, and his two sons and others who came to his rescue received similar treatment from the assembled crowd. Dorsett attempted to swear in special constables, but they refused to serve, and he was forced to take refuge in the house of Josiah Deveaux and send to Nassau for help. In due course, the police magistrate arrived with an armed escort, and "about a dozen of the peacebreakers were convicted, four of whom were imprisoned and the remainder fined."[22]

Sponge Fishing and Pineapple Cultivation

The white inhabitants of northern Eleuthera and Abaco had more economic options than the people of Bimini, Rock Sound, Long Cay, or Port Howe. Ownership of their own vessels and the ethos of hard work and communal sharing also determined that while none became rich, the white Out Island settlements did marginally better than most black communities involved in the sponge fishing and agricultural exporting industries. When times were especially bad or socioeconomic pressure from blacks and coloreds became oppressive to them, the boat-owning Out Island whites could seek a more comfortable existence on a part of the United States coastline very similar to their Bahamian habitat, where local customs decreed an even sharper racial divide than in the Bahamas. As early as 1847, Bahamian "Conchs" were among the first settlers of Key West, Florida, where they continued to engage in boatbuilding, fishing, turtling, sponging, and wrecking but also traded with Cuba and in the Gulf of Mexico.[23] This connection was sustained and intermittently reinforced for at least fifty years, and Key West was largely peopled by white families who had relatives in the Abaco Cays and northern Eleuthera, living a similar lifestyle in houses reminiscent of those in Hopetown, New Plymouth, or Dunmore Town. One early Bahamian migrant, Joseph Curry of Green Turtle Cay, a prolific boatbuilder and trader, became almost the "uncrowned king" of Key West. The Bahamian influence declined, however, first with the immigration of Cubans and later when the road and rail links were completed down the Florida Keys and the city at their southern extremity burgeoned and took on a more American mainland character. The actual migration and movement between the Bahamas and Key West also slowed when the United States government introduced more rigid immigration restrictions in the twentieth century.[24]

Among agricultural enterprises, the pineapple industry was by far the most important, beginning shortly after slave emancipation and peaking between 1885 and 1895 (bringing a short-lived recovery to Rock Sound, Eleuthera), before suffering a sudden decline. The sisal industry began and finished later but brought even fewer profits, especially to the small independent farmers. The large-scale fishing of sponges for export was begun about as early as the commercial pineapple industry and had a similar steady expansion, but it spread even more widely and lasted even longer than either pineapples or sisal, with a peak between 1890 and 1910 and substantial production into the 1930s. Sponging was a permanent feature in many Out Island communities and a mainstay of their fragile economies from 1850 to about 1920. But it was desperately hard work even for the most fortunate fishermen, barely above a subsistence occupation even when world market prices were relatively good, and requiring long absences from their families.

Sponge fishing was done throughout the eight months (October to May) free from the threat of hurricanes. Abaconian spongers made seasonal short ventures each year into the nearby shallows of the little Bahama Bank, but their predominant sponging ground, as for the vast majority of the six thousand Bahamian spongers, was the twenty-thousand-square-mile shallow expanse of the Great Bahama Bank to the west of Andros Island popularly known as the Mud. Each of the three or four annual forays, in which most of the able-bodied men in each settlement participated, lasted six to eight weeks. They left wives and children responsible for homes and farms, with daily dwindling supplies and no news of their menfolk.

Once on the Mud, each sponging schooner with its attendant flotilla of dinghies formed a separate and self-sufficient all-male community. Each schooner carried a captain, mate, and cook and two men for each dinghy, one to scull and one to use the water-glass and hook the sponges. Provisions were carried for the entire voyage: barrels of salt beef, bags of flour, grits, sugar, and dry vegetables, augmented only with fish, the occasional turtle, and green vegetables and fruit from the Andros settlements. Each two-man dinghy crew maintained, and sometimes owned, its dinghy, competing fiercely with the others and working throughout the daylight hours with scarcely a break for eating and the main meal taken after dark. Even Sunday was a working day, though the Abaco spongers at least took breaks to read (or be read) prayers and Bible passages, and nearly all spongers sang hymns and "antums" even as they worked.

Sculling was straightforward labor, but the work of the hooker required great skill and excellent eyesight, as well as strength and endurance. While giving detailed orders to the sculler, he would peer over the dinghy's bows through the wood-sided water-glass, hooking the living sponge free from its coral base with a double-pronged pole up to twelve feet long called a "grains" (also used for crawfishing). Three kinds of Bahamian sponge had commercial value. The most valuable were the "sheep's wool," also known as "checkerboards" from their speckled appearance, the second the "velvets," and the least prized the coarse "grass" sponges, only the best of which were kept. The ablest hookers almost instinctively knew how to locate the largest and best-shaped sheep's wool sponges and rapidly pried them free without damage; the less skilled wasted time on inferior sponges which they often tore.

After the day's catch was complete, the collected sponges were laid out to die, either on a nearby cay or on the deck and in the rigging of the mother ship—preferably the former because the stench was extreme. After a few days, the dead sponges were soaked for a week in a seawater "kraal" made of mangrove stakes driven into sandy shallows before being beaten with flat clubs called bruisers to expel the black organic matter called gurry. After being laid in the sun to dry, the clean sponges were wetted with seawater and crammed into bales in the schooner's hold to be carried for sale at the Sponge Exchange in Nassau. Purchased by sponge brokers representing houses in New York, London, and continental Europe (in a buyer's market), the sponges were sorted, graded, trimmed, and baled for export, mainly to Europe and North America.

Until the great blight of 1938–39, the Bahamas sponge grounds were the most productive in the world, exporting well over a million pounds a year by 1900, with a peak of almost 1.5 million pounds in 1905 (more than twice the average annual world production of natural sponge since World War II). Bahamian sponges, however, had to compete in Europe with Mediterranean production, and in the United States with the sponging grounds in American territorial waters off Florida, centered on Key West, Tampa, and Tarpon Springs. The wholesale price was driven down by competition among the Bahamian sponge fishermen from different islands, who at the peak in 1900 constituted a third of the total Bahamian male workforce. This tendency to competitive overproduction was expertly exploited by the Nassau broker-exporters. Some of these were Bay Street merchants, but the majority were Peloponnesian Greeks whose sponge-fishing traditions went back countless generations and who enjoyed family connections in the metropolitan trading houses. As L. D. Powles disclosed in 1888, however, those who most cruelly exploited the ordinary sponge-fishers were not the foreign-born brokers but the native-born sponge outfitters and boat owners, who enforced the worst iniquities of the truck system on their poorest non-boat-owning black mariner compatriots.[25]

Conditions were worst among blacks from the overpopulated subsistence islands who were drawn into the sponge-fishing trade by near starvation. Many migrated to Andros, where their ramshackle settlements were the most unhygienic and backward in the entire colony. Many boys went into the trade long before the official school leaving age of fourteen, both because of the lack of schooling facilities and because their parents encouraged them to seek a living as soon as possible. Once in the trade they lived lives of almost unbearable harshness and barbarity, usually cut short by illness or accident. The near destitution, ignorance, and wild behavior of black sponge-fishers seen around the docks in Nassau persuaded the Anglican church to establish a seamen's mission on Bay Street where penniless mariners could get food, a game of checkers, even dance, for the price of listening to a religious homily. A missionary was also sent to the sponge-fishing grounds. One priest reported in 1890 that between seven and eight hundred men and boys from Andros were at sea for nine months in the year. Unlike the almost puritanical white Abaconian sponge-fishers, they were innocent of Christian principles and practice. "Blasphemy and swearing, drinking and immorality" were "the order of the day." At much the same time, Governor Shea reported to London that the conditions of work resulted in drastic health problems and that consumption (tuberculosis) was almost endemic.[26]

The system of distributing the income from sponge fishing and the degree of exploitation the system imposed depended on the sponge-fishers' degree of independence, cooperation, and boat ownership. At the healthiest extreme—though they too, of course, suffered from the low wholesale prices—were the Abaconian whites who shared boat ownership, work, and joint income almost equally. But even in Abaco, the income was distributed less equitably when the schooner and (as was the usual case) the dinghies were privately owned. Steve Dodge, closely following the personal recollections and oral tradition account of Haziel Albury of Man-o-War Cay, described the two most common methods of distribution around the turn of the century: "Each hooker-sculler team competed with the others, and sometimes the catch of each was kept separate and sold, with each crewman paying a portion of the bill for provisions and paying 25% to the sponging vessel. This was divided between the owner, the captain and the mate. Another system was to pool the catch and sell it, pay for the provisions, and then divide the receipts into shares, with the owner of the vessel receiving two or three shares, the captain and mate several shares, each hooker one and one-half shares, the owner of each dinghy one-half share, and scullers one share each." An average share around 1900 was between $20 and $30 (£5–6) for a six-week voyage, rarely more and often less. The return of the sponge-fishers, even with this meager emolument (often already laid out on provisions and goods in Nassau), was a momentous event in the distant settlements. As Haziel Albury remembered it: "When the vessel was returning and in sight of home, the flag was a signal to loved ones of a successful trip. Often a new flag had been purchased in Nassau and saved for this moment. When a vessel was due, frequent trips were made to the hill-tops. . . . The first to see the vessel might sing out in a loud voice 'Sail-ho for the *Louise* coming with a big red flag!' They always seemed to know the exact boat when sighted."[27]

Bifurcated, Mixed, and All-Black Settlements

A few Bahamian pineapples were sent as far as England in the 1840s as exotic and expensive rarities, and efforts were made to encourage the cultivation of citrus fruit for export to the American mainland around mid-century.[28] But it was to take advantage of the American market during the age of free trade and distribution by railroad that the Bahamian pineapple industry and the exportation of oranges greatly expanded after 1870. The "red lands" of Abaco, Eleuthera, Cat Island, and Long Island proved most suitable for growing these fruits, but it was the greater availability of local boats and the relative proximity of the American coast that led the first two of these islands to dominate the fruit export trade in the 1880s. All settlements with enterprising inhabitants, access to suitable soils, and their own vessels did reasonably well in the best years. Even the all-black Eleutheran settlements of the Bluff and Gregory Town made some profit from exporting citrus and pineapples as early as 1849, and in 1886 L. D. Powles found Savannah Sound (the most prosperous black settlement in Eleuthera), dominated by the five remarkable Gibson brothers, trading directly with the United States in their three-masted schooner the *Brothers*. Pineapples also brought at least the illusion of prosperity in the 1880s to Rock Sound, which built its own canning factory, to Tarpum Bay (which Powles called "a very flourishing looking settlement"), and, above all, to Governor's Harbour. This township, in the very center of Eleuthera, had originally consisted of a huddle of poor cottages on an islet called Cupid's Cay. But after it was made the seat of the resident justice and the pineapple industry developed, the cay had been joined to the mainland to form a double harbor. The poorest blacks still lived on Cupid's Cay, but the richer inhabitants, mainly coloreds and a few whites, had "established themselves on the mainland on the side of a good-sized hill. The houses on this hill-side," reported Powles, "are white and clean, standing each of them in its own garden, and the whole place . . . looks very like a pretty little English watering place."[29]

More to the point, Governor's Harbour looked very much like the similarly bifurcated township on Harbour Island, which it seemed to be quickly rivaling in size and importance as the "unofficial capital" of Eleuthera. It was, indeed, the northern Out Island settlements with both a mixed population and a mixed economy that gained most from the brief agricultural flourish of the last quarter of the nineteenth century. Dunmore Town, Harbour Island, had always prided itself on being the "second town" of the Bahamas, but its population of around two thousand in the early 1880s was never exceeded. Accurately described by one visitor as "a miniature Nassau," it was prettily laid out on the slopes of a ridge crowned by the commissioner's residence, the second oldest Bahamian Anglican church, an imposing Methodist chapel (largest in the Bahamas), several church and lodge halls, and many two-story houses, a good harbor crowded with sailing vessels, loaded wharves and warehouses, and a general air of commercial prosperity. Harbour Island's location and importance made it an intermediate stop on the sailing routes between Nassau and the outside world and one end of the most active axis of interinsular trade; but it also served as an independent entrepôt, trading directly with the United States, though almost exclusively in sailing vessels. Besides its local and international trade, Harbour Island was second only to Nassau as a boatbuilding center (though both were probably outstripped by Abaco as a whole) and also developed several minor industries, even including in the later 1880s three small sugar mills (Map 7).[30]

Residential and social segregation in Dunmore Town was at least as rigid as in Nassau, though whites and nonwhites were much more equally divided numerically, and a higher proportion of the nonwhites were of mixed ancestry. As in Nassau, the whites lived near the bay or on the hill overlooking it, in houses similar to those in downtown Nassau. Most of the boat owners, substantial farmers, shippers, and shopkeepers were white. The coloreds and blacks lived at the back of the hill or on the lower slopes to the south in small one-story houses or simple wooden shacks raised on limestone rocks. Some owned small boats or shops or were craftsmen or independent small farmers, but most were laborers or mariners working for white employers or were unemployed. Except for a few black Baptists, the races shared worship in the settlement's Anglican and Methodist churches, though the seating, especially in the latter, was rigorously divided. Public school education was nominally integrated, but in practice the whites took advantage of the several

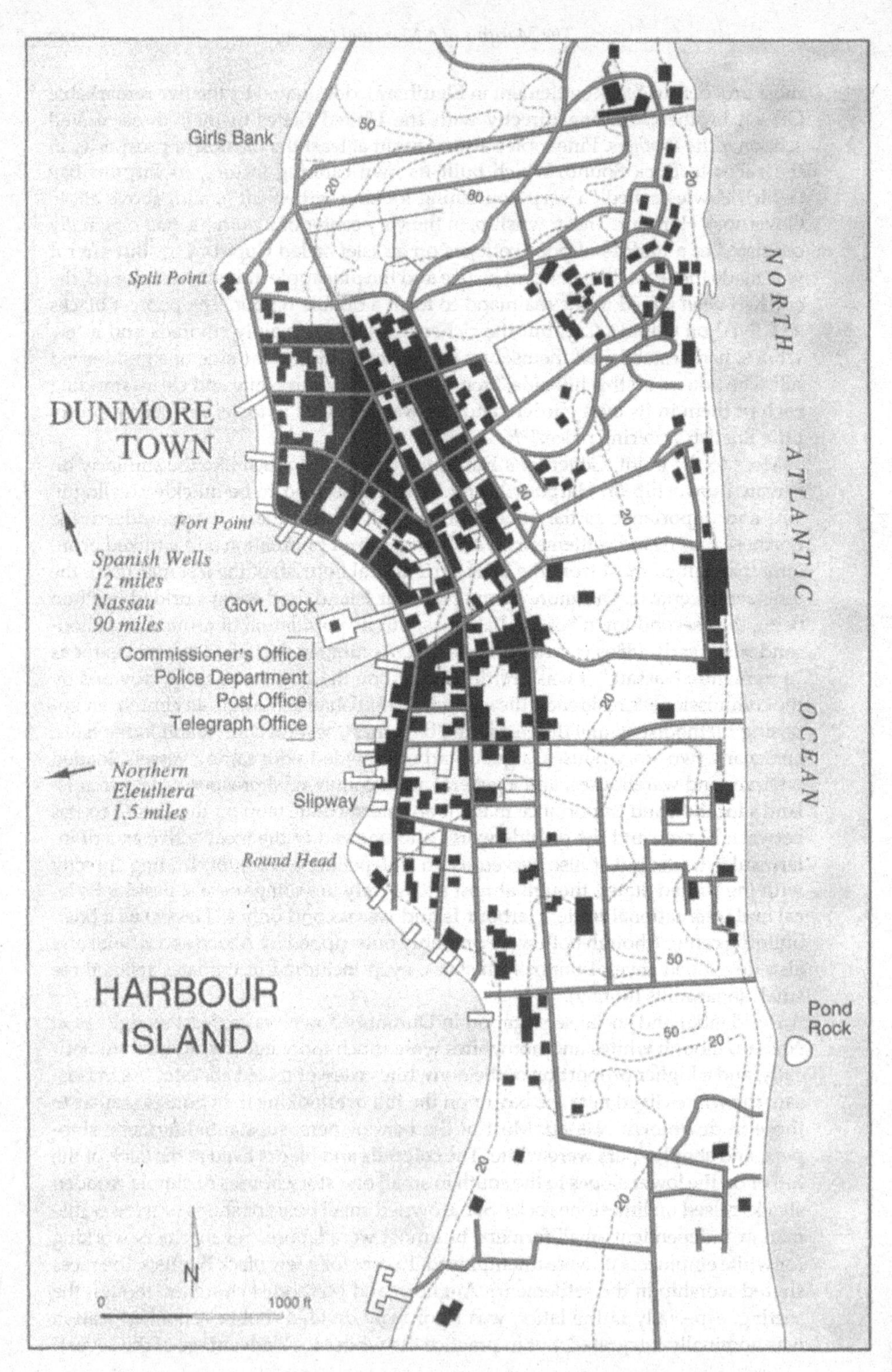

Map 7. Pragmatic Harborside Settlement: Dunmore Town, Harbour Island

private schools on the island and were generally far better educated than their nonwhite fellow "Brilanders." Also related to the socioracial situation may have been the fact that the Harbour Island board school, unlike those elsewhere, was not coeducational. In 1864 it had seventy boys enrolled but no girls.[31]

Custom laid down complex social boundaries over more than two centuries in Harbour Island, though unlike the much less ancient settlement on Green Turtle Cay, Abaco, where the races were more obviously polarized, there was considerable interracial tension.[32] This undercurrent very occasionally erupted into social violence or protest in periods of exceptional hardship or rising expectations or when customary traditions were upset and boundaries overstepped. One such episode occurred in January 1860 over the seemingly picayune question of a new sports ground. Some whites leased a few level acres to indulge in the gentlemanly pursuit of cricket. Both because of the game's proposed exclusivity and because the location chosen for it was an area traditionally used for truck farming by nonwhites, the very first match was interrupted by a crowd of blacks, who drove the players away and took possession of the ground. Charges were laid before the police, and several of the "aggressors" were fined. Most were so angry that they took the option of a jail term instead. Apparently, though, they won a point (or were the ultimate victors of that particular game) because there is no record thereafter of the whites playing cricket at Dunmore Town.[33]

The most significant and notorious incident at Harbour Island, in 1885 and recounted by Powles, was when five colored men tested the custom that whites enter the Methodist church by one door and nonwhites by another. These social radicals (or pioneers), Israel and John D. Lowe, David Tynes, William A. Johnson, and Joseph Whylly—all of them descended from pre-Loyalists and faithful church members who had contributed to its building—quietly entered by the white peoples' door and walked down the aisle. The service was discontinued until they had been ejected, and the following day they were prosecuted before the resident magistrate, who fined them a pound apiece, with the option of imprisonment, for what he termed "brawling." The case was not appealed, and it was many years before the church was desegregated. Many of the nonwhites in the meantime formed a rival congregation.[34]

The population of the second largest biracial township, New Plymouth on Green Turtle Cay, Abaco, increased from 193 in 1815 to 1,000 during the short-lived boom of the American Civil War (when, as an official port of entry it was a convenient jumping-off point and first landfall for blockade runners) and reached a peak of over 1,500 in 1885, during the heyday of pineapple cultivation. At this time, the ratio between whites and blacks was about forty to sixty, with virtually no persons of mixed race because of the customary constraints on miscegenation. Boatbuilding flourished and many inhabitants were still involved in fishing, turtling, sponging, and wrecking. But the chief business had become the cultivation of pineapples on the nearby mainland and their export. In 1890, nearly a million pineapples (as well as large consignments of oranges) were shipped from Green Turtle Cay to the United States, and in the same year the Munro Company established a canning factory that shipped more than three thousand cases of pineapples a year to England.[35] Practically all the businesses, shops, and boats in New Plymouth were owned by the whites, while the blacks were ordinary mariners and agricultural laborers, many of them at sea or working on the Abaco mainland for months at a time. But for a couple of decades at least, enough money filtered through the community to give the settlement a generally prosperous air, and despite disparities of wealth and power and rigid customary segregation, there was remarkably little social tension.

As in the other mixed settlements, the whites at New Plymouth lived together in the best location, by the harborside, in neatly whitewashed or painted stone and wood buildings, while the blacks crowded the fringes, including the swampy and less healthy area at the head of the township creek, in houses of inferior quality. Many of these dwellings, reported T. Wesley Mills in 1887, were ramshackle, unpainted, and overcrowded, though most were kept as tidy and clean as those of the whites. The government school was integrated (and coeducational) and maintained a respectable standard, though it seems to have reached only a fraction of the eligible children. All sections of the community worshiped in the same churches, but segregation by seating was as rigid as that at Harbour Island. Here, too, the Methodist church was by far the largest, attended by most of the whites, with the blacks seated at the rear. The smaller Anglican church had a higher proportion of black adherents, but even there the whites enjoyed the best pews, at the front of the north side.[36]

Mills somewhat euphorically stated in 1887 that at New Plymouth "the two races co-operate in perfect harmony for the general good; the black accepting an inferior status without a murmur." Though Mills's assertion was doubtless exaggerated—the blacks were quiescent because of the greater polarization of the races and the socioeconomic supremacy of the whites was even less open to challenge than in Harbour Island and Nassau—there does indeed seem to have been little overt racial tension in New Plymouth in the 1880s and 1890s. The only riot reported at Green Turtle Cay in the late nineteenth century was a general protest against the government following the seizure of a wrecking prize, the schooner *Pajaro* in July 1880, for a breach of the revenue laws. When the schooner was taken over by the local customs officer, a mixed crowd of blacks and whites went on board, removed the sails, "and committed other acts of lawlessness" in a vain attempt to prevent the vessel from being carried to Nassau for adjudication in the Vice Admiralty Court.[37]

The pineapple industry was far less contentious and more respectable than wrecking, but like so many enterprises in Bahamian history, only a short interlude of relative optimism passed before insoluble problems arose in three crucial areas: cultivation, control of land and shipping, and the perilous and changing international market. The first problem was noted (perceptively as ever) by L. D. Powles, in describing his tour of the pineapple fields near Governor's Harbour, Eleuthera, in 1886. At this point the attenuated island was no more than a mile from shore to shore, and the pines were grown in the longitudinal pockets of red laterite soils rather than on the sandy "white soils" close to the coasts used for growing corn. The methods of preparation and planting were simple. The bush was cleared by burning without any attempt to grub out the roots, and the resulting field was planted with pineapple suckers. These took eighteen months to produce their first pines, which were cut with a stem for the English market but close to the fruit for nearer export markets or for canning. Pineapples were self-propagating if at least one sucker was left on the stem and produced new fruit after only a year. But each "ratoon" fruit was progressively smaller as the soil became exhausted. Because manure and fertilizers were rarely available, the common Bahamian practice was to allow the field to become fallow once the fruit fell below an economic size. This usually happened after four or five years, and the time needed for recuperation was generally from fifteen to twenty years.[38]

This wasteful method of cultivation sufficed where and while the available land exceeded the demands of the export market. But the intensification of the industry not only exhausted all the available land within two decades but gave the larger landowners and those with capital for fertilizer a great advantage over the small peasant farmers who could more easily be wiped out by storm, drought, or disease. These growing conditions made the peasant pineapple grower a victim of the truck system, particularly in Eleuthera. But even more critical was the control of shipping, which posed innumerable problems. The industry was never large enough to justify a regular steamship run (as in the developing banana trade in the West Indies and Central America), and though some pineapples were boated out to passing steamers or shipped on those calling regularly at Nassau, the international trade, as well as interinsular carriage, continued to depend on sailing vessels. Individuals or groups who owned schooners large enough to ship fruit which they grew themselves directly to United States ports had the best chance of making a profit—the converse being true for non-boat-owning peasant pineapple growers. But sailing vessels were subject to long delays in collecting the fruit from different island locations, on the outward voyage, and in the turnaround at American ports, where, of course, the Bahamian shippers (unlike the banana cartel) could control neither onward distribution nor general market conditions. Spoilage of the delicate cargo and disastrously low prices because of glut or poor demand were therefore more common than the occasional bonanzas.

Exports of Bahamian pineapples expanded steadily from 1870 to 1895, but overproduction cut down profit margins, and both Abaco and northern Eleuthera seem to have suffered from the effects of soil exhaustion and plant disease by the 1890s. The establishment of canning plants circumvented many of the problems of transshipment and opened up new areas of cultivation, most notably in Cat Island and Long Island, which had little hope of exporting fresh fruit to foreign markets but could make a marginal profit supplying the canning factories at Rock Sound or Nassau. But even for the mini-capitalist canning plant owners this did not provide long-term profits or save the Bahamian pineapple industry as a whole when it faced its ultimate crisis. The crisis resulted from competition from more efficient American-owned fields in Hawaii and Cuba as well as Florida and Louisiana, the acquisition of Hawaii and the Philippines in 1898 (along with the protectorate over Cuba), and the accompanying protective tariffs applied against tinned as well as fresh fruit. The short-lived sisal industry, which used large tracts of land too stony for pineapple growing in undeveloped islands and offered a quasi-peasant lifestyle to indigent blacks, suffered a similar drastic decline once the Spanish-American War was over and American-funded and protected production reestablished in Cuba and the Philippines.

As early as 1888, L. D. Powles reported that the agricultural soil at Harbour Island and on the nearby mainland commonages was so "worked out" that large numbers of white Brilanders were "giving up their future" and migrating to Key West.[39] Within another dozen years, the collapse of the pineapple and sisal industries—coming on top of the decline of wrecking and the failure of salt production because of crippling U.S. duties—affected the Out Islands as a whole and a far wider swath of their people. Sponging continued to employ many—of necessity, too many—but individual returns were pitiful and never enough to sustain an Out Island family. All Out Islanders, including whites, had to be as self-sufficient in agriculture as possible, but the majority of Out Island blacks had no option but to depend on subsistence farming. For the least fortunate—those without adequate land or any chance of emigration, who had, in any case, gained least in earlier phases—conditions approached destitution. Culturally and socially, many were left in a demoralizing state of limbo. Rooted to a soil that gave heartbreakingly meager returns for the most backbreaking toil, they were neither truly African nor fully Europeanized, torn between an impractical dream of stability, self-reliance, and sturdy independence, a tradition of seizing opportunities, however fleeting and dubious, and a habit of dependency bred in slavery.

Subsistence Farming: Blacks, Whites, and Long Island Whites

There was nothing romantic about Out Island subsistence farming in the late nineteenth century. At best, it was a triumph of necessity against the most unfavorable conditions—poor soil, harsh climate, natural disasters, animal pests—using little more than fire, cutlass, and the occasional hoe. It was reluctantly undertaken, inadequately fulfilled, and all too willingly given up. As a true subsistence activity it involved all members of the family, working as a unit, with minimal age and gender differentiation. Women labored as often as men in the field, just as all shared in the preparation, storing, and cooking of food. Children had agricultural duties from a tender age; men and women continued agricultural toil into old age, sometimes literally dying at work. The system was at its most efficient when the whole family was available, but when the able-bodied men and younger couples were away—at sea, in New Providence, other islands, or even farther afield—the work was carried on by single women, children, and the elderly of both sexes. The household unit was therefore vital for subsistence, though variable conditions led to a considerable range of household patterns at any given time.

In all subsistence agriculture, the availability of enough suitable land was the primary consideration. With the exception of the rare "banana holes" with rich deposits of organic earth, the most sought-after soils for provision crops were the black loams found in island interiors. The sandy white soils on the coasts were ideal only for onions, manioc, and coconuts, and the intermediate "gray soils" were suitable chiefly for corn and potatoes. The general thinness of the earth cover—usually mere pockets in a field of limestone rock—the disjointed location of the various types of soil, competition for access coupled with the preemption of the best and closest fields by formal landowners, and the necessity of rotating the use of the land meant that each family generally owned (or, more commonly, squatted on) several small, scattered fields, often five or even ten miles from their homes so that mere walking and toting took up a large part of each working day, as well as vital energy.

Only a minority of Bahamian Out Island farmers could afford a donkey and far fewer a cart, and they walked to the fields barefoot on serpentine tracks no better than goat paths, over rocks and through bush. Some fields had piled-stone walls. These were generally relics of slavery days rather than true boundaries, though useful to keep out predatory goats or the occasional trampling horse or steer. More commonly, "fields" were irregular expanses, bounded by infertile or fallow areas, rocky outcrops, marsh, or the land worked or claimed by a neighbor and limited in size by the family's needs and capabilities. They were also, to a foreign eye, extremely untidy in appearance. Not only were crops mixed in a seemingly haphazard way, but the apparently casual method of clearing, the patchy nature of the soil and the abundant rocks, and the use of cutlass and hoe rather than any form of plow meant that formal rows and patterns of cultivation were impossible as well as redundant.

The most arduous tasks in Bahamian farming were cutting and preparing the fields for planting, which could be undertaken at any time of the year but preferably in the cooler months between October and March. An area was considered ready for recultivation (often only after a dozen years) once the secondary bush had grown too dense to walk through and main stems were up to two inches in diameter. After such an area had been selected, it was systematically cutlassed several inches from the ground with a machete-cutlass that had to be resharpened every few minutes. The lopped bushes were "lapped," that is, laid in overlapping rows across the entire field, and after a week or two, once thoroughly dry, were carefully fired, upwind to downwind, until completely consumed. The resultant ash, worked into the soil, was the only fertilizer used except where "cave earth" (bat guano) was available. Firing the bush also burned some of the nutrients out of the soil, and planting could not commence until the soil had "cooled" for several weeks; but these disadvantages were offset by the destruction of many insect pests. Likewise, leaving the bush stumps in the ground, a practice condemned by some outsiders as slovenly, had the advantage of providing support for climbing vines.

A typical Bahamian field was dominated by the tall stalks of the chief food staple, corn (either the North American Indian or the more drought-resistant Guinea or Kaffir varieties originally from Africa), interspersed with vine plants such as beans, okra, tomatoes, pumpkins, and squash, all replenished each year. On the periphery were the bushes producing pigeon peas, which were either replanted or self-propagating. Tubers such as sweet potatoes and manioc (for cassava) and other subterranean plants such as peanuts, could, of course, be grown only in areas with a sufficient depth of soil and were usually cultivated in separate fields. Each family would also try to gain access to an area of sandy white soil for growing onions, carrots, peppers, and some manioc, as well as several of the prized banana holes, in the shady, fertile, and generally damp recesses of which grew not only bananas but other fairly soil-greedy food plants like melons, pawpaws, and cabbage, all of which had to be replanted each year. Close to the homestead or on the margins of fields were found long-lived food-bearing trees: coconut palms, oranges and limes, and the semi-wild tamarind and almond trees. Most Out Island families kept fowls, a pig that lived off the meager household scraps, and a few goats, living almost wild. A few owned some scraggly sheep, scarcely distinguishable from goats, though these, like the even rarer steers, donkeys, horses, and mules, were for export rather than for home consumption and use.

Though Out Island fields were rarely weeded more than once a year, nearly all main fields had to be returned to fallow after two or three years and new ones cleared. The repetition of this process for each family in one or more areas virtually every year, with a complex round of planting and reaping many different crops in widely diffused locations, meant that families were engaged in farming tasks almost every day in the year with little or no seasonal relief. The normal daily routine for a subsistence farmer and his family was to rise before dawn and be in the field at first light, carrying only cutlasses, baskets, and water containers. They would work six hours or so until the noonday heat became too intense, with a midmorning breakfast consisting of roasted ears of corn or sweet potatoes. On the long walk back in the early afternoon, they carried field produce in baskets on their heads for the family's main meal, storage, trading with neighbors, or sending to market. The rest of the daylight hours were spent in storing, preparing, or cooking food, tending the small stock, doing household chores, crafts such as plaiting palmetto straw and making baskets, or, if the sea was nearby, fishing from the shore. Dinner, cooked in the open air or the separate shanties behind each house over a small fire with rudimentary utensils, was eaten around sundown without such formalities as a laid table. Though kerosene lanterns were known in the Out Islands (and Harbour Island even had some form of street lighting by 1899), very few black Out Islanders had more than the most primitive homemade lamps and flambeaux, and on normal working days, social life was extinguished by sleep shortly after the sun set.[40]

This mundane routine seldom varied. Those with access to canoes or boats might enjoy day-long fishing, conching, or turtling trips; others might make occasional expeditions to the salinas to rake salt for household consumption or into the bush to gather wild fruits or medicinal herbs. Guns were rare and ammunition difficult to afford, but doves and ducks were sometimes snared in season, and outings were made at night to catch the land crabs on their mysterious peregrinations. Besides, there were weekly breaks for Sunday church services, an occasional Saturday dance, the weekly, fortnightly, or monthly (but irregular) visit of the mail boat, the annual festivities on August 1, December 25, and January 1, and the fortuitous rites of funerals, wakes, and weddings.

Such rituals and festivals were settlement-wide, even island-wide occasions, but subsistence farming was more narrowly family-oriented, with communal cooperation and sharing only in times of mutual need or special hardship. Harvesting, like clearing and planting, was spread throughout the year as need required and could easily be managed by the average family on its own. Only pigeon peas and occasionally plantings of corn came to optimal maturity so quickly that families sometimes recruited the help of willing neighbors or kin. Indian corn was preferred over the grittier but hardier Guinea corn, yet both were grown by most families for insurance. The only types of Indian corn with a fair chance of survival were small flinty local varieties, but Guinea corn could survive prolonged drought and young shoots could survive even the effects of a hurricane that would totally destroy plantings of Indian corn. Theoretically, two crops of corn could be grown each year in the same field, but Bahamian soils made this virtually impossible, and though some farmers spread their plantings as widely as possible or planted two main crops in different locations, the more common practice was to have a major single planting and harvesting each of Indian and Guinea corn each year. Corn should be planted during a rainy season and ideally needs further rain to come to maturity some six months later. But Bahamian rainfall was unpredictable and there were no reliable rainy seasons and a tendency to prolonged drought, especially in the southern islands, so corn cultivation was even more of a gamble than farming husbandry in general, and the risks had to be spread as much as possible. Consequently, Indian corn was planted either in January to February or August to September, and the main Guinea corn plantings were between March and May. In a good year, corn harvests occurred any time from December to August. But for individual farmers it was never so widely spread, and for the majority who had to rely on Guinea corn, the harvesting peak came around the turn of the year.

Corn was not harvested until the stalks and leaves were brown and dry. Husked in the field, the cobs were carried back home, if it was not too far, where they were thrashed by being put in a sack and beaten with sticks until all the kernels were detached. Corn needed for immediate use was taken out, and the rest—for seed and later consumption—stored in metal barrels and pails, covered with a layer of clean sand to keep out rats and weevils. By 1900, hardly anyone knew how to grind corn by stone. Nearly every household owned a metal grinding mill—usually the most sophisticated and valuable household possession—or had the use of a neighbor's mill. Once ground, the corn was placed in a palmetto straw winnowing basket, and by an expert circular motion corn flour was separated from grits and bran chaff from both. In the most self-sufficient, or import-deficient, households, where cassava was not used, corn flour was the only flour used for baking. It took the place of imported white wheaten flour, just as homemade grits displaced imported grits and rice. In the most favored islands in the most fortunate times, Guinea cornmeal was used to feed the household stock, but elsewhere it was the people's staple, and the creatures were fed only the bran, the shelled corncobs, and other residues such as the shelled pods and trashed leaves of peas and beans.

The pigeon pea harvest generally followed immediately after the main corn harvest. As soon as the pods were a uniform brown, they were plucked and shelled and the peas sorted on a sheet or sack, all with amazing dexterity. The green peas were set aside for immediate consumption or sale; the dry brown majority were put up for storage. Pigeon peas, which were at least as hardy as Guinea corn, were almost as vital a Bahamian staple as corn. Though added to stews, which of necessity were far more often based on fish and conch than meat, they were most commonly eaten as a nutritious supplement with cornmeal grits, the forerunner of the almost universal later Bahamian side dish, "peas n' rice."

Cassava, as had been demonstrated since the times of the Lucayan aborigines, had many advantages over other starch crops for Bahamian cultivators, especially in the central and southern islands. The basic manioc root was drought-resistant, grew in mediocre soils, and, like sweet potatoes, could be left in the soil for long periods after maturing until it was needed. Manioc-cassava cultivation and preparation, though, was tedious, technical, and chancy. Besides, in several islands the tuber was extremely susceptible to mosaic disease, just as sweet potatoes were subject to the depredations of a particular species of weevil. For these reasons, both manioc and potato growing seem to have steadily declined, with a resultant emphasis on corn and peas and a greater dependence on imported staples such as rice and grits—and absolute dependency whenever the major crops failed.

Such a dependency was most poignantly illustrated by the intermittent food crises faced by the ordinary black people of Inagua. Some four hundred miles, or up to two weeks' sailing, from Nassau, Inagua had a population that soared from 172 in 1847 to over 1,100 in 1871 because of the development of the salt industry and the use of the island as a collecting point for stevedores on passing steamers or seasonal laborers in Cuba, Panama, and other parts of Central America. Mathew Town, the only settlement, was more neatly laid out than any other Bahamian town on a grid pattern twelve streets by six and at one time was said to be the only Out Island settlement with roads suitable for carriages (Map 8). Most of the inhabitants were drawn by the prospects of wage labor, but once settled, they had no practical alternative. Unfortunately, there was little good cultivable land, and the climate that made Inagua ideal for producing solar salt was extremely unfavorable for peasant cultivation. The Inaguans had always been more dependent on imported foods than most Out Islanders and were consequently subject both the vagaries of the winds that often delayed the sailboats from Nassau and to the handful of white and near-white shopkeepers who dominated local trade and credit. When the salt industry began to suffer from protective American duties in the 1870s and came to a complete stop in 1884 and the steamers called less regularly, preferring Long Cay off Crooked Island instead, the situation rapidly deteriorated. Increasingly driven back on the inadequate agricultural resources of the island, the ordinary black Inaguans faced starvation in times of drought.

As early as 1873, while the salt industry was still active, a Mathew Town resident wrote to the *Nassau Guardian* to report that because of drought followed by unusual floods and the nonarrival of a boat from Nassau for more than three months, both famine and disease threatened. The salt industry had been halted by the rains, the mules that pulled the tramway carts had to be turned loose in the bush for lack of provender, and the "laboring class" was said to be "in a most pitiable condition." Corn was totally exhausted and only a small quantity of rice remained, which few could afford. One woman and her five children had lived for several days on nothing but crabs, which she had walked miles to collect, and many persons were contemplating eating the prickly pears and palmetto "thatch tops" that were said to be the only edible vegetable foods on the island. Moreover, "what with the damp and the famine together," wrote the *Guardian*'s correspondent, "nothing may be looked forward to but distressing fevers among the poor." He begged Nassau merchants to send a boat forthwith, bringing corn and other basic provisions for those who could pay and charitable relief for those who could not.[41]

Eleven years later, in 1883, another letter, perhaps from the same writer, painted an even grimmer picture. A third of the people of Mathew Town were subsisting on crabs, the supply of which was rapidly diminishing. Two recent boats from Nassau had brought only partial relief. Only the few inhabitants who had money could buy the imported provisions, "the prevailing rule under the circumstances being 'no credit' and higher prices!" Sanitary conditions had recently been improved in the settlement but to small avail, for "bodies physically weak from want of necessary and wholesome food cannot resist disease, sanitary perfections in other respects not withstanding. . . . Children especially are suffering acutely. It is painful to witness their haggard faces, and to see the wistful craving looks in their hungry eyes." Again the writer begged for charitable relief. "Money will be of little use at present," he wrote. "Send us corn, rice, pork and sugar, and flour if funds permit, and appoint a representative committee for the distribution of these essentials; thus the present crisis may pass over without consequences which may afterwards involve useless regrets."[42]

The record is silent as to whether the merchants or anyone in Nassau was spurred to charity, but the chances seem slim. Two years later, Powles wrote of

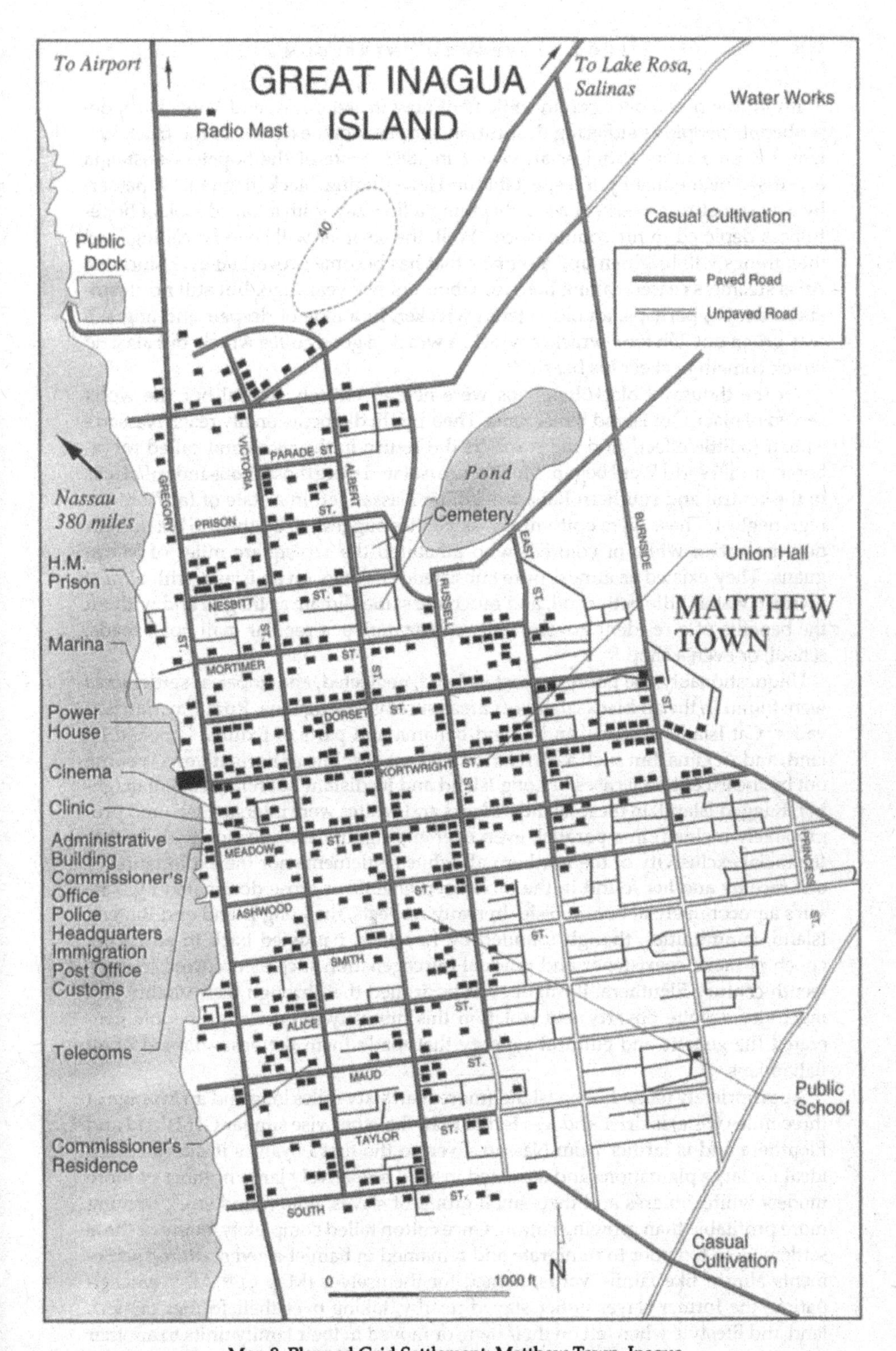

Map 8. Planned Grid Settlement: Matthew Town, Inagua

Mathew Town as a once proud settlement now in sad decay, and Louis Duty described its people as suffering destitution and the worst excesses of the truck system.[43] Even a more Panglossian visitor in 1888 wrote of the hopeless nostalgia expressed by the shabby, if respectable and law-abiding, black Inaguan: "A passer-by may sometimes overhear a sturdy young fellow say, with a forced look of hopefulness depicted in his countenance, 'Well, the steamer will soon be calling, and then things will brighten up,' a remark that has become proverbial ever since the Atlas steamers ceased calling here for labourers five years ago. But still no steamers come. Or, perhaps, an old veteran wrecker, in a tone of despair and anguish may groan out 'Oh for a wrack, a wrack, a wrack, a good coffee wrack' but alas! no wrack cometh to cheer his heart."[44]

Yet the thousand black Inaguans were neither entirely typical nor the worst served of black Out Island Bahamians. Their plight did occasionally reach Nassau's ears, if to little effect. And the steamers did return in the 1890s and called for laborers until World War I began. Much more isolated were those thousands of blacks in the central and southern Bahamas whom Nassau left in a state of far from benign neglect. These were epitomized, as Powles suggested, by the 250 blacks (but not one native white or colored) who inhabited the 110 square miles of Mayaguana. They existed as almost pure subsistence farmers on an island with almost no fresh water, little better soil, and much the same climate as Inagua and without the benefits of a resident government representative, a regular mail boat, roads, school, or even a shop.[45]

Unquestionably, the poorest, most isolated, neglected, and hopeless settlements were found in the all-black islands or areas such as Mayaguana, Rum Cay, San Salvador, Cat Island, Andros, and Grand Bahama and parts of Exuma, Crooked Island, and Acklins. But such a correlation was not absolute or normative as is borne out by the exceptional cases of Long Island and its distant but related small neighbor, Ragged Island. In these islands, blacks and whites were interspersed (and progressively melded) in a parallel, even overlapping, life and lifestyle with neither the racial exclusivity of the northern all-white settlements nor the exploitation of one race by another found in the mixed settlements or those dominated by Nassau's agrocommercial bourgeoisie. In many respects, the Long Island and Ragged Island communities, though founded by Loyalists, harkened back to an earlier epoch of racial coexistence and gradual miscegenation such as occurred in eighteenth-century Eleuthera. It might even be argued that through their vitality and ingenuity despite poverty and isolation this minority of coexisting people generated the genetic and cultural synergy that made them the best adapted of all Bahamians.

Appropriately named Long Island (more than sixty miles long and an average of three miles wide) is drier and less fertile than the otherwise similar Cat Island and Eleuthera and is farther from Nassau. Even to the first Loyalists it did not seem ideal for large plantations and attracted instead a relatively large number of more modest white émigrés and their small group of slaves, who found stock farming more profitable than growing cotton. Once cotton failed completely, many of these settlers were too poor to remigrate and remained in hamlet-sized scattered settlements almost like family yards, named for themselves (Map 9).[46] After emancipation, the former slaves either stayed nearby, taking over their former owner's land and lifestyle when left on their own, or moved in their family units to another

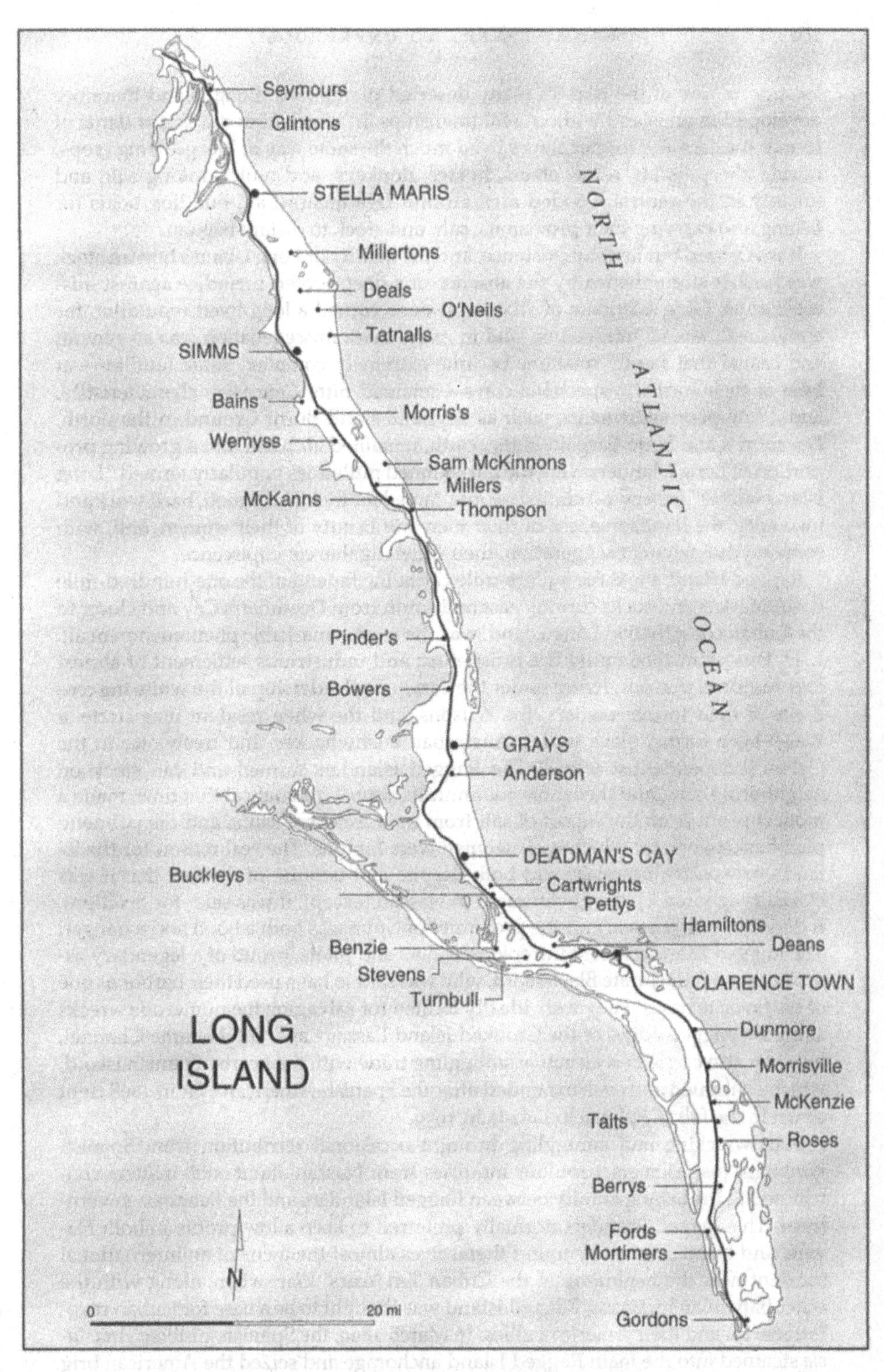

Map 9. Long Island: Family Name Settlements

location in one of the island's many deserted plantations. Long Island therefore developed as an island without real townships, in which both the descendants of former masters and former slaves lived much the same way of life: growing crops, raising sheep, goats, a few steers, horses, donkeys, and mules, raking salt, and (mainly in the central wooded area around Deadman's Cay) building boats for fishing and carrying their provisions, salt, and stock to distant Nassau.

It was a hard but healthy existence, and the quality of Long Island's human stock was further strengthened by the absence of a deep-rooted prejudice against miscegenation. Long Islanders of all complexions earned a long-lived reputation for enthusiastic sexual intercourse, and in many cases miscegenation was so general and casual that family relations became extremely complex. Some families—at least at their formal respectable cores—retained pure Caucasian characteristics, and a few poor settlements, such as Seymour's and Burnt Ground in the north, Dunmore's and Hard Bargain in the south, remained all-black. But a growing proportion of Long Islanders were the fair-skinned mulattoes popularly termed "Long Island whites" or brown-skinned people, famed for their hardihood, hard work and ingenuity, the handsomeness of their men and beauty of their women, and, with some mythologizing exaggeration, their indefatigable concupiscence.

Ragged Island, the three-square-mile cay at the far end of the one-hundred-mile chain of islets and rocks curving east and south from Deadman's Cay and closer to the Cuban coast than to Long Island, was the most remarkable phenomenon of all. L. D. Powles in 1886 found it a prosperous and industrious settlement of almost four hundred persons, living under the easygoing leadership of the white descendants of their former owners, the Wilsons, and the white resident magistrate, a Welsh-born former slave trader, Australian bushwhacker, and freebooter in the Cuban independentist wars.[47] The Ragged Islanders farmed and ran stock on neighboring cays, and the whole community, almost uniquely at that time, made a modest profit from the export of salt from their excellent salina and the palmetto plait basketwork for which their women were famous. The real reason for the island's prosperity, however, was both despite and because of the fact that it was cynically ignored by the government in Nassau (except, it was said, for taxation). It derived from the sea, and the proximity of Cuba was both a boon and a danger. The Ragged Islanders were intrepid mariners and pilots, proud of a legendary association with the pirate Blackbeard, who was said to have used their harbor as one of his favorite bases. They were ideally located for salvaging the numerous wrecks along the ragged edges of the Crooked Island Passage and Old Bahama Channel, but they also carried on an active smuggling trade with the nearby Spanish island, which continued and even expanded after the Spanish-American War in 1898 right down to the fall of Fulgencio Batista in 1959.

Both wrecking and smuggling brought occasional retribution from Spanish gunboats, just as overscrupulous inquiries from Nassau about such matters contributed to the lasting enmity between Ragged Islanders and the Bahamas government. The Ragged Islanders normally preferred to keep a low profile in both Havana and Nassau, but they found themselves almost the focus of an international incident near the beginning of the Cuban Ten Years' War, when, along with the other Bahamian locations, Ragged Island was thought to be a base for Cuban revolutionaries and their American allies. In March 1869, the Spanish gunboat *Andalucia* steamed into the main Ragged Island anchorage and seized the American brig

Mary Lowell, along with Walter Wilson (said to be acting in his official capacity as customs officer) and three other Ragged Islanders. These four men were released, but the American crew was detained and the *Mary Lowell* towed off in the direction of Havana. The Bahamas government responded to Wilson's complaints, probably because the Spaniards had concurrently rounded up several sponging vessels off Andros and seized the much larger American vessel *Yarra* in the Berry Islands. A British gunboat, HMS *Cherub*, was dispatched to Havana to demand an explanation, though little was achieved except the release of the sponge boats. The credibility of the ruggedly independent Ragged Islanders was further undermined when later in 1869 it was reported that three hundred Cuban revolutionaries from the American steamer *Lillian* had been harbored at Ragged Island before making a descent upon Baracoa in Oriente.[48]

Family Life and Customs in Out Island Communities

The emergence on Long Island and Ragged Island of a distinctively Creolized Bahamian person and way of life, melding African and European influences with minimal outside interference, showed that environmental conditions and common needs, including the necessity to seize whatever chance of livelihood offered itself, were at least as important as genetic and cultural inheritance. The ways of making a living in the Bahamas Out Islands before 1900 varied less in type than degree, and the basic forms of subsistence were remarkably similar. To a large extent, similar syncretizing influences were at work in other aspects of life and culture, varied only by degrees of opportunity and isolation: in family life and moral attitudes and in matters of religion, folklore, education, health, and recreation.

More for economic than cultural reasons, tightly knit family units based on the nuclear household, with large numbers of children, were the norm for Out Islanders. Though blacks had a more ingrained taboo against cousin marriage than whites did, their traditional sense of the importance of kinship was very similar to that found, for more racist reasons, in the all-white communities. Kinship ties were further reinforced by the need for economic sharing. Moreover, though the traditional prejudices against cousin mating could more easily be indulged by blacks because of their greater numbers and a concurrent lack of color prejudice (even a preference for "marrying up" to a person of a lighter complexion), inbreeding, with genetic effects similar to those noted by Penrose among the whites, was not unknown among the most isolated black communities.[49] Despite African traditions of polygyny, Bahamian blacks were as concerned as whites to follow both the forms and substance of permanent monogamy, though formal marriage was often made difficult by the scarcity of licensed ministers and families were often disrupted by the prolonged absence of male marital partners. Comparatively relaxed attitudes toward premarital and extramarital sexual activity could be attributed as much to the climate and living conditions as to traditional African mores; as the numbers of illegitimate and colored offspring attested, sexual impropriety was almost as common in mixed as in all-black communities. African custom argued for a more rigid, if somewhat different, set of proprieties than were found in all but the most puritanical and self-regarding all-white communities. Besides, the growing influence of the respectable churches tended to make the Afro-Bahamians increasingly conform to European canons of respectability, while providing the whites and coloreds with a hypocritical shield. In consequence, the accepted courting, marital, and parental practices were increasingly uniform, and there was a much higher level of respectable observance than in the British West Indies even if a decided gap remained between nominal ascription and actual practice.

Courtship for whites and blacks in the Out Islands was formal and not dissimilar to custom in Nassau. If he liked a girl, an Out Island man would consult his parents for their views even before making approaches to his intended and her family. Dowry was not a custom and wealth, not surprisingly, rarely a criterion. Far more important was respectability, health (that is, tacitly, nubility), and sufficient training in domestic skills. No young man would propose marriage with any hope of success who had not an independent competence in the way of land or boat or a house of his own already completed or nearly so. Once a suitor's parents approved of a match, he would write a letter to the girl's parents, requesting visiting rights. If he were illiterate, he would employ a competent scribe for this formal missive, as well as for any love letters he chose to send. Proposals were expected to describe to his would-be betrothed all the points in her moral character he particularly admired.[50] Initially, virginity was highly valued; sexual relations were reserved ideally for those at least betrothed.

After some months, the man would send an engagement letter and ring to the girl's family. A courtship could last as long as three years (often delayed while the man completed his boat and house), though once an engagement was made greater sexual intimacy was permitted. The wedding, arranged at a time or season when a minister and the maximum number of both families were available, though often hastened by pregnancy, was held in the nearest church, with the greatest affordable ostentation in the way of dress and ceremony. This was followed by a reception hosted by the bride's parents in their home, which included flowery formal speeches, refreshments of cake and wine for the women and children, and stronger liquor for the men in a back room. Usually there was dancing, much jollity, and some drunkenness, lasting late into the night, when the married couple was seen off to their new home—situated as a rule in the bridegroom's parents' yard.[51]

Marriage gave both the man and woman a new status in the community, as well as a new household, especially once they began to produce a family. Large families were admired as proof of virility in the man, fertility in the woman, and perhaps the fidelity of both. But children were also recognized as an economic asset. The difficulty of producing enough food and clothing for a sizable family was overcome by the use of children to augment the peasant workforce. They helped in domestic as well as field work as soon as they were able, a situation facilitated by the shortage, even absence, of schools for them to attend. Children were companions as well as essential helpmates to their mothers, especially, as often occurred, when the fathers were away. Thus the bond between children and mothers became especially strong, though all children were regarded as potential insurance to provide support for both parents in old age.[52]

Marriage was considered permanent and final except in extreme cases. Divorce, technically extremely difficult to obtain anywhere in the Bahamas, was virtually unknown in the Out Islands. Husbands often left wives temporarily or for long periods to go on voyages or work projects, but even if men were gone for years, such separations were not considered either a step toward a formal divorce or a license for promiscuity. Even a couple who separated by mutual agreement and lived apart was still considered by the community to be married.[53]

"Outside" (that is, illegitimate) children and unmarried mothers were more common in all-black and mixed than in all-white settlements but were nowhere as numerous as throughout the British colonies in the Caribbean proper and in the Bahamas itself in the mid-twentieth century. The reasons were undoubtedly the widespread high frequency of formal marriages and the customary prejudice and social sanctions against unmarried mothers and their offspring. In 1891, when 30.9 percent of the entire population of the Bahamas was formally married, the figures for all-white Spanish Wells, biracial Harbour Island, and all-black Andros were 36.7, 34.8, and 32.8 percent respectively—all four higher than for the capital island of New Providence. In the adult age range eighteen to seventy, the figures for Harbour Island and Andros were about the same (69.6 and 70.6 percent) and that for Spanish Wells was a remarkably high 76.7 percent.[54]

Though no precise figures for Bahamian consensual or common law marriages are obtainable, such arrangements were uncommon, limited almost entirely to those who could not marry, or remarry, formally. There were, though, a good many single mothers, especially in the black and mixed settlements (as in Nassau), and the official figures disguised or hid a virtual double standard of sexual morality. A young man was almost expected to have premarital sex, and many married men had extramarital love affairs, some even establishing an extraresidential union with a single, separated, or widowed woman. Yet a woman was expected to remain a virgin at least until she had intercourse with her fiancé, if not until her marriage, and after marriage she was expected to be faithful to her husband even if he was away for extended periods. If a wife was unfaithful and it was discovered, the husband was justified in leaving her. Engaged couples often had their first child before marriage, and the baby was usually cared for by the girl's mother. But unespoused women who had illegitimate children were commonly considered "second rate" and usually had difficulty finding husbands. If, however, such a woman did marry, the outside child, or children, were not normally brought into the new union but raised either by the woman's mother or by some other female relative. Though true illegitimacy, that is, children born and brought up outside any form of wedlock, was relatively rare, probably no more than 10 percent in any Out Island, it was a decided social disadvantage, not just because of the stigma attached but because few outside children enjoyed the practical benefits of a full family life.[55]

The resolute commitment to monogamy, the predominance of formal marriage, and the stigma attached to illegitimacy were no doubt influenced by the churches. Yet the uneven and sometimes extremely superficial penetration of the Out Islands by the various churches, their different ideologies, rituals, and social policies, and the competitive conflict between them made their influence less important than other factors. The Methodists successfully challenged the primacy of the formerly established Anglican church in the all-white and mixed northeastern settlements, while in the black Out Island communities the Baptists were by far the most successful with their emphasis on popular participation and practices that were attuned to the people's craving for self-expression and deep-set animist beliefs.

After the Bahamas became a diocese and the Anglican church was vitalized by the ritualist revival, however, the Bahamas became an active field for Anglican missionary activity. Dedicated resident priests such as Rev. F. Barrow Matthews, who spent half a lifetime in Cat Island and Andros, ministered educationally, socially, and medically, as well as spiritually, to widely scattered parishioners and were rewarded with a regard that approached the reverential. The Anglican mission, though, consisted mainly of peripatetic priests, for fifty years sailing from island to island in the yacht called the *Message of Peace* provided by the second bishop, Addington Venables (1863–75), supported almost entirely by the collection plate donations of pious Anglo-Catholics in England. Although the Anglican missionaries undoubtedly brought much spiritual and material comfort, the reports they sent back to their Nassau superiors and English supporters unconsciously revealed a more equivocal role, if not a fundamental ignorance. Naturally, the missionaries stressed the hardships of their travels: uncomfortable, often delayed and sometimes dangerous sea voyages, interspersed with arduous journeys on foot or horseback over roadless rocks. Understandably, too, the missionaries stressed to their supporters the "backwardness" and "superstition" of the people, especially the committed supporters of the rival sects, and exaggerated their own achievements in bringing the gospel light. Their denigrations coupled with realistic descriptions of Out Island conditions had the contrary effect on less susceptible readers: they underlined the remarkable qualities of the isolated Out Islanders, their cheerfulness and hospitality, resourcefulness and resilience, and the way they satisfied their own innate spirituality, as well as developing a proudly independent and self-sufficient way of life.

Anglican missionary complaints about Out Islanders' ignorance extended to white Methodists as well as black Baptists. In 1874, one of the first Anglo-Catholics in the Bahamas, Rev. C. C. Wakefield, vicar of St. Mary's and headmaster of Nassau Grammar School, visited Abaco. Contrary to Penrose a generation later, he reported of the inhabitants of Hopetown, "One could scarcely find a finer and healthier body of people, while the number and appearance of the children proves conclusively that white people will thrive here as well as in England." He went on, though, to ridicule their ignorance of "true religion": "John Wesley is to them what Mahomet is to his followers—almost a god. They know not who he was, when he lived, or how he came to found their religion. They care not to know, nor their preachers to inform them. . . . One man gravely informed me that after Christ left this earth, Christianity was not heard again until Wesley received a direct commission from heaven to found the true religion; another said that the Bible was unknown until Wesley miraculously discovered a copy in Westminster Abbey." Wakefield found Anglican missionary activity more successful in Green Turtle Cay, though Methodist stalwarts claimed that the Anglican church offered no salvation, and white schoolchildren hearing the bell of the small wooden Anglican church sang "unchecked along the roads,

> There rings the bell
> That calls to hell."[56]

On the Abaco mainland, Wakefield visited only Marsh Harbour, where he reported that there was no church or religious service. Presumably he ignored informal or nonrespectable churches, just as he neglected to visit any of the all-black settlements on the Abaco mainland. Anglican missionaries who visited the central and southern Bahamas over the following decades were often just as purblind. A clerical correspondent of the *Bahamas Mission Quarterly,* writing of a circuit of Long

Island in 1888 for an English readership, for example, gave a heartfelt account of the rigors of the journey, the difficulties faced by the few faithful adherents of the Anglican church, and the quaint if not barbaric beliefs and practices of those attending black Baptist chapels or, scarcely worse, no churches at all. Rather than attributing the unstinted help and polite interest shown by the ordinary Long Islanders to an innate ecumenical tolerance and natural courtesy, the writer stressed the competitive jealousy and ignorance of a few obstructionist black pastors and concluded that the poor, backward, credulous, and superstitious folk were ripe for Anglican conversion.[57]

By the 1890s, virtually all Out Islanders were nominally Christian. There may have been a handful of obdurate pagan African survivors, but even the dwindling number of those born in Africa had nearly all become members of some Christian church. African-rooted traditions, though, did remain strong, especially in all-black islands and settlements—probably more so than in any part of New Providence. Powles on a visit to Cat Island in 1887 noted: "The people here are very superstitious, and what is called 'obeahism' is very common among them. I have never been able to find out what the 'obeah-men' are supposed to do, further than they are a species of African magicians, who, for a trifling consideration, will bewitch your enemies and charm your fields, so that anyone stealing from them will be punished by a supernatural agency without the intervention of the policeman or the magistrate."[58] Or, he might have added, of the Christian priest. Even the relatively enlightened Rev. Barrow Matthews, after visiting at least ten settlements along the eastern shore of Andros in the 1890s, commented that the people remained deeply superstitious, and Bishop Henry Churton, visiting Andros in 1902, wrote that the year had been marked with "a bad outbreak of heathenish practices. . . . The old African superstitions die very hard."[59]

Authentic obeah practices were common in mixed settlements but not noted in the all-white communities. Yet some of the more esoteric folklore beliefs and practices there (such as the widespread belief in witches, ghosts, and other spirits) are as likely to have been borrowed from Afro-Bahamian neighbors as derived from a European folk tradition. The use of bush medicine was common in all Out Island settlements and was vital in proportion to the availability of more formal medicine. By the end of the nineteenth century few Out Island settlements ever saw a qualified doctor and only one, Harbour Island, had a resident practitioner. Much medical work was undertaken by the missionaries, clergy, or even resident justices, their informal skills or, even more, any success they achieved, adding to their reputation and charisma among a people who traditionally associated medicine, magic, and authority.

The most vivid account of Out Island bush medicine—a mélange of traditional African practices, native herbal cures, and pure mumbo-jumbo—was given in the early 1900s in Amelia Defries's description of "Aunt Celia" of Eight Mile Rock, Grand Bahama, the largest settlement in one of the poorest, most neglected black Out Islands. Aunt Celia, who, somewhat equivocally, boasted that "nobody never dies of my treatment," picked her medicine in the bush and boiled it freshly for each of her patients. For physiotherapy she used lard or a melted tallow candle, sometimes mixed with cow's gall with a "large, big, rusty old nail." To heal wounds she boiled the shepherd's needle plant, and she administered a concoction of "pepper grass" for inflammations. For toothache, a rusty nail was heated with which

Celia broke the offending tooth and dug out the broken pieces. If there were serious signs of tooth decay, the cure was "hot cobbler's wax" rubbed in daily, to "kill out de worrum what eats de teet away." Celia also claimed cures for tumors and growths, skin problems, headache, sore throats, and typhoid fever. Every Out Island settlement, white and mixed as well as black, had its folk practitioners, each with his or her own specifics, as well as a practical knowledge of the common native pharmacopeia.[60]

Aunt Celia of Grand Bahama also acted as the settlement's midwife, as did many of her black counterparts throughout the West Indies who used similar birth and postpartum methods. If the afterbirth did not come naturally, the midwife would remove it. In some black settlements, the afterbirth was buried in a deep hole along with the umbilical cord. The yard in which an infant's "navel string" was buried was referred to as the child's specific birthplace. After the birth of a baby, the mother and child were not allowed out of the house for nine days and were permitted only family visitors. Some mothers stayed in the house and avoided hard work for three to six months. Black mothers, as in Africa, nursed their children far longer than whites did.[61] Though practices differed considerably, the role of midwives was as critical—and as bound up with folk mysteries—in the white communities as in all others.

Likewise, just as the daily and yearly round hardly varied throughout the Out Islands because of a shared environment and a largely shared economy, there were more similarities than differences in the punctuating events and celebrations—funerals, weddings, Christmas, New Year's Day, and Emancipation Day—though none of these were as elaborate as in Nassau and its suburbs. In spite of economic constraints, though, Christmas was a special time of merrymaking in nearly all the islands. The all-black and biracial settlements celebrated Christmas in a similar way to the Nassauvians, though on a more modest scale. For Androsians, Christmas was one of the few occasions when most of the men and boys were at home. Just before Christmas, whole families visited Nassau, accompanying the men at the conclusion of the last sponging voyages of the year. While the men disposed of their sponges and perhaps caroused in the dockside taverns, the Andros womenfolk did their modest Christmas shopping on Bay Street before returning home. On Christmas Day 1893, Neville Chamberlain, on his father's sisal plantation near Mastic Point, wrote to his sister Ida in England: "Great crowd in all their best clothes with banners flying and great noise of drums and fifes advance up the road from the creek. About half way up a shower soaked them. This did not dampen their enthusiasm." The crowd that invaded the Chamberlain estate then came up to the house, the band playing until their host-employer gave them three-penny and six-penny bits, "which raised their enthusiasm to the highest pitch." They then brought the band closer still, whistling, stamping, and banging, and did a slow march around the piazza, after which they danced. It was clearly a reenactment of the licensed mayhem of the traditional West Indian "planter's Christmas." Chamberlain also told his sister that a "rushing" ceremony was being held by the blacks at nearby Mastic Creek on New Year's Eve, when dancing, "spreeing," and much drinking would take place.[62]

In other islands, the Christmas and New Year's festivities varied slightly. In Eleuthera, Junkanoos were held, but in some settlements the chief amusement was an entertainment given by the various lodges on Christmas Eve. In 1897, for instance, the Gregory Town lodge of the Grand United Order of Odd Fellows gave a program that included "dialogues, recitations, addresses, songs and instrumental music before a large and attentive audience which included the Resident Justice and his wife."[63] In the biracial settlement of Green Turtle Cay, Abaco, New Year's Day was uniquely celebrated by the appearance of the masked figure of "Old Skin or Bunce," who was carried in a wheelbarrow covered in canvas along the streets of the township. A hawker preceded the barrow, telling stories of how Bunce was caught. Money was collected, after which Bunce, who was clothed in a tatterdemalion costume of paper and rags, danced for the donors. No one seems to know the exact provenance or significance of this curious character and performance, but he does seem to be an amalgam of masked and costumed figures found in West Africa and rural England, with some oblique reference to the islands' piratical past.[64]

Not surprisingly, Emancipation Day, August 1, was not celebrated in the all-white settlements, but many black and biracial communities marked the day with celebrations similar to those in New Providence. In Cat Island in 1888, Rev. Barrow Matthews reported that harvested produce and fruit were used to decorate the church—seemingly combining the celebration of emancipation with the older cropover festival from Africa, along with the harvest festival tradition then being revived in the Church of England. Activities organized around Matthews's church included a choral celebration in the morning, a "parish feast" in the afternoon, and sports, including athletics and football. The day ended with a choral evensong in the church. At Harbour Island in the 1890s, the celebration was equally respectable but less church-oriented. Almost the entire black population, smartly dressed, congregated on the whites' harborside area of Dunmore Town, with the friendly society and lodge leading the festivities in a grander version of the band-led parades that occurred at funerals throughout the year.[65]

In the poorer and more isolated settlements, all celebrations were on a far more modest scale and narrowly localized. Christmas was celebrated save in the poorest of settlements at the worst of times, but Emancipation Day often went unnoticed both because it lacked the necessary inspiration from a church and regime that used it to teach social lessons and because it was seen as an extravagant irrelevance, commemorating an almost forgotten event that had changed too little and brought little good. The minimum popular diversions were weekly church services, occasional wakes and weddings, informal dances with the simplest music—in some islands called "rips" from the use of ripsaws as musical instruments—or casual and spontaneous family-sized gatherings for the singing of anthems and the telling of tales. This last folk entertainment is tenuously preserved in Edwards's *Bahama Songs and Stories* (1895), Parsons's *Folk Tales of Andros Island* (1900), and Folkways' long-playing records *The Real Bahamas* (1965).

Above all, Out Island communities shared an unhurried pace, almost a timelessness, that was a consequence and index of their isolation both from Nassau and from the larger world beyond. People everywhere rose at sunrise and usually retired at sundown or soon after. Clocks were scarce or nonexistent, and bells were used to call people to church. At Harbour Island, in lieu of a public clock, the policeman struck the hours from 7 A.M. to 9 P.M. on a large bell outside the police station; the latter hour was the unofficial curfew. "After it has struck," wrote Powles, "no one with a character to lose dare be seen in the streets."[66] In the more developed settlements a few house lights might twinkle into the night, and over wide rock-strewn areas of sea the lighthouses kept their nighttime vigils. But in most settlements, the houses were tightly shuttered soon after nightfall, leaving the night to clandestine lovers, prowling dogs, mosquitoes, and the unfriendly spirits of the dark. And in the more remote islands and settlements, perhaps, the calendar was as unknown, and almost as irrelevant, as the clock.

The nearer and most active Out Island settlements did maintain regular connections with Nassau, many Bahamian mariners sailed between the islands and Nassau on their fishing, turtling, sponging, trading, or wrecking business, and even for the most isolated inhabited Out Islands the mail boats and less frequent visits from circuit magistrates, Anglican missionaries, and the service tenders of the Imperial Lighthouse Service provided tenuous links with the colonial capital. But for most Out Islanders, Nassau—so charmingly sleepy and unprogressive to foreign visitors—was a bewildering, even dangerous metropolis and the world beyond an unimaginable abstraction. Even the few exceptions proved the general rule of the isolation, inertia, and hopelessness of Out Island life before 1900 or World War I. White Harbour Islanders and Abaconians ventured as far as Key West, Florida, but they found there until the twentieth century a similar, if distant, Out Island settlement. A fair number of black islanders also went off to Cuba or Central America by way of Inagua and Long Cay as stevedores or laborers on plantations or the Panama Canal. But they found a narrow and dulling drudgery that soon cast them back, with little gain or incentive to repeat the experience.

A very few nonwhite Bahamians left the Bahamas permanently during the nineteenth century and made successful careers for themselves or provided better opportunities for their children, either in the West Indies or the United States. In doing so they exhibited both the exceptional qualities that had specially frustrated them in their country of birth and the synergy that so often propels immigrants in a new society more strongly than was possible in their homeland or customary among their new ethnic peers. Forerunners of the Toote and the Adderley migrants of the early twentieth century, such distinguished sons (or grandsons) of the Bahamas included Robert Love (1839–1914), who was trained as an Anglican minister in Canada, served as a missionary in Haiti, and settled in Jamaica, where he became an outspoken editor, civil rights organizer, and one of the inspirations for Marcus Garvey. Following different trajectories were Bert Williams (1878–1922), who became one of the most accomplished of all American vaudevillians, and, most distinguished of all, James Weldon Johnson (1871–1938), poet, autobiographer, American consul, and one of the founders of the National Association for the Advancement of Colored People, who was born in Florida to an American father but was great-grandson through his mother of the Haitian-Bahamian free colored pioneer Stephen Dillet.[67]

Such notable migrants and their descendants, however, were so exceptional as almost to prove the rule that Bahamians in the nineteenth century stayed in or returned to the islands of their roots. In addition, virtually all successful early nonwhite migrants were drawn from the relatively privileged (and more widely horizoned) substrata of the nonwhite elite, based on Nassau, not from the Bahamas Out Islands or even the outer reaches of New Providence. Unless driven abroad by absolute want, most Out Islanders were content—or at least inured by a dull inertia—to remain where they had been born and raised. This generalization applied

Governor Shea's failed dream. Two white planters, with good reason, somewhat glumly survey their sisal plantation in Andros, around 1900. Courtesy of Bahamas Archives.

to two of the most remarkable returned Out Island travelers of the nineteenth century. In 1886, Powles encountered near Governor's Harbour, Eleuthera, an "old darky" who had somehow been enrolled in the Royal Navy in 1840 and had lost an arm during the first of the Opium Wars on the coast of China. Ever since then he had received a disability pension of a shilling a day, on the strength of which he had become "quite a rich landowner" in his native place. He told Powles that he did not "regret his arm at the price."[68]

Even more unusual, though epitomizing many of the essential qualities of the nineteenth-century Bahamian Out Islander, white or black, was the amazing anabasis of "Vincent William, alias Old Burton," a Conchy Joe from Cherokee Sound, Abaco, told in the *Nassau Guardian* in August 1885. Two years before, Old Burton had set out alone from Abaco in his twelve-foot open dinghy, hoping to reach Key West. After calling at several islands for water and provisions, he made his destination within several weeks. But not liking the place much, he set out on the return voyage after only a few days. Thus began his adventures. Caught in a violent storm, he was offered assistance by a Norwegian brigantine but would only accept provisions. Shortly afterward, though, he was forcibly taken aboard a Spanish vessel bound for Tobago. In that island he appealed to the British colonial authorities, but they, presumably finding his Abaconian dialect too difficult to understand or even recognize as English, allowed the Spanish consul to ship him to Corunna. From there he was carried to Cadiz, before establishing his British provenance and being placed on a steamer bound for the Thames. In London, he spent more than a year in a workhouse before he was rescued by a clergyman and placed on the steamship *Godalming* to work his passage back to Nassau. This "erratic genius," who had "been quite given up as lost by his relatives," at last thankfully returned to his home in the most isolated and introspective of all-white Out Island townships, where he intended quietly to spend the rest of his days.[69]

II

On the Margins of a Modernizing World, 1900–1973

Women supporting the PLP in George Town, [illegible]. The PLP was the first to mobilize Bahamian women politically, [illegible] to support them in the first general election [illegible] suffrage. From Doris Johnson, *The Quiet Revolution in the Bahamas* ([illegible]), used with permission.

Women advertising the PLP in Grant's Town, 1962. The PLP was the first to mobilize Bahamian women politically but did not convince a majority to support them in the first general election after female suffrage. From Doris Johnson, *The Quiet Revolution in the Bahamas* (Nassau, 1972), used with permission.

6

Structures: Demography and Social and Material Conditions, 1900–1973

Introductory Overview

The beginning of the twentieth century found the Bahamas on the margins of a region itself marginalized by the developing world economy. Even in comparison with the seriously exploited and sociopolitically underdeveloped British West Indies, the colony of the Bahamas lagged behind until after mid-century. The black majority of its people were economically hopeless; they lacked adequate social services and education, and they were subject to a political system that can be characterized as a white Creole agrocommercial oligarchy reinforced by the racial prejudices of white imperial administrators and poor white Conchy Joes and by the timorous conservatism of a small and insecure brown middle class.

The condition of the ordinary Bahamian people was mitigated by the benign environment that made it as difficult to starve as to freeze, by the trickle-down effects of repeated if short-lived economic booms (most notably, the rum-running and tourist investment of the 1920s), and by the persistence of traditional habits of dependency, which had the unconscious and ultimately demoralizing effect of surrendering political power for minimal handouts. For most ordinary Bahamians, emigration provided the only economic amelioration. Long-term or permanent migrations and short-term ventures by migrant laborers had begun in the nineteenth century, but more or less permanent emigration reached its peak, despite U.S. immigration restrictions, during the first two decades of the twentieth century and was augmented by two tidal surges of labor migration during and shortly after both world wars. These movements of people outside the Bahamas, which were accompanied by equally complex internal migrations, had two obviously beneficial effects. They relieved the pressure of a rapidly growing population that was outstripping its native resources, and they provided much needed financial relief in the form of migrant laborers' wages and the remittances sent by Bahamians more permanently settled abroad.

Cumulatively more important than its material impact, though, were the effects of migration on peoples' consciousness and aspirations. Travel, along with steadily improving communications media, opened windows to a far more rapidly developing outside world and increased awareness of disparities and of what Bahamians could, and should, do to redress the balance. The influence of the nearby mainland was more critical than ever, though equally ambiguous. The United States

Thrown back. Patient Andros Islanders at Nassau's Market slip await tide and breeze to return to their homes, around 1900. "Doc" Sands photograph, Gail Saunders Collection.

seemed to Bahamians a land of economic opportunity, the front-runner in modernization, and the fount of democratic ideology. Yet the relative economic benefits of a U.S. connection were tainted for nonwhite Bahamians by the sociopolitical disadvantages of racial discrimination, especially in those states adjacent to the archipelago. Over the eras of the Harlem Renaissance, the Garvey crusade, and the black power movement, Bahamians participated proportionately in the migration by British West Indians which provided benefits to African Americans and colonial stay-at-homes alike. More specifically catalytic, however, were the effects of the two world wars.

World War I was the first British imperial enterprise in which a large number of black Bahamians participated. It made them aware of popular movements elsewhere in the empire (and in Russia) and generated the first demands for sociopolitical advances as a reward for imperial service. These faint stirrings were wiped out first by the illusory benefits of the 1920s boom and then, in bitterness and apathy, by the Great Depression, which brought to the peripheral Bahamas almost as much grief as to the mainline West Indian colonies without a concomitant growth of political parties or organized and coordinated trade unions. World War II also raised Bahamians' consciousness of populist, anticolonial, and Pan-

African movements within the dependent empire, as well as of Britain's increasing imperial debility, though the sociopolitical effects in the Bahamas were more muted and slow-moving than in all the major British West Indian colonies.

The reasons for this sociopolitical retardation were manifold and partly cumulative. It was not just that the Bahamian people were politically unsophisticated as a result of an educational system suffering from fiscal poverty and calculated neglect but that they lacked the fundamental bases for a progressive political movement. Because there was no industrialization in the Bahamas and the industries that did exist were, like the islands and their people, scattered and poor, there was no chance for a forceful proletariat to emerge. Added to this were the negative effects of traditional habits of dependency, particularly the false consciousness that devalued everything African, even for the Afro-Bahamian majority—imprinting the fact that the majority of the poor were Afro-Bahamians and the majority of the Afro-Bahamians poor as a seemingly natural condition.

A third reason was that the period after World War II saw both the greatest and most prolonged economic boom, based on tourism and offshore capitalism and a willingness on the part of Britain to grant political devolution. The benefits of both, however, were preempted and used by the prevailing white Bay Street regime. Despite a slowly rising tide of political activity by a popular nonwhite vanguard, organized as the Progressive Liberal Party in 1953, internal self-government, along with the first substantial improvements in social services, arrived in the early 1960s under the aegis of Bay Street's United Bahamian Party (UBP).

Political progress, though, was inevitable and merely delayed. Britain's imperial retreat, the example of most of Britain's other former black colonies, and the influence of the black power movement in the neighboring United States—all disseminated by hugely improved communications—inexorably led to black majority rule in 1967–68 and the initiation of socioeconomic changes so rapid and wide-ranging as to be almost revolutionary. That the transition was (in a term borrowed by black PLP senator Doris Johnson) a "quiet revolution" was owing to political moderation on both sides, with the economically aggressive Bay Street oligarchy resolutely retaining democratic principles and their black opponents, despite high-flown rhetoric, equally firmly refraining from violence or even retribution. As Colin Hughes has suggested, such an outcome might have been predicted from Bahamian history and an understanding of the essential character of all Bahamians: a national ideology of "symbolic politics" that transcends all party affiliations and even the great visible and invisible divides of color and class.[1]

Even the achievement of full independence by the Bahamas in 1973 seemed at first to have more symbolic than actual significance. Political and fiscal autonomy were already almost complete, and the major socioeconomic changes of the previous quarter-century had occurred steadily almost independent of political action, though they did accelerate after the coming to power of the black PLP government in 1967. To the PLP's only slightly more conservative opponents (by 1973, a majority of them blacks themselves), the shift to independence initially appeared little more than a political ploy designed to deflect attention and criticism from more fundamental problems and policy decisions. The immediate achievement of an individual voice in the United Nations and involvement in the Organization of American States (OAS) and the Caribbean Community (CARICOM), however, along with total responsibility for foreign affairs, internal security, and future development, constituted an accession into the world of adult nationhood that made the question of what it is to be a Bahamian suddenly more important. The necessary national rites of passage also involved the instant invention of a symbolic new flag, a national anthem, even a new name for the new country, the Commonwealth of the Bahamas (a commonwealth of islands within a commonwealth of nations).

It is fitting therefore to use 1973 as the final main divider in this book, setting off the survey of the last quarter of the twentieth century and speculations about the future—the concern of the third and final part—from the more detailed and less subjective study of the factors that affected and shaped the Bahamas and its people from 1900 down to independence. This three-quarters of a century is first viewed overall, in the rest of this chapter, through demographic, social, and material statistics. This necessary structure enables us to return to a staged narrative in the following four chapters, covering in turn the first two decades of the twentieth century (especially World War I), the 1920s and 1930s, World War II and its aftermath, and the decade of unprecedented changes from 1963 to 1973.

Census and Population Trends Before World War II

The more or less decennial Bahamian censuses in the seven decades after 1901 illustrate much more than mere patterns of population change; the beginning of a huge surge in numbers after decades of standstill or minimal expansion coincides with rapid improvements in material conditions and increased political activity. A parallel improvement in the efficiency, breadth, and sophistication of census-taking after mid-century allows for a more detailed and interrelated analysis of the Bahamian people as they stood at last on the threshold of modernization and independence (see Map 10, Table 6, and Figure 2).

The most remarkable features of the Bahamian population at the beginning of the twentieth century were that more than three-quarters of Bahamians still lived in the Out Islands and that what migration had already occurred was either between Out Islands or the beginning of emigration out of the Bahamas rather than the metropolitan effect that was to result in two-thirds of all Bahamians living in Nassau/New Providence by the 1970s (see Table 7 and Figure 3).

On the day of the census, April 14, 1901, only 12,534 of the total Bahamian population of 57,735 were living in New Providence (23.3 percent), though the great preponderance of females in Nassau's island, 128 to 100, suggests that perhaps 1,000 males had temporarily migrated or were recorded elsewhere.[2] Over the previous decade the total population of the Bahamas had increased slightly, averaging only about 1.3 percent per year, and New Providence's population had expanded slightly faster (1.5 percent per year), suggesting a trickle of immigration. Other shifts, though, were more significant. The population of Andros and Eleuthera had increased faster than that of New Providence over the previous decade (by 1,758 and 1,375 compared with 1,620 in total, or 3.8 and 1.9 percent respectively), largely because of migration from other islands to the sponge beds and the sisal and pineapple fields. Conversely, the population of certain islands had fallen, most notably Cat Island, San Salvador, Abaco, and Harbour Island. As Herbert A. Brook,

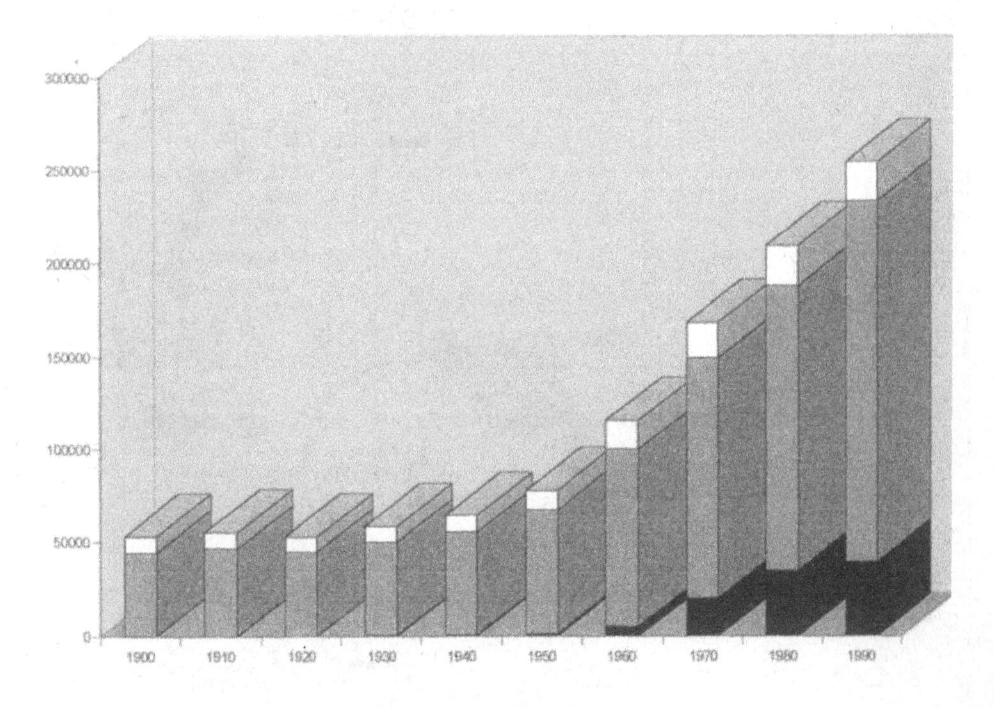

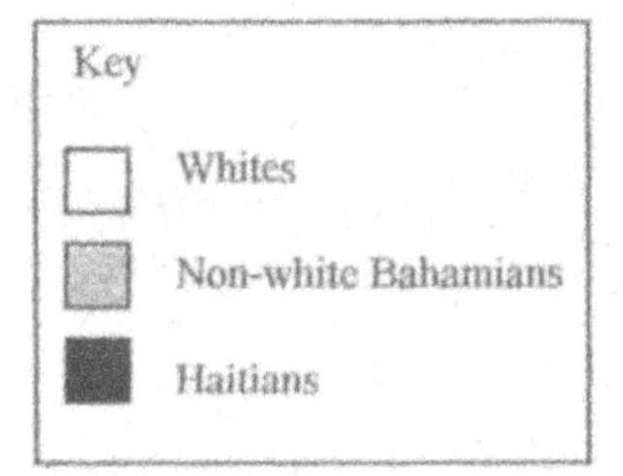

Figure 2. Bahamas: Total Population, 1900–1990

superintendent of the census, pointed out, this decline was mainly a result of internal migration in the first two cases (and some temporary labor migration from Cat Island to Central America) but almost entirely because of emigration to Florida in the case of the Abaco whites and some Harbour Islanders.[3]

The recent small increase in temporary labor emigration was at least partially the reason why the total number of females in the Bahamas at the time of the 1901 census was up by 14.9 percent over 1891, compared with an apparent increase in the number of males of only 10.8 percent, leading to an overall disparity of 115:100 in favor of females. There may, however, have been health reasons for some disparity, with males dying increasingly earlier than females.[4] Certainly, the limited indications in the 1901 census data (which did not include births and deaths, let alone causes of death) suggest a demographically unhealthy population. The number of

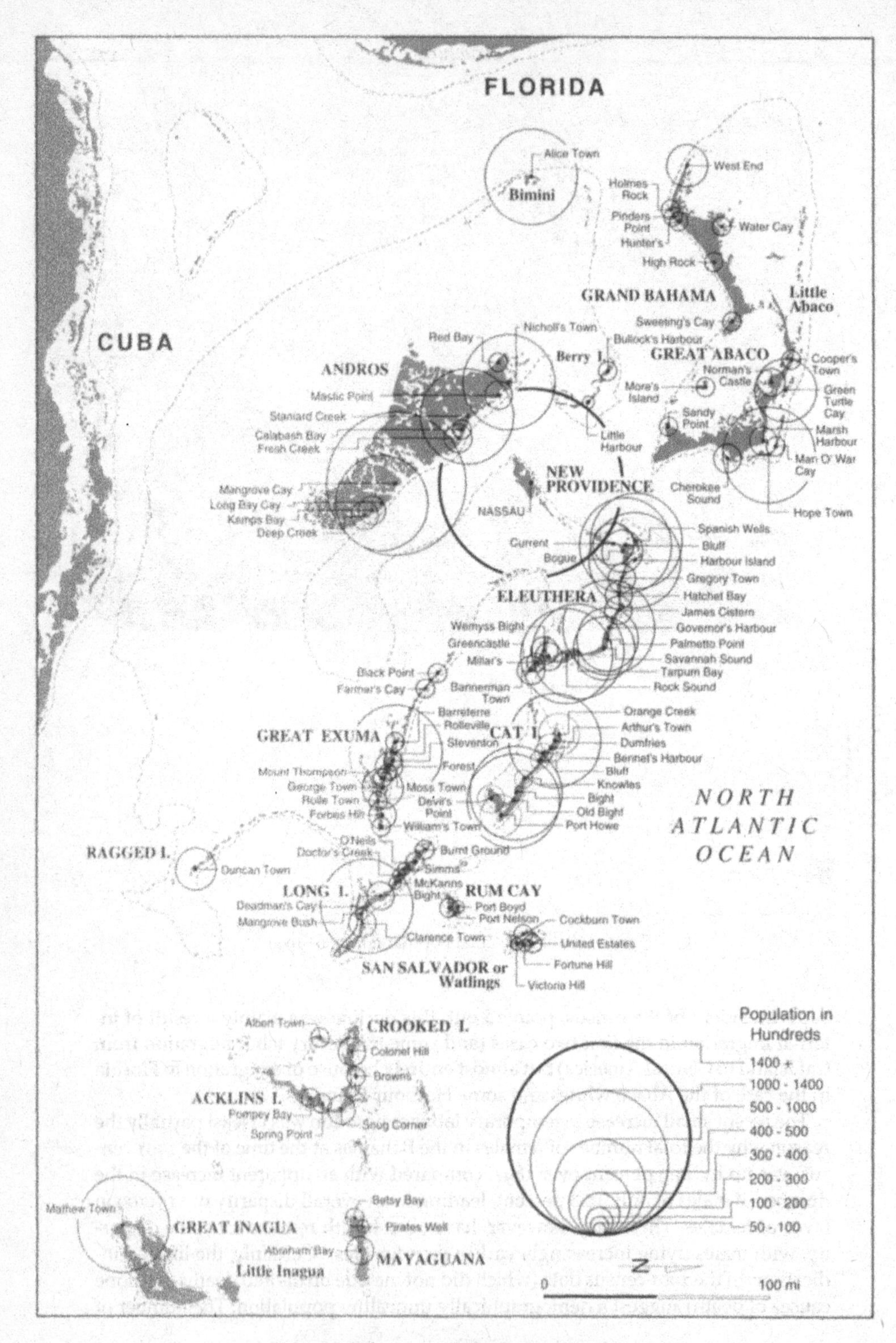

Map 10. Bahamas with Settlements in 1926

Table 6. Total Population and Growth Rates, 1901–1990

Intercensal Period	*Number of years in interval*	*Total population at end of interval*	*Total growth*	*Average annual growth rate (%)*
1901–11	10	55,944	2,209	0.40
1911–21	10	53,031	−2,913	−0.53
1921–31	10	59,828	6,797	1.21
1931–43	12	68,846	9,018	1.18
1943–53	10	84,841	15,995	2.11
1953–63	10	130,220	45,379	4.38
1963–70	7	168,812	38,592	3.78
1970–80	10	209,505	40,693	2.18
1980–90	10	255,095	45,590	1.99

Source: Adapted from Norma Abdulah, *The Bahamas and Its People: a Demographic Analysis* (St. Augustine, Trinidad: CARICOM and ISER, 1987), 15.

persons under eighteen years of age increased by only 9.2 percent in ten years, and their proportion of the total population fell from 52.0 to 50.0 percent, even though the proportion of persons over seventy years of age also fell from 2.7 to 2.2 percent (an absolute net decrease from 1,293 to 1,202).[5]

The number and proportion of people formally married had increased slightly since 1891 (to 16,657 from 14,687, or from 30.9 to 31.0 percent of the total population), though this may have been accounted for simply by the increase in the proportion of the population over eighteen years of age, and the superintendent of the census remarked censoriously that "the status of the population as regards wedlock cannot be viewed with satisfaction." Herbert Brook was also skeptical about the reliability of the statistics for literacy, which also were no great cause for congratulation. Those who claimed to be able to read and write had increased by 5,649 to 19,975 out of 53,735—that is, from 30.1 to 37.2 percent—in ten years. But Brook noted that "a large per cent of those who claimed to be able to read and write, or write, signed their names by making a mark" and that "the spelling of many of the householders is disgraceful and the writing of quite a number is far from good."[6]

Of the 43 percent of the population who declared a profession or occupation in 1901, a seemingly increasing proportion of the majority were in the lower echelons of the workforce and the class hierarchy. The mere 129 "professionals" (including all ministers of religion), though 50 percent more numerous than in 1891, were greatly outnumbered by the 292 termed "officials" (that is, "paid from Colonial or Imperial funds"), whose numbers had remained static. To these two classes were added 748 "traders and clerks," whose number had increased by 116 but whose proportion of the total population had remained almost unchanged.

The 22,014 persons (undifferentiated by gender) listed beneath the 1,169 in the professional, official, and mercantile categories consisted of 3,059 "craftsmen and mechanics," 7,941 "planters and farmers" (mostly small cultivators), 4,271 "seamen and fishermen," and 6,743 "laborers and servants." Altogether, this was an increase of 4,210 since 1891, representing a small increase in the first two and fourth categories but a significant surge in the number of seamen and fishermen—that is,

Table 7. The Metropolitan Effect: Relative Population Growth, Bahamas, New Providence, Grand Bahama, Abaco, and Eleuthera, 1891–1990

	All Bahamas	New Providence	Grand Bahama	Abaco	Eleuthera (incl. Harbour Island and Spanish Wells)	Rest of Bahamas
1891	47,565	10,914	1,780	3,686	9,244	21,941
%	100.0	22.9	3.7	7.7	19.4	46.1
1901	53,735	12,534	1,269	3,314	10,499	26,119
%	100.0	23.3	2.4	6.2	19.5	48.6
1911	55,944	13,554	1,824	4,463	8,119	27,987
%	100.0	24.2	3.3	8.0	14.5	50.0
1921	53,031	12,975	1,695	3,393	7,547	26,821
%	100.0	24.5	3.2	7.5	14.2	50.6
1931	59,828	19,756	2,241	4,233	7,527	26,071
%	100.0	33.0	3.7	7.1	12.6	43.6
1943	68,846	29,391	2,333	3,461	7,864	25,797
%	100.0	42.7	3.4	5.0	11.4	37.5
1953	84,841	46,125	4,095	3,407	7,196	24,018
%	100.0	54.4	4.8	4.0	8.5	28.3
1963	130,220	80,907	8,230	6,490	9,093	25,500
%	100.0	62.1	6.3	5.0	7.0	19.6
1970	168,812	101,503	25,859	6,501	9,468	25,481
%	100.0	60.0	15.3	3.9	5.6	15.1
1980	209,505	135,437	33,102	7,271	10,631	23,064
%	100.0	64.6	15.8	3.5	5.1	11.0
1990	255,095	172,196	40,898	10,034	10,584	21,383
%	100.0	67.5	16.0	3.9	4.1	8.4

Sources: Bahamas Censuses, 1891–1990.

those who could not move into an artisanal occupation, smallholding, regular wage labor, or a salaried post but were subject to the notorious conditions of maritime employment—an increase of 1,737 since 1891, or from 5.3 to 7.9 percent of the total population.

Unfortunately, the 1901 census did not facilitate a full social analysis by making crucial distinctions between employees, self-employed persons, and employers (for example, by lumping traders and clerks), between large-scale planters, smallholding peasants, sharecroppers, commoners, or squatters, or (perhaps most important of all) between whites, blacks, and coloreds. Nor did the census-takers yet consider internal migration an important enough feature of Bahamian life to record the island of birth as well as residence of each person polled. They did, though, make a painstaking record of country of origin, which pointed up the overwhelming (and increasing) degree to which those living in the Bahamas were natives. The Bahamian-born totaled 52,196 persons, or 97.1 percent of the resident population, up from 96.3 percent in 1891.

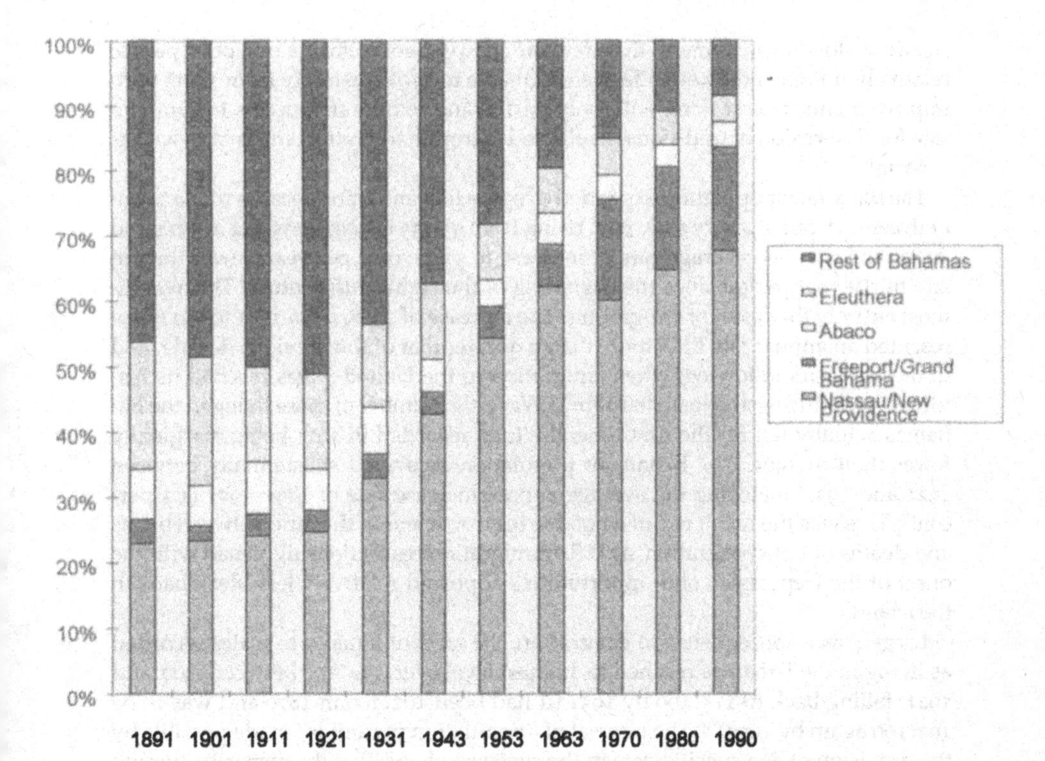

Figure 3. The Metropolitan Effect: Nassau Compared with Other Islands, 1891–1990.

Only 1,529 persons were listed as born outside the Bahamas. The most numerous were the 628 from the West Indies, including a large proportion from the Turks and Caicos Islands (administered by Jamaica), as well as members of the police force recruited from Barbados and Jamaica and the handful of political refugees from Cuba, Haiti, and elsewhere. Of the 356 born in the United States, most were said to have Bahamian-born parents. Those born in England, Scotland, and Ireland totaled 160, with 38 from the rest of Europe, 20 from Canada, and a mere 29 from all other countries. Of the original 6,000 liberated Africans, there remained 308 in 1901, a decrease of 507 since 1891. Sadly, Herbert Brook stated, "In all probability, in a few years, those born in Africa will be entirely extinct in the Bahamas. There will be very few remaining, if any, to witness the taking of another Census in this colony."[7]

To conform to a new Census Act in 1910, the 1911 Bahamian census was more detailed than that of 1901, providing, for example, age-specific data and calculations of household sizes for each district and a fuller list of employment categories.[8] The census method was not improved or much changed over the next two decades. The standard format, despite some wavering over the definition of categories used, therefore facilitates the recognition of demographic continuities, continuing trends, and a few surprising changes between 1901 and 1931.[9] Though some indexes, such as figures for literacy, legitimate births, and life expectancy, show steady if slow improvement, the prevailing impression remains of a poor people relatively untouched by outside events, unable to profit lastingly from short-term improvements, and seeking with only partial and temporary success to compensate for the erosion of traditional livelihoods through migration, internal as well as external.

The Bahamian population expanded over the first and third decades of the twentieth century but at a very slow rate, rising from 53,735 in 1901 to 55,944 in 1911 and 59,828 in 1931—an average rate of increase (0.37 percent per year) lower than in any thirty-year period since the beginning of the eighteenth century. This was almost entirely the result of emigration. The increase of 2,209 from 1901 to 1911 represented an annual rate little more than a quarter that of the previous decade, and in the ten years following, when emigration to the United States reached its historical peak during and just after World War I, the number of those living in the Bahamas actually fell for the first time, the total recorded in 1921 being marginally fewer than in 1901. The Bahamian population recovered substantially between 1921 and 1931, matching the average annual increase rate of 1891–1901 (1.3 percent). This was the result not of a notable improvement in the ratio between births and deaths but of remigration, as U.S. immigration restrictions tightened with the onset of the Depression and opportunities appeared relatively less bleak back in the islands.

Largely as a consequence of emigration, the ratio of females to males recorded as living in the Bahamas reached its highest level ever, 124:100 between 1911 and 1921, falling back to 114:100 by 1931 (it had been 102:100 in 1870 and was to be 102:100 again by 1970).[10] The perusal of "population pyramids" made possible by the provision of age-specific data in the censuses shows that the disparity, though notable among the elderly because of a somewhat higher life expectancy for women, was particularly marked among those of an age most likely to migrate. The demographic diagrams also disclose that while the Bahamian people were slowly but steadily becoming more healthy in respect to fertility, mortality, and life expectancy in every age cohort, there was neither the broad base to the pyramids denoting the high birth rate found in both the late slave period and modern times nor the elongated apex, denoting a large proportion of elderly persons, discovered in the most recent censuses. Such mediocre demographic performance indicators were the combined result, on the one hand, of a harsh work environment (hard work, low pay, unemployment, underemployment), less than adequate diet, and negligible medical facilities, and, on the other hand, of the disruption of families brought about by the frequent and prolonged migration of many adult males (see Table 8 and Figure 4).

In all three censuses, the shortage of males was at its peak among those aged fifteen to forty. The totals were 12,693 women to 7,960 men in 1911, or 159:100; in 1921, they were 11,976 to 7,604, or 157:100; and they recovered only to 13,007 to 10,026 by 1931, or 130:100. By 1970, the sex ratio in this critical age range was to come even closer to parity than the overall population average, at 101:100,[11] with obvious implications for family formation and fertility patterns (see Table 9 and Figure 5).

Though the censuses between 1911 and 1931 provided few relevant statistics, housing was clearly inadequate. Though lacking permanently resident household heads, many houses were overcrowded. The overall average household size in 1911 was 4.7 persons, rising to almost 6 persons in some of the poorest islands such

Table 8. Quinquennial Age Cohort Percentages, 1911–1953

		1911	1921	1931	1943	1953
0–4	m	6.871	7.716	7.729	7.208	7.729
	f	7.325	7.401	7.387	7.084	7.985
5–9	m	7.167	5.886	6.273	6.382	6.330
	f	7.153	5.861	6.354	6.355	6.226
10–14	m	6.778	6.641	6.405	5.484	5.787
	f	6.742	6.689	6.572	5.514	5.708
15–19	m	4.580	4.475	5.502	4.394	4.220
	f	6.524	5.908	6.208	5.274	5.175
20–24	m	2.949	3.062	4.283	4.241	3.580
	f	5.695	5.515	5.539	5.387	4.610
25–29	m	2.631	2.361	2.848	4.155	3.141
	f	4.540	4.179	4.171	4.654	4.004
30–34	m	2.229	2.013	2.049	3.211	2.760
	f	3.289	3.380	2.790	3.769	3.658
35–39	m	2.084	2.488	2.269	2.505	3.082
	f	3.031	3.697	3.283	3.205	3.578
40–44	m	1.987	2.108	1.872	1.836	2.572
	f	2.595	2.668	2.250	2.563	3.096
45–49	m	1.900	1.954	2.000	1.534	1.955
	f	2.251	2.557	2.575	2.213	2.382
50–54	m	1.555	1.648	1.599	1.397	1.404
	f	1.925	1.964	1.655	1.958	1.982
55–59	m	1.278	1.549	1.419	1.344	1.035
	f	1.331	1.645	1.621	1.557	1.431
60–64	m	0.996	1.083	1.018	1.054	0.905
	f	1.165	1.335	1.128	1.283	1.214
65–69	m	0.725	0.871	0.612	0.809	0.733
	f	0.687	1.083	0.825	0.926	1.028
Over 70	m	0.840	0.962	0.874	1.083	1.102
	f	1.176	1.299	1.339	1.620	1.587

Sources: Bahamas Censuses, 1911–53.

as Mayaguana. The average was 3.8 in the demographically healthy and relatively progressive Harbour Island, and the overall average was about 4.0 throughout the Bahamas in 1970—a figure that suggests a gravitation to the optimal norm of the standard nuclear family. Written accounts and photographic evidence attest to the generally small size and poor quality of Bahamian housing before mid-century, especially outside Nassau.

The same categories of employment were used for the censuses of 1911, 1921, and 1931 so some conditions and trends can be followed, though the census-takers were not consistent in their definitions. In 1901 only persons gainfully employed were included in the statistics (some 43 percent of the total population), but later

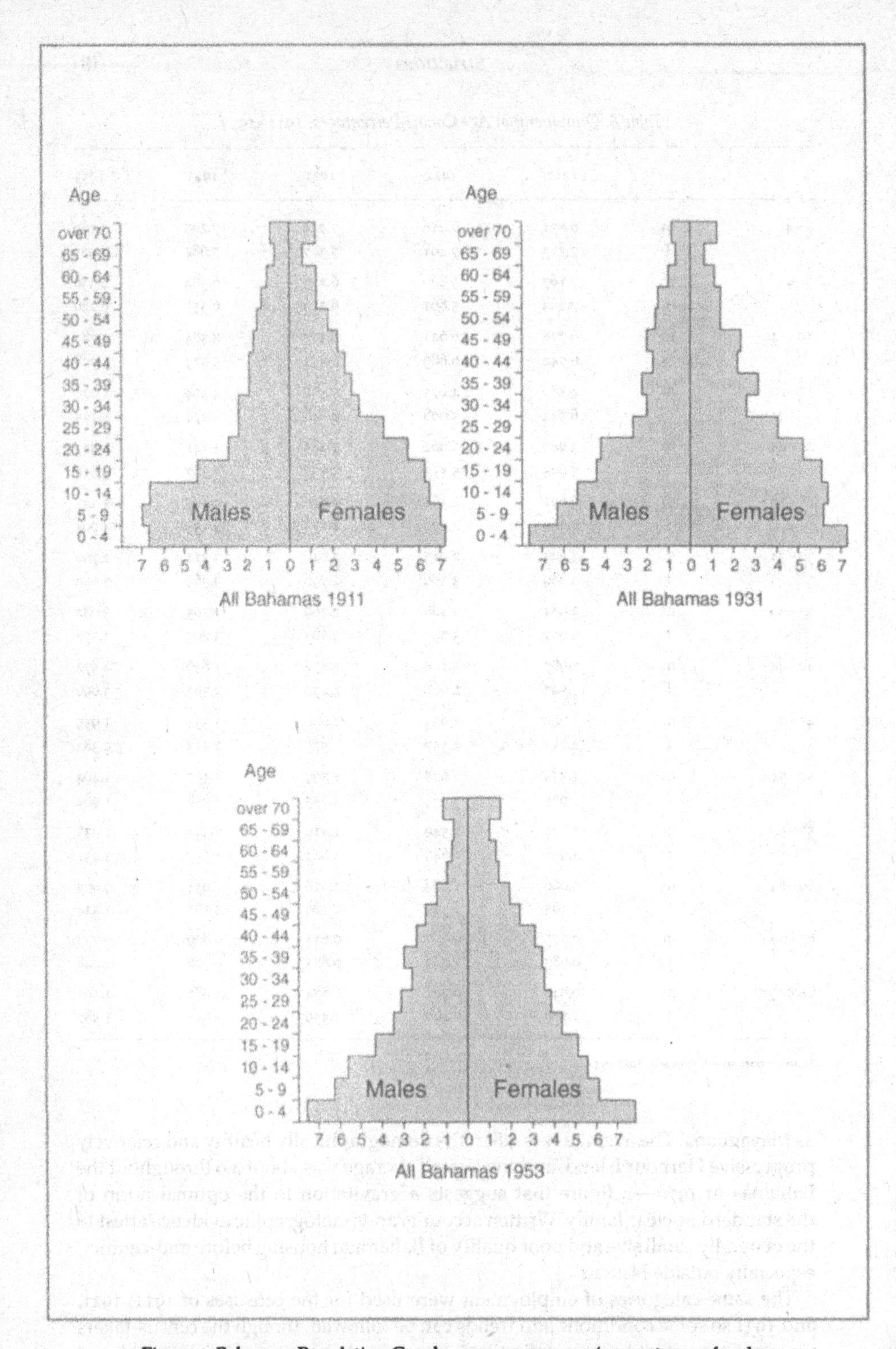

Figure 4. Bahamas: Population Graphs, 1911, 1931, 1953 (percentages of males and females in five-year cohorts)

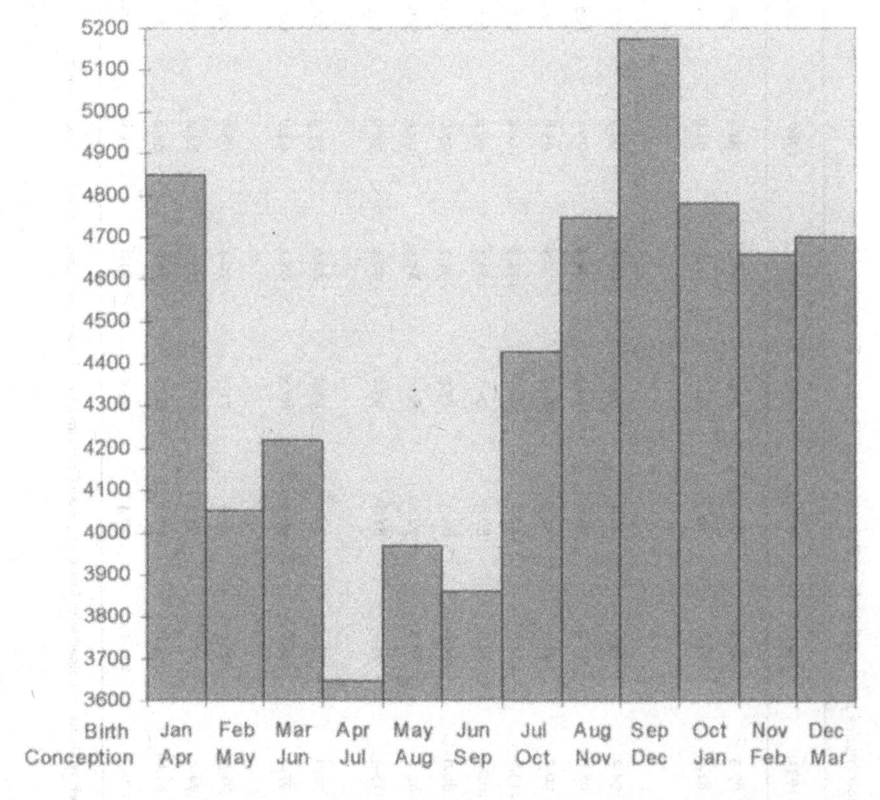

Figure 5. Whole Bahamas: Month-Specific Birth and Conception Totals, 1968–1978

adults without obvious employment and "scholars"—presumably all children between five and fourteen years of age who were in school—were added. Infants were included from the enumeration (about 14 percent of the total population), though percentages were arrived at from the total of those enumerated only.

Over the period 1911–31, the percentage of those classified as officials rose somewhat (from 0.4 to 0.7 percent), though the proportion of professionals stayed more or less constant (a mere 0.2 percent), as did the proportion of those listed as mechanics, hospitalized, or in jail (0.4, 0.3, and 0.1 percent respectively). The percentage of scholars rose roughly in tune with the slow improvement in general literacy, from 20 to 25 percent from 1911 to 1921, with a slight fallback to 24 percent in 1931. Unemployment, rated as high as 26.0 percent of those employable in 1911, officially fell to 18.2 percent in 1921 and 17.3 in 1931, though, needless to say, such figures were easily subject to manipulation.

The census-takers obviously wavered as to how to define tradesmen, general laborers, and domestic servants, but the chief confusion comes from their puzzlement over how to distinguish accurately between agricultural laborers, planters, and different types of farmers. The definition of tradesmen and domestic servants were widened, though the threefold increase in each category might have reflected the partial improvement of the economy in the 1920s. The increase in the number

Table 9. Male-Female Ratios, 1901–1990 (males per 100 females): Bahamas and Separate Islands

	1901	1911	1921	1931	1943	1953	1963	1970	1980	1990
Bahamas	87.0	80.6	81.4	87.3	87.4	86.5	95.1	98.3	94.5	96.1
New Providence	78.0	77.1	77.8	81.6	84.8	86.3	92.8	95.6	91.9	94.2
Eleuthera (incl. Harbour Island and Spanish Wells)	91.0	80.2	86.7	94.2	94.6	93.1	99.0	98.6	98.7	101.1
Abaco	89.8	100.2	91.9	98.9	96.2	94.6	119.3	109.4	105.1	108.5
Grand Bahama	95.4	75.4	75.8	96.2	91.9	114.5	119.7	110.9	95.6	96.3
Bimini	93.5	87.0	130.3	113.6	104.5	112.1	101.0	112.9	114.4	106.3
Andros	101.2	105.6	96.8	102.4	88.6	87.3	91.5	95.1	90.6	101.2
Exuma	80.2	68.3	75.1	80.0	85.6	65.3	87.9	95.2	97.2	106.7
Cat Island	81.4	70.1	70.8	84.1	88.7	72.1	80.9	85.5	93.6	106.3
Long Island	82.5	73.7	76.7	115.4	93.0	81.8	95.2	96.4	95.0	104.3
San Salvador (incl. Rum Cay)	79.0	70.2	75.9	76.6	77.4	89.7	93.0	80.6	75.9	93.3
Ragged Island	111.0	87.8	89.6	97.2	128.8	96.3	87.4	98.1	94.7	140.5
Crooked Island (incl. Long Cay)	84.4	63.1	58.6	61.5	60.4	45.9	71.7	79.4	88.7	98.1
Acklins	81.8	71.9	72.6	74.4	77.8	54.9	72.1	72.7	84.4	83.7
Mayagana	92.5	70.5	66.8	81.8	85.8	85.2	80.8	75.0	91.2	86.8
Inagua	106.1	78.1	99.8	100.3	104.1	99.4	95.6	99.8	101.5	110.9

Sources: Bahamas Censuses, 1901–1990. To provide consistency, Harbour Island and Spanish Wells are combined with Eleuthera, Rum Cay with San Salvador, and Long Cay with Crooked Island.

of tradespersons indicated expansion in the commercial sector in Nassau as well as the lumping together of shop assistants, hucksters, petty retailers, and other shopkeepers with the larger Bay Street merchants. Similarly, the increase in those listed as domestics denoted not just the combining of hotel workers with house servants but an expansion of employment opportunities with the coming of new white settlers and more tourists, accompanied by hotel building, such as the rebuilding of the Colonial Hotel as the New Colonial in 1923 and the building of the locally owned Montagu Beach Hotel in 1926.

The percentage of those listed as general laborers (that is, presumably earning wages at all laboring occupations other than agriculture) fluctuated from 14.5 to 9.7 and back to 11.0 percent without obvious significance. The largest category of all, those who wrested their main living from the soil, was designated in 1911 and 1921 as agricultural laborers, but in 1931 (as in 1901) as planters and farmers. The category of agricultural laborer expanded from 24.5 to 29.1 percent between 1911 and 1921 but then plummeted to 0.4 percent in 1931, whereas the classification of planter/farmer, after falling from 1.8 to 0.7 percent between 1911 and 1921, surged to 28.1 percent in 1931. These statistics almost certainly denote a steady fall in the number of genuine, that is, large-scale, farmers and a concomitant decline in the opportunities for agricultural wage labor. The recategorization of agricultural laborers as planter/farmers thus euphemized the reversion of many Out Islanders to the status of ever more hopelessly poor subsistence farmers.

A parallel and equally serious steady decline was less equivocally indicated by the fall in the proportion of those listed as seamen and fishermen. From a peak of 7.9 percent of the population in 1901, this group fell to 7.4 percent of those tabulated (or perhaps 6.8 percent of the total population) in 1911, to 6.3 percent (or 5.5 percent) in 1931. This proportion, like that of those forced to depend on the soil for a living, moreover, continued to fall steadily, never to rise again (see Figure 6).

Internal migration between 1911 and 1931, as ever, reflected the restless search for a better livelihood or at least fleeting opportunities. Apart from the accelerating drift toward New Providence (and beyond it, while possible, to the United States), the first noticeable internal migration of the twentieth century was that toward the Abaco mainland once the Bahamas Timber Company started operations at Wilson City in 1906. Abaco's population increased by 35 percent between 1901 and 1911 (and its male population by 42 percent), while that of Eleuthera, where pineapple and sisal cultivation was in decline, decreased by 23 percent (and its males by 28 percent).

The Wilson City operation closed during World War I, and by 1921 Abaco's population had declined by 11 percent (and its males by 14 percent). This, though, was only a minor feature of the draining of many Out Islands during the previous few years. Eleuthera lost a further 7.4 percent, Andros (where sponge fishing had passed its peak) 7.5 percent, and Cat Island (suffering probably the worst agricultural decline of any island), 15.8 percent. Most affected of all, however, were those islands hit by the virtual ending of the stevedoring and contract labor trade once the German and American steamships stopped calling during World War I. Inagua's population fell by 30 percent and Long Cay's by 55 percent, the latter becoming almost a ghost settlement within the next few decades. Exuma and Long Island made slight, somewhat anomalous, population gains, and tiny Bimini's population soared by 28 percent because of the start of the rum-running trade. But the

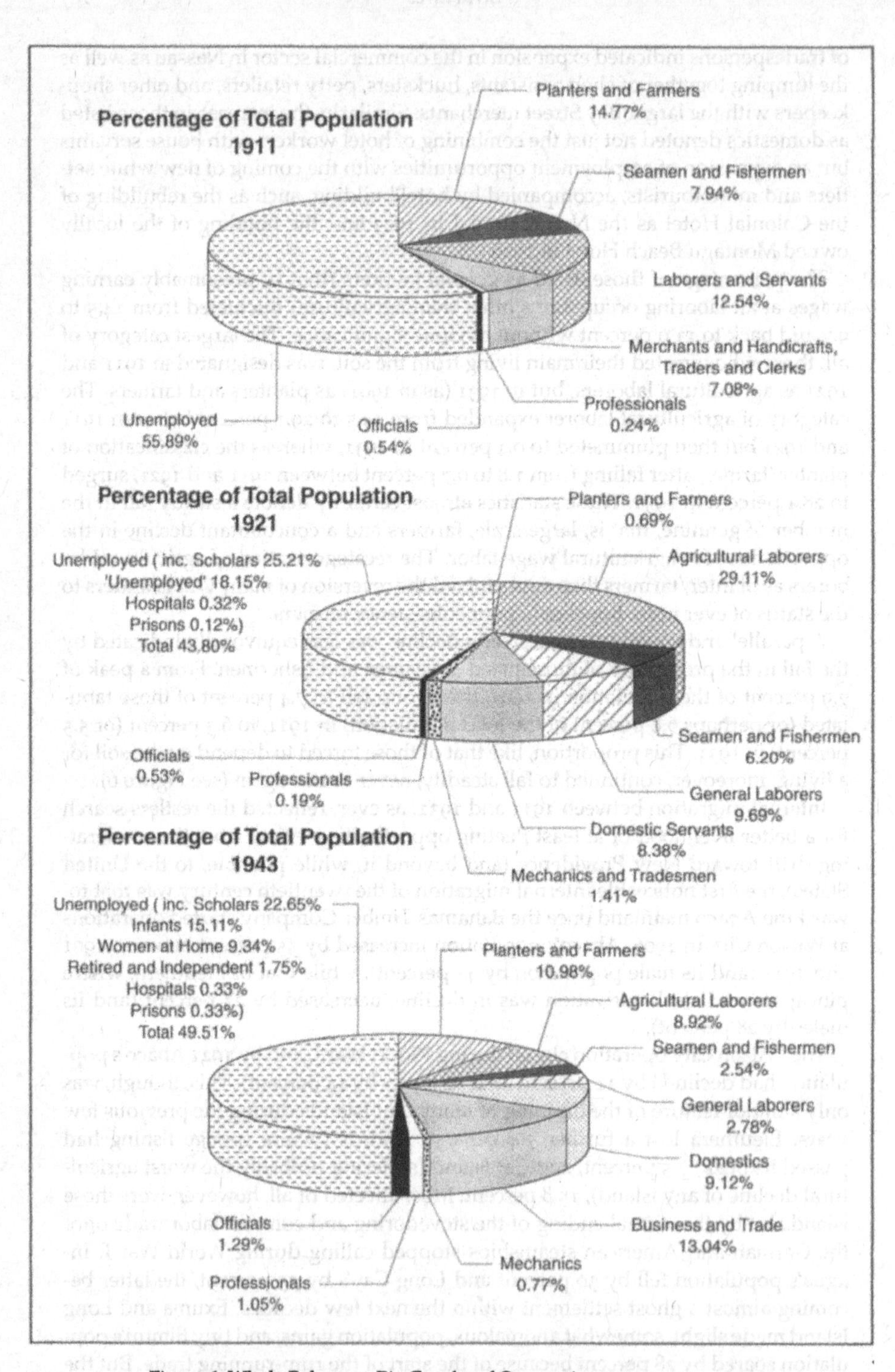

Figure 6. Whole Bahamas: Pie Graphs of Occupations, 1911, 1921, 1943

general tendency to emigration and population decline was emphasized by the fall even in New Providence's population between 1911 and 1921, from 13,554 to 12,975, or by 4.3 percent (losing more females than males).

When the flow of population back to the Bahamas began between 1921 and 1931, New Providence was overwhelmingly the major beneficiary. Nassau's island gained almost exactly the same number of persons as the general increase of the Bahamian population over the decade; 6,781 to 6,797. The population of most Bahamian Out Islands remained more or less static, and the decline continued at Inagua and Long Cay, along with Cat Island, Crooked Island, and Rum Cay, negating minimal gains in other islands. The population of Bimini, though, expanded by a further 18 percent, and Grand Bahama—because of the beginning of lumber operations and rum-running from West End—had a population surge of 32 percent (its male population up by 50 percent).

The Prohibition era of the 1920s and early 1930s had a minor effect on foreign immigration, with consequences that will be detailed in Chapter 8. The first two decades of the twentieth century saw almost no increase in the number of foreign-born persons living in the Bahamas. As an index of the lack of attractions for outsiders, the proportion of Bahamian-born persons reached probably its highest ever in 1921, 98 percent, and even the number of West Indians fell from 408 in 1911 to 249 in 1921. By 1931, however, the proportion of foreign-born, particularly whites, had begun the upward trend that was to accelerate after World War II to reach its maximum in the 1960s. In the 1931 census, 2,268 persons were listed as foreign-born, some 4 percent of the population. Those from the United Kingdom were up by 42 percent to 218 since 1921, those from Canada had doubled to 58, and those from mainland Europe almost trebled to 131. The West Indian–born totaled 590, up by 137 percent since 1921, but fewer than in 1901. The most remarkable rise was in the total number of persons from the United States, which had increased steadily from 245 in 1891 to 356 in 1901, 476 in 1911 and 503 in 1921, but had then jumped by 140 percent to 1,205 in 1931, constituting more than 2 percent of the population of the Bahamas and probably 5 percent of the population of Nassau. As befitted a group who were mainly well-heeled settlers migrating with their families, they were almost evenly divided between males and females. The same was true of the far less numerous officials and settlers from the United Kingdom, though not of the West Indian–born, two-thirds of whom were males.

The Censuses of 1943 and 1953

The onset of World War II delayed by two years the census scheduled for 1941. But neither the 1943 census nor that of 1953 reflected more than marginally the imperial government's increased concern for finding out more about West Indian conditions following the turmoil in the late 1930s, which led to the Moyne Commission, any more than they disclosed changes similar to those initiated for other colonies as a result of the commission's findings. It was not until 1963 that the Census Act of 1911 ceased to determine how the Bahamian census was conducted and tabulated, and this backwardness was not merely symptomatic of the general retardation of Bahamian conditions but indicated the will of the imperial government and the local oligarchy to let sleeping dogs lie.[12]

News from the outside world. Bahamians from Over the Hill line at the general delivery window of the post office in Rawson Square, around 1900. Similar gatherings occurred outside the nearby courts during important cases. To the right is the venerable *ceiba*, which long antedates the public buildings and was known as Blackbeard's Tree. Dying at last, it was cut down in the 1970s. "Doc" Sands photograph, Gail Saunders Collection.

The headmaster of the Government High School and the chief Out Island commissioner, who were the census supervisors in 1943 and 1953, respectively, did what they could to augment and refine the data obtainable under the 1911 act and recommended future changes.[13] The 1943 census for the first time included a breakdown of religious affiliations—a difficult task, for the claims of all denominations added up to a total greater than the entire population. The 1943 census also essayed an interesting, but even more problematic, breakdown of the population by categories of "race"—an exercise that, for self-evident reasons, was not repeated after 1953. Employment categories were confusingly altered twice again but by 1953 had not only been resolved into meaningful categories but for the first time distinguished the workforce from the population at large. Even more valuable, the 1953 census for the first time provided data, albeit imperfect, on housing and sanitation conditions. Despite their partly intentional limitations, the censuses of 1943 and 1953 therefore provide data that not only demonstrate significant trends but also suggest conditions edging toward crisis, social and political.

The Bahamas population in April 1943 was ascertained to be 68,846, an increase of 9,018 in the twelve years since the previous census, or, at an annual average of

1.27 percent, marginally less than over the previous decade (1.28 percent). Though it added in the 1,226 males and 547 females who had recently left the colony for temporary agricultural labor in the United States, it clearly understated the total number of wartime absentees or migrants. This was borne out by the fact that the overall proportion of females to males was 114:100, almost the same as in 1931. The effect of this disparity (or, more accurately, of the absence of males, both temporarily and for longer periods), as well as that of scarcely improved health conditions, on overall fertility and infant mortality rates, is evidenced by the failure of the proportion of the population aged under ten to increase over the previous decade, being 27.03 percent of the total population in 1943 and 27.29 percent in 1931. The proportion of those under five years of age had decreased from 14.67 to 14.29 percent.

The population figures for 1953, eight years after the end of World War II, showed a substantial change. In a decade, the population had increased to 84,841 at an annual average rate of 2.3 percent. The increase was partly accounted for by far more accurate counting of those absent from the colony—mainly the 3,622 agricultural workers (nearly all males) engaged in the organized system of migrant labor popularly called either "the Contract" or "the Project." The disproportion between the number of females and males had also decreased, which suggests that there was still some undercounting of male absentees. But the disparity was now greatest in the ages above normal fecundity, women over forty outnumbering males in the same cohorts by 10,728 to 8,166, or 122:100. The overwhelming cause of the population growth was an improvement in fertility rates. In 1953, 28.27 percent of the population had been born since the previous census (15.14 percent had been born within the previous five years), compared with 14.29 percent at the time of the 1943 census. The gross annual birth rate was thus around 43.0 per thousand, or 201.9 per thousand females aged fifteen to forty, compared with around 32.3 and 145.6 per thousand at the time of the 1943 census.[14] The ending of the war seems to have led not only to a healthier balance between the sexes among younger Bahamians and to healthier conditions in general but also to a greater inclination toward procreation as part of a much more widespread postwar "baby boom." These trends would all accelerate greatly in the years of economic prosperity and political hope that were to follow.

Internal migration and employment patterns and trends already detected continued through 1943 but speeded up notably through 1953. The drift toward Nassau led to an increase of the population of New Providence greater than that for the Bahamas as a whole in the twelve years before 1943. The proportional increase, moreover, was even greater among children of school age because fewer children were left behind in the Out Islands with grandparents by their migrating parents. By 1943, when 42.7 percent of the Bahamian population lived in New Providence, the island contained 35.0 percent of all children aged five to fifteen, compared with 33.0 and 25.7 percent in 1931 and 24.4 and 19.0 in 1921. The continuing trend, occasioned in part by the better education available in Nassau, placed new pressures on New Providence schools and also inevitably led to an even greater disparity between metropolitan and Out Island educational facilities. By 1953, when, for the first time, more than half the Bahamian population lived in New Providence (54.4 percent), Nassau's island also contained 46.1 percent of all Bahamian school-age children (see Table 10).

Table 10. Bahamian Literacy, 1891–1990 (percentages)

	1891	*1901*	*1911*	*1921*	*1931*	*1943*	*1953*	*1963*	*1970*	*1980*	*1990*
Read and write	35.4	43.7	45.6	50.7	71.0	76.0	85.1	91.0	92.5	94.0	95.0
Read only	19.8	13.6	10.1	6.9	3.7	2.2	1.9				
Write only	0.1	0.2	0.3	0.4	0.4	—	—				
Illiterate	44.7	42.4	44.0	42.1	24.9	21.8	13.0	8.0	7.0	5.5	5.0

Sources: Bahamas Censuses, 1891–1990. Figures for 1891–1953 adjusted from census totals to exclude children under five years old. Figures for 1963–90 are for total population over ten years old. No figures for "Write only" after 1931. "Read and write" and "Read only" combined from 1963.

The boost to Nassau's population by migration was made at the expense of the Out Islands as a whole, but the islands suffering most from Nassau's magnetic attraction differed significantly in 1943 and 1953. In the wartime census, the islands losing the most people were Abaco, Andros, and Crooked Island because of the closing of logging operations, the collapse of sponging, and the decay of farming, respectively. By 1953, the rate of migration from the Out Islands had more than doubled, with nearly all the islands traditionally dependent on subsistence farming suffering serious depletion. Acklins Island had lost 27.0 percent of its people since 1943, Ragged Island 23.3 percent, Crooked Island 22.4 percent, Exuma and Long Island 17.7 percent, Cat Island 15.3 percent, and Eleuthera 5.6 percent. Of the smaller islands, Rum Cay, once the most diversified of the subsistence islands, had seen 39.3 percent of its people leave since 1943 and was in danger of losing its viability as a settlement. Only partially offsetting these losses, San Salvador just held its own, Andros and Inagua had made small population increases and Bimini a proportionate surge because of U.S. government installations and other American investments. The population of Grand Bahama had risen from 2,333 to 4,095 (by 75.5 percent) in response to the dynamic logging operation initiated by Wallace Groves—an anticipation of the huge expansion of the late 1950s and 1960s once Groves turned from swathing the pinelands to developing Freeport-Lucaya.

The refined employment statistics of 1943 and 1953 flesh out and help to provide the economic reasons for Bahamian migration patterns. Dividing the entire population into those gainfully employed and those not provides a clearer picture than was formerly available, though juggling the categories (for example, including subsistence farmers, the criminal, and the hospitalized in the former category and including only women who were employed among the workers) both Albert Woods and John A. Hughes were able to claim Panglossian figures for the "unemployed"—0.89 percent in the former case and 1.37 percent in the latter. Neither census-taker, though, was able to disguise the accelerating drift away from traditional agriculture and maritime activities. If one deconstructs the changes in classification categories, it can be ascertained that the proportions of those working the land (whether as "planters and farmers," "agricultural laborers," or simply under "agriculture") fell from 46.0 percent of those "gainfully employed" and 33.1 percent of the total population in 1931 to 21.0 percent and 18.6 percent in 1943. Although the percentage of agriculturalists of those "gainfully employed" remained unchanged in 1953, their numbers represented a rapid fall to 10.6 percent of the total population. Over the same period, the percentage of those listed as fishermen and seamen fell from 5.5 percent of the total population in 1931 to 3.1 percent in 1953, though the percentage of mariners among those "gainfully employed" fell less rapidly and their total number, after a fall from 3,760 in 1931 to 1,746 in 1943, rose to 2,588 in 1953.

The numerical increase in the number, if not proportion, of mariners reflected the expansion of wage-paying opportunities—in this case, to service the burgeoning tourist industry—that drew people toward the Bahamian capital and other developing localities. The Woods census showed an increase in the number and proportion of "domestic servants"—from 3,901 or 6.5 percent of the total population in 1931 to 6,277 or 9.1 percent in 1943—though the continuance of this trend (as well as the steady rise in the number of officials) is disguised by the use of the new category of "Services, including Government" in the Hughes census. The latter totaled 14,536 persons, or 17.1 percent of the total population (compared with 7,168 or 10.4 percent of "domestic servants" and "officials" combined in 1943). Hughes's predilection for a more "modern" classification additionally separated the 449 males (and no females) involved in "electricity, water and sanitary services" from his main services category.

In dealing with the critical question of the numbers engaged in commerce, the 1943 census made the valuable distinction between those who were in business or trade as employees (7,783, or 11.3 percent of the total population) and those who were employers—or self-employed—in business or trade (1,199 or 1.7 percent). This distinction was largely lost in the simple 1953 classification of "commerce," when an apparent decline in numbers (down to 5,744 or 6.8 percent of the total population) disguised a significant expansion. A much more useful refinement in the 1953 census was the substitution of separate categories of "manufacturing" and "construction" to reclassify those previously listed under "general labourers" and "mechanics" (plus, no doubt, others who came under the 1943 "business or trade employees" rubric). The most notable revelation of these changes was that no less than 7,211 persons, or 8.5 percent of the population, were by 1953 engaged in servicing a boom in the construction industry.

Another revealing change introduced in the 1953 employment tables was the gender breakdown. Though no less than 7,467 were listed as "women at home (not otherwise employed)," as many as 5,217 females were listed as gainfully employed in agriculture, compared with only 3,741 males. Although women traditionally had an important role in Bahamian agriculture, this trend toward their predominance was undoubtedly a concomitant of a general decline in agricultural pursuits. Maritime activities were, as they had always been, an exclusively male preserve, and the same gender specificity now applied to the newer occupations in electricity, water, and sanitary services. Males, predictably, also dominated in the construction industry, which employed 6,569 men but only 642 women. More surprising, males outnumbered females by only 1,140 to 1,016 in the "manufacturing" category, though this attests more to the elementary nature of local industry (consisting largely of straw-working and other handicrafts, in which women, as well as children, had always been involved).

The rising tide of internal migration by Bahamians toward employment opportunities, particularly in Nassau, was paralleled, if not quite equaled, by the immigration of foreigners, though the inevitable competitive friction and racial intensification were not to become serious until the 1960s. The number of persons born outside the Bahamas in the 1953 population was up to 5,945, or 7.0 percent of the total, compared with 2,658 and 3.9 percent in 1943 (in 1970 it was to be 29,926 and 14.1 percent). Of the 1953 total, by far the largest number were the 2,534 from the West Indies (including the Turks and Caicos Islands), an increase of 181 percent, followed by 1,871 from the United States (up 73 percent), 793 from the United Kingdom (157 percent), and 220 from Canada (137 percent), with 527 from other parts of the world (80 percent). Of the 46,125 persons living in New Providence in 1953, 45.5 percent had been born in the island, 41.9 percent in the Out Islands, and 12.6 percent outside the Bahamas, though of the migrants in the previous decade probably only two-thirds were Out Islanders and as many as a third from abroad.

The statistics of religious affiliation given in 1953 demonstrate dynamic patterns when compared with those for 1943 and 1963, though exactly what the changes signified is debatable. Over this twenty-year period, the two major traditional churches, the Anglican and Baptist, retained their primacy, though the share of each declined (from 27 to 24 percent and 34 to 30 percent respectively), as did that of the Methodists (from 11 to 8 percent). The major gainer was the Roman Catholic church, which from its American missionary base specialized in education and addressed poor blacks and the upwardly mobile alike, taking over third place from the Methodists by increasing its adherents from 10 to 20 percent of the total. At the same time, minority churches of a theologically radical or pentecostal slant, also emanating from the United States, increased their share from negligible numbers to 13 percent, the Church of God from 5 percent in 1953 to 7 percent, the Brethren from virtually none to 3 percent, Seventh Day Adventists to 2 percent, and Pentecostals 1 percent. In most islands, the sects claimed adherents in proportions similar to the Bahamian totals, with the exception that Baptists were predominant in some of the islands where the population was overwhelmingly black, such as Andros, Cat Island, and Exuma. Anglicans took third place to Baptists and Methodists in Abaco, and in Eleuthera Methodists outnumbered Anglicans, with Baptists third and Catholics a distant fourth.

The statistics for race provided in 1943 and 1953 have more obvious significance, though more as an indication of how people regarded themselves and how the question of racial ascription in relation to class aspirations was a potentially critical issue than as objective realities. In 1943, when Woods's enumerators asked people in which category they placed themselves (and, presumably, their children), 11.5 percent were recorded as "Europeans (white)," 83.3 percent as "African (black)," and 4.7 percent as "mixed." "Mongolians" made up 0.3 percent, "others" 0.2 percent, and 67 persons did not state their race. in 1953, Hughes's enumerators found that 12.6 percent now classified themselves as whites, an increase that was more or less consonant with the recent immigration of Americans, Canadians, Britishers, and other Europeans. The negligible proportions of "Mongolians" and "others" remained much the same as before, but only 72.6 percent now called themselves blacks, while 14.2 percent said they were mixed. In addition, as many as 319 persons now did not place themselves in a racial category (see Table 11 and Figure 7).

The decrease of more than 10 percent in the proportion of self-defined blacks (so that their total numbers had barely risen in a decade that had seen the Bahamian

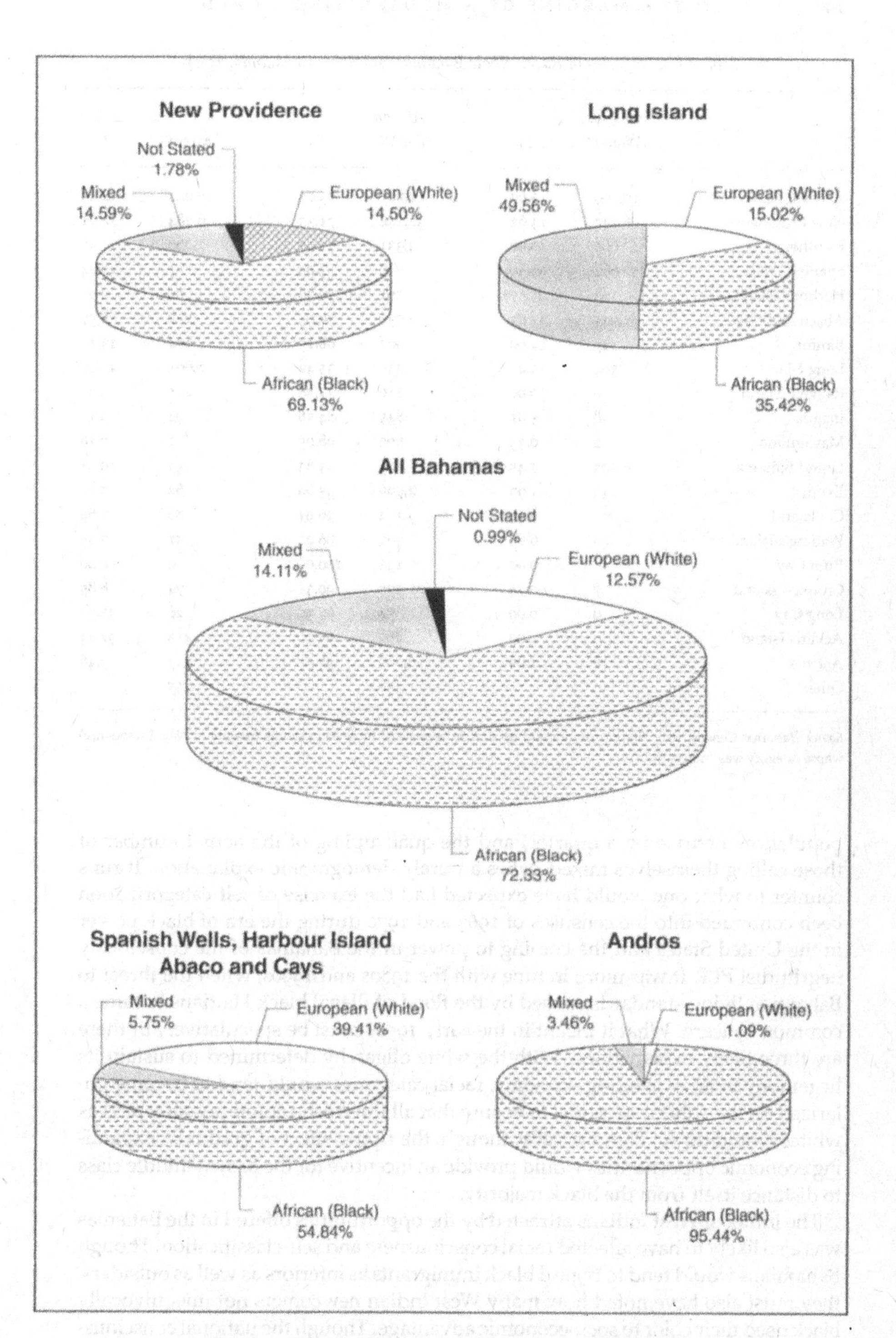

Figure 7. Bahamas: Categories of Race from 1953 Census

Table 11. Categories of Race: Whole Bahamas and Separate Islands, 1953

	"European (White)"	%	"African (Black)"	%	"Mixed"	%
All Bahamas	10,709	12.69	61,627	73.05	12,024	14.25
New Providence	6,742	14.62	32,144	71.35	6,784	14.71
Eleuthera	665	10.96	4,331	71.35	1,060	17.46
Spanish Wells	662	96.50	21	3.06	3	0.44
Harbour Island	198	23.57	591	70.36	51	6.07
Abaco and Cays	1,045	33.61	2,039	59.85	224	6.57
Bimini	147	11.09	903	68.15	174	13.13
Long Island	564	15.2	1,330	35.42	1,861	49.56
Ragged Island	0	0.00	110	34.38	211	65.63
Inagua	58	5.81	845	84.58	94	9.1
Mayaguana	2	0.33	603	98.05	1	0.16
Grand Bahama	305	7.45	3,343	81.63	447	10.91
Exuma	58	1.99	2,799	95.89	62	2.12
Cat Island	13	0.41	3.102	96.91	86	2.69
Watling's Island	46	6.63	597	86.02	51	7.35
Rum Cay	0	0.00	133	100.0	0	0.00
Crooked Island	7	0.74	755	90.31	74	8.85
Long Cay	0	0.00	54	67.50	26	32.50
Acklins Island	0	0.00	860	67.56	413	32.44
Andros	78	1.09	6,809	95.42	247	3.46
Other	119		358		155	

Source: Bahamas Census, 1953. Figures do not add up exactly because of those 843 persons (mainly in New Providence) whose category was "not stated."

population increase by a quarter) and the quadrupling of the actual number of those calling themselves mixed defies a purely demographic explanation. It runs counter to what one would have expected had the exercise of self-categorization been continued into the censuses of 1963 and 1970 during the era of black power in the United States and the coming to power in the Bahamas of the consciously negritudist PLP. It was more in tune with the 1980s and 1990s, when the threat to Bahamian living standards caused by the flood of illegal black Haitians became a common concern. What it meant in the early 1950s must be speculative, but there are three likely explanations. With the white oligarchy determined to sustain its hegemony in an expanding economy, racial categories would tend to become polarized on the American model to ensure that all those who could possibly pass as whites would do so. Paradoxically, though, the ripple effect of gradually expanding economic opportunities would provide an incentive for the brown middle class to distance itself from the black majority.

The influx of West Indians attracted by the opportunities offered in the Bahamas was also likely to have affected racial consciousness and self-classification. Though Bahamians would tend to regard black immigrants as inferiors as well as outsiders, they must also have noted how many West Indian newcomers not unequivocally black used their color to socioeconomic advantage. Though the national consciousness had not yet reached the point that in any walk of life to be a Bahamian was better than being an outsider (let alone the feeling that to be a black Bahamian was best of all), in the 1950s it seems to have been the consensus that if one could not be a white Bahamian, it was better to be a "mixed" or brown Bahamian than a black. In any case, the 1943 and 1953 census classifications indicated that the impending improvement in the Bahamian economy would be bought at the price of increased race and class confusions and tensions, if not also related political conflict.[15]

Takeoff: The Bahamian Population in 1963

As befitted the great social, economic, and political changes then beginning in the Bahamas, the census held in 1963 under the terms of the Census Act of that year was the first to be professionally directed, for the first time generating a wide and invaluable range of nondemographic data. The social historian is especially fortunate that the director of the 1963 census, Jeanette Bethel (Trinidadian-born but married to a Bahamian official), was a trained sociologist and a committed humanitarian, eager to ascertain just how, if not why, the Bahamas lagged so far behind other territories in the region. She was also an enthusiast who, with limited resources, recruited and inspired a remarkable band of young black workers (some of them still students at the Government High School), who pursued information beyond the expectation, and probably the intention, of the white government still in power. The advance in sophistication and scope of the 1963 census was sustained in the first census held under the black PLP government, brought forward to 1970, and further extended by the creation of a separate Department of Statistics within the Ministry of Finance in the mid-1970s, after independence. Since the 1960s, therefore, analysts of Bahamian society have an almost embarrassing richness of socioeconomic data, touching on all aspects of life besides the purely demographic.[16]

The population recorded in the census of the Bahamas soared from 84,841 in 1953 to 130,220 in 1963 and 169,534 in 1970—almost exactly doubling in seventeen years. The increase of 53.5 percent in the first ten years was the greatest proportional increase since the coming of the Loyalists in the 1780s, tailing off only slightly to an average annual increase of 4.3 percent between 1963 and 1970. Given the continuing drift toward greater employment opportunities and a more modern lifestyle, the increase of the population of New Providence continued to exceed the Bahamian average, at least until the mid-1960s, amounting to 75.4 percent in the decade before 1963 and an average of 7.1 percent a year between 1953 and 1970 (compared with 5.9 percent for the Bahamas as a whole). The proportional disparity would have been even greater had it not been for the parallel development of Freeport, Grand Bahama, which though on a much smaller scale, expanded proportionately even faster than New Providence. The population of Grand Bahama quintupled in seventeen years, rising from 4,095 in 1953 to 8,230 in 1963 and 29,943 in 1970, for an average annual increase of 10.1 percent in the decade after 1953 and a startling annual average increment of 37.9 percent between 1963 and 1970. Abaco also had a comparative surge in population in the 1950s and early 1960s because of developments in forestry, agriculture, and tourism; its population rose by 90 percent from 3,407 to 6,490 in the decade after 1953, though the expansion almost halted in the mid-1960s.

Population growth and migration patterns exacerbated existing problems in the

1950s and 1960s and created new ones. The overall population increase was to an extent accounted for by the unprecedented volume of immigration, which presented problems stemming from the overconcentration of New Providence and Grand Bahama, as well as from the ethnicities of the newcomers. At a time when very few Bahamians were emigrating (even temporarily as agricultural laborers as the Project wound down),[17] the proportion of the foreign-born in the population listed in the Bahamian census rose from 7 percent in 1953 to 12 percent in 1963 and over 14 percent (or almost 27,000) in 1970. Though the proportions of foreign-born persons in all but three Bahamian islands were below the overall average and in most were negligible, by 1963 the foreign-born constituted 13 percent of the burgeoning population of New Providence, 21 percent of the Abaconian population, and no less than 31 percent of those in Grand Bahama.

In marked contrast to previous tabulations, the largest number of the foreign-born recorded in 1963 came from Haiti, constituting 3.2 percent of the total population. Even more remarkable, 2.0 percent of those enumerated in the same year were born in the Turks and Caicos Islands, which had been separated from Jamaica since that country had achieved independence in 1962. As a consequence, the numbers of those listed as West Indian–born declined, constituting 1.1 percent of the total. In 1963, 3.4 percent of those enumerated came from the United States or Canada (now listed together) and 1.2 percent from the United Kingdom, leaving a similar number as from all other countries combined. By 1970, the official numbers had changed once more, with 5,226 from the United States now heading the list, followed by 4,741 Haitians, 4,126 from the United Kingdom and Ireland, 2,813 from Jamaica, 1,932 from Canada, 1,492 from mainland Europe, 1,026 from Central and South America, 262 from other parts of the West Indies, 200 from various parts of Asia, 115 from Australia and the Pacific, and a mere 65 from Africa.[18]

More significant than a mere numerical or proportional breakdown was that the immigrants of the 1950s and 1960s broadly fitted into two main categories, polarized in every respect. On the one hand were those who came to settle or to fill the local shortfall in the professions and in managerial and technically skilled positions. Though a few British West Indians came as professionals and specialists, the overwhelming majority of the immigrants in these categories were white; for example, 52 percent of immigrants listed as professionally qualified came from the United States and Canada and 31 percent from the United Kingdom. Such persons, even if not imbued with an ethnic arrogance (as they often were), naturally tended to behave like an elite and, consciously or not, to bolster the traditional Bahamian ruling class.

On the other hand were much poorer and less qualified folk who came to the Bahamas to fill the menial and laboring roles that an expanding economy demanded but a decreasing number of Bahamians were prepared to fill. These immigrants were almost exclusively black, including Jamaicans and Turks and Caicos Islanders, but with Haitians outnumbering all the rest. Haitians living in the Bahamas, indeed, were from the 1940s onward (when the Bahamian economy first became notably better than the Haitian) far more numerous than the official figures recorded. Though the legal Haitian immigrants boosted all figures for the poorest, least educated, and underemployed residents in the Bahamas (as well as of those to whom English was a second language) the expanding number of illegal immigrants (who may have outnumbered the legals by five to one by the 1980s), presented a barely visible specter of a new, ethnically foreign, underclass.[19]

Immigration, however, was only partially the cause for the extremely rapid increase in the Bahamian population between 1953 and 1970. The remainder was the result of a virtual explosion in the birth rate. The resulting pressure on resources, especially in conjunction with the disproportionate growth of Nassau and New Providence, was the salient problem facing the Bahamas government during the economically and politically tumultuous 1960s and 1970s.

The supervisor of the census reported in 1963 that it was almost impossible to arrive at precise figures for the natural increase and fertility of the Bahamian population because of serious deficiencies in the recording of births and immigration, but it does appear that the average annual rate of natural increase between 1953 and 1970 was as high as 37.2 per thousand of the total population and 189.7 per thousand women aged fifteen to forty.[20] These figures, which account for the very broad bases of the population pyramids for the entire Bahamas in 1963 and 1970 (44.1 percent of the entire population was under the age of fifteen in 1963 and 43.6 percent in 1970, compared with 39.8 percent in 1953), were even higher than the previous peak achieved during the transition out of slavery (reaching 32.0 per thousand between 1831 and 1834), discussed in Volume 1. Then it was the result of a combination of strong peasant-style family formation and rapidly improving conditions of health, work, and diet, in conjunction with generally rising expectations.[21] Now a similar rise in economic expectations and even more marked improvements in health, diet, and work conditions were obvious causes, though there were less positive factors associated with the disruption of traditional family life resulting from widespread migration and with a concomitant decline of moral standards (see Table 12).

So general was the natural increase of the Bahamian population in the 1950s that despite an acceleration in the rate of internal migration, the majority of the islands did not suffer a net decrease in that decade (Map 11). Acklins Island, Crooked Island, and Cat Island (which lost 8, 4, and 2 percent of their people respectively) were exceptions to the rule, which saw former losers Eleuthera, Exuma, and Long Island gain 19, 18, and 11 percent more inhabitants respectively. The prevalence of migration, however, determined that the balance of the population in many Out Islands was increasingly distorted, with disproportionate numbers of the very young and the elderly because of the tendency to leave those too young to work for wages in the custody of grandparents who were too elderly to find profitable employment elsewhere. This demographic imbalance, coupled with increasing migration, including that of whole families, decreased Out Island populations again during the 1960s. Between 1963 and 1970, the total population of all islands other than New Providence, Grand Bahama, and Andros (which together increased from 96,597 to 146,817, or by 52 percent) fell from 33,623 to 32,717, or by 2.7 percent, with a decline in the combined population of the islands to the south of Nassau from 16,116 to 14,733, or by 8.6 percent.

Even though internal migrants made up a large proportion of the population of New Providence, the relatively better material if not moral conditions in the Bahamian metropolis determined that the natural increase of its population was almost as large as for the Bahamas overall. Moreover, by the 1960s, the trend of migration toward New Providence was of such long standing that associated groups of migrants had established their own mini-communities in the metropole, a trend that showed signs of replication in Grand Bahama from the beginning. Of the 30 percent of the population of New Providence who had been born in the Out

Table 12. *Population, 1901–1990: Whole Bahamas and Separate Islands*

	1901	1911	1921	1931	1943	1953	1963	1970	1980	1990
All Bahamas	53,735	55,944	53,031	59,828	68,846	84,841	130,220	168,812	209,505	255,095
New Providence	12,534	13,554	12,975	19,756	29,391	46,125	80,907	101,503	135,437	172,196
Harbour Island	1,232	1,031	917	793	769	840	997		1,133	1,219
Eleuthera	8,733	6,533	6,048	6,168	6,430	6,070	7,247	9,468	8,331	7,993
Spanish Wells	534	555	582	566	665	686	849		1,167	1,372
Abaco	3,314	4,463	3,993	4,233	3,461	3,407	6,490	6,501	7,271	10,034
Grand Bahama	1,269	1,824	1,695	2,241	2,333	4,095	8,230	25,859	33,102	40,898
Berry Islands	382	487	328	222	403	327	266	443	509	628
Bimini	563	505	638	756	725	1,330	1,658	1,503	1,411	1,639
Andros	6,347	7,545	6,976	7,071	6,718	7,136	7,461	8,845	8,307	8,187
Exuma	3,086	3,465	3,730	3,774	3,784	2,919	3,440	3,767	3,670	3,356
Cat Island	4,658	5,072	4,273	3,959	3,870	3,201	3,131	2,657	2,215	1,698
Long Island	3,562	4,159	4,659	4,515	4,564	3,755	4,176	3,861	3,404	2,954
San Salvador	667	617	686	675	693	694	968	856	747	465
Rum Cay	529	430	338	252	219	133	77		73	53
Ragged Island	365	353	366	424	417	320	371	208	164	89
Crooked Island	1,597	1,541	1,481	1,329	1,078	836	766	689	518	412
Long Cay	499	376	166	144	101	80	22	26	35	
Acklins	1,565	1,733	1,811	1,765	1,744	1,273	1,217	936	618	405
Mayaguana	335	358	432	518	591	615	707	581	464	312
Inagua	1,453	1,343	937	667	890	999	1,240	1,109	924	985

Sources: Bahamas Censuses, 1901–1990. Harbour Island and Spanish Wells were combined with Eleuthera, and Rum Cay was combined with San Salvador, 1970; Long Cay was combined with Crooked Island, 1990.

Islands in 1963 (somewhat down from 1953), 21 percent came from nearby (though not least impoverished) Andros, 13 percent from Eleuthera, 12 percent from Long Island, 11 percent from Cat Island, and 10 percent from Exuma. Most of these migrants congregated near their fellow islanders in sections of Over the Hill Nassau, if not in the very houses and yards of previously migrated family members. Most of the major islands of origin had spontaneously formed membership associations for socialization and mutual assistance.

Social and Working Conditions Measured, 1963–1973

A more negative aspect of this concerted migration and subtle mosaic building was that migrants, being poor, at least initially, tended to gravitate toward the poorer sections of town and to overcrowd the existing houses and facilities. This process became even more marked in the environs of Freeport as well as the bleakest sections of Over the Hill Nassau among the accelerating numbers of the poorest of the poor immigrants, the Haitians. Despite considerable Out Island solidarity and mutual assistance (and even more remarkable networking among the Haitians), the realities of migration—as is apparent from the growing range of statistics gathered by the Bahamian censuses—led to a spiral of deterioration in social conditions, in which overcrowding, poor facilities, and disrupted families fed on each other.

Though as many as 80 percent of all Bahamians lived in single-family households in 1963 and a further 14 percent in households containing two or more family units, indicators of family dysfunction included the declining percentage of those formally married, the trend toward women having their first child earlier, and the upswing in the proportion of technically illegitimate births that was to reach alarming proportions in the 1980s.[22] In 1963, 29 percent of the total population was formally married, down from 34 percent in 1953. The proportion of common law rather than formal unions and of short-lived marital unions increased steadily. Formal divorce remained relatively rare because of legal complications and expense. As many as 23 percent of formal marriages were of under five years' duration in 1963, but 56 percent had lasted more than ten years; half of all common law unions had lasted no more than five years and only 5 percent more than two decades. Of 5,076 live births recorded in the year before the 1963 census, 3,319 (65 percent) were technically legitimate and 1,937 (35 percent) illegitimate. Of the latter, 24 percent were born to women in stable though common law relationships, 54 percent to women who had never been in a married or common law union, and 16 percent to women no longer living with former partners. By 1963, 31 percent of all mothers had had their first child before they were nineteen years old and 6 percent became mothers for the first time before the age of sixteen.

By 1960 the Bahamas was generating a tremendous amount of wealth. The statistical window-dressers of Bay Street's ruling UBP used such unreliable indexes as annual per capita GDP averages to claim that Bahamians (at U.S.$8,448 per capita in 1960 and U.S.$10,737 in 1970) were enjoying a level of prosperity twice that of Trinidad, between three and four times that of Barbados, four times that of Jamaica, and no less than twenty-five times that of Haiti.[23] Such figures, though, gravely understated the unevenness with which the wealth generated was translated into

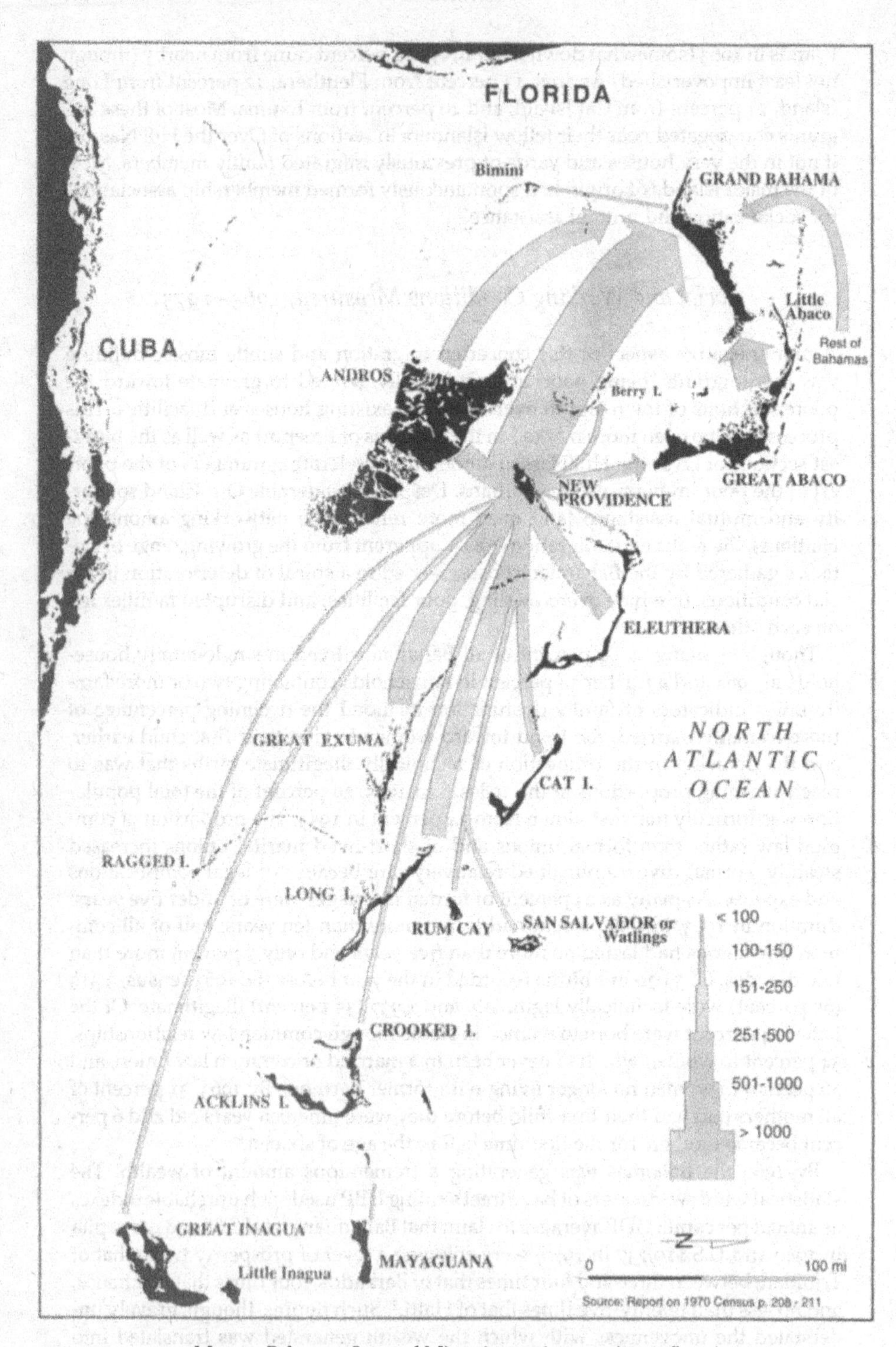

Map 11. Bahamas: Internal Migration, 1960–1970 (net inflows)

material improvements and shared among the people. Material conditions improved more slowly than the Bahamian population and the benefits of improvements were so unequally divided that the gap between the more and least fortunate widened, as is apparent in the statistics of employment and educational levels (and the relationship between them), as well as in those dealing with housing and such related services as water, electricity, and sewerage.

By 1963, the overall literacy level in the Bahamas was as high as in many of the most favored Caribbean territories—91 percent of those over ten years of age—despite the immigration of many illiterate Haitians. But the disproportion between those with basic and those with secondary education or better was very large, and, in the case of the Out Islands, extreme. In New Providence, 71 percent of persons older than ten had received only a primary school education (86 percent spent at least six years in school), 21 percent went on to secondary education, and 2 percent obtained professional qualifications. Only 4 percent had had no education whatsoever. For the Out Islands, however, despite the skewing of the figures by the number of well-educated immigrants in such islands as Grand Bahama, Abaco, and Eleuthera, only 3 percent of those with primary education went on to the secondary level, and less than 1 percent obtained professional qualifications. Twice as many as in New Providence received no education, 8 percent. Overall, the proportions of Bahamians proceeding from primary to secondary and from primary through to tertiary education (1:7 and 1:65), though considerably higher than in 1960, when the Houghton Report claimed the figures were worse than Haiti's, were still among the lowest in the Caribbean.[24]

Substantial educational improvements were made by 1973 (some of them exaggerated by the redesignation of senior as secondary schools), but they were not commensurate with population or economic growth or necessarily related to the needs of Bahamian society. Economic prosperity, paradoxically, brought a regression because the increased availability of jobs at every level made educational achievement less important, particularly in the lower strata of employment. Opportunities in the most prestigious forms of employment had never been better than in the 1960s and 1970s for those fully qualified, and at lower levels many of the best opportunities went to those who had received the best available local education. Although these opportunities drained persons away from the necessary jobs carrying less prestige (such as teaching) or involving harsh labor for mediocre rewards (agriculture, old-fashioned fishing, or laboring on construction sites), in certain respects education was unnecessary or even irrelevant. In the economic expansion of the 1960s, people did well enough financially in many spheres of activity without the benefit of much education, and the demand for persons to fill jobs not requiring any formal education outran the supply. Such conditions and attitudes, however, were to be problematic in the longer term, especially once an economic downturn occurred.

Employment statistics in 1963 and 1970 confirmed significant trends that were already well under way. Though the number of those engaged in fishing stayed steady and the proportion fishing on their own behalf increased to a majority because of the tourist and other increasingly profitable markets, those listed as dependent on agriculture declined at an even greater rate than the general depopulation of the Out Islands. Some major agricultural projects were initiated in Abaco, Grand Bahama, Andros, and Eleuthera, but the majority of those persons listed as engaged in agriculture were small farmers, many living not much above the subsistence level. Yet despite the inclusion of individual small-scale farming as an employment category, the rate of those without any employment listed was the highest in the poorest islands, especially Exuma, Rum Cay, Ragged Island, and Mayaguana, where only 74 percent of men were reported having gainful employment.

Construction, notably in New Providence and Grand Bahama, was the major employer of manual wage labor, along with the lumber industry in Abaco and Andros and salt production in Inagua. But the numbers of those classified as craftsmen and technicians and those engaged in personal and transport services exceeded simple laborers. Those in the third category were mainly servicing the tourist industry, including the self-employed taxi drivers, who were among the most aggressively enterprising of New Bahamians. Tourism also employed, directly or indirectly, as many as a third of all gainfully employed women. Furthermore, tourism, along with the expanding market in general, largely accounted for the steady increase of those engaged in commercial services. The numbers of professionals increased steadily before 1963 and more rapidly thereafter, but there had been a proportionately greater increase by 1963 in the numbers in government employment (aided in part by the inclusion of workers in the government-subsidized Bahamas Airways), and this expansion was to accelerate by the 1970s in proportionate as well as absolute terms.

Official statistics indicated an improving job market responding to a buoyant and expanding economy. Reading between the lines, however, the situation appears less benign and more class-riven than at first glance. Most of the wage labor, mainly recruited from the least educated members of society, was in the nature of casual employment. As is often the case with official statistics, the figures for female employment were misleading if not disingenuous. A very high proportion of women were listed as engaged in "duties in the home," which not only disguised true employment levels but illustrated the way employers could take advantage of traditional gender roles to retard equality and divide the workforce competitively.

A scrutiny of the distinctions made between those employed by others and the self-employed reveals even more insidious situations. The high proportion of the latter indicates an independent and enterprising people who would rather work for themselves, and on their own terms, than for others, which was generally true. But by including all small subsistence farmers, odd jobbers, hucksters, and craftspersons working on their own (such as women engaged in straw work), the classifications disguised the existence of persons who had no options and were victims of the system. A more accurate computation of the self-employed, especially if besides separating the self-employed from businesspersons it distinguished the substantial business owners and employers from the ever-growing number of small businessmen, would show how capitalist class relations prevailed even after the traditional Bay Street oligarchy was overthrown.

Material Conditions Under Majority Rule, 1963–1973

Material conditions, though considerably improved in the 1960s, were even more problematic. This was one of the major revelations of the Bethel census of 1963, and the most euphoric and ingenious later statistics could not conceal the degree to which material conditions lagged behind economic expansion and political change.

In 1953, when, it was claimed, 97 percent of all Bahamian houses were surveyed, 62 percent were said to be of wood or stucco construction and 38 percent made of concrete blocks. In New Providence, the proportion of wooden houses was far higher at 78 percent. At that time, only 23 percent of Bahamian houses had running water, mostly from their own wells or rainwater tanks. In New Providence as many as 71 percent had no running water, nearly all depending on public standpipes. In the Out Islands, the majority drew their water from public wells, and only three islands had public standpipe systems. Though about 22 percent of New Providence houses had some sort of waterborne sewage disposal system, such a refinement was almost unknown in the Out Islands, and less than 8 percent of all Bahamian houses had septic tanks for the disposal of sewage. Figures for electricity connections were not provided, probably because their rarity was an embarrassment. Over the Hill in Nassau a majority of houses were not wired, and most of the Out Islands continued to exist virtually in a pre-electric age.

In 1963, 56 percent of all Bahamian houses were of wood construction, some 14 percent of stucco or loose freestone, and 26 percent of concrete blocks. In New Providence, the proportion of concrete-block houses had risen to 30 percent, and 62 percent were constructed of wood. Some 37 percent of New Providence houses now had piped public water, but 12 percent depended on private wells or tanks, and 50 percent had only the public standpipes. Beyond New Providence, only in Eleuthera, Harbour Island, Spanish Wells, and Grand Bahama had there been notable improvements in the public water supply. The 1963 census laconically noted that the statistics "not only underline the importance of pit toilets in the Bahamas, but also revealed that in some Out Island districts, a large number of households have no toilet facilities at all and are dependent on such commercial arrangements as exist." Electricity supplies "were the exception rather than the rule in many Out Island districts and where the electricity was available it was due to the efforts of private individuals with generators on their premises." Even in New Providence as many as 27 percent of all dwellings were not connected.

Though the number of solidly built concrete-block houses with modern amenities steadily increased through the late 1960s and 1970s, especially in New Providence, Grand Bahama, and Abaco, construction did not keep pace with population growth or necessarily upgrade existing properties. The most notable feature was the rapid rippling out of Nassau into the nearer parts of New Providence, leaving the older areas more crowded and dilapidated than before. The provision of public utilities, moreover, lagged behind the construction of new houses. Considerable efforts were made to increase water and electricity supplies but with inadequate results, and only in central Freeport-Lucaya was anything like a modern sewerage system installed.

Thanks to the addition of distillation plants to the traditional well fields, the water supply to New Providence reached 2.1 billion gallons a year by 1973, but it fell to 1.8 billion gallons by 1980, or by 15 percent, despite a population increase of at least 41 percent. Similarly, the Bahamas Electricity Corporation presented impressive statistics for the increased capacity, production, and number of consumers throughout the Bahamas up to and beyond 1973 but failed to mention relative failures. Between 1971 and 1980 total capacity rose from 228.9 milliwatts to 255.6, or

Surviving eighteenth-century town houses in Nassau. *Above*, Balcony House, Market Street, built of soft American cedar, probably by shipwrights in the early Loyalist period. *Middle*, The Deanery, Cumberland Street, dating from about 1710: a stone core with latticed upper gallery to catch the breeze and shade the sun. *Below*, Georgeside, George Street, built around 1750, with all-round galleries on first two levels and typical Bahamian dormers. All three houses had detached kitchens and domestic slaves' quarters. From Robert Douglas, *Island Heritage: Architecture of the Bahamas* (Nassau, 1992), used with permission.

by 11.7 percent and the number of consumers by 19.3 percent from 42,059 to 50,189, but both these increases were far short of a population rise of 23.6 percent over the same period. Moreover, much of the improvement occurred in Grand Bahama, where the electricity generated almost equaled (and generating capacity exceeded) that of New Providence, with a fifth the number of consumers. Only nine other islands were listed as being supplied with electricity by the public corporation, and the total generated rose only from 34.6 to 59.5 milliwatt hours between 1971 and 1980, no more than 17 percent of the current consumed by either New Providence or Grand Bahama alone.

Because new and larger homes were built, mainly by members of the expanding Bahamian middle class, the average occupancy by number of rooms remained static or improved, but such average statistics disguised the fact that generally the oldest, flimsiest, and smallest houses were most overcrowded. Another disguised statistic with even more significant hidden effects was the increase in the proportion of rented accommodations, especially in the most rapidly expanding areas. In a limited survey, the 1953 census determined that in the Out Islands householders were "to a large extent owners of their dwellings" and that in New Providence 63 percent of householders owned their houses and 36 percent lived in rented premises. By 1963, only 55 percent of all Bahamian houses were owner-occupied, 35 percent were rented privately, and 5 percent were occupied by employees rent-free. In New Providence, moreover, the 43 percent of householders in owner-occupied premises was exceeded by the 47 percent who lived in rented accommodations.

The trend disclosed by these statistics denoted some decidedly antisocial effects. The rentier class was expanding at different levels, at the upper extreme reinforcing the economic dominance of Bay Street capitalists (including the first premier himself) and at the lowest extreme facilitating the rack-renting of the poorest immigrants. Even more insidious, most notably in the case of Freeport-Lucaya, a form of unofficial segregation (albeit, as in South Africa, accompanied by canting paternalist rhetoric) was evident. The highest level of employees (overwhelmingly white) were zoned apart from freeholders but assigned high-quality rental housing; regularly employed laborers and menials (mainly blacks) were housed in company-owned apartments or virtual barracks; and the casual labor force was excluded from company property and crammed into ghettos dominated by rack renters.

From the above information it is clear that the gradual improvement in the quantity and sophistication of social statistics is not necessarily a corollary of an improvement in the quality of life; it often reveals the reverse. With the exception of failing to record accurately the numbers of illegal Haitian immigrants, who, of course, tried to steer as clear of official enumerators as possible (and who may have outnumbered all other foreign-born persons living in the Bahamas by 1973), the Bahamian census-takers and statisticians had ample nondemographic and nonstatistical evidence to recognize all salient problems well before the achievement of political independence in 1973. Whether the steady accumulation of evidence and improvement in its accuracy was ever accompanied by an official capacity or willingness to arrest and deflect dangerous trends or to remedy serious problems, is quite a different matter, as will be discussed in Chapters 11 to 13.

7

New Century, Minimal Changes, 1900–1920

Sketches of Summerland: Nassau in 1901

During the first year of the twentieth century and the last of the long reign of Queen Victoria the first real book was published in the Bahamas. George J. H. Northcroft's *Sketches of Summerland*, printed and published at the office of the *Nassau Guardian*, at the corner of Frederick and East Hill Streets, Nassau, also claimed to be the first book on the Bahamas written by one who had lived in the colony for a considerable time and was familiar with most of the islands.[1] Northcroft, an aspiring poet who touchingly dedicated his work "to her I wooed and won in Summerland," was at pains to preserve "the picturesque crudities of a life fast disappearing" in the face of the "rising tide of modern conventionality" that was sweeping over the islands. His account, however, showed that very little had changed over the previous two decades and painted a picture that was to change only imperceptibly until after World War I. This distant and almost static world, fixed for us by the earliest photographs and picture postcards, is also artlessly conveyed by the forty-eight pages of local advertisements which author and publisher cannily appended to their little volume.

The prevailing impression is of a scattered and impoverished colony completely dominated by its small metropolitan capital city, which was in turn under the economic domination of a handful of white merchants on Bay Street. The decision to advertise in a publication based in Nassau and aimed toward urban buyers and visitors is not an accurate index of the relative importance of New Providence and the Bahamas Out Islands. But it is significant that, with the exception of Inagua, only three Out Island enterprises considered advertising worthwhile. These were a small guest house at Harbour Island called the Sea View Hotel (promising "excellent boating and fishing, picturesque walks in the neighbourhood, unrivalled sea bathing, and a good public library" for ten dollars a week, with "special arrangements made with families"); an Acklins Island exporter with the Bermudian name of Darrell, soliciting orders for "barks, viz. cascarilla, canella alba, snake root," lignum vitae, dye-woods, and sponges ("known to be superior to any other of the Bahamas"); and one José G. Maura (a Cuban immigrant), shipping and commission merchant of Albert Town, Long Cay, who was also the recruiting agent for the Atlas and Munson steamship lines and the Panama Railroad Company.

The recruiting of migrant labor, which, along with the now torpid salt industry, had made Mathew Town a distant second to Nassau in importance, was the object of the remarkable dozen advertisers Northcroft managed to solicit from Inagua.

All were white or near-white merchants, some of Haitian provenance, but most with Nassau connections—a miniature Bay Street clique, who combined the functions of importing provisions and supplies and exporting produce on commission, retail selling on credit, ship broking, and acting as agents for labor employers, shippers, and insurers. Though one D. D. Sargent was consular agent for the United States (and "Correspondent of the American Board of Underwriters"), the most prominent local merchants in 1900 and for the next thirty-five years were the Symonette brothers, Arthur and William. They called themselves ship brokers and commission merchants and advertised the importation of "Provisions, Groceries, Dry Goods, Hardware, Glassware, Tobaccos, &c," the export of "Coffee, Mahogany, Dye-Woods, Lignumvitae, Satin Wood, and Salt," and the furnishing of "Stevedore Labourers . . . to Steamship Lines, and for Contract Work in Foreign Countries." Besides specializing in tortoiseshell (mainly the raw material), they were the proprietors of the impressively named Excelsior Cigar Factory and sole agents for a French wine shipper and a hardware wholesaler from Cleveland, Ohio. Their cable address was that of a merchant house at Port-de-Paix in nearby Haiti.

The mercantile nexus in Nassau was relatively grander and more diverse, though minuscule when compared with mainland American or European ports or even Havana and Santiago in Cuba or Kingston, Jamaica. Clustered round the Bank of Nassau ("Capital paid up £10,000, with power to increase to £25,000") were the twenty or so substantial mercantile establishments, their owners' surnames an almost complete roll call of white Bahamian families and the owners themselves providing the entire masthead of officials and directors of the bank.[2] One of the most prominent merchants was the Hon. R. H. Sawyer, CMG, member of the Legislative Council, president and managing director of the bank, whose firm, besides the usual import, export, and retail business, provided coal and water to visiting steamships and was agent for the major shipping lines between Nassau, New York, Cuba, and Miami and for the recently formed Inter-Insular Mail Line, intended (though it did not quickly succeed) to draw the islands closer and more profitably together.

Other white general merchants were also insurance agents, as was George B. Adderley (not to be confused with the black shopkeeper of the same surname), who, besides exporting sponge, dye-woods, and salt and dealing wholesale in "provisions, breadstuffs, liquor, wines, lumber, shingles & cabinet woods," was agent for the Northern Fire and Life Assurance Company of London. Only one insurance company advertised separately, Sun Life of Canada, foreshadowing the gradual extension of a subimperial capitalistic network, though the local agent, Alfred E. Moseley, son of the English-born founder of the *Nassau Guardian* in 1844, was undoubtedly a member of the Bay Street establishment.[3]

Although the Nassau mercantile oligarchy was dependent on manufacturers and suppliers in the capitalist metropoles (ever eager to exploit the unequal equation between Bahamian export produce and needs for imports), it sustained its power by focusing on and controlling the flow of local imports and exports, dominating local legislation, and exploiting the dependency of Out Islanders on Nassau. With such extensive influence within a restricted orbit, the chief Nassau merchants showed great versatility in exploring all avenues of possible profit, including the extension of tourism occasioned by the recent building of the Colonial Hotel on the site of old Fort Nassau. The pineapple canning firm of J. S. Johnson was one of the few with establishments on more than one island. Its factories in Nassau and Eleuthera produced thousands of cases of its Bahama and Columbian brands of whole, sliced, cored, and grated pineapples and juice. But nearly all the major Nassau houses were involved in the collection and export of Out Island produce and served as wholesale suppliers to Out Island retailers, and many were also outfitters and owners of sponge-fishing boats and (like J. S. Johnson) investors in sisal production.

Even in Nassau itself, many merchants were ingeniously diversified, none more so than the firm of J. L. Saunders & Brother. In their full-page advertisement they somewhat wordily desired

> to call attention to the various businesses in which they are engaged. Their large, amply supplied store at the corner of *Bay and George Streets*, where a full supply of Family Groceries, Provisions and Liquors are always in Stock. Their Dry Goods Store in *Delancy Town* where a line of Staple and Fancy Goods will meet the need and gratify the taste of all.
>
> The Casino at *Hog Island* too well known to require any special commendation here. Their fine Steam Launch *Alicia* which beside serving as a ferry between the shore and the Casino is also available for pleasure parties desiring to visit the *Sea Gardens* or any other place of interest in our waters.
>
> Their *Cigar Manufactory* whose reputation for producing excellent cigars is yearly increasing. They use the best selections of *Sumatra and Havana* tobacco in their fancy lines.
>
> A Barber Shop on Bay Street, three doors from the Colonial, and last but not least their Livery Stables in Union Street, where Rubber Tired Carriages and fine American Horses make driving a luxury and completes the list.
>
> With the exception of their Quarries at *Fort Fincastle* where Stone of any dimensions can be readily obtained, to which they invite the attention and patronage of the public.

A traditional Bay Street shop in 1900 was a modest emporium—a larger version of Out Island general stores—selling foodstuffs, liquor, hardware, and clothing, usually at separate counters, with perhaps a bar out back. But Bay Street showed some faint signs of modernization, both in what was sold and in specialization. Besides imported goods scarcely changed over the previous century, merchants now advertised sewing machines, typewriters, acetylene lamps, ice cream makers, bicycles, and sporting gear for cricket, tennis, and golf, though none of these were novelties to visitors in 1900. Similarly, photography had reached Nassau, but decades after it had become popular in the United States.

Some entire stores were now devoted to groceries (including liquor), to hardware, or to clothing. The Brick Store, opposite the cathedral, owned by T. H. C. Lofthouse, aspired to be a department store in the New York or London fashion, with separate sections for gentlemen's clothing, house furnishings, millinery, notions, and dress goods on the ground floor and ladies' dressmaking and millinery rooms on the second, "presided over by Miss Madden, a first class Modiste from New York, who is prepared to furnish from Ordinary to the Most Elegant up to date Costumes." Further east, on Bay Street, there was a shoe store destined to survive into the 1990s (Williams's), and another that specialized in shoes and hats (a ground floor annex to the Globe House "family hotel, bath houses and boat depot").

Again on the American model, there were no less than four competing drugstores, of which the Bahamas Dispensary was the oldest (founded in 1855), but Cole's Pharmacy, owned by a former director of the Board of Education, George M. Cole, was, like the City Pharmacy, to be much longer lived. Cole advertised "Pure Drugs, Chemicals and Patent Medicines in large variety. Agency for Kickapoo Indian Medicines and Chamberlain's Remedies. Soda and Mineral Waters. Perfumes. Rubber Goods, Sponges & Chamois Skins." The Dispensary added to such stock in trade "Briar Pipes, Cigars, English and American Toilet Soaps and Perfumery, Ladies' Bathing Caps, Sanitary Towelettes, and other Toilet Articles such as are to be obtained at an up to date Drug Store." Less progressively, the Dispensary suggested that "if you want to secure one of the most interesting Photos of some of the old Africans who were formerly slaves in the Bahamas, come and have a look at our collection of beauties."

Clearly the clientele addressed here, local or visiting, was as white as the ownership. The same was true of the two bookstores (one run in conjunction with the *Nassau Guardian,* selling Bibles and "books by standard authors in great variety," as well as *Sketches of Summerland* and guides to the Bahamas), the two photographers, and such tourist attractions as the Naiad, owned by Joseph Kemp ("Has the largest, finest and most varied assortment of Marine Curiosities that is possible to find in the Bahamas"), and Ernest Bethel's seaside pavilion, the Saratoga, which billed itself "For Fruit, Bathing, Fishing and Pleasure." Open every day during the winter season, it was probably the only place in the Bahamas "illuminated at night by electricity." Each evening it acted as a kind of prototype nightclub; its "Foreign and Domestic attractions changed weekly." Besides hiring out steam launches, sailing yachts, and rowboats "at moderate prices," the enterprising Bethel ran the glass-bottomed barge *Saratoga,* said to hold five hundred people, from Rawson Square to the Sea Gardens and back at sixpence a trip.

The Bay Street shops, with their poor-white clerks, catered to whoever could pay—though the black populace was expected to wait politely behind white customers. Nonwhite would-be merchants such as W. P. Adderley, the Dupuch brothers of East Bay Street, Joseph Roker of Duke Street, William B. North, or N. A. Bosfield of Delancy Town could compete with those who commanded the wholesale trade and most of the foreign agencies and offered their customers long-term credit only with great difficulty. Their modest shops were for the most part on the fringes of town. Other nonwhite petty businessmen similarly had to look for interstices in the Bay Street edifice—few of them besides David Patton could advertise—as tailors, carpenters, undertakers, contractors, tortoiseshell craftsmen, or hirers of small boats or carriages.

Almost all advertisers in 1900, of whatever color or class, were Bahamian-born. A Cuban merchant in Inagua, a Spanish-sounding undertaker, and the Cuban Pharmacy in Nassau were evidence of a minor middle-class migration resulting from the political turmoil in Cuba in the last third of the nineteenth century. But the Greeks who were increasingly involved in the buying, packaging, and exportation of sponges were not yet sufficiently established to consider advertising economic, and the itinerant "Syrians" (that is, Lebanese) whom Northcroft had noted peddling their wares in Eleuthera (and who were to be found in many corners of the British and French empires) had not yet graduated to owning shops—with the

Plantains, pumpkins, yams, and thyme. Nassau's downtown market, around 1900.
"Doc" Sands photograph, Michael Craton Collection.

single exception of a Mr. Arteaga, who partnered a Bahamian named Albury selling "all kinds of Aerated Waters."[4] Despite their considerable numbers in other parts of the West Indies, there seem to have been no Chinese or Sephardic Jews yet in business in the Bahamas, though the E. F. Berger listed as owner of the City Pharmacy may have been an Ashkenazi Jew from the United States. The most exceptional American in business, however, was the pioneer photographer Jacob Frank Coonley (ca. 1830–1908).

Coonley was brought up in Syracuse, New York, and trained as a graphic artist but moved into the new profession of photography as early as 1856. At first mainly an imitator of Mathew Brady, Coonley came into his own during the American Civil War and immediately after, working from a studio and gallery in New York City. He first visited Nassau in the 1870s, fell in love with the place as had Winslow Homer and the poet Bliss Carman but, unlike them, moved there to settle. Coonley set up a studio on Bay Street by 1880, then moved into the Masonic Temple building when it was completed in 1885. Coonley specialized in townscapes, landscapes, and genre pictures as well as portraiture and made several trips to Cuba on behalf of the New York Museum of Natural History. He lived in Nassau for the rest of his life but retired from business in 1904, leaving the field open for competition between his chief rival, William Pinder (agent for Kodak in 1900), and the apprentice who was to become one of the most distinguished native Bahamian photographers, the Eleuthera-born James Osborne "Doc" Sands (1885–1978).[5]

Though they made their living chiefly from portraiture, Coonley, Pinder, and

Sands also advertised photographs of "Native Characters, Costumes, Summer and Winter Sceneries" for the tourist market. These pictures, adopted and augmented by postcard makers such as the Detroit Photographic Company, provide the first wide-ranging visual record of the Bahamas to add to—and sometimes correct—written accounts such as Northcroft's. The postcards naturally featured Nassau's most famous landmarks and scenes that tourists would wish to remember and convey to their friends: the brand-new Colonial Hotel, Paradise Beach and the Sea Gardens, the forts and churches, Government House and the statue of Columbus, the Queen's Staircase, the official buildings fronting Rawson Square (before and after the erection in 1905 of the fine white marble statue of Queen Victoria on her throne), and the famous ancient silk cotton tree nearby. The impression conveyed is of palm-lined avenues, white walls covered with bougainvillas, and a sunbaked unpaved white limestone Bay Street, cleared as if for a movie set save for the seemingly almost posed, soon-to-be clichéd motifs of hankie-headed market woman, horse carriage, donkey cart, and blue (later white)-coated policeman officiously directing imaginary traffic.

But when the camera's unbiased eye betrayed the photographer's caution, or the photographer ventured beyond the neat if unsophisticated downtown area and sought to depict the quaint natives and their lifestyle, a harsher reality unconsciously obtruded. Shops in the photographs are smaller and shabbier than their advertisements suggest, the ordinary people are dusty, ragged, barefoot, and not always smiling. The meager wares displayed by the market women suggest a few pennies painstakingly earned, and the fishing, trading, and sponging vessels crowded at the market wharf are tatterdemalion, suggesting a lack rather than plenitude of employment and desperate competition among those who sailed them. In memorable images, a sullen herd of black men and women clip sponges under the watchful eye of a white man in a solar topee, and similarly hatted white owners proprietarily stand amid soldierlike ranks of sisal cactus or pineapples without a laboring black in sight. Pictures of "Bahama natives" taken in their homes Over the Hill accurately show the varieties of house (wattle-and-daub, boxes of boards raised on boulders or sticks, or crude freestone constructions) but poignantly emphasize the hopeless poverty of the people and their home environment—more like the poorest Out Islands than the suburbs of Nassau City and closer to "darkest Africa" than to any parts of the countries from which the tourists came. Such images no doubt were (may still be) comfortable to racists and naive sentimentalists, but they grate painfully against a modern liberal sensibility.[6]

First Hints of Modernization: Before 1901

Snapshots fix the past and its people, but a chronological succession of early photographs and postcards is also like a suitably slow-paced movie illustrating the minimal changes that occurred in Nassau and the rest of the Bahamas between 1900 and World War I. One important innovation was already long in place. The telegraph cable between Cable Beach, New Providence, and Jupiter, Florida, had been operating since 1892, putting the colonial and imperial governments (at least in theory) in almost instant communication, and ensuring that the local newspapers could print important items of world news within days instead of weeks. The cable, however, was expensive to maintain and often faulty and was superseded by the already more reliable system of wireless telegraphy in 1913. Morse code messages were sent and received at the imperial rate of a penny a word until voice transmissions were made feasible by improved radios in the 1930s.[7]

More of a luxury were the first local telephones installed after the passing of a special act in 1906. The initial 150 subscribers, all located around central Bay Street and many on party lines, were connected through a central switchboard, serviced by six operators—all but one of them whites. The system expanded slowly into the eastern and western suburbs until an automatic exchange was introduced and set up in the Vendue House at the foot of George Street in 1916. This exchange had a capacity of 600 lines, but as late as 1918 there were only 400 subscribers in Nassau with 412 telephones, and the average number of calls a day was a mere 1,866.[8]

Electricity became available at much the same time and spread little faster. The Electric Light Act was passed in 1907, but it was not until 1909 that a gas generator was installed in the Vendue House, producing a weak direct current. The ceremonial illumination of the cathedral, kirk, Trinity Methodist Church, Nassau Club, Colonial Hotel, and a few dozen streetlights on June 16, 1909, created quite a stir, but as late as 1916 there were still only 443 subscribers and 276 streetlights, mostly on Bay and Shirley Streets. Because of the slow spread of the service, even some of the wealthiest elite had to wait until a major expansion and reorganization in 1922 before they enjoyed electric power. The middling people and black majority who could afford neither the cost of wiring nor the rates continued to depend on kerosene lamps for another decade or two.[9]

The introduction of electricity, however, made possible at least two other important innovations: the local manufacture of ice and the advent of the cinema. For more than half a century, under a system controlled and subsidized by the government, bulk ice had been imported from Maine during the winter and stored in a thick-walled, partly subterranean ice house located between the Fish Market and Sponge Exchange on central Bay Street. The contract to obtain, store, and distribute the ice was granted by the government to a single Bay Street merchant because only a monopoly (with a government guarantee) was thought to make the business worthwhile. But by 1913, ice was being produced in Nassau, immediately outdating the traditional system. From being a luxury, ice became almost a necessity. Wealthy and middle-class Nassauvians nearly all now had their iceboxes; ice was delivered by dray or collected by servants. At least until private kerosene and electric refrigerators became common in the 1940s, ice was a vital and potentially lucrative enterprise, which government, on the pretext of guaranteeing supply and preventing profiteering, continued to grant to favored Bay Street merchants on a monopoly contract.[10]

Government also became concerned, for different reasons, in the control of the newly introduced moving pictures. The first movies were shown in Nassau in 1911, and in the following year the Cinematograph Act required a license from the police commandant for the public exhibition of films. It also stipulated the type of movie that could be shown and gave the governor power to make rules—suggesting that the concern to censor socially dangerous content was more important than a desire to control a potentially valuable commercial asset. By 1913, Nassau had two motion picture theaters, though only a minority had the money to patronize them.[11]

Fittingly, the person most responsible for introducing the wonders of electricity

Pomp and majesty in the new motor age. Governor Grey-Wilson leaves Rawson Square for Government House in his Rochet-Schneider after the official opening of the House of Assembly in 1906. John Fondas Collection, Bahamas Archives.

to Nassau was an American. Patrick H. Burns, born in Cleveland, Ohio, in 1869, had worked for Western Union as a telegraph messenger, clerk, and telegrapher from 1883 until he was sent to oversee the installation of the telegraph cable from Jupiter to Nassau in 1892. He was appointed official superintendent of telegraphs the same year, responsible for the installation and management of telephones, electric power, and the wireless telegraphy link. When they were amalgamated in 1913, Governor George Haddon-Smith appointed him superintendent of all three services. Burns (who lived the rest of his life in Nassau) left as his most visible monument the rows of pine poles and wires radiating from the ancient Vendue House that disfigure Bay Street in postcards dating from 1907 onward.[12]

Another novelty even more portentous appearing in the same postcards was the automobile. The very first car in Nassau was a tiller-steered three-horsepower Oldsmobile imported by the U.S. vice consul Henry Mostyn in 1905. Every time it passed on the street people ran out to stare. By 1908 there were perhaps six cars in the Bahamas, of which Governor William Grey-Wilson's Rochet-Schneider was by far the grandest—an open four-seater landau, redolent of upholstered leather, purple paint, and polished brass. A postcard of the time shows the vehicle leaving the House of Assembly after the official opening; a flat-capped chauffeur is hunched over the almost upright steering wheel, beside him a white-helmeted police guard, and in the back the uniformed governor and his aide-de-camp, Grey-Wilson sporting his medals and splendid gubernatorial ostrich plumes.[13]

No licenses were deemed necessary until the Motor Car Act of 1908, which decreed a car license fee of £5, driving license fee of £1, and a minimum age of seventeen for drivers. No driving test was stipulated, though the maximum speed allowed was twenty miles per hour and ten miles per hour in town. Cars were required to have a light attached that would signal their approach during the hours of darkness and also illuminate their license plate—as if it were difficult to hear one of these primitive slow-moving vehicles approach, to get out of its way, or to recognize it among such a small number. By 1911 cars had become sufficiently numerous for the *Tribune* to advertise gasoline and tires for sale and cars to hire, but in the year before World War I broke out there were no more than 36 cars licensed throughout the Bahamas, compared with 276 horse-drawn carriages licensed for hire.[14]

Though downtown Nassau had its first electric lights, telephones, cinemas, and motor cars and the inhabitants of Long Cay and Inagua, visited by three or four steamships a week, could read New York newspapers no more than four days old, the only other Bahamian island brought closely in touch with modern developments in the United States before World War I—for good and bad—was mainland Abaco. In 1906, a firm based in Minneapolis registered as the Bahamas Timber Company obtained a hundred-year license to harvest the pinelands of Abaco, Andros, and Grand Bahama and invested £300,000 (five times the annual colonial budget) in a giant operation located at Spencer's Bight, on the eastern shore of the widest stretch of central Abaco.

Out of the uninhabited bush rose Wilson City (named after Governor Grey-Wilson, who had arranged the timber license), described by Steve Dodge as "a marvel in its time." A ship channel was dredged to a three-hundred-foot dock, with a huge loading derrick and conveyor beltways serving a mill that produced up to 18 million board feet of timber a year for markets in the United States, Cuba, and the rest of the Bahamas. Light railway lines radiated ever farther into the hinterland to feed the voracious mill, and the steam engines fueled by pinewood waste drove generators that provided electric light and produced 6,500 pounds of block ice a day—well in advance of Nassau. By 1912, Wilson City was employing an average of 540 persons a day, pumping £28,000 a year into the Bahamian economy in wages.[15]

Wage labor at Wilson City attracted a majority of the able-bodied Abaconian blacks, many of whom came with their families, and a large influx, mainly of single men, from other Bahamian islands. Though the company ran its own stores, it provided a welcome market for Abaconian farmers and fishermen, especially the whites of the offshore cays who did not care to work alongside blacks. Cheap board lumber raised the quality of local housing. Wilson City also promoted a boom among the white boatbuilders of Hope Town, Man-o-War Cay, New Plymouth, and Harbour Island because the cut timber was mainly shipped off in large schooners (up to two hundred feet in length) rather than in steam freighters.

Not all the effects of Wilson City were beneficial, and the operation lasted barely a decade. Accidents in the mill, in logging, and on the railway were common among the largely inexperienced laborers, and the commissioner at Cherokee Sound, commenting on the unexpected number of deaths in his district in 1912 (thirty-one, against only thirteen births), blamed the poor medical facilities as well as the laborers' ignorance of first aid methods. More insidious was the importation of Jim Crow–type segregation from the United States. The managerial staff, five families of white Americans, lived in elegant white bungalows on a hill and enjoyed their own white-painted Methodist church, a private school, electricity and piped water in their homes, and even a tennis court for recreation. The black workers were crammed into "a cluster of 120 houses in four rows," located in a swampy hollow and painted uniform red; in their own church building of the same color the local Methodist minister conducted separate services. Night classes in the red church building were the only form of schooling provided for the workers' families, with very poor attendance and results. Overcrowding, the predominance of male workers, and constant migration also led to social tensions and moral and health problems, especially what were euphemistically termed "social diseases."[16]

Growing frustration among the laborers culminated in a very tense situation just before Christmas 1913. The Bahamas Timber Company was experiencing financial difficulties, had not paid its workers for two weeks, and announced that there was no money on hand to meet the payroll. The workers became mutinous and threatened riot and arson. The problem was beyond the competence of the few local constables, and the general manager of the company appealed to Nassau for aid. Governor Grey-Wilson arranged for an emergency loan from the Royal Bank of Canada and dispatched the money to Wilson City along with the police commandant and a detachment of twenty-two armed policemen. All was quiet and orderly before Christmas and the policemen returned to Nassau, with the thanks of the company officials for protecting the company property from "threatened overt acts" and preventing "a disaster."[17]

Even more than the growing dissatisfaction with the traditional truck and credit systems—including the methods used in the sponge and salt industries and the Bahamian-owned pineapple factory at Governor's Harbour[18]—the labor troubles at Wilson City were a portent of what could happen in a more modern industrialized setting, especially when coupled with American-style racialist employment practices. The scattered nature of the Bahamian working population, its lack of sophistication in labor organization, and its desperate need for cash wages, as well as the general lack of industrialization, prevented more frequent and serious disturbances.

Though in its way a model of the capitalist raping of Third World resources and the exploitation of its workers (using the lures of wages and modern amenities), the Wilson City operation was premature if not misbegotten. Because it was located at a fixed site, it soon depleted its hinterland and its returns diminished. By 1916, the Bahamas Timber Company was employing only 375 men and making so little money that it was ready to pull out. The machinery, rail lines, even some of the houses were dismantled and shipped off. Wilson City became a ghost town, completely uninhabited. A few years later, however, more mobile and obviously temporary timber operations were begun by the Abaco Lumber Company (which inherited the logging leases), based first at Norman's Castle in northern Abaco (between 1926 and 1936) and then at Cornwall and Cross Harbour south of Wilson City in the early 1940s, before transferring to Grand Bahama in 1944, with much more lasting, if indirect, consequences.[19]

The Miami Craze: Migration to Florida, 1900–1920

Similar in its causes and some of its effects to the Abaco migration, though on a far larger scale and longer lived, was the movement of Bahamians to and from

Florida. In several phases, indeed, Bahamians were among the pioneer developers of south Florida, though for numerical reasons alone, the effects of the migration were proportionally greater on the Bahamas than on Florida—as well as generally less positive.

For a hundred years after the United States acquired Florida in 1819 (it became a territory in 1822 and a state in 1845), the southern half of the peninsula had more in common and better communications with the Bahama Islands than with the rest of the United States. This situation was reversed only with the completion of the north-south railroad (which reached Miami in 1896 and Key West in 1912), the substantial peopling of the southern counties of Florida with Americans, and the related tightening of immigration restrictions, culminating in the Johnson-Reed Act of 1924.

The first, or Key West, phase of the Bahamas-Florida connection, which lasted from the 1840s to 1900, has already been mentioned[20] but requires somewhat more detail. The first migrants from the Bahamas were whites from the northern settlements, drawn by the opportunities for wrecking, sponging, fishing, and trading with Cuba but driven both by the poverty of the Bahamas and by dissatisfaction with having to compete with the newly emancipated blacks. Governor Bayley said in 1860, when two-thirds of the population of Key West was made up of "Conchs," that the Abaconians had migrated because they were "disgusted at the civil and religious equality of the negroes" and were conversely attracted by the fact that Florida was a slaveholding state resolutely adhering to "Southern values," where they could "gratify their contemptuous dislike without stint and without reprisals."[21]

But if it remained a bastion of white racialist supremacy, Key West came to be a mixed community when many black Bahamians migrated after American slavery ended in 1865. The attraction of wider opportunities and better wages (relatively free from the crippling parasitism of the truck and credit systems) offset the harsh realities of segregation and discrimination.[22] The initial development of the Florida sponge fisheries in the 1870s was an extension of the Bahamian industry that provided relatively better returns for the fishermen because of underfished sponge beds, an open-ended domestic market, and a shortage of skilled and hardworking sponge fishermen. Such conditions, predictably, did not last; but in the 1880s, political turmoil in Cuba and U.S. import restrictions led to the transferral of Cuban cigar manufacturing to Key West, which spurred a second wave of black Bahamian migrants. Many women and children came for employment in the cigar factories, despite the pitiful wages. Governor Blake reported in 1885 that black Bahamians had begun to migrate, periodically or permanently, to Key West, "which the expansion of cigar manufacture for the American market has raised from a village to a comparatively wealthy town. Six schooners are now engaged in this passenger traffic."[23]

By 1892, when the population of Key West had reached twenty-four thousand, at least eight thousand were of Bahamian origin, of whom a majority were nonwhites (compared with nine thousand Cubans). The deterioration of conditions in the Bahamian pineapple, sisal, and sponging industries, accelerated by U.S. protectionism and the not unrelated acquisition of alternative sources of supply after 1897 (notably the Philippines and Hawaii) increased the number of Bahamians eager to migrate. But the virtual acquisition of Cuba by the United States made Key

West no longer either a necessary naval base or the best place to make cigars or fish for sponges, and it declined in attraction and importance as a migrant destination. Fortunately, however, an even more attractive area for Bahamian blacks was beginning to open up, 150 miles to the north.[24]

The migration of Bahamians to the southern Florida mainland was a reciprocal outcome of the southward thrust led by Henry M. Flagler, whose Florida East Coast Railroad made possible a lengthening chain of winter-defying farms and resort hotels that leaped the Gulf Stream with the purchase of potential farmland and the building of the Colonial Hotel in Nassau in 1899–1900. The fertile tracts of southern Dade County, opened up once the railroad reached Florida City in 1905, were particularly promising, and Bahamian blacks migrated eagerly to fill a labor shortage that guaranteed them between $1.25 and $1.50 (or between 5 and 6 shillings) a day, compared with the going rate in New Providence for what little wage labor was available of between 1 shilling and sixpence and 2 shillings.[25]

The prevailing need was for manual laborers to clear bush and dig drainage channels and agricultural toilers to plant and reap. An overwhelming majority of such migrants were males, most of whom stayed in Florida for less than a year at a time, traveling by the frequent mail boats for no more than $5 each way. But once Miami and other towns began to burgeon with sun-seeking whites and Bahamian conditions reached depression proportions, more Bahamians came as families and stayed permanently. Fishermen, carpenters, masons, domestics, and even members of the nonwhite middling classes joined the flood that became popularly known as "the Miami Craze."[26]

The nadir of the Bahamian slump and the peak of the Miami migration came in 1911. In April of that year the British ambassador in Washington reported that there was a seemingly insatiable demand for Bahamian workers in southern Florida and that the migration was assuming "such proportions as to cause anxiety to the Government and inconvenience to the sponge outfitters and employers of labour" in the Bahamas. In the previous three months alone, 875 Bahamian males and 221 females had landed in Miami and only 210 males and 87 females traveled in the opposite direction. So many Bahamians were now settled in Miami that the ambassador recommended the appointment of a British vice-consul there to look after their interests and to relieve the governor in Nassau of much of the work and trouble they were causing him.[27]

Governor Grey-Wilson (who at the same time was conjuring up the desperate plan of having Canada annex the ailing colony) was aware of the causes of the migration but was at a loss as to what to do about it. He was torn between deploring the loss of Bahamian laborers and seeing the migration as a safety valve and source of valuable cash remittances. As he told the House of Assembly in October 1911, a temporary migration would relieve hardships caused by the decline of the salt, sisal, and tomato industries, the failure of crops through two successive droughts, and the inability of government to provide labor in public works. But the exodus to Florida seemed to be entering a "new and by no means satisfactory phase. For whereas formerly the 'home' remained in this colony, now emigration is of a more permanent character, and wives and families in too many instances are joining the pioneers."[28]

Though exact numbers are almost impossible to calculate because of the mixture of temporary and permanent migration, probably 5,000 black Bahamians were permanently settled in mainland Florida by 1914.[29] In 1920, when their numbers probably peaked, Bahamian-born blacks in Miami totaled 4,815, constituting no less than 52 percent of the city's blacks and 16.3 percent of the entire population. Bahamians congregated in two main areas, Coconut Grove on the south Miami waterfront, and northeast of the railroad tracks downtown in what was first called simply "Colored Town" but later Overtown (an area reduced by the more or less enforced migration of blacks to Liberty City in the late 1930s and almost erased by the building of Interstate 95 in the 1960s).[30] Outside Miami, smaller segregated Bahamian communities were found in Florida City and Homestead to the south and northward in Dania, Fort Lauderdale, West Palm Beach, Fort Pierce, and even as far as Daytona Beach—all places connected with Miami by the Florida East Coast Railroad.

Bahamians were welcomed for their skills, their willingness to work hard for comparatively low wages, their general cheerfulness, and because they caused less trouble than American blacks. But their reputation was based on a careful social calculus on their own part, an ability born out of long experience of coexistence with whites in a harsh ecology to steer the delicate line between independence and accommodation, to turn "knowing their own place" to their own advantage.

Overcoming "the usual concept of the Southern States people" was a perennial problem, and the vice-consul, once appointed, spent much of his time establishing the special rights of British-born blacks. Several incidents of white mob or police brutality between 1907 and 1927 involved the British ambassador in Washington and almost threatened international incidents.[31] But even the system of Jim Crow segregation had some advantages for Florida Bahamians. It provided the sense of community, effective integration between permanently settled and more temporary migrants, and extensive networking already found in Over the Hill Nassau. Although attempts by Anglicans and Methodists based in Nassau to establish missions to black Bahamians in Miami had limited success because of white opposition (and the practical difficulty of finding black pastors), migrants eagerly formed their own churches, as well as friendly societies, lodges, and, after 1917, branches of the Universal Negro Improvement Association (UNIA).[32]

Bahamians brought their culture to all their Florida settlements, not just a distinctive style of housing, "two story wooden frame houses, with wide, two-tiered balustraded porches designed to take advantage of ocean breezes," but also their festivals and dances. Besides modest Junkanoos at Christmas and New Year, Bahamians partied for Emancipation Day and Queen Victoria's birthday each August, and in 1911 migrant farm workers in West Palm Beach combined these celebrations with a parade and dance in honor of the coronation of George V. Even more puzzling to Americans of all shades was the annual procession and burning of the effigy of Guy Fawkes on November 5, a custom that continued until the 1930s, when Floridian whites, discovering that Fawkes was a man of their own color, put a stop to the custom. At much the same time, however, the famous black folklorist Zora Neale Hurston wrote, in an unpublished manuscript for the Works Progress Administration, of the pervasive musical folkways brought to much of the east coast of Florida "by the flood of Negro workers from the Bahamas." Bahamian music, wrote Hurston, "is more dynamic and compelling than that of the American Negro, and the dance movements are more arresting; perhaps because the Bahamian offerings are more savage. . . . Nightly in Palm Beach, Fort Pierce, Miami, Key West and other cities of the Florida east coast, the hot drum heads throb and the African-Bahamian folk arts seep into the soil of America."[33]

In Florida, not only were many jobs (admittedly, mostly menial) customarily reserved for blacks in a labor seller's market, but because of strict customary segregation, craftsmen and specialists such as tailors, cobblers, hairdressers, and morticians found a large, clearly defined, and relatively prosperous clientele among people of their own color. Similarly, those who ventured into shopkeeping found that they had their own reservoir of customers without the competition from privileged white merchants they would have experienced in Nassau. That a large proportion of the wholesalers were northern Jews rather than southern whites was also an undoubted, if intangible, advantage.[34]

Another notable, though even less tangible, benefit of Jim Crow segregation for Bahamians was mentioned in an official report on migration from central Eleuthera in 1909: "In Miami the black man has to be extremely careful as to how he conducts himself, otherwise his liberty and even his life are endangered, and for this reason alone he abstains from liquor, saves his money and remits to his people at home."[35]

A final advantage of residence in segregated ghettos like Miami's was that it gave Bahamians a foothold in the United States, along with an experience that would encourage them to migrate onward to what seemed, at least after World War I, almost a Promised Land to southern blacks—the modern and industrialized cities of the northern United States. A few black Bahamians, along with other West Indian migrants, had already blazed the way to New York considerably before the Harlem Renaissance of the 1920s. They included the Adderleys, whose family produced two famous jazz musicians, and the son of "Sankey" Toote, who was to become one of Marcus Garvey's chief lieutenants.[36]

The great majority of the Miami migrants, however, either moved frequently between Florida and the Bahamas or retained close familial links. Undoubtedly the migration relieved the pressure of Bahamian underemployment and the desperate plight of those bound to subsistence agriculture in the Out Islands, and the infusion of Florida money was important to the Bahamian economy. Most of the money was remitted in registered letters (rather than in postal orders, as, for example, from Panama to Barbados and Jamaica) so totals are difficult to arrive at. But the amount sent by registered mail and postal orders and carried by returning migrants may have totaled U.S.$100,000 a year by 1920, when the commissioner in Exuma estimated the remittance of U.S.$15,000 to that island alone. The importance of the money to those remaining in the most beleaguered islands was indicated by the report of the commissioner at the Bight, Cat Island, in 1912: "The introduction not only of the dollar bill, but the fives, tens and twenties, into the district from Miami has made many a heart glad. It is a common occurrence for registered letters to contain $40 and $50 coming to wives from their husbands and to parents from children."[37]

As Howard Johnson has pointed out, though, the Florida migration also had short- and long-term disadvantages. Most obviously, it speeded the depopulation of the Out Islands, leaving many with hardly any able-bodied men and most with a disproportion of women, old people, and the very young. "The island is almost denuded of young men," wrote the commissioner at Cockburn Town, San Salvador, one of the most affected islands, in 1920: "Throughout the whole of the year both men and women have been going to Florida. I regret to report that at the time of writing there is not a single man on the whole island. It seems incredible but it is nevertheless true. If something out of the ordinary doesn't turn up soon, the district will be manless, because the married as well as the single are going."[38]

Moreover, the money generated by the migrants went "primarily to satisfy consumption needs rather than for productive investment" or was dissipated even more quickly in conspicuous consumption and display. In either case, it found its way into the pockets of grateful Bay Street merchants without bringing permanent benefit to the poorer islands and islanders. This process helped to create a typical "remittance society" in which external money raised aspirations and increased the taste for foreign goods while further narrowing and weakening the indigenous economic structure and actually widening class divisions.

Like the returnees sporting their Panama money in Bridgetown, Barbados, or Kingston, Jamaica, the symbol of Florida wealth was the black "dude from Dade" in outlandish clothes (said to be changed twice a day, three times on Sundays), strutting a style ironically in contrast to the meek, industrious sobriety practiced abroad. The apparent success of such persons provided a model for other blacks to follow, but their imported behavior and ideas disturbed local whites. The most prosperous and respectable returnees might hanker to build new homes and retire to their Out Island birthplaces, but clearly none of the migrants would willingly return to wresting their living from the soil or be satisfied with Bahamian wage levels.

Most serious of all, prolonged migration produced social dislocation and distress. Women deserted by their husbands sometimes took up with other men for support or comfort, and children lacked paternal discipline. The absentee men themselves—despite their reputation for hardworking frugality and temperance—also formed other liaisons, and even more temporary sexual encounters (at the work camps and the seedier edges of Miami or Nassau) led to unprecedented levels of venereal disease.

Medical Conditions, 1900–1917

The prevalence of such antisocial diseases helped to point up the backward medical conditions in the Bahamas: poor in Nassau and appalling in the Out Islands, with only marginal improvements between 1900 and 1920. One lasting problem was the shortage of qualified doctors. An act in 1906 aimed to eradicate quacks but could set only minimal standards. No one could practice medicine without a license, but two types of practitioner were recognized, the qualified and the unqualified. The former had to have a degree or diploma from an accredited British medical school or from a non-British institution specifically recognized by the governor in council; the latter were allowed to practice within limitations laid down on their licenses, which could be revoked at any time. Though there were some private qualified practitioners in Nassau as well as several medical officers attached to the hospital, in 1912 there were only three qualified doctors throughout the Out Islands, official medical officers based at Inagua, Harbour Island, and

The realities of a drudging life. Nassauvian blacks clipping and baling sponge under the eye of a white supervisor, around 1900. "Doc" Sands photograph, Michael Craton Collection.

Green Turtle Cay, Abaco. Of the forty-two thousand persons in the Out Islands, only five thousand lived in the districts directly served by these doctors; the remainder either went to Nassau for treatment or depended on the unqualified practitioners.[39]

As in the remoter British American colonies, commissioners, ministers of religion, and schoolteachers were often expected to act as unqualified medical practitioners. In 1904, the Methodist minister at Harbour Island, who had attended a hospital course in his college years, complained that not only did he spend much of his time in medical work but a large proportion of his salary went to providing medicines. After an Out Island tour in 1913 revealed a drastic shortage of proper medicines, the chief medical officer prepared a list of concentrated mixtures and tablets and a pamphlet of instruction for their use for simpler ailments, and the Pharmacy Act of the same year gave permission for a limited number of unqualified persons to sell drugs in the Out Islands. The system of unqualified practitioners and untrained pharmacists continued largely unchanged into the 1940s and 1950s, especially in the islands to windward, as the fascinating memoirs of "Dr." Evans W. Cottman illustrate.[40]

Because of its origins as a poorhouse (founded in 1809), its cumbersome management, and the dubious quality of its services, the hospital in Nassau entered the twentieth century with the reputation of being a place of last resort for the poorest sections of society. It was divided into four sections, one each for the sick, the indigent, lepers, and the insane, though the total number of beds was only 167. In the sick wards there was insufficient differentiation between the young and old and between the sexes or between surgical, obstetric, chronic, and infectious cases. The insane asylum had no accommodation for private patients and acute and mild cases were often not segregated. Consequently, those who could afford it arranged for treatment at home, even for leprosy and insanity.[41]

The Medical Department Act of 1911 and the Public Health Act in 1914 were attempts at modernization, though good intentions were hamstrung by meager allotments in the colonial budget as well as by the persistence of old attitudes. Under the 1911 act, the hospital was placed under a superintendent and a board of seven commissioners (of whom four had to be from the House of Assembly) appointed annually by the governor. The medical supervision of all hospital services was made the responsibility of a chief medical officer, whose duties were clearly specified, along with the minimum qualifications required for a resident surgeon and other doctors, a matron, nurses, and midwives. All midwives practicing in the colony were supposed to be examined by the resident surgeon before being licensed, and student nurses were required to serve a three-year apprenticeship before they were granted a certificate of proficiency. Such measures were positive, but they had little immediate success because the majority of doctors and all matrons continued to be expatriates (few of them highly qualified) until the 1950s, and it was even longer before an effective school for training local nurses was established, let alone a system of internship for qualifying doctors. In the shorter term, the gulf between ideal and reality was cruelly emphasized by the revelation by a former matron to the Nursing Association in England in 1914 that the first chief medical officer under the 1911 act went mad from chronic alcoholism and was confined in a private room in his own hospital.[42]

The well-intended actions of the strengthened Board of Health met much the same fate. A rigorous system of quarantine for incoming ships, using Athol Island to the northeast of Nassau harbor, and a systematic program of vaccination had been in place for decades and were likely, though not certain, reasons for the cessation of cholera, yellow fever, and smallpox epidemics. But occasional typhoid outbreaks, dysentery, tetanus, and worm infestations defied attempts to improve sanitation, and the increase in other serious diseases reflected ignorance and inefficiency as well as deficient diet. As early as 1872, officers of the Board of Health had been authorized to enter premises to inspect sanitary conditions, but this had been largely a dead letter. In 1911 a sanitary inspector was officially appointed to the board and charged with making quarterly reports to the chairman, and by 1913 the board had instituted a systematic clearance of accumulated garbage, regular house-to-house inspections, and the cleaning or closing of suspect wells.[43]

The Public Health Act of 1914 attempted to reinforce these preventive measures. The Board of Health was charged with advising the governor on everything pertaining to the health of the colony and given the power not only to inspect houses and yards but to oversee the cleaning of streets, drains, latrines, and the public markets—duties previously assigned to the Board of Works. The Board of Health was also to inspect and condemn food unfit for human consumption and to impose fines for infractions, including the sale of adulterated milk. The 1914 act also included minatory regulations against the spread of infectious diseases. If infectious patients could not be effectively isolated at home, they were to be removed to the hospital. Those with chronic infections were forbidden to practice as bakers, barbers, boatmen, stevedores, bootmakers, butchers, cooks, dairymen, domestic servants, fishmongers, carriage drivers, straw vendors, nurses, tailors, dressmakers, or washerwomen—almost the entire gamut of service occupations—on the threat of a £10 fine or a month's imprisonment. Children with infectious diseases were banned from school, and infected persons were forbidden to use the public library. Potentially even more disruptive was the prohibition of holding a wake over an "infected" corpse.[44]

Perhaps most important, the 1914 act (in line with English "liberal" reforms which some thought invaded individual liberties) made it compulsory for teachers to report children suffering from infections and to bar them from school and household heads who believed a family member was suffering from an infectious disease to call a medical practitioner. Doctors were bound to notify the Board of Health if the patient died from one of these diseases. The Board of Health had the authority to enter private homes to fumigate them and to remove and destroy an infected person's belongings.[45]

Though public resistance to revealing diseases to which social stigmas were attached meant that some of the most dangerous diseases were not specifically listed as notifiable, the general principle of notification applied by the 1914 act and official inquiries during World War I did help to expose the startling extent of serious health problems among the black and colored population, particularly the scourges of tuberculosis (TB) and venereal disease (VD). Many people suffering from TB—which flourished in conditions of poor nutrition and slums but was regarded with shame—were neither hospitalized nor segregated. But 12 percent of persons admitted to hospitals in 1912 and 1913 were suffering from TB, and more than half died because they had applied for admission in the advanced stages of the disease.[46]

The situation concerning VD was at least as serious. Syphilis superseded the less dangerous gonorrhea to assume epidemic proportions in the first two decades of the century. The figures given in the 1912 Health Report for both VD and TB were so shocking that the House of Assembly refused to print them for fear of damage to tourism. Once again, only severe cases reached the hospital, but 27 percent of all patients hospitalized in 1913 (that is, 146 persons) were suffering from VD. The English matron and chief nurses objected to having to minister to such cases, particularly to being in attendance at operations performed on the male genital organs. In 1916, the acting chief medical officer, Dr. William Pitt (a black West Indian), told Governor William Allardyce that he believed 90 percent of Bahamian "coloureds" were affected "in one way or another by this terrible curse." Though this was an obvious exaggeration, Dr. Pitt's successor reported: "So widespread are the ravages of venereal disease that I am afraid the wage-earning capacity of the labouring classes is likely to be seriously impaired."[47]

The governor and white assemblymen were not unduly concerned about the health of nonwhites in general (and quite content to draw conclusions about their morals), but a perceived threat to the viability of the labor force struck closer to home. In 1917, Governor Allardyce appointed the Commission on Venereal Disease to investigate the growth of VD over the previous two decades. It reported in the following year. Recommending the appointment of a government bacteriologist to

Stoic endurance. African-born sponge clipper, Nassau, around 1900.
"Doc" Sands photograph, Gail Saunders Collection.

conduct detection tests and take advantage of the latest advances in medicine, the commission predictably looked for scapegoats for the epidemic. It blamed returning migrants who had contracted disease in Florida, foreign workers who had come to Nassau during the building of the Colonial Hotel, and waiters who worked in the hotel during the tourist seasons. Most important, though, was the spread of disease through prostitution, which was found to be prevalent in Nassau despite the passage of the Immoral Traffic Act in 1914. Any night, it was said, "women of the lowest classes" could be found openly soliciting in the vicinity of the principal wharves or at the dance halls, where liquor was sold and "vulgarity prevailed." The dance halls—popular forerunners of the tourist nightclubs of a later era, which featured much more systematic prostitution—were claimed to be "principally places of assignation and centres for the dissemination of venereal disease. They appear to be Meccas for the worst type of prostitute and the happy hunting ground for characters of ill repute. The women go there for the purpose of soliciting and the men for the purpose of 'picking up a woman.'"[48]

The 1917 commission noted that the stigma attached to VD was so great that persons kept it as secret as they could and sought cures from bush doctors and quacks rather than regular practitioners. The commissioners attributed much of the problem to wartime conditions and doubtless saw the importation of diseases as analogous to the infection of dangerous new ideas, which also came from foreign travel. But they were honest enough to point out that the causes of the VD epidemic were of longer standing because a shocking number of men who had volunteered for war service had been found to be suffering from disease—quite apart from those who contracted VD in Nassau while awaiting transportation or picked up infections once abroad. Had its mandate been wider (or its members less biased), the commission might have concluded that the very high number of nonwhite Bahamian recruits to the colors between 1915 and 1918 who were rejected on a wide variety of medical grounds was an indictment of the very colonial system those recruits, with such ill-earned loyalty, had volunteered to defend.[49]

The Bahamas and World War I

The Bahamian response to Britain's declaration of war on the Central Powers on August 4, 1914 (news of which was received the same day in Nassau and Inagua, up to two weeks later in the remoter settlements), was as unquestioningly patriotic as in most other parts of the empire. Patriotism survived the first phases of the war, which had little direct effect on the Bahamas. But once shortages and other hardships began to bite, especially after the United States entered the war in 1917, enthusiasm waned and was further qualified by the chilling experiences undergone by Bahamian volunteers in the fighting zones and in the wartime work camps in the American South. Though the celebrations in November 1918 showed a general relief that a horrible war was over, many nonwhite Bahamians considered it had been a white man's war fought over imperialistic issues.

Certainly, the Bahamian white elite waved the flag first and hardest. The legislature met immediately and passed two emergency acts giving the governor in council unlimited powers for defense purposes and voting £10,000 from public funds for the war effort, which was augmented to nearly £50,000 by the end of the war. Governor Haddon-Smith hosted a public meeting in Nassau's Rawson Square to explain the conflict, reassuring the people that they were in no direct danger and encouraging them to increase food production in case imports were restricted. A more formal patriotic gathering was convened in St. Andrew's Hall at which the governor also presided. An unusually wide spectrum of Nassauvians was present, though, predictably, the center seats were reserved for the all-white Imperial Order of Daughters of the Empire (IODE), clergy, and public officials, while the representatives of the various colored and black friendly societies and lodges and the general public were seated at the sides and back of the hall.[50]

Two committees were struck: one for recruiting, which consisted of the English police commandant, two local whites, a colored, and a black, and one for raising funds and war material, in which local whites predominated. In the initial drive, nearly all Bahamians contributed money, even beyond their meager means—such as the people of Mangrove Cay, Andros, who raised £17.5.0 (or $86), mostly in pennies. Many ordinary Bahamians, boasted the governor, had "not only denied themselves luxuries, but in many cases, the necessaries of life. . . . There have been instances of seamstresses and market women earning a few shillings a week insisting on giving either three or two shillings."[51] Throughout the war, such organizations as the IODE and Bahamian Red Cross were tireless in raising funds and making and shipping garments and other supplies. The white proprietress of the *Guardian* (Mary Moseley) and the colored owner-editor of the *Tribune* (Gilbert Dupuch) competed in raising funds for the West India Regiment, though the latter complained as early as November 1914 that some Out Islanders were being forced to donate and printed a letter saying that the Assembly grant of £10,000 might have been better used to mend the roads.[52]

The recruiting committee was aided by the eagerness of all Bahamians to join up and the readiness of those unable or unwilling to go to subscribe to the cost of sending others. Among the volunteers were stevedores unemployed by the sudden ending of visits by ships of the Hamburg-America Line and sailors and farmers affected by a temporary slump in the prices of sponge and sisal. Most, however, were simply adventurous or idealistic, if not to the extreme of fifteen-year-old Etienne Dupuch, who "thought that this was an answer to my dream of carving my name in glory by giving my life for a just and glorious cause."[53] But for the first year of the war, the Bahamians ready to serve—whether or not from loyalism pure and simple—were thwarted by the unwillingness of the British government to accept nonwhite colonials. The intensification of the fighting revised this policy in 1915, when the War Office called on the West India Regiment, though making it clear that no nonwhites would be commissioned as officers. On the first anniversary of the outbreak of war, the new governor, William Allardyce, made a renewed appeal for recruits. Well aware of the delicate color situation, he tactfully guided a resolution through a public meeting at St. Andrew's Hall providing for raising a small contingent in the colony, its expenses defrayed by public subscription, to accompany the West India Regiment from Jamaica to England, whereas those of purely European descent who wished to volunteer should make their own way to Canada to join Canadian forces.[54]

Legend has it, however, that the very first man to respond to the official recruiting drive in August 1915 was the white William F. Albury, who was placed in charge of the First Contingent without the benefit of any rank and was later commissioned. The official photograph long enshrined in the Nassau Public Library suggests that six of the thirty men in the First Contingent were Bahamian whites.[55] The so-called Gallant Thirty—reduced from seventy volunteers by the winnowing out of the unfit and the underaged—included a wide cross section of the Bahamian population, including civil servants, tradesmen, mechanics, farmers, and fishermen of all shades of color. They were roughly kitted out, given rudimentary drilling, and provided with a splendid send-off. Two days before they left, impressive ceremonies showing off the volunteers for all Nassau to see took place on the Eastern Parade Ground. On the day before their departure, Lady Allardyce hosted a reception at Government House, usually out of bounds to coloreds and blacks. Gifts, mainly of cigarettes and tobacco, were provided. The farewell ceremony on September 10, 1915, was held at Rawson Square, which, like the rest of downtown Nassau, was colorfully decorated. Nearly the entire population turned out to hear the governor speak and present instructions to Private William F. Albury. Bands played and cheers were given as the contingent left on the specially leased schooner *Varuna* to join the British West Indies Regiment at its depot in Jamaica.[56]

The largest Bahamian contingents, 105 and 87 men, followed the Gallant Thirty in November 1915 and May 1916 and were augmented by five further drafts—of 78, 53, 51, 50, and 32, respectively—between August 1916 and September 1917, totaling 486 recruits in all for the five battalions of the British West India Regiment. Altogether, 1,800 Bahamians (some 10 percent of the adult male population) offered themselves for service, of whom approximately 700 served overseas. Besides the contingents sent to Jamaica, 53 Bahamians living in England, the United States, and British Honduras enlisted, as did 50 Bahamian laborers then in Panama. Except for the half dozen whites in the Gallant Thirty, virtually all those serving in the British West India Regiment were colored or black. The small number of white Bahamians volunteering for the war included about 36 old scholars from Queen's College, most of whom joined the Canadian forces. A few also entered the United States Army after April 1917. Compared with those of the major belligerents, which included the white self-governing colonies, Bahamian casualties were relatively light. Fewer than 50 died. Of those enlisted in the Bahamas, 6 were killed in action, 3 died from wounds, and 28 from other causes.[57]

The waning of enthusiasm for the war among ordinary Bahamians was discernible in the steadily declining number of recruits for the armed forces. After the first adverse effects, the Bahamian economy made a modest revival as the wartime demand raised sponge and sisal prices and the internal market for foodstuffs improved. Nassau was hardly affected by the war until 1917. The Development Board created in 1914 was held in abeyance until after the war, as were public works such as the deepening of the main wharf to take tourist steamers. But while the United States remained neutral the tourist trade continued, and the numbers for the winter seasons of 1915 and 1916 exceeded the twenty-six hundred who came in 1914. The chief wartime restriction, the blackout, was regarded as simply a tiresome joke as long as the only warships seen were occasional vessels of the Royal Navy making social calls.[58]

From early 1917, when submarines began to prowl the ocean passages through the Bahamas, the threat became more sinister, and strict shipping restrictions imposed after the United States entered the war in April 1917 cut off the tourist

For King and Empire. The "Gallant Thirty" first contingent of volunteers for World War I. *Above*, paraded at the police barracks. *Below*, the public send-off to Jamaica, aboard the sloop *Varuna*, September 9, 1915. Courtesy of Nassau Public Library.

trade and seriously curtailed food imports, especially flour. Some Out Islands felt positive effects. "Death has stared the Long Cay people in the face," wrote the local black schoolteacher in 1917 of those most affected by the loss of the stevedoring traffic, "and in awful fright they started to cut down land, light fires, and put in corn, potatoes, and peas, and they are rejoicing in the prospect of the best harvest in the history of the island."[59] For Nassau, though, the crisis was less remediable, and panic set in as shortages grew and prices rose. During the last year of the war there was rarely more than a week's supply of flour in Nassau, and on several days in August 1918 there was no bread for sale in Nassau's bakeries.[60]

Governor Allardyce went to Washington to negotiate for food supplies and urged the Assembly (consisting, of course, largely of merchants) to organize the judicious distribution of imported food, to suppress profiteering, and to encourage reduced consumption. The response can be gauged by the fact that the governor, in explaining why the Bahamas was not sustaining its pledge under the War Contingent Act of 1916 to provide two hundred fresh recruits a year, reported that the Assembly was no longer willing to pay all the costs of kitting and shipping the recruits and their separation allowances.[61] The failure to receive promised allowances was one of the reasons why fewer black Bahamians were volunteering for service at the front. Another was that wartime opportunities for well-paid labor in the United States were beginning to offer a far more attractive alternative. Most important was the recruitment of three thousand Bahamians for short-term labor contracts on the port facilities at Charleston, South Carolina. This project, organized in July 1918 by the Mason and Hangar Construction Company for the U.S. War and Labor Departments, offered contracts for three months, renewable for a second three months, with basic rates of pay of $3.30 (or 13 shillings and 7 pence) per ten-hour day, at least four times what could be earned in Nassau.[62]

A more deeply seated disinclination was privately conveyed by Governor Allardyce to the British government some months before the South Carolina project materialized. The main reason was almost certainly that news of conditions in the fighting zones, including pernicious racial discrimination, had filtered back to the Bahamas. In July 1917, after an Out Island tour, the governor candidly wrote the British minister in charge of recruiting that he found some of the people "unpatriotic, not to say disloyal." The coloreds and blacks were beginning to see the struggle as "a white man's war." Those in the biracial settlements of Governor's Harbour and Rock Sound, Eleuthera, were particularly hostile, while most in the black settlements in Andros and Cat Island appeared indifferent to the war and adamantly opposed to enlisting. Overall, there was now "a general desire on the part of the coloured generation in the Colony to escape from military service."[63]

Exactly what the Bahamians volunteering to fight for king and empire experienced and how it affected them is wonderfully conveyed in the autobiography of Sir Etienne Dupuch, *Salute to Friend and Foe* (1982), the only published firsthand account, by the person who was to be the very last survivor of the 1915–17 Bahamian contingents.[64]

Etienne, the now seventeen-year-old light-skinned son of the ambitiously middle-class (if critical of the government) owner of the *Nassau Tribune*, falsified his age to be accepted into the first Bahamian reinforcement draft early in 1916. At first it was no more than a youthful adventure, providing valuable new experiences and no more hardships than might have been anticipated. For the somewhat sheltered and naive Dupuch, it was an unusual opportunity to mix on close terms with ordinary Bahamians and to meet West Indians and Europeans for the first time in their own countries. He made lifelong friendships with many of his black fellow draftees and encountered educated West Indians with liberal ideas, including a few white officers such as the Trinidadian Captain Andrew Cipriani and the Anglican chaplain J. C. Wippel, future principal of Codrington College, to whom Dupuch was batman for a time. The handsome and personable young man was treated kindly by white civilians, especially French women, who were relatively unprejudiced racially and may have been intrigued by his partly French ancestry. Other experiences were more shocking and cumulatively traumatic. For a proud islander, the immensity of the imperial army organization and his own insignificance within it were dashing. Throughout his military service, Dupuch remained a private in rank, subject to discipline that was often petty and callous. He also endured the casual brutality and pointless inefficiencies inseparable from life in the ranks, some danger, much discomfort, and a great number of racialist indignities.

After some easy preliminary training at the Nassau police barracks, during which they could spend nights at home, and a splendid formal send-off at the dockside in Nassau, the contingent crammed into the schooner *Zelleas* was becalmed in the southern Bahamas, suffering from hunger and thirst and scared by the schools of circling sharks. Soon after they arrived at Port Royal, Jamaica was hit by a hurricane, which delayed further training by several weeks. Dupuch was bored by the formal drills and annoyed by the severity of one of the noncommissioned officers who had been a former employee of his father. But he was most shocked by the behavior of some of his fellow recruits, who seized every opportunity to drink the cheap Jamaican rum and visit the Kingston brothels. No less than twenty-four of the Bahamian contingent were returned to Nassau as medically unfit, mainly suffering from alcoholism and venereal disease.

Enrolled in the Fifth Reserve Battalion of the British West India Regiment consigned to Alexandria, Egypt, Dupuch endured with the others appalling conditions on the transport SS *Magdalena*. A fire on board nearly got out of control, the food was disgusting, sleeping quarters were squalid, and the ship carried no proper medicines. When the tropics-bred troops encountered cold weather, many succumbed to pneumonia, and one morning Dupuch woke up next to a corpse. The extremes of heat and cold in the desert, the subsequent mud and ice of the western front, along with poor food and cynically inadequate medical attention killed many West Indians, including some Bahamians. Dupuch attributed his own survival mainly to spending his entire pay, a shilling a day, on cod liver oil.

An initial disappointment—quickly qualified once the senseless carnage at the front was encountered—was the British policy of not using the West Indians (or any nonwhite colonials not regarded as "warlike races") as fighting troops. Except for the first contingent, which was formed into a machine-gun detachment and fought in Southern Palestine, the Bahamians were employed as manual laboring pioneers, building roads, gun emplacements, and trenches just behind the lines on the western front. This work exposed them to the discomforts, horrors, and dangers of the battle area without the chance for glory. Dupuch's unit often underwent prolonged bombardment while at their backbreaking labors, and he himself narrowly missed extinction from a shellburst while accompanying Rev. Wippel up the line.[65]

Far worse was the blatant discrimination and prejudice the proud Bahamian volunteers had to endure. Though they were painfully aware of the class-race prejudices at home, it was galling to suffer humiliations from non-Bahamians whom they had come to serve alongside. Even the lower-class whites had picked up racism toward black colonials from their social superiors. Symbolic of the situation were the frequent signs reading "Out of Bounds to Native Troops." Through conversations with Indians, especially Sikhs, they learned of the nationalistic feelings fomenting in India against the British, how Indians felt about holding "inferior positions in their own country," and the sentiment of many that they were showing loyalty mainly in the hope of moving more rapidly toward independence. Many of the Indians seemed admirable to Dupuch, and he was especially shocked to see the way the lowliest English treated the highest-ranking Indians. In Dupuch's words, "It was then for the first time that I realized that the lowest, dirtiest, scrubbiest Englishman was considered superior to the finest Indian."[66]

Despite their ordeals, the Bahamians (as in Florida) gained a general reputation for cheerful hard work and exemplary behavior, receiving somewhat condescending citations from both General Edmund Allenby and Field Marshal Douglas Haig. Toward the end of the war, however, many began to share the disillusion, disgust, and anger that led the Tenth Battalion of the British West India Regiment to mutiny at Taranto early in 1918. In sympathy, some of Dupuch's battalion, including fellow Bahamians, refused to relieve a squad of English pioneers on latrine-cleaning duties, were placed under arrest, court-martialed, and sent to army prison. One of these men, Johnny Demeritte, though suffering from wounds that led to his losing both legs, was also involved in a race riot in Liverpool, England, before his demobilization.[67]

Immediate Postwar Repercussions

Etienne Dupuch returned from Europe shorn of his earlier idealism. "I was a changed person when I returned to my island home at the age of 20 after seeing the people of Europe wallowing in a cesspit of human degradation," he wrote more than sixty years later. "I was a very bitter man and swore that never again would I lift a finger, certainly not risk my life, in defence of King and Country, or of anything removed from my limited sphere of activities."[68]

This statement is unequivocal enough; yet even a cursory examination of Etienne Dupuch's long career and his psyche reveals seeming contradictions that help to show that Bahamian race and class identity were more complex and ambiguous matters than conveyed by the quoted words of a twenty-year-old veteran of World War I in 1919. Throughout his life, Dupuch was adamantly opposed to racial discrimination among Bahamians and was always critical of racialist attitudes that stemmed either from British officials or the local white elite. His proudest claim (retailed with monotonous regularity in his later editorials) was to have been the author of the landmark antidiscrimination regulation passed by the legislature in 1956. Yet this did not preclude a strong sense of the importance of class distinctions and a personal snobbery that made more of the Dupuches' white European than their black African antecedents.

Politically, Dupuch (like at least some of his peers) was always disturbed by the prospect that racial polarization would lead to social conflict and disruption. This concern led him sequentially to oppose actions by the Bay Street oligarchy that might provoke dangerous political reactions among the blacks, to attempt (with very limited success) to establish a multiracial middle party, and to oppose black power politics so adamantly that he ended by supporting Bay Street once it was in opposition. Even more remarkable was Dupuch's apparent volte-face over imperialism and the imperial monarchy. He developed a highly personalized ideal of the British Empire and Crown indistinguishable from conservatism and not unrelated to his lifelong hankering for the symbols of rank. Thus he saw racism as an aberration and policies he disliked as stemming not from the Crown but from evil ministers, though he could criticize the monarch if (as in the case of Edward VIII) he deviated from Dupuch's lofty principles.[69]

Much the same might be said about Dupuch's conversion from Anglicanism to Roman Catholicism during the 1920s. Quite apart from theological considerations, like others of his class he seems to have been attracted by a nonestablishment faith that was nonracialist yet hierarchical and deeply conservative. Dupuch's prominence among the laity of the Catholic diocese of the Bahamas bore fruit in his achievement of two papal knighthoods. He seems, though, to have obtained equal satisfaction from what he regarded as close personal friendships with two British lords even more egocentric than himself, Beaverbrook and Mountbatten, and he came closest to earthly bliss when awarded a British knighthood in 1965. In sum, Etienne Dupuch represented three important strands in Bahamian race-class attitudes and relations: the feeling that race and class were best divorced and that race should be kept out of politics; the belief that there was a natural balance in Bahamian society which only enlightened Bahamians such as himself could understand; and the motivating ambition or solipsism that felt that anything was evil that kept men of destiny like himself out of the ruling class.[70]

Similar complexities and ambiguities attended the racial tensions that over much the same period spread to the Bahamas from the opposite direction: the U.S. South. Race relations in the Bahamas were not simply polarized, as outsiders have often presumed. One example followed the scandal attached to the collapse of the Bank of Nassau in 1916. When it was revealed that it was not just inefficiency but dishonesty on the part of the bank's directors and auditors—all members of the Bay Street oligarchy—that had led to the disaster, Governor Allardyce pusillanimously was reluctant to prosecute the culprits. He pointed out to London that "the status of whites in the Bahamas was not what it ought to be. Whites have not the respect nor the standing with the dark population." If the bank officials were brought to court, he believed that their close blood relations with other members of the legislature and the groundswell of public opinion would at the least lead to mass resignations and make the colony almost impossible to administer.[71]

Allardyce's fears proved exaggerated. The directors and auditors were prosecuted and convicted. Yet in commenting on the case, Gilbert Dupuch's *Nassau Tribune,* proud to be known as "the organ of the coloured population," extended its sympathy to the "honourable gentlemen" convicted and chided the judge for his "harsh and scathing" comments on the incompetence of the auditors. The governor responded by explaining that one of the prosecuted directors, W. C. B. Johnson, deputy speaker of the Assembly, had considerable influence over the editor of the *Tribune* and was a close political friend of the black MHA Leon Walton Young.[72]

Letters and editorials on race-class issues were fairly common in the Nassau press during the second decade of the twentieth century and did not always follow predictable lines. In November 1917, in response to suggestions that the Bahamas might (like the Danish Virgin Islands) be annexed to the United States, a strongly anti-American letter was printed in the ultra-conservative *Nassau Guardian*. "The United States on the whole cannot be considered a civilized country," it claimed, because of the discriminatory policy that compelled Negroes to "submit by law to residential segregation, and to 'Jim Crow' travel." American Negroes had "an inferior franchise, labour limitations, and insecurity of property," compared with those in the Bahamas, and suffered from "insecurity of life" from the threat of lynchings. Clearly the letter writer felt that race relations in the Bahamas were quietly fixed by custom without the need for legislation and feared the strife that might come from greater polarization under influences from the American South.[73]

That this was no idle threat was borne out by the experiences of Bahamians in Florida and South Carolina during World War I and shortly afterward and the repercussions reaching Nassau. The revival of the Ku Klux Klan in 1915 and such incidents as the near lynching of the Irish priest of St. Agnes Bahamian Anglican church in Miami were countered by the rapid spread of Marcus Garvey's Universal Negro Improvement Association after its formation in 1917. Bahamians were not directly implicated in the widespread interracial violence that occurred in the "red summer" of 1919, but many were attracted by what the UNIA offered and became involved in the movement. The most notable of these were Frederick Toote, Garvey's chief organizer in Philadelphia, and Captain Joshua Cockburn, an enterprising if somewhat rascally Androsian who had gained his master's certificate as a pilot on the West African coast and was commander of the ill-fated SS *Yarmouth* of the Black Star Line in 1919 and 1920. But hundreds of émigré Bahamians joined the twelve UNIA chapters in southern Florida and perhaps as many the three in the Bahamas during their heyday.[74]

This movement caused perturbation at home and abroad. In May 1921, the white Methodist minister in Miami, reporting that he was being forced to close the mission to migrant Bahamians for lack of a black pastor, wrote that the most distressing aspect was that it revealed "the tendency of a strong section of the Coloured people to throw off the friendship of the Whites." This, he claimed, was the result of agitation by the UNIA and the influence of Marcus Garvey, who had recently visited both Miami and Key West.[75] Just two months later, the Methodist minister in Nassau wrote to the Wesleyan Methodist Missionary Society in London:

> To give you some idea of the undercurrent flowing in this colony, coming from America, via Miami, let me tell you what I saw yesterday in a magazine in the vestry of our Wesley Church [Grant's Town]. . . . On the question of some race turmoil in the West this statement was made—"The Negro must look upon every White man as his POTENTIAL enemy." I do not know how widely this magazine is circulated in this colony, but of this I am sure, there has been much propaganda work done and I can see that the attitude of the Negro is very different indeed from the attitude when I first came here in 1905. This is undoubtedly due to the emigration to Florida, and the vile treatment the Negroes have received there.[76]

Such problems continued but were muted, and the direct influence from Florida was already well on the wane because of the virtual closing of migration to Florida after 1920. The first attempt at restriction had been made in 1917 by the requirement that those requesting entry to the United States demonstrate their literacy.

This proviso was suspended because of the wartime demand for Bahamian laborers but reintroduced in 1920—the first stage of a policy of general exclusion (less a tiny quota) by the Johnson-Reed Act of 1924.[77] But as previous Bahamian booms had demonstrated, improved economic chances were the most effective palliatives for social unrest. The onset of the prosperity accompanying the rum-running era of Prohibition in the United States therefore more than offset the effects of curtailed emigration. One writer has even gone so far as to state that "the passing of the Volstead Act by the United States Congress in December 1919, was to be more important to the Bahamas in its effects than the events of 1914–1918."[78]

8

Limited Benefits: The 1920s and 1930s

Volstead's Gift: The Bootlegging Era

So obvious and arguably beneficial were the effects on the Bahamas of bootlegging during the era of American Prohibition (1919–33) that Governor Bede Clifford, with typical jocularity, suggested that a statue of Prohibition's enforcer, Senator Andrew Volstead, be added in Nassau to those of Christopher Columbus and Queen Victoria. More perceptive analysts, including Governor Clifford's successor, Charles Dundas, recognized that the benefits of the economic boom were unevenly spread and transitory and that the Bahamas was saved from the depth of unrest experienced by the rest of the Caribbean during the late 1930s less by the delayed onset of the Great Depression than by the colony's intrinsic conservatism and inertia.[1]

The year after the Great War ended was a time of recession in the Bahamas. World prices of Bahamian sponge and sisal tumbled when the wartime demand ended abruptly, and remittances dried up as servicemen and migrant workers returned to swell the labor market. Tourism did not recover quickly because passenger shipping was in short supply, and an unfavorable currency ratio between sterling and the dollar penalized a colony that was more than ever dependent on imports. These setbacks were exacerbated by natural disasters. Prolonged droughts hampered efforts to increase food production, and a hurricane in September 1919, though missing Nassau, scourged many Out Islands, destroying crops and seriously damaging the sponge fisheries.[2]

The effects of the Volstead Act rapidly lifted the gloom, particularly for Nassau and those Bahamians most able to benefit from Americans' desire to evade Prohibition. The Bahamian capital was ideally situated as an entrepôt, easily capable of expanding its normal inflow of West Indian rum, English gin, and Scotch whiskey, which was then filtered through the northern islands to an American coast almost impossible to blockade effectively—especially by way of Bimini and West End, Grand Bahama, only fifty miles from Florida. The flow of illicit liquor became a flood, and the infusion of new wealth into the Bahamas was immediate. The existing colonial customs tariff placed a relatively high import duty on liquor, and though the Tariff Amendment Act of 1920 allowed an 80 percent drawback on reexports and another act three years later reduced the liquor import duties by 50 percent, these reductions were offset by the increase in volume.[3]

As early as March 1920, the *Times* of London reported that Prohibition had "transformed the Bahamas Government's financial position as if by magic from a deficit to a comparatively huge surplus, provided labour for large numbers of

Rum waiting to be run. Cases and barrels of liquor on Nassau's dockside, early 1920s. "Doc" Sands photograph, John Fondas Collection, courtesy of Bahamas Archives.

unemployed Bahamians and put more money into circulation in this little British colony than has been the case for many years."[4] Even before the Volstead Act came into force, Nassau's harbor was more crowded than at any time since the blockade-running 1860s, with ships unloading barrels and cases of liquor that piled up on the wharves and filled available warehouses. Women as well as men were employed as stevedores, and many private individuals leased out their cellars. By February 1921, Governor Harry Cordeaux wrote that there were thirty-one permanent or temporary bonded warehouses, needed to store the 13,700 barrels and 37,400 cases imported so far. The Bahamian revenue from liquor imports and reexports soared from £81,049 (already anticipating Prohibition) in 1919, to £204,296 in 1920, and £1,065,899 in 1923. Despite the reduction in duties, the increased vigilance of U.S. agents, and Bahamian customs evasion, this revenue did not fall below £500,000 a year before 1930.[5]

Though United States officials fumed at Bahamian connivance with American bootlegging, moralists such as Mary Moseley complained of the corruption it brought in its wake, and an immeasurable (and probably increasing) quantity of liquor passed through the Bahamas without duty being paid, most Bahamians could engage in rum-running without danger or even technical illegality. As Hugh McLachlan Bell wrote in 1934, "It was not the business of the dealer who possessed liquor to inquire whither it was bound; that was the business of the Customs and the buyer. The men who made the greatest fortunes in Nassau never sailed a ship nor sold to any person in the United States a pint of booze. They did not have to go so far; buyers flooded their offices, took the liquor direct to chartered ships and sailed away."[6]

As a comparison between Bahamian business directories in 1900 and 1930 discloses, Prohibition brought an almost quantum jump in the number of Bay Street merchants (invariably white and nearly all Bahamian-born) engaged in the already flourishing liquor business. The most common method of transshipment was for a Nassau merchant to land the liquor, paying the duty less drawback, to bottle the majority of the liquor that came in barrels rather than cases, and then to consign it on behalf of an American customer to an obviously fictitious destination. The favorite was the tiny French colony of St. Pierre and Miquelon off the southern coast of Newfoundland, exports to which were nil before 1920 and amounted nominally to £1,208,718 in 1922, two-thirds of the Bahamian total. The liquor was normally transferred to smaller and faster vessels somewhere in the no-man's area between Bahamian and United States territorial waters. It was, incidentally, in the cause of suppressing bootlegging that the United States government extended the limits of territorial waters from three to twelve miles.[7]

Even more questionable practices of which Bahamian officials were accused involved the illegal transfer of ships' registries to disguise American ownership and the issue of two sets of clearance papers. A U.S. federal agent quoted a Bahamian informant, a Mr. M. Cole, about how the latter practice worked. The first documents were issued with the liquor shipment. An hour or so later, the person to whom they were issued would return and declare that he had discharged his cargo of liquor on the high seas and be given papers clearing his ship "in ballast." Thus armed, an American rum-runner could legally carry liquor to the edge of United States territorial waters and also, once he had transferred his cargo to speedboats and reentered a home port, claim to inquisitive customs officers that he had been in ballast for the whole voyage. As for the corrupt connivance of Bahamian officials, the U.S. agent could only state that "Mr. Cole did not say there would be any money required outside the regular fees but intimated that he and the boys expected to be taken care of."[8]

Private Bahamian individuals undoubtedly showed equal or greater ingenuity in profiting from the liquor trade as close to the line of legality as they dared, although, as in the drug-running era six decades later, American accusations of wrongdoing evoked fervent official denials, and the actions of overzealous U.S. agents within Bahamian territorial waters several times threatened diplomatic incidents. In 1921, Governor Cordeaux, enjoying the increased revenue flow and clearly influenced by the legislature, argued that the amount of liquor run into the United States from the Bahamas was infinitesimal compared with the total consumed on the mainland and that both the risks and profits involved in bootlegging accrued to American citizens. And in 1927, after complaints through the office of the United States consul, Governor Henry Orr reported that he had made a surprise inspection of the customs at West End, Grand Bahama, but had found no irregularities. The collector of revenue, F. H. Bowe, was zealously doing his duty and if any American vessels were carrying false papers, they were forgeries by private individuals.[9]

Both such pleas were clearly disingenuous. Governors had only to use their eyes and ears to know what riotous times bootlegging had brought to Nassau, and the action on the rum-running "front line" along the northwestern edge of the Bahamian archipelago was an open secret. The American Anti-Saloon League and its supporters even advocated that the United States should seize Bimini, which before Prohibition had been a worthless outpost but now brought the Bahamian government a fortune from the liquor stored and transshipped there. Like Nassau,

Bimini, along with West End and Cat Cay, had become the resort not only of international smugglers but of trippers eager to enjoy the delights of drinking in a raffish atmosphere.

As early as February 1920, permission was granted for the consignment to Bimini of an amount of liquor hugely in excess of local needs. The owner of the liquor, Charles Vincenti, an American of dubious character, was virtually kidnapped by U.S. federal agents and taken to Miami for trial on smuggling charges. Following protests by the Bimini commissioner and the Bahamian government, Vincenti was released and the federal agents were accused of illegal arrest. In a confidential report, however, the commissioner described the usual transactions at Bimini. Liquor, in unrealistically large amounts, was taken out of the bond warehouse for the "ostensible purpose of meeting the requirements" of a legitimate local trade and placed in a dealer's store. When night fell, the liquor was transferred to a boat and disposed of for a cash payment some miles off the harbor, by prior arrangement. Since the boat was not bound for any port, either within or without the colony, no official clearance was necessary.[10]

Activities at Gun Cay and Cat Cay, just south of Bimini, were even more flagrant and just as invulnerable. As a report from the United States Treasury Department stated in 1927, Bahamian schooners owned by licensed liquor dealers in Nassau such as Allan H. Kelly anchored inside the cays almost permanently. From such vessels, whiskey and other alcoholic beverages were sold, and schooners and power boats from Nassau constantly replenished the stock. One notorious vessel owned by two "Englishmen," a hundred-foot barge or scow without sails or power called the *Dreamland*, lay permanently at anchor behind North Cat Cay. Equipped with electric lights and refrigeration, it held thousands of cases of liquor and was frequently visited at night by unlighted American motorboats, which took on hundreds of sacks of liquor. Besides one of the owners and three other whites, the *Dreamland* had a seemingly superfluous crew of seven blacks. Their main task, like that of many Nassauvians, male and female, was to sew the bottles of liquor into conveniently portable, floatable, and disposable sacks of five.[11]

A few Bahamians of buccaneering spirit were directly engaged in rum-running, more to corner all the profits that could be had than in a lust for adventure. Most notable of these was a poor young "passing white" from the Current, Eleuthera, Roland T. Symonette, whose dangerous adventures during Prohibition laid the basis of one of the largest Bahamian fortunes, earning him entry into the Bay Street oligarchy and its eventual leadership. He was knighted and became the first Bahamian premier in 1964. Symonette was listed in a secret memorandum in 1922 as one of the most active Bahamian ship captains engaged in smuggling, and in the following year his first wife, Nellie, with a candor that was unimaginable forty years later, testified that he had made a million dollars in three years, mainly by running liquor between Nassau and the American mainland.[12]

A handful of opportunistic Britons and Canadians were also involved in rum-running. But the more dangerous aspects of the trade were dominated by Americans. Most notorious of these—mainly from his own account—was William McCoy, whose bootleg whiskey had such an excellent reputation that it was called "the Real McCoy." After arriving in Nassau in August 1920, McCoy purchased a local fishing schooner named the *Henry L. Marshall* and claimed to have made a profit of $15,000 on his first voyage and $35,000 on the second. Registering as the innocent-sounding British Transportation and Trading Company in November 1921, he claimed to have run over 175,000 cases of liquor from the Bahamas into the United States. McCoy's chief supplier was a tough Irish-American, George Murphy, who headed the Bahamas Island Import and Export Company, said to be the largest bootlegging firm in Nassau. Though McCoy returned to the United States when Prohibition ended, Murphy remained in Nassau to become a prominent member of the Bay Street clique. He promoted the real estate developments of Shirley Slope and Tower Heights in Nassau, launched horse racing at the Hobby Horse Hall track, and became the manager of the Montagu Beach Hotel, built with Bay Street money guaranteed by the legislature in 1926. Representing Exuma in the House of Assembly from 1935 to 1946, Murphy ended his career as a respected member of the Legislative Council.[13]

By 1921, sleepy Nassau seemed to have taken on almost the ambience of a Wild West town. As his biographer quoted William McCoy, the town was

> well launched on her third and most prosperous era of activity [that is, after piracy and blockade-running]. . . . The big money clan rushed in upon her. Adventurers, businessmen, soldiers, including a renegade officer or so, sailors, loafers, and at least one minister, they sought to make their fortunes by keeping America wet. Bay Street . . . was no longer a sun drenched idle avenue where traffic in sponges and sisal progressed torpidly. It was filled with slit-eyed, hunch-shouldered strangers, with a bluster of Manhattan in their voices and a wary truculence of manners.

According to the same source, Bill McCoy had been joined by equally colorful and even shadier characters, with nicknames such as "Tampa," "Ranger," "Squinty," "Goldie," and "Suggsy," who were in Nassau to buy liquor, to prevent fraudulent sales to the organizations that employed them, to harass and delude undercover federal agents, or simply to roister.[14]

Though the prim editor of the *Nassau Guardian* complained that the English and American press seemed intent on "blackening the character of the Colony" by exaggerating the collusion of Bahamians in bootlegging and by asserting that "gangs of American crooks were allowed to wander about Nassau . . . with a gun on each hip" with impunity, other sources, including the contemporary local newspapers, provided a racier picture. As H. M. Bell recalled the year after Prohibition ended, the Lucerne Hotel on Frederick Street, Nassau, was the unofficial headquarters of the bootleggers. It included among its clientele Sir Daniel Tudor, the chief justice, and other English officials. Letters to the *Tribune* also attested that much drinking, dancing, and noisy partying took place at the Lucerne and at the nearby Hotel Allan and Bucket of Blood nightclub, and Etienne Dupuch, the editor, wrote disapprovingly of the incursions of the "flapper" generation, of "the orgy of the Lucerne," and of the crowd of hedonists who, dancing all night and every night, had introduced a new "dance abomination" called the Charleston to Nassau.[15]

The climax of the partying season was the Bootleggers' Ball, held in late July. Attracting mainly foreigners, it began on a Saturday afternoon and ended climactically late on Sunday, to the scandal of local sabbatarians. According to H. M. Bell, "Mother," the owner-manager, kept relative peace in the Lucerne with the help of Tom Lavelle, a large, rough Irishman who carried guns in his hip pockets. Nassau as a whole was also generally peaceful, bubbling but not quiet boiling over. "Bootleggers played poker for $100 on the piles of empties, competed at pitch and toss with gold pieces on the wharves, roared loud choruses as they trekked to their boats for outward runs," wrote Bell. "Timid folk stayed home o'nights, preachers threatened all and sundry with the wrath of God, an attempt was made to draw social lines between the 'best people' and the newly rich liquor families. But money ruled." Yet, Bell added, "there was no roughness to speak of and no killings. . . . The majesty of the British law held trouble in the waterfront bars down to fist fights and the order was 'No guns in Nassau'—meaning that none were to be pulled there."[16]

American Influx: Tourists, Money, and Ideas

Though the two newspaper editors bewailed Nassau's creeping materialism and the neglect of traditional industries, not all was simple accumulation or thoughtless dissipation. However much individuals hoped to make their private fortunes, canny governors and a Bay Street–influenced Development Board saw that most of the colony's windfall wealth was deployed in financing public works, improving communications, and making the Bahamas more attractive to tourists and well-heeled immigrants and investors.

By the end of the decade, Nassau had a modern water system, with water pumped from well fields west of the city to a prominent new concrete water tower on Fort Fincastle hill, and its first system of piped sewerage, though it served only a limited area north of the ridge and city water was available Over the Hill only from public standpipes. Similarly, the reorganization and expansion of electricity supplies in 1922 (with diesel generators producing 2,300 volts at high tension and 200 or 115 volts at low tension, alternating, American style, at 60 cycles a second) provided a general service at least for the well-to-do, who were also the main beneficiaries of the greatly improved cold storage facilities.[17]

In 1923 the government made a start to the long-discussed plan to make Nassau harbor suitable for deep-draft vessels such as passenger liners. Even when seas were calm, all large ships had previously been forced to anchor off the harbor bar, from which cargoes were transshipped by lighters and passengers landed by tenders. In rough weather, when the surge made the bar impassible, ships had to anchor off Clifton in southwestern New Providence, and passengers traveled sixteen miles to Nassau on a very bad road. Now, over a five-year period, the bar and harbor were blasted and dredged to allow entry, turning, and mooring for vessels with drafts up to twenty-seven feet. A concrete dock six hundred feet long and one hundred feet wide, connected to Rawson Square by a steel bridge, was completed in July 1928 and named for Prince George, Duke of York (later King George VI), who visited Nassau later that year.[18]

The multiplication of motor vehicles in New Providence was a symbol of the new affluence. Whereas only 6 cars had been imported in 1918, the number rose to 297 in 1922, and by the end of the decade nearly a thousand were registered throughout the colony. Despite the passage of a new Motor Car Act in 1922, the growth in the number of cars, the complaints about speeding and reckless driving, and the rise in traffic accidents stimulated public criticism and the need for more traffic regulations. There was also much demand for the government to improve the roads. Even in 1922, New Providence boasted thirty-three and a half miles of roads within the city and suburbs and sixty-five miles of country roads, and by the end of the decade most of these had been tarred. Except for a few miles of drivable road in and around major settlements such as Harbour Island and Governor's Harbour, and a reasonable "earth" road seventy miles long down the length of Eleuthera completed by the government in 1930 to encourage agriculture, such improvements did not extend to the Out Islands.[19]

Similar disparities existed in all other aspects of communication. Whereas the telephone system extended fairly widely in Nassau during the 1920s, only the major settlements in the main Out Islands were linked by primitive party line systems. By 1925, rudimentary wireless telegraphy stations were installed at Harbour Island, Governor's Harbour, Hope Town, and Norman's Castle, Abaco, Mathew Town, Inagua, and (for obvious reasons) Bimini and West End, Grand Bahama. But for most other settlements, transmission even of urgent messages took almost as long as ever. Haziel Albury, for example, noted that anyone at Man-o-War Cay who wished to send a telegram had to travel to Hope Town by sailboat, at the whim of the wind, while those receiving a telegram via Hope Town had to pay an extra four shillings, or a dollar, for its delivery by boat. Ordinary mail, of course, took far longer, though Abaco was served by a motor mail boat as early as 1924, and sailboats had been replaced by government-subsidized motor mail boat services to most other islands by 1929.[20]

Many other improvements, concentrated in Nassau and New Providence, were directly or indirectly the result of promotion by the Development Board, authorized in 1914 and activated from 1920. Under the energetic but far from disinterested chairmanship first of R. H. Curry, member of the Executive Council and the chief Bahamian steamship agent, and then H. G. Christie, MHA, most successful of all Bahamian real estate agents, the board spent thousands of pounds on advertising to attract wealthy Americans and Canadians as visitors or settlers and tirelessly encouraged government and individuals to make certain that material and social conditions were improved to make the incomers comfortable. Besides the incomparable climate and swimming beaches (such as the newly christened Paradise Beach on Hog Island), advertising stressed such elite sporting activities as yachting, duck and pigeon shooting (as close as Lakes Cunningham and Killarney and the Pine Barrens of New Providence), grass court tennis (at the all-white Nassau Lawn Tennis Club or the hotels), and golf, for which courses were constructed at Fort Charlotte and the newly created (and racially exclusive) Bahamas Country Club at Cable Beach. Algernon Aspinall's *Pocket Guide to the West Indies* (1923) also mentioned that the Nassau Club and the luxurious Porcupine Club on Hog Island extended hospitality "to visitors suitably introduced," the latter, of which all the charter members were wealthy Americans, charging a subscription of $15 for two weeks or $25 for the season.[21]

Along with being more involved than ever in facilitating communications to and from the Bahamas, the government was concerned to improve hotel accommodations. A contract with the Munson Steamship Company guaranteed Nassau direct passenger and freight service from New York at least once a week during the season and every two weeks in the summer, compared with the monthly connecting service to and from the United Kingdom as part of the line connecting Halifax, Bermuda, Nassau, Jamaica, and British Honduras, which was the best that could be negotiated with the Canadian Steamship Company. The great majority of visitors, however, came by way of Miami. Several passenger ships competed in comfort and speed, though the fastest took fifteen hours each way and none was as grand as the Munson or Canadian steamers. For example, although the weekly sailing SS *Nassauvian,* pride of the minuscule Allan Line (managing owner Captain Allan U. Johnson, also proprietor of the Allan Hotel), enjoyed the government mail contract and promised "First-Class Accommodation to Fifty First Class Passengers," it was built of wood and not much bigger than the timber schooners of the day or the largest modern Family Island mail boats.[22]

The richest and most sought-after visitors came in their own yachts, but an increasing number of the more adventurous and wealthy came by air. Seaplanes had first been seen in Nassau in July 1919 before the troops returned from overseas, and in 1923 Aspinall's *Guide* claimed that the Bahamas was "The first West Indian Colony to enjoy aerial communication," with "opportunities for aviation between Nassau, the 'out islands' and Miami." Two pioneers of regular flights who competed for the distinction of having started the oldest scheduled airline in the world had early flights to the Bahamas: the Kentuckyian A. B. Chalk, whose miniature airline, formed in 1921, was still flying between Miami, Bimini, and Nassau more than seventy years later, and the Puerto Rican Juan Trippe, founder of the eventually huge (though not immortal) Pan American Airways, which made its first flights to the Bahamas in the same year as Chalk's and on January 2, 1929, initiated a regular daily flight during the winter with twenty-four-passenger seaplanes.[23]

Most remarkable was the speed with which Henry Flagler's Colonial Hotel was replaced after its spectacular destruction by fire on March 31, 1922. The Development Board immediately negotiated with the Munson Steamship Line over rebuilding and the terms of a new lease, and the government advanced a loan of £430,000 at a very low interest rate to a Munson subsidiary construction company, with incentives for an early completion. Cuban and British West Indian laborers and craftsmen were imported to finish the enlarged and modernized New Colonial Hotel within six months so it was ready for the record-setting tourist season of 1923. It was advertised in 1926 as "an absolutely fireproof hotel, which has won the reputation of being the finest in the South. Set in tropical gardens overlooking Nassau's picturesque harbor. The center of Nassau's social and sport life. Splendid orchestra, unique grills, dancing in the tea gardens. Hundreds of rooms commanding magnificent panoramas of islands, sea and sky. New eighteen hole golf course—championship tennis courts—famous bathing beach—fishing, sailing, delightful trips to nearby islands—and the society of people of distinction." All this could be enjoyed at rates advertised in Aspinall as "£1.0s.10d. ($5) per day and upwards," though the more budget-minded might find accommodation at the Allan Hotel for from 8s.4d. to 16s.8d. ($2–$4) per day or in boardinghouses for between £2.1s.8d. and £5.4s.2d. ($10–$25) per week.[24]

So successful was the American-owned New Colonial that in 1926 a consortium of Bay Street merchants successfully negotiated a similarly favorable loan from the government to build an only slightly less grandiose replica behind ancient Fort Montagu and its excellant sandy beach at the other end of Nassau. Both hotels were constructed in the Spanish-American manner developed in Florida and Havana rather than in Nassau's traditional neo-Georgian style and were on a scale disproportionate to the existing public buildings. The New Colonial Hotel boasted 250 bedrooms and the Montagu Beach Hotel 200, compared with the Royal Victoria's 90 and the 20 each of the Lucerne and Allan. In keeping with what the clientele would find familiar and comfortable and would intuitively decode "the society of people of distinction" to mean, all of Nassau's hotels were more rigidly segregated than ever before. In tune with the flagrant racialism of Frank Munson, its owner (who was anti-Semitic as well as negrophobic), the New Colonial attempted to exclude blacks from all but the most menial work, employing Cubans or other Latin Americans in the absence of suitable and willing local whites. A majority of the workers in the other Nassau hotels were blacks, but the very few nonwhite tourists in the 1920s and 1930s were forced to find accommodations in the limited range of black-owned boardinghouses, some of them Over the Hill.[25]

The private clubs that sprang up to serve the well-heeled visitors and settlers were equally exclusive. The Porcupine Club, formed as a privileged retreat before World War I by American Whitneys, Doubledays, Morrows, and Drexels, served its own plutocratic kind. Similar island retreats were the Bimini Rod and Gun Club, built by the American investor Thomas J. Peters at a cost of over a million dollars and opened in January 1920, and the members-only Cat Cay Club set up on the leased Crown land of South Cat Cay in the late 1920s by another wealthy and enterprising American, C. J. Martin. On New Providence, American and Canadian residents and visitors could dine in luxury and play roulette and poker at the Bahamian Club, the first establishment to be granted a gaming license, owned by yet another American, C. F. Reed.

Though many elite white Bahamians were honorary members of the Bahamian Club (perhaps the hidden price of the gaming license), few of them chose to patronize it. Their preferred social locations were the Nassau City Club, whose Saturday night turtle dinners in the 1920s Sir Alan Burns was to remember with relish a quarter-century later, and the Royal Nassau Sailing Club beyond Fort Montagu. Even there, Nassau's complex social hierarchy (already, needless to say, male-dominated) enforced itself. The Royal Nassau Sailing Club catered mainly to the white officials and the crème de la crème of local whites, augmented by visitors "suitably introduced." Nouveaux riches, however well-off, were not entirely welcome, particularly if they were not of unimpeachable white provenance. Paradoxically, even too much skill at sailing might be held against an applicant as prima facie evidence of a lowly Conchy Joe background. Frustration at this situation is said to have been the chief reason why the young Roland Symonette and others like him formed the rival—and in its way equally exclusive—Nassau Yacht Club in 1931.[26]

As a sign that the Bahamas was becoming an exotic extension of Florida—with the additional advantage of being untrammeled by Prohibition—was the beginning of the boom in real estate sales to Americans which, though intermittently slowed by the overdevelopment in Florida at the end of the 1920s, by the worst of the Great Depression, and by World War II, was to reach its peak in the 1960s. From the Bahamian side, this boom promised to be a new bonanza for well-placed white entrepreneurs. Of the half dozen who advertised realty services in the *Bahamas Handbook* of 1926, most were merchants who were opportunistically adding real estate to their traditional business, just as they had recently expanded their involvement in the liquor trade. Selling off Bahamian land to foreigners initially had almost as unfavorable an image as shipping booze to them. But this was no impediment to the man who, starting as much a poor white outsider as Roland Symonette, was destined to become almost synonymous with Bahamian real estate, as Sir Harold G. Christie, MHA. Christie began operations in 1922 on a shoestring and opened proper offices on Bay Street in 1926, but he nonetheless advertised "the best residential locations that Nassau and the outer Islands afford . . .

water front properties . . . small islands." Although he rode the plea—if not quite inventing it—that foreign investment in land meant prosperity for all Bahamians, for Christie real estate was no more or less than a commodity—a natural resource of tremendous potential for personal wealth and power. His choice of a telegraphic address, "Chrisland," betrayed an unconscious ambition to take over the entire Bahamas, if only to divide it up again for sale and profit.[27]

Christie and his emulators took advantage not only of the demand (as time went on, cleverly stimulated by advertising) but of immensely favorable local circumstances: the shortage of money, the failure and hardship of traditional agriculture, the local farmers' ignorance of the value to others of their beachfront lands, muddled and tenuous titles, and an inefficient if not actually corrupt Surveyor General's Department and Registry. Over the years, Bahamian realtors built up a veritable land bank of properties, some bought at windfall prices but most being items on which options and agency agreements were held. Specialized knowledge of land tenures, registration, sales, and covenants gave them the confidence to offer almost any tracts or islands a buyer might want. Realtors were, however, somewhat hampered or restrained by a colonial administration that was as ambivalent toward them and the value of their activities to the colony at large as it was toward the rum-runners and fought a long battle with them to retain command at least of the two and a half million acres of as yet ungranted Crown lands.

The colonial administration was not averse to controlled development and was not very tender toward the rights of peasant squatters, but it could be jealous of private aggrandizement by as yet unestablished local whites and almost paranoid about surrendering what it regarded as Britain's imperial patrimony to foreigners. "I don't like the idea of parting," wrote Governor Cordeaux confidentially of Crown lands in August 1925, "though it's difficult to refuse genuine development schemes. Americans are buying every available inch of private land in New Providence and paying enormous prices for it—and there will soon be nothing British left except the Flag!" Small grants of Crown land were made provided houses were built almost immediately, and leases were granted for huge tracts as long as agriculture or other forms of development occurred very soon. Clauses were inserted in leases at this time to the effect that the lands were not to be used in any way to assist the illegal export of liquor to the United States. But at the same time lessees were given assurances that they could evict native farmers even if they claimed to be annual tenants of the Crown—immediately and without compensation if they were casual farmers and with two years' notice and rent-free occupation or compensation for immediate vacation if they were living permanently on the land. Even more insidious, developers of Crown and private lands alike were empowered to apply any restrictive covenants they pleased.[28]

Besides Cat Cay, Governor Cordeaux himself was responsible for leasing several cays in the Abacos, including Murray Cay to Charles J. Alexander and the much larger Grand Cay to Dr. Charles S. Dolley, an American long resident in the Bahamas. Cordeaux also negotiated the huge lease to an Anglo-American corporation called the Grand Bahama Development Company of 430 square miles of Grand Bahama, on grandiose promises to build a network of roads and a deepwater port at West End. Nothing came of this scheme, though it foreshadowed the development of Freeport-Lucaya by Wallace Groves some thirty years later.[29]

Most of the successful land sales in the 1920s were of private rather than Crown land, and the majority of these were, as Governor Cordeaux noted, in the most populous and partially modernized island of New Providence. In several cases, the speculative purchase and subdivision of former estates, on which only a scattering of houses were built in the 1920s, merely set patterns and laid the groundwork for later expansion. The most notable transaction was the sale of the extensive pineapple and sisal fields owned by the J. S. Johnson Company to the west of Nassau, which skirted some of the island's loveliest beaches. At Westward Villas, roads were built and water laid on, with lots 60 feet wide and 130 feet deep sold for £100 and houses built and furnished for between £2,700 and £4,000 On Cable Beach, the prime location, very few houses were built for years because of the collapse of the Florida building boom, though within three decades patient speculators were to be rewarded at least a thousandfold. Even more visionary was the purchase by the Miami firm of Nelson and Bullock of the Clifton, Old Fort, and adjacent estates in the far west of New Providence. Only one or two houses were built during the 1920s, including the impressive concrete Old Fort and Carmacoup mansions illustrated in the 1926 *Handbook*, but in this area Lyford Cay and its satellites were, within forty years, to outshine even Cable Beach as an enclave of millionaires.[30]

Closer to town, on the eastward and westward extensions of Nassau's north-facing ridge, building was already extensive in the 1920s. Close to downtown, George Murphy's Shirley Slope was advertised in March 1923 as "Nassau's first restricted Realty Development." Nearby, another American migrant, Edward Toote, began the similar Buen Retiro subdivision, where a house built in 1923 for £4,700 was sold three years later for £10,000. A mile or so further east, the first fine houses were built on Village Road behind the Montagu Beach Hotel, and the Bahamian bootlegger Allan Kelly constructed three houses on the seaward side of what was to become the San Souci Estate.[31] Most heavily promoted of all was the Vista Marina development just west of Fort Charlotte. Situated on the fertile estate called the Grove, once owned by James Moss, the colony's greatest slave owner, this was now the property of an expatriate Englishman, G. R. Baxter, who engaged H. G. Christie as exclusive sales agent. Targeting rich Americans and the local elite, Vista Marina's advertisements read: "Nassau's Ideal Residential Section, adjoining the Country Club and Golf Course, with half-a-mile of Bathing Beach, this beautiful suburb, with its hills sloping towards the sea, affords every advantage to home builders that the city affords." Less attractive, however, were the confidential conveyance documents, which ordained that "no lot or any part thereof or any interest therein in the Vista Marina Subdivision of the GROVE Estate shall be sold, leased or otherwise conveyed to any person other than a full-blooded member of the Caucasian race."[32]

The Underside of the Boom of the 1920s

The inflow of American people, money, and ideas in the 1920s reinforced and extended Nassau's patterns of residential segregation. But at the same time there was a trickle-down effect both of money and the ways of making it that helped to divide the relatively fortunate nonwhites from the impoverished black majority and thus prevent an explosive polarization. Nonwhite businessmen made significant if modest advances during the 1920s and were also to a degree involved in property developments. The preferential areas north of Nassau's ridge were those most obviously affected by the 1920s boom and were most attractive to white native and American developers. Yet the immigration of Out Islanders and West Indians and the remigration of black Bahamians from Florida, as well as the general growth in the black population, expanded the sections of Nassau Over the Hill even more, offering chances for more modest developers, many if not most of them nonwhite Bahamians.

Grant's Town filled its boundaries during the 1920s, thanks largely to the black assemblyman Leon Walton Young, who had useful political allies, and probably financial backers on Bay Street. Young was responsible for Kemp's Addition and Walton Ville in the area south of Young Street and north of Wulff Road between Market and East Streets, both opened up in 1923. Another area developed to house Out Island migrants was Mason's Addition, the work of the less well-known Origen Mason, who sold fifty-by-one-hundred-foot lots for £25, on which wooden houses could be built for £100 each. In the area of bush just outside the city boundaries south of Fort Charlotte, the white non-Bahamian H. N. Chipman developed Rainbow Village, later called Chippingham, which became the home of immigrants from Long Island and Inagua, Barbados and Jamaica. Besides those white Americans and Bahamians (notably including W. C. Johnson and R. T. Symonette) who used ambitious, amenable blacks as front men, there was at least one white American who openly sought to develop a residential area for blacks. This was Captain J. S. Engler, a Miami merchant well aware of the influx of returning Florida migrants, who in 1924 purchased and subdivided a large tract of uninhabited bush south of Wulff Road, Grant's Town's southern boundary, named it Englerston, "Nassau's Master Suburb," and hopefully offered "homes on easy terms." That an area adjacent to this became known as Coconut Grove (or simply "the Grove") pointed up the Miami origins of many of its first settlers, as well as providing an ironic titular counterpoint to "the White Grove" on the waterfront three miles to the northwest.[33]

The great advances in material conditions and health in the most favored parts of New Providence advertised by the Development Board were in stark contrast to those parts of the Bahamas—and even of Nassau—which visitors seldom saw. Nothing illustrates this better than a filling in of the gaps in Mary Moseley's disingenuously promotional *Bahamas Handbook* with the clinically objective findings of Sir Wilfred Beveridge's *Report on the Public Health and on Medical Conditions in New Providence, Bahama Islands,* published in the following year, and the contemporary more or less confidential reports on other social problems, particularly the incidence of crime.

Beveridge, an eminent doctor and health scientist who taught at the London School of Hygiene and Tropical Medicine and served as medical and sanitary adviser to the Colonial Office, was polite to Bay Street, stayed in Nassau a mere four weeks, and saw nothing of the Out Islands. But what he did see was damning enough. Though he affected to be encouraged by the fact that it was the Bahamian legislature that had sought "the advice of an expert from Home," Beveridge also quoted as a warning the recent statement of "an eminent Public Health authority" that "the Bahamas are past praying for."[34]

Beveridge praised Nassau's new waterworks and sewerage system, then under construction, though he deplored their limited extension. He had some good to say of the efficient and cleanly way in which the police barracks, prison, poorhouse, and parts of the hospital were run. Many schoolteachers and nurses did the best they could, though he believed that they were undertrained, overworked, and disgracefully ill supplied, serving in schools that had space for only half the eligible children and a hospital that those who could afford to avoided like the plague. Other parts of the report were grimmer—almost a horror story. Lepers were not isolated in a proper leprosarium, and in the aptly named Isolation Ward of the Lunatic Asylum, "The so-called wards consisted of dark, bare rooms in a dilapidated building. Each room was devoid of hospital equipment beyond in some cases a bedstead and small table. The door of every room was secured on the outside. There was no visible sign of any attempt being made for the comfort of the patients." Beveridge found one aged woman suffering from senile decay and partial paralysis lying on the floor completely unattended, while in an adjacent room a corpse awaited removal to the mortuary.[35]

Overall, Beveridge was horrified by the combination of public indifference, poverty, and ignorance that led to so much substandard housing, overcrowding, and lack of cleanliness. The sanitation clauses of the 1914 Health Act were obviously ineffectual. Photographs backed up by restrained but graphic prose depicted hovels and slummy yards in pockets even in Nassau's northern suburbs, to the west within a few yards of the New Colonial Hotel, and not far east of Rawson Square in the areas around Dowdeswell Street and the Pond. Conditions in Grant's Town and Bain Town were worse: uncollected garbage festered in piles among which pigs, dogs, and fowl rooted, and open privies polluted wells and cooking areas.

The consequences were clear. Those attempting to promote Nassau and the Bahamas as the health resort of the Western Hemisphere should have been shocked by statements about the prevalence of diseases, largely eradicated elsewhere, that stemmed from preventable conditions. Some products of overcrowding, ignorance, poor nutrition, and lack of hygiene—TB, VD, pellagra, worms, neonatal tetanus—were simply a reproach to the colonial regime and affected only residents. But other diseases were directly dangerous to visitors. Venereal disease was, of course, a threat to casual sexual adventurers and, like TB, was thought to be even more contagious than it is. But at least one other disease threatened the most innocent and careful visitor. Even more telling than the photographs in Beveridge's report was the map that showed the wide dispersion of the eighty-one cases of typhoid reported between February and September 1927. Predictably, the largest number, thiry-four, were from Grant's Town and Bain Town, but twenty-one were from the crowded housing north of the ridge between Victoria Avenue and Hawkins Hill, a dozen from the Pond and further east, seven from Delancey town, five from the western suburbs, and four from the downtown core.[36]

Several American tourists had contracted typhoid fever in Nassau in 1925 and 1926, which was one of the reasons for the summoning of Dr. Beveridge in 1927. Over the same period, administrators and legislators were more concerned than they openly admitted about the rising incidence of crime, including juvenile offenses, resulting from the bootlegging era and social conditions Over the Hill. It was true, as H. M. Bell said, that killings were comparatively rare, that guns, if carried, were rarely pulled, and that major crimes were so infrequent that the public regarded them as fascinating phenomena. When murder trials occurred, such as that of Octavius Forbes in November 1924, they were treated almost as public theater and the Supreme Court and the square outside were crowded daily with an avid audience. Similarly, when three Bahamians (two of them clerks in the Audit Department, the other a taxi driver) used dynamite to break into the public vault on the night of March 16, 1926, and stole gold and silver worth £15,850, the public was as agog as if Butch Cassidy and the Sundance Kid had suddenly descended upon Nassau. The colonial secretary, A. C. Burns, however, made light of the affair, saying the vault was ancient and weak because "when it was built no one dreamed that it would ever contain so much money or anyone would be so depraved to break into it." The three robbers were caught and convicted, the vault rebuilt more robustly, and the police instructed to be more vigilant in future.[37]

Underlying trends and their causes were undoubtedly more serious and worrisome to Bay Street and Government Hill, which feared that the forces of law and order were insufficient. Incidences of stealing, housebreaking, burglary, and violent crime rose steadily throughout the 1920s, and the bootlegging trade led to the dangerous dissemination of firearms. In addition, it was thought that Bahamians returning from the United States (some of them previously engaged in bootlegging and other illegal activities) were bringing with them methods learned from American gangsters. The prison became overcrowded, and serious incidents there during 1928 suggested that Sir Wilfred Beveridge's favorable remarks in the previous year had been misplaced.

On July 25, 1928, a prisoner called James Johnson, alias Snowball, while being subdued for violent disorder, called out to the other prisoners that he was being murdered and a riot ensued that was put down with great difficulty. Shortly afterward, ten ringleaders in the riot escaped from an infirmary room being used as a cell because of overcrowding, released the other prisoners, and took over the prison. When besieged by armed police under senior officers, some surrendered but others remained defiant and pelted the police with broken bottles and conch shells. Before they were persuaded to give themselves up, one of their number, Milton Storr, rushed an officer with an ax and was shot to death.

A commission of inquiry on the riots discovered much slackness at the prison. Prisoners mixed freely both inside the prison and on the work gangs. They were given mind-numbing and pointless work. Despite serious overcrowding and the failure to segregate the more and less dangerous prisoners, a white prisoner, one Captain Reeves, was given preferential treatment. The chief jailer, Clarke, a Barbadian, used prisoners to perform personal and domestic services. He and his family lived within the compound, and the main gate was not locked until the last family member returned at night, sometimes after 9 P.M. The commission report recommended that because of the increase in criminal activity and behavior, steps be taken to tighten discipline and security, particularly by introducing a more rigorous form of solitary confinement and ensuring that no prisoners be allowed to retain unauthorized articles in their possession. It also suggested that they be provided with more useful work.[38]

The steady rise in juvenile crime was an even more basic social problem, though the regime was slow to recognize it and, rather than tackle the root causes, merely fulminated about moral decay and the decline of the work ethic and proposed stricter discipline. As early as 1921 a reformatory for juveniles was proposed, and A. F. Adderley, the black MHA, even advocated an institution that was not a prison but one "where love and tender care reigns." The majority in the House, however, turned down the idea as a waste of public money. By 1923, the situation had so deteriorated that the question resurfaced, and a commission of inquiry was held. The report bore out contemporary newspaper accounts to show that juvenile vagrancy and crime were common, accompanied by drinking, bad language, and vandalism, and that there were numerous female as well as male offenders. Between August 1921 and February 1923, 112 juveniles aged between nine and fourteen charged with vagrancy or larceny were brought before the Magistrates' Court (there was no special court for young offenders), of whom about twenty were habitual offenders who gave the police constant trouble. While most delinquents, especially boys, came from Nassau, a large number, particularly girls, came from the Out Islands, with or without their parents. In search of a livelihood if not a fortune, some of the girls, aged between sixteen and eighteen, came to Nassau alone. If they had no family or friends, they often rented a room in a disreputable area. Some shared lodgings with other girls, and to make ends meet or to supplement their earnings, they turned to prostitution.[39]

Cleveland H. Reeves, an exceptionally civic-minded colored Nassauvian who was relieving officer at the General Hospital, blamed worsening social conditions in Nassau on the liquor traffic. But he claimed that besides those who flocked to Nassau for work, many of the opportunistic migrants were idlers who slept in people's backyards and on the wharves, got into fights and overcrowded the hospital, and caused a nuisance by begging for money or food. The report also took a moral stance by attaching much blame to the rising incidence of illegitimacy and family breakdown, thereby almost inadvertently identifying related and more fundamental problems. Though the rate of illegitimacy in the Bahamas was well below that in Jamaica, in the southern district of New Providence (that is, Over the Hill) it was 72 percent. Fathers of "outside children" were not legally compelled to contribute toward their maintenance, and many mothers of children by different fathers were destitute and could not properly care for their offspring. While such mothers were out working or looking for work, they had little control over their children, who wandered the streets half-starved, almost bound to get into trouble.

Numerous children, described as "waifs and strays," were left by emigrating parents with family or friends who were too poor to care for them properly. Out Islanders who remained in Nassau did not always register their children in school, and these had no option but a life on the streets. Truancy was common even among children registered in schools; of sixteen hundred children registered in New Providence in 1922, no more than six hundred attended regularly. Parents were accused of being indifferent to their children's education and of preferring to pay the small truancy fine so they could send them out to look for work. In fact, a great number of parents, particularly single mothers, had little option between that and starvation.[40]

Despite the manifest evidence of the growing problem of juvenile delinquency and its underlying causes, progress was slow and limited. Almost nothing was done as a result of the 1923 inquiry, and it was not until 1928 that the government established the Boy's Industrial School (euphemism for a reformatory) and made efforts to corral and reform some of the most persistent offenders. In the following year, of the 289 cases of truancy brought before the courts, 31 of the worst offenders were whipped and 14 sent to the Industrial School. Though this institution had a worthy record over the following decades, it was always overworked and underfunded, understandably confused as to whether it was intended primarily to isolate and punish young offenders or to reform them and make them useful citizens. Nothing was done for years for young female delinquents, and it was to be more than thirty years—when problems were almost out of hand—before special juvenile courts were established and social workers specifically trained to deal with children and related family problems. Symptomatic of the situation was that the truancy officers were regarded as a hated and despised arm of the law, almost human rat catchers.[41]

Women in Bahamian Society in the 1920s and 1930s

One mixed blessing of the Prohibition era and its aftermath was a slow but steady shift in gender roles. The relatively greater opportunities opening up to women probably contributed to discord in the family and the increase in juvenile delinquency as well as to the amount of money in circulation and greater material expectations. In general, women in the post–World War I years had more responsibilities, and an increasing number joined the paid workforce. In Nassau, the developing tourist industry drew women, especially black women, into domestic work as cooks, laundresses, and cleaners. The steady growth of the Bahamian servant population between 1911 and 1943, as in Jamaica, was both a cause and a concomitant of the rural-urban migration and the steady expansion of the middle class. But although these changes affected women's roles in relation to men across the social spectrum, they did far less to change the class structure in relation to differences in color.[42]

The trend in North America that women, not men, filled the increasingly important occupation of secretary-stenographer affected the Bahamas, though white elite women led the way. Elite women had the opportunity in the postwar years to learn shorthand and typing from Mrs. Percy Lightbourne, who had trained abroad. This training qualified them to work in private offices and as clerks in the civil service and at the Royal Bank of Canada. Many other elite women entered the workplace as owners and operators of small dry goods stores or assistants in larger establishments, as caterers, fancy shell workers, librarians, and teachers in private schools. Their doyenne was Mary Moseley, the redoubtable proprietor and editor of the family newspaper, the *Nassau Guardian*, which she took over in 1904 at the age of twenty-six. Moseley, who went to England to serve during World War I, was a Bahamian patriot who also upheld old imperial ideas, above all the notion of white supremacy. She was for many years the dominant trustee of the Nassau Public Library, and her tireless promotion of the Bahamas and her view of Bahamian history and traditional values were best expressed in the *Bahamas Handbook*, published by the *Nassau Guardian* in 1926.[43]

Just as preference was given to men over women in nearly all forms of employment, so the rigid color line and racial discrimination that Moseley epitomized barred the great majority of nonwhites from office jobs in private businesses and within the civil service. The expansion of the Bahamian middle class that occurred as the result of Prohibition, American prosperity, and the increase in the number of American visitors and residents most benefited Bahamian whites and Bahamian white males over females. The relatively large white minority in Nassau and the increased migration from Harbour Island, Abaco, and Long Island provided almost enough personnel of the most acceptable color to satisfy those responsible for employment in the civil service and Bay Street proprietors catering to white American tourists. Yet there were trickle-down effects, especially in the 1920s but even during the 1930s, which benefited nonwhites of both genders as well as all color shades.[44]

One of the most immediate effects of Prohibition was the increased availability of at least menial wage-paying jobs for black women. Women were hired by the liquor merchants to decant the liquor from casks into bottles and to sew the bottles into the burlap sacks used for the onward traffic, and women were even seen rolling the casks to and from warehouses as supplementary stevedores. As bootlegging profits declined, so did this area of employment. But few women returned willingly to work at home. They were employed in larger numbers than ever as domestics (in hotels and restaurants as well as private homes), in petty shopkeeping, and as market women.

Though the majority remained housewives, in Nassau as well as the Out Islands, black women more than ever before dominated the petty retailing and crafts scene in downtown Nassau and the few important Out Island townships. This trend was especially notable in the fledgling straw industry, in which not only nearly all the workers but also most of the organizers and entrepreneurs were black women. During the late 1920s and early 1930s straw and sisal-work craftswomen, such as Estelle, Melissa, and Manette Davis, Eunice Demeritte, and Rebecca Jarvis from Fox Hill, began to congregate to sell their wares in Rawson Square (referred to as the Park) in central downtown Nassau. In the late 1930s and early 1940s, enterprising vendors from the fruit and vegetable market, notably Albertha Brown, Rebecca Rahming, and Eva Adderley, greatly expanded the trade to satisfy tourist demand by sewing and fashioning at their stalls the rolls of palm straw plait provided from Over the Hill, New Providence, and the Out Islands into mats, baskets, and hats.

By the late 1940s, when tourism skyrocketed, this tiered industry had become highly organized and widespread, though it remained a female preserve. Women and children throughout the islands processed the palmetto straw and sisal fiber and wove the plait to send to Nassau. There, popular items were almost mass-produced in workshops Over the Hill and decorated with Bahamian shells and imported colored raffia for sale at specialized stalls that outnumbered those selling fruit and vegetables. For several decades Bahamian straw and sisal work was exported for sale as local produce in other Caribbean tourist centers until Bahamian tourist demand outran the supply and the flow of raw material and even finished items was reversed, especially by imports from Haiti and the Dominican Republic. Although some exceptional Bahamian craftswomen remained dedicated and original artists whose work commanded premium prices (but made none of them rich), the cost-cutting dealers and entrepreneurs such as Myrtis Thompson, Albertha Brown, and Florence Pyfrom profited most. Pyfrom, a white American married to a white Eleutheran, for example, was an agent for an American hat company and at one time employed as many as two hundred female workers in her straw-work factory.[45]

For the black women in families with higher aspirations than weaving plait and street vending, the 1920s and 1930s provided improved though limited opportunities, and those of lighter complexion, as always, tended to achieve most. Along with enjoying a markedly improved standard of living, more became aware of educational opportunities, especially abroad. For example, several colored middle-class girls, such as Yvonne North, Carmita DeGregory, and Alice Hill, studied nursing in New York. Yvonne North, a light-skinned graduate of Queen's College

More horses and bicycles than cars. Bay Street in the early 1920s. *Above*, the eighteenth-century Adderley Building on the eastern edge of Rawson Square. *Below*, the twentieth-century Royal Bank of Canada, next to the Out Island Produce Exchange. "Doc" Sands photographs, Gail Saunders Collection.

in Nassau, studied at Lincoln Hospital (a black institution) before returning to Nassau and entering private practice. She was one of the early officers of the Bahamas Nurses Association. Alice Hill, also educated in Nassau, was trained at the predominantly white Buckley Training School in New York. After completing the state board examination in 1926 she worked for some years in New York before returning to Nassau as a private nurse in 1934 and becoming the first government welfare nurse in the 1940s.[46]

Without leaving home, a very few light-skinned colored women such as Mary Anderson and Naomi Dupuch found modestly paid clerical work in the civil service, and some, like Rowena Hill Eldon (future wife of the near-white controller of customs and mother of both the Anglican bishop and the president of the College of the Bahamas), in offices and downtown shops. The majority of nonwhite women who found paid employment, however, became nurses, dressmakers, music teachers, public school teachers, and stenographers and usually, in the absence of local training facilities, had to teach themselves. As early as 1918, Governor Allardyce was sufficiently impressed by the enterprise and reliability of this small subclass of pioneers to remark that "with few exceptions, the local [male] youth is past praying for. The young women have a much larger sense of responsibility."[47]

Yet as Bahamian women made perceptible socioeconomic advances (at different paces according to the color calculus) their organization as a distinct class was very slow, not just in comparison with Bahamian men but compared with their female counterparts in the region at large, particularly those in the Spanish-speaking Caribbean. In the British Caribbean, women's self-help societies and home industries organizations were the forerunners of women organizing in their own interest. Evidence is scanty for the early stirrings of a similar movement in the Bahamas, although an oral history source has mentioned that there was a self-help shop in downtown Nassau that provided an outlet for upper-class women to sell their preserves, candies, and handiwork. Women who sent articles remained anonymous, indicating that the shop hoped to "provide income-earning possibilities for gentlewomen who had fallen on reduced circumstances." To aid women more generally, the Bahamas Home Industries Association was formed in the 1920s as an offshoot of the Imperial Order of the Daughters of the Empire, with Annie Finlay as secretary, a committee of white elite women, and meetings held at Government House.[48]

As in the British West Indies generally, upper-class and colored and black middle-class women focused on social work and charitable organizations that gave them opportunities for public activity as well as satisfying their sense of noblesse oblige, with subtly arranged social layers of activity. The general effect of such organizations was to reinforce, not upset, the social order, though they did contribute to the improvement of social conditions, provide elite women with useful experience in organization and leadership, and set up models for those below them in the social order eventually to emulate. White elite women established the Bahamas Red Cross Society in 1915 and a decade later organized the Infant Welfare Centre, primarily to serve the colored and black population. Clinics were opened at three Over the Hill locations with the aim of controlling the high mortality rate. Besides treating children, the centers issued supplies of dried milk to mothers, who were also given talks and pamphlets on "mothercraft."

Similarly, Lady Cordeaux, wife of the governor who served from 1921 to 1927, founded the Oleander Club, which aimed to train black laboring-class women in housewifery skills, including cooking, sewing, smocking, crocheting, and knitting. Among those recruited to assist at the club were such prominent members of the nonwhite elite as the wives of the two leading black lawyers, Ethel Adderley and Rita Toote, Rowena Eldon, and Mamie Worrell, the latter the well-educated American wife of a black doctor and owner-operator of the chief guest house for nonwhite tourists during the 1930s. Adderley and Toote also formed a Ladies Committee to collect money and clothing and organize relief work for the victims of the hurricane at Bimini and Grand Bahama in 1935, which became a permanent organization to help the needy, called the Christmas Cheer Committee.[49]

There is little evidence that the Bahamian chapters of Marcus Garvey's UNIA, which at their peak boasted a thousand members, including a fair number of women, ever developed a distinct feminine component even though the Miami and Key West UNIA chapters had flourishing women's auxiliaries, of which many of the officers and members of the (male) advisory boards were Bahamian expatriates.[50] Yet there was a small and short-lived Civic League Working Women's Club in Nassau in the 1920s, established "for the improvement of young girls," to sponsor exhibitions of "native products" and to arrange talks by prominent blacks. Moreover, at least two black women were very active in trying to promote the interests and welfare of ordinary black women. Frances "Mother" Butler and Lettie Tinker had both traveled and been exposed to other cultures, particularly among the black communities of the United States. On returning to Nassau after living for some years in Miami, Mother Butler, with Lettie Tinker's assistance, founded the Mother's Club in 1929, originally (like the later Ladies Committee) to relieve hurricane victims but becoming a permanent organization to collect used clothing and furniture for the needy and to provide Christmas cheer for the aged. Having resolutely remained almost exclusively a black, nonelite, and Over the Hill organization, the Mother's Club built its own headquarters building on Gaol Alley off East Street in 1940.[51]

At most, the Mother's Club and similar more transitory organizations were more popular and self-driven versions of the welfare activities organized by the aspiring nonwhite middle class and the white elite. Though it is tempting to read into them greater significance than they warrant, it should be remembered that they were not concerned with fighting for increased political rights and that they played a passive role in the first faint stirrings of trade union organization that occurred in the late 1930s. There is little evidence that their members were aware of American and British feminist movements, let alone influenced by them, even to the limited degree that this occurred in Cuba, Puerto Rico, and the more developed British West Indian territories. There was no Bahamian woman equivalent to Audrey Jeffers in Trinidad or Amy Bailey and Mary Morris Knibb in Jamaica in the 1920s and 1930s who spearheaded the struggle through social and labor organizations for increased political rights and participation for women. The small advances Bahamian women had made in the 1920s and 1930s, however, did provide them with the reinforcement of the traditionally important role of women within the beleaguered Bahamian family and an increasing self-confidence—albeit learned from the top downward and with socioethnic distortions—that was to stand them in remarkably good stead once the Bahamas made its long-delayed social and political advances from the 1960s onward. In this respect, therefore, it is just that Frances "Mother" Butler should occupy as distinguished a place in the

Bahamian pantheon as does her son Sir Milo Butler, the first great black populist politician and first black governor-general.

New Immigrants, Incipient Nationalism

Though migration, poverty, ill health, and sheer ignorance had serious effects on the majority population, especially those crammed into Over the Hill Nassau, the delicate equilibrium was sustained by other factors than subtle social and ethnic subdivisions, even (perhaps especially) when economic conditions deteriorated in the 1930s. One of these factors was an emerging protective xenophobia that to a degree was shared by all Bahamians. There was never a general aversion to WASP American or Canadian visitors or even migrants, and even less to their money, a small amount of which filtered down to the poorest Bahamians. There was a degree of antipathy to Britons, both because they tended to assume imperialist attitudes and were notorious for being more careful with their money than North Americans.[52] But this aversion was overridden by a generally ingrained loyalty to the mother country and, on the part of nonwhites, by a sense that Britons, if not actually nonracist, tended to be as indifferent to or dismissive of Bahamian native whites as they were of native blacks. The dominant forces in the Bahamian legislature, however, were able to gain widespread support from the nonwhite assemblymen and the general populace alike for a much more active antipathy toward several classes of immigrant they regarded as less desirable: Greek, Lebanese, Jewish, and Chinese traders and black West Indian craftsmen and laborers. Such self-interested sentiments, which naturally grew as economic conditions deteriorated and competition heightened, can perhaps be delineated as a form of Bahamian proto-nationalism, however riddled and confused by class and ethnic contradictions.

The antipathy to Greek migrants was as old as the Greek migration itself, dating back to the 1880s. The very first arrivals seem to have been simple sponge fishermen, sponsored by mainland Greek sponge merchants seeking to expand their business worldwide. The original migrants could be characterized as poor predators, seeking to steal bread from the mouths of black Bahamian sponge fishermen, and were easily excluded.[53] The second wave of Greek immigrants—Aegean islanders marginally less impoverished but still sponsored, whose intended function was to act as sponge processors, agents, or middlemen for the Greek-dominated international market—were disliked by the Bahamian sponge fishermen because they drove down wholesale prices and feared by Bay Street because of the likelihood that they sought to invade the most lucrative aspects of Bahamian sponging, the ownership and outfitting of sponging vessels. When this perceived danger had been averted, the Bahamian oligarchy at least tolerated the Greeks for their efficiency in providing connections with the necessary larger markets. In the early decades of the twentieth century the resident Greek community grew steadily, partly through its own fecundity, partly through the immigration of more distant family members. By the mid-1920s, Greeks were said practically to control the buying, packing, and exporting of Bahamian sponges. But through hard work and enterprise they had also diversified from the sponge trade into other commercial ventures, including restaurants, bakeries, fruit and vegetable retailing, and even real estate. In these activities they encountered renewed and persistent opposition from entrenched Bay Street merchants, along with competition from the aspiring brown and black petit bourgeoisie.[54]

Regarding themselves as whites, though clearly of an intermediate class, the Bahamian Greeks distanced themselves from the black majority and brown middling class alike and were generally rejected as outsiders by the local white elite. A very few of the Bahamian Greeks eventually made their way into the Bahamian elite by astute business deals and resolute ascription to acceptable social norms. Others, as doctors and lawyers, gained popular respect and even affection for committing themselves to the interests of ordinary black Bahamians. But for the most part, the Bahamian Greeks remained a distinct minority, resolutely endogamous (almost absolutely so in the case of their women), their original language, culture, and religion sustained by family ties and even strengthened once prosperity enabled them to build their own church and pay for the support of a priest brought in from Greece.[55]

Smaller in numbers, from cultures that were either more adaptive or less obtrusive, the Lebanese, Jews, and Chinese experienced at least as much opposition as the Greeks once they seemed to challenge the dominance of Bay Street or the aspirations of the nonwhite would-be traders and craftsmen. Lebanese first came to the Bahamas at much the same time as the first Greeks as part of the diaspora that saw as many as a million people escape from Turkish misrule in Syria. Typically, Lebanese migrants started off as peddlers, itinerantly selling pins, buttons, cheap textiles, trinkets, even rice, sugar, and grits, in tiny quantities and at the lowest prices. With their exiguous profits as well as a network of suppliers and backers, successful Lebanese peddlers graduated to owning shops, concentrating on dry goods rather than groceries. As late as the 1920s, Lebanese were to be seen peddling goods in the Out Islands or on the sidewalks and wharves in Nassau. But by then, three or four Lebanese-owned businesses—which had already occupied fixed premises by the turn of the century—had begun to dominate the lower end of the dry goods market in Nassau. Most remarkable in its way was the Ouwade family, which had opened a shop in Nassau as early as 1894, changed its name to Baker, and within three generations had managed to join the Bay Street oligarchy, with two brothers in the House of Assembly.[56]

Far less assimilable but most commercially successful was the Amoury family business. The patriarch, Joseph Kalil Amoury, came to the Bahamas in 1891 and owned a shop by 1895. By the 1920s, the J. K. Amoury store, along with those owned by the Bakers and another Lebanese, K. S. Moses, had soared ahead of native dry goods retailers by dint of low profit margins, rapid turnover, frequent sales, and aggressive advertising. As early as 1923, J. K. Amoury was involved in the wholesale as well as the retail trade and was the licensed commission agent for a range of major American products (particularly cash registers, adding machines, typewriters, pianos, and radios), cutting out a whole level of middlemen thanks to a family network that extended from New York, through Nassau, to Bahia in Brazil. Even more provocatively, the Amourys, unlike the other Lebanese (and Jewish) traders, attempted to move from the popular to the high-quality and tourist end of the market which established Bay Street firms regarded as their preserve, beginning by opening a high-class boutique, M. Sraeel, in January 1926. Not surprisingly, J. K. Amoury (who died the month after the opening of M. Sraeel) suffered much commercial obstructionism, and neither he nor his sons ever scaled the heights of Bahamian society and politics (or, for that matter, seemed to have wanted to).[57]

Jewish traders were virtually unknown in the Bahamas before 1923, when Moses Garfunkel opened the Home Furniture Company, branch of a firm established in Miami. But Garfunkel and Jewish businessmen who came on his heels, though popular with their poorer customers, suffered even more severely from commercial opposition and personal criticism than did Amoury, Armaly, Moses, or the Bakers, who were at least Christians. In a spirited response to accusations that he was a foreign invader, unfairly undercutting established competitors to drive them out of business, Garfunkel claimed that he had no ambitions to sell anything but reasonably priced furniture to satisfy an obvious local demand. He did not undercut through "meanness" as he was accused of doing, but through good business methods, taking advantage of dealing direct with the manufacturers and bulk buying in conjunction with his Miami operation. Moses Garfunkel and the son who succeeded him on his death in 1924 were personally liked and respected for their chirpy sense of humor, their fund of stories, and their liberality. Their cause was not helped, however, by two aggressive Jewish-owned firms that opened in 1926. One made an oblique stab at Bay Street by calling itself "the Store with a Conscience." The other, by claiming to be a branch of a London West End tailor who guaranteed to undercut Nassau prices by 50 percent, challenged both local "quality" stores and local tailors, who were exclusively members of the nonwhite middle class.[58]

The Chinese migrants to the Bahamas, though they suffered antagonism and opposition as did the Greeks, Lebanese, and Jews, were part of a larger, more prolonged, and complex problem because they came to the Bahamas by way of the West Indies. They first arrived in Nassau as early as 1879, when a migrant from Cuba, Pan Yuong, opened a small restaurant on East Bay Street, and the *Nassau Guardian* noted: "It is astonishing how the Chinese settlers are thriving in our midst. We now have about a dozen Celestials who are patterns of industry, ingenuity and perseverence."[59] These pioneers seem to have remigrated, for most of those Chinese who found a permanent place in the Bahamas came in the 1920s, when the ending of the "dance of the millions" in Cuba suddenly made Nassau, with its bootlegging boom, a more attractive prospect. As in the West Indies in general, the Chinese used their famous frugality, hard work, ingenuity, and family networks to discover, fill, and expand certain niches in the colonial economy. In Jamaica, Trinidad, and British Guiana they came almost to dominate the grocery trade in the peasant sector, but in the Bahamas there was neither a suitable market nor a willingness on the part of the Bay Street wholesalers to allow them entry. A few Chinese eventually owned small groceries in Nassau, but most were at least initially involved in the equally traditional restaurant and laundry businesses.

Two families predominated in the early years of Chinese migration, the Cheas and Wongs. Though they spoke only Chinese and a little Spanish, money they made in Cuba enabled Luis Chea and the brothers Samuel and Henry Wing Wong to open three restaurants and a lunch counter in the Bay Street area and two laundries between 1923 and 1925. In the following year, when Chinese took over the Sunlight Bakery, the Wongs made the bold step of entering the dry goods and tourist markets when they opened the Chinese Republic Silk Store, selling Christmas presents, toys, and French toiletries as well as Chinese silks. Most of the Chinese immigrants who came to the Bahamas in this period, even if they were not family members, worked in some capacity in the businesses owned by the Cheas and Wongs. But a few Chinese sought employment outside, including Lim Pah and Pancho Wong, who in 1925 claimed to be "contractors, carpenters and painters, furniture and wood polishers with many years experience in Austria," and Cham Wong, who advertised himself in the same year for a position with a private family as cook or footman.[60] Thus those who resented or feared the Chinese influx could claim that the "Celestials" were not only invading Bahamian business, at several different levels, but were threatening to take jobs from ordinary Bahamian employees. By an insidious extension, it was also suggested that the competitive influx into the Bahamas of other West Indians was exacerbated by the way they were being excluded from their native territories by the Chinese, who had been allowed far too much license by the colonial governments. This neatly yoked at least two strands of local xenophobia, while at the same time implicitly recommending a solution: the Bahamas for Bahamians.

There were two complementary means of controlling immigration: general acts of the legislature and the more subtle and flexible orders in council, applying to particular cases and short-term situations. Since 1920 the principle had been established that anyone coming to settle or work in the Bahamas had to have the approval of the governor in council. This proviso was relaxed, though, in times of need, most notably when the Purdy and Henderson Company was allowed to bring in hundreds of Cubans and other West Indian laborers and artisans among the workforce of eighteen hundred used to reconstruct the British Colonial Hotel in 1922. Many of the British West Indians employed at that time stayed and settled in Nassau, including such persons as Clement T. Maynard, a Barbadian with experience in France, Brazil, Panama, and Cuba (who was the father of a future Bahamian cabinet minister), and Lionel Leach, a Trinidadian who had helped in the reconstruction of Kingston, Jamaica, after the 1907 earthquake and had also worked in Cuba.[61]

The first serious attack on foreign migrants was led by a near-white businessman, R. J. Bowe, the MHA for Exuma, who in April 1925 made a proposal in the House for an ordinance that would allow only first-class passengers to land in the colony and would totally exclude all "Chinese, Syrians, Turks, Arabs, Gypsies, Hindoos and Egyptians." Bowe's plea, though intemperate, combined concerns about a flood of unsuitable migrants and a takeover of Bahamian business with a solicitude for the plight of the poorest blacks, including those in his own Out Island constituency. "Is there any wonder that you have Jamaicans coming into this country in such large numbers?" he asked in a letter to the *Guardian:* "They are being pushed out of their own country by Celestials from the Far East and 'Jewestials' from the Near East. I have seen Jamaicans in nearly every place I have visited even on the Isthmus on Tehuantepec, driven to seek a living in an alien country by foreigners, permitted to enter by a Crown Colony Government much against the wishes and protests of the native Jamaican." Bowe was quoted as having stated in the House that "before they knew it there would be a colony of Chinese here that would capture the entire grocery and dry goods trade of the Colony." The sponge industry, he claimed, was already "entirely in the hands of Greeks and there were a number of Syrians here some of whom used to live in stables when they first arrived and could now buy the whole property."[62]

Ingenuously, Bowe stated that he would have no objection to such immigrants as the Chinese being allowed in if they undertook the kind of farming to which they were accustomed in their homeland. They could then take the place of the poor Out Island farmers, who were thwarted in their wishes to migrate by the foreigners' preemption of the work the Out Islanders sought in Nassau. "The class of immigrants that I proposed to exclude are not producers but extractors of wealth," he explained in another letter to the *Guardian:* "We would welcome tomorrow any enterprising people who would go in for farming, or any other industry, but will this element go in for hard work? No, I am afraid not, altho' I have seen Chinamen in Mexico cultivating fruit and vegetables in large quantities. If they would do so here we would not object to their presence." After the devastating hurricane of 1926, Bowe, citing notices that had been posted in the Out Islands on government orders warning Out Islanders against migrating to Nassau because of overcrowding, again wrote to the *Guardian* on behalf of the "poor spongers who maintained the principal industry of these Islands all their lives, the ex-pineapple growers who also contributed in bygone years to the wealth of the Colony." Despite the recent disaster, he asserted, none of these were "allowed to come in their hour of distress to seek means to rebuild their devastated homes or even to work for sufficient to relieve their hunger, yet the city is allowed to be over-run by aliens and outsiders taking the bread from the mouths of our own people."[63]

Though Bowe's 1925 motion was seconded by the black MHA Leon W. Young, he received little support from the rest of the House. In the debate, his fellow near-white Roland Symonette—not at that time a fully accepted member of the Bay Street cabal—was quoted as saying that he "thought that if people came here and took business away from the local people they ought to be given credit for doing it. He would like to see some more live business men come here."[64] Symonette was even more outspoken about objections to the immigration of West Indian workers. When the House of Assembly debated a motion by the black MHA S. C. McPherson in March 1926 that a committee be struck to consider whether the British Colonial Hotel and other large employers should be compelled to employ more Bahamian and fewer foreign workers, the future premier (then in his first year as an MHA) was quoted as saying,

> We have the worst class of labour in this colony it is possible to have. Our labour is beyond anyone's imagination. I speak from actual knowledge. Take the average working man in the Colony. It doesn't take much for him to live and he doesn't want much. If his pay is 10s a day for a week of six days and you raise it to 15s he only works four days. Give him long hours in one day and increase his pay and he will quit work right now. The next thing is there is very little they can do. I am not one to run down our own people—I have tried in my business to help them in every way but they make it impossible.[65]

As immigration from all directions and at all levels continued in the later 1920s, however, opposition to it became a general chorus, rising in volume as economic conditions gradually deteriorated with the decline of bootlegging profits, the double disaster of the 1929 hurricanes, and the knock-on effects of the Wall Street collapse of 1929 and the Great Depression of the 1930s.

As early as January 1927, the governor, on the advice of his Bay Street–dominated Executive Council, issued a one-year ban on the entry of West Indians (specifically, Jamaicans, Belizeans, Bermudians, and Cubans) unless they came as first-class passengers. This act aroused unfavorable comment in the *Nassau Tribune,* and exceptions continued to be made for well-qualified artisans and some relatives of West Indians already settled. During 1928, however, the ideas of R. J. Bowe gained much wider acceptance. The proclamation of 1927 was extended and widened to include persons from the Turks Islands, a previously open gateway to many West Indians. In August, a motion very similar to Bowe's of three years earlier was proposed by A. K. Solomon, the most prominent Bay Street merchant-politician, gained support from nearly all MHAs, including the black lawyer T. A. Toote, and resulted in restrictive legislation in September 1928.[66]

The 1928 act ostensibly excluded only "undesirable aliens," mentioning "lunatics, criminals, prostitutes, seditious persons," and anyone "whose presence in the Colony would not be conducive to the public good." But the legislation was cunningly designed to make it difficult for any illiterate or poor person to fulfill the requirements and to give the immigration officer great latitude in excluding anyone he wished. This did not satisfy such prominent Bay Street merchants as MHA Asa Pritchard (later, long-serving Speaker of the Assembly), who claimed that the act would not necessarily prevent "any stranger coming into the Colony to conduct business as heretofore." "Half measures are often useless," wrote someone using the suitable pseudonym "Bay Street" in the *Nassau Guardian.* "If the tenor of the Immigration bill read 'preventing an immigrant engaging in business here', instead of 'preventing the landing of undesirables', the mists of obscurity would have been lifted from this most important matter." Similarly, the downturn in business and the retrenchment in public works programs in 1929, which saw a sudden rise in unemployment (along, of course, with a decline in local sales), led to widespread support for tighter restrictions on the immigration of foreign laborers.[67]

In October 1929, when it was suggested that immigration restrictions be eased to allow in artisans and laborers to help with rebuilding after the recent hurricanes, a group of local builders and contractors (ironically including the fairly recent West Indian migrants Maynard and Leach) petitioned the acting colonial secretary (member of a prominent merchant family) that such a move was unnecessary and potentially damaging. They pointed out that there was an abundance of local laborers and claimed that there were also already sufficient skilled workers to complete the work in a reasonable time. Remembering their audience, they concluded that employing local workers would also help to keep down wages. Foreign artisans would not only demand higher wages but would "take away from this community money which is sorely needed for local Circulation."[68]

Early in 1930, Governor Orr followed the advice of the Executive Council and announced that the restrictions excluding West Indians and other migrants seeking work would be extended indefinitely. Shortly afterward, Etienne Dupuch, now an MHA, ostensibly championing the native worker, proposed in the House a committee "to consider the advisability of licensing all skilled mechanics in this island who are not Bahamians." Dupuch justified his proposal in the *Tribune* on the grounds that the Immigration Act and government proclamations had already effectively controlled the labor market by closing the door to West Indians and that controls on the immigration of skilled workers were a logical extension. At the same time, the Bay Street merchants who controlled the legislature intensified their campaign to exclude foreign business competitors. Demonstrating a turnabout similar to Dupuch's was Roland Symonette, who was one of the most outspoken delegates from the House of Assembly who called upon Governor Orr in November 1930 to ask for executive measures against "the alien invasion in business." The governor's response was specifically to prohibit the entry of persons intending to set up shops or stores without a special permit from the governor in council. Between 1930 and 1933 this prohibition was reinforced by laws to license commission merchants, operators of boats, and shopkeepers, though a move among the mercantile element in the Assembly to impose differential licensing fees on non-Bahamians was thwarted, and an extremist position that foreign businessmen already established should be expelled was opposed by both major Bahamian newspapers.[69]

Post-Prohibition Tristesse: The 1930s

Successive blows in the 1930s doomed the traditional elements in the Bahamian economy and made the shift from productive to service industries almost inevitable. The profits from bootlegging had already declined greatly before Prohibition came to an end in 1933. Government revenue plummeted from a high of £1.5 million in the middle 1920s to less than a third of that in 1929 and to a sixth by 1935 and was accompanied by progressive cutbacks in public works, services, salaries, wages, and employment. Concurrently, even stiffer U.S. immigration and tariff policies almost completely cut off the outflow of Bahamian migrants and the inflow of migrants' wages and remittances, while choking off traditional exports (pineapple exports, for example, once worth £200,000 a year, fell to nil in 1935). The institution of limited forms of imperial preference to a degree revived the tomato and sponge industries through exports to Britain and Canada (whose share of Bahamian exports doubled during the decade). But successive hurricanes and droughts and the mysterious blight that destroyed 99 percent of all Bahamian sponges in two months in 1938 made it seem that the elements were conspiring to reinforce the effects of the worldwide Depression.[70]

Government efforts to encourage Out Island agriculture were, to say the least, lukewarm. An agricultural inspector was appointed in 1931, but Governor Orr wrote pessimistically about the "conservative characteristics of the local farmer, and his suspicion and dislike of outside influence and advice." His successor, Clifford, professed encouragement at the enterprise shown by farmers' associations in Exuma but complained of the "lack of leadership and necessary sense of cohesion." His suggestion that help was needed to bring produce to market was greeted in the Assembly with almost as little enthusiasm as his proposal to introduce an income tax. A bill to create a produce exchange in Nassau was introduced in 1934, but it took two years to be enacted, and the system set up never worked effectively. Almost needless to say, the income tax idea was choked in its cradle.[71]

The Bay Street solution to the economic crisis, wholeheartedly endorsed by Governor Bede Clifford, was more or less to give up on the Out Islands and make Nassau attractive to those able and eager to escape the asperities of the Depression. As Clifford told the Executive Council on being forewarned by his friend Franklin D. Roosevelt of the ending of Prohibition in 1933: "Well gentlemen, it amounts to this—if we can't take the liquor to the Americans we must bring the Americans to the liquor."[72]

Governor Clifford and the Development Board worked closely together to improve communications, accommodations, and entertainment for tourists, with a decided preference for the wealthier ones. New contracts were negotiated for more frequent steamship services for smaller subsidies; a weekly Cunard sailing from New York was added to the fortnightly Munson service, and larger and more luxurious ships made the Miami run. A pier for liners was constructed at Clifton, better facilities for seaplanes built, and a direct telephone link arranged between Nassau, New York, and Canada so that businessmen could keep in touch with their offices. Most important, the government took a direct interest in Nassau's main hotel and its facilities, first enforcing a stiffer contract on the ailing Munson Company, then, when this was not fulfilled, taking over hotel, golf course, and Paradise Beach and leasing them back to another American on condition that major renovations would be made.[73]

A sports enthusiast as well as a surveyor, Clifford personally supervised the layout of polo and cricket grounds under Fort Charlotte (which was also tidied as a tourist attraction), sponsored international tennis and golf tournaments under the aegis of what was now called the British Colonial Hotel, and encouraged George Murphy in his plans to develop horse racing at Hobby Horse Hall near Cable Beach. Clifford's parallel acquisition of the valuable Prospect Ridge was also approved by the Assembly, though only after an agreement behind the scenes to allow its subdivision and sale by the chief Nassau real estate agents. As Clifford proudly noted in his autobiography, the campaign succeeded beyond expectation. The number of tourist visitors (still limited to the winter season) rose from 10,295 in 1932–33 to 25,000 between December 1934 and March 1935. Even more gratifying was the quality of the visitors, who, at the upper end of the international social scale, included a heady mix of celebrities of stage, politics, and literature, American money, and British titles. In April 1935, Nassau was referred to as "the social centre of the South," where "the society set of Palm Beach and other Florida resorts mingled with the fashionable colony here in a gay whirl of parties prompted by the visit of Their Royal Highnesses the Duke and Duchess of Kent." A few of the transients dropped anchor and built substantial winter homes on newly developed Prospect Ridge, Cable Beach, or the Eastern Bay. A smaller number of the more reclusive bought their own Out Island cays.[74]

The promoters aimed to provide a stay that fulfilled the tourists' expectations without threatening either their persons or their prejudices. Besides beaches and sports, historical attractions, and a range of sophisticated shops, visitors to Nassau were offered picturesque native crafts and entertainment. Catering to the expanding market (and laying the groundwork for patterns that were to become general after World War II) were not only the white commercial elite but a range of nonwhite entrepreneurs, entertainers, craftspersons, and servants who delivered what the white foreigners sought even if it meant running the risk of demeaning themselves and debasing their culture. At the benign end of the scale were those black men and women who volunteered eagerly for training as house or hotel servants in the euphemistically named "civic centre," established in 1931 by the future governor Dundas while he was colonial secretary. Musicians, singers, and dancers, many of whom had learned their skills in Harlem or Miami before remigrating,

Black men playing for whites only. The Chocolate Dandies at Nassau Yacht Club, 1930s. Leonard White, second from right, front row, was the bandleader. Immediately behind him, Lawrence Francis, known as "Shorty the Serenader." In the center at piano, with trademark grin, George Symonette, later a famous solo entertainer. Gail Saunders Collection.

eagerly sought work in the hotels, where one of the most popular local bands went by the degrading label of the Chocolate Dandies. Tourism also offered opportunities for boat, taxi, and surrey drivers, straw and shell workers, small boys diving for coins, young women selling themselves for little more, and outright beggars.[75]

The center of tourist activity was, of course, the respectable seaward side of downtown Nassau. One significant institution more or less born in this era was the Over the Hill nightclub. Such open-air dance halls surrounded by roofed balconies as Weary Willie's, the Zanzibar, or Silver Slipper were developed out of traditional drinking and dancing places by enterprising blacks with American experience such as Felix Johnson and Edgar Bain to cater to the tourists' condescending will to "slum" among "picturesque natives." This was a more manageable and regular, and less spontaneous, version of the occasional attendance by tourists since the nineteenth century at open-air native dances at Fox Hill and other country locations. The new nightclubs were, nonetheless, important social crossing places, not just for tourists but for different levels of local society, where authentic native music and dance were sustained and developed.[76]

A similar ambiguity affected the traditional Junkanoo parades, when residents of Over the Hill riotously descended on downtown Nassau before dawn on

"Trow us a penny, Boss." For a century, boys diving for coins were the first Bahamians encountered by tourist visitors, 1920s. "Doc" Sands photograph, Gail Saunders Collection.

December 26 and January 1. These were vivid and exciting spectacles for the tourists on their Bay Street balconies, perhaps for the very reason that they teetered on the edge of being uncontrolled. In 1932 and 1933 the authorities were concerned about the number of paraders who neglected to wear costumes and were clearly drunk, and after 1934 the Boxing Day Junkanoo was banned because of the disruption it caused both on Christmas Day and the following working day. The New Year's morning Junkanoo continued, the focus of police attention as well as popular participation but also attracting increased commercial support. By 1938, when Boxing Day became an official holiday and the Boxing Day Junkanoo was allowed to revive, both parades were much better sponsored and controlled, setting the pattern for the modern extravaganza: a magnet for tourists yet at the same time regarded as the most important of all manifestations of traditional Bahamian culture.[77]

The most memorable and worthy of those who entertained the tourists of the 1930s were the troubadours—including Phillip Brice of Fox Hill, "Cowboy," "Shorty the Serenader," "Blind Blake" (Alphonso Blake Higgs), and George Symonette—who not only popularized the goombay rhythm and traditional Bahamian songs such as "Brown Skin Gal," "Pretty Boy," and "Hoist Up the John B. Sail" but gently satirized themselves, their fellows, and the white folks they serenaded. This was a subtle and dignified revenge against such customers as Governor Clifford and his titled and monied friends, who could (as Clifford's autobiography attests) make fun of local ceremonies and dignitaries, treat black religious services Over the Hill as amusing entertainment, and even refer to Nassau blacks as "coons." What gives an extra savor to former governor Clifford's anecdote about being greeted on his arrival in Nassau in 1932 by the playing of the national anthem almost in counterpoint with "Mama Aint Got No Peas, No Rice" is that he himself was the unconscious butt of a sly local joke.[78]

Even more important than the tourists and winter residents were the effects of encouragements given to American, Canadian, and British investors eager to escape what they regarded as punitive taxes in their own countries as a result of the Great Depression and to take advantage of the cheap land and labor available in the Bahamas. Enterprising lawyers initiated what was to become the most lucrative business of all for them, the setting up of locally registered companies as tax shelters. The local bank—ironically a branch of the Royal Bank of Canada, headquartered in one of the countries from which tax refugees were escaping—was involved in the setting up of the pioneer tax refuge, the Bahamas Trust Corporation, registered in 1937. Though keeping a low profile, the first president and largest investor was the American Arthur Vining Davis, also president of Alcoa, who was later to develop a large agricultural estate at Rock Sound, Eleuthera.[79]

The refugee tycoons, of whom the most famous (or notorious) was Harry Oakes, offered economic palliatives but at the same time exacerbated social problems and divisions once it was clear whose benefit they chiefly served. One notable exception was Austin Levy, a New England textile manufacturer, who was not only Jewish but seems to have had a genuine desire to benefit the Bahamas and its people from the time he first visited Nassau on his honeymoon in 1915. Finding "no agriculture in the Bahamas as the term is generally understood in the United States" and the colony damagingly dependent on food imports, he managed to acquire two thousand acres at Hatchet Bay, Eleuthera, in 1936 and poured much of his fortune into creating a model dairy farm and chicken hatchery. Communication with the Nassau market was facilitated by the construction of an excellent sheltered harbor and the building of four motor vessels in local yards, which (along with later wartime shortages) helped to moderate the obstructionism Levy suffered from Nassau food wholesalers. Nearby Alice Town became something of a company town, though this was not resented because of the water supply Levy provided, the reasonable prices in the company-owned store, and the employment given for two hundred local people. Levy even paid wages slightly above the Bahamian average—for which he was to be chided by the governor, the Duke of Windsor, as setting a bad example.[80]

More typical in its practical profit motivation and in the sociopolitical tensions it generated was the government-encouraged rescue of the Inagua salt industry by the Erickson brothers, who were also from New England. The Ericksons' West India Chemical Company built new salinas, rebuilt the dock, and raised salt production sixfold between 1935 and 1937. Employing up to one hundred local laborers, their enterprise saved the island from destitution. But the wages they paid, two shillings a day, were half the going rate in Nassau, and their company store was unpopular with established merchants whose business it cornered, if not also with customers tied by credit. Because of Inagua's good communications with Jamaica and the rest of the British West Indies during the increasingly disturbed late 1930s, these conditions were to prove inflammatory.[81]

In crowded New Providence, employment was so scarce that laborers competed with each other for the available work and unquestioningly undertook whatever work was required of them. The bootlegging millionaire Ralph G. Collins, for example, was regarded almost as a philanthropist when he employed hundreds of workers (most of them semistarving Out Island migrants) for a shilling a day plus a hot midday meal. They were set to build an unbroken two-mile, ten-foot wall around his huge property close to downtown Nassau, stretching south from Shirley Street almost to Wulff Road. Collins's motives were mainly commercial and not necessarily racist, though over the years his wall was to assume great symbolic importance. It protected from encroachment and sustained the market value of subdivided properties in what was to become the white and brown middle-class enclave of Centreville. But it also literally walled in the whole of Grant's Town from eastward expansion or even communication—a visible class and subethnic barrier built by the duped black underclass itself.[82]

Grander still in scale and less immediately problematic were the operations of the American-Canadian-British mining magnate Harry Oakes during the eight last years of his life that he devoted to the Bahamas. Oakes had made a huge fortune from the Kirkland Lake gold mine in northern Ontario and was easily persuaded by Harold Christie to take up residence in New Providence in 1934 to avoid Canadian taxes. A man of rough manners, whose energy, ambition, and acquisitiveness equaled his fortune, he descended on the island with a force that proved almost more than Bay Street could handle. Easily Christie's best customer, he acquired ten thousand acres in New Providence, a fifth of the island—a huge swath southwest and west of Nassau, including prime lakefront, beachfront, and ridgeland. Oakes built his main house, Westbourne, on Cable Beach and another mansion at the Caves, then started a farming project, leveled a polo field, and began the construction of Nassau's first airfield. Legend has it that he acquired the British Colonial Hotel almost on a whim, out of pique at poor service, but the acquisition was commercially astute as well as entirely consonant with his tireless self-aggrandizement. Three successive governors believed that even if he was personally crass, his Croesus-like wealth was a tonic the colony needed. He obtained naturalization, virtually bought a seat in the Assembly, and was moved upward to the Legislative Council in rapid succession. He then leapfrogged all the local elite by obtaining a hereditary title as Sir Harry Oakes, Baronet, thanks, it is said, to the strategic gift of £50,000 to St. George's Hospital in London.[83]

Though his personal demeanor was dictatorial and his motives always suspect to the more perceptive, Oakes seemed a godsend for the underemployed ordinary people of New Providence. On his farm, in his many building projects, and in the creation of Oakes Field, he employed as many as fifteen hundred men at one time, paying unskilled labor a shilling a day above the statutory four shillings established in 1936 and providing free dinners and transportation. This relief, however, was equivocal. It antagonized other employers of labor and gave the proletariat a view of the wages and work conditions employers could offer. But being available to only a fraction of those seeking work, it could not solve the general problem of unemployment and divided the potential proletariat into a fortunate minority and an increasingly frustrated majority.

Faint Stirrings: Unrest During the Great Depression

Much more than Governor Bede Clifford (whose behavior and attitudes as they appear in his own memoirs make him seem almost a P. G. Wodehouse creation), the more serious and professional Governor Charles Dundas, who was the colonial secretary in the Bahamas when the Depression first hit, was well aware of the desperate state of the Out Islands and the explosive potential of New Providence and was extremely concerned that the colony in his charge not follow the lead of the British West Indies in generating "socialist discord." The signs were significant, but the dangers were not realized.

Demands for political change in the depressed 1930s were scarcely more articulated than in the relatively prosperous 1920s. Between 1925 and 1929, a heterogeneous assortment of reformists—ambitious brown and black businessmen and even a few progressive whites—had formed a loose alliance termed by some the Ballot Party, with the specific aim of weakening the power of the Bay Street cabal by introducing the secret ballot and the more general aim of reducing racial discrimination. The proposed measures were not truly radical and were aimed more at promoting the middle class against the upper than at replacing Bay Street with a true democracy, let alone changing the political system altogether. The most that could be said for the spokesmen for change was that they wanted a fairer share of the benefits of prosperity for themselves and resented the way the political system, preferential discrimination in jobs, and the segregation of schools (as in clubs, places of entertainment, and even such purportedly neutral organizations as the Boy Scouts and Girl Guides) militated against them.[84]

Perhaps most typical of the advocates of moderate changes was the tailor and musician R. M. Bailey (1875–1960). Born in Barbados, he had studied classics at Codrington College, but his hopes of a career in the law had been thwarted by poverty and discrimination and he had migrated to Nassau in 1898. There he was able to make a living but found that discrimination because of his color was compounded by distrust of his West Indian origins. Bailey never sat in the House of Assembly, but he strongly supported the nonwhite Bahamian MHAs C. C. Sweeting and S. C. McPherson in their campaigns, and throughout the 1920s and 1930s his tailor shop next to W. P. Adderley's Big Store on King Street was an informal political academy. The greatest achievement of Bailey and his associates was to persuade the government to set up the racially mixed Government High School in 1925 and to sustain it in subsequent harder times. But the informal Ballot Party, of which Bailey, Sweeting, and McPherson were notable members, lost impetus during the height of the Depression, when people were forced to look to their own survival, psychological depression took hold, and, not coincidentally, the number of nonwhites in the Assembly fell from the record of nine in 1928 (a third of the total) to four in 1935.[85]

The ideas of the secret ballot and the outlawing of formal discrimination were kept alive during the Great Depression, along with calls for higher minimum wages and an income tax for the rich by a mere handful of idealists, a surprising number of them whites or near-whites. Among them were Henry Taylor and Cyril Stevenson (who had to be especially cautious because of their jobs as Bay Street employees), Percy Christie, the "black sheep" brother of the realtor Harold Christie, and another white, Holly Brown, son of a Grenadian father and Bahamian mother, member of the Gallant Thirty in World War I, who was cast back by the Depression from a life in Canada and founded the radical newspaper the *Herald* with J. Stanley Lowe in May 1937. These socialist moderates, publicly labeled "communists" and privately regarded as social renegades by Bay Street, did not constitute a formal party and had no representative in the legislature. But they were encouraged, or armed, by news of sociopolitical unrest elsewhere in the British West Indies and by a steady rise in more or less inchoate civil disturbances and Depression-related crime in their own colony—at least to the degree that these manifestations argued for moderate change as an antidote to outright social revolution.[86]

In July 1935, when Roland Symonette was building the Prince George Hotel, between three and four hundred men turned up looking for employment, and as soon as it was evident that most were to be disappointed, a near riot broke out, accompanied by stone throwing. Later in the year, eight hundred unemployed men turned out for forty advertised jobs at Fort Charlotte. Many of those who could not find work took to begging and a few to crime, including arson as well as theft. Within two weeks in the late summer of 1937 both the Nassau Theater and Montagu Theater (which practiced seating segregation for those who could afford to patronize them) mysteriously burned down. By July 1938, Governor Dundas reckoned that there was a "Nassau mob of about 1000 persons," consisting of "young loafers, criminals and riff raff of that type."[87]

A so-called labor union was formed by Percy Christie in 1936, which within a year boasted eight hundred members. The union may have had some influence in persuading the Assembly to pass the Minimum Wage Act of 1936 and the administration to ordain the minimum daily wage of four shillings, which Christie had been publicly advocating since 1931. But Christie proved no equivalent of the Trinidadian white labor leader Captain Cipriani, just as Charles Rhodriguez, the black merchant who ousted Christie in 1938 largely on the grounds of his color, lacked the charisma of Trinidad's Uriah "Buzz" Butler (who similarly ousted Cipriani) or Jamaica's Alexander Bustamante. Nor, for that matter, was there yet the necessary proletariat to lead. Craftsmen and the permanently employed shunned the union, and for unemployed laborers even the dues of a shilling on joining and a penny a week proved too much. The union, hampered even more by an inability to operate without membership dues than by an absence of labor legislation, soon petered out.[88]

An even less effectual union movement had been begun in Inagua in 1934 by Theodore Farquharson, an Acklins Islander who had returned to the Bahamas from the United States to manage a family store at Mathew Town in 1928. Neither Farquharson nor his followers were the instigators of the incidents at Inagua in 1937 that seemed at first examination—and were exaggerated in the international press—to be a Bahamian extension of troubles in the British West Indies. There was indeed labor unrest at Inagua in 1936, directed first against the chief local merchant, Arthur Symonette, for the way he operated the truck and credit system and then, more or less in alliance with Symonette against the newcoming Erickson brothers once they had opened their own company store, taken over the stevedoring contract from Symonette, and refused to raise wages. But the actual trouble stemmed from a more general social malaise and the existence of a gang of desperadoes styling themselves the Band of Inaguan Terrors, led by two brothers named Duvalier.[89]

In August 1937, motivated by personal grievances and general disaffection against the Ericksons and their friend the local commissioner, Arthur Fields (a colored Trinidadian, a doctor by profession, who had been in Inagua more than a decade), the Duvaliers attacked and wounded Fields and one of the Ericksons, killed a salt company employee, set fire to several of the company buildings and the government radio station, and forced the Ericksons, Fields, and others to take flight in the Ericksons' yacht. The rest was as much farce as tragedy. The Erickson yacht broke down and drifted to Cuba, where its passengers were arrested and briefly detained for carrying arms. The authorities in Nassau, alerted by radio, attempted in vain to charter an aircraft and then sent an armed detachment of police in a mail boat, which broke down and marooned them at Rum Cay. When the police eventually arrived at Mathew Town after eight days, the Duvalier brothers had fled in a sailboat to Haiti. Arrested there two months later and extradited to Nassau, they were tried for murder, convicted, and executed by the end of November 1937.[90]

Despite extensive and alarmist coverage in the British and American press, the Inagua incident blew over like a summer squall. The black West Indian Fields was replaced by a white Abaconian much more independent of the Ericksons. When the chief Out Island commissioner John A. Hughes (who was by now also the colony's labor officer) visited Matthew Town early in 1938, he reported everything quiet. Though the Ericksons did not like Japheth Malone, the new commissioner, calling him arrogant and racially prejudiced, Hughes claimed that Malone had garnered respect and that the settlement was calm. No trace of the truck system remained, the salt operations were back to normal, and many of the inhabitants had quietly returned to the business of smuggling with Cuba.[91]

Much more significant, though unnoticed in the overseas press and eventually anticlimactic, were the disturbances in Nassau associated with the by-election that placed Harry Oakes in the House of Assembly in July 1938. The by-election for one of the two seats in the Western District of New Providence was occasioned by the elevation to the Legislative Council of the distinguished (and quintessentially moderate) black lawyer A. F. Adderley. Banking on the support of one of the largest black electorates in the colony and the tradition that this seat normally went to a nonwhite, the dynamic but relatively poor and uneducated black shopkeeper Milo Butler (son of the founder of the Mother's Club) offered himself in opposition to Harry Oakes.

Oakes was not in the Bahamas during the election, which was managed for him by his attorney Kenneth Solomon, who also happened to be the leader of the government in the House of Assembly. Behind the scenes, Butler's credit was stopped at the Royal Bank of Canada under Bay Street pressure, while at the polls the Oakes party openly distributed money and liquor, under the eyes of the police stationed to prevent disturbance. When it was clear that Butler was so decisively beaten that he would lose his deposit, he announced that he would lodge a protest against the glaring bribery. A drunken and unruly mob attacked the police when they closed the polling station, slightly injuring two white officers with missiles. Among those arrested were two of Butler's most ardent supporters, who were convicted and imprisoned for six months.[92]

The day following the election, Milo Butler led about forty supporters downtown to the colonial secretary's office, where he excitedly voiced his grievances. Rumors began circulating that there was to be a major riot to coincide with Emancipation Day, August 1. While a police investigation was being undertaken at the orders of the colonial secretary, Butler formulated a petition to the governor, calling for the secret ballot, the establishment of an election court of appeal, and the fairer representation of blacks on public boards and in the civil service. The Emancipation Day demonstration, however, was orderly and peaceful. Between seven and eight hundred people paraded the city streets with banners calling for the secret ballot, listened to speeches at the Southern Recreation Ground, and then dispersed without marching on Government House.[93]

Governor Dundas, though, believed that conditions remained explosive "and might with slight provocation have become critical." Just as his predecessor had sought to avert unrest by advocating the Minimum Wage Act in 1936, Dundas became convinced that the secret ballot was the minimum now necessary to defuse the situation. Announcing his intention to dissolve the House of Assembly, he threatened to make secret balloting the issue of a general election. Apprehensive that such an election would inevitably become a color issue, many legislators began to adopt a less hard-line attitude and in June 1939 passed an act for the secret ballot—though this was said to be merely for a five-year trial period and was limited to New Providence. For the Out Islands, where a third of Bahamian electors returned two-thirds of the members and Bay Street remained paramount, the secret ballot was to be delayed until 1949.[94]

Another palliative minor measure for which Dundas was responsible was the appointment of a labor officer, but it is significant that the person he chose was not an expert and combined his job with that of being chief Out Island commissioner. For Dundas firmly believed that the root of the trouble lay in the Out Islands and that only by reviving Out Island agriculture and reversing the trend of migration could the problems apparent in New Providence be solved. "Only thereby," he wrote in a confidential memo early in 1940, "can the great majority of the people be helped and Nassau itself saved from becoming a gathering ground for a parasitic element and possibly a centre of dissatisfaction and slum existence with disproportionate incidence of petty crime."[95]

The imperial government considered the Bahamas so different from other West Indian colonies and its economic, social, and political problems so much less serious that it did not include the colony on the itinerary of the Moyne Commission, which surveyed conditions throughout the British West Indies in 1938–39. But just as one of the salient features of the Moyne recommendations was the revival of the West Indian peasant sector as a counterweight to industrial modernization, so Dundas's plea fell on ready ears, and the Colonial Office sponsored a report on the development of agriculture in the Bahamas by E. A. McCallan, who had been director of agriculture in Barbados from 1920 to 1934. Published in Nassau in May 1939, this report painted a dismal picture of backwardness and neglect and made sweeping recommendations—some but by no means all of which were subsequently implemented.[96]

Before World War II broke out, Governor Dundas had appointed a general Out Island committee under the chairmanship of George Murphy, set up a marketing committee to improve the Out Island produce exchange, and arranged for the appointment of eleven agriculture inspectors, two of whom were employed in teaching agricultural husbandry in the schools. The creation of a proper agricultural department, though, had to wait until after the war, and such proposals as economic protection for Out Islanders' produce (which cut across the interests of Bay Street importers, wholesalers, and retailers of American produce) never came close to realization. The even slimmer chances of the creation of a true Bahamian peasantry and the limits of Dundas's vision for the ordinary black Bahamian can be gauged from a confidential report he made just before he was displaced to make way for the Duke of Windsor in 1940: "It is my considered opinion that the Bahamas coloured people are by nature and inclination essentially employees and that they are little fitted to be independent producers. . . . There are of course exceptions, but as far concerns the mass of the people, experience of them forces me to the conclusion that they will do far better as agricultural labourers than as producers."[97]

Equivocal Refuge: Jews in the Bahamas in the 1930s

It was as well for Dundas and his Bay Street associates that making a livelihood was far more important than political ideals for nearly all nonwhite Bahamians in the late 1930s. Nonetheless, the racist discrimination they faced from an increasingly capitalist and Americanized white regime was a growing irritant. They were subject to forces that were an extension of worldwide trends—racist and antidemocratic in the sacred name of nationalism—of which the German and Italian fascist regimes were merely the most obnoxious manifestations. In this sense, the colony of the Bahamas, under the control of commercial oligarchs who were allied with—even financially dependent upon—wealthy refugees from what they regarded as dangerous socialism in their own countries, was ill-prepared to participate in the war against European fascist dictators that began on September 3, 1939.

That this interpretation is not entirely fanciful is borne out by the deeply ingrained racism, anti-Semitic and anti-Chinese as well as negrophobic, maintained by the ruling Bahamian regime. Some of this racism stemmed from that snobby chauvinism that led Mary Moseley in the early 1920s to disparage West Indian blacks in the *Nassau Guardian* and to complain that the price of progress apparently included the experience of seeing a Jew selling hot dogs and hamburgers from a van in Nassau. "Shortly we may expect to see a Chinese quarter and a Ghetto, perhaps with foreign language papers," she wrote in 1923. Such, of course, never materialized, chiefly because ways were found to exclude nearly all Jews and Chinese as well as black West Indians. Anti-Semitism, moreover, was reinforced by those who took the lead from Allen Munson, owner of the New Colonial Hotel from 1922 to 1932, and were determined to ensure that Nassau, in contrast to Miami Beach, be a resort for gentiles. As Michael Pye reports in his negative book on the Bahamian regime of Governor Windsor, at the end of the 1930s Lorraine Onderdont, manager of the Royal Victoria Hotel, wrote to a Miami travel agent: "We were very much annoyed today when your party arrived in Nassau and I found that they were Jewish. . . . It is up to agents to see that they keep at least one place a Christian resort."[98]

Austin Levy was allowed (after what might be termed a probation of twenty years of mere visits) to establish and develop his model farm at Hatchet Bay on the principle, surely, that money bought exemption, provided it was also understood that Levy intended a noncompetitive business in an Out Island and had no intention of establishing a group of his coreligionists, let alone a ghetto. Far more tragic was the way Bahamian society had become so infected with American-style anti-Semitism that, in its own small way, it colluded in the unwillingness on the part of

Britain, Canada, and other Western nations to accommodate penniless refugees from Hitler's pogroms in the 1930s and thus helped to condemn at least some Jews to the Holocaust.

In the late 1930s, the Bahamas was desperately short of qualified doctors, particularly in the Out Islands. In 1939 Governor Dundas reported that there were as many as three vacancies on the small hospital establishment. For these positions there were no white applicants, and in the existing political climate it seemed unwise to appoint nonwhite West Indians as had sometimes been done in the past. Hearing of the Bahamian dilemma, the British Co-ordinating Committee for Refugees put pressure on the Colonial Office to appoint from among the many highly qualified Jewish doctors desperate to escape from the clutches of Nazism. Governor Dundas consulted with his councillors and gained extremely reluctant permission to appoint two such persons on the understanding that they would be district medical officers for Out Island service, on one-year terms, and strictly forbidden to practice privately.[99]

Three weeks before Hitler's invasion of Poland, the Colonial Medical Appointments Sub-Committee interviewed candidates at the Colonial Office in London. Two German Jews, Francis Klein and Ulrich Oberworth, were appointed, each with a string of degrees, wide experience, and enthusiastic references. Arriving in Nassau before the end of 1939, they served, mainly in the Out Islands, throughout the war, though apparently neither settled permanently in the Bahamas. Far more poignant were the cases of two of those who failed to be appointed. Dr. V. E. Klare, a twenty-seven-year-old German working in Austria who termed himself a quarter Jewish, traveled from Vienna to London for the interview. Unsuccessful because other candidates had more experience, he returned home on August 11, 1939, bravely telling his interviewers that he was satisfied that the jobs should go to others with more genuine refugee status. Ludwig Reinheimer, aged forty-four, was such a person. A World War I veteran with brilliant academic credentials, he had risen to be chief medical officer of Frankfurt before being sacked under the Nuremburg Decrees in 1936 and reclassified as an agricultural worker. In a pathetic and self-abasing letter addressed to the Colonial Office in May 1939 (which tells us as much about Reinheimer's perceptions of the imperial and colonial regime to which he was applying as about that which he sought to escape) he described himself as of "an irreproachable but unlucky family . . . pensioned off as having Israelitic grandparents." His wife, he pointed out, "is entirely free of nonaryen [*sic*] ancestors . . . our two daughters (being 6 and 5 years of age), and I enjoy an excellent health. By the by children and father have blue eyes and blond hairs as the photos enclosed shall demonstrate."[100]

The photographs of the worried father and his smiling daughters, one hugging an even more "Aryan"-looking doll, remain in the Colonial Office's Bahamas files, ghosts to bring unexpected tears to the researchers of later times. Ludwig Reinheimer was turned down by the Colonial Office on the grounds that he had not been able to appear in London for the interview. It is highly unlikely that he, Klare, or their families, survived a war that was never to be much more than a distant rumble to the Bahamas and Bahamians.

9

World War II and Its Aftermath, 1939–1962

Phony War: The Start of the Windsor Era

Britain declared war on Nazi Germany on behalf of itself and its empire on September 3, 1939. Though nominally involved, the Bahamas was hardly affected until the United States went to war in December 1941, and even then the effects were unexpected and not all negative. American tourism continued to flourish from 1939 through 1941, augmented by the arrival of well-heeled refugees from Europe, led by the former King Edward VIII, now Duke of Windsor, and his American Duchess. From 1942 to 1945 the Bahamas assumed considerable strategic importance as an antisubmarine and aircraft staging base, and New Providence became an important training ground for aircrews. The immediate effects of these developments, however, were dwarfed by the more general and longer-term changes that gathered speed during the late 1940s and 1950s: the increase in the flow of people, money, and ideas thanks to improved air, sea, and media communications; a steady improvement in Bahamian standards of living and political awareness; and the substitution of an informal but seemingly irreversible trend toward American economic and cultural hegemony for war-battered British imperialism. Conservatism continued to reign, however, and even reached its apotheosis with the heyday or last hurrah of the Bay Street oligarchy.

In very different ways, the collapse of the sponge industry and the arrival of the Duke of Windsor as governor were of more moment to the people of the Bahamas than anything that happened in the wider world before the Japanese attack on Pearl Harbor brought the United States into the war. The sponge industry had been making a modest recovery since 1935 until a mysterious fungus suddenly struck late in 1938, almost totally destroying the Bahamian sponge beds. An industry that at its peak had employed nearly three thousand men in 220 sloops and schooners and 1,300 dinghies was closed down in 1939. The industry had given employment in clipping, sorting, and packing the sponges and indirectly in boatbuilding and sailmaking. Though reopened to a degree in October 1946, the sponge industry never recovered fully. Most of the best-quality sponges did not return, and Bahamian sponges could not compete with greatly improved synthetic substitutes.[1]

In Andros the effects of the sponge blight were devastating and not much less so in Abaco and Acklins. Many spongers migrated to Nassau, desperate for work in a depressed labor market; those who stayed turned back to the already overworked soil. Cases of starvation occurred and destitution was so general that the hard-pressed colonial budget set aside £15,000 in 1939 for the relief of Andros. For the less unfortunate in New Providence chances for employment in the tourist industry improved until the end of 1941, and in addition to those working for expatriate settlers, a few hundred people found laboring jobs on the small United States Navy installations set up in Exuma and New Providence as a result of the Churchill-Roosevelt bases-for-destroyers deal in August 1940. Such benefits, however, were offset by the inflation in prices that followed from dependence on imports in conjunction with shipping difficulties, as well as from opportunistic profiteering. Some essential commodities, including flour, rice, cooking oil, and kerosene, tripled in price between 1939 and 1942 although wages for unskilled work remained static at the level decreed in 1936.[2]

Though the number of tourist visitors recorded by the Development Board fell from 48,432 in 1939 to 21,328 in 1940, this decline was accounted for entirely by the loss of "transient" passengers because of the virtual cessation of visits to Nassau by cruise liners. The number of "stopover" tourists increased from 12,905 to 13,656 between 1939 and 1940 and rose to 14,741 for the war-shortened winter season of 1941 (when the total number of visitors was up from 21,328 to 28,219, before falling to 6,054 in 1942, 3,652 in 1943, and negligible figures in 1944 and 1945).[3]

Next to Sir Harry Oakes, the most notable new employer of Bahamian labor was the enigmatic Swedish industrialist Axel Wenner-Gren, multimillionaire owner of Electrolux. Arriving in the late 1930s as a tax refugee, Wenner-Gren had purchased the central tract of Hog Island through Harold Christie and built a mansion named Shangri-La after the Himalayan utopia of James Hilton's currently best-selling novel *Lost Horizon*. An enthusiastic yachtsman, Wenner-Gren also employed Bahamian laborers to dig a canal across Hog Island and construct a hurricane-proof marina on its leeward side. The employment, though, was short-lived. Wenner-Gren's well-attested business connections with Nazi Germany, rumors of his quasi-fascistic political and social ideas, and sheer gossip (which made the Hurricane Hole and Shangri-La canal a potential base for German U-boats) led to his being declared persona non grata by the United States and British governments in 1942 and moving the center of his operations in the Americas from Nassau to Mexico. Curiously, however, he retained close business connections with his white associates in the Bahamas, not least with Governor Windsor, whom Michael Pye scandalously implicates in a conspiracy to evade British taxation and "launder" money through Mexico, if not in more sinister and traitorous projects.[4]

Such speculations were consonant with the almost surreal atmosphere in Nassau of the early war years. Many of the refugees were ambivalent about the war, American tourists were uninterested and it was considered bad manners to discuss the situation in Europe in their presence, and the ordinary people were too desperately poor to feel even the limited patriotic loyalty evinced in World War I, let alone to ask searching questions about the ideas of those visitors and refugees offering them employment. The early patriotic gestures of members of the Bahamian elite, of which they unselfcritically boasted once the war was over, were therefore almost comic, if not pathetic. Very few Bahamians volunteered for service before 1942, and no attempt was made to recruit drafts of volunteers as in the previous conflict. Though more than one thousand were to serve before the end of the war, far fewer went overseas (or died in the cause) than in World War I. The Assembly, it is true, voted an interest-free loan for the duration of £250,000—about half the annual revenue at that time—but the sums raised by private contribution were, even by the standards of an impoverished colony, minuscule: £26,500 for Spitfires, £250 for tanks, £1,079.9s.3d. for a damaged ward of the Malta Hospital.[5]

Etienne Dupuch, who had rallied to the imperial cause despite his postwar disillusion in 1919, took special pride in his memoirs of being both chairman and the only nonwhite on the War Materials Committee formed in June 1940 (a month after Dunkirk). As the *Annual Report* for the Bahamas straightfacedly reported in 1946:

> As a result of its efforts the Committee was successful in salvaging almost £90,000 worth of materials from waste. Of this some £20,000 worth was given free to military workshops in the islands or sold to local industry, while £61,643 worth was sent to Britain as a gift from the people of the Colony. Twenty shipments were sent to Britain during the War and all got through. The material sent included metal of all grades prepared according to specifications of the Ministry of Supply for smelting on arrival, medical and surgical equipment, field glasses and telescopes, compasses, firearms and cartridges to help arm Britain's Home Guard; wool, sisal, lignum vitae, and other local products; canned tomatoes, pineapples, guava marmalade, honey, specially prepared for submarine crews, and numerous other canned goods.

So pleased were Dupuch and his committee with their efforts that in 1945 they reconstituted themselves as an Aid for Britain group to help relieve the postwar food shortages in the mother country.[6]

Though it did not please Governor Dundas, who was unceremoniously shipped off to Uganda, or Etienne Dupuch, who as a Catholic royalist deprecated the abdication and its cause, the arrival in August 1940 of the former king-emperor Edward, Duke of Windsor, to govern the Bahamas was greeted with enthusiasm and hope by nearly everyone in the colony. Ignorant that the British government was eager to remove an embarrassing personage as far as possible from the threat of his being used as a Nazi puppet to a post of minimal importance, the local elite and the socialite refugees were gratified by the arrival of one of the century's most glamorous figures. Windsor's American Duchess was equally fascinating, particularly to her compatriots, and at the least the pair's presence was seen as a boost to Bahamian tourism. As Windsor himself confidentially reported soon after arriving: "Local interests have already quite naturally begun to use both the Duchess and myself to boost the American trade for the coming winter season. I will not go so far as to say that they have as yet done so in an undignified manner, and as Governor I have a certain amount of control."[7]

The general tendency to regard the Windsors as a distinguished romantic couple was expressed by Blind Blake in a hugely popular goombay calypso:

> It was love, love alone
> Cause King Edward to leave de trone. . . .
>
> I know King Edward was noble and great
> But it was love that cause him to ablicate.[8]

The ordinary people, moreover, had vague but optimistic expectations from the great-grandson of the queen whom they regarded as having freed the slaves (and whose statue Windsor faced as he landed in ceremony in Rawson Square on August 17, 1940). They probably had an inkling of the myth that Edward was not only a rebel but had sympathy for the plight of the poor, based on his reported response

Governor HRH Duke of Windsor and his wife performing their duty at a march past, Rawson Square, Nassau, 1942. Courtesy of Bahamas Archives.

to conditions among the South Wales miners; "Something must be done for these people."

The opening to the public of most of the Duke's official correspondence after thirty years and the publication of some of the Duchess's letters by Michael Bloch and her own memoirs a little later revealed the limits of his capabilities and concern and her almost limitless hatred and contempt for the Bahamas and its people. "The heat is awful," wrote the Duchess to her Aunt Bessie late in 1940. "I long for some air that isn't caused by electric fans. . . . I hate this place more each day. . . . Where did you stay when you came to this dump and why did you come here? . . . We both hate it and the locals are petty-minded, the visitors common and uninteresting." Here she was concentrating her venom on whites. As an American southerner, her attitudes toward nonwhites were at best condescending, at worst racially prejudiced.[9]

It was fortunate that both of the Windsors were adept at keeping up appearances. The Duchess, smartly accoutered in designer uniforms, graciously lent her prestige to worthy causes such as the Red Cross, the Infant Welfare Clinic, and a canteen for white servicemen. Her patronage, indeed, made such charities chic, though a local woman not generally known for her waspishness later remarked that had a fete been held for Hitler's birthday it would have been well attended.[10] The Duke, accustomed to a life of privilege and adulation, was a weak and slothful character enthralled by his wife. But he could not entirely discard deeply imbued lessons of duty and correct behavior and had also learned from his father the art of self-projection. Even if motivated mainly by fear of the consequences, he did express concern for the welfare of the people under his governance; in emergencies he was capable of acting decisively (if not always wisely), and, following the example of his father, King George V, he was the first Bahamian governor to use the radio as a means of projecting a firm and agreeable image of the ruler to the ruled.[11]

The Duchess was later to refer to the Windsors' Bahamas years as a Napoleonic exile. She called Nassau her husband's St. Helena, though had she been better read in history her ambitions for his return to power might have led her to prefer the analogy of Elba. For the Duke, seemingly, his Bahamian tenure was one last tiresome duty in a protracted abdication, a temporary stage in the progress toward a life as self-indulgent monarch of the international social set with no duties. The Windsors were quintessentially transatlantic figures, and the one positive aspect of their spending much of their tenure in the Bahamas in visiting the United States was that the Bahamas benefited from the negotiations in Washington—for example, to facilitate food supplies or employment opportunities—that were the frequent pretext. Indeed, for all its banalities, the Windsor regime in the Bahamas could be regarded as symbolizing, almost personalizing, a transitional phase before the great changes brought about by far more important underlying forces: World War II, the concomitant decline of British imperialism, and the increasing Americanization of the hemisphere.

Counterposed Views: Rosita Forbes and Sidney Poitier

The twilight zone of prenationalist limbo of the late 1930s and early 1940s Bahamas, located between peace and war, poverty and prosperity, the traditional and the modern, Britain and America, is neatly encapsulated from opposite viewpoints in the accounts of two utterly different autobiographers: the English aristocratic socialite Rosita Forbes and the black Bahamian actor-to-be Sidney Poitier.

Mrs. Arthur McGrath, who used the pen name Rosita Forbes as a travel writer and social correspondent, was a wealthy and restless world traveler who was persuaded to visit and perhaps settle in the Bahamas by Sir Charles Dundas, whom she had met in Lusaka, Northern Rhodesia, in 1937. They were both old-fashioned British imperialists who shared the ideals of Cecil Rhodes and naively seem to have regarded the Bahamas Out Islands as little different from the "White Highlands" of British East Africa: beautiful farmlands undeveloped by their picturesque "primitive" native inhabitants.

After her first visit to Nassau in the winter season of 1938–39 on the invitation of Governor Dundas and the Development Board, Rosita Forbes rewarded her hosts with a promotional potboiler entitled *A Unicorn in the Bahamas*, published in London and New York in the early summer of 1939.[12] Secretly, however, she disliked Nassau and its society, deprecated Bay Street's neglect of the Out Islands, and believed that tourism was an insecure and impermanent basis for the economy. As she wrote in her more candid (if still somewhat florid) memoir *Appointment with Destiny* (1949), the Out Islands were "the real Bahamas, carrying the main population with unlimited space to cultivate." Yet the local regime lacked the means or will "to break down the growth of centuries and put back into cultivation land which in the days of slavery and the Loyalist settlers bore good crops. . . . With few exceptions," she claimed, "Nassovian [*sic*] interests are concerned with shopkeeping and land values. Agriculture means nothing to the merchants of Bay Street. They would rather import canned goods from America than encourage difficult local production."[13]

The only lasting prosperity possible for the Bahamas, Forbes believed, lay in farming, preferably on large estates. Caribbean history had shown the impermanence of "buccaneering, piracy, wrecking, gun-running and boot-legging," which "came and went with hurricane force." Tourism likewise was an uncertain business, she pointed out, adding what turned out to be an inaccurate prophetic warning: "When peace returns and New York to Europe means a nine hours' flight, with planes regular as suburban trains, it may be that clerks on a fortnight's holiday—as well as millionaires—will go further afield. What then will be left to the Bahamas except their sunshine and their silken seas and the simple living that can be made—year in, year out—upon the land?"[14]

According to Rosita Forbes, "All this Sir Charles [Dundas] knew. He was a wise man and did not mind being unpopular among those who wanted to make fortunes in synthetic exploitation. Into my mind he put the idea of an old-fashioned manorial settlement upon an Out-Island." The chief Out Island commissioner, John Hughes, was converted to this anachronistic venture and, after Andros had been rejected as too flat and backward, picked out a splendid site between Governor's Harbour and Palmetto Point in central Eleuthera. Bush was cleared and a sort of Hans Christian Andersen manor house built on a hilltop by local laborers under the stern and skilled direction of a somewhat surprising devotee, Roland Symonette, who proved his versatility by turning himself into a chef when the Duke and Duchess of Windsor made an unheralded visit.[15]

Rosita Forbes called her dream house Unicorn Cay, and she seems to have lived there fairly happily, if intermittently, thereafter. But her vision of starting a replica of the society on the slopes of Mount Kenya never materialized. Several titled and monied expatriates followed her lead but immediately became mired in the problems of resolving titles to land that was either held under "generational" (extended family) tenure or claimed by squatters' rights—neither of which Forbes understood or regarded as anything but a confusing nuisance. Despite the increasing shortages of food as the war developed, Rosita Forbes's grandiose farming plans were also thwarted by what she regarded as official indifference and obstruction, as well as by the lack of sufficiently skilled and willing laborers. Her particular adversary was W. H. Heape, the colonial secretary, with whom she carried on an acrimonious paper battle over an alleged undertaking to provide a drivable road to serve the settlers' domains.[16]

Besides her ability to charm most people, Rosita Forbes had the invaluable quality of noblesse oblige, getting on with a wide range of mutually disparate types because she regarded almost all but fellow English aristocrats as social inferiors. Besides Roland Symonette, she usefully befriended the black lawyer T. A. Toote (for his skill in unraveling land titles and his wife's expertise with tropical plants) and the Jewish landowner Austin Levy (whose well-stocked freezers at Hatchet Bay kept Unicorn Cay well supplied). She had less success with the black local people, finding them unwilling permanently to act the part of faithful retainers. Wavering between a patronizing tolerance and frustration, she was puzzled by their moods, finding them on different occasions quaint, superstitious, friendly, cheerful, funny, emotional, vocal, fickle, feckless, casual, and proudly stubborn. She went so far as to quote almost wistfully the Duchess of Windsor on social life in the United States South: "We Southerners always flatter ourselves we know best how to deal with coloured people," adding, "Perhaps they do. The Southern States certainly achieved a dignity and spacious grace of living which they maintained through the desperate poverty following Abolition. They were put to all sorts of expedients, but they kept the respect of their own people, who had been their slaves."[17]

Though eager for wage labor in the lack of alternatives, black Eleutherans understandably did not share Rosita Forbes's quasi-feudalistic conception of their role. Domestic work or farm labor for others was clearly second best to living as independent peasant farmers, working on their own lands and in their own houses. The lack of opportunities for such an existence explained their tendency to migrate, particularly once well-paid jobs opened up during wartime. Forbes, increasingly critical of the unreliability of her workers, selfishly complained that the government did nothing to discourage emigration to Nassau and actively encouraged the black Eleutherans to go off to the United States to work as agricultural laborers rather than persuade them to stay to farm their own islands. She did not seem to realize that the migrants were drawn by far higher wages than she was able or prepared to pay. Nor did she recognize the dilemma that if the government did provide help for Out Island agriculture, this would draw most back into independent peasant farming rather than increase the number prepared to offer permanent wage labor to expatriate whites.

The other side of the coin was illustrated in the Cat Island of Sidney Poitier's early years, where there were virtually no whites, native or expatriate. The future first black film superstar was born by chance in Miami, to which his Out Island farmer father and pregnant mother had sailed in a schooner with a hundred cases of tomatoes they had grown, for sale at the Miami Produce Exchange. It was February 1927, after the door had been closed to immigration and just before new

Farming couple returning from the field. Rock Sound, Eleuthera, late 1940s.
From postcard in Michael Craton Collection.

protectionist tariffs would effectively exclude Bahamian produce as well. As soon as Evelyn Poitier had recovered from Sidney's premature birth, the forty-three-year-old father and twenty-eight-year-old mother returned with the baby to northern Cat Island to rejoin their other six children (left in the care of the maternal grandparents) and renew their backbreaking toil as peasant farmers.[18]

Out Island peasant life in an all-black community during the Great Depression was the enveloping experience of Sidney Poitier's first ten years. Both parents were uneducated, Reginald having married Evelyn when he was twenty-eight and she thirteen. But they owned some land and had access to more, were healthy, tireless, adept in a multitude of practical skills, and proudly self-sufficient, earning themselves respect and some standing in the scattered community centered on the small village of Arthur's Town—with its simple church and chapels, all-age school, lock-up, and wooden courthouse awaiting the infrequent visits of the island's commissioner. Schoolteacher, constable, visiting Anglican priest, and even commissioner were all nonwhites. In adjacent yards and nearby houses were grandparents, uncles, aunts, and numerous cousins, but the essential working unit was the close family, with mother in charge of the house but also toiling alongside her man in the fields. Children too labored and had household tasks as soon as they reached six years of age, just as in slavery days.

In Sidney Poitier's spare but graphic account, his father was a proud perfectionist fighting a heroic and ultimately losing battle against a pitiless economy. "He planted by the moon and reaped his harvest at a moment dictated by a combination of rain and sunshine, and the unpredictable sailing schedule of interisland cargo freighters." The bony limestone of his tomato fields was nurtured with bat earth scoured from distant caves and transported on the back of the family donkey. Adjacent to the prized tomato lands (the tenure of which provoked quarrels, fisticuffs, and a permanent estrangement between Reginald Poitier and his brother) was a two-acre subsistence plot on which the family raised an expert mix of "string beans, sweet potatoes, navy beans, yams, okra, onions, pepper and corn." Corn, though, was the daily staple, the center of every meal, only occasionally relieved by rice, a Sunday luxury for the comparatively well-off because it had to be imported. Corn was "roasted, toasted, baked, boiled, stewed, and ground into grits by a small hand-operated grinder, but first it had to be plucked, shucked, and dried in the sun until the kernels, hard as pebbles, could be easily rubbed from the cobs. Grits and fish, roast corn and fish, grits and eggs, chicken and grits—cornmeal cereal and condensed milk. Whatever the time of day, whatever the meal, corn made its appearance."[19]

In the fields with her husband and children every weekday from shortly after daylight, Evelyn Poitier would tell from the sun the time to prepare the family midday meal. From a straw carry-all basket she drew a cast-iron pot, some dried fish, grits, and seasonings. Deftly building a fire around three stones, she set the pot, dropped in a nugget of hog lard, onions, tomatoes, green beans, and okra, let it stew and simmer, then added dried fish, grits, water, and seasoning. When the sun was at its apex she called the family to lunch. Fashioning a plate from a seagrape leaf, she dished food and served her husband first, then did the same for the children, and herself last of all. All ate with their fingers or a scoop made from another seagrape leaf. After the meal, the pot was washed and put away, the used leaves buried beneath a tomato plant to act as compost, and all returned to their tasks in the field.

Evelyn started the long trek back to the house around four o'clock, a full hour ahead of her husband. She was followed by the older children, gathering firewood along the five-mile route. Back home, she completed the chores of washing, ironing, mending, cooking the evening meal, and baking with the help of the children, who fetched water, fed the fire, shucked corn, shelled peas, slopped the hogs, and fed the fowls. They also learned from their mother how to make straw work from palmetto leaf and rope from sisal. "She taught them early and quickly the lessons that had been hammered into her and her mother before her by a hard life in a semiprimitive society," wrote Poitier. "Survival requires everybody to carry a load. Her intention was simple: discipline imposed on the children now not only will help the family but will also benefit the children in later years."[20]

These timeless lessons were vital in a life that even in normal times skirted disaster from hurricane, drought, or sickness and grew harsher and more hopeless throughout the 1930s. The children seem to have had minimal schooling, there was no modern medicine, and the crowded conditions led to problems of sexual promiscuity that Poitier scarcely disguised by joking about them. For some reason, he chose to say nothing about the role of the churches, which played a large part in the lives of most Out Islanders. Yet even to the millionaire film actor the Cat Island of his first decade had its irreplaceable, now long-lost values that (from the perspectives of Hollywood, New York, and Nassau in the 1980s) he celebrated without romanticism:

> There was no welfare on Cat Island. Everybody worked except those who were too old or sick, and in such instances, of course, younger, healthier members of the family supported them with their labor. Older people were an integral part of the family structure,

with tasks appropriate to their advanced ages, until things got too difficult for them, at which time they would sit down and do nothing, assured of their continued—and revered—place in the family unit. . . . Young people were required to be honest, live up to their responsibilities, and respect their elders. My father always harped on that. There was no juvenile delinquency, no marijuana, no gang membership, no drinking, and no prostitution.[21]

A similar nostalgia for traditional Out Island life and values was expressed in the 1930s by a remarkable white Bahamian commissioner, Elgin Forsyth, who spent much of his career on another all-black island, Andros (which Rosita Forbes was to reject in favor of Eleuthera). "Today," he complained in 1930, "no one makes sugar, syrup, candy, preserves, starch, bay rush flour, benny paste, or any of the numerous small items that two generations ago went so far to make Bahamian life self-supporting and comfortable." Yet Androsian peasant farming still had its idyllic phases. Twice a year, at harvest time, wrote the eloquent Forsyth,

whole families disappear into the bush for the space of two or three weeks. It is really a semi-annual "Jamboree", when the men accompany their families to camps deep in the woods, a sort of back to nature movement; and here for a time all are happy, reaping and clearing the field by day, and at night assembled round huge camp fires in the sombre shadow of the forest, roasting potatoes, corn and crabs, to the melody of native songs, while great stars look down, and eerie night noises lend wings to the imagination of an imaginative people, who throng the woods with fearsome beings, among whom the yahoo, chanchilee, lusea, boccamice, and chic sharney hold high place. . . . After a few weeks of this, all return home, bringing back pleasant memories, and perhaps a sack or two of corn or peas, and leaving behind a few nearly cleared patches set with crops to furnish forth the raw materials of another sylvan idyll.[22]

Elgin Forsyth also wonderfully conveyed the way that the sea was a perennial lure to Bahamian subsistence farmers. "Every boy longs to leave school and fly to it before he is twelve years old," he wrote in 1931,

he sees himself gripping the helm, eyes fixed on the taut luff and smoking lee, while far behind the foaming wake the sails of his rivals, hull down, are rapidly slipping below the blue horizon. With such a picture lit with the matchless colours of the Bahamian landscape dyed into every fibre of his being, what charmer can lure him to the hot briar-filled fields, the dull bovine existence of a farmer's life?

Truly these are men
Who never see the ocean
But they feel its hand
Pluck like a Syren at the heart
To drag it from the land.[23]

Forsyth expressed a timeless feature of the Bahamian national psyche. But at the height of the Depression nothing was further from the thoughts of most Bahamians than the joys of ocean racing. Forsyth's lyricism would have struck a sour note among the Androsian sponge fishermen, whose maritime livelihood was erased by the sponge blight of 1938. Sporting events, such as the Out Island Regatta at Georgetown, Exuma, sponsored by wealthy yachtsmen, mainly expatriates, for "native working sailboats," were to be the luxuries of easier economic times. If Out Islanders felt the call of the sea in the later 1930s, it was an avenue of escape, to Nassau and beyond. This was certainly true of the Poitiers, first for Reginald, who was forced to give up the struggle to survive in Cat Island and migrated with his family to Nassau in 1937, and then for Sidney, who in 1943 took the mail boat across the Gulf Stream to Miami and a new life in the United States.

The experience of the Poitiers was typical of hundreds or thousands of Out Island migrants. The parents had occasionally traveled to Nassau and Miami, but Sidney was seeing cars, electricity, and more common modern wonders for the first time. Reginald, Evelyn, and the five younger children crammed into a three-room wooden rented house already occupied by an older daughter, her husband, and two babies, on Ross Corner, an Over the Hill area favored by Cat Islanders. Family, kin, and fellow islanders cooperated as much as they could, but the switch from a self-sufficient peasant lifestyle to a money-wage economy was traumatic. "Unlike Cat Island," wrote Sidney Poitier,

> Nassau required the selling of one's labor for a price, and using the returns from the sale of that labor for the food buying and the rent paying and the clothes buying and the doctor's bills. The new neighbors did not exchange corn for beans, yams for peas, or papayas for sugar apples. Nor did they use the free age-old root medicines; instead when sickness came, they bought from a pharmacy the medicine that probably originated from the very root that used to be free but was now packaged and refined and cost money.[24]

For months while Reginald was looking for a job Evelyn took to the most degrading convict work, breaking limestone rocks into pebbles with a hammer for mixing with cement: eight hours' work for twenty cents a day. Reginald found work in a bicycle shop owned by a black Bahamian but after three years of low-paid work was laid off without explanation or recompense. The family moved to an even smaller and cheaper house further south in Grant's Town, and Reginald, at the age of fifty-nine, attempted to return to the work he knew best, farming a scrap of Crown land in the center of the island as an untenured squatter. This venture was doomed, not producing enough food for the family, let alone a surplus for sale.

Though Sidney Poitier referred to the social system as patriarchal, his account underlined the heroic supporting role of a Bahamian mother, especially in hard times. Evelyn valued the proud independence of her man above all and was confident that the "new, ruthless, sophisticated system of tourism and colonialism, however relentless," would never totally dismantle the displaced farmer's pride. But better than anyone she knew the signs of impotence and despair that came from joblessness, and though she sometimes railed at circumstances, she kept a cheerful face, toiled and scrimped, ingeniously managed the family finances, and kept the worries of her economies to herself.

These troubles were scarcely sensed by Sidney and his siblings and friends, rapidly growing up in a carefree, amoral, open-air life on the streets. "That place Nassau was not good for raising tomatoes or children," reminisced Poitier when he was in his fifties. Though mother could be a fearsome scold and both mother and father whipped discovered miscreants, their own distractions and the crowded slum conditions led to a steady erosion of Out Island morals and morale. For example, when the marriage of Sidney's sister Teddy broke up and she started to consort with a disreputable character nicknamed "Blood," Reginald Poitier applied physical correction as long as she continued under the family roof but washed his hands of responsibility once she left home, even when Blood maltreated her. Sidney himself was saved more by luck than good sense from graduating from petty theft and vandalism to the serious crime, violence, and alcoholism that landed a brother and friends in jail and led to tragic early deaths.

Losing his virginity (acquiring a severe dose of the clap in the process) and leaving school as soon as he became a teenager, Sidney began to contribute to the family finances as a laborer, working on Axel Wenner-Gren's canal, in a Bay Street warehouse, and on the new airfield base once the United States entered the war. But a combination of restlessness and dissatisfaction with dead-end jobs, the false attractions of America pictured on Nassau's movie screens, and his father's intuition that if he stayed he might follow the downward path of some of his associates led to an agreement that Sidney should take advantage of his fortuitous American birth and follow his older brother Cyril (an illegal immigrant who obtained citizenship by marriage) to Miami. Accordingly, on a January morning in 1943, Sidney, a few days short of sixteen years of age, said good-bye to his mother at home, walked with his silent father to the dock, and set out with a battered suitcase and three dollars in his pocket as a third-class passenger on the wooden motorship *Ena K*, to make his fortune in the land of opportunity.[25]

The Burma Road Riots, 1942

Sidney Poitier was much younger than most migrants when he left the Bahamas for the United States, and he was to be exceptionally successful. All the same, his move was part of the general stirring that followed the entry of the United States into World War II—a prelude to irreversible changes to the Bahamas and its people.

The effects of the war were much more immediate and explosive than anyone in the regime anticipated, having something of the nature (albeit premature and abortive) of a revolution of frustrated expectations. Within a few weeks of Pearl Harbor, plans had been laid to make New Providence a major air base, expanding and upgrading the airport close to Nassau which Sir Harry Oakes had already donated to the government (and which bore his name), and adding the even larger Satellite Field (later to be named after the Duke of Windsor) next to Lake Killarney at the western end of the island. The building contract was awarded by the United States government to the giant Pleasantville Corporation, which brought in modern equipment and advertised for twenty-five hundred local laborers.

This construction project promised a relative bonanza for the local unemployed, a chance to sell their labor for something like the rates they knew were normal on the mainland—some $3 (or twelve shillings) a day. Unknown to them, however, the Bahamas government had agreed to peg local wages for unskilled labor at the rates established in 1936: four shillings for an eight-hour working day, despite wartime inflation. Even more cynically, or foolishly, this rate was applied to semiskilled as well as unskilled work (a tenth of what the few American workers at the sites were earning for identical work), and the labor gangs were placed under the direction not of American or local nonwhite foremen but of two white Bahamians, on the erroneous principle that they would know best how to control black Bahamian workers. John Hughes, the labor officer, candidly expressed the regime's complacency when he told a concerned nonwhite political candidate in the impending general election, due for June 1942, "Go on, Mr. Cambridge, you will never have any [labor] trouble in the Bahamas."[26]

Organized proletarian action certainly seemed unlikely. There was much talk, and Charles Rhodriguez reactivated the unskilled workers' labor union, announcing the formation of a Federation of Labour that would also represent skilled workers. A modestly attended public meeting was held on May 22, 1942, after which the union and federation executives drafted a petition with the help of their attorney, A. F. Adderley, calling for a minimum wage of eight shillings a day. So little concerned was the administration that Governor Windsor left for an appointment in Washington May 28. The following day, the petition was delivered to the labor officer and passed on to the acting governor, Leslie Heape, who made a vague statement that an advisory board would be appointed to consider the question of wages on what was already being called the Project.[27]

This assurance seems to have satisfied Rhodriguez and his fellow executives but not the workers. On Sunday, May 31, a group of laborers at the Satellite Field went on strike. Karl Claridge, one of the white supervisors, persuaded most to return to work. But a small group remained obdurate, led by a vocal young Androsian, Leonard Green, alias Storr, who had just joined the Project. When Storr tried to call the other workers back out, he was taken by the American field manager to the Pleasantville Corporation headquarters at Oakes Field, where under interrogation he asserted the obvious fact that it was impossible to live on four shillings a day. While Storr was being questioned, an increasingly angry group of about four hundred workers gathered outside, some loudly calling, "We want more money."

None of the labor organizers was present, but when John Hughes appeared, the workers expressed two complaints: the inadequacy of the minimum daily wage and the unfairness of the system whereby they went unpaid when rain prevented them from working. Hughes promised that the matters would be dealt with as soon as possible and persuaded all but a few of the younger workers to go home. At this juncture, though, the situation was inflamed when a detachment of four policeman, under the command of the white Bahamian Captain Edward Sears, confronted Storr and his remnant and tried to disperse them by force. When the other workers noticed that Storr had a cut above his eye, they presumed that it had been inflicted by the Conchy Joe captain and the situation grew ugly. Claridge's car was overturned, and the crowd was broken up only when Sears drew his revolver and fired it in the air.[28]

Still Hughes was convinced that the workers could be mollified. Having obtained an agreement with the Pleasantville operators over pay for rainy days, he persuaded Rhodriguez, Adderley, and Dr. C. R. Walker (a black candidate for New Providence South in the forthcoming election) to talk to the workers early on Monday morning June 1, 1942. Adderley gave a brief speech to the Satellite Field workers at their transportation point on West Bay Street, calling for a return to work to "preserve harmony," but they refused to move. At Oakes Field, where more than a thousand workers had gathered, Dr. Walker was even less successful, the men refusing to clock in and calling out, "No Work Today!"[29]

Not anticipating serious trouble, the "labor representatives" left Oakes Field for their own workday. But the crowd swelled and boiled, and the presence of Captain Sears and a police detachment had the opposite of a calming effect. The crowd reached more than two thousand, and Sears sent for reinforcements. But by that time, large groups of laborers, many carrying sticks and machetes, had left the field and were marching north through the crowded Southern District toward downtown Nassau. As they went, they sang "patriotic" songs such as "We'll never let the old flag fall," though legend has it that they also sang what was to become the symbolic anthem of the ensuing riot: "Burma Road declare war on the Conchie Joe, Do Nigger, don't lick nobody, don't lick nobody."[30]

More volatile and disorganized than the traditional parades descending on Bay Street from Over the Hill, the laborers and their family supporters were still merely looking for someone in authority to whom they could express their grievances and from whom they might obtain some satisfaction. Many hundreds gathered noisily in front of the colonial secretary's office, where, instead of Leslie Heape (who presumably was safely inside Government House), they were addressed at 9 A.M. by the expatriate attorney general, Eric Hallinan. His request that the workers elect a formal delegate to present complaints, which would then be given immediate attention, was regarded as a stalling tactic; and his ill-judged remarks that the American authorities had been reluctant to employ Bahamian laborers and it had only been through the Duke's intercession that they had work at all were misinterpreted as a threat that if they did not return docilely to work they would lose their jobs.[31]

Within minutes, the crowd had exploded, raging up and down Bay Street breaking windows and looting stores. A parked Coca-Cola truck provided convenient missiles. By noon, downtown was a shambles, though most of the crowd had left the scene with their loot—cleared by the police and a detachment of Cameron Highlanders from the garrison. The damage was not totally indiscriminate; such shops as those owned by the Speaker of the Assembly and the wife of one of the white Project supervisors were almost gutted, but the shoe store owned by Percy Christie, the white would-be labor organizer, was left untouched. Particular targets were the white-owned liquor stores, the stock of which fueled the aggression of rougher elements in the crowd.[32]

The reaction of the white administrators and Bay Street merchants was a mixture of belligerence and panic, while the brown and black middle class expressed shock and disowned the actions of the mob. Anticipating trouble, one of the white supervisors from the Project had stayed home; the other went fishing for several days. Though Mary Moseley boldly walked the street until chased indoors, many whites ran for shelter from the downtown area, and some parents (including a few nonwhites) came into town to "rescue" their children from Queen's College. An angry "Delegation of Citizens," including Roland Symonette, Speaker Asa Pritchard, and Stafford Sands (whose car had been wrecked), went to Government House, demanding more forceful action. Pritchard called Acting Governor Heape a fool and threatened that if nothing was done he would appeal directly to the military. Hallinan later testified that one delegate asked why machine guns had not been turned on the crowd, and another, hearing shots from the direction of Grant's Town, said, "That's the stuff to give them."[33]

In fact, Heape had already acted, calling those who were regarded as the representatives of labor to Government House at 10:20 A.M. and instructing them to do what they could to pacify the rioters. A. F. Adderley and Bert Cambridge claimed to have persuaded some of the crowd to return from Bay Street Over the Hill, but when they attempted to speak to a clamorous mob of two thousand gathered on the Southern Recreation Ground, their efforts were countervailing. Confused by the radical rhetoric of Milo Butler and fired by liquor, the crowd shouted down Adderley, called Cambridge a "white man's pimp," and physically assaulted the black politician (and rentier) Leon W. Young and the owner of Weary Willie's nightclub, Leonard White. Reporting back to Acting Governor Heape, the failed "labor leaders" were told that wages would not be discussed until the rioting was quelled.

The disturbances had not yet reached their climax. Though leaderless, the crowds were inspired by a few of the most outspoken and aggressive, who later laid claim to hero status. Leonard Storr Green, who seems to have been born in the Turks Islands, had a confrontation on Bay Street with Captain Sears. When Sears told Green that he would have him deported to his birthplace, Green retorted that he would make sure that the police officer returned to his native Abaco. Another rioter, Alfred Stubbs, alias "Sweet Potato," set light to a picture of the royal family, and Napoleon McPhee publicly burned a Union Jack. When questioned, McPhee memorably stated: "I willing to fight under the flag. I willing to die under the flag. But I ain't gwine starve under the flag."[34]

From the turbulent meeting on the Southern Recreation Ground, the crowd fanned out, attacking and looting bars, particularly those owned by the white Bethell brothers. When the commissioner of police, Reginald Erskine-Lindop, arrived with an armed detachment of police and soldiers, the crowd pelted them with stones and bottles. Erskine-Lindop read the Riot Act outside the plundered Cotton Tree Inn on Blue Hills Road, but this did not halt the brickbat barrage that hit several policemen and Cameron Highlanders. Though no general order to fire was given, shots were fired in the ensuing melee. One man, Roy Johnson, was killed instantly and six seriously wounded, of whom one, David Smith, died later that day in the hospital. Forty rioters and several of the forces of law and order were treated for minor injuries.[35]

Just after noon, in an atmosphere of deceptive quiet, the police and military withdrew from Grant's Town, except for the four junior policemen left at the Southern Station. As the word of the killing of Johnson spread, however, an incensed crowd of several hundred attacked the police station, burned the fire engine and wrecked an ambulance, broke into the Grant's Town post office and public library, and went on a rampage of general looting throughout the Southern District. Quiet returned only after all the police and garrison were mobilized, pickets established in a ring around Grant's Town, and a military curfew declared.

Even this was merely a lull. As soon as the curfew ended at 6 A.M. on the following day, Tuesday, June 2, a crowd of several hundred laborers and other troublemakers marched to and fro, singling out several specific targets for attack: the white-owned Cole Pharmacy on Shirley Street downtown, the home of a black policeman, and (with less obvious motivation) a black-owned shop Over the Hill. A looter shot by the shopkeeper was one of the other three fatalities following from the riots and curfew infringements.[36]

The Duke of Windsor flew back to Nassau as soon as he could after hearing news of the riots, arriving on the evening of Tuesday, June 2. He was preceded by a detachment of seventy-five U.S. Marines disguised as military police, ostensibly to protect American military installations but available to support local forces. In the event, they were not required. After consulting with his officials, the Duke confirmed the curfew and the ban on public meetings and added censorship of the press. On Wednesday morning he met with several black leaders, one of whom, Dr. C. R. Walker, using biblical terms, told him that the ordinary people, aware of his reputation as a humanitarian, looked to him as their savior against oppression, inequality, and poverty. That evening, the Duke broadcast to the colony, urging calm and a return to work so that wage negotiations could proceed.[37]

The following morning, Thursday, June 4, more than half the workers reported for work on the Project, and by the end of the week work was proceeding as before. True to his word, the Duke immediately negotiated a raise of a shilling a day in the minimum wage, with a free midday meal and a less formal understanding that those engaged in specialized work would be paid above the minimum rate. He went on the radio again on June 8 to announce these concessions and the lifting of the curfew. The police and military, however, remained on alert, and the embargo on public meetings continued through the general election on June 19–22. The election went off without incident and proved something of an anticlimax, leaving the composition of the House of Assembly essentially unchanged.[38]

A greater distraction was a major fire in downtown Nassau less than four weeks after the riots. A failed shopkeeper resorted to arson, and the conflagration spread over more than two blocks. Only the frantic efforts of volunteers (including the Duke of Windsor himself) and the fortunate presence of extra fire engines at the Base prevented Bay Street's complete destruction. Apprehended, the white incendiary was in due course sent to jail for seven years, a sentence that ironically balanced the stiffest sentences meted out to the black rioters who had assaulted Bay Street one month earlier. In all, eighty persons appeared before the courts as a result of the riots, twenty-two before the Supreme Court and fifty-eight in Magistrates' Court, of whom sixty-seven were convicted. The maximum sentences of eight years at hard labor were passed on Leonard Storr Green and on Harold Thurston, both of whom already had lengthy criminal records.[39]

These court cases provoked no popular demonstrations, though undoubtedly the shock waves ran deeper through all sectors of society than appeared on the surface. One latent effect was the exacerbation of tensions between the colonial administration and the Bay Street oligarchy. To head the almost inevitable commission of inquiry the Duke of Windsor chose Sir Alison Russell, former chief justice of Tanganyika, along with two white merchants not involved in politics. Regarding both the Duke and his nominees as too broadminded, and to forestall criticism, the majority in the Assembly voted for setting up their own Select Committee. Though it included the pro-trade-union Percy Christie and the black lawyer T. A. Toote as token liberals, this committee was dominated by hard-line Bay Street figures: Asa Pritchard, Roland Symonette, and the rising ultra-conservative lawyer Stafford Sands. At the same time, the Assembly voted to indemnify all those who had suffered damages in the riots.

Not surprisingly, the reports of neither commission nor Select Committee mentioned race issues, though privately everyone from the Duke of Windsor and the American vice-consul downward believed they played a large part in the outbreak. Even more predictably, the House committee found no fault in the policies of the legislature. The administration was blamed for negligence in not informing the workers of the wage situation and for mismanaging the crisis. White employees of the Pleasantville Corporation were said to have spread false information among the workers about the rates of pay and even to have encouraged black Bahamians to demand higher wages and better conditions, while native labor leaders were accused of stirring up trouble for their own advantage.[40]

The Russell Commission was much more thorough and less self-serving. Besides citing the immediate wage dispute and the part played by rumor in the outbreak, it recognized that there were deeper-seated causes: the economic depression, political inequalities, and deficiencies in social and labor legislation. Some of the commission's recommendations verged on the radical but had scant hope of immediate implementation. There was a call for tax reform, less dependence on import duties and the introduction of an income tax, death duties, and a tax on land sales. There should be greater control over the sale of land, particularly cultivable acreage in the Out Islands. Agriculture and fishing should be much more strongly encouraged to slow, halt, or reverse the dangerous drift toward Nassau. Believing that some of the social unrest stemmed from overpopulation because of the rising birth rate (particularly among the black majority), the commission provocatively encouraged birth control. Politically, it suggested some reform in the outdated constitution, the permanency of the secret ballot in New Providence, and its extension to the Out Islands.[41]

The two reports concurred only in recommending appropriate labor legislation. Viewed positively, this can be seen as an only slightly delayed reaction to the suggestions made by Major George Orde-Browne after visiting the Bahamas in 1939 as part of his survey of labor conditions in the British West Indies. More realistically, it might be viewed as an operation of the hegemonic principle that minor adjustments are adopted (more often, indeed, by conservative than liberal regimes) to forestall radical change. In the Bahamas case, if the so-called labor leaders were not quite Bay Street pawns, they were innately moderate intermediate figures, with whom achieving a working relationship was clearly preferred by the ruling regime to the threat of mob violence. Certainly, the Trade Union and Workmen's Compensation Acts passed in March 1943 were minimal as well as overdue. Although the former provided for the registration of trade unions and established the legality of strikes, work stoppages were held to be illegal if construed as coercing the government or inflicting undue hardship on the people. Moreover, all civil servants, domestic servants, and hotel and agricultural workers were debarred from forming or joining a union. Even the Duke of Windsor warned the legislature late in 1943 that the two acts fell short of acceptable modern labor standards.[42]

The Russell Commission's recommendations on taxes and birth control went no further than discussion in the Executive Council. Although Governor Windsor was personally in favor of birth control from "a humane point of view," he was advised by the council that it would be unwise to broach the issue publicly because blacks were likely to regard it as "a subtle way of gradually eliminating their race." Tax reform was much more vehemently opposed, particularly by Councillors Harold Christie and Ralph Collins, who argued that it would discourage wealthy foreigners from investing in the Bahamas. Their basic motives, of course, were more blatantly selfish and not unique to themselves. Even the nonwhite MHAs concurred in opposing new taxes, illustrating the lasting principle that financial self-interest united the upper and middle classes and divided them from the poor, regardless of race.[43]

The Contract: Bahamian Laborers in the United States, 1943–1963

The 1942 riots, though a warning, did not precipitate major constitutional, political, or social reforms. Even the Ballot Act, which made the secret vote permanent in New Providence and extended it to the Out Islands, was not passed until 1946 and came into effect with the general election of 1949. Much though later commentators, including Doris Johnson and Randol Fawkes, teleologically saw the Burma Road Riots as initiating a popular movement, they were merely a spontaneous reaction to underlying conditions, triggered by the wage issue. As economic conditions improved steadily during the war and spectacularly afterward, nothing so serious erupted again until 1958. By then, the other necessary ingredients for political change had been added, especially popular awareness and greater political sophistication and populist leadership under the banner of Black Power.[44]

For a decade and a half, improved incomes—increasing faster than inflation—were a sociopolitical palliative. No one was more aware of the importance of wage employment than the Duke of Windsor and his wife. As the Nassau bases rapidly approached completion, there was a fear of the effects of renewed unemployment. As early as September 1942 the Duchess wrote confidentially to her Aunt Bessie: "The negroes are busy *complaining* now that the base is nearing completion and some of them are being laid off. I should not be surprised to see more trouble—but this time one is somewhat prepared and there is enough fire-power on the island to deal with the situation." By March 1943, though, her husband had found a more long-term alternative, having negotiated an agreement in Washington for the recruitment of up to five thousand Bahamians as agricultural laborers in the United States. This important development—popularly called either the Project as an extension of the work on the bases or the Contract, after the binding agreement the workers signed—lasted more than twenty transitional years and had significant social effects. It was the most momentous achievement of the Duke of Windsor's regime.[45]

Recruitment for the Contract began in April 1943 at the specifically created Labour Bureau in Nassau, which later sent out recruiters to several Out Islands. By May, 2,500 Bahamian laborers had been dispatched to join other West Indians, particularly Jamaicans and Barbadians, in the United States, and by August the full quota of 5,000 had been reached. At the peak in July 1944, 5,762 Bahamians were employed on the Contract, almost a twelfth of the entire population, perhaps a sixth of all adult Bahamian males, and more than a third of all able-bodied male Out Islanders. Initially, the Bahamians were employed on Florida farms, and 850 were housed in a single camp at Belle Glade near Lake Okeechobee in July 1943. But soon groups of 300 to 400 were transferred further afield, migrating according to seasonal needs as far north and west as New York State and Minnesota. As time went on, Bahamians were dispersed in smaller groups, especially where farmers became familiar with them and encouraged their return. At first, nearly all the migrants were black male laborers, but an increasing minority were women, some traveling as couples. Besides helping to harvest "tobacco in Tennessee, apples in New York, corn in Minnesota, peanuts in North Carolina, citrus or sugar cane or beans in Florida," some on the Contract were employed in tending livestock, cooking for other workers, and occasionally operating farm equipment. In 1945, 91 poor whites from the Out Islands were specifically recruited for work on dairy farms, though almost all, disliking the climate more than the hard work, returned within the year.[46]

The formal agreement between the United States and Bahamian governments stipulated that the workers could be employed only in agriculture and would not be liable for military service. They had to be eighteen years of age and pass a medical examination conducted by the American authorities. Transportation from their homes to the port of entry in the United States would be at the expense of the Bahamas government, but travel costs within the United States would be paid by the U.S. government. Wages were to be set according to the rates and methods in the areas of work and might include piecework in preference to hourly rates. In any case, the minimum wage was to be thirty cents an hour, at least twice the usual rate in the Bahamas. Workers were guaranteed employment for three-quarters of the period of their contracts, not counting Sundays or one other day off in each set of seven days. Somewhat speciously, the agreement promised that the workers would not be discriminated against on account of their race, color, or creed.

Each worker signed a personal contract, giving specific details of pay and working conditions. The term was either for six or nine months, with one month's notice of termination on either side. The usual pay was between $3 and $5 for a twelve-hour working day, with free lodging, transport, and midday meal, though the pay could be augmented when piecework rates applied. It was understood that seventy-five cents would be withheld from each day's pay (later raised to twenty-five cents in each dollar), to be paid as "a family allowance to the worker's family in the Bahamas, or deposited on behalf of the worker in the Post Office Savings Bank of the Colony." Many workers voluntarily remitted extra money to their dependents or their own savings accounts so that of the £300,000 earned by migrant workers in the nine months after April 1943, £60,000 was transferred to the Bahamas as family allowances or savings. By the end of the war, the annual amounts earned and transferred were about £500,000 and £150,000. Family allowances, averaging about £10, were paid each month in the Bahamas, while single migrants built up nest eggs sometimes of hundreds of pounds in their savings bank accounts.[47]

Although the Contract increased the earning power and ability to save for thousands of black laboring Bahamians (most of whom had lived on the margins of a cash economy all their lives), it also took a toll on the Out Islands. The majority of workers spent six or nine months on the Contract in the United States and then returned, at least for a spell. Many, though, deserted their communities, settling permanently in the United States or Nassau. Out Island settlements were therefore left with a scarcity of men in their most productive years. Women and children, along with the oldest men, were left in charge of the farms, forced to cope with the heavy work of clearing, planting, and cleaning the fields. The net result was a neglect of farming except for subsistence. In the absence of their spouses, women undoubtedly gained more independence, but the effects on family life were not entirely positive. Women were at least temporarily heads of their households, responsible for the financial management and child rearing as well as their traditional domestic chores and the additional farmwork. This responsibility strengthened and gave increased confidence to many women but for others proved too much strain. The role and authority of the father tended to be diminished, and in many cases, the traditional family broke down altogether.

Those women who could, or willed to do so, husbanded their remittances and kept careful records for their husbands' return. Others found that what was sent was barely enough to keep starvation at bay or spent what was sent, careless of the future. Feeling deserted, many also took up with other men. At least one writer has claimed that the Contract profoundly disrupted Bahamian family life, "with men returning from the United States to find their wives carrying children for other men, or even to find, after they had sent home large portions of their earnings, neither their wives nor earnings." And though many men on the Contract lived with admirable frugality, saving and supplying their families with funds and buying only goods such as clothes, useful back home, others were wasteful. As one thrifty Cat Island veteran remembered, "Some fellows they just go over there and just squander away with the money and have a big time, you know, [spend] as they make it. They figure they got allowance coming home to the family and they ain't worrying with the money that they make. What they make they just blow it out."[48]

Experiences gained through the Contract were significant in shaping the Bahamian view of America and life in general. Out Island laborers, some of whom had never visited Nassau, let alone the United States, found the journey itself as important an event as the Middle Passage had been to their slave ancestors. "It [the Contract] made a one hundred and fifty degree turn in my life," declared Samuel Miller in 1991. "I'm sure—I'm not goin' to say that I'm guessin', I'm sure—that if I was in The Bahamas and didn't come to the United States, in the time period that I was in, I wouldn't have nothing [to] compare with what I have now."[49] "It made it good for us, workin'," remarked Calvin Bethel in 1992. "We didn't actually, say, enjoy [working on the Contract]. But the way t'ings was home, it beat home. Any way you was livin' better than you was home. . . . An' then it gave you chance to grab at somethin' bigger."[50]

Once in Nassau, the Out Island recruits to the Contract were signed up, photographed, and given their first passport. To some, their compulsory vaccination shots were a strange ordeal. Virtually all had traveled by boat, but some had scarcely heard of airplanes, which were to take them to the United States. Once there, most were housed in army-style labor camps, which, though spartan by American standards, were plush to Bahamian Out Islanders, with serviceable tables, chairs, and beds, efficient stoves, running water, inside flush toilets, showers, and laundry facilities. Radios were a common feature rather than an occasional wonder, and cinemas (though segregated) were easily accessible, as were less wholesome diversions such as bars, brothels, and gambling places.[51]

Even more important, Bahamians accustomed to the narrow horizons of their own islands, the limited company of their family, kin, and near neighbors, and an unchanging diurnal and annual routine were brought into the proximity of strangers, from other islands, other colonies, and many parts of the United States, and into work, leisure, and cultural patterns and customs that were initially alien. Though Bahamians were inured to hard work, their new regimens were very different, especially where a piecework system applied. Instead of being responsible for all phases of farming, they were now employed for the most part simply for harvesting. Though not often given the responsibility of operating machinery, the migrant laborers were frequently worked in conjunction with harvesting equipment and were in effect animate parts of a larger machine. Instead of the usual Out Island system whereby most of the fieldwork was undertaken between dawn and early afternoon, laborers were worked far later, especially when there were the inducements of piecework earnings. Piecework, moreover, gave the Bahamian laborers a novel appreciation of the relationship between the amount of work expended and the cash return they could expect. Though there was a residual nostalgia for the familiar pace and routine of Out Island methods, as well as an unassuaged longing for working land of one's own, nearly all these changes in the long term undermined traditional Bahamian farming. The Contract was seen as a means of bettering oneself, of making money to live better in the Bahamas, to buy land and build houses, but rarely as a prelude to returning to the traditional subsistence farming with hoe and cutlass.

Though the laborers on the Contract ranged more widely over rural America and encountered a wider variety of American people than the agricultural migrants of the early part of the century, only a small minority endeavored to stay permanently in the United States. For most, their experiences somewhat contradictorily both reinforced their preference for their homeland and seeded a determination eventually to change it for the better. In addition, travel inevitably gave Bahamians a greater sense of their own uniqueness and a confidence that they were at least as worthy as any foreigners.

Some on the Contract had very positive relationships with their American employers, even in the Deep South. Usually this was because either partner in the relationship exceeded the expectations of the other. Remelda Bodie said of her white Virginia employer, "He was very nice to us. We used to take our food on the farm and cook and then he used to say, come in the house and look around. He was the best white man I ever see to be that nice." More remarkably, H. R. Bethel became the virtual protégé of an employer in Vero Beach, Florida, who not only made him manager over several hundred other employees but in time gave him the power to sign checks on his behalf and even trade securities on the New York Stock Exchange.[52]

In the northern states, though the Bahamians encountered racism, sometimes subtle, they gained a sense of the potentialities of a constitution that was technically egalitarian and that gave blacks political power in proportion to their numbers, especially in the cities. In the South, however, the customary prevalence of Jim Crow practices made a mockery of the promise in the agreement that the black Bahamians would not suffer from discrimination. The worst excesses of the Jim Crow system were mitigated by the Bahamians' sense of self, however: a combination of keeping to themselves, a sense of humor, a long-practiced skill in deflecting or bypassing the racialism of the whites, and a sturdy contempt for the majority of American blacks.

As one Cat Islander remembered, the southerners were "kind of mean on colored people. Oh, in Florida they used to lynch colored people. Colored people had no right in Florida. . . . In fact, you couldn't go to no fun, to no dances around. In Florida the law would be there to get you. Take you to jail and make you pay some money . . . after I see that, I stay in my camp."[53] Nearly all those who worked in the

South chafed at a system that, in contrast to the more easygoing or more scrupulous Bahamian style, allowed all whites to call them "nigger" or "boy" or redneck sheriffs to enforce a curfew on blacks in the white sections of town after 6 P.M.; that made blacks go round to the back of liquor or grocery stores, always served them last and often ungraciously, refusing to let them try on shoes without wearing stockings or hats without a head covering; and that while they were traveling sometimes denied them places to eat or sleep and at best gave them facilities that were separate but never equal.

To proud Bahamians, gratuitous harassment by white overseers was especially intolerable. "We had this fella," recalled Samuel Miller forty years later, "he would come and go and he would check each [piece of] fruit. [He] had to see if you had the right size. . . . So what would he do, he would kick the box—you done pick a whole box of fruit—kick it over, check 'em, an' he leave 'em on the ground till you pick 'em up. He wouldn't put his hand [in the box], he'd kick it over, check every one o' 'em, then he would [say] 'Pick that up, boy.'" Another informant recalled an occasion when, as a brash youngster fresh on the Contract, he had been prepared to draw a knife on a white overseer who similarly kicked over a box of gathered fruit. A grizzled veteran restrained him (perhaps saving his life), encouraging him to allow the thought of the money he was earning to override the indignity. Bahamians, indeed, had a reputation for being less troublesome as well as more conscientious workers than American blacks and in exceptional cases were recognized as not being cowed as a consequence. Sidney Poitier tellingly recounted how as a greenhorn Miami immigrant in 1943 he affected to misunderstand a white police officer who called him "boy," stating his name and provenance instead. Amused rather than angry, the officer dismissed him as a "crazy Bahamian." It is unlikely that a white policeman would have treated an American black so expansively or that the black would have answered a white policeman so boldly. It was an index of the difference in their status and acquired characteristics that Bahamians generally despised American blacks (at least in the South) as both lazy and craven, and this attitude produced tensions between them and fights that sometimes ended fatally. The American blacks worked "just to get a couple of dollars and go to the beer joint," claimed a Cat Island veteran of the Contract. "Bahamians don't leave till sundown. They's work [because they are] away from home. They come to make money."[54]

Social Effects of the War: The Murder of Sir Harry Oakes

From the beginning of 1942, the war brought wage employment, relative prosperity, and wider horizons to many more Bahamians than those involved in the Contract. As in World War I, there was no early inclination to use nonwhite troops, and conscription was never introduced. From the beginning of the war a predominantly black Bahamas Volunteer Force (later renamed the Bahamas Home Guard) was formed for local defense, to which was later added the Bahamas Air Service Squadron, to serve as a local auxiliary to the Royal Air Force (RAF). At first, the only Bahamians to serve overseas were a handful of whites who joined the air force in Canada or England. But as the worldwide conflict extended, a racially mixed authentic military unit was raised called first the Bahamas Defence Force and then, once sent for final training in Jamaica in 1944 as part of the North Caribbean Force, the Bahamas Battalion. A detachment of this unit, under the command of the colored Lieutenant Wenzel Granger, saw active service in Egypt and Italy between 1944 and 1945. In all, more than a thousand Bahamians (including a few whites who joined the American forces, women who joined the Women's Army Air Force, civilians attached to the RAF and U.S. Engineers in the Bahamas, and fifteen men recruited to work in British munitions factories) served with the armed forces, of whom some three hundred went overseas and fifteen lost their lives.[55]

Even more than in World War I, those who went overseas were exposed to a range of new and sometimes radical ideas, the realities of class conflict that did not include a racial component, the vulnerability of the British Empire and the notion of white superiority, the inevitability of change in the wake of a war ostensibly against imperialism, and the demand for social and political equality among colonial peoples, most appositely those of the British West Indies. More immediate, however, were the social effects of the transformation of New Providence into an important air base and the temporary residence in Nassau of many thousands of ordinary foreigners—albeit almost all white males. To the small garrison of Cameron Highlanders (later superseded by Pictou Highlanders from Canada) and army engineers and other servicemen manning the U.S. bases, three thousand personnel were added by the end of 1942 to man the Operational Training Unit (OTU) stationed at Oakes Field and the 113th Wing Transport Command unit based at the Satellite (Windsor) Field. Somewhat later, once the Florida Strait and other Bahamian channels were regularly prowled by German U-boats, Windsor Field became the base for two squadrons of antisubmarine patrol planes. At the Oakes Field OTU, some five thousand pilots already qualified for single-engined planes were trained to fly twin-engined Mitchells and four-engined Liberators, along with about six hundred bomber crews—another five thousand men—while untold further thousands of airmen passed through New Providence in ferrying aircraft from American factories to North African and European war theaters, by way of South America.[56]

Inevitably more social mixing occurred than the Bahamas had ever known before, though the women of the white regime did their utmost to ensure that the traditional proprieties were maintained and the white servicemen kept from moral delinquency. The IODE opened a temperance canteen and sponsored decorous monthly dances, and the local clubs offered members' privileges to officers and held occasional social evenings for other ranks. The Duchess of Windsor opened a rival canteen that purveyed liquor as well as tea, though her liberality did not extend to allowing in nonwhites. This deficiency was remedied by a third canteen operated by a committee of middle-class nonwhite women, though the standards of decorum they expected were at least as rigorous as in the other establishments. In addition, the service units organized their own entertainments, held in the large gymnasium at Oakes Field: parties, dances, and occasional visits by touring singers and comedians. At such events nonwhite personnel were segregated, and policy decreed that only whites be invited from off the bases. The color line, however, was slightly more relaxed than in Nassau society in the case of handsome young women without "pronounced negro features." Other local nonwhites also visited the Oakes Field base to watch sporting events such as boxing matches or to participate in table tennis competitions.[57]

Officers moved freely to and fro, but other ranks were allowed off the bases only once every two weeks and were specifically instructed not to "consort with colored women." Consorting was carefully defined as walking in the company of a colored woman, standing about and talking with her, or visiting her in her house. Servicemen were allowed to be served by a colored woman at a reputable cafe or shop and were not held to be "consorting" if they happened to be sitting next to a colored woman in a bus or church. These injunctions, of course, were largely ignored, despite the vigilance of the Military Police. Roy Smith, who was posted to Nassau as a radio operator in 1942 and later settled there, for example, recalled in 1978 that "trips to town were not used to the best advantage . . . invariably most of our pittance of service pay was dispensed to various bartenders in such genteel places as the Quarterdeck." This establishment, still in business in the 1960s, was an upstairs bar frequented by unaccompanied colored females and had convenient adjacent rooms in a shabby wooden building on East Bay Street—just one of a number of disreputable bars and virtual brothels. In October 1943, the Executive Council noted that prostitution was becoming a menace and that the police had been ordered to clear women of ill repute off Bay Street. At the same time, the incidence of venereal disease among RAF servicemen became a matter of concern, though mitigated by the novel wonders of penicillin.[58]

Despite the limited opportunities for more polite intercourse, more than a dozen servicemen made Nassau their permanent home by marrying local women—about as many as those Bahamians serving abroad who brought back wives after the war. In very few cases did these marriages breach established color lines, though more often they crossed lines of class and culture. Of much more general moment were probably the effects on all Bahamians of seeing the behavior and listening to the social (sometimes socialist) ideas of visitors from several strata below those of the customary tourists. In a more practical way, the presence of the bases in New Providence, with their special lines of supply, not only ensured that the Bahamas did not suffer serious wartime food shortages but actually helped raise the standard of living among the majority population. Temporary shortages of canned goods, fresh meat, and grits late in the war were not sufficient to make rationing necessary. Though dwindling supplies of kerosene led to long queues in Nassau and long, dark nights in the Out Islands, the limited supply of gasoline was not a general hardship where cars remained a luxury and the majority were accustomed to walking or riding a bicycle.

That there were almost no negative effects of the war and the horrors of the worldwide conflict made little impact on Bahamian life is borne out by the fact that the most shocking wartime event was the brutal unsolved murder of Sir Harry Oakes on the night of July 7–8, 1943. The sensational acquittal of the only person charged, Oakes's estranged and outlandish son-in-law, the Mauritian Alfred "Count" de Marigny, and the absence of a clear motive, have allowed for endless, and excessive, speculation over fifty years—including two somewhat conflicting exculpatory autobiographies by Marigny himself.[59] Probably more important than finding the solution to the mystery of who killed Oakes, however, is the light the assumptions, hypotheses, and debates about the murder shed on Bahamian society and social attitudes during the 1940s.

The Duke of Windsor was certain in his mind and what he wrote in secret dispatches as to who was guilty and what should be done, but he was ill-informed.

Victory March, Nassau, September 1945. Royal Air Force airmen celebrate impending return home, before a sparse Bay Street crowd. Courtesy of Bahamas Archives.

He acted with unaccustomed firmness and undue haste and consequently was responsible for totally bungling the case (by mistrusting local policemen and bringing in American detectives, who fabricated evidence and were found out, leading to Marigny's acquittal). "The older and more conservative elements and the whole negro population suspect de Marigny's guilt," Windsor wrote in August 1943, "but above all wish to see the murderer, whoever he is, pay the supreme penalty for so dastardly a crime which caused the death of a fine old man and great benefactor—the best friend the Bahamas ever had." The Windsors' snobbish, or prudish, distaste for Marigny and his circle, however, led the Duke to call him the leader of "a quite influential, fast and depraved set of the younger generation, born of bootlegging days, and for him they have an admiration bordering on hero worship. This unsavoury group of people would therefore like to see Marigny escape the rope at all costs, whether guilty or innocent—but if the coloured people are ever given the slightest reason to suspect the jury, then the consequences may be grave."[60]

In fact, Marigny had very few friends, and these included as many nonwhites as whites; and if the "more conservative elements" had reasons to dislike Marigny, they may well have had more motive to fear and hate Sir Harry Oakes. Quite apart from the suggestion that Oakes was threatening to transfer his investments from the Bahamas or the more extravagant theory that he had crossed Meyer Lansky and the Mafia in their plans to make Nassau a new Havana, Oakes was an overbearing newcomer whose wealth, power, and influence challenged the established Bay Street regime. Also, as a self-made man and foreigner, Oakes was notoriously careless about the niceties of Bahamian social convention.

The Duke of Windsor, who seems to have been more friendly and intimate with Oakes than with any Bahamian, also seems to have misread the attitude of ordinary blacks toward the American-Canadian adventurer. Much as the wage employment he offered was appreciated, Oakes's dictatorial manner and temper (which mixed summary sackings and verbal and even physical abuse with casual generosity) made him enemies in all walks of life. Significantly, his death was an occasion for wonder and speculation, not universal grief. More likely, Oakes was seen as but another rich and powerful white patron, and one rather less socially adept than the traditional Bay Street "buckra." He was a person to be respected for the power he wielded and gratified for the patronage and protection he afforded; but he was not loved. Indeed, as was true with slave owners and their powerful white descendants, he was the object of a deep-seated and disguised resentment that could turn to peculation, hatred, or even violence once the wind changed or the tide was right.

For all his personal mediocrity, the Duke of Windsor, as a royal aristocrat, could rise above and ride upon the petty social counterpoint of the colony he governed, identifying with none, befriending whom he chose, and more likely to establish a rapport with the lower than the ruling classes. This quality explains his personal popularity and the confident way in which he both expected and cultivated cooperation, despite his private disdain for all Bahamians, his frequent misreading of social conditions, and his paucity of positive achievements. He was also fortunate in that the last phase of his time in the Bahamas saw an economic upturn that was to continue and accelerate throughout the postwar years, disguising and delaying the resolution of the fundamental problems of underdevelopment, overdependence on tourism and imports, inflation, inequality, and political inertia.

The Beginnings of Airborne Tourism

In summing up his reluctant tenure of the governorship at the end of 1944, the Duke of Windsor wrote euphorically, and with some exaggeration, that since the United States had entered World War II, "there had developed a state of prosperity as has never been experienced, and the remarkable feature of this prosperity is that it has come mainly through the labour of the working classes who never before in the whole history of the Colony have earned as much money as in the last two years."[61] Victory in Europe and over Japan was properly celebrated in May and August 1945, but there must have been some trepidation among all classes that peace, along with the departure of the Duke of Windsor, would mean a return of the Bahamas to its prewar condition as a depressed backwater. Such fears proved groundless because the Contract was renegotiated with more generous terms, and both tourism and foreign investment not only revived but achieved hitherto undreamed-of dimensions. In the first respect, the Bahamas was able to benefit hugely and be on the front end of a new wave of airborne tourism by the possession of two large modern airfields once they were vacated by the RAF early in 1946; in the second, the colony actually benefited from Britain's economic woes, as higher taxation to pay for the war, harsh domestic restrictions in 1947, and finally the devaluation of the pound two years later made the Bahamas a favorite haven for a new generation of financial émigrés.

The initial influx of British money, signaled by the opening of a branch of Barclays Bank in 1947, was soon dwarfed by refugee dollars, as sophisticated accountants and lawyers pointed up the advantages of offshore "suitcase" companies and tax-sheltering Bahamian trusts to Americans wishing to avoid the attentions of the Internal Revenue Service (IRS). As long as sterling remained a currency officially watertight through exchange controls, the Bahamas was not only an invaluable official earner of dollars for the benefit of the pound (worth up to $30 million a year), but it also served as a convenient, if clandestine, leakage point of further untold millions between the sterling and dollar blocs. Even when the sterling bloc was dismantled, the Bahamas continued to prosper as a haven from an increasingly severe United States IRS, including among its increasing range of expertise the "laundering" of money of dubious provenance.

By the late 1940s, Bay Street lawyers' office fronts featured checkerboards of locally registered offshore companies in the thousands, just as the number of banks and trust companies rose from one of each in 1939 to dozens in the 1950s and more than seventy in all in the mid-1960s. Only with the spectacular and discreditable collapse of the Canadian Nassau-registered Atlantic Acceptance Corporation was a reasonably rigorous Companies Registration Act passed, in 1965. Absolute bank secrecy—like that in Switzerland—lasted much longer. One result of the surge of foreign investment and flow of foreign funds was a rapid rise in the value of Bahamian real estate—properties on Bay Street rose in value by 300 percent in the first decade after the war and those in the Out Islands, starting from a lower base, proportionately even more. By 1964, land on Cable Beach was realizing as much per front foot as it had cost per acre forty years earlier. This spurred a general inflationary process—with the cost-of-living index rising from 100 immediately before British devaluation in 1949 to 160 in 1958 and 190 in 1965—the negative effects of which were felt as disproportionately as were the benefits of the investment boom.[62]

The chief beneficiaries were white lawyers and realtors, epitomized by the brilliant and ubiquitous Stafford Sands and the less flamboyant Harold Christie. Company flotation was an extremely lucrative business, not just through setting up and maintenance fees but because Bahamian law required local representation on the board of any locally registered company and substantial equity involvement if the company actually carried on business in the Bahamas. The profits from sales and leases of Bahamian real estate and such concessions as the forty-eight thousand square miles of oil exploration leases awarded in 1946, the one hundred thousand acres granted to Wallace Groves in 1955 for the building of his dream city in Grand Bahama, or the "sweetheart" forestry deal with the Owens-Illinois Company in 1959 were probably even larger, even without the undercover fees that were exacted for the mere privilege of access which was practically under the control of Bay Street politicians. Even more than the traditional plums of commercial hegemony—import and export trade, wholesale and retail business—these new, less visible activities were monopolized by a handful of entrepreneurs, whose greed and concomitant need to control the reins of power led to intensifying the Bay Street system despite growing demands for its reform.

Three of the means by which Bay Street sustained its hegemony were the control of patronage, the trickle-down effect of economic prosperity, and the promulgation of the myth that it alone could sustain the flow of wealth. Bay Street never fully controlled the media, but this was more than made up by the way its dominance in the legislature allowed for the underdevelopment of education—thus guaranteeing both a lack of popular political sophistication and a shortage of nonwhite professionals—and by the perpetuation of age-old habits of dependency and a lack of self-confidence on the part of the black majority. Most culpable of all, perhaps, were the nonwhite middle classes or those among them who turned their back on the chance to lead a sociopolitical revolution by preferring to look to their own relative advantages—failing to acknowledge that they were thereby likely always to occupy at best an intermediate and secondary position.

The most important agent of Bahamian postwar prosperity and Bay Street power was the Development Board, which under the chairmanship of Stafford Sands came to take a larger share of the colonial budget than the entire education system.[63] Its chief concern was the development of tourism and the encouragement of foreign investment, and it appeared to be impressively successful—though skeptics might well argue that the improvements for which it claimed chief credit were inevitable or fortuitous.

Oakes Field served as the first commercial airport in the Bahamas, under the direction of the director of civil aviation, first appointed in 1946. At first, Pan American Airways provided only one flight a day in the winter season, to and from Miami. But this service increased eightfold by 1950, with three daily flights in the summer months. Longer-haul flights were also inaugurated, with British South American Airways pioneering the London-Bermuda-Nassau route in 1946, taken over by the restructured British Overseas Airways Corporation with Lockheed Constellation and Boeing Stratocruiser aircraft in 1950, when there were also flights to and from New York and Montreal at least once a week, by BOAC and Air Canada.

Oakes Field remained the premier airport—with the sluggish London-bound Stratocruisers taking off directly over Government House—until superseded by Nassau International Airport (Windsor Field) in November 1957. By that time, both air traffic and the number of airfields had hugely proliferated. In 1958 there were twenty-three thousand aircraft movements in New Providence alone, doubling again by 1965. By 1959 there were nineteen airports and landing strips in the Bahamas, of which seven were owned and operated by the Bahamas government, eight privately owned, and four of the largest—in Grand Bahama, Eleuthera, San Salvador, and Mayaguana—built and maintained by the United States government, as a result of the missile tracking bases agreements of the mid-1950s. By 1965, the total number of airports and airfields had risen to forty-one—twenty-eight of them privately owned—serving, in all, twenty-six islands and cays. By that time, six airlines connected the Bahamas with Miami, Fort Lauderdale, New York, Montreal, Toronto, Bermuda, Jamaica, and Mexico City, while Bahamas Airways—with its elegant De Havilland Doves and workhorse Douglas Dakotas—served the Out Islands with the help of various charter airlines.[64]

The increase in air traffic matched the surge in tourism, which became more than ever dominated by North Americans. Mass tourism, particularly the concept of the package tour, however, was pioneered by a visionary Briton, Billy Butlin, who purchased a site at West End, Grand Bahama, in 1948 and planned a superior version of his popular British holiday camps, with five hundred rooms and accommodations for a thousand. Doomed by his patriotic wish to use British capital, materials, and expertise and to seek British as well as American vacationers, Butlin was dogged by a dock strike in Britain, building delays on accommodations and airstrip, and the shortage of qualified local staff. It was rumored that Butlin was also impeded by trying to remain too independent of the Bay Street oligarchy, which was concerned that the operation might fall into the hands of American gambling interests. Though it attracted eighteen thousand visitors at the cost of $99 a person for a week's holiday, Butlin's Vacation Village was closed by its nervous creditors in the fall of 1950 after operating for only one season. In the estimate of Grand Bahama's historian Peter Barratt, it was "essentially the right development in the right place—but . . . ten years too soon."[65]

Learning much from Butlin's ideas and his failures, the Development Board—chaired by Stafford Sands from 1949 until he became minister of tourism and finance in 1964—declared a year-round season in 1950, set up offices in key American cities, spent millions on advertising that targeted ordinary Americans, and did its utmost to encourage hotel building, air transportation, and the training of hotel staff. A key factor was the passage of the Hotels Encouragement Act in 1949 and its subsequent amendments that not only promised investors a ten-year tax holiday but allowed them to bring in materials and food duty-free and foreign staff without the normal immigration restrictions. Hotel builders also were led to believe they would be allowed casino licenses once the time, and the terms, were right. As a result, the Bahamas was able to become the first overseas sun-holiday destination to benefit from the postwar American economic boom—a priority never relinquished, at least in terms of numbers.

From a total of 32,000 holiday visitors in 1949, the Bahamas attracted 132,000 in 1955, 342,000 in 1960, and almost three-quarters of a million in 1965—for an expenditure by the Development Board that had risen from less than £100,000 to not far short of £2 million. In 1959, more than 22,000 visitors arrived in July, compared with 29,000 in March, the busiest month, drawn largely by "economy" summer rates. In 1964, 87 percent of all visitors to the Bahamas came from North America; those from Britain totaled no more than 9 percent. Of the visitors in 1960, six out of seven went to Nassau, though the share of the Out Islands had risen to a third by 1965 with the development of Grand Bahama. About two-thirds of all visitors were "stopovers"—those staying more than forty-eight hours. Most of those traveled by air; the remainder were mainly cruise ship passengers staying less than two days and using their ship as a hotel.[66]

Between 1960 and 1965, exchange control records showed that United States tourists spent the huge total of $227,414,000 in the Bahamas. This sum was exceeded by Bahamian expenditures in the United States (mainly for food and consumer goods) of $382,720,000, but, as the official Annual Report for 1965 noted, this apparent dollar deficit on the part of the Bahamas had been "more than made up by the inflow of investments by U.S. companies and individuals, and the income from Bahamian-owned U.S. portfolios"—not to mention the many other invisible profits to fortunate Bahamians from the American connection.[67]

Some of the fruits of prosperity filtered down naturally or were cannily dispensed in the form of legislated or administration-introduced improvements, but these were scarcely enough to guarantee the maintenance of Bay Street's hegemony into the 1960s. What happened in fact was a slow tactical retreat under external as well as internal pressures that postponed the inevitable victory of the black majority for perhaps a decade.

At the economic level, the late 1940s and 1950s saw a steady if modest improvement in the fortunes of the Bahamian middle class, represented by better job opportunities in the civil service, improved chances on the lower slopes of business, the greater availability of borrowed money because of the inflow of capital and the proliferation of banks, and more opportunities for the younger generation to go abroad for higher education or professional qualifications.

Of the last of these trends, the counterposed examples of two of the many outstanding alumni of the Government High School stand out as of more than symbolic significance. Kendal Isaacs, quintessential product of the moderate brown middle class, volunteered as a teenager for the Bahamas Battalion in the last year of the war. As an officer veteran he obtained a place at Cambridge, where besides his LLB he obtained a Blue for representing the varsity at tennis (though, as he wryly recalled, he had to win the university singles championship before the white-slanted committee selected him). Financially supported by his family, Isaacs went on from Cambridge to the Inns of Court and was called to the bar in 1950. Returning to Nassau, he found briefs and profitable commercial business almost nonexistent in the face of the obstruction of white Bay Street lawyers, nearly all of whose qualifications had been obtained through the convenient provision that allowed for bar admission after local apprenticeship. The establishment, though, was prepared to shunt him into the less rewarding role of stipendiary magistrate and later even appoint him attorney general.

As a black from a less privileged background, Isaac's slightly younger schoolmate Lynden Pindling had a harder route upward and reacted in an emphatically more radical style. The son of a Jamaican policeman turned Over the Hill shopkeeper and an Acklins Island mother, Pindling also trained in England as a lawyer at his family's expense. At the London School of Economics, where he studied before the Inns of Court, he met many other black British colonials and seems to have been influenced both by the socialist Harold Laski and Laski's far more conservative successor, Michael Oakeshott. Returning home in 1953, Pindling found neither rich briefs nor official employment and turned instead to litigation on behalf of poor clients and to popular politics. Pindling was to become the first black premier and prime minister, and Isaacs, once the white regime was vanquished, the leader of the opposition—knighted, respectively, in 1982 and 1993.[68]

A postwar occurrence that was equally telling, if more symbolic than significant, was the founding of the first formal black-owned bank in 1952. The People's Penny Savings Bank was the brainchild of Leon McKinney, originally from Long Cay but educated in Miami, where he gained experience as an insurance agent to a nonwhite clientele. Returning to the Bahamas in 1937, McKinney worked first for the Erickson salt company in Inagua and then as assistant manager of the Community Industrial Life Insurance Company. McKinney's dream—shared by a handful of the most prominent and relatively prosperous dark-skinned colored Bahamians—was to shortcut the capitalist system by establishing a bank that would cater to middle- and lower-income nonwhites, few of whom owned bank accounts and were mostly overawed by Bay Street banks, if not actively discriminated against.

Strategically located in the heart of Grant's Town, opposite the Southern Recre-

Bay Street dressed up to legislate. The House of Assembly, around 1950: four black and three brown faces out of twenty-seven. To the left of the ancient mace, Roland Symonette, with Etienne Dupuch on his right. Harold Christie is fifth from the right. Stafford Sands in the doorway, looking away from the camera. Courtesy of Bahamas Archives.

ation Ground, where the major political meetings took place, the People's Penny Savings Bank was opened with optimistic rhetoric on November 21, 1952. On a platform that included impassive representatives of the Royal Bank of Canada and Barclays Bank as well as his brown fellow directors and the nonwhite members of the House of Assembly, Leon McKinney stated: "We are not seeking what is profitable for a few. . . . We are thinking in terms of the many . . . this institution, at present, does not boast of being a bank but rather a school of 'thrift' where any man, woman or child may take the first step towards self sufficiency by opening an account with an amount as small as a penny." The People's Penny Savings Bank undoubtedly achieved these limited aims at a time when blacks were hardly ever seen inside Bay Street banks, on either side of the counter (there was not a single nonwhite teller before 1958), though it always struggled as an authentic bank and was liquidated in the 1980s.[69]

Trickle-Down Prosperity and Political Stirrings

In line with the British Labour government's efforts to bolster social services in its colonial territories, and following some of the recommendations of Professor Henry

Richardson's government-sponsored *Review of Bahamian Economic Conditions and Postwar Problems* (1944), the Bahamas did experience some improvements in health and educational services in the first decade after the war—though agriculture continued to be almost ignored and political concessions resolutely resisted.

The infant welfare clinics sponsored by the Duchess of Windsor were continued and extended, with volunteer, mainly nonwhite, helpers making valiant efforts to reduce infant mortality through better pre- and postnatal care. In response to the revelation of a government-sponsored survey by Dr. W. Santon-Gilmour in 1944 that the incidence of tuberculosis in the Bahamas was the highest in the British West Indies, the former thirty-three-bed RAF hospital at Prospect Ridge was converted to an isolation hospital for TB patients. In 1953, the dilapidated General Hospital in downtown Nassau was replaced by a new building with two hundred beds, and the primitive and prisonlike lunatic wards were relocated in more modern and humane premises at Fox Hill, six miles out of town. Conditions for Out Islanders, however, were scarcely improved—though the gradual improvement of air communications did enable Nassau-based doctors and nurses more easily to serve the Out Islands and some emergency cases to be brought to Nassau.[70]

The small and slow educational advances were even more equivocal. In 1946 two elite scholarships of £400 a year for university study abroad were instituted, and over the following five years the Board of Education organized in-service training for teachers and nurses in the United Kingdom. After much debate, a director of education was appointed in 1947, with a suitable white expatriate filling the post, a small technical school opened in 1949, and a similarly modest teacher training college with thirty trainees started in 1950. Suggestions for affiliations with the new University College of the West Indies were deflected.

The 1951 Education Act broadened the powers of the Board of Education but purposefully denied it control over secondary schooling, which remained largely in private hands. Probably to ensure it was more directly controlled, the Government High School was made a separate government department. Although steadily enlarged, the Government High School remained in cramped non-purpose-built quarters until 1960, with a white headmaster of the old colonialist stamp and expatriate British and Canadian teachers rigidly constrained by Colonial Office regulations.[71] Increasing demand, especially among the growing colored and black middle classes, led to the establishment of three church-sponsored high schools. In 1945, the Augustinian monastery on the Fox Hill road was enlarged to include a boys' high school, St. Augustine's College, to which a girls' school, St. Francis Xavier's Academy, was added on the other side of town a few years later. Though single-sex schools, both were racially mixed, following for years an American rather than British curriculum. The coeducational St. John's College, opened by the Anglican diocese just Over the Hill on Market Street, Nassau, in January 1947, however, drew only nonwhites and adhered to the British tradition.[72]

Under pressure from the Methodist authorities in England, as well as from those who objected to the fact that a denominational and exclusive school should receive as much aid from the government as did Government High School, the white-favored Queen's College gradually became more integrated. This was opposed by many parents, particularly those concerned about the "threat" to their daughters in a coeducational school. The result was the founding of the private St. Andrew's

School in 1948 which—fittingly in an establishment that was essentially a Bay Street creation—was actually a limited company, with the parents of all the children enrolled as shareholders. By this means, the school was exclusively run for white children and was not integrated until the 1970s.[73] All high schools, however, despite their subtle racial differences and different affiliations, remained essentially elitist, serving only a fraction of the children of secondary school age.

Such deprivations, as well as discrimination, helped to fuel the growing sociopolitical discontent, though dissent was diffused or deflected by the tactics of the regime, by division among the opposition forces, or by too much concern for comparatively trivial matters or purely sectional interests. It was not a politician but a black Methodist minister who led the opposition on the part of the black majority to the hegemonic tactics of the Bay Street regime. In a remarkable sermon delivered at Governor's Harbour, Eleuthera, on January 14, 1946, Rev. H. H. Brown made a clarion call. "I doubt if there is anywhere else on earth masquerading as 'democracy' a less representative government," he asserted.

> Instead of "government of the people, for the people," we have "exploitation of the many, for the privileged, by the few." That a people has the kind of government that it deserves is almost axiomatic. A criticism of the local government is therefore a criticism of the entire population. Until people awaken to their own responsibilities, they will not have a responsible government. But nothing can possibly justify the attempt of any government to keep the people asleep. Who has learned the lesson of the [1942] riot? Not the Governor with his recent appalling appointment [of Stafford Sands] to the Executive Council. Not those members who repeatedly block the simpler efforts for economic improvement, political development, or educational expansion. Not an administration which sends thousands of men overseas on "projects" and does nothing to prepare for their return home.

Essaying a prophecy, Rev. Brown also stated that unless the regime became less selfish and the ordinary citizens awoke to the responsibilities of democracy, the riot of 1942 would "seem pale and insignificant in comparison with its successor."[74]

The opposition to the regime was united in favor of the secret ballot, but the passage of the Secret Ballot Act in July 1944 broke up the loose alliance of reformists. A perceptible split occurred between the continuing populist radicalism of Stanley Lowe's biweekly *Herald* and the more cautious reformism expressed by Dupuch's daily *Tribune* and such short-lived papers as the *Voice* in the late 1940s and the *Citizen's Torch* in the early 1950s. This last was a publication of the Citizens' Committee formed in 1950 by a group of middle-class nonwhites concerned about discrimination and such issues as the banning of films regarded as racially sensitive (including *No Way Out*, starring Sidney Poitier) and the opposition of the regime to any closer alliance with the British West Indies, then moving cautiously toward some form of federation. The constitution of the Citizens' Committee expressed the moderate (and damagingly imprecise) aims to "generally protect, improve, preserve and defend the economic, educational and political rights of all Bahamians."[75]

By 1953, moves were afoot to organize a formal political party to oppose Bay Street and its practices, though the opposition remained weakened by a lack of cohesion and concerted aims. Early in 1953 the conservative *Nassau Guardian* announced that a Christian Democratic Party had five hundred members, but it disappeared within the year. Equally abortive and shadowy was the People's Political Party, which was variously claimed to be an offshoot of the Citizens' Committee, the creation of two black activist newcomers, or even the creature of the white Speaker of the House of Assembly, Asa Pritchard, whose devious object was alleged to be to bring the black people back to the "old practice of following the lead of white representatives."[76]

Much better organized, with a well-formulated platform that addressed burning issues in a calm and deliberate manner, was the Progressive Liberal Party, the formation of which was announced late in October 1953. It stemmed from tactical discussions held in September 1953 by the seasoned campaigners Henry Taylor, William Cartwright, and Cyril Stevenson—the latter two having become the owner and editor respectively of the *Herald* after the death of Stanley Lowe in January 1953. The PLP's initial manifesto seemed a direct response to the 1946 challenge of Rev. H. H. Brown: "The Progressive Liberal Party hopes to show that your big man and your little man, your black, brown and white man of all classes, creed and religions in this country can combine and work together in supplying sound and successful political leadership which has been sadly lacking in the Bahamas." More specifically and cogently, the party's policy statement in June 1954 called for wider representation in the House of Assembly, the enfranchisement of women, and the reduction of the life of the House from seven to five years. It vowed its opposition to communism and promised a more equitable social system. It pledged support for equal employment opportunities, better education, lower prices, low-cost housing, and strong immigration controls. It also promised a "New Deal" for the most neglected Out Islands, the development of agriculture, and improved social services.[77]

Despite its broad-based appeal, the PLP made slow progress at first, facing even more internal than external problems. Most of its leading members suffered from Bay Street obstructionism—loss of jobs, printing contracts, or credit at the bank—that made the more cautious middle-class nonwhites hesitate to join them. More insidious was the subtle campaign to suggest that their policies would eventually lead to socialism if not outright communism. This fear was probably reinforced by the way PLP officials referred to some of the more prosperous middle-class nonwhites as Bay Street lackeys.

Most problematic of all, though, was the question of color. The founders of the PLP were mainly whites or near-whites, who genuinely believed that their party should be transracial, possibly because a large proportion of them were also Catholics. This predominance grated against some of the second rank of party adherents, blacks with a deeply bred distrust of coloreds as well as whites, who were easily influenced by the beginnings of black power rhetoric emanating from the United States and the West Indies. The two key figures were Milo Butler, with his emotive Baptist-preacher style, and the more cerebral Lynden Pindling, who recognized that besides appealing to the oppressed black majority, a successful opposition party would have to mobilize a Bahamian proletariat.

In moves that are still the subject of heated debate and scholarly analysis, a caucus of blacks of whom Lynden Pindling emerged as leader gradually took over control of the PLP beginning in 1955. In preparation for the general election of 1956, the party also attracted the dynamic young black lawyer Randol Fawkes, who, as the founder of the Bahamas Federation of Labour in May 1955, was now the acknowledged leader of Bahamian trade unionists in succession to Charles Rhodriguez. Deploring the reverse racism of the party leaders if not the proletarianization of the party, the first chairman of the PLP, Henry Taylor, was increasingly treated as a figurehead, sidelined, and eventually (in 1963) forced into resignation and virtual exile, though he was to end his career as governor-general. Meanwhile, moderates of all shades, as concerned about the racial polarization threatened by developments within the PLP as they were of the dangers of Bay Street extremism, formed a kind of Bahamian Fabian Society called the Bahamas Democratic League (BDL), the first actions of which were to present liberal petitions in the House of Assembly through its most prominent member, the near-white (and Catholic) newspaper editor Etienne Dupuch.[78]

The first of these petitions, against the restrictive Collins Wall, was a failure. The wall was not breached until 1959. But the second, against discrimination in public places, was successful early in 1956 after dramatic episodes in the House of Assembly. At one stage, the colored musician MHA Bert Cambridge stated, "I have worked in hotels on this island and I know that common prostitutes are admitted to places in Bay Street because they are white and decent coloured people are refused admission." Though at least two white MHAs joined the nonwhites to support Dupuch's mild original resolution—stating that discrimination was "not in the public interest" and calling for a commission of inquiry—the white majority voted instead for a select committee. When the Speaker announced a committee consisting of five white Bay Street stalwarts and only two nonwhites, Dupuch vehemently protested and was threatened with arrest. "You may call the whole Police Force," he told the Speaker, "you may call the whole British Army. . . . I will go to gaol tonight, but I refuse to sit down, and am ready to resign and go back to the people."[79]

Uproar in the public gallery was calmed only by a hasty adjournment of the House. Spurred by statements from all Nassau hotels but one (that operated by its Bay Street creditors) that their doors were open to all regardless of race, the committee decided to adopt the first part of Dupuch's resolution. It was passed unanimously by the House on February 29, 1956. As Colin Hughes commented, "Probably the majority in the House concluded that passing such a resolution was less of an evil than risking a commission appointed by the governor, possibly even a non-Bahamian commission, which might open up wider questions." The PLP, however, criticized Dupuch for not pressing for a commission and binding antidiscriminatory legislation.[80]

The polarization of politics on color rather than purely class lines was expedited by the general election of May 1956. Advertising the undoubted economic growth under their leadership and circulating the rumor that their opponents planned an income tax and large salaries for their representatives, the Bay Street candidates shamelessly deployed their own wealth in traditional ways to ensure reelection, concentrating on the hugely overrepresented Out Islands. Numerically, their victory was overwhelming, but more significant was the election of six black members of the PLP, four for Nassau seats and two from all-black Andros. The two near-white radicals most opposed to racial polarization suffered notable defeats: Henry Taylor, though he was still nominally chairman of the PLP, and Etienne Dupuch, who shared the fate of all but one of the candidates of the BDL. With the small PLP group acting for the first time as a coherent parliamentary opposition, the Bay Street clique was constrained to organize itself as a political party, though its United Bahamian Party (UBP) was not formally constituted until March 1958.[81]

Regarding electoral reform as more important than the constitutional advances that even Bay Street favored (for the independence from the Colonial Office and governor they would afford), the PLP immediately demanded the redistribution of seats, the abolition of plural voting and property qualifications, and enfranchisement for women. While consolidating their gains by membership drives and encouraging labor organization, PLP leaders raised the political temperature by outspoken journalism and public speeches, sometimes theatrical behavior in the House of Assembly, and sponsoring public demonstrations in downtown Nassau while the House was in session. Frequent cables and a delegation of protest were also sent to the Colonial Office in London (which, though under a Conservative British government, was rightly seen as edging toward reform in the wake of the Suez debacle of 1956). The PLP's biggest opportunity for forcing change through confrontation, though, came with the general strike and related turmoil of January 1958.[82]

The 1958 General Strike and the Rise of the PLP

Though as owner-operators they were hardly proletarians, the Nassau taxi drivers were a tightly knit group, almost exclusively black, that strongly supported both the PLP and the union movement. A long-standing dispute over the carriage of tourists to and from the hotels between the independent taxi men and the Bay Street–owned tour companies touched on basic issues of race and class, and the imminent opening of the new international airport at Windsor Field (which, being fifteen miles from town, made transportation much more important and lucrative than ever before) made a showdown almost inevitable. Forthright action by the Taxi-Cab Union, moreover, would fulfill one of the axioms of trade union tactics, especially in the early stages of unionization, that success was most likely to follow from work stoppages in the most vital sectors of the economy.

On November 1, 1957, a hundred taxi drivers used their vehicles to block access to the new airport, causing flights to be canceled and effectively blocking all tourist traffic for twenty-four hours. Although some drivers were charged with obstruction and assault, a truce was arranged for eight weeks to allow for arbitration, during which time the taxi men enjoyed a virtual monopoly of airport transportation. Most of the disputed issues were resolved by December, but PLP and Bahamas Federation of Labour tacticians decided to make a stand on the remainder and called a general strike to coincide with the opening of the House of Assembly on Tuesday, January 13, 1958. A wide section of workers in key industries responded, whether unionized or not: construction workers, hotel staff, airport porters, bakers, garbage collectors, Electricity Corporation employees, and even privately employed domestics. Anticipating the fulfillment of Rev. Brown's 1946 prophecy, Bay Street and its minions responded with panic. "Rumors of impending riots were everywhere as the city prepared to erupt," reported the *Nassau Guardian* two days later. "Along Bay Street merchants threw up storm windows in the first measure against the expected blow. Police said they expected trouble. Gangs of men were reported drinking heavily preparatory to marching on Bay Street. Looting was feared. Riot squads were alerted. Injury and bloodshed seemed inevitable." This was irresponsible alarmism, but a large and heated crowd did indeed turn out at Rawson Square, cheered the PLP members as they filed from the House to the Council chamber, and, when Milo Butler called out, "These are your representatives. . . . Get rid of white man rule in this country," booed both the white MHAs and the governor as he inspected the guard of honor.[83]

Shaken by this unprecedented lapse of manners, Governor Sir Raynor Arthur (whose previous responsibility had been the governorship of two thousand whites and seven hundred thousand sheep in the Falkland Islands) called for a British army detachment from Jamaica and a Royal Navy frigate, which were conveniently standing by. A company of the Worcester Regiment flew in the next day, carrying sidearms and prepared to preserve order but discreetly housed outside town at Oakes Field. No naval personnel were landed once the frigate docked, though technicians were said to be available to help maintain essential services. All bars were closed by magisterial order, but martial law was not declared, or even a curfew.[84]

Since the Taxi-Cab Union, Bahamas Federation of Labour, and PLP all enjoined no actions but peaceful picketing, the governor's reaction was undoubtedly precipitate. There were tense moments during the sixteen-day strike but no bloodshed. The most serious incidents were almost symbolic; a scuffle on the picket line outside Asa Pritchard's shop (three picketers were charged with intimidation and Pritchard's son was charged with running at the lines with his car), the alleged discovery of sticks of dynamite at the waterworks and in the grounds of a hotel, and mysterious fires that damaged the Worcesters' canteen and destroyed the offices of the *Nassau Guardian*. But Governor Arthur's dramatic recourse to the army and navy did help to draw the attention of the world press to the Bahamas, and even if it did not in itself indicate a decision on the part of the Colonial Office that something had to be done, it certainly made it impossible for the British authorities to sit on the fence over Bahamian conditions from that time forward. The unprecedented level of imperial concern was indicated by the week-long visit to the Bahamas in April 1958 of the secretary of state for the colonies, Alan Lennox-Boyd.[85]

Shocked by the first setback to tourism since the war, Bay Street itself (now formally constituted as the UBP) was jolted into accepting some long overdue changes, while at the same time redoubling its efforts to divide and discredit the opposition. With the fledgling Bahamian unions being given financial aid and advice by British and West Indian trade unionists and the labor experts at the Colonial Office mixing advice with persuasion, the House of Assembly at last passed the Trade Union and Industrial Conciliation Act in July 1958 that brought the Bahamas in line with Jamaica, Trinidad, and Barbados. Besides laying down the rules for union organization and industrial action, the act set up a Labour Department headed by a chief industrial officer and a Labour Office responsible for dealing with all matters connected with workers' wages, insurance, welfare, and family allotments, as well as continuing to recruit and organize workers on the Contract—all under the ultimate authority of a Labour Board appointed by the governor.[86]

These labor reforms satisfied most workers and PLP members but (to the secret satisfaction of Bay Street) not the most ardent labor activists, especially their chief spokesman, Randol Fawkes. Carried away with his personal popularity as a public speaker, Fawkes was disappointed both in his motion to have the party's name changed to the Progressive Labour Party and in his own ambitions to be chosen its leader. Even more serious blows were the failure of a twelve-day strike of construction workers at a new hotel site when a hundred workers crossed the picket line and the formation of a splinter Bahamian Trades Union Congress with the tacit support of the PLP's official *Herald* newspaper. Because the PLP leaders seemed to concur with the governor's warning to the BFL's 1958 Labour Day parade not to mix labor business with politics, Fawkes left the PLP to form his own Labour Party.[87]

For the PLP and the new UBP the two most contentious matters were electoral reform and the increased involvement of the legislature in the executive branch of government, though these were underlaid by the more important issue of the increased racial polarization of politics. Goaded by the threat of a royal commission, the UBP accepted the principles of widening the electorate and redistributing the seats but beat a rear-guard action over the details. As for extending the powers of the elected branch of the legislature, they countered Governor Arthur's use of the royal prerogative in 1959 to strengthen the Legislative Council as a counterweight to the House of Assembly by demanding an increase in the powers of the government boards which the House effectively controlled. Nonwhites, including PLP members, were tactically invited to join the boards, among them the all-important Development Board. Some broke ranks to accept appointment, but most PLP supporters refused on the realistic grounds that they would be only token members, easily outvoted by the Bay Street majority. The PLP's preference was to accept the governor's appointment to the reformed Legislative Council, at least until the power of the UBP was broken in the lower house and a system of responsible government (with an executive cabinet drawn from the majority party in the elected assembly) instituted—on the British model and along lines already followed in Jamaica, Trinidad, and Barbados.[88]

During 1960, the PLP made important recruits among the small group of middle-class black professionals and almost doubled its representation in the House of Assembly, which increased political, racial, and class tensions. The elevation of a UBP incumbent to the Legislative Council occasioned a by-election at Grand Bahama in February, where a black PLP candidate was elected (over an Independent and a Labour as well as a UBP opponent) after an energetic and bitter campaign, a recount, and an appeal to the Elections Tribunal. Much more important were the results of the by-elections in May following the creation of two new double-seat constituencies in New Providence. In the solidly black Southern District, the two PLP candidates each gained two-thirds of the votes, Labour candidates came in third and fourth, and the two blacks nominated by the UBP (one a former MHA) obtaining a derisory 5 percent of the votes apiece. In the less homogeneous Eastern District, where the Labour Party made only a nominal showing, the results were far closer, but both of the PLP candidates were successful, receiving a total of 3,967 votes to their UBP opponents' combined 2,874.[89]

Under renewed pressure, the UBP accepted the principles of universal adult suffrage and five- (rather than seven-) year parliaments, though it resisted other electoral changes that would threaten its predominance in the Out Islands. It also went to great lengths to alter constituency boundaries in New Providence to its own advantage, as well as to commission an economic survey that stressed recent progress but cleverly slid over the many remaining problems and failures. As the fulfillment of a decade-long campaign led by Doris Johnson, Georgina Symonette, and Eugenie Lockhart, women obtained the vote in 1961, when both parties organized themselves for the crucial general election set for November 1962. Despite heartfelt pleas by Governor Arthur on leaving the colony that interracial hatred was un-Bahamian and that party divisions on racial lines would be self-defeating if not disastrous, the campaign exhibited an unprecedented racial polarization and bitterness—intensified on the one side by UBP hard-liners and on the other by a ginger group of young black radicals calling themselves the National Committee for Positive Action.[90]

Much of the inspiration for the PLP radicals came from the black power movement then rising to a climax in the United States and from the political successes recently achieved by black majorities in other British colonies in Africa and the West Indies. The countering propaganda of the UBP relied on the Bahamian traditions of racial coexistence and distaste for social conflict and the ambivalence toward Africa and its legacies felt by nearly all nonwhite Bahamians. When the *Herald* uncovered a secret policy report from an American journalist working for the *Nassau Guardian* that flatly stated, "This is a white man's society," the UBP's paper unrepentantly counterattacked:

> Think carefully. Does anyone seriously think that it is not? Is it an African society? Anyone who says so is insulting the people of the Bahamas who for centuries have been British—in name, in language, in custom, education and culture. In everything, in fact, except origin. Does the *Herald* advocate that the streets of Nassau should echo to the beat of the tomtom, or witness the primitive rites of voodoo and black magic? Not even the *Herald* advocates that.
>
> And why? Because the people of the Bahamas have had centuries of civilization. There can be no comparison between them and their brothers across the ocean who are for the most part only one generation removed from savagery.[91]

In response to the question, "Is the P.L.P. a Negro Party?" Henry Taylor regretfully concluded that it had to be because no whites could be found with the courage to support it. Jim Crow policies were still effectively maintained in the Bahamas, which were "un-democratic, un-British, un-Christian and against the principles of the United Nations Universal Declaration of Human Rights." Defending a reverse racist stance (though still making token efforts to recruit from others than blacks), the PLP's *Herald* asserted:

> There is no desire in this Party to persecute people because of the colour of their skin. It is not the desire of the Party now or at any time after it has attained majority status to persecute people of the white race. It is not our desire to bring the white race down; it is our desire to raise our people up.
>
> We preach race because it is necessary in order to educate our people in the proper way. It is necessary to make our people realise that there are some good things about the Negro. . . . Over the years the whites have been taught to support their own people, politically and otherwise. This is all we are asking our people to do.[92]

The 1962 general election confounded both the PLP optimists and the most pessimistic UBP supporters, giving Bay Street a renewed lease on power through the fastest five years of economic expansion and condemning Bahamian society to an intensified and long-lasting state of racial polarization. The two main parties' manifestos were curiously similar in content, though the UBP's was the shorter and more punchily written. The *Guardian*, moreover, cleverly turned the violent stump oratory of Milo Butler—full of references to the lasting evils of slavery and calls for revenge—against itself. Subtly playing on the fears of violence and violent change, the paper referred to current conditions in Ghana, Guyana, Cuba, and the Congo, where the people had fallen for "the demagogic claptrap of political opportunists who promised them freedom, glory and riches," and asked if "so many happy, well-fed, and in many cases self-employed 'slaves'" could be found if the white Bahamian's foot was in fact "placed squarely on the neck of his countryman."[93]

Though the PLP could claim to have polled more total votes than the UBP and to have lost simply because its opponents had a stranglehold on the Out Islands (which had twenty-one seats to New Providence's twelve), its defeat was shattering. Overall the PLP had lost two seats and even in New Providence won only half of the seats, four going to the UBP, one to a conservative Independent, and one to Randol Fawkes (Labour-Independent). In the Out Islands, the PLP had retained only the two Andros seats, to the UBP's fifteen and the four won by Independents. The overrepresentation of the Out Islands—where many of the voters were away on the Contract and the UBP with its wealth could campaign more effectively than the PLP—along with the manipulation of the New Providence constituency boundaries, undoubtedly played a major part in the defeat. Analysts have subsequently pointed out the advantages that the UBP gained from improving economic conditions and from a general climate of fear engendered by the situation in Cuba, particularly the Missile Crisis of October 1962.

The main reason for the PLP's 1962 setback, however, was almost certainly a fear of the consequences of black majority rule, shared not only by the white minority and the nonwhite middle classes but by many blacks themselves. The most bitter pill of all, these included a majority of the recently enfranchised women. This lack of confidence in their fellow blacks (or, as PLP pundits would prefer to define it, lack of self-confidence or false consciousness and self-hatred) was perhaps best expressed in two letters printed in Etienne Dupuch's daily *Tribune*, which in the run-up to the election resolutely came out against the PLP. One letter almost echoed the *Guardian* line in asserting that the UBP alone had the experience and means to maintain stability and prosperity. The PLP, it claimed, wanted "to break down all the safeguards that have guaranteed us stable government" and went on to ask readers to "examine their records and see how many have made any brilliant success of their own affairs. These people don't want to come in to learn government. . . . They want to take over a happy and prosperous country with perhaps the most delicate economy in the world. . . . They want to experiment with your bread and butter."[94]

The other letter, just two days before the election, dug even deeper into the psyche of Bahamian blacks, touching on the spirit of dependency and distrust of their fellows that had hampered the thrust for independence since slavery days. "Let us look and see where we get our bread from," wrote a person signing himself

"Coloured Carpenter": "Not coloured people because the blind can't lead the blind. We are all poor and we have to go to the white man for jobs. We know that if we work for a coloured man he can't pay us off, so don't let us look at where we fall. Now to you ladies, every morning you have a job to go to and somebody will do you a favour, but for whom are you working? . . . So if the P.L.P. gets the majority of seats in the House of Assembly, you know that only they and their families will be taken care of."[95]

10

Free at Last? A Decade of Radical Changes, 1963–1973

Modernization Comes to Abaco: Jack Ford's Account

No other ten-year period in Bahamian history saw so much economic, political, and social change as that which began with Bay Street's last general election victory and ended with the achievement of Bahamian independence under the all-black PLP government. By all economic indexes except the equitable distribution of wealth and the amounts spent on social services, the steady improvement of the economy after 1942 accelerated to reach undreamed-of heights—if at the cost of an even greater dependence on tourism and imported goods and the novelty of a sizable national debt. Nassau and New Providence continued to lead the way in expansion and modernization, and most Out Islands continued to fall behind. But a new pattern was introduced with the enthusiastic and almost entirely private development of Freeport, Grand Bahama, which, with Abaco, threatened to become a cultural if not also demographic extension of Florida.

Material, demographic, and cultural changes, though, were overshadowed by political developments and their social effects. The UBP reinforced its surprising success in the 1962 election by accepting internal self-government in 1964 from an imperial power eager to devolve authority and responsibility. But the prolonged anomaly of white minority rule was brought to an end in 1967, as much by Bay Street's follies, or greediness, as by the overwhelming force of the black majority and the charisma of its leaders. Once in power, however, the PLP government spent so much money and put so much emphasis on black power ideology, Bahamian nationalism, the centrality of the party, and the personal cult of the leader that new divisions arose. These were not just between newly dominant blacks and now marginalized whites but between nonwhites of different classes, interests, and ideologies. The achievement of independence in 1973, though of huge symbolic importance, resulted from the search for a unifying cause that would provide a tonic for the ruling PLP rather than from universal popular demand. Independence, as we shall see in the last part of this book, also left manifold problems that remain to be resolved at the end of the century.

All parts of the Bahamas, even those least developed and those voluntarily clinging to traditional values, underwent remarkable changes in the decade 1963 to 1973. This transformation is epitomized in the account given by Jack Ford, a teacher from England based in Green Turtle Cay from 1948 to 1953, of the changes he observed when invited by former students and friends to revisit Abaco in 1968.[1]

Jack Ford was a forty-five-year-old Essex village schoolteacher when he answered an advertisement for Out Island head teachers placed by the newly appointed Bahamian director of education in 1947. Ford and his wife, Eve, reached Nassau in July 1948 by ship to New York, train to Miami, and a short airplane hop. In contrast to the drabness of postwar Britain, the colonial capital seemed a place of dazzling sunshine, white walls, and brilliant flowers; it was also expensive, charmingly quaint, and frustratingly inefficient. The entire education administration was housed in a single room in the upstairs of a ramshackle wooden building, one side shared by the director and chief inspector, the other by "two or three clerks jammed tightly together."[2]

The Fords learned that they had been assigned to a tiny island 125 miles from Nassau which could be reached only by the weekly mail boat. It had a one-room all-age school, no running water or electricity, and no licensed doctor closer than the capital. The posting, described as "only fit for a single man," involved not just teaching at the New Plymouth school on Green Turtle Cay but the supervision of all schools throughout Abaco, an area "about as big as England south of the Thames," accessible only by sailing boat.

The baptism was rough. The Fords set out for Abaco on July 20 in company with the Welsh Methodist minister and his wife on the rickety, cockroach-infested mail boat *Richard Campbell* (nicknamed "Wretched Campbell"), with its Conchy Joe captain and mate and all-black crew. They slept on the deck in choppy seas, at dawn passed Hole in the Wall, the rocky southern headland of mainland Abaco, and reached the dockless settlement of Cherokee Sound just after sunrise. There the dinghies unloaded "crates of soft drinks, sacks of sugar and flour, and many boxes of goods with only a set of initials on the top to show who they were for," taking some fine watermelons, crates of empties, and further orders in return.[3]

Cherokee Sound was only the first of the six Abaco settlements at which the *Richard Campbell* called, following a routine that, though tedious, greatly raised Jack Ford's admiration for the seamanship, efficiency, and toughness of Captain Russell and his crew. From Cherokee, they bucked northward over the ocean, to enter the more sheltered Abaco Sound through the white water of Little Harbour Bar. At Hope Town on Elbow Cay, the chief Abaco settlement and home of the commissioner, half the houses were unoccupied because of migration and the remainder unpainted and showing the effects of a recent hurricane. Here they said good-bye to the Methodist couple before crossing over the Marsh Harbour on the mainland, described as "a row of unpainted houses running in a single line along the shore," without a usable dock.[4]

The last two stops before their destination were the settlements of Man-o-War Cay and Guana Cay, after which the *Richard Campbell* detoured to avoid shoals into the always dangerous and sometimes impassable ocean outside Whale Cay, reentered Abaco Sound through the tricky Whale Cay Channel, and chugged the last five miles to the calm haven on Green Turtle Cay. Exhausted, the Fords were greeted more with curiosity than warmth in the mixed but segregated settlement and shown to the house they had been assigned: a rough-cast concrete shack lit by kerosene lanterns and unscreened against mosquitoes, without proper kitchen or

Abaco's mail boat lifelines in the 1940s and 1950s. *Above,* Captain Sherwin Archer's old sponge schooner *Arena,* the last of the sail mail boats. *Below,* one of the early motorized mail and freight boats, the sturdy *Stede Bonnet,* named after a notorious pirate who was hanged at Charleston in 1718. Photographs courtesy of Ruth Rodriguez.

bathroom, or adequate furniture, bedding, or utensils. Drinking water was drawn from a well less than fifteen feet from an outdoor earth privy.

Appalled by the accommodations, the lack of facilities at the school, and the obvious resentment of the local teacher, Jack and Eve Ford returned immediately to Nassau on the *Richard Campbell.* There they found that their crate of personal belongings had arrived from England badly damaged. Ford applied pressure to the Board of Education, however, and the couple was soon back at Green Turtle Cay with more clearly defined instructions and a houseful of furniture and other necessities, including a roll of mosquito netting and a kerosene refrigerator. These were later followed by cartons of used textbooks from the Essex education authorities, Ford's previous employers.

Jack Ford reassured his subordinate teacher that she would continue in her job at her former salary while he concentrated on the senior students and his supervisory duties over the rest of Abaco. During his five-year tenure he ceaselessly harried the Board of Education to extend and improve the New Plymouth school building and built a model new head teacher's house, complete with rainwater tank and flush toilet. Deeply involving themselves in community affairs, the Fords became accepted, respected, and then regarded with affection by both sections on Green Turtle Cay. As much as for his teaching, Ford gained respect for his practicality and his efforts to become a competent seaman, first in a secondhand local sailing dinghy and then in the sixteen-foot *Mickey,* a wooden motorboat he commissioned from one of the simple family boatyards then found in almost all Abaco settlements.[5]

Ford came to esteem the hardihood, enterprise, and old-fashioned values of the Abaconians, especially those living on the cays and making their livelihood from the sea. Though not an obviously religious person, he saw the importance to the isolated islanders of church services, weddings, and funerals. The Fords also enjoyed the secular celebration of the burning of Guy Fawkes on November 5 and the even more arcane ritual of the parade of "Old Skin" (alias "Bunce") on New Year's Day. Though they had a greater natural affinity for the Abaco whites, the Fords came to appreciate the subtlety of the cultural differences between whites and blacks and marveled at the way the customary separation was maintained in a peaceable tension, through interdependence and long practice. What most impressed them, however, was the enthusiasm with which all the people of Green Turtle Cay celebrated the coronation of Queen Elizabeth II on June 2, 1953. That the people of so isolated and neglected a settlement should feel such loyalty was puzzling but also poignant.[6]

At least materially, conditions in the settlements of the Abaco mainland were, with one exception, even more backward than on the cays. Jack Ford discovered this in his first inspection visit, when he sailed both sides of Abaco in company with the Anglican minister Father Bob Dobson in the church-owned native-built schooner *Star.* The three-hundred-mile voyage took almost two weeks, visiting the string of black settlements on the rough ocean side of northern Abaco before sailing both ways across the leeward bight inside the huge bow-shaped island. At best, the mainland settlements were quaint but dilapidated, at worst no more than huddles of shanties with an air of impermanence. Some, like Norman's Castle, the former lumber center, were deserted and tumbledown; others, like Cedar Harbour, seemed purposely hidden to escape attention. "These are relics from the bad old days of slavery," thought Jack Ford. "The slaves would escape and live a life of seclusion at the back of very awkward channels where the way through the mangroves was so devious that strangers would become lost or easily ambushed. . . . When strangers came the whole population took to the bush, a habit that still continues if a boat coming in is not recognised."[7]

The schools, Jack Ford's chief concern, were in disgraceful condition. Except for one unfinished concrete block building, all consisted of wooden structures in late stages of decay. None of the teachers was trained and some were illiterate. No reading matter was available, and many of the children wrote only on slates with pieces of limestone rock. Though in one school the pupils serenaded him with more verses of the British national anthem than Ford himself knew, he encountered a female teacher who could read and write no more than she had learned by rote from the Bible and Prayer Book and whose teaching consisted solely of having the children copy the Lord's Prayer from the blackboard. A male head teacher kept school so infrequently that Ford, arriving unannounced, caught him at midmorning running ahead to open up the building, laces untied and trousers unbuttoned. This was in sad contrast to such dedicated teachers in the white settlements as Walter Sands of Cherokee Sound and Haziel Albury of Man-o-War Cay, who, though technically untrained, produced impressive results.[8]

The contrast, though, was not purely between the black and white settlements. The black pupils of the mixed settlements of Marsh Harbour, Hope Town, and New Plymouth did far better than most of their Abaco mainland brethren, and the southern mainland all-black settlement of Sandy Point was regarded as a model throughout the Bahamas. Though indifferently served from Nassau, the Sandy Point people were hardworking and prosperous. They built their own boats and made an excellent living from fishing, carrying their catch the sixty miles south to Nassau. The communal spirit was strong, and there was even a cooperative store. The houses were neat, well painted, and comfortable, well spaced along a wide sandy street, and Jack Ford, after almost a week aboard the *Star,* enjoyed an evening meal "laid out like at an English table" and the luxury of clean sheets and a mosquito net.

Little more than twenty miles to the northwest of Sandy Point, Moore's Island and its people presented a stark contrast. The chief settlement, appropriately named Hard Bargain, lay between a poor anchorage and a swamp so polluted that its stench carried well out to sea. "The old school building had literally fallen to pieces," reported Jack Ford. "A new one was promised but how much does a promise mean to the Board of Education?" According to the somewhat gullible Englishman, most of the black people of mainland Abaco believed in obeah if they did not actively practice it, and their promiscuity was legendary. But the people of Moore's Island were by Jack Ford's account drunken and larcenous besides. "That night the men built a huge fire on the shore," he wrote of his first visit in 1948,

> and after dark bottles of rum and moonshine were placed in a circle a short distance from the fire. The men began a dance and when they got thirsty, reached for a bottle to take a swig. As the heat increased they drank more; as they drank more, the dance grew faster and more furious. Eventually they cast off their clothes, and ended up like naked demons, shadowy in the red light of the fire. One by one they became exhausted and dropped to sleep off their drunken stupors. The fire died down and at last all was still. The women took no part until morning when they arrived to take their befuddled spouses home. A mad orgy of moonshine and savagery was over!

In the early 1950s, the black crewmen of the *Stede Bonnet* deliver supplies to the whites of Man-o-War Cay, Abaco, but get no further than the dock. Photograph courtesy of Ruth Rodriguez.

Because of the Moore's Islanders' reputation for stealing from visiting ships, those attempting to sleep aboard the *Star* had remained half-awake all night. Hearing suspicious noises on deck near daybreak, Jack Ford woke the captain by tugging the string attached between his toe and the spare anchor for this purpose. They rushed on deck to see a dark figure about to climb aboard slide back in the water and glide away like a shark. At daybreak they were glad to weigh anchor and leave.[9]

A quarter-century later, Jack Ford, now retired, was thrilled at the offer of an expenses-paid return trip to Abaco, though he had to be convinced that the poor people he had known in the 1940s could now afford to pay for the trip. In December 1968, he and Eve flew on a BOAC Boeing jet from London to Nassau, where they were the guests of Patrick Bethel, a former pupil teacher now teaching at the Teacher Training College. They found the town, with its modern office buildings and jammed traffic, much changed, and Paradise Island, its huge hotels and casinos joined to the mainland by a high-flying bridge, almost unrecognizable. Bay Street, decorated for Christmas, seemed like London's West End transferred to the tropics, crowded with tourists and local shoppers. A half dozen cruise liners filled the expanded docks, and only the many sailboats crammed with Out Island produce moored at the Market Range (unfortunately soon to be shifted far down the harbor) provided a link with the past and with what such old hands as the Fords regarded as "the real Bahamas."[10]

Two days later, the Fords flew to Abaco on a Bahamas Airways DC-9 jet in as many minutes as the *Richard Campbell* had taken hours. They landed briefly at Marsh Harbour, now the hub city of Abaco, with "well laid out streets and large buildings" and soon to boast five banks, five doctors, four supermarkets, and Abaco's one and only traffic light. Then they made the short hop to the new airport serving the extensive development at Treasure Cay, former site of the Loyalists' first settlement in Abaco, on the mainland directly opposite Green Turtle Cay. Though the cay now boasted a short airstrip, it was privately owned, and New Plymouth was still served by water taxi. The spirit of the place and the warmth of their welcome the Fords found almost unchanged. But the changes wrought by prosperity were manifest. There was even a car on the settlement's diminutive Main Street. Most of the traditional wooden houses had been painted in bright colors and lovingly restored, and there were many luxurious new houses of concrete and native stone—for the most part retirement homes or holiday retreats for islanders making their living elsewhere. Electricity and piped water were now general and telephones and gas cookers common.

Many islanders returned to the cay for a holiday reunion, the Fords were feted by blacks and whites, and the celebration of Old Skin on New Year's morning was by common consent one of the most enthusiastic in living memory. But for Jack Ford the most heartening experience was making a trip along the new Abaco Highway that joined Crown Haven with Sandy Point 120 miles to the south and seeing the changes in the mainland villages and especially their schools. Jack Ford had passing regrets that a small cay he had been offered for £50 in the 1940s but lacked the money to buy had recently changed hands for £35,000. But thanks to land sales, tourist developments, lumbering, and large-scale farming, many settlements, accessible to each other in minutes or hours by car rather than days by boat, now rivaled Sandy Point in obvious prosperity, and the large American car was a far more common sight than the traditional Abaco dinghy. Most of the schools had been changed beyond recognition and had much better teachers, buildings, and supplies—start of a transformation that was in due course to see the twelve all-age schools serving five hundred pupils in 1950 become a total of twenty-four schools, including two high schools, with a total enrollment of twenty-four hundred children.[11]

"The educational system which Jack Ford came from England to help supervise has changed dramatically," understated Patrick Bethel in 1992, before going on to question whether in the process of growth and improvement "some of the 'values' of 40 years ago" had been lost. Ford would certainly have regretted the worst aspects of modernization while approving the benefits of change, but in 1968 he seems to have been blinkered by euphoria. Most remarkable of all, his account gives no hint either of the dramatic political changes that had occurred in the year before his return to the Bahamas or of any social ferment beneath the surface of Abaconian life.

Despite all his struggles with the government departments in Nassau, Jack Ford was no more a politician than he was a conscious racist. The only reference to local politics during his service in Abaco was to the "farce" of the general election of 1949. Abaco was (until 1968) a single three-member constituency, and by Ford's account,

> The candidates arrived before election day on a charter boat and distributed bottles of liquor to the whole of the male population. Speeches were made with the usual impossible promises and then the politicians disappeared, leaving the rest to their agents. One had to own property in order to vote. A vote was worth five pounds and a new dinghy boat sail. On voting day each voter was asked who he wanted to vote for, and the choice was recorded. Nothing was secret for the whole township was gathered around to hear the pronouncement. When the voter left the polling area he openly received his reward from the agent.[12]

Despite universal suffrage and the secret ballot, as late as the general election of 1967 Abaco returned UBP members for all three of its seats by a very wide margin. But only a year later, when Abaco had been split into two single-member constituencies, the PLP won Cooper's Town (the northern mainland townships), leaving only Marsh Harbour (southern Abaco and the offshore cays) with a UBP representative.[13] Yet Jack Ford's account gives no more than a hint that the Abaconian whites were coming to regard their home settlements as refuges after the overturning of Bay Street by the PLP and no indication at all that the Abaconian blacks were poised for takeover and revenge. No doubt he was misled by the universal warmth with which he and his wife were welcomed back and by the material and moral improvements he discerned. But he was also broadly correct in his implied assessment of attitudes in Abaco at that time: that the changes between 1967 and 1968 had been radical enough until the PLP proved itself or showed its true colors; that far more important than political conflict was material well-being; and that in any case the politics fought out in Nassau probably still had limited relevance for distant Out Islands like Abaco, bound to their own time-worn traditions.

Taming the Bush: The Origins of Freeport-Lucaya

Many of the Abaconians who had left home to make a living had not gone abroad or to Nassau but to the other major island of the northern Bahamas, Grand Bahama, where the astounding development of Freeport-Lucaya orchestrated by the American Wallace Groves (with Bay Street's connivance) promised, or threatened, the creation of a new polity and society only nominally Bahamian.

The natural connection between the two geographically similar islands of the Little Bahama Bank had been reinforced when the Abaco Lumber Company moved its operations from central Abaco to Pine Ridge, Grand Bahama, during World War II. In 1946 the struggling company (along with its valuable logging leases) was bought by Wallace Groves, a Virginia financier eager to leave the United States after serving a term in federal prison for mail fraud. Groves revived the operation by renegotiating the lease terms to allow the logging of smaller trees and contracting with the British coal industry to supply millions of pit props. At its peak the company boasted two permanent and six mobile steam-driven sawmills and several miles of railway line, employing eighteen hundred persons, nearly all migrants. The shantytown of Pine Ridge had three times the population of the next largest Grand Bahama settlement, West End, with uncomfortably juxtaposed sections of Abaconians, Cat Islanders, Turks, and Caicos Islanders and the first small influx of Haitians. Wallace Groves himself lived some way off in the splendid isolation of Little Whale Cay in the Berry Islands, where he built a mansion (or manor house), marina, airstrip, tropical garden, and aviary.[14]

By 1955 the demand for pit props had come to an end, and in any case the supply of timber in the concession area was almost exhausted. Nonetheless, Wallace Groves managed to sell the Abaco Lumber Company and its rights to cut timber (though not, it seems, the lease rights to the land itself) to the National Container Corporation, soon to become a subsidiary of the mammoth Owens-Illinois Company. Thanks to another undercover agreement with the Bahamas government, Natcon plundered the pineforest mainly for pulpwood to make cardboard, turning its attention back to Abaco in 1959.[15] Meanwhile, the ingenious Groves had plowed the $4 million he had received for the Abaco Lumber Company into the first stage of a far more grandiose enterprise: the creation of a free port, industrial complex, and luxury hotel and residential area extending over the central third of Grand Bahama.

Buying the cooperation of Stafford Sands and other major Bay Street figures and winning the enthusiastic support of the governor, the Earl of Ranfurly, Wallace Groves obtained the largest concession involving the Bahamas since the grant to the Lord Proprietors in 1670, the modestly titled Hawksbill Creek Agreement, signed on August 5, 1955.[16] This agreement concentrated on the plans of Groves's recently constituted Grand Bahama Port Authority to build a deepwater harbor on swampy Hawksbill Creek as the focus of an industrial area, but it included the grant of fifty thousand acres (eighty square miles) of land and tax and other concession of breathtaking generosity. The Port Authority was given the right to administer, plan, and develop the port area and to license persons and businesses. "Undesirables" were to be excluded, but Port Authority and licensees could bring in any workers they needed without consulting the colonial immigration authorities. The Port Authority and its licensees were exempted from excise, export, and stamp duties for the ninety-nine years that the agreement was to run. They were also guaranteed that for at least thirty years there would be no real estate or personal property taxes and no taxes levied on earnings. On the pretext of bringing industrial development to the Bahamas and the promise of employment and prosperity to at least some of its people, the Bahamian government had subcontracted its responsibilities, if not virtually surrendered its sovereignty over one of its largest islands.

The Hawksbill Creek Agreement had inbuilt performance guarantees, and to fulfill these and cover the huge costs of the projected independent empire, Wallace

Groves and the Port Authority took on a bizarre range of partners and licensees, some of them unsavory and few with any commitment to the long-term welfare of the Bahamas. Of such passing predators the leviathan was Daniel K. Ludwig, the billionaire owner of National Bulk Carriers. The chief initial requirement of the agreement was the provision of a deepwater harbor, and though Groves had persuaded Natcon to build a dock in Hawksbill Creek as part of the Abaco Lumber deal (later buying it back cheaply), it was insufficient. At this stage, Ludwig, who was engaged in disputes with Japanese shipbuilders, proposed to set up a shipyard to build his giant oil tankers in Grand Bahama. This project evaporated when Ludwig made peace with the Japanese but not before Hawksbill Creek had been enlarged to take ships with a thirty-foot draft and six-hundred-foot turning circle.[17]

The late 1950s saw other initiatives, not all of them successful. An oil bunkering operation off Hawksbill Creek was planned and started, and a construction company, half owned by the Port Authority, began what was eventually the Grand Bahama Highway and Freeport International Airport and built the first roads and buildings in the area grandly styled Freeport City—the population of which was no more than 150 by 1960. One of the first licensees, Bahamas Seacraft Limited, that planned to build motor cruisers by the hundreds, soon failed, as did the thousand-acre farm at Pine Ridge growing cucumbers and tomatoes in vain anticipation of frosts in Florida. The small scale and tenuous viability of the operation at this time is measured by the fact that Charles Hayward, chairman of the British industrial group Firth Cleveland, bought a 25 percent share of the Port Authority for £1 million—a deal that had important and beneficial results when Hayward's son Jack settled in Freeport and made its development his chief life's work. Jack Hayward, popularly nicknamed "Union Jack" for his philanthropy and British patriotism (symbolized by donations to the British National Trust and the rescue of the SS *Great Britain* from the Falkland Islands), served as something of a British (though not Bahamian) counterweight to Freeport's Americanization, as well as providing a more humane slant to its rampant capitalism.[18]

Enough had been achieved by 1960 for the Grand Bahama Port Authority to obtain the important Supplemental Agreement, signed on July 11, 1960, which laid the basis for the takeoff of development during the early and mid-1960s. In recognition of having fulfilled its initial commitments, the Port Authority was granted a further 150,000 acres for a nominal payment. In return, it was committed to build a two-hundred-room luxury hotel by the end of 1963 and to provide free education for schoolchildren living within the Port Authority area. The right of the Port Authority to continue to license lawful businesses and import workers not demonstrably undesirable was reaffirmed, and a vague reference was made to the possibility of setting up a future municipal government as a way of formalizing the devolution of local authority.[19]

As an extension of the boom in the United States and worldwide of the 1960s, developments at Freeport accelerated on every side. A substantial increase in U.S. oil import duties in March 1960 at the behest of Texan producers made the project of offshore storage and bunkering of foreign oil hugely more attractive. Ideally located between the Florida Straits and Providence Channels, the Hawksbill Creek oil terminal suddenly began to receive up to a million barrels a month of Venezuelan oil. This was then transshipped to fuel American and other coastal and oceangoing vessels wishing to avoid U.S. taxes and cut down on bulk by fueling in mid-voyage. Almost inevitably, a refinery was built to process imported crude oil, with the hope of petrochemical spin-offs. The refinery did not succeed in the face of competition and the eventual worldwide oil slump, which also slowed down the bunkering operation. Nor did the guaranteed availability of cheap gasoline throughout the Bahamas sufficiently offset the air and sea pollution from the refinery and discharging tankers or that whatever profits were made accrued to the operators, not to the Bahamas government and people.

At first, it seemed that D. K. Ludwig had moved on, leaving the Port Authority a free gift of the needed deepwater harbor. But the truth was less comfortable. The shipping magnate had sold his harbor-front land to a subsidiary of United States Steel for more than his total investment in Grand Bahama and had also expanded what was left of his original grant of two thousand acres by preempting prime acreage in the residential center of Freeport, a few miles from the harbor. By 1961, United States Steel, in cooperation with Ludwig and the Port Authority, had constructed a huge cement plant on the Hawksbill Creek waterfront, designed to produce at least a million tons of cement a year. If not directly suborned, the authorities were sufficiently impressed by the scale of the operation and the cost benefits of locally produced cement to guarantee United States Steel a monopoly of all cement production in the Bahamas for a dozen years. The unstated price to the people and ecology of Grand Bahama, however, was (despite the most modern technology) serious air pollution.

Ludwig was also instrumental in helping to shape downtown Freeport. In 1962 he came to an agreement with the Port Authority for the joint development of a thousand acres of pineland scrub half a mile south of the infant city. He planned to build a major hotel and casino, a tourist shopping center, and an eighteen-hole golf course that would, Florida-style, raise the value of surrounding real estate. Ludwig and Port Authority later parted ways, but not before the Bahama Princess and Princess Tower Hotels had become the largest resort complex in the Bahamas, the lushly relandscaped area called Bahamia one of the most prestigious residential locations, and El Casino and the International Bazaar less tastefully set the tone for Freeport's tourist boom. The arterial crossroad at the heart of this conglomeration, fittingly (and without satiric intent) christened the Ranfurly Circus, bade fair to be Freeport City's new focal center.[20]

The Lucayan Beach Hotel, more suitably located three miles distant on Freeport's splendid beachfront and with the associated marinas and canals that were a distinctive feature of local developments, had already preceded the Princess Hotels in fulfilling the Port Authority's requirements under the 1960 Supplementary Agreement. Though initially lacking the casino, which came to be regarded as necessary for success, the new hotel gained an almost incredible piece of fortuitous publicity when divers uncovered the remains of a Spanish treasure galleon just off its beach. The wreck yielded ten thousand silver coins said at first to be worth $9 million—a literal jackpot. The discoverers, however, made little profit, thanks to the depredations of "experts" and "advisers" and Bay Street's predictably prompt passage of a treasure hunting act requiring local partnership and the surrender of 25 percent of all finds to the government.[21]

Other hotels, clubs, and marinas came in rapid succession as optimistic investors were more attracted by the concessions of the Hawksbill Creek Agreement than they were discouraged by the Port Authority's licensing fees and profit-sharing requirements. But just as important as strictly tourist developments was the creation of a real estate twin to the Port Authority called the Grand Bahama Development Company, which (though also involved in the building of the Lucayan Beach Hotel and new areas of downtown Freeport City), by subdividing one hundred thousand acres of the outlying concession area, was to add the hyphenated "Lucaya" to Freeport's official name.

The Grand Bahama Development Company was a typical product of Wallace Groves's entrepreneurial wizardry. At first it was a joint venture, with the Port Authority providing the land and a consortium headed by a shadowy Canadian financier named Louis Chesler putting up $12 million in much-needed cash. Under the terms of the partnership the investment was swallowed by building works without an immediately profitable return, and by 1965 the Port Authority had assumed 54 percent of the shares of the Development Company (later 57 percent), taken full control of the board, and effectively squeezed out Chesler and his associates. At this stage, land sales soared, first encouraging a profitable reflotation of Chesler's surrendered shares and then providing a bonanza for Groves and the Development Company. Precise figures were never disclosed (thanks to clever accounting and the secrecy possible through the Hawksbill Creek Agreement and favorable Bahamian company laws), but it was widely reported that land sales in Freeport-Lucaya realized $30 million in 1966 alone.[22]

Most of the land sales were of large blocks to subdevelopers tightly regulated by contract and tied by income sharing to the Development Company—a capitalistic version of medieval subinfeudation. Too many of the sales—of individual lots as well as large tracts—were purely speculative. But thanks to the investors' optimism, the requirements inserted in land buyers' contracts, and Groves's vision of the potential and needs of Freeport-Lucaya, progress in the middle 1960s was spectacular, especially in the provision of infrastructures. Such amenities as a fine modern clinic, library, private schools, and churches were obtained by attractive private donors and institutions with free land grants, but the Port Authority and Development Company led the way in providing the best roads in the Bahamas, the largest and most modern electricity, water and sewerage facilities, and, along with its deepwater harbor, an airport capable of taking the largest jets. Publicity handouts claimed in the late 1960s that Freeport-Lucaya, with two thousand hotel beds, hundreds of marina berths, docking for cruise liners, and five eighteen-hole golf courses (more than in all the rest of the Bahamas), was already capable of handling a million tourists a year. It was also boasted that there was more than sufficient space, power, and fresh water for a residential population of half a million.[23]

Quite apart from any hypothetical future problems from hosting as many tourists as the rest of the Bahamas and having twice as many permanent inhabitants, Freeport-Lucaya already faced at least two serious sociolegal problems: what to do about the enclaves of privately owned land within the boundaries of the concession and where to house all the necessary workers. Though most severe in Grand Bahama, both of these problems applied almost everywhere foreign-owned developments occurred throughout the Bahamas.

Land Development: Two Key Tenure Cases, 1959–1967

Given the natural affinity of Bahamians for the land where they had their roots, however casual they were in cultivating it or obtaining formal title, and especially given the strength of the customary system of family tenures called generational property, the equally entrenched concepts of common usage, and the obscurities of squatters' rights, conflict was inevitable with those who wished to sell or acquire Bahamian land for development. A contradiction existed between, on the one hand, an attitude derived from the notion that land is tribal or kinship territory simply for usufruct, the use by members of the tribe or kin according to need, found in Africa and many premodern cultures throughout the world; and on the other hand, the concept of real estate, leading from royal ownership to permanent freehold possession and transmission by individuals that was essential to the development of Europe and its imperial expansion in modern times.[24] But more practically and specifically in the Bahamian context, it involved a conflict between poor islanders (almost exclusively black), who relied on custom and usage and rarely had written titles, and lawyers (until the mid-1960s, nearly all whites) eager to establish precise boundaries, formal title, and uninterrupted possession on behalf of individual clients. These clients as often as not were themselves Bahamians, sometimes persons wishing to protect their property against encroachment, but more usually those aiming to sell land to foreigners.

Nor surprisingly, the key enactment and the most precedental court cases involving Bahamian land titles occurred during the period when Bay Street was presiding over the most rapid phase of land dispersion in Bahamian history, between 1959 and 1967. The Quieting of Titles Act of 1959 for the first time laid down the rules and process by which unimpeachable freehold title to Bahamian land could be established, incidentally limiting the number of persons who could claim joint title to three. By making certainty of tenure possible, it also made it vital. But it remained a complex and protracted business, involving long searches in the records, much paperwork, and frequent recourses to the courts, increasing the importance and professionalism of lawyers specializing in land transactions and also multiplying their fees.

Two of the most significant Bahamian land tenure cases during the 1960s did not involve Grand Bahama but Exuma and Paradise Island, which were in the process of being "developed" much like Freeport-Lucaya. The first landmark case under the 1959 Quieting of Titles Act involved the Bowe Estate of the Forest Exuma, in 1961–62.[25] The case came forward because the documentary titleholder, a black Exumian named Maxwell Bowe, then aged seventy-one, petitioned the court to establish his undisputed freehold to the land so he could sell it to a Florida real estate developer for a very large sum of money. The act required a petitioner to advertise his intentions in the newspapers to give any adverse claimants opportunity to come forward to dispute his right. In the event, Bowe was confronted by no less than twenty-eight adverse claimants, who contended that they had a generational right to the land in common, which in practice meant that they had to establish their rights as squatters.

The Forest Estate was an almost four-thousand-acre tract of typical scrubby limestone in the center of Great Exuma, adjacent to the Rolle commonages of Mount Thompson and Ramsey's. Identical in its boundaries to an old Loyalist slave plantation, it consisted of some fifteen roughly walled "fields," mainly covered in bush but intermittently used for farming and grazing. These fields totally surrounded a settlement, which in 1960 had a population of two hundred in thirty-seven households, two churches, and a school. The Forest had been sold by its original owners, the white Adderley family, to Max Bowe's father in 1903, bequeathed to Bowe and his three siblings in 1920, and devolved on Bowe alone in 1948. The Bowe family lived just outside the settlement, in a small house on the site of the old plantation great house, nicknamed the "Slave House," which had been destroyed in the hurricane of 1926 (Map 12).

The rights of the inhabitants of the settlement were not disputed by Bowe. As the presiding judge, John G. F. Scarr, noted, "At one time the Settlement itself reputedly belonged to the Estate, but with the end of slavery it was given to the freed slaves, whose descendants are represented by the present inhabitants." All of them referred to the settlement as "generational property," and some applied the term to the Forest Estate as a whole. "It was, however," added Scarr (unintentionally showing the bias of professional lawyers against such customary tenures) "quite impossible to ascertain exactly what was meant by this expression except that in some way the property passed from parents to children."[26]

Max Bowe claimed that his family had farmed the estate for at least forty years, raising horses, sheep, and poultry and growing provisions, and that the residents of the settlement had "merely provided labour on the Estate . . . occupying moveable small-holdings for which the rent consisted of annual thirds of the crops produced." The adverse claimants asserted that for well over thirty years they had used and enjoyed the whole of the Forest Estate "at will, farming where they wanted, moving when they wanted, and keeping what they called their 'creatures' (that is to say poultry, sheep, goats, pigs and so on) where they wanted." They emphatically denied ever working for Bowe, paying him shares of their produce, or even asking his permission to work the land. They did acknowledge that Max Bowe and his father had lived in the Slave House and its successor and that the Bowes had raised much stock, including race horses, on various parts of the estate. But they claimed that the Bowes were allowed to do this merely "as a matter of sufferance on their part." In obvious emulation of the Exuma Rolles, the inhabitants also claimed that the affairs of the Forest were "watched over and supervised by a small self-elected body which they called the Committee," a practice which Judge Scarr admitted was "fairly common throughout the Bahamas in places where there are settlements and common land."[27]

Despite overwhelming evidence of customary usage over generations, the inhabitants had no chance against the resources of the law. As Judge Scarr pointed out, they had to prove that the owner had either abandoned the land or been dispossessed, that adverse possession had been taken by another (or others), and had been continued without interruption for twenty years. Quite apart from the impossibility of denying that Bowe had lived on and worked at least part of the land for forty years, wrote Scarr, there was no evidence that any effort had been made to oust him. English precedents decreed that the "smallest act would be sufficient to show him that there was no discontinuance," and Bowe had provided innumerable proofs of his contributions toward the Forest Estate as a whole (including the maintenance of wells, walls, and gates and the donation of land for the churches and school). "I would not go so far as to say that Mr Bowe ignored the residents completely in these matters," said Scarr, "or that the local committee was never involved, but what I do say is that all these things clearly and abundantly show that Mr Bowe regarded himself as the owner in possession and behaved as such and was by general repute such until at least 1960 when this trouble started between him and his tenants."[28]

The very solidarity of the adverse claimants worked against their case. To be

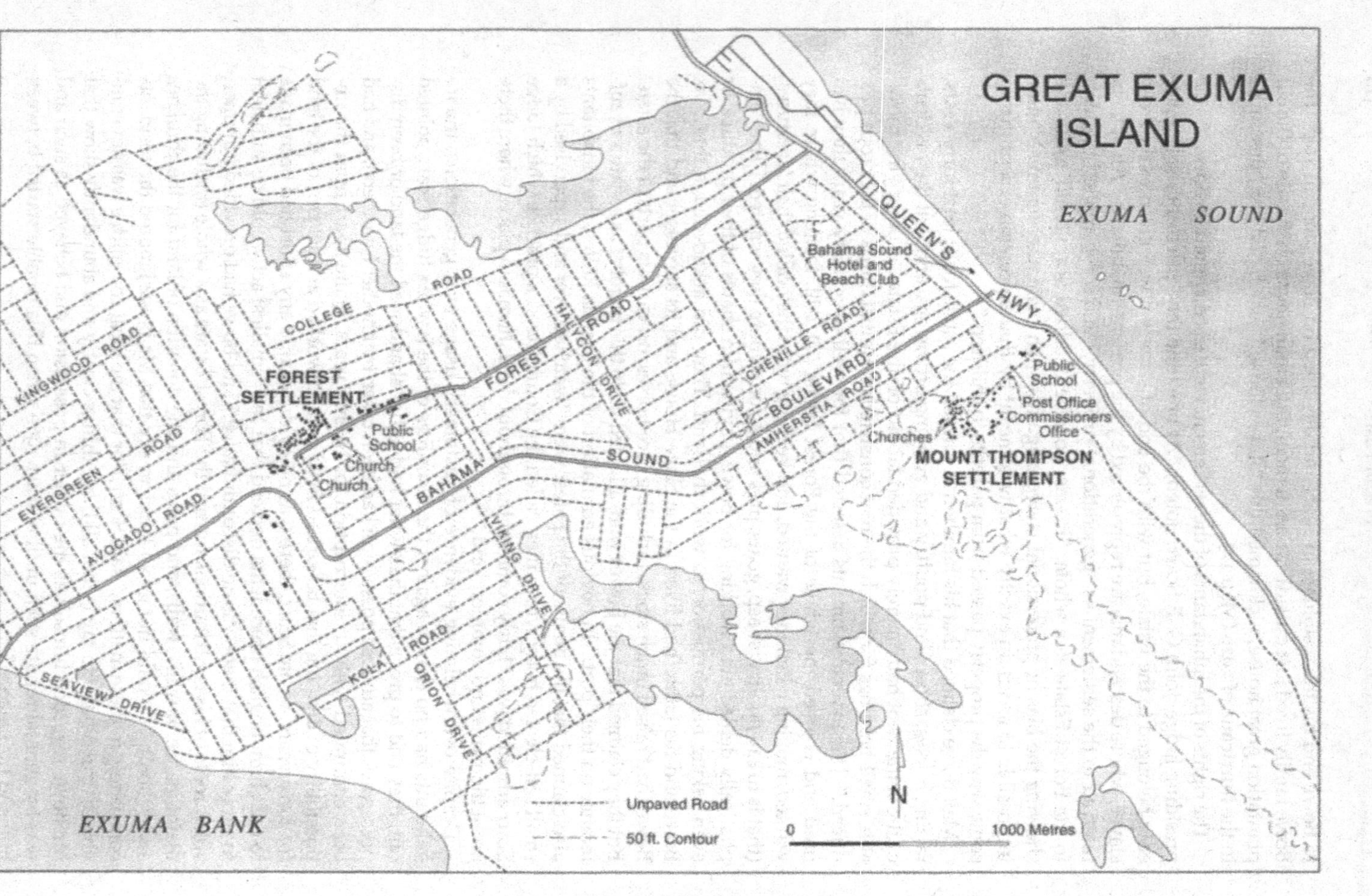

Map 12. The Forest, Exuma, 1980

effective, a joint claim would have to apply to the same piece of land, continuously occupied by the claimants in common, that is, acting as "a unified body . . . as mutual agents the one for the other." Such proof was obviously impossible because it was clear that each separate family worked different parts of the Forest Estate independently. Moreover, even if the claims had been made singly, it would have been impossible for any one family to prove continuous working of any area for the necessary twenty years. The poverty of the soil and the traditional system of slash-and-burn determined that no area could be farmed for more than two or three years and had to be left fallow for at least an equal period. Even the claim that animals grazed the fallow land was inadmissible, decreed Scarr, since "the evidence that this was done continuously for 20 years in the case of any one single pasture on the estate is most unreliable (as well as being unlikely)."[29]

In proof that the adverse claimants were in fact sharecropping tenants, Judge Scarr cited ten times from the voluminous evidence presented by both sides. Perhaps the most damaging facts came from a case heard before the local magistrate the previous year, when three of the present adverse claimants had provided details of sharecropping arrangements in an effort to upset a charge of trespass brought against them by Bowe—a melancholy example of the "catch 22" principle. Despite remarking that Maxwell Bowe was a poor witness in his own defense and that over the previous twenty-five years the general system had been "run in a very loose and unbusinesslike manner," Judge Scarr concluded that "whichever way one looks at it, and taking the most benevolent view of the Adverse Claimants' case, it is entirely devoid of merit and fails completely."[30]

Bowe was granted clear freehold title, and in due course the land was sold to the American developer. Bulldozers crisscrossed the bush to build roads given fancy names, and hundreds of lots, priced according to elevation and proximity to the sea, were sold to gullible foreigners. The Forest settlement was left a landless enclave. Apart from the short-term benefit of earning wages from the developer, the only positive feature, ironically, was that the projected end product never materialized. As happened in all but a few cases throughout the Bahamas, nearly all lots were bought speculatively by persons without the real intention, or even means, to build. Within twenty years, the Forest Estate had reverted to bush, except for a dozen scattered new homes and gardens occupied a few months a year and the areas cleared, planted, and grazed by a new generation of squatters from the original settlement.[31]

The Price-Robinson case concerning Paradise Island was very different from that of the Forest but equally important. Even more complex and therefore protracted, it dragged on from 1960 to 1968 and went all the way to the Judicial Committee of the Privy Council in London. Though it ended unequivocally in favor of native Bahamians against the developers, it was not on the surface a simple confrontation between the two. More subtly, it pitted family members determined to retain their land against others eager to sell out. Interestingly, the lawyers representing the successful side against the developers were white, while those arguing on behalf of the adverse claimants were black.[32]

In 1960 the hugely valuable but still underdeveloped cay enclosing Nassau Harbor to the north (still called Hog Island but soon to be rechristened Paradise Island, after its world-famous Paradise Beach) was sold to the heir to the A&P grocery chain, Huntingdon Hartford. A tycoon with unusually good taste, Hartford established a gourmet restaurant, the Café Martinique, and built the elegant Ocean

Club, graced by a complete antique cloister and statuary imported from Europe. Also an eager sportsman, he added a world-class golf course and splendid tennis courts, even introducing to an indifferent world a new game called Paradise Tennis. None of these ventures paid their way, and Hartford ran out of money or interest. The destiny of Paradise Island was to become a hotel-casino, marina, and complex of millionaire's homes, owned and developed by the seemingly incongruous corporation Mary Carter Paints (widely suspected of being a Mafia "front") and its successor, called Resorts International, registered in Atlantic City, New Jersey.

Huntingdon Hartford and the subsequent developers needed the entire eastern two-thirds of Hog/Paradise Island, but they found that the land they had bought was awkwardly split by a narrow strip of disputed land running north to south from sea to harbor. This land was claimed by a Nassau family (mainly surnamed Robinson) with a centenarian matriarch, Mrs. Price. In heroic contrast to the proposed developments, Mrs. Price had spent much of her life living on the island and working the land as a traditional Out Island peasant farmer, bringing produce to the Nassau market by boat. The right of old Mrs. Price and her immediate family to the strip of land was incontrovertible, by squatters' rights if not also by documentary proof, which tied the land through a succession of owners all the way back to the time of the Lord Proprietors' Governor Nicholas Trott in the 1680s.[33]

The issue was complicated because when Mrs. Price's immediate family refused offers to be bought out and moved to quiet their title under the terms of the 1959 act, more distant family members who had come to preliminary terms with the developers appeared on the scene as adverse claimants. Not only claiming rights under the principles of generational property, they asserted squatters' rights, on the grounds that they and their immediate family had also lived on and worked the land some time in the fairly recent past. The matters under adjudication were not just the veracity of these claims but the precise area worked and thus the proper boundaries of the area belonging to Mrs. Price and her family. In successive decisions, two judges decreed, and the Privy Council agreed, that whatever the adverse claimants had done on Hog Island was independent of Mrs. Price's activities, probably on adjacent land, and in any case was neither in a single area nor continuous. Therefore, their claims to squatters' rights and generational property rights to the land in question were alike dismissed, and absolute freehold title was affirmed (or "quietened") in favor of the Price-Robinson family.

Much if not all of the disputed land was sold to the Paradise Island interests once the money offered had reached a level almost impossible to refuse, but not before ownership of it had been tactically used as a kind of collateral. For example, it seems that the right to build the necessary connecting roads across the strip was parlayed into lucrative jobs for the Price-Robinson family with the hotel-casino complex, though in appointing the brilliant Olympic athlete Tommy Robinson to the post of director of public relations, Resorts International, perhaps by a lucky accident, got one of the most suitable Bahamian candidates.

Boom Town: Freeport-Lucaya in the 1960s

Elements of both the Exuma and Paradise Island cases were replicated in Grand Bahama during the same period. Almost all of the huge tract of land granted to the

Port Authority and Development Company—stretching thirty miles from Hawksbill Creek in the west to Gold Rock Creek in the east—was originally Crown land, uninhabited and uncultivated. But there were some small exceptions scattered along its southern seashore—minuscule villages, "yards," or single habitations and patches of present, recent, or long past cultivation. The resolution of land titles, the buying out of those willing to sell, evictions, and the pursuit of difficult cases through the courts employed almost a complete department of the Freeport-Lucaya administration throughout the 1960s. The Port Authority and Development Company were usually generous in compensating those who agreed to surrender their claims but implacable in treating those whom they regarded as trespassing on their land. The extreme example of the latter was the razing by the Development Company of the Anglican chapel at Smith's Point in 1962 on the grounds that it blocked the eastward extension of Lucaya. The company later made partial amends by allowing a relocated replacement to be dedicated by Bishop Bernard Markham in 1968 and by donating a small Baptist church for the nearby Mather Town community in 1970. In one or two cases individual smallholders achieved a David-like success in the courts against the Freeport-Lucaya Goliath, with the more or less altruistic help of black lawyers in Nassau.[34]

That most of the more substantial villages within the Freeport-Lucaya boundaries survived was, though, less the result of the people's court victories than calculation on the part of the Freeport-Lucaya authorities of the actual and social cost of litigation in the courts when generational and squatter claims were made by so many people and of the practical benefits to the developers of having "dormitory" enclaves for their workers for which they had no legal responsibility. The hamlets of Russell Town and Williams Town, on valuable beachfront due south of Freeport City center, and Smith's Point and Mather Town near the Fortune Bay marina development in central Lucaya were definite inconveniences but were allowed to remain, though strictly fenced in and given only limited access by road. The remnants of an old loggers' camp called Old Freetown (formerly Raccoon Town), fifteen miles further east, was too distant and isolated to be either a serious problem or a convenient place for workers to live (Map 13).[35]

Quite different, however, was the scattered strip of habitation within the Freeport-Lucaya boundaries just east of Hawksbill Creek, consisting of the settlements of Pinder's Point, Lewis Yard, Hunter's, and Mack Town. Though originally containing hardly more people than the four extended families after which they were named, these settlements became first contiguous and then almost a single unplanned township, overcrowded with migrant workers, including illegally landed Haitians. Though they had several churches, shops, bars, and a nightclub, they enjoyed none of Freeport's amenities except for electricity. "Very little of the residential building is in any way distinguished," wrote Peter Barratt with careful understatement, "and some of the recent 'housing', if it may be called that, constructed for the immigrant labourers, is of very mean appearance."[36] Hemmed in between harbor, sea, and the BORCO oil refinery (and, from the Port Authority's viewpoint, luckily almost hidden), this extended slum also suffered air pollution—constantly from the refinery and, when the wind came from the north, from the cement works too. These penalties were endured by the more menial, casual, and lowest-paid workers wanting to be as close as possible to available work because of the unwillingness of their employers to house them in Freeport-Lucaya.

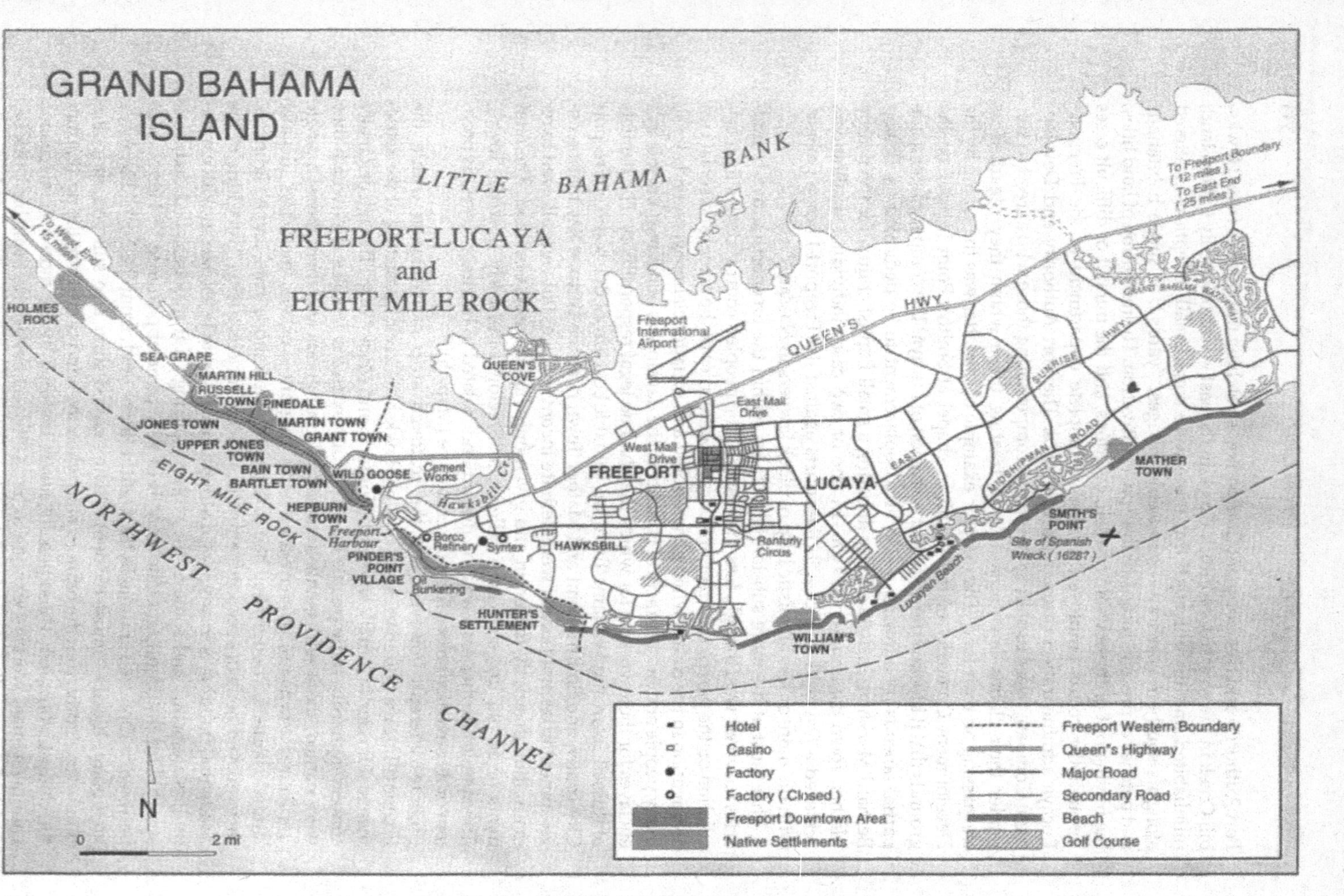

Map. 13. Freeport-Lucaya, Grand Bahama, with Enclave Settlements, 1958–1990

A few of the regular Port Authority employees lived in areas of Freeport City from the beginning, particularly the subdivision called Marco City. Also, the cement company attempted to provide decent housing for its workers by buying up and improving the area called Silver City (alias "Tin City," after the shacks constructed of metal siding), where the first Freeport laborers lived. But the growing emphasis on real estate development after the formation of the Development Company, not to mention that the Port Authority was responsible for education if not other social services within its boundaries, meant that the majority of workers always lived outside Freeport proper. At the very least, this arrangement meant that Grand Bahama's "dream city" had a very awkward and unbalanced social composition.

The unfortunate class situation, moreover, was exacerbated because nearly all those living in Freeport-Lucaya were wealthy or well-paid whites, whereas the workers living outside the boundaries were almost exclusively blacks. Most dangerous of all was that many of the more skilled laborers and white-collar workers employed by the Port Authority and Development Company and living within the concession area—whether American southerners recruited without restrictions under the terms of the Hawksbill Creek Agreement or white Bahamians drawn by the opportunities offered—needed no encouragement to use the advantages that their color brought or to exercise an inbred racism. Long practice had made the more educated whites adept at smoothing over racial inequalities, but there were ignorant American "rednecks" who were far cruder. Most irksome of all to proud nonwhite Bahamians (and to the West Indians employed in some numbers by the Port Authority) was the way such persons conflated all nonwhites as "nigras" or, provoking a more subtle annoyance, called all manual workers, even the anglophones, "Haitians."

The net result was that Grand Bahama during the 1960s, without any formal policy or subtle planning and perhaps without even any intention on the part of the Port Authority and Development Company, developed a form of class and racial separation and a general racialist tone not very different from South African apartheid. Grand Bahama's Sowetos were the slums behind the BORCO oil refinery and, even more, the elongated jumble of settlements farther west collectively called Eight Mile Rock. Making a mockery of the boast of Freeport (from about 1962) that it was the "second city" in the Bahamas was the fact that as many persons lived in the two unplanned strip conurbations outside the concession boundaries on either side of Hawksbill Creek as in the whole of Freeport-Lucaya; Eight Mile Rock alone had as many people as Freeport City and did so throughout the 1970s and 1980s.[37]

Eight Mile Rock was somewhat less constrained for space than the Pinder's Point–Mack Town cluster but was still a dire example of the effects of spontaneous growth, for which initially neither Freeport-Lucaya could, nor the Bahamian government would, be held responsible. Originally (as the name implied), Eight Mile Rock was a disjointed necklace of seven or eight poor hamlets at roughly one-mile intervals along the rocky seashore. It was the location of the grand Bahama commissioner's office until it was moved to the West End during the Prohibition era. The first change came when most of the Turks Islanders from Pine Ridge, along with their wooden houses, were relocated at Seagrape after the sale of the Abaco

Lumber Company in 1955. But once Freeport began to develop and the government built the twenty-four-foot-wide highway between Hawksbill Creek and West End a mile inland, migrants flocked to settle along the new road and spill out from it in both directions until even the inhabitants themselves barely knew where one former settlement ended and another began.[38]

Hopelessly deficient in water, sewerage, and power facilities and with totally insufficient schools, health services, and policing, Eight Mile Rock had, and long retained, something of the ambience of a mining town. "From an aesthetic point of view," Peter Barratt reckoned it "a candidate for the ugliest community in the Bahamas," though he added that "paradoxically it is probably one of the wealthier of the out-island village settlements." This description may have applied to commuters with well-paid guaranteed jobs in Freeport-Lucaya, to the enterprising owners of local shops, bars, and other small businesses, and most of all to the fortunate owners of land on which they could build rental housing. But it certainly did not apply to those forced to pay the high rents charged, to the underemployed or unemployable, or, above all, to the illegal Haitian immigrants whom Dr. Adolph Richter, the district medical officer, claimed in 1967 made up around 50 percent of the population of both Eight Mile Rock and Pinder's Point. Despite the almost inevitable proliferation of churches and the valiant social work of some priests, particularly the Catholics serving the Haitians, Dr. Richter and others noted that there were many social, health, and moral problems. Besides tension between old inhabitants and new and Bahamians and non-Bahamians (Jamaicans and Turks Islanders as well as Haitians), these people were plagued by alcoholism and diseases resulting from inadequate sanitation, malnutrition and ignorance, casual promiscuity, domestic violence, and juvenile delinquency.[39]

It was partly in an attempt to resolve these problems—embarrassing to both parties—that a second Supplemental Agreement was negotiated between the Bahamas government and the Freeport-Lucaya authorities in 1965. The document began by acknowledging that the provisions of the previous agreement had been fulfilled, though this time it added more requirements than it made concessions. To modify Freeport's image as a purely expatriate community by encouraging more lower-income workers to live there, the Port Authority covenanted to build a thousand "low- and middle-income" houses within the concession area, beginning with two hundred within eighteen months. Work began on a housing estate called Hawksbill in April 1966. Other provisions called for the Port Authority to build school accommodations for a total of fourteen hundred pupils and two clinics to serve not just Freeport but the surrounding area as well. Further, the Port Authority was charged to extend its water lines to the settlements of Pinder's Point and Eight Mile Rock and to contribute £10,000 toward a town planning study for the area from Eight Mile Rock to Holmes Rock.[40]

Though no progress was made in providing municipal government in Grand Bahama, the second Supplemental Agreement implicitly acknowledged the existence of a "Greater Freeport" for which the Port Authority and the Bahamas government had at least some shared responsibility. For the first time, too, cracks appeared in the authoritarianism of the Port Authority because the new agreement had to have the approval of four-fifths of the licensees to become effective. The required 80 percent of licensees had given their assent by Christmas 1965, and the document was signed by Governor Sir Ralph Grey and came into effect on March 1, 1966.

Self-Government Under Bay Street Leadership, 1962–1967

The limited changes imposed on Freeport were some of the last effective actions of a government and administration already under scrutiny from outside the Bahamas, as well as under continuous and increasing fire from the political opposition at home. A climax and showdown were approaching.

The UBP took advantage of its surprising electoral victory at the end of 1962 and of the willingness of the British government to devolve imperial authority to press rapidly toward internal self-government under the responsible government system. Shortly after the general election, Duncan Sandys, the British colonial secretary, was in Nassau to attend the vital Lyford Cay talks at which President John F. Kennedy and Prime Ministers Harold Macmillan and John Diefenbaker defined the special relationships between the United States, Great Britain, and Canada within the NATO Alliance. Sandys found time to discuss constitutional issues separately with UBP and PLP leaders and with members of the Executive Council, inviting them to London for constitutional talks. When these were held later in 1963, the PLP strongly supported the major changes and dissented only on the proposed powers of the governor in choosing senators, the ratio of Out Island to New Providence seats in the lower house, and the continuance of double- and triple-member constituencies.[41]

After much fine-tuning by Colonial Office lawyers drawing mainly from West Indian precedents, the new constitution came into effect on January 7, 1964. Though the British government retained control of foreign affairs, defense, internal security, and further changes in the constitution (and the British Treasury continued for some time to have financial powers through the membership of the Bahamas in the Sterling Bloc), the effective powers of the governor were greatly diminished. The real power was unequivocally invested in an executive consisting of a premier and cabinet of ministers drawn from the majority party in the House of Assembly. The executive was responsible to the people through the House of Assembly in the sense that it was bound to resign and call a general election (that is, in formal terms, the premier was to "advise the Governor to dissolve the House") if it lost a vote of confidence. Otherwise, the House was to last for a term of five years, unless the premier, for political reasons short of an unfavorable confidence vote, chose to "advise" the governor to dissolve it sooner.

The existing House was expected to continue until the end of its term in 1967, when its thirty-three members would be augmented by five and redistributed to give New Providence seventeen against twenty-one Out Island members (compared with the previous twelve and twenty-one). Elections to the House of Assembly were, of course, to be by universal adult suffrage and secret ballot, though for a time it remained possible to have a second or third vote in the two- and three-member constituencies, and British residents continued to be able to vote until Bahamian citizenship was more precisely defined. A more formal upper house of the legislature was created in the form of a fifteen-person Senate, formally appointed by the governor, but only after consultation and advice and with merely delaying, not vetoing, powers. Eight senators were to be nominated by the governor "after consultation with the Premier and any other person he may in his discretion decide to consult," five were appointed "on the advice" of the premier, and two on the "advice" of the leader of the opposition.[42]

The achievement of internal self-government was a proud moment for all Bahamians, despite the disappointment of many that the change occurred with the UBP still firmly in charge. The ambivalence of public sentiments was perhaps best indicated by the amendment made by an anonymous graffiti artist who painted in the word "BLACK" before "Premier" on a poster reading "Congratulations to the first Premier of the Bahamas." Sir Roland Symonette announced a cabinet consisting of fourteen of the twenty-three members of the House of Assembly, plus the leader for the government in the Senate, with Stafford Sands (himself soon to be knighted) holding the significantly twinned portfolios of tourism and finance. The widely respected nonwhite Eugene Dupuch (who had joined the UBP just before the election) was given ministerial responsibility for welfare services, on which increased expenditure was promised in the new budget. But reforms were no more than token. While proudly pointing to rising tourist figures and a £2.5 million current account balance in the treasury, Stafford Sands announced a deficit of £1 million in his first budget for increased capital spending. Increased shop license fees and real estate taxes were levied, but a proposed new tax on gambling was, perhaps expectedly, stalled in the Senate and dropped. A proposal by the premier that ministers be voted salaries was also discarded after strong PLP dissent. But this proved a Pyrrhic victory for the opposition because it provided the Bay Street ministers with justification to continue the practice of combining private commercial with government business.[43]

Conflict of interest among members of the ruling party and the control of gambling were two issues on which opposition to the UBP government increasingly focused, along with racial discrimination or insensitivity, immigration and citizenship concerns, and (above all in the public forum) the vital question of the equitable redistribution of parliamentary seats before the next general election. Though stunned by its 1962 defeat, the PLP soon regrouped its forces and became more systematic in its populist tactics. The divergence of aims and ideology from those of the labor movement (particularly with its dynamic leader) was a continuing problem. But disagreements with the more moderate (and mainly lighter-skinned, middle-class) nonwhite reformists were resolved either by voluntary defections or by squeezing them out—leading some to form yet another third political grouping, the National Democratic Party (NDP), in 1965. Speeding the quest for authenticity as the party of the black majority, the PLP learned from the rhetoric and tactics of the black power movement and received particular encouragement, reflected kudos, and even financial support from such acclaimed figures as Norman Manley of Jamaica, Kwame Nkrumah of Ghana, Martin Luther King, Adam Clayton Powell Jr. (a frequent visitor to Bimini), and that increasingly politicized son of the Bahamas, Sidney Poitier.[44]

Out-and-out demagogues like Milo Butler could always be relied on to provide a racialist slant to political discourse. But far more thoughtful, and cumulatively effective, were debates carried on in the newspapers about racially questionable texts found in the schools. These included a standard geography text and Richard Le Galliene's Bahamian adventure story *Pieces of Eight*, which said disparaging things about Africa, Africans, and Afro-Bahamians. Harriet Beecher Stowe's *Uncle Tom's Cabin* also came under attack for its objectionable portrayal of a black hero far too compliant to the dominant whites and their culture.[45] In June 1966 an Afro-Bahamian Club was formed with the aim of influencing the authorities as well as

Sir Roland and Lady Symonette celebrate the coming of internal self-government in 1964, with scarcely a nonwhite face in sight. On Symonette's left, Governor Sir Robert Stapledon. Courtesy of Bahamas Archives.

raising public consciousness. Among other activities, it lobbied the Ministry of Education for a more enlightened history curriculum. Implicitly (probably justly) criticizing the pioneer *History of the Bahamas* published by one of the present authors four years earlier, the club's spokesman wrote in a letter to the *Guardian* in April 1966: "Our children are compelled to study about the European brightmen (the conquerors so to speak) and nothing about themselves. After 300 years our schools do not have a proper history of the Bahamas. Why? I will tell you why. It is impossible to write a proper history of the Bahamas without mentioning Africa and a proper and true history of the Bahamas might begin with the great men of Africa and lead up to the achievements of our own black people."[46]

Controlling the flood of migrants attracted by rapidly increasing opportunities in the Bahamas had become an even more contentious issue than it had been in the 1920s, and with different overtones. The 1928 Immigration Act, although inspired both by employment concerns and an incipient nationalism, had given the authorities the more or less arbitrary right to exclude persons but did not include either a definition of Bahamian citizenship or specific employment controls. The new Immigration Act, which became law on January 6, 1964, added to the absolute status of "Bahamian-born" the intermediate and almost unique category of "Bahamian Belonger," to include those persons born elsewhere who had dedicated their lives and fortunes to the Bahamas. The act also provided for certificates of permanent residence which might be endorsed to prohibit employment without approval of the Immigration Board and for shorter-term entry permits for specific jobs.[47]

The UBP advertised the 1964 Immigration Act as more clearly defining what it was to be Bahamian and making it easier to exclude undesirables, and as such it was generally welcomed by Bahamians. But many decisions under the act remained arbitrary, giving the regime the power to exclude persons it did not want while opening the door wider to those it favored. The PLP was particularly concerned about the implications of "Belonger" status and the exemption of Freeport-Lucaya from the act's provisions. They charged that Bay Street, far from preserving Bahamian identity, was eager to change it—specifically by encouraging the settlement of expatriate whites while effectively excluding all blacks, Americans, and British West Indians, as well as Haitians and Cubans.

The PLP gained much more political capital, though, over the UBP's evident gerrymandering of the new constituencies. The opposition charged the regime with an eagerness to keep the Out Islands overrepresented and as politically unenlightened as possible, with undue haste in establishing new boundaries (especially in New Providence) before up-to-date census figures were available, and with dragging its feet over voter registration. But the fact that a large proportion of those qualified to register were slow to put themselves forward apparently also convinced the PLP of the need for some dramatic action that would galvanize all its potential supporters. The results were the parliamentary histrionics that climaxed on what became known as Black Tuesday, April 27, 1965.

The drama began with near comedy. In the debate on the report of the Constituencies Committee on April 4, the loud-voiced heavyweight Milo Butler refused the order of the Speaker (the premier's son) to limit his speech to fifteen minutes and was forcibly carried from the House by four equally burly policemen. Not to be outdone, the more diminutive but equally vociferous deputy leader of the PLP, Arthur Hanna, followed suit and suffered the same indignity. Daily increasing and more restless crowds of PLP supporters outside the House were not quietened by the speedy reinstatement of Hanna and Butler—the latter of whom immediately pressed his advantage by speaking for forty-five minutes. Nor were they calmed when Premier Symonette spoke over radio station ZNS on April 26, since while begging the people not to jeopardize their prosperity by being drawn into disorder, he blamed the disturbances on irresponsible agitators and promised (or threatened) that his government would not be intimidated.[48]

On Tuesday, April 27, a huge crowd of PLP supporters, scarcely contained by a large detachment of police, booed the UBP members as they entered the House. The noise of the crowd was clearly heard within the chamber as PLP members opened the windows on the plausible pretext of letting fresh air into the overheated room. Motions made by opposition leader Lynden Pindling to defer the decisions of the Constituencies Committee and by PLP member Spurgeon Bethel to set up a national registration campaign more accurately to determine voter distribution, followed by the redefining of boundaries under United Nations supervision, were decisively defeated. At this juncture, Pindling fierily accused the government of a dictatorship with which he and his party could have no truck. In an action reminiscent of Oliver Cromwell in the seventeenth-century House of Commons, he strode over to the mace in front of the Speaker's chair, shouting, "This is the symbol of authority, and authority in this island belongs to the people." He then lifted the mace, carried it to the window, and threw it down. "Yes, the people are outside," he said to the stunned Speaker and UBP, "and the mace belongs outside too!" Not to be left behind (and perhaps on cue), Milo Butler seized the hourglasses used by the Speaker to time members' speeches and threw them after the mace, as the crowd chanted "PLP, PLP" over and over again.[49]

To forestall arrest, Pindling led his PLP members out of the House, which was left in confusion while Randol Fawkes argued with the Speaker (R. T. "Bobby" Symonette) that business could not be continued without the symbolic mace. Pindling addressed the crowd from the roof of a post office van, gave his version of what had happened, and called for volunteers to join him in a sit-down demonstration. Hundreds complied, the police moved in to seize demonstrators, and there were many scuffles. After twenty minutes, the Riot Act was read by a magistrate, the riot squad kept in readiness moved in, and the crowd dispersed—most moving toward the Southern Recreation Ground. Having recovered the shattered mace, the House approved the Constituencies Committee report and was adjourned, though the UBP members cautiously stayed in the building till assured that Bay Street was safely cleared.[50]

The almost certainly premeditated actions of the PLP's leaders at first seemed to have split the opposition. But actually they polarized Bahamian politics as never before, convincing many uncommitted blacks that the PLP was the only party with the dynamism to achieve substantial change. The PLP disowned further violent and unlawful actions and maintained that it was opposed to the composition and conduct of the legislature, not to the parliamentary system as such, but it effectively boycotted the House for nine months. Three of its more moderate members resigned, to take the lead in forming the National Democratic Party. Like the PLP, the NDP made representations to the Colonial Office but received merely a polite hearing and the response that disputes were now matters of internal Bahamian politics. The PLP, however, took its complaints to a far wider audience and a more powerful international tribunal, achieving something of a coup when an official party delegation of eight persons, with Lynden Pindling as spokesman, was allowed to petition the United Nations Committee on Colonialism on August 23–24, 1965.[51]

Speaking to the full UN committee of twenty-four as official leader of the Bahamian opposition, Pindling made a calm, comprehensive, and convincing indictment of the social, economic, and political condition of the Bahamas under the UBP. He accused the regime of hobbling the labor movement, of controlling immigration to its own advantage, of purposely retarding the education system, and of holding back on social welfare. He presented damning arguments that inequitable taxes and the lack of conflict-of-interest legislation helped members of the regime to grow ever wealthier, while the ordinary people (who carried most of the tax burden through import duties and were informally taxed by Bay Street merchants) remained relatively poor and struggled against inflation. The bulk of Pindling's speech, however, concentrated on the disproportionate allocation of parliamentary seats by which the UBP sustained its power and on the impediments placed in the way of effecting changes. Though Pindling said nothing about specific constitutional changes and stressed that his party did not seek independence at that stage, he accused the British government of unduly favoring the existing regime. His only reference to the incidents of April 27 was the statement that had it not been for the moderation of the PLP leaders the situation would have turned far more serious and that he believed the governor would have been only too happy to call for British troops once more.[52]

Answering questions even more impressively on the second day, Pindling obtained implied or actual endorsement from the representatives of several former colonies, though the fact that the strongest support came from Viktor Shakhov of the USSR was of more questionable value. Once the Bahamian delegates had withdrawn from the committee chamber, the British delegate repeated the official line that since the Bahamas enjoyed internal self-government under a responsible government system and universal adult suffrage, it was clearly a democracy, and such matters as the redistribution of parliamentary seats were properly and best settled internally. As expected, the UN committee did nothing formally about the Bahamian petition, though the PLP and its leader achieved invaluable publicity and were palpably strengthened.[53]

The Coming of Majority Rule: The PLP Victory, 1967–1968

Fair parliamentary representation was a basic political issue, but the PLP gained moral superiority over Bay Street on the questions of conflict of interest and political corruption, especially in respect to gambling concessions. At the 1963 constitutional talks the PLP had agreed to ministers keeping their private businesses, but it strenuously objected when they took advantage of their offices to extend them. Sir Roland Symonette had felt no compunction when accepting a position on the board of Mackey Airlines at the same time he was made premier, and Sir Stafford Sands even more brazenly combined his posts of minister of finance and tourism with an appointment to the board of the Royal Bank of Canada. Yet these were only part of a general pattern described by Lynden Pindling to the UN committee on August 23, 1965. The fifteen Bahamian ministers

> all belonged to the merchant oligarchy, which had been in control since 1729 and was of European extraction. The ministers owned large shares in the majority of local enterprises and benefitted from government contracts, all with the tacit approval of the United Kingdom Government. For example, the Prime Minister [strictly, premier] was perhaps the biggest road-builder in the country. The Minister of Maritime Affairs was a major supplier of lumber and hardware goods to the Government and perhaps the biggest ship-owner in the country. The Minister of Agriculture had large farming interests and supplied air-conditioning material to the Government as did the Minister of Electricity. The Minister of Finance and Tourism was head of a food chain, an insurance company and a law firm which often represented his Ministry and his clients at the same time.[54]

Behind the scenes, moreover, even grosser greediness and corruption existed, the nature and extent of which were only gradually and partially revealed in the American press and through a royal commission investigating casino gambling concessions after the PLP came to power.[55] Casino gambling had always been a controversial and emotive issue, dividing the UBP as well as the country at large. Casinos were seen to be a useful magnet to draw well-heeled tourists, immensely profitable for their operators, but difficult to supervise so that all the profits stayed within the country and organized crime was kept at bay. Casinos were also strongly opposed by churches, particularly Catholics and Baptists—to whose churches a majority of PLP members belonged. Their lobbying organization was the Bahamas

Christian Council, and one of their most vocal spokesmen, the Baptist minister H. W. Brown, was one of the official PLP delegates to the UN in August 1965. Though cynics and those favoring casinos accused the churchmen of being most concerned about distractions from the Sabbath and the depletion of collection plates, this was unfair. Familiar with the ordinary Bahamians' love of petty gambling and the well-established effects of the local "numbers game," foreign lotteries, and horse racing at Hobby Horse Hall, churchmen had always deprecated the way the quest for instant riches militated against industry and thrift, draining money from poor families for the benefit of the gambling operators, and now they feared an even greater demoralization and impoverishment if casinos were generally introduced.

There had been two limited exceptions to the rule against casinos, granted through "exemption certificates" to small private clubs in Nassau and on Cat Cay. The author of the exemption idea was none other than Stafford Sands as a young lawyer in 1939. Sands personally made several unsuccessful applications between 1946 and 1959 for exemption certificates to the Executive Council, of which he was then a member, on behalf of himself and others. Similarly scotched were the initial attempts to obtain casino licenses for hotels on Paradise Island and at Lucaya by Huntingdon Hartford and Louis Chesler and a later attempt by a group headed by a daughter of Sir Harry Oakes to purchase the Nassau exemption. On April 1, 1963, however, it was announced that the Executive Council had granted an exemption certificate to a company called Bahamas Amusements to operate an unlimited number of casinos in the Freeport-Lucaya area for a ten-year period. Despite the furor raised by this grant, ardent campaigning by the Bahamas Christian Council, and, it seems, the personal opposition of Premier Symonette, Sir Stafford Sands—at the same time he was changing the Bahamian currency from "pounds, shillings and pence" to "dollars and cents"—managed to negotiate a similar exemption certificate on behalf of the American-owned Paradise Island Enterprises early in 1966.[56]

On October 5, 1966, a bombshell article appeared in the *Wall Street Journal* alleging that the Freeport gambling license had been corruptly obtained and that Mafia figures were involved in the operation of the casinos. The two authors (who subsequently won a Pulitzer Prize) showed that the casino manager at Freeport was wanted in the United States for tax evasion, having previously operated an illegal bookmaking operation in New York with two associates who were also with him in Grand Bahama. Behind these front men was said to be the sinister Mafia kingpin, Meyer Lansky. It was asserted that a secret planning meeting had been arranged by Wallace Groves at the Fontainbleu Hotel on Miami Beach on September 26, 1961, attended by prominent Bahamians and underworld figures, and that in due course the casino license was obtained by Groves's companies through bribing members of the Executive Council and other government figures. Among those named as having received princely "consultancy fees" from Freeport-Lucaya were Stafford Sands and four other members of the Executive Council, the Speaker of the House of Assembly, Bobby Symonette, and the self-righteous owner-editor of the *Nassau Tribune*, Sir Etienne Dupuch. It was also stated that the New York public relations firm employed by the Ministry of Tourism had purchased and destroyed the manuscript of a damaging book of revelations called *The Ugly Bahamian*.[57]

The Mafia connection was never conclusively proved (for Paradise Island or for Grand Bahama), and the *Wall Street Journal*'s allegations about local corruption were not unequivocally substantiated until the royal commission made its report in March 1967. But the rash of publicity (amply backed up by articles in *Life, Time,* and the *Miami Herald*) was too much for Bay Street to suppress or the *Guardian* and *Tribune* to play down. Hoping to defuse the issue or at least postpone unfavorable developments until the UBP was safely reinstated, Premier Symonette announced on December 1, 1966, that the general election would be brought forward to January 10, 1967. Three weeks later, after the governor had been to London, the colonial secretary announced in the British House of Commons that the Bahamian government would welcome an inquiry into allegations about gambling—though after the impending election.[58]

The UBP clearly hoped that by calling the election so suddenly it would catch the opposition unprepared and that by scheduling it so soon after Christmas and New Year's the electorate would be distracted by holiday celebrations. But these proved to be miscalculations. By stressing the spiritual rather than material side of the holiday season, the PLP was able to reinforce the moral ascendancy provided by the gambling and "conflict of interest" revelations. Even more inept (almost incredibly so in retrospect) was the UBP's choice of the election date. As the biblically attuned PLP leaders gleefully pointed out, the "tenth day of the first month" was the day of Passover, when Pharaoh ordered the Israelites in Egypt to be released from bondage and their Exodus began. Thus the theme from the movie *Exodus* joined "We Shall Overcome" as a PLP anthem, along with the "Amen" song from Sidney Poitier's recent Oscar-winning movie *Lilies of the Field.*

Standing on their claim that they had done nothing unconstitutional or even undemocratic and relying on their hold on the Out Islands, the still incomplete voting registers, the votes lost by the PLP to the NDP, and the support of those who believed the PLP was both inexperienced and dangerously radical, the UBP remained confident to the last. Convinced that the unreformed constituencies, the competition from the NDP, and the sheer financial muscle of Bay Street were too much to overcome, even the PLP was amazed at the outcome on January 10, 1967.

It was one of the closest elections in history. By one computation (totaling the votes in the two triple-seat and three double-seat Out Island constituencies), the UBP polled slightly more total votes than the PLP. Though the total votes each received were almost equal, the UBP also fared somewhat better relative to its rival in the Out Islands (with 13,431 votes to 3,500) than the PLP did in relation to the UBP in New Providence (13,048 to 5,987). As expected, the difference in total votes was made up by those cast for the NDP. But what surprised everyone was that the total cast for the NDP was a derisory 826, with all three incumbent candidates heavily defeated and the rest losing their deposits for receiving less than 10 percent of the vote. The eradication of the NDP meant that the splinter vote did not damage the PLP as expected and had less effect on the outcome than the 1,292 votes cast for Randol Fawkes's Labour Party and the 2,858 cast for Independents.

As predicted, the PLP was triumphant in New Providence, taking twelve of the seventeen (all single-member) seats, some by overwhelming margins. In unequivocally black constituencies, the UBP put up black candidates, but they fared almost as poorly as the NDP nominees. For the UBP, Stafford Sands won convincingly in his Nassau City stronghold, as did the less controversial Geoffrey Johnstone

Victory on the tenth day of the tenth month. The crowd celebrates the PLP's triumph, 1967. Courtesy of Bahamas Archives.

for the white suburban Fort Montagu district. But Premier Symonette squeezed in by a mere 47 votes in middle-class Centreville, and the only other UBP victory was by Foster Clarke (like Symonette, a white of partial black ancestry) in neighboring Palmdale, by 592 votes to 527. Randol Fawkes, unopposed by the PLP, was elected for working-class St. Barnabas district by a huge margin over his black UBP opponent.

What was more surprising was that the PLP made significant inroads in the UBP-dominated Out Islands. The subterfuge of splitting Andros and adding another seat to include the Berry Islands paid off to give the UBP one of the three. But the splitting of Grand Bahama into two constituencies misfired when the PLP won both, despite a strong showing by the candidate for Labour in the constituency including Freeport-Lucaya (where, of course, few of the expatriates voted). The UBP swept the triple-seat constituency of Abaco and the double-seat constituencies of Long Island and Exuma. But it narrowly lost one of the two Harbour Island seats to the idiosyncratic Independent Alvin R. Braynen (who came from the same settlement and from much the same mixed-race Methodist background as R. T. Symonette) and did worse than expected in triple-seat Eleuthera. Here the voters, on whom the PLP had expended much of its limited Out Island election resources, put PLP candidates first and third in the poll—though the strong showing of another moralistic Independent may have had an important influence on the outcome.[59]

The net result of the election (which to the credit of all parties was conducted more scrupulously than ever before and without serious violence) was a heart-stopping tie between the two major parties—eighteen to eighteen, with one Labour member and one Independent. Both parties immediately wooed the Labour representative, Randol Fawkes, with offers of a ministerial post, and the UBP added other inducements. But though Fawkes relished what was to be the high point of his turbulent career, it was no real contest. Cleaving to the party he thought most likely to fulfill his political and social ideals, if not also remembering that it had not opposed him in the election, he announced the following day that he had agreed to a coalition of the PLP and Labour Parties and had accepted the post of minister of labor in a PLP government. When the sole Independent, Alvin R. Braynen, refused to join with the UBP he had come to abhor, both parties agreed to his election as the neutral Speaker of the House.[60]

For more than a year, the PLP government was on trial. But it came through triumphantly, thanks to the moderation and shrewdness of its leaders, the almost uninterrupted improvement in the economy, and the widespread disgust at the findings of the Bacon investigation into casino licensing. As Colin Hughes has written, the events of 1967–68 saw "a convergence of the two parties, the U.B.P. becoming more liberal in pursuit of votes, the P.L.P. becoming more conservative in pursuit of business support." Over the longer run, moreover, it might be argued that the PLP and its leaders did not sufficiently distinguish themselves from their predecessors in either ideology or practice, though it would be an obvious exaggeration and simplistic to claim (as some were to do) that they were simply outdoing their former masters and giving Bay Street a new complexion. Time proved that the majority of Bahamians wanted their own distinctive identity, not one borrowed from radical black Americans or from the communist regime in neighboring Cuba.

Old Bay Street did not succumb without a fight in 1967, backing up warnings of a decline in investment and an increase in unemployment by planting a fabricated document in the *Guardian* which alleged that the PLP planned to introduce swingeing taxes, to open immigration freely to Haitian, British West Indian, and American blacks, to close or take over all private schools, and to nationalize and raise the cost of Out Island transportation. The UBP also made much of the PLP's almost immediate voting of princely salaries to the legislators (which rewarded the premier with more than the governor) without implementing the conflict-of-interest legislation for which it had previously clamored. The UBP even won a moral victory in the reheld election at Crooked Island when its candidate, Basil Kelly (previously unopposed when the NDP candidate withdrew under suspicious circumstances), was returned, even though the PLP adjourned the House for seven weeks to fight the election and used electioneering tactics for which it had long attacked its Bay Street opponents.[61]

For his part, Premier Pindling hardly put a foot wrong. Counseling hard-core PLP supporters against reprisals, he made reassuring speeches about his government's commitment to free enterprise and the continued expansion of the tourist industry. The governor's speech at the opening of the new legislature (which, following British parliamentary practice, expressed the government's official policy) was similarly anodyne. It spoke of the need for immediate improvements in education and health services and for economic diversification but stressed the vital importance of tourism and foreign investment. As for the burning questions of Bahamianization and immigration, it promised stricter but fairer immigration controls and committed the government to training Bahamians to fill as many posts as possible but pointed out the need for qualified expatriates for the immediate future. Implementing the governor's speech, the first PLP budget greatly increased expenditures for education and health, leaving the allocation to the Ministry of Tourism strongly in third position.[62]

More important in practical terms were the findings of the Bacon Commission, the redrawing of the electoral map by the reconstituted Boundaries Commission, and the work by PLP organizers behind the scenes to sign up new members and to register all voters. Stafford Sands had resigned his seat in the House, disposed of his law practice, and announced his intention to spend most of the year outside the Bahamas, but, contrary to expectations, he appeared to answer questions before the Bacon Commission. This act of bravado—not without a heroic dimension in being undertaken, as soon transpired, under sentence of imminent death from cancer—proved unwise in the light of what it both revealed and concealed. Sands would not disclose details of his bank accounts on the grounds that they involved the private affairs of clients and refused to say anything about a mysterious check for half a million dollars paid to him, for fear of self-incrimination. But he freely admitted to receiving a consultancy fee of $10,000 a month from the Grand Bahama Port Authority. He claimed that this money went into UBP funds along with other sums given to him for the party, although the statement went counter to the Port Authority's denial that it had directly funded the UBP. Self-righteously, Sands claimed that in 1960 or 1961 he had turned down an offer of $2 million from Meyer Lansky for the Nassau casino exemption, skating over the fact that he had been instrumental in obtaining the same concession for others of equally dubious provenance some five years later.

As to the £200,000 fee that Sands was shown to have received from the Grand Bahama Port Authority for obtaining the Freeport exemption certificate, the Bacon Report concluded that it was "even by Bahamian standards, out of proportion to the legal services he had rendered. . . . The enormity of the fee demanded and the speed and manner with which payment was effected, coupled with every circumstance of his handling of this application, leave . . . no doubt that he was selling his services primarily as an influential Member of the Executive Council and not as a lawyer." Similar strictures were levied concerning the "consultancy fees" or outright payments paid or contracts made by the Port Authority to seven other present or former members of the Executive Council and House of Assembly (including the premier and his son, the Speaker) and to the commissioner of police at different times between 1961 and 1966. Though even the PLP was shown to have received a contribution to party election expenses through its leader from a shady American operator in return for vague promises of a future deal (never delivered), the Bacon revelations allowed Premier Pindling to propose a motion in the Assembly on January 24, 1968, passed two days later, that those found "to have received consultant fees and other questionable payments were guilty of a crime against the people of the Bahamas, and ought to be and are hereby condemned."[63]

The police commissioner immediately resigned, and most of those named in the Bacon Report more or less voluntarily departed from public life. The most notable exception was Sir Roland Symonette, who continued to be elected until 1977 and gave up his seat shortly before his death in 1979. Sir Etienne Dupuch, forever

Governor Sir Ralph Grey, Premier Lynden Pindling, and the first PLP cabinet, 1967. Second from left, Milo Butler, first governor-general (1973–79). Fourth from right, Randol Fawkes, the Labour leader, who was not reappointed after the PLP landslide in 1968 and went into opposition. On Milo Butler's right, Cecil Wallace-Whitfield, who left the PLP to form the opposition FNM in 1971. On Butler's left, Arthur Hanna, deputy premier, who resigned in 1984 over the Drug Commission findings. Of Pindling's 1967 ministers, only Clement Maynard (far right) still sat in the cabinet in 1992. Courtesy of Bahamas Archives.

protesting innocence, moved to Florida, though his editorials in the *Tribune* continued to infuriate and amuse his enemies and admirers until his death in 1991. Sir Stafford Sands, having sold up most of his Bahamian assets, including the selling of the Nassau Market grocery chain to the American Winn-Dixie corporation, left the Bahamas to live his last few months in affluent ignominy in Spain. A more glorious ending was destined for the PLP backbencher Uriah McPhee, who also died from cancer, on February 16, 1968. Relying on the Bahamian people's traditional love of splendid burial ceremonies, the PLP accorded him the first ever Bahamian state funeral on February 23. Four days later, Premier Pindling announced the snap general election for April 10, which he hoped would bury the UBP.

The premier's optimism was justified, and the PLP's landslide victory was prelude to an all too brief period of socioeconomic euphoria and popular content before the international recession of 1970 brought the PLP's honeymoon period to an end. Before the election, the PLP published an economic progress report that disproved the UBP's negative predictions, showing soaring rates for tourism, education, and the provision of utilities. The electoral rolls had been expanded to fifty-five thousand from thirty-eight thousand just one year earlier, and official PLP membership was at a peak. With some exaggeration, the PLP claimed that instead of looking for payment for their votes, electors were offering contributions for the party's war chest. The UBP still had the richer campaign resources but was undoubtedly harmed by the addition of three new seats for New Providence and by the splitting of the remaining four multiple Out Island constituencies and their reduction by two seats. The credibility of the UBP was further damaged by accusations (at least partially founded) that a half dozen of its black candidates had criminal convictions and some had even been to jail. Several UBP speakers were interrupted by rowdies or stoned, and at least one election meeting, at Fox Hill, was broken up. But these unfortunate instances merely represented PLP dominance and were unnecessary.[64]

Digging In: Optimistic Reforms in the Early Pindling Era

In the fifteen months since the last election there had been a 20 percent swing to the PLP. This time, the party polled 21,908 votes to the UBP's 5,842 in New Providence and, more remarkably, 10,183 to the UBP's 6,455 in the Out Islands. In Nassau City (where no more than 40 percent of the electors were white) the black UBP candidate Cleophas Adderley somewhat surprisingly retained Stafford Sands's vacated seat; Geoffrey Johnstone substantially increased his margin in Fort Montagu; and former premier Symonette wrested Uriah McPhee's former seat of Shirlea from the PLP. In the predominantly black constituencies, however, the PLP margins were overwhelming. Milo Butler, for example, polled 1,549 votes in Bain's Town against 49 for the UBP. In the Out Islands, the races were often close, though the PLP won easy victories in Andros (where Premier Pindling polled four times as many votes as his opponent), in Grand Bahama, and in northern Abaco. The combined effect was that of the thirty-eight seats in the House the PLP won twenty-nine to the UBP's seven. In New Providence, the disparity was sixteen to three, and in the Out Islands thirteen to four. The one Independent, A. R. Braynen, the Speaker alleged by the UBP strongly to favor the PLP, was elected by 341 to 222 without PLP opposition. Randol Fawkes was also reelected for Labour in St. Barnabas unopposed by the UBP and without official PLP opposition, though he charged that his Independent opponent (who polled a respectable 35 percent of the vote) had strong PLP support.[65]

The first priority of the now supreme PLP was further constitutional advance short of Bahamian independence. After preliminary discussions in Nassau, an all-party conference was held in London from September 19 to 27, 1968. The results considerably strengthened the colony's independent authority while augmenting the power of the ruling party within it. Despite UBP opposition, the Senate was to be enlarged to sixteen members, appointed by the governor for the duration of the lower house. Nine senators were to be nominated by the prime minister (as the premier was now more grandly titled), four by the leader of the opposition, and three were to be independent.

The imperial government retained control over foreign affairs and defense, though the governor was expected to consult with the prime minister before making decisions. For the first time the Bahamian government was given the right to negotiate trade and migration agreements with other governments. Police and internal security were placed under the control of a cabinet minister, with the governor retaining only the ultimate responsibility. To reduce the chances of political interference, however, a Police Service Commission appointed by the governor was to have a monitoring role. Similarly, an ostensibly independent Civil Service Commission was to be appointed by the governor, with the aim of reducing the chances of government patronage, favoritism, or undue influence.

In the first clear definition of Bahamian citizenship, the contentious Belonger Status introduced by the UBP was amended. In future, only those persons born in the Bahamas and those given "Bahamian status" through a certificate of naturalization from the governor could be Bahamian citizens. More symbolically, having become a virtually self-governing entity within the British Commonwealth of Nations, the Colony of the Bahama Islands, in an amendment five years later, was accorded the more dignified (if somewhat confusing) official title of the Commonwealth of the Bahamas.[66]

Underpinning the political changes that constituted Britain's declining imperial role in the Bahamas were the financial changes that reflected the decline of sterling and the ascendancy of the dollar. In October 1968 the Bahamas Monetary Authority was created (a forerunner of the Central Bank set up in 1974), with control over currency, exchange regulations, and the operation of banks and trust companies. The process that had begun with Stafford Sands's adoption of a decimal coinage led through the complete divorce of the Bahamian dollar from sterling, to the establishment of a clever if cumbrous machinery by which the local currency was nominally sustained at par with that of the United States. This change slightly slowed the pace of inflation, just as the survival of a viable local currency helped to minimize the consequences of an economy so dependent on tourism (the annual visitors were already five times and eventually twelve times as numerous as the resident population), in which the vast majority of tourists were from the United States.

A more glaring and less easily soluble problem was the inadequacy of the Bahamian educational system. The booming economy and new political regime provided unprecedented opportunities in the public service and private sector for the black majority. The few who had qualified under the deficient and elitist previous system rose with sometimes dizzying rapidity. But because less than 10 percent of school leavers attained the minimal requirements for clerical employment, there was a serious and increasing shortfall. This was especially true in the lower-paying, less-glamorous public sector and worst of all in the critical area of teaching—leading to a continued reliance on expatriates, mainly whites, that was galling to many of those now in power.

In the second PLP budget, education was the main priority, followed by health services and public works, with tourist promotion falling to a still prominent fourth place. As for the islands' main industry, the PLP was simply encouraging a trend that saw the annual flow of tourists surpass a million for the first time in 1968 and was to continue to rise, save for short-lived declines in 1970 and 1974–75, toward three million in the 1980s. The rise in the number of Bahamas-based banks and trust companies from 78 in 1966 to 120 in 1969 and 164 in 1970 also indicated that UBP scare tactics had failed to halt a rising tide of investment and offshore banking. Similarly, in the improvement of health facilities and roads, the party was to an extent merely increasing the pace of moves initiated by the UBP, expanding, indeed, with an enthusiasm that was not easy to sustain. The designation of the Princess Margaret Hospital as a teaching school for doctors as well as nurses and its recognition as one of the premier hospitals in the region in the 1970s was the proud climax of a steady expansion since the 1950s, which was followed by a period of consolidation if not decline in the quality of services because of the relative shortage of money and personnel. With even more energy, the PLP fulfilled election promises to improve the roads. In New Providence, giant Barber-Greene mechanical spreaders replaced the familiar Public Works Department patching gangs (themselves a fairly recent innovation) as the symbol of the new PLP dispensation. More fundamentally, the Public Works Department's operations were for the first time extended to the Out Islands, where hitherto private contractors had reigned, including the former premier. By July 1971, the PLP's finance minister was able to claim that the party had spent $12 million on five hundred miles of road—notably on new highways in the neglected Out Islands.[67]

It was in the vitally important area of education that the new regime made the most basic, widespread, and lasting changes, beginning under the direction of a dynamic and idealistic minister of education, Cecil Wallace-Whitfield. The PLP's aim was not only to expand and improve but to Bahamianize the system, from bottom to top. Unprecedented capital expenditures were made to upgrade school buildings and teachers' accommodations in the Out Islands. With incredible rapidity many new secular (and coeducational) secondary schools were added to the single Government High School (which claimed among its alumni both Lynden Pindling and Stafford Sands) and the several private, mainly church-affiliated high schools. This was achieved by upgrading the existing senior schools and building several new schools in New Providence and by creating central high schools in all the major Out Islands for the senior pupils in the scattered all-age schools. At the same time, the traditional bias toward purely academic learning was moderated by a stronger emphasis on technical training, while, against a similar colonialist inertia, attempts were made to increase the relevance and Bahamian content of academic curricula, including the use of local rather than metropolitan examples in classroom teaching if not in texts and the teaching of West Indian and Bahamian history at every level.[68]

At the tertiary level, progress was limited at first to the foundation of an evening institute for continuing and adult education, the appointment of a resident tutor from the University of the West Indies, and the creation of a second teacher training college on a surrendered U.S. tracking station at San Salvador. Of necessity, the majority of Bahamians aiming for the professions continued to be trained abroad, a situation the government accepted, if not wholeheartedly endorsed, by multiplying the number of scholarships granted for foreign study. The destination of scholarship holders was, to an extent, an ideological issue. A majority of the most qualified high school graduates continued to choose the United Kingdom for study, but the number who went to the predominantly black campuses of the University of the West Indies (UWI) or to Canada increased steadily. More students than ever before, though, went to the United States, especially to all-black schools in the southern states. This was as much because of their less exacting entrance requirements (and in some cases their eagerness to recruit outstanding athletes) as for reasons of racial preference, but it did have noticeable cultural effects.

Grandiose statements of intent to repatriate Bahamian tertiary education came

School's out. Haziel Albury's all-age all-white school at Man-o-War Cay in the late 1940s. Photograph courtesy of Ruth Rodriguez.

closer to reality in 1974 with the foundation of the College of the Bahamas (COB), which, within a decade, in close affiliation with the UWI and several U.S. schools, had more or less assimilated all tertiary-level teaching, including technical and teacher training, providing university-level and associate degree courses, among them those in such relevant subjects as hotel management and catering. The COB was also, along with the Department of Archives, to lead the way in the promotion of black, West Indian, and Bahamian history, including a growing emphasis on social history topics and oral history methods.[69]

Most of the problems of Bahamian education under the PLP stemmed from the very rapidity of its expansion and from underfunding once the 1960s economic boom passed and budgetary allotments failed to keep pace with the bulge in the school-age population—itself the product of those optimistic years. Undoubtedly mistakes were made through overenthusiasm, inexperience, and mismanagement. Among them were the building of several extremely expensive experimental primary schools in New Providence based on United States models and unproven theories. The overexpanded, unprestigious, and unrewarding Education Ministry, moreover, was from the beginning one of the least efficient of the new ministries. The overwhelming problem, however, was the continuing shortage of willing and able Bahamian teachers. Though the number of teaching candidates multiplied sixfold within a decade, the preference of the more able high school graduates for the professions and training abroad was signaled by the fact that the proportion of entrants to the teaching colleges with the original requirement of five "O" level examination passes had fallen within ten years from 90 to less than 10 percent. Just as symbolic was the unpopularity and failure of the second training college, which—though it closed ostensibly for reasons of expense—trainee teachers, especially from New Providence, saw, with some justification, as an inferior institution set on a backward Out Island almost like a Bahamian gulag.

It was an unfortunate irony that an educational system idealistically dedicated to Bahamianization from the grass-roots level remained even more dependent on expatriates than the economy as a whole. The expatriate teachers, who were mainly white Britons with a minority of Canadians and black West Indians (the latter mostly in Out Island posts) enjoyed tax-free salaries up to twice what they received at home and generally more than their Bahamian counterparts. But they did not enjoy job security beyond the terms of their contracts, were constrained by the increasing restrictions against expatriates, and understandably were rarely attuned to the ideals of the new Bahamian order. Undoubtedly, too, the compensatory rhetoric of black power and Bahamianization made life difficult in the classroom and staffroom as well as outside school for all expatriate teachers. Many of those who were not already timeservers or racists were soon disillusioned by the conditions, gave less than satisfactory value, were accordingly resented, and left the Bahamas with neither the proud achievements nor the fond memories of such pioneers as Jack Ford of Abaco.

Bahamianization and Crisis in Freeport-Lucaya

In no area of the Bahamas was the conflict between the idealistic demand for Bahamianization and the reality of a continuing dependence on expatriates and foreign capital more apparent than in Freeport-Lucaya. The part the casino revelations had played in the PLP victory made it inevitable that there would be both demands for greater government control and nervousness approaching panic on the part of Freeport-Lucaya residents and licensees. Matters were not helped by the worldwide recession that began in 1969 and deepened in 1970 and the rumors that Wallace Groves was pulling out and that all his assets in Grand Bahama were on the auction block. What actually happened was more complicated but almost as disconcerting. Groves did resign as he approached seventy in July 1970, but by that time majority ownership of the Port Authority and Development Company had already changed hands and was soon to undergo another almost equally obscure mutation.

Despite his denials of an impending sale only a month earlier, Wallace Groves announced in February 1968 (on the eve of the Bahamian general election) that the Port Authority and Development Company were merging with Benguet Consolidated, a giant mining company based in the Philippines and listed on the New York Stock Exchange. Despite the suspicion that Freeport might be falling under the control of the corrupt Marcos regime, the majority of licensees welcomed the opportunity to buy shares for the first time and the rules that decreed that New York Stock Exchange–listed companies' actions be public and regulated. Even the subsequent splitting of the Grand Bahama operations from Benguet's mining concerns by the creation of a Panamanian holding company called Inter-Continental Diversified was not resisted because the latter was also listed and traded on the New York Stock Exchange. The licensees were less happy, though, when it was revealed that the Bahamas government has used the Benguet merger both to buy into the company (with a 7.5 percent million-dollar stake) and to insist on greater government surveillance of Freeport-Lucaya. Henceforward, the Port Authority was to consult with Nassau over town planning and layout, any change in utility charges, the exclusion of persons, and—most contentious of all—the licensing of new business enterprises. Against initial resistance from the Marcos regime (which held up ratification until early in 1969), the Bahamian government also insisted on the right to audit the Port Authority's books and to appoint a director to the boards of the Port Authority and the new parent company.[70]

In the first phase of PLP rule, new projects were begun, most notably the opening of the refinery, the groundbreaking for a film studio, and the construction by Firth-Cleveland of the tallest building in the Bahamas, a nineteen-story apartment block. The Freeport-Lucaya authorities also made diplomatic overtures toward the new government, such as inviting Marguerite Pindling, the premier's wife, to launch the fourteen-thousand-ton ferry–cruise ship MV *Freeport* in Germany. At the beginning of 1969, however, the Freeport-Lucaya licensees became agitated when all work permits were called in for reissue and the payment of a fee, and the government tightened up procedures regarding the payment of customs duties and the rounding up and deportation of illegal immigrants. The Freeport-Lucaya Chamber of Commerce claimed that the government was infringing licensees' rights under the Hawksbill Creek Agreement, threatened to go to arbitration, and provocatively retained the maverick Randol Fawkes (no longer minister of labor) as legal counsel. In face of what Peter Barratt has called the Licensees' Revolt, Prime Minister Pindling made one of his most incisive and important speeches at Pinder's Point in September 1969. "In this city where, regrettably, almost anything goes," he stated, "some economic opportunities have come to Bahamians . . . [but they] nevertheless are still the victims of an unbending social order which if it now refuses to bend must be broken."[71]

At the following PLP convention, token support for the licensees by the two Grand Bahama MHAs was silenced and Prime Minister Pindling promised to speed up the Bahamianization of Freeport-Lucaya. In February 1970, the Port Authority declared that at the insistence of the licensees it would pay the legal fees for all arbitration proceedings. Within hours, the government countered what it saw as an act of defiance by an announcement that it was moving to amend the Hawksbill Creek Agreement in respect of "the sovereign right of the Bahamas to control immigration," passing an act to this effect the following month. Many longtime Freeport residents found that they could not obtain work permits, and Bahamian customs and immigration officials became noticeably more officious. The damaged morale of foreign residents was exacerbated by the serious downturn in the economy and consequent social problems. The slump in tourist arrivals and land sales was accompanied by the flight of some licensees and the bankruptcy of others. Among the business failures were the largest plumbing firm and the chief local mortgagor, the Freeport Savings and Loan Association, which was saved only by a takeover by First National City Bank. Layoffs and unemployment led to friction between labor and management and to a wave of petty larcenies, emphasizing the absence of adequate policing.[72]

In September 1970 a royal commission chaired by Sir Hugh Wooding, former chief justice of Trinidad, was appointed to examine the critical state of Freeport-Lucaya and its relationship to the rest of the Bahamas. The thorough and judicious Wooding Report was published in March 1971. The right of the Bahamas government to control immigration was affirmed, for security reasons as well as to give job priority for qualified Bahamians. It was revealed that 99 percent of sales of real estate had been to non-Bahamians. Of 1,400 current Freeport licenses, only 155 were held by Bahamians. Of the labor force, only 34 percent was Bahamian, of clerical workers 22 percent, of administrators, executives, and managers, 14 percent, and of professionals and technicians, a mere 11 percent. The report recommended that work permits should be granted to expatriates only if no qualified Bahamian was available and only for as long as it took to train one. The Port Authority was reminded of its contractual obligation "to train Bahamian-born persons to fill positions of employment," and the report announced that certain unnamed licensees had agreed to contribute an initial $1 million and $250,000 a year for a training and educational fund. It also encouraged the government to provide more scholarships for Bahamians in key areas of shortage: business management, accountancy, engineering, and surveying.

For what was often advertised as a model city for the Bahamas, Freeport-Lucaya exhibited some, if not all, of the problems familiar in Nassau and its hinterland. Although the Wooding Report concluded that the descriptions of a crime wave in Freeport-Lucaya were exaggerated, it did recommend ground rules for better policing and the establishment of a prison. It criticized the Port Authority for failure to live up to its promises regarding low-cost housing and agriculture, pointing out that the obligation to provide a thousand housing units had not been fulfilled and that because of the failure of local farming projects the bill for imported foodstuffs was a stunning $47 million a year.

The general conclusions of the report, though, were positive. It stated that Freeport-Lucaya stood as "a monument to the vision, the optimism and industry" of its founder, Wallace Groves. It pointed out that the Bahamas government did not wish to obstruct Freeport-Lucaya's development but merely to change its direction. It said nothing about the often mooted devolution of local authority but recommended more dialogue between government and local representatives. Above all, however, the Wooding commissioners affirmed in conclusion that Freeport-Lucaya, "not being a foreign outpost but an integral part of the Bahamas community, should carry the Bahamian image, maintain a Bahamian loyalty, promote Bahamian security and uplift the Bahamian economy."[73]

Honeymoon Over: Depression and Discord, 1970–1973

Statements of moderate principles and intentions were all very well, but they could not in themselves restore investors' confidence, any more than they could reverse the downward trend in the world economy that began in 1969. Though Freeport-Lucaya was the area most obviously affected, the early 1970s were a period of economic and political crisis for the Bahamas as a whole. The record number of tourist arrivals in 1969 was followed by a slump that was made worse because tourists had less to spend. Despite ever-increasing amounts spent promoting tourism, the number of arrivals, after a small recovery in 1971, slipped again in the mid-1970s and did not made a substantial surge again until 1978, when the increase in the proportion of cruise passengers and "package" tourists over the more lucrative "stopover" and individual visitors resulted in a further decline in average spending in the Bahamas. The government did add to its revenue by taxing the casinos, but almost certainly the amount taxed was less than that drained out of the Bahamian economy by being alternatively spent in the casinos and associated hotels to the profit of their foreign owner-operators. The opponents of gambling such as the Bahamas Christian Council argued that despite government auditing attempts and regulations that decreed that no Bahamian should play the casinos or even be a croupier, the casinos were also inherently demoralizing, offering illusory promises of unearned wealth and temptations of corruption that far outweighed the benefits of ancillary employment or increased government revenue.

As the quality and tone of tourism were being lowered by attempts to make the Bahamas a kind of subtropical Atlantic City, so the reputation of Bahamian offshore banking was eroded by the government's unfortunate combination of slackness and interference and by the infiltration of less than impeccable financial operators, money, and methods. Several of the weaker banks failed in 1970, and others, alarmed by hints of changes in government policies (and perhaps by incipient corruption) transferred to more efficient, reputable, and safer jurisdictions, notably Bermuda and the Cayman Islands. For a time, their place was filled by one of the sinister giants of international malfeasance, Robert Vesco. A fugitive from the U.S. Securities Exchange Commission who, as later transpired, was engaged in stripping the huge assets of Investors' Overseas Services, Vesco bought up a Nassau bank, Butler's, as the linchpin of his operations. Renaming Butler's the Bahamas Commonwealth Bank and claiming that it could become a truly national bank, Vesco virtually bought himself safety from extradition and earned local popularity by spreading around some $25 million in investments and soft personal loans before moving on to Panama, Costa Rica and (somewhat bizarrely) Cuba in the late 1970s and 1980s.[74]

A more immediately shocking occurrence was the sudden collapse of Bahamas Airways on October 9, 1970, with the loss of eight hundred jobs. The ostensible reason was the refusal of the Bahamas government to take up BOAC's offer to sell a majority stake in a losing operation. Rumor had it, though, that BOAC's decision to pull out was precipitated by the overambitious plans of Everett Bannister, a personal friend of Prime Minister Pindling and alleged associate of Robert Vesco, to form a rival private airline. Bannister's Bahamas World Airline was formed in December 1970, but underfunding, lack of expertise, and, above all, the failure to obtain authorization for scheduled international flights meant inevitable failure and liquidation within two years. The chief losers were the Out Islands, which for three years were deprived of the regular air service on which they had come to rely. During this chaotic period of free enterprise, two other small independent local carriers, Out Island Airways and Flamingo, tried but failed to fill the gap, and it was not until Bahamasair was formed as the government-sponsored national airline in 1973—with permission for scheduled flights between the Bahamas and the United States—that reliable and adequate air service was restored to the Out Islands.[75]

Such failures and barely concealed scandals led to the suspicion that too many in government were intent on feathering their own nests rather than tackling basic ills. Accusations that while increasingly authoritarian, the new regime was ideologically null and in practical terms little different from its predecessor (and less polished) did as much as economic woes to place the PLP and its leader under stress. In fact, by trying to continue to satisfy a majority, Pindling and the PLP faced mounting attacks from left and right. Labor leaders and party radicals accused them of reneging on election promises and falling short on reforms or went further and demanded a revolutionary rather than reformist posture. That Randol Fawkes should play his usual gadfly role within the labor movement was no more than a familiar nuisance, but young socialist idealists—anticolonialist admirers of black power activists and Fidel Castro's Cuba—were also increasingly disaffected and disruptive. In its earlier phase, the PLP had been positively energized by the ginger group called the National Committee for Positive Action, but that body's successor, Unicomm, was often politically embarrassing in its extremist rhetoric. Fortunately for the PLP, however, Unicomm was neutralized when its most extreme members eventually left the party to form the tiny Vanguard Nationalist and Socialist Party.[76]

Far more damaging to the PLP were the defections toward the right, which gradually led to the reorganization of the parliamentary opposition. The process began at the party convention in October 1970, when Cecil Wallace-Whitfield attacked "creeping totalitarianism," asked whether the PLP had "room in it for the questioning youth or only for a few of the old-timers and hordes of bootlickers and yes-men," and resigned from his ministerial post by quoting Martin Luther King: "Free, free at last, my soul is free at last." Three other ministers resigned or were sacked. A few weeks later, when Randol Fawkes introduced a no-confidence motion listing the Bahamas Airways failure and several other conflict-of-interest matters, eight PLP members (including the four former ministers) voted with the UBP and two others pointedly stayed away. The eight rebels were suspended from the PLP for two years but hesitated to make a complete break, staying in the House and calling themselves the Free PLP. Within a year, however (somewhat chastened by a massive by-election defeat), they had come to terms with the few remaining UBP members and formed a new party called the Free National Movement (FNM). This became the official parliamentary opposition early in 1972, in time for the next general election.[77]

The beleaguered government took strenuous and sometimes chancy measures to resolve its manifold problems, not least of which were survey findings that three-quarters of the houses in Bain Town still had no running water, that 85 percent of Over the Hill incomes went for rent and food, and that a quarter of tourists were dissatisfied with service in hotels and disinclined to return to the Bahamas. In March 1971 the government introduced price controls on food, against the opposition of black businessmen as well as Bay Street members of the UBP and accusations by Wallace-Whitfield that it constituted incipient communism. The announcement of massive borrowing to improve social services and plans to introduce pensions likewise led to accusations of financial improvidence and warnings of the dangers of stagflation—that is, of rampant inflation in a stagnant economy—or of the more specific horrors of an income tax.[78]

The institution of a campaign of courtesy toward tourists was more widely applauded, though at least one writer emphasized that there should be no return to the cringing forelock-tugging of the past and that white Americans should not expect Bahamians to be servile like southern American blacks.[79] More contentious were the continuing problems of Bahamian nationality and the pressures placed on expatriates. The first roundups and deportations of illegal Haitian immigrants aroused slight sympathy, but the treatment of Belongers and licensed workers was much more criticized. In July 1971, Belongers not continually resident for twenty years were arbitrarily charged $500, and the fees for work permits were raised substantially. Expatriate workers now had to pay an initial $250, plus an annual fee varying from $25 for laborers and domestics to $500 for professionals and managers. Permits were not to be renewed beyond five years except in special circumstances. Later in the year, the government announced that non-Bahamians without special skills would be weeded out, that non-Bahamian husbands of Bahamian women would not be given the same residence rights as the non-Bahamian wives of Bahamian men, and that Turks and Caicos Islanders would not receive the preferred status their government had requested. In November 1971 the general policy of the government was said to be to prevent large numbers of expatriates from settling permanently because they were likely to "exert considerable change which would be alien to the traditional social and political norms of the population."[80]

Symbolic Climax: Bahamian Independence, 1973

Astutely, Prime Minister Pindling and the PLP simplified the issues and deferred many problems by concentrating the minds of the people on the question of national independence. Though there had not been hitherto a widespread demand for immediate independence, Pindling announced in the speech opening the legislature on June 14, 1971, that independence would be sought immediately after the next general election, which was brought forward by six months to September 1972. An official Green Paper published in March 1972 eloquently laid out the government's arguments.[81] PLP members dutifully rallied to the cause, while the parliamentary opposition, somewhat wrongfooted, argued that while it was not against independence on principle and in due course, the Bahamas was not yet ready for it.

Much the strongest opposition to independence came from Abaco, where the traditional loyalty to the British Crown was reinforced by the whites' fears of reverse discrimination and the complaints by almost all Abaconians of Nassau's relative neglect of Abaco since 1968. Abaconians claimed that though their island and its cays provided $3 million a year to government in taxation revenue, it received less than a third back in local expenditures—specifically citing Nassau's delay in providing promised high schools and a tarmac surface for the Abaco Highway. Errington Watkins, a black UBP supporter, and Leonard Thompson, the white developer of Treasure Cay, formed an organization called the Greater Abaco Council and sent a petition to the queen, said to be signed by three-quarters of adult Abaconians. It asked that in the event of Bahamian independence Abaco (along with Grand Bahama if its people wished) be allowed to separate and continue to be a British dependency, much like Bermuda, the Turks and Caicos, or Cayman Islands. The petition fell on stony ground when the Commonwealth Relations Office responded that the British government (as the queen's advisers) could only consider applications that came officially from the Bahamas government. Watkins, Thompson, and the Greater Abaco Council were therefore compelled to wait and see whether the 1972 election would give them a mandate for further action.

As the 1972 election drew closer, the government attempted to offset an estimated shortfall of 13 percent in the budget with grandiose plans to revive Bahamian agriculture and fisheries. Bahamian pride was invoked (and security reinforced) by the creation of an armed marine division of the Bahamas Police. Moderating the effects of a minatory Conspiracy Act passed in March 1971, in a symbolic gesture of togetherness it was announced that the Out Islands would henceforward be known as the Family Islands. The PLP government also made its bravest gamble with public opinion by announcing that the casinos would be more heavily taxed, progressively Bahamianized, and fully taken over by the government by 1977.[82]

The general election held on September 19, 1972, was an astounding victory for the PLP, a vindication of its preelection tactics, and above all an unequivocal mandate for Bahamian independence. For the first time the opposition openly acknowledged that the Bahamas belonged to the black majority and attempted to fight the election on issues other than race: only seven of the FNM candidates in the thirty-eight constituencies were whites (little more than the statistical proportion of whites in the Bahamian population).[83] The PLP, though, managed to submerge its failures or convey that they were the result of factors beyond its control and sustained its image as the authentic black peoples' party confronted by an opportunistic coalition of UBP die-hards and PLP renegades. Attacking FNM "terrorism," it stressed national unity and campaigned on the slogan "Peace, Love, Prosperity."[84]

In the consequent landslide, the FNM won only nine seats to the PLP's twenty-nine. Every one of the eight former PLP candidates for the FNM was defeated, as were Randol Fawkes and the other seven candidates of the reconstituted Commonwealth Labour Party and all nine Independents. Only one seat was lost by the PLP to the FNM—Crooked Island, where Basil Kelly had stood down in favor of a black FNM candidate. Overall, the election proved that only in constituencies where white voters were in a majority could an anti-PLP candidate succeed. Even the one exception, St. John's (northern Eleuthera), was equivocal, since the white FNM victor over the Speaker, Alvin Braynen (Independent), did not have to face an official PLP candidate.[85]

Perhaps the most surprising result was that the PLP won three of the four seats for Grand Bahama and Abaco. The total vote was close, 3,408 to 3,310, and in Abaco 62 percent of the voters favored the FNM. Errington Watkins won easily at Marsh Harbour (covering the southern Abaco mainland and white-dominated cays), but the PLP retained its two Grand Bahama seats, and Leonard Thompson lost Cooper's Town (northern Abaco) by a mere four votes because, he claimed, of the PLP's gerrymandering that had attached the all-black suburbs of Marsh Harbour to Cooper's Town.[86]

Though dashed by the election result and even more by the FNM's decision to accept independence on the grounds that the election result had indicated the majority will, the Greater Abaco Council redoubled its efforts to keep Abaco within the British Empire. To his eloquent disgust, Errington Watkins was expelled from the FNM, but allies and advisers were obtained from the Tory ranks in the British Parliament, representation was obtained for a multiracial delegation from Abaco at the London independence talks, and the separatists, now reorganized as the Council for a Free Abaco, drew up a second petition—this time signed by half the Abaco voters—aimed at influencing the debates on the Bahamas Independence Bill in the British House of Commons and Lords. Though the two original activists, Watkins and Thompson, resolutely opposed armed revolution, more ardent separatists, led by Chuck Hall and Arnold Albury, opened up negotiations with the virulently anticommunist arms supplier Mitchell WerBell of Defense Systems International, Powder Springs, Georgia, the swashbuckling British mercenary soldier (and Conservative MP) Colonel Colin "Mad Mitch" Mitchell, and the eccentric millionaire Michael Oliver of Carson City, Nevada, who had already made an unsuccessful attempt to set up an independent "libertarian" state on a Tongan atoll.[87]

The Abaco separatists were disappointed by the authorities in London and outflanked by the government in Nassau. London's attitude was probably best expressed in the testy remark allegedly made to Leonard Thompson by Lord Balneil, the minister in charge of negotiations: "We just want to get rid of you, rid of you, we'd like to get rid of the colonies."[88] At the same time, Nassau's political skill and confidence were demonstrated by some of Prime Minister Pindling's most emollient speeches and by the calculated gamble that allowed a well-publicized visit to Abaco by "Mad Mitch" Mitchell on the eve of independence which led Mitchell to ridicule and disown the alleged revolutionaries.[89] Abaco separatism did not die with Bahamian independence, but it became increasingly desperate, divided, and futile, containing elements of farce. Reorganized as the Abaco Independence Movement (AIM), which spurned Westminster as resolutely as it had rejected Nassau, it was most active in the mid-1970s and had its own well-written newspaper. But the AIM was discredited, the *Abaco Independent* ceased publication in 1977, and the separatist movement finally petered out when the member of Parliament representing AIM's successor, the Abaco Home Rule Movement (successful by four votes in 1977) was defeated and replaced by the first white Abaconian PLP member, Edison Key, in 1982.[90]

Meanwhile, having stymied the separatists and obtained the official approval of the FNM, Pindling and the PLP had calmly but triumphantly led the Bahamas into independence. Following a White Paper laying down the principles and format of independence published immediately after the general election, government departments frantically geared up to face logistical problems such as the formation of a proper defense force and diplomatic corps and the renegotiation of existing treaties.[91] The multiparty Independence Conference held at Clarence House in London during December 1972 was mostly concerned not with principles but with the minutiae of the new constitution. The consequent Bahamas Independence Bill passed its third reading in the British House of Commons by seventy-four to four and in the House of Lords by fifty to eleven, becoming law on June 12, 1973.

The independence of the Bahama Islands, arguably the climactic achievement of the Bahamian people, came into effect at midnight on Sunday, July 9, 1973. The Union Jack was slowly lowered to the sound of the Last Post, and in its place, to the jaunty beat of the new national anthem, "Lift up your heads to the Rising Sun,

Independence Day, July 10, 1973. Prime Minister Lynden Pindling displays the constitutional document to the people while Prince Charles ponders. Courtesy of Bahamas Archives.

Bahamaland," the new national flag was hoisted proudly, its black triangle on stripes of aquamarine and gold said to represent "the vigour and force of a united people determined to develop the rich resources of land and sea." The following morning, a dramatic ceremony was held at Nassau's Clifford Park in which Prince Charles, the heir to the British throne, handed over the independence instruments to Prime Minister Pindling, who immediately held them up to the crowd like a Wimbledon champion showing off his trophy. In symbolic counterpoint, Sunday's official national day of prayer and thanksgiving and Monday's ceremony were followed by a joyful Independence Junkanoo on Tuesday morning.[92]

Forgetting for the euphoric moment the unresolved problems of nationality, color, and class as easily as those of the economy, Bahamians endorsed the proud claim of one of the chief framers of their brand new constitution: "We have gone out of the way to protect the rights of the under-privileged while not losing sight of the human apprehensions of the privileged. We have endeavoured to give equality under the law to the majorities and the minorities, the rich and the poor alike. We have preserved and affirmed the fundamental rights and freedoms of the individual, irrespective of race, place of origin, political affiliation, creed or sex, subject only to the rights and freedoms of others and the public interest."[93]

Besides its noble declaration of fundamental rights and freedoms, the document which Lynden Pindling proudly displayed to the Bahamian people affirmed that though matters of internal security, external defense, and foreign affairs had finally been handed over to the elected government, the Commonwealth of the Bahamas remained resolutely within the British Commonwealth, with the queen as head of state. The monarch, however, was represented by a governor-general, who, it was tacitly assumed, would henceforward be a Bahamian, appointed on the advice of the ruling party. Fittingly, the first holder of the post was Sir Milo Butler, hero of the PLP's struggle and outspoken advocate for ordinary black Bahamians since the Burma Road Riots of 1942—though it was Lynden Pindling, the indispensable helmsman, who spoke at the United Nations when the Bahamas was admitted as the UN's 138th member on September 18, 1973.[94]

III

On the Eve of the Twenty-First Century: The Present and Future of the Bahamian Past, 1973–1999

Pauline Davis, Savatheda Fynes, Chandra Sturrup, and Eldece Clarke, Olympic Games silver medalists in the sprint relay, Atlanta 1995. Debbie Ferguson was alternate on the squad, running in the preliminary heats. Photograph courtesy of *Nassau Guardian*.

11

A Quarter-Century of Independence: Events, Changes, and Their Social Effects, 1973–1999

Conspectus

Early in 1993, following the PLP's defeat at the polls after six consecutive electoral victories and twenty-five years in power, former prime minister Sir Lynden Pindling was asked to summarize his party's achievements. "Heading the list," he claimed

> was to have convinced a subjective, submissive, retarded black population that they were, in fact, somebody, and they could do some things and achieve some things. They were convinced to see the pride in themselves. Self-reliance developed and they did, in fact, achieve stature. I think that was one of the primary psychological goals which we set out to achieve. Secondly, now having done that, was to move from a colonial state to a state of national independence in a nonviolent way and develop a thriving democracy in the process. Then, thirdly . . . would be to move what would have been a majority of the population living in an unhappy state and move them into the middle class. This has happened with most phenomenal growth during the period.[1]

Not even Pindling's bitterest opponents would deny the PLP's role in ending the long political dominance of the white minority in 1967 and of making the final break with British imperialism in 1973. Despite his enemies' accusations that he was a dictator heading a party devoted to a spoils system, his concession speech in August 1992 had a magnanimous, almost noble, ring: "The people of this great little democracy have spoken in a most dignified and elegant manner. And the voice of the people is the voice of God."[2] The PLP's quarter-century in power, moreover, coincided with remarkable socioeconomic changes and developments in Bahamian consciousness.

Many, though, would take issue with aspects of Pindling's 1993 laudatory self-evaluation. Both his disparagement of the "submissive, retarded" psyche of Bahamian blacks before the PLP was created and his suggestion that they were only now proudly self-reliant were clearly exaggerated, though not so hyperbolic as the claim that the PLP had been instrumental in moving almost all Bahamians out of poverty into the "middle class." There certainly had been phenomenal growth, but most commentators would attribute it to factors other than partisan politics, achieved, indeed, despite rather than because of black majority rule. Pindling's statement ignored the influence of internal and external forces beyond the control of legislation: demographic shifts, migrations, world market forces, and radical improvements in communications.

Above all, though, Pindling's statement verged on the euphoric. It ignored, as we cannot, the manifold problems still besetting the independent Commonwealth of the Bahamas, whether or not they are attributable to, or remediable by, political action. Accordingly, this last part of our history of the Bahamian people will look, as dispassionately as possible, successively, at political and diplomatic events since 1973, trends in economics and education, demographic changes, material improvements, and the problems posed by disease, drugs, crime, and the need to diversify the economy and the ways that these have, and have not, wrought changes on Bahamian traditional lifeways and culture. Finally, the process of conscious Bahamianization and dealing with illegal immigrants, particularly Haitians, the preservation of traditions and historical artefacts, and the conscious creation of a national myth will be described in a way intended to answer the crucial question of what it is to be a Bahamian at the end of the second millennium.

Establishing a Nation: A Diplomatic Corps and Foreign Policy

As a newly independent country with limited resources, the Bahamas had the problems of aligning itself according to its new status and the wishes of its people, while setting up a diplomatic corps virtually from scratch. Having its own say in issues that concerned its interests was, indeed, one of the chief arguments for independence, and on at least two counts 1973 was a fitting year to make the crucial move. As Deputy Prime Minister A. D. Hanna argued in January 1971:

> We are not free to make all our own trade or other treaties with other nations that would be beneficial to the Bahamas; we are powerless to extend our national boundaries . . . or our fishing zone beyond the three mile limit and we watch idly by in anger and sadness while the poachers come, as they did this season, and lay bare our craw-fishing grounds. We watched without a voice while the British and the United States Government agreed to drop deadly poisonous gases off our shores. We have no power to negotiate or conclude international air routes between the Bahamas and any other country.[3]

Later in the same year, Prime Minister Pindling explained to the Bahamian Students' Association at the Jamaican campus of the University of the West Indies:

> Not only is 1973 the year when the United Kingdom is due to become a full member of the European Economic Community, but we now see that it is also the year when the most important world conference on the Law of the Sea will be held. . . . It is my view that the Bahamas would be at a great political and economic disadvantage if at that time it were not independent, and theretofore not able to fully put its own case, and not able to decide for itself what decisions it must take in its own best interest. Such are the implications.[4]

The Bahamas had had a nominal Ministry of External Affairs since 1969, but it did not function like other branches of the executive. The prime minister combined the external affairs portfolio with his other duties, but most important decisions were handled by London through an expatriate secretary to the governor (external affairs), and the quasi-ministry was, at most, regarded as a training ground for future diplomats. The Bahamas' only representation abroad was tourist offices in England, Germany, Canada, and eight American cities and a High Commission in London, consisting solely of a commissioner without any staff. As independence approached, however, the prime minister gave up the external affairs portfolio to Paul L. Adderley (who was to serve in the post more than twelve years), the governor's external affairs secretary was temporarily seconded to the ministry for training the staff, and the permanent secretaryship was given to Oris Russell, a white Bahamian regarded as the most accomplished and professional local civil servant, who continued to serve the PLP government as loyally as he had the UBP until his retirement in 1982.[5]

Despite much energy and enthusiasm, the Bahamas greeted independence with a largely inexpert diplomatic corps, hampered by a minuscule budget and inheriting a legacy of nearly three hundred treaties previously negotiated in its name. Following the precedent of other newly independent Commonwealth countries, the Bahamas had the privilege of retaining those former treaties which it favored as well as the right to renegotiate those it did not, but the shakedown process was complex and protracted, especially because of the need for new treaties.[6] The somewhat amateur aspect of early Bahamian diplomacy—if not the will to thumb its nose at its former masters—was exemplified by the 1973 appointment to the key position of high commissioner in London of the maverick white Bahamian Alvin R. Braynen, whose defection from the UBP had led to the ascendancy of the PLP in 1967 and who was said to have welcomed independence because it would rid the Bahamas of "obnoxious Englishmen." Candidly acknowledging that his appointment was a patronage reward for services rendered to the government, Braynen ran his office with a genial and benign insouciance. Claiming that in his four years' service he received only one letter from the Ministry of External Affairs, he did more or less as he pleased, much like an old-fashioned Out Island commissioner, making decisions pragmatically and only when absolutely necessary, acting as host to visiting Bahamian dignitaries, distributing largesse to needy students, throwing the occasional party, promoting tourism, and recruiting. When he returned to the Bahamas, he reported not to his ministry but directly to the prime minister.[7]

The foreign policy of the new Bahamian nation can be generally characterized as expressing the desire to seem completely independent of its former imperial master without falling under the alternative sway of its dominant neighbor to the west and north or, more subtly, to downplay both the lingering cultural, historical, and sentimental ties with Britain and the geopolitical and economic realities that tie the destiny of the Bahamas to that of the United States. Such motives explain the vital importance to the Bahamas (as to many similar small new nations) of its role within the United Nations, its solidarity with the so-called Third World or developing nations, and its adherence, at least rhetorically, to the principles of nonalignment. Actual foreign policy decisions, though, have always tended to be affected by ambiguities if not contradictions. The Bahamas joined most important international organizations that came under the umbrella of the UN or UNESCO, or were unequivocally neutral, soon after independence. But it delayed its membership in the Organization of American States (OAS) for almost a decade, largely because that organization was perceived to be virtually run by the United States. Conversely, though much lip service was given to the need for links with other Caribbean nations, particularly those within the Commonwealth, membership in the Caribbean Community (CARICOM) was delayed even longer, not only because of the fear that the Bahamas might be financially drained or flooded by people from poorer and more populous countries in the region but because some of these countries (particularly Jamaica under Michael Manley) were thought to be dangerously left-leaning if not, like Cuba and Guyana, actually socialist.[8]

In this respect, the Bahamas was exhibiting its ideological correlation with the United States, as well as its dependence on American tourists, investors, and military protection in the event of a foreign attack. Its continued fidelity to the ideal of the Commonwealth and to some British institutions and symbols, particularly the monarchy, was similarly practical, if more abstract. The Commonwealth possessed the intangible qualities of being a sort of club for consultation and cooperation, incorporating nations of all sizes and stages of development, from North and South alike, and it served both as an alternative or supplement to the United Nations and something of a counterweight to the United States. Theoretical arguments can be made for the value of retaining a hereditary figurehead as head of state just as they can for the retention of the Judicial Committee of the British Privy Council as the ultimate court of appeal, though the most important reasons that the Bahamas resolutely remains a monarchy are that the majority of the people continue to relish the associated pomp, circumstance, and charisma and their leaders mostly value the monarch as the fount of reputable honors. Though awarded only on the advice of the government, these include, besides the ultimate accolade of knighthood, titles that retain references to the long-defunct British Empire.[9]

The pragmatic heterogeneity of Bahamian external relations, as well as the ideal climate and facilities the Bahamian capital possesses for large international gatherings (not to mention the media attention brought to the country and the kudos accruing to the ruling political party) are shown by the fact that besides hosting Her Majesty Queen Elizabeth II five times (1966, 1975, 1977, 1985, and 1994) and sundry lesser royals on other occasions, Nassau has been the meeting place for the Commonwealth Heads of State (1985) and the plenary sessions of CARICOM (1991) and of the OAS (1992). Several diplomatic episodes or events, however, have had much more direct relevance to the Bahamas a fledgling nation and people. Most notable of these have been involvement in the evolution of a new Law of the Sea in the mid-1970s, the formation of the Bahamian Defence Force in 1976, the serious international incident of the sinking of HMBS *Flamingo* by Cuban warplanes in 1980, and the effects on Bahamas–United States relations of the activities of Cuban-American crawfish poachers and Drug Enforcement Agency (DEA) agents in the 1970s and 1980s, the invasion of Grenada in 1983, and the long-standing question of U.S. bases in the islands.

Bahamian participation in the negotiations of the third United Nations Commission on the Law of the Sea (UNCLOS III), which started in 1973 and were not concluded until the convention signed at Montego Bay, Jamaica, in December 1982, was of fundamental importance in establishing the territorial extent of the new nation and its rights over adjacent waters and the sea floor. But it had an even wider significance in showing how this new nation of less than a quarter-million people could play an effective role in world diplomacy and, in cooperation with similar former colonial small nations, argue and sustain not only its own interests but general principles, even against the interests of the major powers.

Geographically, the Bahamas is unique, being an archipelago scattered over one hundred thousand miles of sea, only 6 percent of which is land, but a very large proportion is shallow banks. As a colony, it was subject to the three-mile territorial limit agreed to by Britain in 1878, as well as to the recognition of international shipping lanes and navigation rights established during that age of laissez-faire (or laissez-aller). Following the lead of Trinidad-Tobago and other newly independent Caribbean states, the Bahamas declared a twelve-mile exclusive fisheries zone in 1969 and talked of extending it to two hundred miles. It also strongly supported the idea put forward by Malta in 1967 that a small insular nation's adjacent seabed be protected to avoid exploition by more technically advanced nations and the "archipelagic principle" that a nation's territory be delimited outward from a baseline drawn between each of its outlying islands. For these reasons, the Bahamas naturally gravitated toward the "archipelagic bloc" of delegates from the Philippines, Mauritius, Fiji, Tonga, and Indonesia when UNCLOS III opened in 1973.[10]

After protracted debates, conducted for the Bahamas under the direction of Minister of Foreign Affairs Paul Adderley but largely on the spot by the chief Bahamian delegate, George Stewart, the archipelagic principle was established in 1978. It stated that a country might employ as territorial baselines "any non-navigable continuous reefs and shoals lying between the outermost point" of its "dry land or drying reefs." The Bahamas, moreover, gained the key additional concession (probably based on the original grant to the Lord Proprietors in 1670, which included banks as well as cays) that the huge Bahama Banks be specifically recognized as dry land for the purposes of drawing archipelagic baselines and calculating the land-to-water ratio. The Bahamas thus gained the privilege of being defined an archipelagic nation denied to the Philippines, as well as a land and sea extension greater than that of any Caribbean island nation, including Cuba.[11]

In 1977, five years before UNCLOS III concluded, the Bahamas declared a two-hundred-mile exclusive fisheries zone under the Fisheries Resources (Jurisdiction and Conservation) Act, at the same time that the United States made a similar declaration, leading to much potential overlapping.[12] The final act of UNCLOS III, a convention signed at Montego Bay, Jamaica, in December 1982, besides establishing a twelve-mile limit to territorial waters, endorsed the principle of a two-hundred-mile exclusive economic zone, including ocean floor mineral rights. This agreement sat well with the Bahamas (because of the possibility of oil leases and royalties as well as the protection of fishing resources) but not with either the United States or the United Kingdom, both of which declined to sign the convention. Though the Bahamas did concede the free international navigation through all Bahamian sea passages inherited from colonial days, as well as the right of peaceful overflight, the 1982 convention was regarded as a victory for such ministates as the Bahamas over the major economic powers.

Regarding adjacent territories less than four hundred miles distant—the Turks and Caicos Islands, Haiti, Cuba, and the United States—the Bahamas followed the normal international practice, endorsed at Montego Bay, of tracing a median line to delimit its maritime boundaries. This line was well out into the Atlantic Ocean, through the Caicos Passage, around Great Inagua, along the middle of the Old

The Lobster Fisheries Talks, 1975. Minister of Foreign Affairs Paul Adderley forcefully puts the Bahamian case to U.S. negotiators. Courtesy of Bahamas Archives.

Bahama Channel, around Cay Sal and northward along the midline of the Florida Straits. There, however, it came into conflict with the claim of the United States to hold a special jurisdiction over its entire continental shelf, specifically, in this area, the so-called Blake Plateau, extending off the coast of Florida well within two hundred miles of the nearest Bahamian cays or reefs. This was the chief reason why the United States was not a signatory of the 1982 Montego Bay Convention. The chief immediate areas of contention, however, were the fishing grounds around the Cay Sal atoll and along the southern fringes of the Great Bahama Bank, where Bahamian interests clashed with both those of fishermen out of Florida and from the ports of another nonsignatory at Montego Bay, the United States' sworn enemy, Cuba.[13]

Though establishing the extent of Bahamian territory in international law with minimal diplomatic forces was a proud early achievement of the new nation, effectively patrolling and policing such an immense area was to prove a daunting task. In colonial times smuggling, poaching, and other forms of illegal traffic generally went undetected and the rare emergencies or territorial issues in the Out Islands—such as the suppression of the Inagua disturbances in 1937 or the arrest in 1956 of a small group of Cubans who had raised the Cuban flag on Cay Sal—were dealt with by the police based in Nassau only with great difficulty.[14] Largely because of the increase in crawfish poaching by Cuban and Cuban-American fishermen and a first awareness of the problem of illegal Haitian migration, the tiny marine division of the Bahamas Police Force formed in 1971 was greatly enlarged and detached as the maritime Bahamas Defence Force (BDF) three years after independence. Trained by officers seconded from the Royal Navy and initially provided with four fast armed motor vessels named after major Family Islands, the BDF was soon engaged in warning off and rounding up poachers, smugglers, and illegal immigrants.

At the height of the so-called Lobster War, dozens of Cuban-Americans were charged with illegal fishing within the newly declared territorial zone and their boats confiscated, and in September 1978 the Bahamas government was threatened with a $15 million damage suit when a fourteen-year-old Cuban-American boy was shot and critically wounded.[15] This incident, though, was overshadowed by the *Flamingo* episode. From December 1979, Cuban MIG fighters several times "buzzed" BDF vessels patrolling the fishing grounds of the Great Bahama Bank, especially while they were in the process of making arrests. Around 5 P.M. on Saturday, May 10, 1980, the HMBS *Flamingo* intercepted two Cuban vessels engaged in fishing some two miles south of Cay Santo Domingo, fifty miles north of the Cuban port of Gibara. The Cuban boats fled but were quickly overtaken and ordered to stop, which they did only when shots were fired across their bows. The BDF boarded the boats, arrested their eight crewmen, and towed the boats toward the nearest settlement, Duncan Town, Ragged Island.

Within an hour, two Cuban MIG fighters appeared and fired bursts of machine-gun fire to the side and in front of the *Flamingo*. When the BDF vessel did not halt, the MIGs flew off to rearm, returning an hour later. The *Flamingo* was sunk with a rocket and the crew machine-gunned as they attempted to escape in their rubber dinghies. Most of the marines made it safely to the arrested fishing vessels, but four men were lost, presumed shot and drowned.

The survivors, several of whom were slightly wounded, set one vessel adrift and escaped to Great Ragged Island with their prisoners in the other. Landing on the southern end of the cay in the early hours of Sunday morning, they walked into Duncan Town and radioed Nassau. At 9:30 A.M., before help arrived, more MIG fighters and a larger plane carried out simulated attacks on the settlement, and a Cuban helicopter briefly landed near the seized fishing boat in a vain effort to rescue the arrested fishermen. In midmorning a chartered DC-3 approached from Nassau with BDF reinforcements and police officials. The plane was harried by MIGs as it came in to land, and its departure with prisoners and wounded was delayed more than two hours by the threatening presence of Cuban planes and the helicopter. On the following morning, BDF marines readying to sail the seized fishing vessel to Nassau and a U.S. Coast Guard helicopter joining in the search for the missing men were both dangerously harassed by MIGs.[16]

Though not extensively reported in the international press and naturally downplayed by Cuba, the episode aroused great anger among all Bahamians, especially when the Cuban government suggested that the MIGs were simply counterattacking presumed pirates, called for the arrest and trial of those attacking the Cuban fishing boats, and accused the U.S. Central Intelligence Agency of setting up the incident as a provocation. The Bahamian authorities behaved impeccably in releasing the eight Cubans on an $80,000 cash bond, made a formal complaint to the UN Security Council, and demanded from Cuba a full apology, reparation for the dead marines' families, and compensation for the lost patrol boat. A high-level Cuban delegation sent to Nassau stalled and blustered for a time, but within six months the Cuban government acceded to the Bahamian demands, apologizing for "an unfortunate mistake" and paying $400,000 for each of the dead marines' families and nearly $4 million to replace HMBS *Flamingo*.[17]

Whether the Cuban government was genuinely repentent, wanted not to seem to bully smaller neighboring nations (Castro, like a lesser Joseph Stalin, preferred the image of benign elder brother or uncle to ogre), or hoped to detach the Bahamas from its close allegiance to the United States, the resolution of the *Flamingo* incident was seen as an important independent success for Bahamian national diplomacy. Since tension immediately eased around the fishing grounds and no further incidents occurred, this was seen as a tacit acknowledgment by the Cuban government of Bahamian territorial claims.

Somewhat surprisingly, though U.S.-Bahamian relations continued to have their ups and downs, Bahamian relations with Cuba steadily improved but never became really close. Though trade and private visits to Cuba remained minimal, the Bahamas never joined the American economic embargo or ban on travel there. On many occasions cultural and sporting delegations visited Cuba and a small number of Bahamians took advantage of scholarship offers to study at Cuban tertiary institutions, though delegates and students usually complained of their spartan accommodations, attempts to indoctrinate them, or that they were treated as dollar tourists. There was also considerable skepticism because scholarships were allocated through the Vanguard Party and its newspaper, both widely believed to be subsidized by the Cuban government. Whatever motives the host nation had, though, participation in festivals and international athletic contests sponsored by Cuba—in which the Bahamas often came second to its hosts—had the positive effects of promoting feelings both of Caribbean solidarity and of pride in being Bahamian.[18]

Even more important, the *Flamingo* incident served as a national rite of passage. It was a fortunately minor example of the blood baptism said to be necessary to formulate the national consciousness of all emergent nations, for the first time giving the Bahamian people an inkling of their unique place in the world and what was needed to defend it. Public demonstrations against the sinking of the *Flamingo* (boycotted by the Vanguard Party) included fervent statements about being ready to serve against national enemies, and the well-orchestrated and moving memorial service for the dead marines held at Clifford Park provided an obvious surge of patriotism and resolve. Four subsequently commissioned BDF patrol vessels were christened with the names of the lost marines. That these were no passing sentiments, moreover, is borne out by the fact that the story of the *Flamingo* and its martyrs was the basis of a nationalist opera called *Our Boys*, written by Cleophas Adderley, Winston Saunders, and Phillip Burrows and first performed in 1987.[19]

Bahamas–United States Relations in the 1970s

Relations with the United States were uneven, ideologically ambivalent, and subject to partisan politics. Besides the issues of fishing and mineral rights in disputed areas, periodic exchanges occurred over such matters as air routes and Bahamian bank secrecy laws. In most cases the U.S. government acted tactfully and did not force conclusions, particularly when the interests of American individuals and companies rather than those of the government were involved. Fishing disputes were generally left to the courts, applications for seabed exploration in disputed areas firmly deflected, air route negotiations left for resolution between interested companies and the International Air Transport Authority (IATA), and the illicit movement of money regulated internally by the U.S. Internal Revenue Service where possible. Arrangements that were mutually beneficial were usually made readily, such as the U.S. Customs and Immigration preclearance of departing tourists at Nassau and Freeport International Airports set up in 1978. Much more problematic, however, were cases involving both Bahamian sovereignty and United States strategic interests, of which much the most important were the continued existence of U.S. bases on Bahamian soil and the independent activities of U.S. agents in Bahamian waters.

The British government had conceded several tracts of Bahamian land on ninety-nine-year leases for American bases in 1940, and these concessions were greatly extended between 1950 and 1963, with little or no consultation with the Bahamian government. Long-range proving ground facilities for guided missiles were set up in Grand Bahama, Eleuthera, San Salvador, and Mayaguana (as part of an arc from Cape Canaveral that extended through Grand Turk, Antigua, and Barbados to Ascension Island in the South Atlantic), an oceanographic research station was established in Eleuthera, and, most important, the Atlantic Undersea Test and Evaluation Center (AUTEC) was located near Fresh Creek, Andros, on the mile-deep Tongue of the Ocean, for the secret testing of Polaris submarines and other sea monsters. These bases were regarded as of crucial importance by Britain as well as the United States throughout the Cold War and were accepted by the minority of Bahamians to whom they brought employment or who were convinced of the value of the protective umbrella of the United States. Most of the bases were still important for the Americans in the earlier stages of NASA's Space Shuttle program, though, with the exception of the AUTEC facility, their obvious value declined in the later 1970s, except for the surveillance of sea and air traffic approaching American shores.

Bahamians, however, were always divided on the value of the American bases and with the coming of independence saw them, at best, as bargaining counters for the receipt of privileges from the American government and at worst as invasions of sovereign territory. The most obvious benefit to the Bahamas was the provision of first-class airstrips open to civil aircraft in central Eleuthera, central Andros, San Salvador, and Mayaguana (that at Gold Rock Creek, Grand Bahama, was superfluous to Freeport's own airport) and for bringing employment and service income to certain impoverished Out Islands. Certainly, the bases had radical effects on the economy and society in their immediate areas, and for the entire islands of Mayaguana and San Salvador, as long as they operated, they were the chief sources of cash and links with the modern world.

The impact of the bases, as in New Providence during the war, was most noticeable in the earliest phase. In October 1956, for example, the commissioner at Governor's Harbour, Eleuthera, complained of the "tremendous change in conditions" the guided missile base brought to the nearest native settlement. "Most of the men from the Base frequent James Cistern because of its proximity to their living quarters," he wrote, "and more so because of the fact that a large number of prostitutes from Nassau have made this settlement their place of business." Dances were carried on all day long, the sale of liquor was booming, and there were drunken brawls even on Sundays. It was reported that 350 more American servicemen were imminently expected at the base, news of which brought more prostitutes on each mail boat. Keeping order was beyond the ability of the single local constable (second grade), and the commissioner pleaded that at least one regular police officer be sent to James Cistern to take charge.[20]

Life in distant San Salvador and Mayaguana, with far fewer inhabitants than Eleuthera and not easily within the range of Nassau's opportunistic streetwalkers, could be even more disrupted. At Abraham's Bay, Mayaguana, for example, the commissioner accused the teacher of disorderly conduct, the illicit sale of liquor, and the encouragement of prostitution among the women, many of whose husbands were away on farming contracts.[21] Some of the American personnel on long-term postings entered into liaisons with local women, a few of whom bore them colored offspring. Generally, though, the U.S. personnel, nearly all of whom were white, regarded the Bahamas Out Islands as hardship postings and treated the people as backward and primitive, if not with out and out racism.

As time went on, the U.S. authorities did what they could to restrict their men to the bases and to provide them with more frequent stateside rest and recreation periods. Certainly, all the bases had far better air connections with the United States than with the rest of the Bahamas or even with each other. Security around the most hush-hush installations—Gold Rock Creek, Grand Bahama, and the AUTEC base in Andros—was particularly tight. But near all the bases there continued to be some social interchange, valuable if intermittent employment opportunities, and the more or less licit distribution of American goods. These features were welcomed at least by the nearest natives, though more perceptive Bahamians feared the effects of the stark disparities between the living styles and material expectations of the American personnel and those of their ostensible hosts, particularly if and when the bases were to be closed. Once more in Bahamian social history, the spirit of independence was compromised by the trammels of dependency.

Worse even than the insensitive ways in which the U.S. government acquired and used its Bahamian bases was the almost casual manner in which it closed them down once they were no longer useful. As the Atlantic missile tracking stations became outmoded and the Cold War gradually faded, the U.S. government cynically made a moral point out of its national convenience by offering back to the Bahamian government the use (though not invariably the technical leaseholds) of its unwanted bases and even the possession of the installations and equipment that it would have been more costly to dismantle or remove. On San Salvador, two installations were handed over by negotiation in the 1970s; one turned for a time into the second Bahamian teacher training college, the other leased as a field research station for a consortium of American colleges. After the college closed and the field station lost sponsorship, the island suffered a bleak decade before the building of a Club Mediterrané facility in the year of the Columbian Quincentennial. Gold Rock Creek and Governor's Harbour were drastically trimmed in the 1980s, leaving the Bahamas in possession of decaying buildings and a huge inventory of outdated equipment that it had neither the will nor skill to use.[22]

Probably least fortunate of all was Mayaguana, which the Americans deserted in the late 1970s. It was left with a runway far beyond its needs and a few decaying roads but with no useful remaining facilities at the former base and a way of life hopelessly disrupted by the years of relative plenty. As Jerome Lurry-Wright showed, the 605 persons still living on the island in 1987 existed in a state of limbo, having almost lost contact with the traditional farming-fishing subsistence peasant ways but with no realistic hopes of obtaining the alternative benefits of modern life with which they had become familiar. Religion and traditional folklore still played an important part in their lives, but family life had lost its coherence, conflicts between persons and groups were endemic, crime was on the increase, and a general spirit of anomie prevailed.[23]

AUTEC and general surveillance facilities remained the chief U.S. interests in the Bahamas, and the Bahamian government carried on a long fight to sell its sovereignty in these respects as dearly as it could. As early as 1973 the Bahamas had negotiated rental payments for the bases (hitherto granted free) and obtained a $10 million loan to start the BARTAD agricultural scheme in Andros, but it later asked for increased payments and more development loans, as well as a firmer long-term commitment and guarantees of local employment. The U.S. government stood on its earlier treaty agreements and claimed that the Bahamas was not eligible for soft development loans because its people enjoyed an annual per capita income (then $2,000) more than twice the limit for U.S. foreign aid. A low point in relations was reached in 1976 when External Affairs Minister Adderley said that the United States would be asked "to disband and leave their installations" if no agreement could be reached. Two years later, Prime Minister Pindling eased the situation by announcing that the government did not intend that the United States "should get out and leave our country or anything like that" and expressed patience. Not until July 1983 was it announced that agreement had been reached in principle over the continuing leases on the AUTEC base and the greatly reduced installations in Grand Bahama, Eleuthera, and San Salvador—termed a missile tracking station, an oceanographic research center, and a navigational radar station respectively.[24]

The Drugs Agony of the Early 1980s

By this time, however, U.S.-Bahamian relations were dominated by the far more serious sovereignty issues revolving around drug trafficking through Bahamian waters to the United States. Bahamian charges of serious infringements by U.S. agents were countered by American accusations that Bahamians from ordinary civilians, lawyers, and bankers, through police, customs and immigration officials, up to senior politicians, including Prime Minister Pindling himself, were involved.

As the 1984 Commission of Inquiry revealed, the traffic in cocaine and marijuana through the Bahamas had been escalating steadily since independence and had reached staggering proportions by 1983. At the very least, the Bahamian authorities were inadequate to stanch the flow, their inadequacies had been ignored, and the traffic consequently almost covered up. More seriously, a very large number of Bahamians—if not the entire Bahamian people—stood accused of profiting from a clandestine business in a manner that echoed the immoral opportunism of piracy, blockade-running, and rum-running days but far outstripped them in scale and evil effect. What was involved was thus not merely a question of sovereignty but a questioning of the national way of life, psyche, and morale and their roots in Bahamian tradition.

The Police Drug Squad had been formed as early as 1968 but dealt only with the comparatively small number of drug offenses in New Providence until the Police Marine Division (PMD) was set up in 1971. From 1974, mainly under the command of Assistant Superintendent Lawrence Major, the PMD made systematic patrols, seizures, and reports on the widening scope of the traffic, which involved the use of remote islands and landing grounds as transshipment points for cocaine and marijuana, mostly originating in Colombia. The highlights of this phase were the seizure by Major's men of 247 pounds of cocaine, said to have a U.S. street value of $2 billion, and of a cache of marijuana at Black Rock, Grand Bahama, somewhat implausibly said to be six feet high and two miles long.[25]

The replacement of the Police Marine Division by the Bahamas Defence Force in 1976 provided something of a hiatus. But the police continued to work closely with the BDF, and in March 1979 Superintendent Alonzo Butler and Assistant Superintendents Lawrence Major and Avery Ferguson made a dramatic report which identified a network covering the entire archipelago; the chief operations were in the Exumas, Andros, Grand Bahama, and Bimini, major activity in Abaco, the Berry Islands, Cat Island, Crooked and Acklins Islands, and the Ragged Island chain, and some trafficking in Inagua, Mayaguana, San Salvador, Long Island, and Eleuthera. As much for fear of alarming the law-abiding as alerting the traffickers, this report was not published until 1984. Figures also not published until 1984 showed that the Bahamian authorities between 1980 and 1983 (not counting the undetected traffic or the seizures made by agents of the U.S. Coast Guard and Customs services, DEA, or FBI) seized hundreds of tons of marijuana and thousands of pounds of cocaine.[26]

There was partial and intermittent cooperation between U.S. and Bahamian authorities, but much more tension, confusion, and obfuscation because of the overlapping activities of the American agencies, their employment of double agents and other "dirty tricks," and their often casual invasion of Bahamian territory. U.S.-Bahamian official relations seriously deteriorated after an exposé of the drug traffic in the *Wall Street Journal* in January 1982. But relations reached a nadir in September 1983, when an NBC news program (probably U.S. government–inspired) alleged that Prime Minister Pindling was involved in widespread drug corruption. The program was closely followed by a series of articles in the *Miami Herald* entitled "A Nation for Sale: Corruption in the Bahamas" (informally banned in the Bahamas but widely circulated) and the revelation of an abortive "sting" operation carried out by U.S. agents aiming to entrap a Bahamian cabinet minister.[27]

The response of most Bahamian people was shock and of the government, outrage. At his own request, Prime Minister Pindling appeared on NBC television to deny the charges but cut his interview short and threatened the network with a million-dollar lawsuit for defamation. Behind the scenes, the case against the ambushed cabinet minister was apparently dropped at the request of the U.S. ambassador for fear of jeopardizing the AUTEC negotiations. But much closer to the surface, the alleged infringements of Bahamian sovereignty clearly influenced the unexpectedly anti-American stance of the Bahamian government over the invasion of Grenada, which occurred just a month after the NBC and *Miami Herald* bombshells.

Grenada's prime minister, Maurice Bishop, was overthrown on October 13 and shot on October 19, 1983. Prime Minister Pindling attended the CARICOM meeting in Trinidad on October 22 which condemned the coup, suspended Grenada from CARICOM, and declared a severance of air and sea links with the island. Yet when the United States (ostensibly at the request of the Organization of Eastern

Caribbean States [OECS] and the embattled governor-general of Grenada) invaded Grenada with massive forces just three days later, the Bahamas joined Cuba, Surinam, and Trinidad in condemning the American action.[28] In a special meeting of the Permanent Council of the OAS in Washington on October 26, External Affairs Minister Paul Adderley made a fiery speech:

> A new morality of international law is sought to be imposed upon us by those who would seek to justify the military intervention in Grenada. . . . We believe in the rule of law, we believe in the rule of international law and we are irrevocably committed to the principles of non-intervention. Any intervention in any form is abhorrent to us whether by direct military force or more subtle forms of aggression which have the effect of destabilization and which are intended to overthrow a government. Grenada is a fellow Commonwealth country and a fellow Caribbean nation. These are bitterly sad times for us. Grenada and the other members of the Organization of Eastern Caribbean States, Jamaica and Barbados, are our brothers; the other participant, the United States of America, is a valued friend. But we cannot ever condone a double standard of international morality. . . . We take this opportunity to record in the most positive fashion our national abhorrence to any act of foreign intervention designed and calculated to affect the sovereignty or independence of any state.[29]

Adderley addressed the General Assembly of the United Nations in New York on November 15, 1983, calling for the immediate "removal of all foreign combative forces" from Grenada.[30]

The government's stance drew strong support from a not too welcome source. John McCartney, leader of the tiny Vanguard Nationalist and Socialist Party, normally the strongest critic of the PLP, echoed the words of Maurice Bishop in claiming that the Bahamas was "in nobody's backyard" and that the U.S. invasion of Grenada was but a dress rehearsal for planned invasions of Cuba and Nicaragua. The majority of Bahamians, however, with exaggerated fears of Cuba and convinced of the value of the American defense umbrella, tended to support the U.S. action in Grenada. Not surprisingly, the opposition party, the FNM, did not support the government's rhetoric and saw it as a tactic to deflect attention from the more immediate and pressing questions of drug-running and corruption. FNM leader Kendal Isaacs sent letters of congratulation and support to Prime Minister Eugenia Charles of Dominica, chair of the OECS, and to President Ronald Reagan, thanking him for the evidence that the United States would "positively stand with small nations such as ours in keeping democracy alive." A former leader of the opposition, Norman Solomon, even wrote in the *Tribune* that he would be willing to accept an American invasion of his homeland if circumstances similar to those in Grenada ever occurred in the Bahamas, though he more equivocally added that "the Bahamas is as independent as the United States wishes it to be."[31]

The question of national sovereignty was vital, but the problems of drug trafficking and corruption could not be swept under the carpet. At the end of November 1983 the PLP government called a commission of inquiry "To Inquire into the Illegal Use of the Bahamas for the Transhipment of Dangerous Drugs Destined for the United States of America." Consisting of a former chief justice, Sir James Smith, the Bahamian bishop of Barbados, Drexel Gomez, and a senior officer of the Royal Canadian Mounted Police, Edwin Willis, this body was dominated by the chief investigator, Robert Ellicott QC, former attorney general of Australia. Given the specific mandate to look into drug transshipment, the involvement in drug-

Signifying that the Commonwealth of the Bahamas remains a monarchy by common consent. Queen Elizabeth II, flanked by her consort, Prince Philip, and Prime Minister Pindling, graciously replies to a loyal address of welcome on her arrival in Nassau, February 1975. Courtesy of Bahamas Archives.

running of ministers, MPs, and civil servants, the adequacy of Bahamian law enforcement and penalties, and relations with U.S. enforcement agencies, the commission convened on December 7, 1983, and sat for 146 days, spread over nearly a year, with 95 days of public testimony and 40 days of closed sessions in Nassau and 11 days of closed sessions in Miami.

Though the report of the commission did not unseat the prime minister or oust the PLP government, it was far from a whitewash, and the evidence brought forward revealed that in some respects the NBC and *Miami Herald* accounts were understatements. Quite apart from the diplomatic and political implications, it was dramatically clear that drugs posed some of the most serious social problems the Bahamas had ever faced, made all the worse by the economic effects. Drug corruption was multidimensional. While drug-traffic-related profits were so vast and easily acquired at all levels that too many Bahamians had wanted a part in the game, the drugs themselves had become so readily available and relatively cheap in the islands that many Bahamians became addicted and the wrong sort of tourist was attracted to the islands. Drug-related profits, moreover, distorted the economy, the easy ill-gotten wealth not simply upsetting material and moral values but facing Bahamians with the dilemma of having to weigh the economic cost of suppressing the trade.

The Drug Commission uncovered trafficking in virtually every one of the Family Islands, but three areas stood out both in their importance in the scale of the trade and in illustrating the dimensions of the problem. Largely because of its proximity to Miami, one of the busiest and most affected areas was Bimini and its neighboring cays. According to the commission's most colorful and voluble witness, the "turned" trafficker Luis G. Garcia, nicknamed "Kojak," Bimini was a major transshipment area between 1978 and 1983 but required complete participation by the local population and eventually proved too vulnerable to U.S. and Bahamian police surveillance. Planes from Colombia would either land at night on the unlighted South Bimini airstrip or drop their cargoes in bales and packages in shallow waters to waiting local boatmen. The drugs would then be transferred to high-powered speedboats for the fifty-mile dash across the Florida Channel. Large quantities were stowed in the bushes on South Bimini awaiting shipment, and many unclaimed packages found floating in the water were appropriated by local fishermen. The ratio of marijuana to cocaine was approximately ten to one by weight, though probably three times to one in favor of cocaine in value. "Kojak" Garcia estimated that in 1979–80 an average of three to four planes came in each month, carrying cargoes of four to five thousand pounds apiece, an annual traffic of at least twenty tons.[32]

The chief local distributor was said to receive $90,000 for each run, school-age children were being paid $500 for one night's work, and one witness testified that he had seen "children between 10 and 12 years of age with five or six thousand dollars in their pockets." The amount of money in U.S. dollars transferred from Bimini to the Central Bank in Nassau escalated from $544,360 in 1977 to $1.4 million in 1978, tripled again in 1979, and reached the astounding total of $12.3 million in 1983—from a total population of some two thousand persons. The local police and customs officials were ineffectual if not actively involved themselves, and though 191 arrests were made for drug offenses in the Bimini area between 1978 and 1983, only one of those arrested was a Bahamian. When the Nassau Drug Squad under Superintendent Stanley Moir and Assistant Superintendent Paul Thompson made a raid in December 1979 and arrested a dozen traffickers, the police detachment was stoned and abused "by children, adults and elderly people" alike. Saddest of all, schoolchildren were said to be receiving payment in drugs, 80 percent of all young persons above school leaving age were reputedly "free-basing" cocaine, and there were already between fifty and sixty confirmed addicts in the Bimini settlements.[33]

More isolated transfer points were obviously preferable to foreign traffickers, and a small island with an airstrip and controlled access was considered ideal. Gorda Cay, on the southeastern edge of the Little Bahama Bank, promised such conditions, though it proved an ill-starred magnet for a range of desperadoes, Bahamian as well as foreign. Working through complaisant Nassau lawyers, several shady characters in succession obtained a lease on the five-hundred-acre cay, not seriously developing the promised resort or citrus groves but building an airstrip, either for their own drug transshipments or to charge others for its use. Chief of these operators was an American named Frank Barber, later convicted of drug smuggling and jailed in Texas. Associated with Barber was the ubiquitous "Kojak" Garcia, who claimed that he had a hot-line connection to senior officers at police headquarters in Nassau, providing him with daily information on the movements of the Drugs Division. Frank Barber's Bahamian caretaker at Gorda Cay, Barry Thompson, though nominally employed at $500 per week, was said to have cleared $3 million in eighteen months while working for Barber.[34]

Frank Barber's operation ran into trouble through competition from unexpected sources: the black fishermen from the nearby model settlement of Sandy Point, Abaco, and a renegade boat operator from the ultra-conservative and respectable all-white settlement of Spanish Wells, off North Eleuthera. Enterprising Sandy Point residents, accustomed to visiting Gorda Cay for casual cultivation or on fishing trips, discovered a cache of marijuana by accident, treated it as treasure trove, and ransomed it back to the drug-runners. Then, denied a formal share in the operation, a few foolhardy men from the settlement, armed only with cutlasses against automatic weapons, hijacked a planeload of cocaine. Selling the haul at $25,000 a pound was not difficult but highly dangerous, and the hijackers became hunted international fugitives. One survivor told the commission an almost incredible, tragicomic, but ultimately pathetic tale: Family Island fishermen who had scarcely before left the Bahamas lived for a while in Florida like millionaires, then fled hit men from one country to another carrying suitcases of cocaine and hundred-dollar bills, exorcising their terror by snorting the drug until they were addicted. At the far point of his own picaresque odyssey, the witness applied for sanctuary in one of the Arabian Gulf states. But he was denied entry, not because he was now a cocaine junkie and emphatically not because of the dubious provenance of the money he carried, but because he could not convincingly prove himself a Muslim.[35]

Frank Barber was arrested in the United States in 1982, and Gorda Cay was sold to Abner Pinder of Spanish Wells, ostensibly for farming. The drug-running, however, increased in volume, and whether or not he was directly involved in trafficking, Pinder was plausibly said to have exacted $1,000 a kilo of cocaine and $20 a pound of marijuana for the thousands of pounds of drugs passing through Gorda Cay. Never formally charged either in the Bahamas or the United States, Pinder eventually escaped to a luxurious retirement in his native Spanish Wells. That he was able to do so in such a reputedly law-abiding and God-fearing community was variously interpreted as an admirably Christian acceptance on the part of the locals of a returned and reformed prodigal, an example of local tendencies to turn a blind eye to, or even admire, enterprising ways of moneymaking, however questionable, or—least likely of all in a settlement already growing immensely rich from crawfishing and other respectable enterprises—as evidence that Pinder was only one of many "Sigillians" engaged in the drug-running business.[36]

The island most closely controlled by Colombians—for four years almost the hub of their drug-running through the Bahamas—was Norman's Cay, just fifty miles southeast of Nassau, at the northern end of the Exumas. Norman's Cay was beginning to be developed as a legitimate resort in the 1970s, with an airstrip and two harbors, when it apparently was tested as a drug transshipment point by Colombians in 1976. Two years later, most of it was leased to an innocent-sounding Nassau-registered company fronting for Carlos Enrique Rivas, also known as Joe Lehder, already notorious as a major Colombian drug baron. The airstrip was extended and two hangars built, and by early 1979 Lehder's thirty or more well-armed retainers had made the cay secure by persuading the few resident homeowners to leave the island and lease them their houses and by dissuading innocent yachtsmen from using the harbors or coming ashore. Among those turned away was the opposition politician Norman Solomon, who reported to the police in July 1979 (and to the commission in 1983) that he had been threatened by armed men when he tried to explore and that yachtsmen and islanders on neighboring cays told him of almost nightly plane traffic to and from the airstrip. A convicted drug-runner, Edward Ward, testified in 1983 that he alone had made almost a dozen flights from Colombia during 1979 in a plane he had bought with a loan from Lehder. On each flight he carried up to 520 kilos of cocaine, worth $50,000 a kilo wholesale in the United States, for which he was paid $400,000 a trip.[37]

The zealous Assistant Superintendent Major had made a damning report on the activities at Norman's Cay in March 1979, but a police raid was not organized until November that year. Then it was delayed a further two weeks and its command transferred from Major to the more senior Superintendent Howard Smith, who was the same man "Kojak" Garcia later named as his informant at police headquarters. The November 14 raid was almost a full-scale invasion, involving ninety armed police officers, but, not surprisingly, it came up almost blank. Thirty men were arrested, a majority of them Colombians, and a large number of arms confiscated, including automatic weapons. But no more drugs were found than might have been for the personal use of Lehder's entourage. Joe Lehder himself was off the cay, having left in his yacht with his family just before the police arrived, allegedly to make a call on his friend and associate Robert Vesco, whose yacht was anchored at Cistern Cay, a few miles further down the Exuma Cays.[38]

Lehder and his family returned to Norman's Cay and stayed there intermittently until July 1982, long after Vesco had been finally deported from the Bahamas in December 1980. Apparently, the drug traffic continued almost unabated, despite ineffectual police raids on November 28, 1980, January 29, 1981, and September 8, 1982. It may even have continued after the police established a permanent post on Norman's Cay in 1983. Witnesses before the commission reported that besides sundry Nassau lawyers, builders, and businessmen, among those who visited or were guests of Joe Lehder at Norman's Cay were the MP for Exuma, George Smith, and other, more senior, PLP politicians.[39]

The Drug Commission unequivocally demonstrated what all close observers sensed: that though very few Bahamians were direct traffickers or engaged in criminal activities, many had been so beguiled by the profits to be made that they had become accomplices in the traffic. These included ordinary individuals willing to perform simple but illegal jobs for payment many times what could be earned by honest toil; lawyers, investment consultants, and other fixers with the right connections and expertise, prepared to do business with companies and individuals of murky provenance who processed without question monies that likely came from drugs and properly belonged to the U.S. Internal Revenue Service; and immigration, customs and police officials who took bribes to allow entry and residence to known criminals, to let packages, even planeloads and ship cargoes, pass without inspection, or to add the supply of useful inside information to the neglect of proper law enforcement. Throughout the islands, sometimes in the poorest and unlikeliest locations, palatial new homes signified the most successful, unscrupulous, and ostentatious operators, though admittedly the number of half-finished palaces also testified to the risks and vagaries of the game. Less visibly, untold millions of dollars flowed into the Bahamian economy, either the intermediate takings from the trade or the ultimate profits laundered through notoriously complaisant Bahamian banks.

The commission was not a judicial body, but it provided ample evidence to enable the Bahamian and U.S. courts to prosecute the most flagrant offenders. Three individuals came in for special censure. Of the Exumian-born lawyer Nigel Bowe (who was eventually extradited to the United States, tried, and imprisoned for fifteen years) the commissioners laconically reported that "his consistency in denying any involvement with drug trafficking is exceeded only by the frequency of allegations against him" and that they "took grave exception to his frequent excursions into the vulgar and profane." Prime Minister Pindling's close associate Everett Bannister (whose extradition was still being sought by the United States ten years later) was quoted by Mrs. Edward Ward as claiming, "Our Prime Minister and other people are just figure heads and it's actually people like us who run the government. We have all the say so. We are the ones that do all the work." And of Senator Andrew "Dud" Maynard the commission noted that "whilst he was Chairman of the PLP, he acted on the premise that party members should receive preferential treatment where they met the same qualifications as other people," quoted his statement that though he was opposed to influence peddling, he saw nothing wrong with payments "for obviating red tape and delays," and commented that "the irony of this position escaped Senator Maynard during cross examination."[40]

Maynard resigned from the Senate and his party chairmanship, and there were other political casualties. Most prominent was the minister Kendal Nottage who, earlier, when politicians' assets had to be made public, had almost boasted of the $10 million he had acquired since entering politics and now stood accused of doing business with a known American gangster and drug merchant. The minister and Exuma MP George Smith resigned after evidence was shown that he had accepted a BMW car as a bribe from Joe Lehder. Three other ministers also left the cabinet if not the PLP. The deputy prime minister Arthur Hanna resigned in disgust at the revelations before the commission, and two others were sacked for favoring the prime minister's resignation, one of whom, Hubert Ingraham, went on to join, then lead, the opposition and become Pindling's successor as prime minister in 1992.

The prominent lawyer-politicians Arthur Hanna, Livingstone Coakley, Henry Bostwick, and Clement Maynard (who succeeded Hanna as deputy prime minister) were cleared of allegations by the commission. The commission's clearing of Prime Minister Pindling, though, was more equivocal. A rigorous scrutiny of his finances showed that Pindling had received approximately five times his official salary between 1977 and 1983, including a $750,000 gift from the chief executives of the Grand Bahama Port Authority, $474,000 from Everett Bannister for purely nominal services (including "finder's fees"), $250,000 from an American benefactor called Barber (subsequently returned), and $181,000 from "unidentified sources." Two of the three members of the commission concluded that it had not been proved that any of these monies were drug-related. Bishop Drexel Gomez, however, entered the following minority report:

> It is certainly feasible that all of these payments could have been made from non-drug related sources. But in my opinion, the circumstances raise great suspicions and I find it impossible to say that the payments were all non-drug related. Some could have been but . . . it certainly cannot be contested that the Prime Minister did not exercise sufficient care to preclude the possibility of drug-related funds reaching his bank account or being applied for his benefit. In the absence of inquiry he could have unwittingly received drug related funds. . . . To this extent, at least, he left himself, in my opinion, open to criticism for lack of prudence by a person holding the high office of Prime Minister.[41]

The police force as a whole came out relatively well from its examination, though the commission concluded that its resources were inadequate to solve the drug problem. The statistics presented of seizures of drugs and arrests of persons on drug charges were superficially impressive. But it was clear that the seizures represented only a fraction of the traffic through the Bahamas (said at one time to amount to a third of all illegal drugs destined for the United States), and though the number of persons charged and convicted remained fairly steady (around 1,100 and 560 a year respectively between 1980 and 1983), those awaiting trial trebled in three years (from 151 in 1980 to 452 in 1983). The majority of persons charged with drug offenses, moreover, were comparatively minor offenders from Nassau rather than the major drug barons and profiteers. There also was disquieting evidence of imperfect security and poor accountancy of the quantities of drugs seized, of seized drugs subsequently disappearing, and of policemen at all levels taking bribes, if not actually selling drugs back into the market. Resolute attempts, however, were made to cleanse the police of its few corrupt officers by demotions, transfers, and outright sackings, just as similar moves—on a smaller scale—were made in the customs and immigration services.[42]

On the burning issues of U.S.-Bahamian relations, the activities of American agents, and the infringement of Bahamian sovereignty, law, and individuals' rights, the commission was extremely thorough and fairly conclusive. Although clearly uncomfortable with having to examine witnesses who were already convicted criminals, turncoats, or undercover agents and objecting to the failure of certain key witnesses (including the U.S. chargé d'affaires in Nassau) to appear to testify, the commission concluded that U.S. participation in the inquiries was not (as some of those implicated accused) an attempt to discredit the Bahamas or a calculated plot on the part of the U.S. government to destabilize that of the Bahamas. U.S. agents had become convinced from their observations and informants that many Bahamian private individuals, officials, and politicians (including perhaps even the prime minister) were involved in the drug trade and the laundering of drug money, and they had no confidence in either the ability and willingness of the Bahamian police to arrest, or the courts to convict, the most serious offenders. Consequently they had overstepped their orders and agreements made with Bahamian authorities, cut corners, and even transgressed Bahamian law in attempts to find evidence that could be used to convict transgressors in U.S. courts. The most objectionable undercover scheme, code-named Operation Grouper, was set afoot by the DEA with the intention of entrapping a minister known to be close to the prime minister. This scheme, though, had been conceived and carried out independently by junior members of the DEA and was ultimately called off by superior authorities. Clearly, to achieve the main mutual purpose, the effective suppression of the drug traffic through the Bahamas, far greater trust and cooperation between the U.S. and Bahamian forces were needed as well as an expansion of the Royal Bahamian Police Force and the Royal Bahamian Defence Force.[43]

In the late 1980s and 1990s both the police and defense forces were enlarged and made more professional (through the creation of a Police College, the institution of a special drug training course, and the expansion of the defense force's flotilla to a dozen vessels), and relations and cooperation with the U.S. agencies greatly improved. But these changes did not occur quickly and did not necessarily stanch the flow of drugs. The police proudly pointed to increased totals of drugs seized

(13,000 pounds of cocaine and 37 tons of marijuana in 1985, rising to an all-time peak of 20,500 pounds and 76 tons in 1987), but it was not clear how much this reflected greater police effectiveness or whether it even indicated an actual increase in the overall traffic.[44]

U.S.-Bahamian relations were not improved by the appointment of the assertive Carol Boyd Hallett as ambassador to the Bahamas in 1986, though one positive effect of her outspoken campaign against drug trafficking was the publication of more information about the actions of U.S. agencies. In 1990, as minister of national security, Paul Adderley claimed that the cocaine traffic had diminished in 1989, citing a 42 percent drop in seizures over 1988. But to the 2.28 metric tons seized by the police and defense forces on their own had to be added the 3.19 tons taken in cooperation with the Americans. The climax was past, however, and Adderley's successor, Darrell Rolle, was able to announce a further drop of 82 percent in seizures in 1990.[45]

By the mid-1990s, once the Bahamas was more confident of its national sovereignty, the U.S. government became more sensitive to sovereignty issues, mutual distrust had almost faded away, and the DEA, FBI, U.S. Coast Guard, and the Bahamas police and defense forces worked closely together. They were not often engaged in combined operations, but they shared information and a surveillance system that included sophisticated radars hovering in captive balloons over Grand Bahama, Exuma, and Inagua. An important symbol of this era of better U.S.-Bahamian relations was the appointment in 1994 of the comparatively relaxed former football player Sidney Williams as the first black U.S. ambassador to the Bahamas.

After two decades it seemed at last that the drug flow through the Bahamas had slowed to a trickle, though it was not certain whether this was mainly because of the coordinated efforts of Bahamian and U.S. forces or whether the major drug producers were finding other routes, if not other markets. Moreover, the U.S.-Bahamian surveillance system was now at least as much concerned with the control of illegal immigrants and illicit fishing and with security in general as it was with the suppression of drug-running. For Bahamian politicians, too, the emphasis gradually shifted. From corruption stemming from trafficking through the Bahamas to internal drug problems and from drugs in general to other forms of corruption, slackness, and mismanagement in the face of serious economic recession (though the recession was highlighted by the loss of drug money), they became concerned over radical shifts in the patterns of tourism and foreign investment and over the problems associated with hugely increased Haitian migration.

Pindling Under Siege: The Last Phase of the PLP, 1987–1992

It was probably fortunate for Prime Minister Pindling and the PLP that the 1984 Drug Commission report came out three years before a general election was scheduled. The ruling party and its astute leader were able to use the interim to mend fences, regroup, fan the last embers of the sovereignty issue (accusing the opposition of being subservient to the United States), and otherwise exploit the divisions among their opponents. The PLP still enjoyed the remnants of the mystique of being the party of the black majority, the vanquisher of Bay Street, the achiever of independence. Though at levels far below those elsewhere in the hemisphere, the PLP had also entrenched its supporters through patronage and used the government-dominated radio station for propaganda. It also did what it could to alter the constituencies and registration systems to its own advantage—in the process increasing the number of parliamentary seats from forty-four to forty-nine. But it was the qualities of its leader which were the PLP's chief remaining assets. A masterly, even ruthless, tactician, Pindling was a brilliant manipulator of the Bahamian ethos, an inspiring orator in the folk tradition, a black whom other blacks admired because he had outdone Bay Street "at their own game," yet who still retained the common touch. As Susan Love Brown noted when observing him campaigning in Cat Island in 1990, Pindling came across not just as charismatic orator but also, depending on his audience, as "deferential younger person, equal sibling, gentle father."[46]

Such qualities had carried the PLP and its leader to victory in 1977 (at a time of serious recession) and in 1982 (when rumors of corruption were already rife) but were thought to be wearing thin by 1987. The general election of June 19–20, 1987, was even closer than the PLP's thirty-one-to-eighteen margin suggested, and the election was followed by accusations of gerrymandering, registration irregularities, and voting fraud. The gentlemanly Kendal Isaacs (who managed to retain his seat in one of the most obviously altered constituencies) resigned for reasons of health from the leadership of the FNM, to be succeeded by the fire-eating Cecil Wallace-Whitfield, who told a large public rally that if the wrongs were not righted in the election, the people should go to the streets and he would be the first to call for "revolution." This rhetoric turned out to be bluster, compounded by tragedy as Wallace-Whitfield's health rapidly declined and he succumbed to cancer, leaving the leadership open to Hubert Ingraham, who had (to Pindling's chagrin) been elected as an Independent against a PLP candidate but soon moved over to the FNM.[47]

Despite desperate efforts to sustain their old bright image, Pindling and the PLP were living on borrowed time between 1987 and 1992. In the 1987 election they had lost the support of most of organized labor, but their opponents multiplied at every stage in the economic decline and every new revelation of government mismanagement, waste, and corruption. As the 1992 election approached, Pindling and his ministers made optimistic statements that the recession had bottomed out and promised action to restore tourism, find new investment, and create more jobs. The government initially also made an attempt to capitalize on the coincidence of the election with the five-hundredth anniversary of Columbus's landing in the Bahamas. A Quincentennial Commission was set up and elaborate events planned that would divert, perhaps distract, the ordinary people. The public, however, remained largely indifferent to the proposed celebrations, if not actively opposed to them because of the backlash throughout the hemisphere, which preferred to regard Columbus as the first of the European conquistadors, the destroyer of the Indians, and the initiator of plantations and Afro-American slavery.[48]

Of far more moment were the soaring national debt, which passed $1 billion early in 1992, the effects of the worldwide recession on Bahamian tourism and employment, and the dire performance of government-controlled corporations. Difficulties with agricultural schemes and the national airline were familiar problems but reached scandal proportions when it was revealed that cattle in Andros were starving for lack of money to pay for imported foodstuffs, that four new planes were grounded because the losses incurred from running them were greater than the mortgage payments, and that despite its financial troubles Bahamasair was drastically overstaffed. Slack ticketing and accountancy procedures and outright peculation at Bahamasair, along with overstaffing, were matched or exceeded at the national telephone corporation, BATELCO. But these failings and losses were dwarfed by information that was gradually revealed about the contracts for extending Nassau International Airport and the operations of the government's Hotel Corporation. The original contract for the airport had, curiously, been awarded to a Brazilian builder, with a generous budget of $58 million and permission to bring in foreign artisans. The government then let the costs escalate to $82 million but reneged on its payments, causing a halt in the project which threw 458 Bahamian laborers out of work.[49] The hotel crisis was even larger in scale. During 1991, Resorts International, which controlled Paradise Island, and Carnival Cruise Lines, owner-operator of the byzantine Crystal Palace Resort-Casino on Cable Beach (between them, the largest employers in the Bahamas), both announced crippling losses, and in January 1992 Carnival threatened either to pull out or declare bankruptcy. The Hotel Corporation, already accused of making an initial "sweetheart deal" with Carnival and using the Crystal Palace to "featherbed" PLP supporters, agreed to yet another bailout. Adding to massive debts, incurred through an unbusinesslike combination of takeovers and extravagant new building, the Hotel Corporation took a 40 percent stake in the Crystal Palace for $70 million. Though the government cited the drastic decline in tourist stopovers resulting from the worldwide recession as the cause of the Hotel Corporation's woes, the opposition charged the corporation with gross irresponsibility as well as corruption and accused the government of virtually printing money to disguise its failures. More generally, the FNM was able to use the disastrous misuse of public funds as an argument for privatization and to project itself as the party of private enterprise rather than government spending.[50]

The PLP postponed the election as long as it could and claimed a somewhat empty victory in two by-elections which the FNM did not contest because they were "a waste of public money." Asserting that the government's five-year term came to end on September 2, the anniversary of its convening, rather than on June 20, when its predecessor was dissolved, Prime Minister Pindling delayed prorogation until July 9, announcing August 19 as the election date. The extra time hindered rather than helped the PLP's cause. As early as April, the *Nassau Guardian* had predicted that the PLP would "get out that old racial horse and flog it into full sprint towards election day," and though Radio ZNS did not repeat the cliché of rerunning *Roots* as part of its campaign, it did broadcast "racially inflammatory programmes" accusing the FNM of being the old UBP in disguise. Many Bahamians, however, expressed disapproval of this tactic, stating that Pindling and the PLP were insulting their intelligence. Public PLP meetings, moreover, could not match those of the FNM in numbers and enthusiasm, and the chief opposition leaders outmatched the traditional PLP style of biblical rhetoric.[51]

Liberation and jubilee were the FNM themes, but FNM supporters were nonetheless unprepared for the extent of the victory declared on August 20, 1992. The number of parliamentary seats, thirty-two to seventeen, was almost exactly reversed, with the FNM polling 63,181 (or 55.7 percent) of the votes to the PLP's

50,104 (44.2 percent) in a very large turnout. Though Sir Lynden Pindling outpolled his FNM opponent almost four to one (compared with Hubert Ingraham's victory by 1,045 votes to 793), his former chief ministers, Clement Maynard, Paul Adderley, and Bernard Nottage, barely squeezed back in, and many established PLP figures, including Arthur Hanna, Kendal Nottage, and Milo Butler Jr., lost by varying margins. The formerly discredited George Smith was easily returned for Exuma over a white female FNM candidate, Lynn Holowesko, but one of the only two white PLP candidates, Marvin Pinder of Spanish Wells, initially declared elected for northern Eleuthera by two votes, lost the seat by seven votes after an appeal and recount. The successful candidate was another white, Noel Roberts, son of Sir George Roberts, a former Bay Street magnate and president of the Senate. Perhaps even more symbolic of the attempt to expunge the past, Prime Minister Ingraham appointed to the Senate and included in his first cabinet as minister of tourism Brent Symonette, the son of the first premier, Sir Roland Symonette, leader of the UBP.[52]

A portent to the superstitious, and underlining for all the difficulties the new FNM government would face, was the rampage through the northern Bahamas of one of the worst hurricanes ever recorded, just three days after the general election. No more than eight miles wide but generating tornados around its edges and winds even higher than those that devastated Homestead, Florida (allegedly a world record 230 miles per hour), Hurricane Andrew providentially bypassed New Providence and caused hardly any loss of life. But it virtually obliterated the Current, Eleuthera, damaged every building in Spanish Wells, and wiped Cat Cay clear. That the government in Nassau—painfully lacking in resources and resourcefulness—was slower to respond to the plight of the afflicted areas than individuals and agencies in the United States, Canada, Britain, and even tiny Bermuda was a poor augury for the immediate future.[53]

The FNM had been elected on a platform promising a complete turnaround—the eradication of corruption, patronage, and slackness, the replacement of government overspending by new investments in the private sector, the revival of tourism, and, above all, the creation of more jobs. But the new government found problems even greater and more difficult to solve than imagined. Within weeks of the election, a series of commissions of inquiry began, looking into each of the government corporations in turn. These investigations dragged on painfully for more than a year, revealing so many shady dealings and so much mismanagement and waste that the public grew tired and clamored for more positive action. Instead, the government seemed hamstrung. Handed colossal debts and problems still growing, it had to take out more loans rather than being able to reduce the deficit. The revelations from the commissions increased skepticism abroad about business opportunities in the Bahamas, and new investments were slow in coming. Diversification proved very difficult, and tourism suffered from the continuing trend toward cruise ship and package holidays, which expatriated most of the profits. Even more disappointing to ardent supporters of the FNM than the failure to find new sources of employment was that the government, for fear of further unemployment and the breakdown of services, was unable to sack more than a handful of employees and officials who owed their jobs to PLP affiliation. At the same time, many of the FNM's own people, so long in the wilderness, showed their inexperience or naiveté in expecting to emulate their forerunners and reap the rewards of

Bahamian agriculture, traditional and modern. *Above*, land at United Estates, San Salvador, cleared by slash-and-burn for cultivation of pockets of soil in honeycomb rock surface. *Middle*, market gardening on reclaimed coastal swale on Rolle commonage land at Mount Thompson, Exuma. *Below*, orderly row of pawpaws for U.S. market grown on crushed-rock soil with fertilizers and modern irrigation methods, near Rock Sound, Eleuthera, 1980s. Photographs courtesy of Neil Sealey.

success. Though the FNM's leader made a virtue out of necessity by preaching magnanimity in victory and reconciliation, as well as attempting to set an example by reducing parliamentary salaries, as long as the worldwide recession continued and the burden of the national debt grew, the cry inevitably soon arose of plus ça change.

The fundamental problem was that ideologically the FNM government was much less different from its predecessor than its election rhetoric proclaimed; the political process, in fact, was much less important than its self-important practitioners claimed or believed. An outside observer might even consider that just as twenty-five years of uninterrupted rule had seen the PLP assume and entrench much of the style and method of the hated UBP, which it had superseded, it would be only a matter of time before the FNM followed suit. The Bahamas between 1973 and the 1990s might be said to have achieved a recognizable national identity and political independence. But, as ever, it remained subject to three forces beyond its political control: the dictates of geography, of the world economy (especially as it related to the United States), and—for our purposes most important—the peculiar and timeless, insular and familial, independent but resourceful and pragmatic character of the Bahamian people.

This last factor was exemplified by the experience related in 1994 by a middle-class brown Nassauvian in his early seventies, a native whose memories stretched back to encompass the Great Depression and the changes brought to the Bahamas by World War II and the events of 1967, 1973, and 1992, one who had been born poor but had grown comfortable if not rich. With a close family relationship to the leader of the opposition, this person (we will call him Edwin) had always been resolutely opposed to the PLP and its leader, though his daughter and her husband, government employees, had become PLP supporters and members of the Pindlings' court. A PLP stalwart, recent millionaire, distant cousin, and old associate of Edwin's had a daughter due to be married, and Edwin was naturally invited to the splendid celebrations.

At the wedding reception, held at the Ocean Club on Paradise Island, Edwin picked an empty table and went to select from the plenteous buffet. When he returned, he found that the spare places at his table had been taken by the daunting quartet of Sir Lynden Pindling, Everett Bannister, Sir Clement Maynard, and his brother, former senator Andrew "Dud" Maynard. Though the four moguls might have been in conclave about high finance and politics and the political and economic future of the country, the former prime minister welcomed the newcomer into the circle with a request to elucidate an arcane point of local history and genealogy: "Come, Eddy. You'd know this. You're a Mason's Addition boy. Where was it exactly that old Ezekial Thompson lived during the war, and what Family Island did his family hail from?" Edwin (a walking Bahamian encyclopedia) gave the answers, and for an hour or so the five Bahamians and others passing by genially discussed family and island matters, the good old days, and the current price of conch.

12

The Conflict of Change and Tradition: Demography, Economy, Material Life, and Morality, 1973–1999

Demographics, 1973–2010

Demographic statistics delineate the body if not the soul of a people, and though the Bahamian census data are now so complex, detailed, and costly that half a decade passes before they are published, from them one can not only discern the changing size, shape, and condition of the Bahamian population but make projections into the future and foresee some of its problems.[1]

In the last quarter of the twentieth century the number of those legally living in the Bahamas continued to swell, if at a rate considerably less than predicted in the first years of independence.[2] The population is expected to reach a third of a million by the year 2010, though the rate of increase has slowed with a steady decrease in the birth rate, the aging of those born during the 1950s and 1960s boom, and the continued tightening of immigration controls. In population, the Bahamas will remain only a medium-sized country in the region, with large areas apparently underpopulated. But the problems of accommodating a legal population tripling in fifty years (let alone a further 20 percent of illegal immigrants) are exacerbated by limited natural resources and the relatively slow increase in facilities at a time of a rapid rise in material expectations and the natural tendency of the population to migrate to the more favored islands and choose the most lucrative and less toilsome occupations.

The last Bahamian census before independence (1970) counted a total of 169,534 people. The census of 1980 showed an increase to 209,505 and that of 1990 to 225,095. The average annual growth rate, which was 5.4 percent between 1953 and 1963 and 4.3 percent between 1963 and 1970, was only 2.3 percent during the 1970s and 2.2 percent between 1980 and 1990. With the annual growth rate during the 1990s expected to fall well below 2.0 percent and little above 1.0 percent by the end of the first decade of the twenty-first century, projections suggested a Bahamian population total of 292,200 for the year 2000 and 324,600 for 2010 (see Table 13).[3]

Besides the controls on immigration, the chief reason for the slowing Bahamian population growth rate is a steady decline in the crude birth rate—from as high as 40 per thousand in 1960 to about 28 per thousand in 1980 and a projected 20 per thousand in 2000—as a result of the voluntary birth control accompanying "middle-class values" and of the steady aging of the population following the un-

Table 13. Bahamas, New Providence, and Northern Islands: Population Growth, 1901–1990, and Projected Growth, 1990–2020

	Bahamas total	New Providence		Northern Islands (New Providence, Grand Bahama, Abaco)	
1901	53,735	12,534	(23.3%)	17,628	(32.8%)
1911	55,944	13,554	(24.2%)	19,841	(35.5%)
1921	53,031	12,975	(24.5%)	18,663	(35.2%)
1931	59,828	19,756	(33.0%)	26,230	(43.8%)
1943	68,846	29,391	(42.7%)	35,185	(51.1%)
1953	84,841	46,125	(54.4%)	53,627	(63.2%)
1963	130,220	80,907	(62.1%)	95,627	(73.4%)
1970	168,812	101,503	(60.1%)	133,863	(79.3%)
1980	209,505	135,437	(64.6%)	175,810	(83.9%)
1990	255,095	172,196	(75.0%)	223,128	(87.5%)
2000	292,200	220,600	(75.5%)	264,000	(90.4%)
2010	325,000	247,000	(76.0%)	300,000	(92.3%)
2020	350,000	274,800	(76.5%)	327,000	(93.4%)

Sources: Bahamas Censuses, 1901–1990; Norma Abdulah, *The Bahamas and Its People: A Demographic Analysis* (Trinidad: CARICOM, 1987), 17–26; authors' own revised projections, 1995.

Note: Percentages are of total Bahamian population in given year.

precedented "baby boom" of the 1950s and 1960s. Bahamian population growth is also slowed somewhat by the relatively slow decline in the crude death rate (also affected by the general aging process) and by the continuing relatively high infant mortality rates compared with those in most other countries in the region. Despite undoubted improvements in health care for the youngest and oldest alike, infant mortality remained at 21 per thousand in 1990, twice that of the United States and higher than in Cuba, Barbados, and Jamaica, though only a fifth that of Haiti. Between 1963 and 1990, Bahamian life expectancy at birth rose from 65 to 68 years for males and from 73 to 75 years for females. This was considerably below the rates for Barbados (73/77), Cuba (73/78), Jamaica (75/79), or the United States (73/80), though far higher than those for Haiti (52/55). Indeed, almost all Bahamian demographic statistics would be further affected were all Haitian immigrants to be recorded—with their much higher birth rate (despite high infant mortality), larger proportion of the young, and lower life expectancy (see Tables 14 and 15).[4]

In any case, the Bahamian population continues to be too large, in the sense that it presses against available resources and facilities, is increasingly poorly distributed, and suffers from other features of unregulated modernization, expansion, and internal migration. The population of New Providence continues to grow far faster than that of the Bahamas as a whole, and its disproportionate share of the total Bahamian population is moderated only by the growth of Grand Bahama and Abaco. The share of these three islands continues to soar, and many islands' populations continue to decline in absolute as well as relative terms (see Map 14).

The enumerated population of New Providence (excluding, of course, many illegal immigrants), 101,503 in 1970, rose to 135,437 in 1980 and 172,196 in 1990, annual increase rates of 3.3 and 2.7 percent respectively. Thus the population density

Table 14. Bahamas: Estimated Live Births, Reported Deaths, and Indicated Gross Natural Increase, 1980–1992

Year	Live birth occurrence	Rate (per 1,000 pop.)	Deaths	Rate (per 1,000 pop.)	Gross natural increase	Rate (per 1,000 pop.)
1980	5,934	28.3	1,344	6.4	4,590	21.9
1981	5,759	26.9	1,153	5.4	4,606	21.5
1982	5,826	26.6	1,185	5.4	4,641	21.2
1983	6,030	27.2	1,104	5.0	4,926	22.2
1984	5,752	25.5	1,150	5.1	4,602	20.4
1985	6,325	27.3	1,341	5.8	4,984	21.5
1986	5,791	24.5	1,407	5.9	4,384	18.6
1987	5,439	22.7	1,376	5.7	4,063	17.0
1988	5,747	23.5	1,319	5.4	4,428	18.1
1989	6,140	24.7	1,459	5.9	4,681	18.8
1990	6,117	24.0	1,343	5.3	4,774	18.7
1991	6,192	23.9	n/a	n/a	n/a	n/a
1992	6,759	26.5	n/a	n/a	n/a	n/a
Totals						
1980–90	64,860		14,181		50,679	
Averages						
1980–90	5,896	25.6	1,289	5.6	4,607	20.0

Source: Preliminary Report on the 1990 Bahamas Census (Nassau, 1994).

for the eighty-square-mile island (of which less than half is habitable) is 2,152 per square mile—far higher than Barbados (1,547) and not far short of Bermuda (2,768).[5] New Providence's share of the total Bahamian population, which declined somewhat during the years of Freeport's most rapid growth, rose from 60.1 percent in 1970 to 64.6 percent in 1980 and 67.5 percent in 1990. Even with the decline in the rate of increase, this trend suggested that by the year 2000 the population of New Providence might be 205,000 and reach a quarter million by 2015, representing at least 72 percent of the total Bahamian population.

During the period 1970 to 1990, the populations of Grand Bahama and Abaco also rose, but less rapidly than New Providence's. That of the former expanded from 25,859 in 1970 to 33,102 in 1980 and 40,898 in 1990 (average annual rates of 2.8 and 2.4 percent) and of the latter from 6,501 in 1970 to 7,271 in 1980 and 10,034 in 1990 (average annual rates of 1.2 and 3.8 percent). These trends suggested populations around 47,000 in 2000 and 55,000 in 2010 for Grand Bahama and as high as 12,000 in 2000 and 15,000 in 2010 for Abaco. The share of the Bahamian total represented by the combined populations of the two northern islands actually rose slightly from 19.2 percent in 1970 and 1980 to 20.0 percent in 1990, but a continuing increase (projected as high as 22.3 percent by the year 2020) was based on a further draining of the other islands rather than by a faster rate of growth than that of New Providence.

The three islands of New Providence, Grand Bahama, and Abaco accounted for 79.3 percent of the total population in the Bahamas in 1970, rising to 83.9 percent

Table 15. Bahamas: Abridged Life Tables for Males and Females, 1989–1991

Age interval	*Proportion dying*	*Of 100,000 born alive*		*Stationary population*		*Average remaining lifetime*
Periond of life between two exact ages stated in years	*Proportion of persons alive at beginning of age interval dying during interval*	*Number living at beginning of age interval*	*Number dying during age interval*	*In the age interval*	*In this and all subsequent age intervals*	*Average number of years of life remaining at beginning of age interval*
$x - x + n$	$n^{q}x$	l_x	$n^{d}x$	$n^{L}x$ (T_x − $T_x + 5$)	T_x	$e^o (T_x) l_x$
Males 0–1	0.022205	100,000	2,221	98,392	6,831,756	68.32
1–5	0.003069	97,779	300	421,251	6,733,364	68.86
5–10	0.003245	97,479	316	487,189	6,312,113	64.75
10–15	0.002288	97,163	222	485,276	5,825,523	59.96
15–20	0.004072	96,941	395	483,900	5,340,248	55.09
20–25	0.011390	96,546	1,100	480,183	4,856,348	50.30
25–30	0.014310	95,446	1,366	473,899	4,376,165	45.85
30–35	0.015848	94,080	1,491	466,883	3,902,267	41.48
35–40	0.025516	92,589	2,362	457,365	3,435,384	37.10
40–45	0.033769	90,227	3,047	443,723	2,978,019	33.01
45–50	0.038404	87,180	3,348	427,958	2,534,295	29.07
50–55	0.060805	83,832	5,097	406,978	2,106,338	25.13
55–60	0.076758	78,735	6,043	379,095	1,699,359	21.58
60–65	0.105141	72,691	7,643	345,240	1,320,264	18.16
65–70	0.158697	65,048	10,323	300,111	975,024	14.99
70–75	0.199001	54,725	10,890	246,777	674,913	12.33
75–80	0.276693	43,835	12,129	189,055	428,135	9.77
80–85	0.374037	31,706	11,859	128,433	239,081	7.54
85–90	0.502326	19,847	9,970	73,310	110,648	5.58
90–95	0.714306	9,877	7,055	30,172	37,338	3.78
95–100	0.852402	2,822	2,405	6,713	7,166	2.54
100–105	1.000000	417	417	453	453	1.09
Females 0–1	0.016467	100,000	1,647	98,808	7,527,860	75.28
1–5	0.003482	98,353	342	423,410	7,429,052	75.53
5–10	0.001494	98,011	146	490,412	7,005,641	71.48
10–15	0.000780	97,864	76	489,153	6,516,009	66.58
15–20	0.002587	97,788	253	488,379	6,026,855	61.63
20–25	0.004272	97,535	417	486,711	5,538,476	56.78
25–30	0.006421	97,118	624	484,152	5,051,765	52.02
30–35	0.010207	96,495	985	480,141	4,567,613	47.34
35–40	0.012987	95,510	1,240	474,577	4,087,472	42.80

Table 15. (continued)

Age interval		*Proportion dying*	*Of 100,000 born alive*		*Stationary population*		*Average remaining lifetime*
Period of life between two exact ages stated in years		*Proportion of persons alive at beginning of age interval dying during interval*	*Number living at beginning of age interval*	*Number dying during age interval*	*In the age interval*	*In this and all subsequent age intervals*	*Average number of years of life remaining at beginning of age interval*
$x - x + n$		$n^{q}x$	l_x	$n^{d}x$	$n^{L}x\ (T_x - T_x + 5)$	T_x	$e^{o}\ (T_x)\ l_x$
Females	40–45	0.016946	94,270	1,598	467,527	3,612,896	38.33
	45–50	0.022342	92,672	2,070	458,501	3,145,368	33.94
	50–55	0.034427	90,602	3,119	445,529	2,686,867	29.66
	55–60	0.041135	87,482	3,599	428,892	2,241,339	25.62
	60–65	0.064418	83,884	5,404	406,692	1,812,447	21.61
	65–70	0.093695	78,480	7,353	374,890	1,405,755	17.91
	70–75	0.134804	71,127	9,588	332,966	1,030,865	14.49
	75–80	0.220978	61,539	13,599	274,774	697,899	11.34
	80–85	0.307832	47,940	14,757	202,986	423,125	8.83
	85–90	0.435735	33,183	14,459	128,906	220,139	6.63
	90–95	0.567571	18,724	10,627	65,344	91,233	4.87
	95–100	0.773577	8,097	6,263	22,993	25,889	3.20
	100–105	1.000000	1,833	1,833	2,896	2,896	1.58

Source: Preliminary Report on the 1990 Bahamas Census (Nassau, 1994).

in 1980 and 87.5 percent in 1990—a trend that predicted an almost incredible share of 93.4 percent by the year 2020. Of the less modernized and favored islands, only those closest to Nassau/New Providence (and the United States) showed any population increase between 1970 and 1990, and the more southerly islands suffered absolute declines, some of them catastrophic. Bimini and the Berry Islands made a small increase of 16.5 percent between 1970 and 1990, and the population of Eleuthera (with Harbour Island and Spanish Wells) rose by 12.3 percent during the 1970s, though remaining static throughout the 1980s. Andros, after reaching a historical peak (8,845) in 1970 fell by 6.1 percent during the 1970s, with a further small decline (1.4 percent) during the 1980s. The population of Exuma remained almost level from 1970 to 1990 (falling from 3,767 to 3,556), but that of Long Island declined by 23.5 percent (from 3,861 to 2,954) and of Cat Island by 36.1 percent (from 2,657 to 1,698, compared with a peak of 5,072 in 1911). Inagua's population—though never large and clustered near the Mathew Town salt pans—fell by 11.2 percent,

NEW PROVIDENCE
ISLAND
North Cay
Long Cay
Silver Cay
Salt Cay
PARADISE ISLAND
Athol Island
Paradise Island Airport
Montagu Bay
NASSAU
Stapleton Gardens
Englerston
Blair Estate
Sandilands Village
Camperdown
Winton Heights
Winton Meadows
Highbury Park
Sea Breeze Estates
Yamacraw Beach Estate
Millar Heights
Carmichael Village
Coral Heights
Coral Harbour
ADELAIDE
Clifton
Lyford Cay
Mt. Pleasant
Love
Gambier Village
NASSAU INTERNATIONAL AIRPORT
Lake Killarney
Commercial
Residential and Hotels
Woodland, Scrub and Reclaimed Land
Agriculture
Recreation
Industrial, Airport and Public Use
Swamp and Mangrove
Lakes
P Port
M Marine Facilities
Schools
National Park
Supermarkets
N
0
4 km.

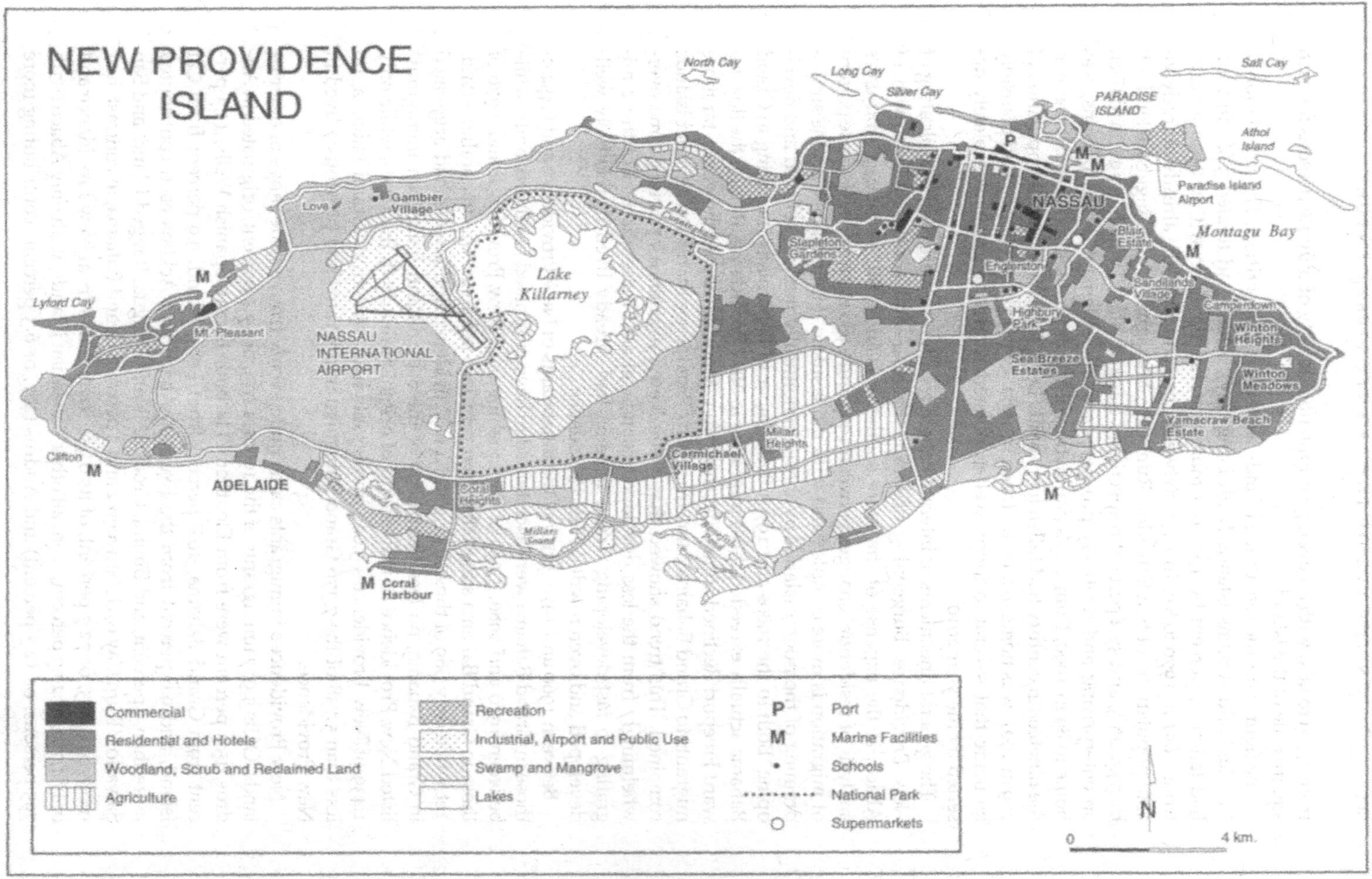

Map 14. Nassau and New Providence: Land Use, 1995

from 1,109 to 985, with an average population density of only 1.6 persons for each square mile of the island.

The figures for the remaining islands were even more critical. The population of Crooked and Acklins Islands (with Long Cay), which had totaled 3,661 in 1901, had fallen 55 percent by 1970 but more than halved again within twenty years, from 1,651 in 1970 to 817 in 1990. Between 1970 and 1990, the already scarcely viable populations of San Salvador/Rum Cay, Mayaguana, and Ragged Island fell by 39.5, 46.3, and 57.2 percent respectively. Ragged Island, which in 1931 had been an enterprising and relatively prosperous small settlement of 424 persons, was home to 89 in 1990; Rum Cay's population of 850 at the height of the salt trade in the nineteenth century had fallen to 53 while Long Cay, which had a population of 499 in 1901, was home to a mere dozen in 1990. In 1990 projections could plausibly be made that several formerly well-populated islands might be completely deserted by the year 2010.

The general lineaments of internal Bahamian migration are clear: the bloating of New Providence, burgeoning of Grand Bahama, and considerable growth of Abaco, at the expense of the more southerly islands. But as Norma Abdulah's analysis of residential changes between 1960 and 1980 showed, the precise pattern of migration is more complex and with more subtle implications than the simple draining of the poorer islands by those economically more developed and developing. Both in the 1960s and 1970s the number of Bahamians migrating to Grand Bahama actually exceeded those migrating to New Providence, though the flow toward Freeport declined somewhat thereafter. More significant, however, far more migrants to Grand Bahama came from New Providence than from all other islands combined. This trend showed that while New Providence's recruits came overwhelmingly from the less developed islands, almost three-quarters of those migrating to fast-developing Grand Bahama had already lived in relatively well-developed and overcrowded New Providence.

Between 1960 and 1970, 5,917 of the inhabitants of New Providence and 6,454 of those in Grand Bahama were ascertained to have originated in other islands, while between 1970 and 1980, 5,027 of the inhabitants of New Providence and 7,376 of those in Grand Bahama stated that their previous residence was in another island. Yet while only 669 of those living in New Providence in the 1960s had originated in Grand Bahama, no less than 4,695 of the 6,454 Grand Bahamian immigrants listed New Providence as their island of origin. Similarly in the 1970s, while only 1,439 of New Providence's 5,027 immigrants had come from Grand Bahama, no less than 5,758 of the 7,376 Grand Bahamian immigrants had previously lived in New Providence.

New Providence's immigrants came quite evenly from a wide range of other islands. Of its 5,917 immigrants of the 1960s, 1,035, or 17.5 percent, originated in Andros, 15.3 percent were from Eleuthera/Harbour Island/Spanish Wells, 11.3 percent from Grand Bahama, 10.8 percent from Long Island, 9.9 percent from Cat Island, and 9.6 percent from the Exumas. Abaco and Acklins each contributed more than 5 percent, and Bimini, Crooked Island, Inagua, Ragged Island, and San Salvador/Rum Cay each between 2 and 5 percent. Grand Bahama, in contrast, had received 4,695, or 72.7 percent, of its 6,454 immigrants from New Providence and only 1,759, or 27.3 percent, from all other Bahamian islands, with only Abaco (with 795 persons, or 12.3 percent) and Andros (407, or 6.3 percent) contributing more than 2 percent each. The figures for the 1970s were equally telling, with 78.1 percent of Grand Bahama immigrants having previously lived in New Providence, 6.5 percent in Abaco, 6.2 percent in Andros, and only 9.2 percent in all other Bahamian islands combined.[6]

Thus, whereas Nassau was the perennial magnet for economic refugees from the poorer Family Islands, Freeport mainly attracted a different kind of migrant. The minority who came directly from the poorer islands (along with the legal or illegal migrants from Haiti, the Turks and Caicos Islands, and other parts of the West Indies) were drawn by the chances of relatively well-paid manual labor. The majority who came directly from New Providence, however, were either those disappointed by Nassau and optimistic of Freeport's greater opportunities, who tended toward the service industries, or the upwardly mobile taking advantage of the Bahamianization of salaried jobs, professional posts, and commerce in Freeport-Lucaya that began with the PLP's accession to power and accelerated after independence.

Though the age and gender profiles of the Bahamas as a whole and of the most populous islands exhibit healthy characteristics, those of the less fortunate islands continue to show the results of migration and the consequent social disruption. The population pyramids derived from the 1990 census for the entire Bahamas, New Providence, and Grand Bahama show an attenuation toward the pattern found in fully developed countries, following the easing of the birth rate and the increase in life expectancy since the 1970s, while the lack of emigration outside the Bahamas tends toward an equalization of the sex ratio—except in the middle and later years—because of the markedly longer life expectancy of women. The proportion of the population under the age of fifteen, an uncomfortable 44 percent in the 1960s, had fallen to 38.4 percent in 1980 and 32.2 percent in 1990, though the actual increase in numbers (as well as the growing numbers of Haitian children) did not noticeably lessen the pressure on schools, especially in New Providence.

The attraction of New Providence and Grand Bahama for Family Islanders as places to work and school their children, as well as the aging of the "baby boomers," are reflected in a comparative thickening of the profile in the middle cohorts for those two islands. Though 33.3 percent of the New Providence population and 36.0 percent of Grand Bahama's remained under school leaving age in 1990, the proportions of those persons aged twenty to fifty had risen from approximately 27 and 30 percent in 1970 to 45.8 and 46.0 percent in 1990, respectively. A similar trend in the middle age cohorts is detectable in Abaco (with 44.1 percent aged twenty to fifty and 34.4 percent below school leaving age in 1990), thanks to immigration for job opportunities and retirement remigrations. As befits a recently developed area, Freeport's island differs significantly from both Nassau's island and Abaco in the comparatively small proportion of elderly persons. In 1990, in fact, Grand Bahama had the lowest percentage of people over the age of sixty in the Bahamas, 3.95 percent, compared with 6.12 percent for New Providence, 7.55 percent for Abaco, and 6.79 percent for the Bahamas as a whole (see Figure 8 and Table 16).

For the other islands, though there is an increased tendency for migration in families and something of a trend (demonstrated, for example, in Susan Love Brown's 1990 study of Cat Island) for obdurate nonmigrants to retain standard family patterns, the general population decline is exacerbated by the disproportion of the young and old (particularly old women). The bare statistics also disguise a

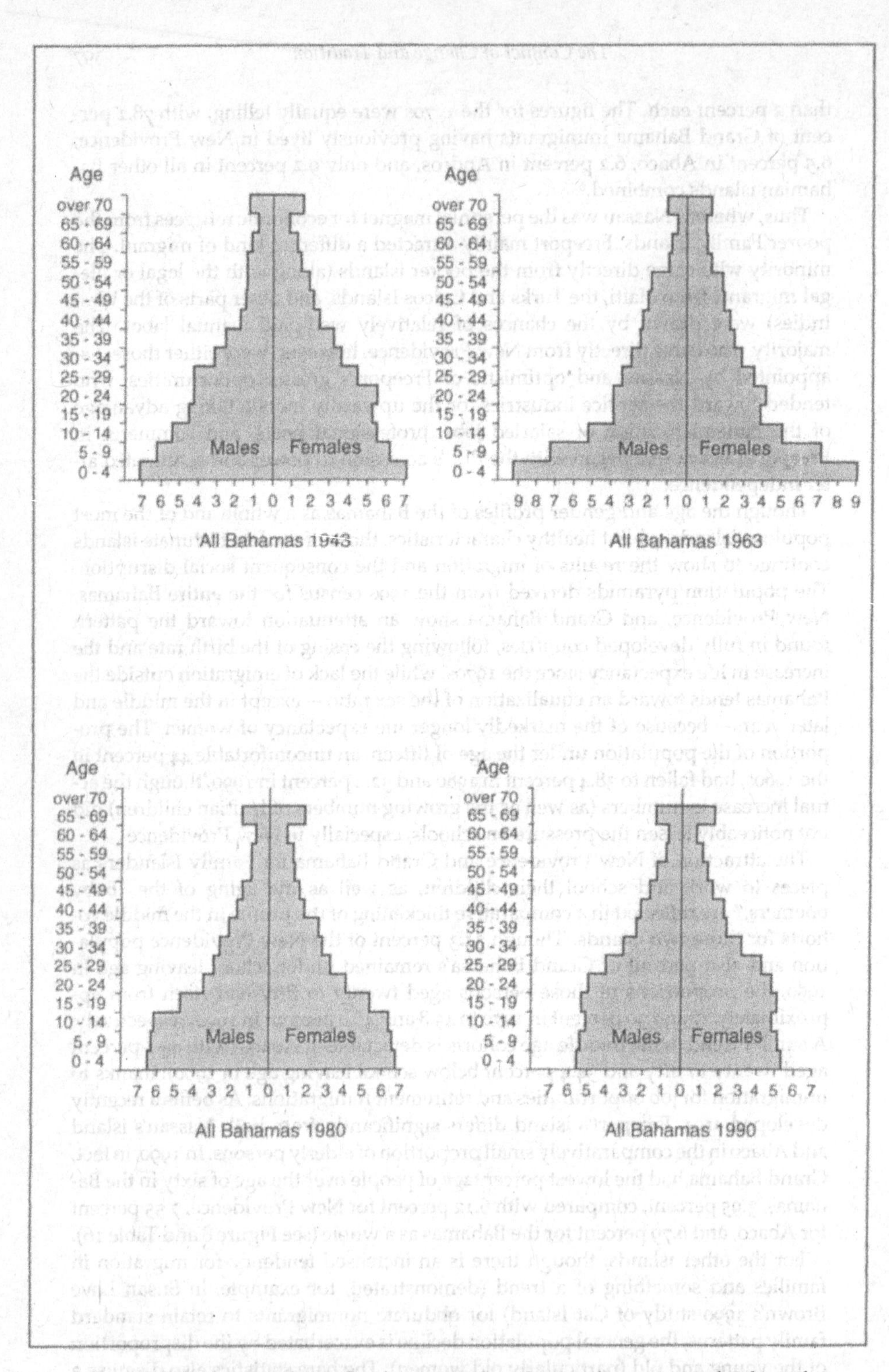

Figure 8. Bahamas: Population Graphs, 1943, 1963, 1980, 1990 (percentages of males and females in five-year cohorts)

Table 16. Bahamas: Quinquennial Age Cohort Percentages, 1943–1990

Age cohort		*1943*	*1953*	*1963*	*1970*	*1980*	*1990*
0–4	m	7.208	7.729	9.468	8.078	6.238	5.726
	f	7.084	7.985	9.356	7.828	6.206	5.587
5–9	m	6.382	6.330	7.474	7.893	6.622	5.431
	f	6.355	6.226	7.515	7.610	6.651	5.244
10–14	m	5.484	5.787	5.236	6.062	6.299	5.135
	f	5.514	5.708	5.195	6.128	6.355	5.041
15–19	m	4.394	4.220	4.025	4.210	6.231	5.284
	f	5.274	5.175	4.149	4.448	6.231	5.297
20–24	m	4.241	3.580	4.060	3.676	4.810	4.963
	f	5.387	4.610	4.337	3.828	5.150	5.035
25–29	m	4.155	3.141	3.694	4.056	3.653	5.034
	f	4.654	4.004	3.868	4.060	3.967	5.171
30–34	m	3.211	2.760	2.962	3.494	2.923	4.052
	f	3.769	3.658	3.068	3.304	3.213	4.396
35–39	m	2.505	3.082		2.763	2.664	3.036
	f	3.205	3.578	m 4.664	2.723	2.942	3.300
40–44	m	1.836	2.572	f 5.159	2.221	2.219	2.400
	f	2.563	3.096		2.279	2.412	2.524
45–49	m	1.534	1.955		1.786	1.766	2.105
	f	2.213	2.382	m 3.858	1.891	1.895	2.257
50–54	m	1.397	1.404	f 4.099	1.689	1.399	1.660
	f	1.958	1.982		1.791	1.577	1.849
55–59	m	1.344	1.035		1.352	1.048	1.280
	f	1.557	1.431	m 1.875	1.336	1.225	1.402
60–64	m	1.054	0.905	f 2.352	0.885	0.975	0.939
	f	1.283	1.214		1.139	1.151	1.121
65–69	m	0.809	0.733		0.647	0.778	0.685
	f	0.926	1.028	m 1.409	0.861	0.956	0.880
Over 70	m	1.083	1.102	f 2.173	0.748	0.948	1.265
	f	1.620	1.587		1.215	1.497	1.898

Sources: Bahamas Censuses, 1943–1990.

tendency of the fittest to migrate, leaving those less healthy and less educated behind for the difficult task of sustaining traditional Family Island life. Among the Middle Islands, Eleuthera retained a relatively healthy age and gender balance despite an overall loss of population, and the independent-mindedness, self-sufficiency, and prosperity of Spanish Wells were reflected in its demographic profile—with a decidedly "middle-class" decline in the number of children born. In contrast, severely depopulated Cat Island and Mayaguana alike, while in the 1990 census having fewer children in the 0–4 year range than in either the 5–9 or 10–14 cohorts, still had a disproportion of their people under the age of 20, and the number of those in the 20–49 age range (414 for Cat Island, 64 for Mayaguana) was actually exceeded by those aged 50 to 79 (427 and 88), of whom 59 and 53 percent, respectively, were females (see Figure 9).[7]

Material Conditions and Employment, 1973–1992

Although many statistical indicators conditions in the Bahamas were steadily improving, averages notoriously disguise extremes, and more careful analysis discloses a far less optimistic general picture. Average figures for population density have limited meaning because of the extreme variations. The average rise in living standards and decline in the birth rate also allow for encouraging figures in respect to household sizes and available facilities, but these are undermined by extremely uneven distribution and by such factors as the tendency of the poorest and least educated to have the most children and the continuing trend for family disruption to occur in the poorest and most crowded areas. Sickness and crime also, of course, tend to be more prevalent in relation to low employment and poor living conditions. Figures can be "massaged" to provide a Panglossian view (the PLP, not surprisingly, providing a generous budget for a Statistics Department staffed largely with its own supporters), but they can also reveal (as with Norma Abdulah's 1987 UNESCO/CARICOM/ISER study) far more disquieting realities.

The *Preliminary Results* of the 1990 census, published in 1992, included statistics that showed that the number of Bahamian "households" had risen faster than the population between 1980 and 1990, from 48,233 to 67,594, and that the average household size had fallen from 4.34 persons to 3.77. The largest average household size in 1990 was found in Andros (4.33) and the smallest in Spanish Wells (2.46), but every Bahamian island recorded a decline in household size. In many cases this was obviously caused by depopulation through migration, with Ragged Island and Rum Cay being the extreme examples (falling from averages of 5.47 and 3.71 persons to 3.07 and 2.52, respectively). Yet in some islands where the population had stayed static or increased, household sizes still declined. Exuma's, for example, despite virtually no drop in total population, fell from an average of 4.55 persons in 1980 to 3.74 in 1990. In New Providence, the average household size had declined from 4.61 persons in 1980 to 3.88 in 1990, in Grand Bahama, from 3.99 to 3.60, and in Abaco, from 3.95 to 3.32.[8]

Analysis of these statistics is complicated by the fact that, as Norma Abdulah noted, "household" was virtually equated with "dwelling" as late as the 1980 census yet by 1990 had come closer to being differentiated to mean, more accurately, a bonded group of persons or an individual living in one premises. Though not generally so, an apparent increase in the number of households might actually denote greater crowding in the case of different families living on the same premises. The difficulties of identifying or defining "household heads," as well as the tendency to correlate "family" with conjugal households, moreover, seriously complicate the analysis of family, marital, and parental patterns and trends.[9] Nonetheless, Abdulah's unraveling and reweaving of the 1980 census data and a careful look at the statistics available by 1994 from the 1990 census are revealing, particularly in respect to the relative roles of men and women.

The great majority of Bahamian households in 1980 were single conjugal families living in separate houses, though one in five households had no families at all

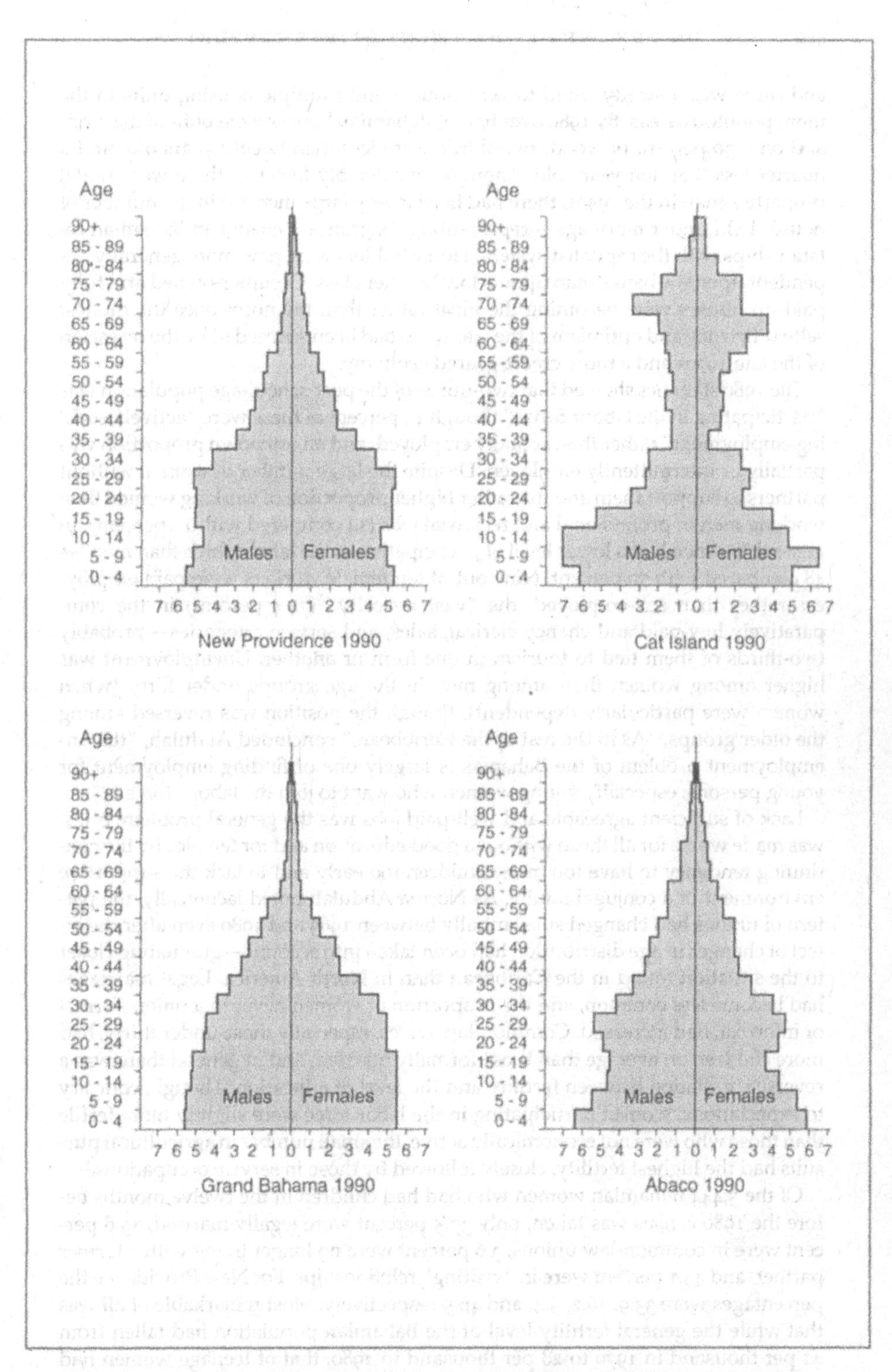

Figure 9. Bahamas: Population Graphs, 1990: New Providence, Cat Island, Grand Bahama, Abaco (percentages of males and females in five-year cohorts)

and there was a steady trend toward double and multiple housing units in the more populous areas. By 1980 over half of Bahamian houses were built of masonry and only 30 percent of wood, two-thirds were less than twenty years old, and a quarter less than ten years old. Though considerably fewer of these were rental properties than in the 1950s, there had been a very large increase in the number of houses held under mortgage—representing a significant change in Bahamian relationships with the capitalist system. Householders were now more generally dependent upon the banks than upon a local rentier class. Occupier-owned and fully paid-up houses were becoming the ideal rather than the norm once the modest self-sufficiency and optimism of the late 1960s had been succeeded by the recession of the late 1970s and a more credit-geared economy.

The 1980 statistics showed that two-thirds of the post-school-age population was "participating in the labour force," though 15 percent of these were "actively seeking employment" rather than actually employed, and an unknown proportion was partially or intermittently employed. Despite the large number of women without partners to support them and the rather higher proportion of working women than working men in professional and technical jobs (14 compared with 11 percent), in general "women had a lower level of participation in the labour force than men"—48 compared with 70 percent. Nine out of ten female workers were paid employees rather than self-employed, the "vast majority" (74.4 percent) in the comparatively low-paid and chancy clerical, sales, and service categories—probably two-thirds of them tied to tourism in one form or another. Unemployment was higher among women than among men in the age groups under forty (when women were particularly dependent), though the position was reversed among the older groups. "As in the rest of the Caribbean," concluded Abdulah, "the unemployment problem of the Bahamas is largely one of finding employment for young persons, especially young women who want to join the labour force."[10]

Lack of sufficient agreeable and well-paid jobs was the general problem, but it was made worse for all those without a good education and for females by the continuing tendency to have too many children too early and to lack the supportive environment of a conjugal family. As Norma Abdulah noted laconically, the pattern of unions had changed substantially between 1963 and 1980 even after the effect of changes in age distribution had been taken into account—gravitating closer to the situation found in the Caribbean than in North America. Legal marriages had become less common, and the proportion of women never in a union, formal or informal, had increased. Common-law wives, especially those under thirty, had more children on average than those formally married, and in general there was a reverse correlation between fertility and the level of education. Though, contrary to expectations, women participating in the labor force were slightly more fertile than those who were not economically active, the small number in agricultural pursuits had the highest fertility, closely followed by those in service occupations.[11]

Of the 5,444 Bahamian women who had had children in the twelve months before the 1980 census was taken, only 37.5 percent were legally married, 15.8 percent were in common-law unions, 3.6 percent were no longer living with a former partner, and 43.1 percent were in "visiting" relationships. For New Providence the percentages were 33.9, 16.2, 3.4, and 46.5 respectively. Most remarkable of all was that while the general fertility level of the Bahamian population had fallen from 41 per thousand in 1970 to 28 per thousand in 1980, that of teenage women had stayed level (around 90 per thousand females aged fifteen to twenty) and the proportion of live births to teenage mothers had risen from under a seventh to over a fifth. Of the teenage mothers, who bore 21 percent of all children born in 1979–80, no less than 78 percent were in visiting relationships. The average age at which all mothers had had their first child fell from 21.0 years in 1970 to 20.6 years in 1980, while teenage mothers had on the average first given birth at only 16.6 years.[12]

A limited fertility study of women in New Providence, produced at about the same time as Norma Abdulah's report, showed that while the largest category of women were those with one to two children who had had only one partner, almost half of those women were single at the time of the survey. While once-married still-married women on average had the largest families, they were outnumbered by single women, and their fertility as well as their numbers was almost matched by those of single women who had had multiple partners. Though modern methods of contraception were widely used (abstinence, bush medicine, and the rhythm method being reported by only 3, 4, and 5 women respectively out of the 638 surveyed), more than a quarter of the women, and half the teenagers, reported using none at all. Interestingly, of the three religious affiliations that accounted for three-quarters of the women surveyed, the Roman Catholics reported the greatest use of contraception, with Anglicans close and Baptists substantially behind. Given this finding, it was perhaps not surprising that the Baptists tended to have the largest number of children.[13]

Ten years later, the social conditions deducible from the census data had not generally improved and in some cases had regressed. Moreover, the overall picture would certainly have been worse had all illegal immigrants, characterized by generally shifting unions, higher birth rates, lower incomes, and poorer and more crowded houses, been included in the census. The rate of building had slowed and the increase in the provision of electricity, water, and sewerage fallen even further behind the increase in population. Though the greater acceptance of the notion of common-law unions had narrowed the definition of "technical illegitimacy" and the rate of births to unwed teenage mothers was marginally down, this was largely owing to the decline in the proportion of teenagers in the population. The highest level of fertility continued to be among uneducated and underemployed females, and a disturbing number of single-parent or broken homes prevailed.

During the 1980s, the Bahamian annual crude birth rate continued its steady fall, from 28 to about 25 per thousand, but the decline in the crude death rate below 6 per thousand was slowed by a perceptible increase in the number of deaths in the young adult range, particularly for males. The average number of deaths recorded of persons aged twenty to forty for the period 1989–91 compared with 1980–83 showed an increase of 49 percent overall and of 60 percent for males, a rise plausibly attributed to the increase in AIDS, as well as to drug- and crime-related deaths and traffic accidents.[14] There was a slight rise in the number of marriages (which not coincidentally followed the intermediate vagaries of the economy) from a crude average of 7.7 per thousand between 1970 and 1973 and 5.9 per thousand between 1974 and 1977, to 8.9 per thousand between 1988 and 1992. This, however, was offset by a greater increase in the number of legal divorces, from fewer than 100 per year in the 1970s to as many as 425 a year in the 1980s. In 1990, 2,797 of Bahamian private households were headed by divorced persons, compared with 4,995 by those informally separated, 5,629 by widows and widowers, 15,683 headed by single persons, 6,075 by those in common-law unions, and 26,469 by those formally married. Though the census still failed to recognize family relationships within households, the number of single-headed families seems to have continued to increase, with a third of all households female-headed.[15]

The preliminary results of the 1990 census (the last held during the regime of the PLP) included evidence of the continuing general improvement in housing and other facilities and especially of the great changes since 1963, though, perhaps naturally, they did not emphasize failings, shortfalls, or the more problematic trends. By 1990, 53.7 percent of all Bahamian household/dwellings had public water piped into the house and 3.3 percent into the yard (compared with a combined total of 37 percent for New Providence and almost none for the Family Islands in 1963). A further 24.0 percent of households, however, used privately piped supplies, 10.3 percent still depended on public standpipes, and 8.6 percent on wells or tanks (7.7 percent private, 2.1 percent public).[16] Moreover, both the quantity and quality of public water supplies presented problems, particularly in New Providence, where piped water was normally brackish and often discolored, and supplies were increasingly dependent on water barged in from Andros.

By 1990, far fewer Bahamian houses had inadequate or shared sewerage facilities, though only 9.9 percent of all dwellings enjoyed flush toilets linked to a public sewerage system. Some 77 percent now had flush toilets (clearly one of the great demands on the water supply), but 67 percent of all dwellings were still dependent on cesspits or septic tanks. Approximately 10.4 percent of dwellings still shared toilet facilities, 16.1 percent used pit latrines, and 1.8 percent (almost certainly an undercounting, given the number of illegal immigrants living in shanties in the bush) were listed as having no toilet facilities at all.[17]

The vast majority of Bahamian houses had some electricity by 1990, and the distribution system in New Providence, Grand Bahama, and some other islands (notably Spanish Wells, with its community-owned generators) was impressive. But the total amounts generated continued to fall short of the population growth, and the unit cost rose higher than the general rate of inflation. As Susan Love Brown showed for Cat Island, Family Islanders suffered in proportion to their isolation, either from a comparatively inefficient public system, with frequent interruptions, or from a dependency on private generators, which probably trebled the unit cost and left users additionally dependent on chancy fuel supplies. In a society ever more geared to the use of electricity for refrigerators and televisions as well as for lighting and cooking, this was a far from insignificant factor in explaining the drift away from the less modernized islands.[18]

The three consumer items that became virtual necessities as the Bahamian people entered the mainstream of the modern world (and the world of consumer debt) were automobiles, later, TV sets, and to a slightly lesser degree, telephones. The statistics for vehicle registrations, indeed, were the most accurate index of the expanding economy. In 1956, the total number of cars, trucks, taxis, buses, and motorcycles licensed was 5,641, or an average of one to every sixteen Bahamians. The total had risen to 8,016 by 1958 but took off in the last years of the UBP and first of the PLP in the 1960s, soaring from 28,232 in 1966 to 53,713 in 1969 (one for every three Bahamians). In the latter year there were 32,000 licensed vehicles in New Providence and over 16,000 in Grand Bahama—or two for every three persons on the average—compared with about 6,000 for the rest of the Family Islands put together. The recession of the 1970s saw a decline, to 48,342 in 1974, with New Providence staying level but the number of vehicles in Grand Bahama falling to under 10,000. The numbers surged upward again to total 70,255 in 1984 (50,192 for New Providence and 20,063 for all the other islands), and over 100,000 ten years later. By then, New Providence, with its 58,000 private cars, 950 taxis, 640 trucks, and 580 buses, on roads largely dating from donkey-cart days, was suffering from serious traffic and parking congestion and a high accident rate, as well as the problem of disposing of derelict vehicles.[19]

The Bahamas had telegraphic communication with the rest of the world as early as 1892, and Nassau had a limited telephone service from 1906. The local telephone networks were gradually widened and radio replaced the overseas cable, but quantum leaps were made with the installation of a forward-scatter radio system in 1959, the introduction of interinsular and overseas direct dialing in 1978, the switch to earth satellite routing by the INTELSAT system in 1987, and the introduction of cellular telephoning in 1988. By the 1990s, at least a third of Bahamian homes had telephones, with 49.6 telephones per 100 persons overall. Most Bahamian islands were in almost instant touch with each other and with the rest of the world, and Nassau, Freeport, and some other centers had hookups for faxing, teleconferencing, and computer networking.[20] Important as they were, however, these improvements in communications did not noticeably slow the drift from the Family Islands and had less social and cultural effects than those wrought by television.

Before 1977, only the Bahamian islands just across the Gulf Stream from Florida were able to receive television. On July 4, 1977, though, the Bahamas Broadcasting Corporation started its own transmissions; the station was officially opened by Queen Elizabeth II on October 20 that year. With color from the beginning and an effective range of 130 miles, ZNS TV within a short time made a television set in the house as common as a car in the yard for a majority of Bahamian homes, however poor. Since, like the United States and unlike Britain, the Bahamas did not institute licensing for TV sets, precise numbers are unavailable, but there were probably sixty thousand sets by 1990. Although it had started proudly autonomous of outside commercial networks, in 1983 ZNS widened its offerings by adding the facility to retransmit satellite transmissions and later added a second channel, increasing programs from the original sixty-five to almost two hundred hours per week. Even more important stages in what was clearly a cultural as well as communications revolution were the proliferation of private satellite receivers during the 1980s and 1990s (which not only made it possible for TV to be seen anywhere in the Bahamas but brought the Bahamas as a whole into a worldwide network), the widespread addition of video machines to TV sets, and the introduction of cable TV, beginning in Grand Bahama in 1989. All of these developments linked the Bahamas even more directly to the culture and commercialism of the United States (see Tables 17 and 18).[21]

Among the most interesting details available from the 1990 census were those for religious affiliation, showing the continuation of trends already noticed from the period 1943–63, though their precise significance remains open to debate. The three chief churches remained the same, though their relative importance had shifted considerably. The Baptists (strongly identified with the PLP for much of the period) had increased their share of the total population from 30 percent in 1963

Table 17. Gross Domestic Product per Capita: Bahamas Compared with Other Countries in Region, 1960–1988 (1988 U.S. dollars)

Country	1960	1970	1980	1988
Bahamas	8,448	10,737	10,631	11,317
Chile	1,845	2,236	2,448	2,518
Argentina	2,384	3,075	3,359	2,862
Uruguay	2,352	2,478	3,221	2,989
Brazil	1,013	1,372	2,481	2,449
Paraguay	779	931	1,612	1,557
Bolivia	634	818	983	724
Peru	1,233	1,554	1,716	1,503
Ecuador	771	904	1,581	1,477
Colombia	927	1,157	1,595	1,739
Venezuela	3,879	4,941	5,225	4,544
Guyana	1,008	1,111	1,215	995
Suriname	887	2,337	3,722	3,420
Mexico	1,425	2.022	2,872	2,588
Guatemala	1,100	1,420	1,866	1,502
Honduras	619	782	954	851
El Salvador	832	1,032	1,125	995
Nicaragua	1,055	1,495	1,147	819
Costa Rica	1,435	1,825	2,394	2,235
Panama	1,264	2,017	2,622	2,229
Dominican Republic	823	987	1,497	1,509
Haiti	331	292	386	319
Jamaica	1,610	2,364	1,880	1,843
Trinidad & Tobago	3,848	4,927	8,116	5,510
Barbados	2,000	3,530	3,994	4,233

Source: World Almanac, 1988.

back to 33 percent, but the proportion of adherents to the formerly established Anglican church had fallen further from 24 to 17 percent. Though the total of Roman Catholics had fallen somewhat (reflecting doctrinal and organizational discord), this decline was much less than that of the Anglicans, whose number of adherents the Roman Catholics now equaled almost exactly. The Methodists, third behind Baptists and Anglicans as late as 1943, had fallen further in popularity, to seventh. From commanding 8 percent in 1963 to 5 percent in 1990, Methodists (who were plagued by serious internal splits) were now outnumbered by the adherents of both Pentecostalism and the Church of God.

That the total of reported church affiliations in 1990 was 7.5 percent less than the total population, the converse of previous statistics, may or not indicate a slight decline in Bahamians' traditionally avid rate of church attendance. Perhaps arguing against a decline in spiritual activity, the "radical" or "spiritualist" churches were the greatest gainers between 1963 and 1990. Though the share of Brethren and members of the Church of God had not grown, that of formal Pentecostals had burgeoned from 1 to almost 6 percent of the total population. When the 3 percent of

Table 18. Comparative Life and Material Indices: Bahamas and Selected Countries, 1990

	Bahamas	*Bermuda*	*Barbados*	*Jamaica*	*Cuba*	*Haiti*	*United States*
Area (sq. m.)	5,382	21	166	4,244	42,803	10,714	1,937,725
Population (th.)	255	58	255	2,456	10,608	6,513	249,224
Blacks/whites	85:15	61:39	80:4:16[a]	76:3:15[a]	11:37:51[a]	95:5[b]	12:85
Arable land (%)	1	0	77	19	23	20	20
Agricultural employment (%)	5	2	8	32	20	66	n/a
GDP per capita (US$)	9,875	23,000[c]	5,250[c]	1,529[c]	2,000[c]	380[d]	21,082[d]
Unemployed (%)	12[e]	2[f]	18.6[d]	18.7[d]	6[c]	50[d]	5.2[c]
Births (per th.)	17	15	18	21	18	45	15
Deaths (per th.)	6	7	8	5	7	16	9
Infant mortality (per th.)	21	12	16	16	12	107	10
Life expectancy (yrs. at birth, m/f)	68/75	72/78	73/77	75/79	73/78	52/55	73/80
Marriages (per th.)	7.9[f]	13.7[e]	5.8[e]	4.6[e]	7.9[d]	n/a	9.7[d]
Divorces (per th.)	1.6[e]	3.7[g]	1.4[e]	0.4[e]	3.1[f]	n/a	4.8[d]
Physicians (per th.)	9.8[i]	7.0[j]	9.4[i]	4.9[h]	19.1[h]	1.6[h]	21.4[h]
Literacy (%)	95	98	99	74	98.5	23	99
TVs (per th.)[e]	223	617	259	105	202	4	813
Radios (per th.)[e]	515	864	863	400	335	30	2,126
Phones (per th.)[f]	49.6	n/a	37.2	n/a	5.4	n/a	n/a
Cars (persons per car)	4.9[i]	3.7[j]	6.9[f]	n/a	46.2[f]	304.3[e]	1.8[f]

[a] Blacks/whites/mixed.

[b] Blacks/whites and mixed.

[c] 1989.

[d] 1988.

[e] 1986.

[f] 1987.

[g] 1985.

[h] 1984.

[i] 1983.

[j] 1982.

Source: Canadian Global Almanac, 1992.

Seventh Day Adventists (up from 2 percent in 1963), the almost 2 percent of members of the Assembly of God, and the more than 1 percent of Jehovah's Witnesses were added, the combined share of the nonmainline churches was more than 20 percent, compared with 13 percent in 1963. Perhaps indicating a bias toward Christian churches among the enumerators, no figures were given in the 1990 census for either the followers of Mohammed or the adherents of Vodun.[22]

Not entirely unrelated to church affiliation, but of great significance, were the 1990 figures for employment and education. Most clearly problematic—though even more than ever obfuscated by incoherent categories—were the latest available figures for employment (1993). If one ignores Norma Abdulah's recommendations to use definitions that would distinguish salaries, wage, and self-employment, recognize underemployment, and reveal more clearly the dependence on tourism and offshore banking, these figures suggest the continuance of disturbing trends. The total of those listed as employed, 118,950, was the highest ever, and the proportion of women, 47.3 percent, was significantly greater than in previous computations. But because the proportion of the total adult population said to be employed had not increased, apparently at least a third of the adult population was still not in the workforce and the proportion of unemployed males had increased. Though age-specific figures were not provided, almost certainly this situation was especially critical among those closest to school leaving age.

The categories of employment, though difficult to decode, were annoyingly further muddied by the use of two methods of computation, distinguishing "industrial" from "occupational" groupings. Yet both tables unequivocally show the serious further decline in traditional occupations and jobs involving manual labor, a continuing shift toward urban, office, and government employment, and a failure to diversify the economy. In the "industrial" table, a mere 6,435 persons, 5 percent of the working population (88 percent of them males) were still engaged in agriculture, hunting, forestry, and fishing combined. Mining, quarrying, electricity, gas, and water (a curious combination) accounted for 2 percent, manufacturing only 4 percent (shared equally between men and women), and construction 6 percent. These categories were outweighed by the 7 percent in transport, storage, and communication, 10 percent in financing, insurance, real estate, and other business services, 15 percent in hotels and restaurants, 16 percent in wholesale and retail sales, and 38 percent (14,141 males and 17,093 females) in "community, social and personal services." The "occupational" table counted only 4,417 persons, 4 percent, as skilled agricultural and fishery workers, considerably fewer than the 7,682, 6 percent, of "legislators and senior officials," and outnumbered even more by the 17 percent of professionals, technicians, and associate professionals, the 14 percent of clerks, 19 percent of craft and related workers, plant and machine operators and assemblers, 22 percent of service workers and shop and market sales workers, and the 17 percent in what were unhelpfully categorized as "elementary occupations" (see Figures 10 and 11).[23]

Educational Achievements and Problems in the 1980s and 1990s

More helpful and impressive than the employment figures, though still problematic, were the 1990 education statistics. Although the figures did not fully indicate the quality or practical relevance of the schooling or relate to enough variables, they did disclose a remarkable improvement—almost an explosion—in Bahamian education since the 1960s, bringing it seemingly ahead of all territories in the region except perhaps Barbados, Bermuda, and Puerto Rico. By 1990, only 2.69 percent of the adult Bahamian population totally lacked schooling, 92.26 percent even of those over forty-five having had at least some elementary education. Compared with the disgraceful figures before the PLP came to power, 76.25 percent of the adult population (and almost half of those over forty-five) could boast some secondary education or better; 44.40 percent had gone beyond fourth grade in high

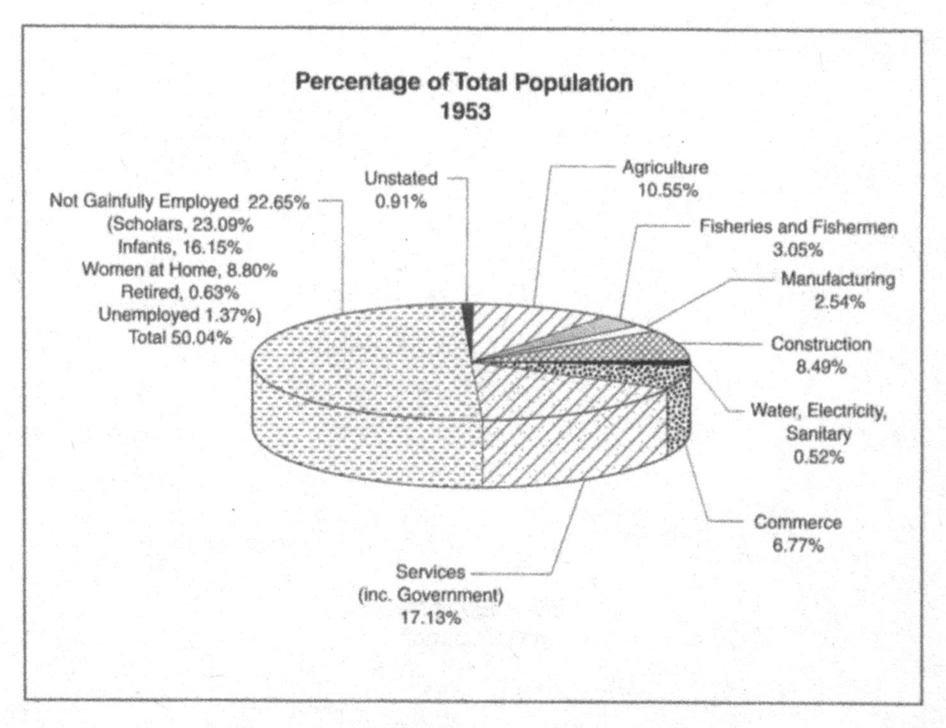

Figure 10. Whole Bahamas: Pie Graph of Occupations, 1953

school, 10.64 percent into tertiary education, and 6.85 percent (9,179 persons) had achieved three or four years in college or university—at least two-thirds of them abroad.[24]

Other educational statistics also seem to give grounds for national satisfaction. By 1986, $82 million, or 19 percent of the national budget, was allotted to education, some four times that given for the promotion of tourism. The Ministry of Education operated 187 schools, of which 149 were outside New Providence, and the single government secondary school when the PLP came to power had multiplied to thirty, no less than nineteen of them in the Family Islands. The teacher-pupil ratio, once as high as one to seventy in some schools, had been reduced to an average of one to twenty. The College of the Bahamas, opened in 1975, boasted almost two thousand students by 1986, when its budget received a 19 percent boost and there was widespread talk of upgrading it to university status. A closer look at the history of Bahamian education during the PLP years (such as that given in 1989 by Dean Collinwood, a white American social scientist who taught for some years at the College of the Bahamas) and of the system taken over by the FNM in 1992, however, reveals a far from peaceful or fully successful process of improvement and fundamental problems, some of which would seem to be almost insoluble (see Table 19).[25]

The expansion of educational facilities seemed to have outrun the ability to fund them, especially as the recession that began in the early 1970s took hold. Mismanagement and planning failures—inevitable in any new nation—can be blamed for

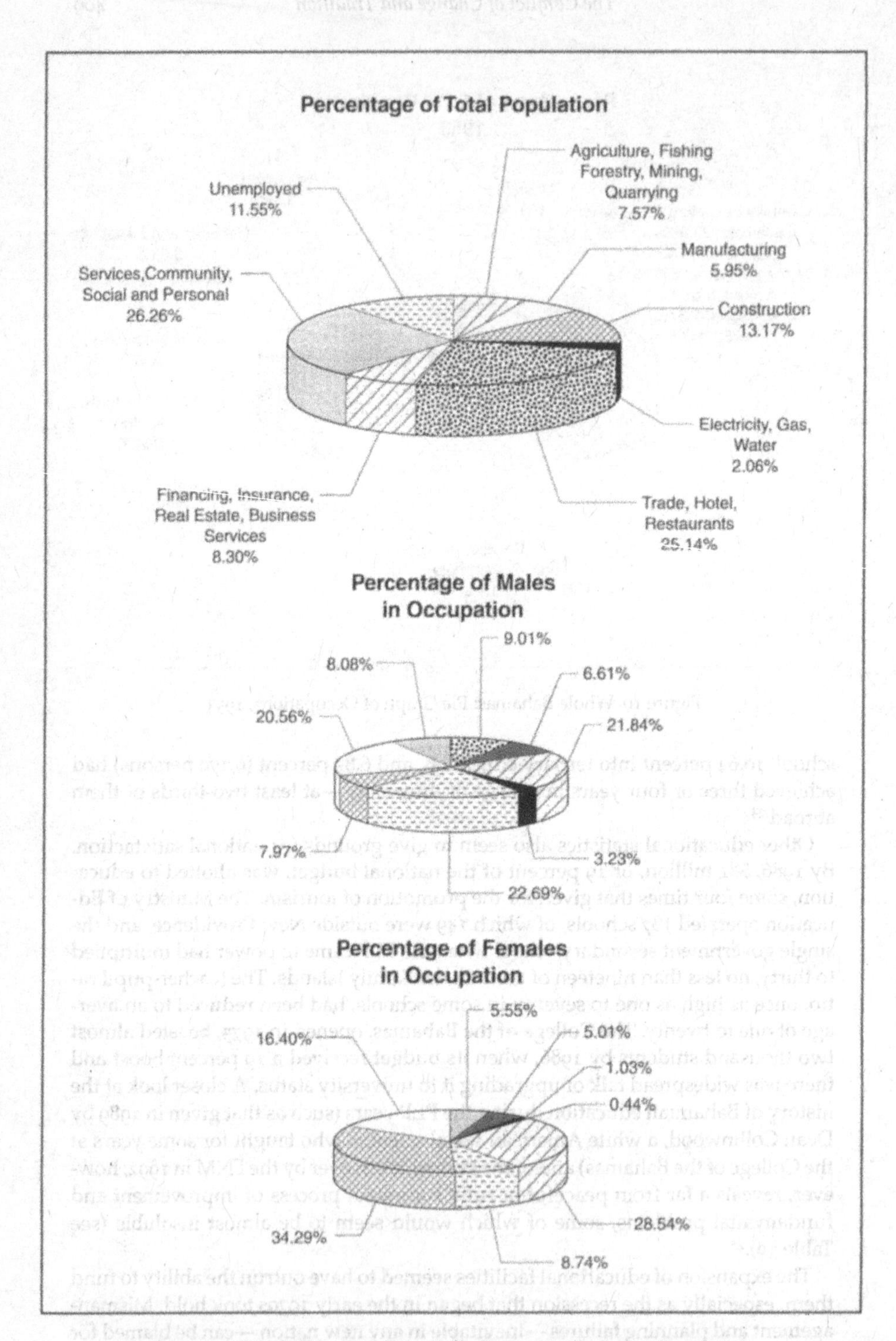

Figure 11. Whole Bahamas: Potentially Economically Active Population over 14 years of Age, 1970

Table 19. Bahamas: Population Aged over 20 Not Attending School, by Highest Educational Attainment, 1990

Category	All aged 20–24	All aged 45+	All Males aged 20+	All Females aged 20+
Total	84,667	40,003	59,846	64,834
No schooling	1,982	1,496	1,866	1,608
	2.34%	3.74%	3.12%	2.48%
Kindergarten	193	256	206	243
	0.23%	0.64%	0.34%	0.37%
Elementary	9,097	18,236	13,023	14,310
	10.74%	45.59%	21.76%	22.07%
High school grades 1–3	15,393	8,620	12,105	11,954
	18.78%	21.55%	20.23%	18.44%
High school grades 4+	45,536	7,479	24,905	28,110
	53.78%	18.70%	41.62%	43.36%
College or university	5,118	1,225	2,834	3,508
1–2 years	6.04%	3.06%	4.74%	59.41%
College or university	1,716	475	973	1,218
3 years	2.03%	1.19%	1.63%	1.18%
College or university	5,124	1,844	3,592	3,376
4+ years	6.05%	4.61%	6.00%	5.21%
Other	256	295	268	283
	0.30%	0.74%	0.45%	0.45%
Not stated	162	81	123	120
	0.19%	0.20%	0.21%	0.19%

Source: Bahamas Census, 1990.

some of the problems. Yet probably more crucial were simple and unavoidable dilemmas: falling into the no-man's-land between ingrained traditions and unrealistic aspirations and lack of knowledge about what education the Bahamas needed, wanted, or could achieve.

The lack of money for maintenance, coupled with sheer slackness, meant that even new buildings and facilities quickly ran down, while the inability of the government to sustain salaries at the rate of inflation caused a serious decline in the morale of teaching staff and an increased unwillingness of the more able and ambitious Bahamians to enter or stay in the teaching profession. To the general dissatisfaction with the continuing dependence on expatriate teachers were added complaints by pupils and parents of the minority of expatriates who were slack, incompetent, or openly contemptuous of Bahamians and Bahamian culture. Unenthusiastic or disaffected teachers, whether native or foreign, could hardly be expected to inspire their pupils with the practical purposes (let alone the joys) of

Hugely expanded and improved since the 1960s, Bahamian government schools remain overcrowded, underfunded, and short of teachers. Each school, though, retained its distinctive uniform. Courtesy of Bahamas Information Service.

education, galvanize those who thought that being in high school was an end in itself and an automatic route into the middle class, or discipline the minority who were unwilling to be in school at all and were disruptive. To the "us" and "them" of teachers and pupils (and their parents) was added the far more serious (and sadly traditional) dichotomy between teachers and administrators. On its side, the government tended to see cutbacks in education as a soft option in a straitened economy and to disregard dissent, especially if it emanated from expatriate staff, while an Education Ministry not notable for internal economies or efficiency, too easily assumed, according to Dean Collinwood, an elitist indifference familiar from the bad old colonial days.[26]

The situation reached crisis proportions in the early 1980s. In January 1981, the Bahamas Union of Teachers (BUT), representing most public school teachers and some teachers at the college, staged an unprecedented strike for improved pay and conditions which lasted three weeks, despite the appearance of Prime Minister Pindling on television demanding that they return to work. An agreement was patched together but did not last. The college was placated by substantial improvements, with help from the World Bank, including library and computer resources, a cafeteria, student center, and faculty lounge; but nothing commensurate was done for the schools. In mid-1982, the majority of BUT members voted for further industrial action, despite the government's position that that they were civil servants and that striking was illegal under the terms of their contracts (a clear legacy of colonial times). In the event, action by the teachers was anticipated by students. In February 1983, pupils from two high schools formed the Students National Action Party (SNAP). For two weeks they boycotted classes and demonstrated in Rawson Square, calling for the resignation of the minister of education, Darrell Rolle. Besides support from the BUT (and the Vanguard Party), this action was, not surprisingly, endorsed by the opposition FNM, whose then leader, Cecil Wallace-Whitfield, was himself a former minister of education.[27]

The student demonstrators were temporarily suspended from school, but the government's ire was concentrated on a headmaster, Leonard Archer, who was both the outspoken president of the BUT and secretary general of the Trade Union Congress. At the height of the storm, suspicious fires broke out in four different schools, one of which totally destroyed the administration building of St. Augustine College. In June 1983, the permanent secretary to the Ministry of Education recommended that Archer be "retired in the public interest" on the grounds that he had incited the students and publicly scorned the civil service regulations. The response of the BUT was to burn the regulations page by page in public and to invite the socialist prime minister of Jamaica, Michael Manley, to address a union meeting. After two days of debate in parliament and an unsuccessful appeal to the Civil Service Commission, Archer was prematurely retired, albeit on a full pension. This action occasioned further downtown demonstrations, during which the prime minister was booed and several teachers arrested.

Thereafter, the dispute cooled somewhat, partly because the government and people were distracted by the drugs scandals, partly because of a power struggle within the BUT between the radicals and moderates. According to Dean Collinwood (following the ideas of his fellow sociologists Harriet Lefley and Albert Memmi), it also related to the tendency of Bahamians, like many formerly colonized people, too readily to accept the structures of authority and (more specifically Bahamian characteristics) to accept the status quo as long as it was accompanied by good interpersonal relationships, to shy from leadership in preference for an easy life, and to be too easily satisfied with material or superficial improvements.[28] The government certainly seemed able to defuse and control dissent by piecemeal disbursements—concentrating on the college, a few showpiece new buildings, and such trendy innovations as computer terminals, while comparatively neglecting such less publicly visible resources as books and other basic teaching resources.

In a way that few persons seemed to realize, primary, secondary, and tertiary education and the problems they faced were interrelated and interdependent in fundamental ways. Though the preparation of young children for the secondary schooling that was now the Bahamian norm was at least as important as preparing high school students for tertiary education, ingrained hierarchical prejudices not only tended to allocate budgets in reverse proportion to the level of schools but accorded status to teachers according to the level at which they taught. Family Island school postings were likewise rated lower than those in New Providence. All schools continued to depend on expatriate teachers whose commitment to and empathy with the Bahamas was likely to be less than total (paradoxically, any disdain they felt for their Bahamian pupils and colleagues as often triggered by a perception of their failure to be politically progressive as of either their cultural backwardness or sheer laziness). But the fruits of this dependence were further soured by the tendency to post expatriates to the less prestigious and unpopular schools, mainly in the Family Islands. Almost as bad as the old monitorial system and probably worse than the former dependence on white colonialist Britons (such as Jack Ford in Abaco during the 1950s) were the results of reliance on disgruntled teachers from Canada, the United States, or the Commonwealth Caribbean (not to mention India, Pakistan, or the Philippines). The failures of the government schools, moreover, led to an escalating preference for the private schools.

High school teachers complained that an increasing number of children obtaining entry were barely able to read and write (very few of them Haitians, whose parents ensured that those attending elementary school got the best possible results out of the system). Yet this failure at the primary level was no more startling than the steadily declining standards of attainment in government high schools. To an extent, this had been covered up—and almost certainly exacerbated—by the abandonment of the Bahamas Junior Certificate (BJC) in 1975. It had originally been designed as a leaving certificate for those going no higher than the former "senior" primary or "all-age" schools but became merely an intermediate examination at the eighth grade once a division was made at that level between junior and senior high schools. There was thus a pedagogic rationale for its discontinuance, but skeptics attributed it mainly to the abysmal results being obtained. In 1973, for example, of 1,937 candidates taking the BJC (a notoriously easy examination), 40 percent passed in no subjects at all. Of 1,057 who took four or more subjects, only 66 actually passed four or more subjects.[29]

Fifteen years later, however, the results in the far more critical tenth grade "Ordinary" level Overseas General Certificate of Education (OGCE) examinations (taken in preference to the allegedly tougher Caribbean Examinations Council alternative), which for the majority of Bahamian high schoolers was the nearest equivalent to a school leaving certificate, were equally dismal. In June 1991, a confidential analysis was made by E. Stubbs of what were expected to be the last OGCE "Ordinary" level results for all Bahamian schools, private as well as public. Only a minority of age-qualified high schoolers (60 percent of them girls) took any subjects at all, and there was great selectivity in what subjects were attempted. Not surprisingly, perhaps, religious knowledge was one of the most popular. Yet the percentage of failures (that is, marks below 35 percent) was 40.3 percent. Of the five levels of pass, only 3 percent of subject passes were in the A range and 8.1 percent B's, with 19.3, 11.8, and 17.5 percent in the C, D, and E range, respectively.

Comparison with the private schools' results placed the achievement of government schools in an even sorrier light, and that of most Family Island high schools was bleak indeed. The failure rate of government schools was 51.4 percent against 26.2 percent for private schools. Though government high schoolers outnumbered private school pupils five to one, the total number of subjects taken was almost exactly equal, and yet the total of passes in the A and B categories was 778 to 255 (22.8 to 5.8 percent) in favor of the private schools. Though South Andros High School did notably well with twelve A grade passes (many of them in religious knowledge), the next best result from the Family Islands was the eighteen B grade passes from Governor's Harbour, Eleuthera. The best results from the government high schools at Cooper's Town, Abaco, and San Salvador were seven and four C grade passes respectively. Over the entire high school system, the proportion of pupils who stayed in school even to attempt the three subjects in the twelfth grade OGCE

"A" level examination needed for entry to universities in Canada and the United Kingdom was no more than one in thirty.[30]

At this time of dismal educational achievement the education portfolio was given to Paul Adderley in place of the embattled Darrell Rolle in 1984, and in 1988 the new minister of education (foremost among all Bahamian nationalists) announced the planning of a national curriculum and an examination system more attuned to Bahamian needs and conditions. Somewhat ironically, the ministry's main planner was a consultancy based in Cambridge, England. But the already well-established Commonwealth Caribbean–based Caribbean Examinations Council (CXC) curricula and examinations were rejected along with the British OGCE system because they were almost as externally oriented. Instead, it was announced that the Bahamas Junior Certificate would be reintroduced and a radically new and carefully indigenized Bahamas General Certificate of Secondary Education (BGCSE) for school leavers was painstakingly designed, for initiation in 1993.

In principle, the new BJC and BGCSE were admirable, geared to orderly progress through secondary to tertiary education. The BJC was designed to ensure that those entering the high schools would at least be trained in the basics, while the syllabus leading to the BGCSE contained a rational core of required subjects, included practical as well as theoretical work, and laid stress on Bahamian content. In intention, the BGCSE history syllabus and rationale provided a model example. The primary aim of the history syllabus was "to stimulate interest in and enthusiasm for the study of the past," to "develop knowledge and understanding of past events and experiences, linking them with the present," and "to ensure that candidates' knowledge is rooted in an understanding of the nature and use of historical evidence." Even more than the 20 percent optional component of the CXC alternative, Bahamian history became the primary element in the Bahamian-Caribbean "core content" of the new history syllabus, with an emphasis on the students' own research. To this requirement were added two optional subjects chosen from a short list of relevant "Aspects of World History," which initially included both modern U.S. domestic history and the history of race relations in the United States and South Africa but pointedly excluded the British history that was once the staple of Bahamian history syllabi. Whether this new syllabus was to succeed and the new system to revivify the old, however, depended on the willingness and ability of the teachers to adapt, and such practical matters as the availability of a sufficient supply of suitable and affordable texts. Although the Ministry of Education expressed satisfaction with the first results in 1993, the major problems still awaited resolution in the mid-1990s (Table 20).[31]

Though the College of the Bahamas was far less involved in the planning of the new secondary school syllabus than might have been expected, the shape and quality of Bahamian education very much depended on the college, not least because it was largely responsible for training and upgrading Bahamian teachers. The college had achieved much to be proud of in its first twenty years, though it remained hampered by more difficulties than chronic underfunding.

Because of its modest initial outlay, the college had to recruit largely local teachers—mainly from high school staff—for its first faculty. The advantage was a comparatively high ratio of Bahamian teachers from the beginning (40 percent in 1978, rising to only 45 percent within the next decade) and also an enviably high proportion of female to male teachers (59 percent in 1978). The disadvantages, of

Table 20. Bahamas: School Enrollments, 1994–1995

	Government Schools									*Independent Schools*								
	Primary			*All-Age*			*Secondary*			*Primary*			*All-Age*			*Secondary*		
	No.	*Enrol.*	*Av.*	*No.*	*Enrol.*	*Av.*	*No.*	*Enrol.*	*Av.*	*No.*	*Enrol.*	*Av.*	*No.*	*Enrol.*	*Av.*	*No.*	*Enrol*	*Av.*
New Providence	24	15,558	648	—	—	—	12	12,402	1,034	14	5,005	358	3[a]	2,629	876	10	4,290	429
Grand Bahama	10	3,285	329	2	236	118	4[b]	3,878	970	4	950	238	2	969	485	3	1,039	346
Other Family Islands	57	4,155	73	38	3,740	98	8	2,825	353	4	273	68	4	130	33	2	132	66
Totals	91	22,998	253	40	3,976	99	24	19,105	796	22	6,228	283	9	3,728	414	15	5,461	364

[a]Queen's College, the oldest secondary school, with an attached junior deparment, is listed as an all-age school. Five special schools were listed, one each for the deaf and learning disabled in New Providence and Grand Bahama and one for the blind in New Providence. The total enrollment was 268.

[b]One junior high school.

Source: Directory of Schools, 1994–1995 (Nassau: Ministry of Education, Planning Unit, 1995).

course, were the faculty's comparative lack of experience and postgraduate qualifications. Of the 130 faculty in 1978, 100 had bachelor's degrees and 62 master's, but only 7 had achieved a doctorate (8 others were working toward one). The attempt to upgrade the faculty encountered several impediments. Salaries and contract provisions were inadequate to attract highly qualified expatriates, and Bahamian faculty were either worked too hard or had insufficient incentive, financial or other, to undertake further study. Though prepared to provide more than four hundred scholarships at a time for undergraduate study overseas during the 1980s, the government was less generous in making grants for postgraduate studies and even slower to acknowledge the need for leave or funding for independent research by college faculty. According to Dean Collinwood, this inadequacy stemmed from ignorance about the proper role of a college in promoting research as well as teaching and also, perhaps, from a fear that the research might delve too deeply into the nature of Bahamian society and government and facilitate criticism.[32]

The government was hampered in developing a truly national college even more by the financial cost and the associated need to improvise. The most obvious result was that the College of the Bahamas developed under the wing, if not the domination, of more firmly established institutions abroad. Of these the oldest and strongest link was with the University of the West Indies, which had trained many Bahamians (notably in medicine and law) since the 1950s and had sent resident tutors to prepare students for entry to UWI since the 1960s. The connection climaxed with the setting up in Nassau of the UWI Centre for Hotel and Tourist Management to provide the last two years of a bachelor's degree and postgraduate diplomas in hotel and tourist management. Partly as a result of internal difficulties at the UWI (the three campuses of which came close to sundering in the 1980s) and partly because of the will to independence that led to Paul Adderley's rejection of the CXC examinations, the government provided the School of Hotel Training and Management with splendid new premises in 1993.

That the revivified hotel school was made virtually autonomous of the College of the Bahamas (though directly adjacent to it) was seen by some as a sign of a waning commitment on the part of government to the ideal of a Bahamian university.[33] A parallel charge was that while government policy was weakening the vital West Indian connection it was too readily encouraging a more insidious cultural affinity to the United States. The college had enjoyed fruitful direct links with the University of Miami and Florida International University almost since its foundation. Yet, just when Bahamian high schools switched from the British to the American grade system in the 1970s, so policy decreed that the college aspire, at least as a preliminary stage, simply to the status of a junior liberal arts college. By 1985 it did indeed offer two- or three-year programs leading to an associate degree in any of its seven academic divisions. Unfortunately, though, this was a qualification fully recognized only in the United States and even there tended to lead to association only with universities of the second or third rank.

With considerable funding from outside agencies, the College of the Bahamas has greatly expanded and improved its facilities. Especially meritorious among its achievements (and very relevant to this present work) have been the creation in the Faculty of Arts of a Bahamas Studies program in which students in their second year produce solid work on Bahamian history from primary sources. An ambitious Research Unit for Historical and Anthropological Studies has also been set up, with a four-person team engaged in an oral history project exploring such subjects as internal and external migration, ethnic and cultural diversity, and styles of socialization and assimilation. An encouraging few fully qualified Bahamians have returned to make a long-term commitment to the college. Yet as the experience of other small young nations in the region has shown, the sheer cost of setting up a full range of faculties and facilities for teaching and research, the full machinery of examinations and degree-granting, and an adequately qualified and recompensed staff is so immense that realists have come to predict—even given the existence of a more enlightened, wise, and trusting government and bureaucracy—the postponement of the elevation of the College of the Bahamas into a national university of the Bahamas well into the twenty-first century.

Crime in the 1980s and 1990s

The state and destiny of the nation which the educational system is attempting to serve and shape—but in fact is more shaped by than shaping—is most clearly shown through an examination of the growing incidence of crime, the intractable problems of health and welfare, and the immutable imperatives of a fragile and ill-balanced economy.

Blithely ignoring or romanticizing their historical involvement in international lawlessness, including piracy, buccaneering, privateering, blockade running, and various other types of smuggling, Bahamians had always regarded themselves as a relatively law-abiding and peace-loving people. The colonial crime statistics—arrests, convictions, prison occupancy—generally bore out the belief that Bahamian persons, property, and households were safe from criminal assault. This situation changed dramatically in the second half of the twentieth century so that the Bahamas (and, above all, Nassau) came to be near the top in world tables of serious crimes per capita, including thefts, thefts with assault, rapes, rapes with violence, and murders. The Bahamas also rated high in crimes that went unpunished. Much of the escalating crime was blamed on drugs but could equally be attributed to unemployment, the disappointment of rising expectations, and the replication of U.S. patterns too readily displayed in the media. Others more generally blamed the decay in morality and discipline associated with the breakdown of traditional family and other unfortunate features of modernization in the Bahamian context.

Whatever the causes, the symptoms were frightening. Whereas as late as 1961 the number of criminal cases brought to court was less than 3,000, or one for every 43 persons in the population, by 1981 this had risen to 14,000, or one for 15 persons on the average, though only 434 persons ended up in prison. That crime was escalating faster than even an expanding police force and overworked judiciary could cope with can be borne out by a comparison between what was intended to be a nonalarmist summary of the crime situation made by Adrian Day, the editor of the *Bahamas Dateline* in 1984, and the purportedly objective annual report of the Royal Bahamas Police Force for the same year.[34]

In April 1984, the *Bahamas Dateline* quoted Interpol figures that showed that the Bahamas had the highest per capita crime rate in the world in 1979 and 1980, being placed in the top in all categories of major violent crime and twelfth in burglary, and the statistics were still rising. Most middle-class homes were now fitted with burglar bars and alarms, and tourists were far from immune. Day quoted the assistant commissioner of police: "Living in our beautiful country is becoming more and more hazardous every day," and added the advice: "One traveling to the Bahamas must take the same precautions one would take in traveling at home. Stay on well lighted streets, keep valuables in a secure place such as a hotel safe, walk in a confident manner, plan your excursions ahead and eliminate the possibility of getting lost in unfamiliar areas. It is best to travel in groups whenever you can and if trouble should arise, don't play the hero. I do not mean to alarm you, just make you aware of being careful."[35]

A few months later, Adrian Day drove home his point with some chilling examples. Nine homes belonging to doctors resident behind the hospital (close to Over the Hill) had been robbed fourteen times during the previous year. Within a single month three masked gunmen held up five couples, raped one of the women after beating her boyfriend, tied another couple up and left them by the side of the road, and shot at another couple who refused to open their car door to them; two masked gunmen held up six persons, locking a couple in their car trunk and shooting the man when he pleaded with them not to hurt him; two masked men held up three couples, raped one of the women, and robbed the other two; two masked men armed with U.S. .45 automatics robbed six golfers on the South Ocean Beach course, taking wallets and jewelry valued at $8,000; Camperdown residents reported five shotgun robberies and a rape; and a Chinese food store owner was shot to death outside her Cordeaux Avenue store by two gunmen, who escaped with a mere $500.[36]

Of the 13,099 criminal cases handled by the police in 1984, 9,795, or 75 percent, were in New Providence, and 1,130 directly involved drugs (65 percent in New Providence, 16 percent in Grand Bahama). The police report was coy about the proportion of cases brought to court and leading to convictions and imprisonment (maybe as few as 5 percent) but did complain of understaffing and overworking, especially of the Criminal Investigation Department (CID). In a force now totaling 2,000 persons (only 104 of them women), there were only 70 men in the CID branch at headquarters, no proper forensic laboratory, and no forensic scientist on staff. Though serious crime occurred mostly at night, most CID officers were on day duty, many of them assigned to protect VIPs; those on night duty served thirteen-hour shifts as many as seven nights in a row. Yet despite these personnel shortages, police officers still had time to prosecute no less than 20,451 traffic offenses in the year (15,531 in New Providence, 4,734 in Grand Bahama, and 186 in all the other Family Islands put together). The police report also proudly announced the performance of a myriad of formal and ceremonial duties, usually involving the splendid Police Band, providing protection and displays for a royal visit, a CARICOM summit conference, the PLP convention, the Red Cross Fair, ten changings of the guard at Government House, four openings of the Supreme Court, Independence Day, Remembrance Day, two church parades, and three military funerals.[37]

Largely as a result of government and public concern about the drug problem, by the 1990s the police budget had doubled, its numbers increased by 25 percent, and its facilities greatly improved. A victory in the drugs war was beginning to be claimed, but other forms of crime continued to increase and show new manifestations.

Major drug trafficking had slowed, and there were signs that the fear of "a whole generation of Bahamian youth lost to addiction" was exaggerated. Yet supplies of marijuana and cocaine (mainly "crack" crystals) remained plentiful and far cheaper than in the United States, bringing with them the Bahamian equivalent of all the social evils familiar to American cities: gangs of pushers and enforcers, unemployed youth driven to crime by their addiction, criminals in whom drug use released hidden demons to add senseless vandalism, violence, and rape to simple burglary. The situation was made far worse because the drug traffic was augmented by an unprecedented trade in guns—from the cheapest "Saturday night specials" to sophisticated semiautomatics. Despite periodic gun amnesties during which the police culled hundreds of unlicensed firearms, the problem escalated so that by the mid-1990s one police magistrate spent nearly all his time in courts sentencing gun offenders and lived in fear of his life and property at the hands of the desperadoes he punished.[38]

Crimes of physical violence, particularly rape, touched raw nerves in a society brought up to believe that verbal abuse was the normal limit of violence, that women, even if subordinate, deserved respect, and that policemen had no need of firearms. Several strands of popular revolt were represented in the campaign against crimes of sexual violence spearheaded by the outspoken opposition MP Janet Bostwick, who proposed to crowded meetings in 1984 a bill that would subject first offense rapists to the cat o' nine tails and imprisonment at hard labor and give life imprisonment to second offenders. The PLP countered with a Sexual Offenders Act that increased penalties but did not reintroduce corporal punishment. The PLP government also wavered over whether to retain the death penalty for even the most heinous types of murder, leaving twenty-nine men on "death row" for an FNM decision on their fate when their party left office in August 1992.[39]

Lawlessness, including murders, increased by about 40 percent between 1980 and 1992. Speaking to a church congregation in August 1994, a stipendiary magistrate pointed out that the 1992 crime figures represented a daily average of 50 crimes throughout the year. On the average there were 11 stealing offenses, 10 break-ins, and 4 robberies each day, 3 reported rapes a week, and a murder every eight days. Of the 44 murders and 138 reported rapes in 1992, 33 of the former and 58 of the latter were solved, "in the sense of persons arrested and charged." But 64 percent of the 4,112 stealing cases and 80 percent of the 3,900 break-ins remained unsolved. At the end of 1992, moreover, a backlog of 10,000 cases awaited trial in the courts. "This means that for the criminal out there," said the magistrate, "he knows that if he commits a crime other than murder there is a 70 per cent chance he will not be caught, and even if he is, there is a long time before he goes to court for trial."[40]

Along with the problem of detaining illegal immigrants and housing juvenile offenders, the increase in crimes gave rise to gross overcrowding and scandalous conditions in the prisons. Not surprisingly, much was revealed during the acrimonious election campaign of 1992. The Fox Hill facility, designed for 500 inmates, held more than four times that number. The maximum security area, designed for 220 prisoners, contained over 700 and lacked sufficient or adequate beds, toilets, or washing facilities. Food, sanitary, and medical conditions were substandard throughout the prison, and there were accusations of savage abuse, favoritism, and corruption on the part of the overworked and undertrained staff. Drugs and

An ever-expanding feature of modern tourism. Seven cruise ships almost fill Nassau's capacious harbor in the 1990s. Though boosting official tourist figures, cruise ships employed few Bahamians, and cruise passengers, to an extent deterred by reports of crime and incivility, rarely explored beyond the nearer reaches of Bay Street. Likewise, in the 1990s the money spent by the increasing number of "all-inclusive" package tourists benefited the tour operators and hotel owners more than it did Bahamians at large. Roland Rose photograph, courtesy of Bahamas Information Service.

weapons were said to circulate freely, and there were tales of internal gangs and inmate violence, including homosexual rape, that were as bad as those told of the worst prisons in the United States.[41]

In April 1992, opposition leader Hubert Ingraham called upon the minister of security (the once more embattled Darrell Rolle) to institute a commission of inquiry into prison conditions, following the escape from Fox Hill of the Cuban drug trafficker Alejandro Rodriquez Bohorques. This well-heeled villain had walked out when false release papers were presented by two men posing as police officers. Subsequent police inquiries disclosed that the papers were forged by prison officers and that those on duty at the time were party to the deception. Seven prison officers were sacked and charged, but Minister Rolle was able to deflect calls for his resignation by announcing the takeover of command at Fox Hill by the redoubtable former assistant commissioner of police Lawrence Major and the recruitment of twenty-two new prison officers from Canada.[42]

The prison revelations allowed Police Chief Bernard K. Bonamy once more to make the plea that the force was overworked and underfunded. In May 1992 he told fellow members of the Caribbean Association of Police Commissioners that less funds meant more pressure because criminal technology was outdistancing that of police forces. He did advocate working more closely with the people in community policing but at least equally stressed the importance of frequent meetings of police chiefs because of the internationalization of criminal activities.[43]

Of even greater concern to thinking Bahamians was the sudden proliferation of violent gangs among the youth in New Providence and Grand Bahama. In May 1993, Assistant Superintendent Alladyce Strachan, the first woman to reach such a senior rank in the police force, described and explained how this had come about in an interview with the *Nassau Guardian.* Strachan said that neighborhood groups had started in the 1960s and 1970s because of "the need to belong." The chief groups were the rival Farm Road Boys and Kemp Road Boys. They had engaged in disruptive but not often criminal behavior. In 1987 or 1988, two better organized and more destructive rival groups emerged, calling themselves the Syndicate and Rebellion. The young gangsters would stay away from school, ride around in jitneys drinking alcohol, smash windscreens, scrawl graffiti, and commit petty robberies. The Rebellion in particular was a structured organization, with distinctive clothes, armed with firearms, short cutlasses, knives, and bats. Besides disrupting parties and attacking people at Junkanoo parades, they became more and more involved in organized crime. The model caught on and spread like a disease throughout New Providence, with the creation of the Gun Hawks, the Border Boys, the Jungelist, the She Hawks, the South Beach Gang, the Kemp Road Posse, and the Elizabeth Estates Gang.

Strachan perceptively saw the gangs as providing a separate subculture for youth whom the wider society had failed. Relationships among members were of primary importance, and the gangs provided organization, a sense of belonging, security, loyal friends, and recognition for individuals, even if their morals were twisted and their behavior increasingly criminal and antisocial. She said, "What was considered a banding together of harmless or [merely] disruptive delinquent groups has developed into dangerous criminal minded youth in a short period of time. The growth of these gangs has expanded at an epidemic rate." Strachan gave the opinion that the root causes were the growth of dysfunctional families and the alienation of the youth from the formal institutions of the society. The breakdown of the traditional Bahamian family structure had "resulted in youngsters having an abundance of unsupervised time. The presence of a father in the home to help discipline the children is irregular. There are few role model fathers to pattern after. In cases of single family homes, the mother is often at work during critical times of the day and children are left to supervise themselves." Besides the lack of guidance within the family, there was a lack of communication or dialogue between the youth and the police, church, government, and civil leaders. In addition, Strachan cited "the decline in religious values, the lack of respect for others and their property, the lack of national pride and the general acceptance of criminal activity." Two other factors were the too ready availability of alcohol, marijuana, and cocaine and the prevalence of movies and videos such as *New Jack City, King of New York,* and *Boyz n' the Hood* that celebrated the gangster lifestyle.[44]

In October 1992, the Discovery Day celebrations were marred by lawless and violent behavior by groups of young hoodlums, and the *Nassau Guardian* claimed that some gangsters were so lacking in fear of the law that they were planning attacks on the police. To overcome these gangs, it wrote, required more positive government action but also greater cooperation between ordinary Bahamians and the police. These, announced as priorities by the new FNM government, led to such initiatives as the provision of sporting facilities and youth clubs Over the Hill in which police officers like Strachan were involved, though Strachan herself had to admit that the more enlightened officers (particularly the few women) had to overcome the confrontational and male macho ethos that still persisted within the police force.[45]

Perhaps the most sobering aspect of Bahamian crime in the 1990s, though, was the spread of gang violence to the high schools in a fashion all too reminiscent of conditions in the inner cities of the United States. In January 1992, the *Tribune* reported that violent acts were being reported daily from New Providence schools, with gang rivalry within and between the worst of them. At Donald Davis High School a teacher had been beaten up and five handguns confiscated. The BUT called emergency meetings and its former president Leonard Archer called on the government first to acknowledge the problem and then do something about it. In a remarkably candid response, the minister of education, Bernard Nottage, admitted that violence in the schools was a grave concern and went on to attempt an explanation. Students organized in gangs and exhibited violent behavior because they feared other students and watched too much violence on television. But violence sometimes occurred because of an inappropriate curriculum; students became bored and uninterested in some of the subjects being taught in school.[46]

Besides the drive for curriculum reform, the government made resolute attempts to improve security in schools and to punish offenders. The problem was the total inadequacy of the probationary courts and the youth correctional system. The reformatory ethos of the old boys' and girls' industrial schools was outmoded if not discredited and their facilities hopelessly overstretched. The only practical alternatives were more or less to ignore the least criminal offenders—recycling them back to the ordinary schools—and to send the more hardened cases to adult prison. Given the state of the prisons, this last was a desperate measure indeed. As in most of the "developed" countries, prisons were both schools for crime and agents of brutalization. Horror stories circulated not just of squalid conditions and abuse by wardens but of the forceful sodomization of young offenders by inmates infected with HIV.[47]

Medical Services: AIDS and Other Problems

The specter of AIDS was for the Bahamas (as for much of the Western world) more than just a serious health or social problem; for many Bahamians it was a paradigm of the general decay of social norms, perhaps even an apocalyptic warning of God's wrath. In an ugly way, it also fueled popular prejudices against Haitians and homosexuals, who were held to be the principal transmitters of the disease. AIDS was without doubt a serious scourge, but the public's panic tended to mask the threats from other medical problems and the general inadequacy of health and welfare facilities, just as the obsession with the "Haitian threat" and concern for the alleged increase in homosexuality disguised the underlying economic and social factors involved—not least the persistent male orientation of explanatory analysis.

One perennial Bahamian health problem that tended to be overshadowed by the drugs and AIDS scares, though it was not unrelated to both and was similarly both product and exacerbator of underlying social conditions, was alcoholism. In 1971, Dr. Timothy McCartney, the most prominent Bahamian psychologist, called alcoholism the number one health problem, both from the physical and mental health points of view, noting that the Bahamas ranked third in the world in alcohol consumption per capita (11.3 liters per year) and maybe highest in the world for admissions to mental hospitals on account of alcoholism (110 per 100,000). Assuming that it was an almost exclusively male affliction, McCartney attributed alcoholism not just to the sheer availability of liquor and the traditional Bahamian bar culture but to fundamental social failings: the fatherless home and the often dominant and aggressive behavior of women in female-headed households, familial tensions, and overcrowding, leading to the need to escape from reality, to relieve tensions, or to restore a macho self-esteem.[48]

Sandra Dean-Patterson, a decade later the director of the Crisis Center in the Department of Social Services, in her 1978 doctoral thesis used statistics to stress how alcoholism stemmed from hedonism as well as escapism. Thus it was a product both of rising prosperity among the more prosperous and of hardship among the less fortunate. In contrast to the United States, though, it was the lower income groups in the Bahamas that had the higher intake of alcohol and greater incidence of alcoholism. Dean-Patterson also pointed out that alcoholism was particularly damaging in middle age, was seriously increasing among women, and had actually increased as a result of the government raising the tax on beer—driving the Bahamian drinker back to the traditional Bahamian demon, hard liquor.[49]

Long before the drug epidemic of the 1980s, Timothy McCartney showed the similarities between drug abuse and alcoholism in the Bahamian context, accurately predicted a trend toward the crisis already raging in the United States if the drug flow through the Bahamas increased, and advocated differential policies toward pushers and users, expanded treatment facilities, and a program of public education. The drug crisis, however, hit the Bahamas with the force of an unforecasted hurricane. "Without doubt the single most pressing health issue for 1984 was the growing epidemic of drug abuse, particularly the smoking of free-base cocaine," wrote Dean Collinwood in his review of the year. The number of drug-related admissions to Sandilands Hospital (which treated drug and alcohol victims as well as more straightforward "mental" patients) had jumped from twenty in 1983 to over two hundred in 1984. Dr. David Allen was appointed chairman of a National Task Force on Drug Abuse, which energetically publicized the problem, set up a drug hot line, advocated a special drug court to speed the prosecution of drug pushers, and urged the immediate improvement of rehabilitation facilities.[50]

Public awareness was raised, though the drug storm raged on almost uncontrolled until it began to burn out of its own accord. Almost a decade later, however, it was still seen as a major problem, and its causes still related to persistent Bahamian social conditions. In January 1992, for example, Dr. Richard Adderley addressed a Healthy Lifestyle Seminar hosted by the Young Liberals on the topic of the crisis surrounding the Bahamian male. The lack of good male role models was one reason why so many young Bahamian men were in prison or living with drug problems, he said. Echoing Timothy McCartney, and probably angering the growing number of Bahamian feminists, he also described mothers in single-parent homes as domineering, overly aggressive, and controlling. The males either reacted violently to this control by females, he claimed, or resorted to drugs as a compensation for low self-esteem. In December 1992, with equal pessimism but more practical liberalism, Terry Miller, chairman of the newly formed Bahamas Association for Social Help (BASH) declared that the problem of drug addiction was worse than ever and called on the new FNM government to hand over the buildings of an abandoned primary school to serve as a halfway house for drug addicts and alcoholics and a rehabilitative center for women.[51]

By this time, however, much greater concern, if not much more action, was being directed toward the AIDS crisis. From the first awareness of the problem in 1985, public anxiety had been heightened, as in the rest of the Western world, by the lethal effects of HIV infection and the absence of a cure and also by ignorance and misinformation. Since awareness of the outbreak came on the heels of the drug revelations, dirty needles among drug users were at first said to be the chief agents of the spread of HIV, even though intravenous drug-taking was comparatively rare in the Bahamas. Reports from the United States that the disease was epidemic among the male gay community focused attention and public disapproval on the small and hitherto more or less ignored gay subculture in the Bahamas, impugning the lifestyle of all those known, or believed, to be AIDS victims. For a time the perception remained that AIDS was an affliction limited to deviant males—homosexuals and drug addicts—with casually promiscuous homosexual tourists being cast as the major villains. The discovery toward the end of the 1980s that those testing HIV positive and suffering from full-blown AIDS included undoubtedly heterosexual males, females, and infants came as a serious shock. Now the causal agents were said to be casually promiscuous sex in general, particularly when unprotected by the use of condoms, while the few statistics available provided an all too plausible new scapegoat: the Haitian immigrant.

Around 1990—when the conventional wisdom was that the AIDS epidemic originated in Africa and was consequently most prevalent in the tropical nations of the African diaspora—it was claimed that more than a thousand, or 10 percent, of all Haitians in the Turks and Caicos Islands had tested HIV positive. Bahamians pointed to what they claimed was the general promiscuity of Haitian immigrants and the allegation that the majority of the prostitutes throughout the Bahamas were Haitian women. By 1992 the situation was indeed grave, and the greater availability of statistics made it clear that the incidence of HIV positive and AIDS cases was scarcely higher among the Haitians than the people of the Bahamas at large. In March 1992, the minister of health, Charles Carter, announced that at Fox Hill Prison, where 10 had died from complications of AIDS in the previous year, 100 out of 1,000 inmates had tested HIV positive, as had 3 percent of 4,825 pregnant women tested at the Princess Margaret Hospital between September 1990 and October 1991. Carter called for better health education and closer involvement by community organizations and churches but was not able to announce extra spending by the hard-pressed PLP government.

Much more alarmist and urgent was the perspective of head of the Infectious Diseases Unit at the hospital, Dr. Perry Gomez. In December 1992 he warned the new government that the worldwide AIDS epidemic seemed out of control and quoted predictions that 110 million people might be infected by the year 2000. Already in the Bahamas, he claimed, AIDS-related illnesses were probably the leading killers of people between the ages of twenty and forty—purposely not singling out the

Haitians or making a distinction between male and female victims. Despite the shortage of money in developing countries such as the Bahamas, the government should allocate far more than it had already toward preventing HIV infection, for the costs of treating the projected epidemic would be truly staggering.[52]

The FNM did increase allocations over the following two years, but without immediate effect. During AIDS Awareness Week in November 1994, Dr. Gomez announced that the Bahamas had the unenviable distinction of having the highest incidence of HIV per capita in the English-speaking Caribbean and the third highest rate in the world. Since 1985, when the disease was first monitored, there had been 1,660 AIDS cases, of whom 961 had died. In the same nine-year period, 3,354 persons had tested positive for the HIV virus in the Bahamas, a rate of 1.3 percent of the entire population, or one person in 78. "AIDS is everybody's business," said Gomez, "and it behooves all of us in our families and the wider context of what is a family, to do the utmost we can to help reduce the impact of this problem on all of our brothers and sisters in this country."[53]

One positive result of the AIDS scare was that it led Bahamians, like the people in other threatened countries, to reassess their sexuality and sexual attitudes and the relationship of both to social problems. Immediate responses, though, tended to be pragmatic or emotional, not necessarily enlightened, and certainly not amounting to a sexual revolution. More publicity, more openness, coupled with fear, doubtless led to safer sexual practices, at least among the more educated sections of society. As part of the FNM's general campaign of public hearings into the state of the nation, the Senate Select Committee on Culture included a discussion of Bahamian sexuality in May 1994. Besides clinical analyses from a psychologist at Sandilands Hospital and Sandra Dean-Patterson of the Social Services Crisis Center, an Anglican priest, while making a gesture toward liberalism, did little more than affirm what he regarded as traditional family values, while making a sectarian sideswipe at the laxer morality of the Baptists. Even less helpful was the testimony proffered by a born-again Christian. Claiming authenticity as an outside child who had herself engaged in extramarital relationships before she saw the light, she made a swingeing condemnation of promiscuity, blaming it on the sinful indulgence of the men and the lax compliance of the women.

As to homosexuality, she said the Lord had cautioned her to be silent for fear of antagonizing any in the audience who might have such proclivities. But she did not feel bound to overrule the diffidence of the Almighty, saying bluntly that it was not even a debatable issue. The Bible was clear: homosexuality was an abomination in the sight of the Lord.[54] The audience laughed in shock while the professional experts winced, though it was by no means certain that even the experts' evidence had really gone to the nub of the question of sexual orientation. The male-biased analysis made by Timothy McCartney in 1971 still seemed the acceptable orthodoxy. Overt male homosexuality, or what Bahamians called "sissy" or "funny" behavior, was said to be of purely psychological origin. It occurred partly because of the stereotyping of male roles in the society, which led to a sense of inadequacy in those who found themselves unable to live up to the image, but mainly through faults in the family. Salient among these was the reversal of parental roles, either with a "very strong, dominating, masculine mother, and a quiet, non-masculine father" or "a possessive mother, over protective and overattached to her son, creating a dependency relationship from which the son may never be able to free himself ('mama's boy')." Another cause was said to reflect on the social and living conditions specific to a large section of the Bahamian population, "the easy access to sexual gratification with members of the same sex, especially in childhood and adolescence," which could result "in habit patterns which can persist throughout an individual's life." To complicate the issue further, McCartney subscribed to the notion that the aggressively heterosexual behavior exhibited by many Bahamian males could be a form of latent homosexuality, an overcompensation for sexual insecurity.

Not recognizing the circular logic or contradictions in his own analysis, McCartney treated homosexuality as deviant behavior or "social maladjustment." It was a problem without a certain cure, but "much could be done to minimise its incidence." Though he did advocate a better climate of opinion that would allow open discussion of sex problems and discouraged punitive and hostile attitudes toward homosexuality, he concentrated on a two-point program for its "minimisation":

> A structured, stable family unit, in which a child can go through the process of sexual identification appropriate to his various life stages, is of prime importance. (Again and again, we come back to the overriding importance of the family structure, this 'society-within-a-society', and the fundamental effect of the soundness—or the instability—of this small unit on the mental health of the whole community.) Enlightened sex education, particularly by way of pre-marriage guidance for young people, could do much to create an awareness of the importance of sex identification, interpersonal relationships between parents and children of the same and the opposite sex, etc., to the adequate psychosexual development of the child.[55]

McCartney's analysis might truly reflect predominant Bahamian views of male homosexuality and plausibly suggest some of its causes within the faulty structures of Bahamian society. But its exclusively male orientation provides neither a full explanation of gender identification nor a fully useful solution for the problems of fractured, female-headed families. If Bahamian males were reluctant to acknowledge the place, even the existence, of homosexuality, in the society or in themselves and were eager to blame its manifestation solely on Bahamian women, their attitude toward female homosexuality was even more Victorian in the sense that, like Queen Victoria, they seemed unwilling to believe it even existed, let alone might reasonably stem from failings in the Bahamian male. The possibility that male sexual license, involving canons of reputation, might have ancient roots in Africa and the certainty that a strong role for women in the family has a long and honorable history in the Bahamas has no more part in the McCartney equation than do the emergence of women's liberation and the influences of modern sexual hedonism borrowed from the developed world, which encompasses all varieties of sexual permutation, including homosexuality, male and female, and bisexuality.

A feminine if not feminist viewpoint was clearly needed to make the debate more in tune with modern reality. In the predominant concerns and debates over alcoholism, drug abuse, and AIDS, the existence of other diseases and social problems among the poor, the interrelationship of different health and social problems, and the growing inability of the Bahamian medical and welfare resources to cope with them tended to get lost.

One exception to the tendency to treat such problems as alcoholism, drug abuse, and AIDS as isolated phenomena, debated without their full social context and with a traditional male bias, was provided by Bahamian Dr. Sonia Lunn, founding director of the Drug Action Service, in a talk in January 1992 on the impact of alcohol and drugs on the health of Bahamian women. She stressed that women's health depended largely on the choices that women made for themselves. Under the influence of alcohol or drugs, women might not make healthful choices. For example, alcohol or drugs could impair a woman's decision to use a condom during sex. As a result, she might contract a sexually transmitted disease (STD) such as AIDS or gonorrhea. Conjuring up further interlocking circles of cause and effect, Dr. Lunn also pointed out that alcohol and drugs were a particular problem among the poorer sections of the population and were related to unemployment, youth crime, and teenage pregnancies.[56]

The failure to take positive action and the unavailability of resources, however, remained. Under the PLP, the principles of medical treatment available to all, free if necessary to the poor, and a national welfare system were theoretically maintained. But facilities increasingly fell short of the ideal, so that by 1992 the opposition FNM was able to state, "Bahamians are acutely aware that public health in our country is in a deplorable and frightening state." The psychiatric hospital at Sandilands was hopelessly overburdened by the addition of drug-related cases to alcohol victims and the clinically deranged, while the main Princess Margaret Hospital was almost overwhelmed in ministering to the victims of AIDS and other resurgent STDs, tuberculosis and childhood diseases previously thought to have been wiped out, and the increasing number of victims of violence and traffic accidents. Most visible to the public was the chaotic overcrowding at the Out Patients Department, as at the government clinics in the Family Islands, though this was caused by inadequate ambulance and general welfare services. Public ancillary services, such as dentistry and optometry, were also sorely deficient.[57]

Doctors, nurses, social workers, and staff were generally dedicated, even heroic, but morale inevitably slipped as conditions deteriorated below those of a developing nation toward a Third World level. In 1992 it was said that doctors in the Out Patients Department were treating an average of forty patients a session, that at nights even in the major acute wards the ratio of nurses (often students) was one to twenty, and that the attendants in the inadequate number of ambulances had no more than advanced first aid training. Staff were grossly underpaid, nurses, for example, having had no general increase for seven years. Not surprisingly, fewer would-be doctors and nurses opted for local training, and those trained abroad showed increasing reluctance for government service, even if bonded to do so under the terms of their scholarships. Much of the shortfall, as in the teaching profession, was made up by doctors from some of the poorer Commonwealth countries.[58]

The public almost reverted to the attitude prevailing in the worst of colonial days, considering the government hospital, medical, and social services places of last resort for the poorest of the poor. Perhaps inevitably, the fact that a large proportion of those who clamored for medical treatment were Haitians prejudiced many Bahamians against the public facilities. Though the Princess Margaret Hospital continued to give preferential treatment to fee-paying patients treated by private doctors with associate status, those Bahamians who could afford it increasingly opted for private treatment at the lavishly equipped Doctor's Hospital in Nassau, Freeport's Antoni Clinic, or, for an ever-increasing number, in one of the numerous hospitals in south Florida. This trend (though it impoverished some) inevitably reopened and widened the distinction between "haves" and "have-nots," a class division, even if no longer determined solely by color.

As part of the 1992 election campaign, Prime Minister Pindling promised major expenditures and reforms, including a second major hospital and a national health insurance scheme that would "pay all doctors' and hospital bills."[59] Defeat at the polls freed the PLP from having to show whether it would have been able to carry out these promises. The FNM had been more cautious. Though it pledged in its election manifesto to "provide high quality health care for all," as befitted a party infused with Thatcherite (or Reaganite) principles of minimal government spending, it simply promised to "ensure that affordable private Health Insurance is available and monitor the insurance industry to make certain that reasonable and appropriate premiums and fees are in effect" and to "encourage Bahamians to take charge of their own health care, lead healthy and non-abusive lives, and provide for their old age." The FNM was more forthcoming about social welfare, pledging that "child welfare and protection, probation, and public assistance will be provided as a matter of right on a national basis to those having need thereof."[60]

In any case, increased government funding proved almost impossible, at least in the short term. In December 1992, the new minister of health, Ivy Dean-Dumont, announced that because of financial stringencies the government would not proceed with the building of a new hospital. Instead, it would simply upgrade some of the wards at the Princess Margaret Hospital, while at the same time compiling a register of Bahamians studying to be doctors "in order to encourage them to work where they are needed rather than where they make the most money."[61] Whether the FNM government would be able to fulfill its pledges to improve other branches of the social services rather than, in true neoconservative style, rely on the long-suffering Bahamian people to provide help for themselves seemed equally unlikely at that time.

In the Social Front Line: The Testimony of Delia Mason-Smith

The interrelationship between the problems of health and welfare and the nature of Bahamian society in the process of modernization are perhaps best illustrated anecdotally, using the testimony of an exceptionally dedicated and well-trained but overworked female relief worker and focusing on one of the most typical and telling cases with which she has had to deal. While giving a realistic impression of the situation in the 1990s and how it came about, this approach has the merit of providing a much more optimistic view of the future, of the positive role of women in Bahamian society, and of the resilience of the Bahamian spirit than might otherwise occur.

Delia Mason-Smith (as we shall call her) is a brown woman now in her fifties, born Over the Hill in Nassau to parents who kept a small shop and, though poor in relation to the Nassau elite, were in the upper socioeconomic stratum of their East Street neighbors, respectable Anglicans and ambitious for their children. Delia proved an exceptional student from primary school days but was also fortunate to be in the Bahamian cohort luckiest for upward mobility. She easily passed the examination for entry to Government High School in 1956, just as the school was receiving its first surge of government spending. Performing well in the tenth grade Overseas School Certificate examination, she was one of the first class in the Bahamas to go on to the Higher School Certificate, concentrating on the three subjects necessary for entrance to university in the United Kingdom. Obtaining a place at the University of Leicester to study for a bachelor of arts degree in sociology and winning a government scholarship (which bridged the gap between the cost and what her family could afford, in return for an engagement to government service for a similar length of time), she graduated in 1968. With the PLP now in power, she returned to a post in the recently formed Department of Social Services in the Ministry of Labour and Welfare.[62]

Delia found her first degree of little practical importance in a department responsible for public assistance, child welfare, and family counseling, but in 1970 the ministry sent her to study for a master's degree in social work at the University of Michigan, Ann Arbor, just outside Detroit. Studying alongside many blacks then involved in the protests over the sacking of the black radical Angela Davis and consigned to practical work in the poorer areas of an American city still staggering from the effects of the black power riots of the 1960s were shocks to Delia's consciousness far greater than her three years in the English Midlands. Lectures and discussions with her classmates gave her a better awareness of the African heritage, freeing her from that Bahamian prejudice which regarded Africa with embarrassment, as barbaric and primitive, its superstition and tribalism redeemable only through Christianity and "civilized" institutions. Even more, her experiences in the Detroit slums gave her a vivid awareness of the effects of poverty, race-class oppression, and hatred and refueled her commitment to help the unfortunate in her own society.

The Detroit experience also reassured Delia of the special value of being a Bahamian, even for the poorest of the blacks. She was convinced that the ideological message of many lectures and rap sessions that the socioeconomic malaise in the United States was the lasting product of class and race oppression dating back to slavery did not apply with equal force, if at all, to the Bahamas. However Bahamian slavery had been, it had not left Bahamians as bitter, demoralized, and hopelessly unenterprising as she found most American blacks. However feckless and unreliable in the family context they might be, Bahamian men were cheerful, proud, and ingenious in adverse circumstances. Whether or not slavery had done permanent damage to black family patterns (and she was not aware of the counterargument that American slaves had far stronger family patterns than modern American blacks), Delia emphatically denied that the tradition of strong feminine roles was anything but a positive feature of Bahamian family life.

Delia carried these convictions back to Nassau, and they were reinforced in the subsequent twenty-five years of her career with the Department of Social Services. For all that time she struggled in an underfunded system, available to give counseling for all who applied but able to provide financial assistance only in the most desperate cases. With school leavers ineligible and a strictly enforced family means test (fixed in the mid-1980s at the near-starvation level of $40 a week), she mainly dealt with those unemployed with dependents, or the unemployably old, sick, alcohol- or drug-addicted, or mentally ill. The overwhelming majority of her clients were women, most of them single mothers. Haitians were not excluded, and their legal status was not an issue to the department, but very few applied.

Delia was frustrated by her inability to help all the needy and angry at some aspects of Bahamian society and government policy. She condemned the irresponsible behavior of many Bahamian men and regretted the absence of a strong family planning program such as seemed to have been successful in Barbados and Jamaica. She was disappointed by the failure of the government either to provide a relevant education program or to show sufficient concern for placing school leavers in employment, but even more by its failure to recognize that for most Bahamians school was simply a path away from the Family Islands and a life of menial toil. Even if they had succeeded in school, she knew from what they told her and from experience that they would never go back. Nonetheless, she also knew that family life and family relationships, especially but not exclusively the bond between mother and child, were of crucial importance to all Bahamians, not only vital to the continuing health of Bahamian society but proof against almost all adversity.

In evidence, Delia mentioned that "love children" were almost never abandoned, however negligent the father might be in providing support, that despite the huge incidence of teenage pregnancies there was a very low call for terminations, and that the demand for children to adopt far outran the number of children available for adoption. Equally impressive was that in the vast majority of cases of hardship, Bahamians were able to rely on the help of family members, not just the immediate circle but emphatically including the grandparent generation and stretching back and forth to distant kin. The welfare system would immediately collapse if it were not so. It was a hallowed custom dating back to harsher economic times, through slavery, almost certainly back to African roots.

Above all, and also with ancient roots, was the importance of the mother in the household and of women in the society at large. Mothers even in two-parent homes took part in all important decisions and exercised discipline—often more firmly than the fathers. The man might provide, and he had special roles almost exclusive to himself, such as fishing and traveling afar to where wages could be earned. But whether the man was supportive or not, or away, the mother was quite capable of turning her hand to earning too; women were traditionally active as hucksters, straw vendors, seamstresses, and retail shopkeepers. Bahamian women were strong, independent, and inventive because they had had to be. Even at the least bad of times, and with optimal family cohesion, their contribution was essential, materially as well as morally.

This tradition had stood Bahamian women in good stead in the modern world, when almost as many women as men (and far more than in most countries) had risen through the education system to the top in politics, administration, business, and the professions. But men were not marginalized thereby. The ideal remained the close immediate family in the wider kin, with marriage as a partnership. Elaborate weddings were intended to be the sign and seal of this ideal. Delia's own parents had run the shop together, through bad times and better. She herself had risen to the top in her profession; yet she too was a wife and mother (and by the 1990s a grandparent also). In the late 1960s she had married Basil Smith, a classmate of hers at Government High School, whose academic route had taken him to the University of the West Indies and the United States on his way to a successful career—neat counterpoint to Delia's—in life insurance.

The story of the Mason-Smiths was a trajectory upward into the new Bahamian middle class. That of most of the women whom Delia met in her professional function was far less fortunate. Most of them were victims of the deterioration of family and the demoralization of both men and women that were the consequences of modern upheavals. Yet most of her clients' histories were instructive about parallel perennial features of Bahamian society, lifestyle, and customary behavior. One tale she told by way of illustration was that of an unnamed woman (whom we will call Bernice) whom she had been counseling during the weeks before our first interview (in December 1983).

Bernice was a black woman in her middle twenties, born in Andros but brought to Nassau as a child around 1960. Living in the poorest section of Bain Town, she had not done well at school and left at age fifteen when pregnant. Able to find only intermittent work as a domestic, she did manage to land a regular man, and they married in 1975, when Bernice already had three children. The recession hit the couple hard, and in 1978 they left for Grand Bahama, hoping for better opportunities. For a time their circumstances improved. But Bernice had two more children and when the husband fell out of regular work, the marriage began to founder. By the time Bernice was pregnant with her sixth child, the husband was often absent and when at home was increasingly abusive. When her new baby was only a few days old, Bernice took the mail boat back to Nassau with her children, virtually destitute, and appeared at Delia's office the following week.

Delia was impressed by Bernice's resolution and authorized a payment from the emergency assistance fund. But how had Bernice managed so far in Nassau, with a tiny baby and five other children, no money, house, or job? And how did she expect to resolve her predicament in the longer term? Delia was not surprised to hear that Bernice and her family had been taken in, if not exactly welcomed, by her mother and an aunt in their already overcrowded houses. They were all well fed, though the children lacked clothes to go to school. Bernice was confident she could get work as a maid in the new hotel opening up on Cable Beach; she had "good references and connections." This proved true. Family members in good standing with the ruling party and union vouched for her at the hotel, and she went to work while her mother cared for the infant and younger children and saw the others off to school. Within a few weeks, Bernice had found a small wooden house for herself, close enough to her mother's.

But not all was yet resolved. The hotel work was too strenuous for a woman who had so recently given birth, with long, inconvenient hours and meager pay. Bernice had been off sick. Telephone calls to Grand Bahama appealing to the father for support had proved in vain. She appealed once more to the department for financial assistance but met underlings skeptical of her honesty and commitment. Delia had overruled them and given more temporary aid, while Bernice negotiated through her "connections" at the hotel for lighter work. Delia had just heard that Bernice had been offered a position on the night security detail, at least until she was stronger. We asked to be kept in touch with further developments. "Oh, I don't expect to see Bernice again," said Delia. "What we see here in the office—the long-term cases dragging on for years—are mostly those with far more serious problems; women with dependents but no husband, job, or hope of either; sickness, a drinking problem, serious mental disturbance. Above all, though, it's those without family to help, or whose family have finally got disgusted and given up."

In turning to other aspects of modern Bahamian society and social life, Delia was equally well informed and realistic but guardedly optimistic too, citing her personal case, as well as examples she encountered in her professional work and day-to-day experiences. She strongly denied that modern influences and socioeconomic problems had been accompanied by a decline in religious activity and commitment. Since independence there had been a surge amounting to a revival. You had only to see the new churches lining the central ridge of New Providence, along Harold Road and Independence Avenue, bursting with activity most days of the week, to realize that "religion was big business." A host of new churches were evangelizing the ordinary black people (including the Haitians), along with the more dynamic pastors and preachers from the traditionally respectable churches—Anglican, Catholic, and Methodist, if not Presbyterian. The churches of the black poor, Baptists and Church of God, were gaining wider acceptance and respectability under a new generation of education and dedicated young leaders.

Delia's sister, who had once scorned all churches, had become a born-again Baptist, treasurer of a church now full of middle-class adherents, who were now complaining that their dynamic young minister was too active in evangelical work and ought to pay more pastoral attention to his immediate flock. An even greater change had come over the Church of God under the statesmanlike leader Bishop Brice Thompson. As recently as Delia's youth, they had been the object of outside curiosity and amusement. Now their puritanical moral standards were widely respected, their congregations included wealthy middle-class blacks, and (despite some dissent within the flock) their annual convention for years had been attended by the prime minister and his wife. With a smile, Delia mentioned that she and Basil had gone back to being regular members of St. Agnes Anglican church after fifteen years' nonattendance. Asked why this had happened, she readily admitted that it related to having a family of their own and wanting their children to enjoy the church influences they themselves had had when young. It had occurred to them that they had always used the church when they needed it: when they were married, when their children were baptized, when they were troubled and needed counsel. Now was the time to give something back. Most important, perhaps, now they were getting on in years, was the question of who was going to bury them—give them the good send-off all true Bahamians wanted—when their time came to die.

Delia remarked on the great social changes in the economy during her half-century of life. She rejoiced in the material improvements in which she and Basil shared and generally approved of the reshuffling of class relations which saw so many prosperous and wealthy nonwhites. But she deprecated the obvious ills that came along with these changes—the materialism, the great disparities of wealth, the violence, crime, and family breakdown. Like many middle-class and educated Bahamians, she and her husband particularly regretted the imbalance of the modern economy, the overdependence on tourism and offshore banking, the over-urbanization of Nassau and Freeport, the depletion of the Family Islands, and the decay of traditional livelihoods, as well as of traditional family values.

As evidence of a common nostalgia for the past and of hope that all is not yet lost, Delia cited three heartening examples that may or may not illustrate wider trends: the vitality of such spontaneous organizations as the Hanna-Heastie-Tynes family consortium that existed mainly to arrange trips back to their ancestral islands (in this case, Crooked Island and Acklins); the prosperous revival of fishing centered on Spanish Wells and Sandy Point, Abaco; and the renewed commitment to farming represented by two young men who had given up well-paid government jobs to start Sunshine Farms in the New Providence interior, using sophisticated rock crushers, fertilizers, and water sprayers. The Mason-Smiths had in a small way shared in the latter enthusiasm. Around 1976, they had obtained a grant of three acres of Crown land off Cowpens Road, in southeastern New Providence, which had been turned into a market garden to supply tomatoes, squash, melons, onions, and corn for the ever-ready Nassau market. Not unexpectedly, however, they had not found Bahamians ready to perform the necessary hard toil for economic wages. Basil instead had come to rely on the Haitians living in the nearby bush, despite minatory notices in the press against employers of illegal immigrants, threatening initial fines of $600 and $1,200 and prison for a third offense.[63]

13

The Bahamian Self and Others: Achievements, History, and Mythology in the Creation of a National Identity

Bahamian Nationality: The Law of Citizenship and Belonging

As the tumultuous twentieth century draws to its close and our long book to its conclusion, it is clear that more than a quarter-century of political independence, even a conscious policy of Bahamianization by the two counterpoised political parties, have not been enough in themselves to provide Bahamians with a coherent sense of national identity. Internal divisions (of color or class or even between the subcultures of different islands) and powerful external influences (of modernization in general and the United States, Britain, and the West Indies in particular) confuse and diffuse. The uniqueness of the Bahamian people, however, we believe, is immanent. As we hope to show in our final chapter, a sensitive review of the common elements shared by all those born and living in the islands, and particularly a summary and reevaluation of the shaping forces in their shared history and environment, will reveal this uniqueness.

In respect to changes that can be made and aims realized by policy decisions and enactments, Bahamian governments since 1967 (and even more since independence) have done their best to ensure that the Bahamas and its resources belong to Bahamians, that Bahamian property is not easily alienable to non-Bahamians, that the status of being a Bahamian is not granted easily to outsiders, and that residence and work permits do not jeopardize the chances of employment or commercial profit for Bahamians.

The Independence Constitution of 1973 was ostensibly generous in granting Bahamian citizenship, but the subsequent Nationality Act (1973) and Immigration Act (1975) added hedging provisos and clearly separated permanent residents from citizens. Enactments, policy, and practice also virtually closed the "back door" to Bahamian citizenship by making it illegal for visitors to take up employment and almost impossible for those on work permits to be employed for more than a term, let alone become permanent residents or citizens. The difficulty for many lower-class arrivers of obtaining authentic documentation and the determination that decisions at all levels could be made almost arbitrarily on grounds left purposely vague by immigration officers and a board not bound to provide explanations or constrained by a clear appeal procedure further controlled the numbers and types of new Bahamians.[1]

The Independence Constitution declared eligible for citizenship all persons born in the Bahamas before July 10, 1973, as well as those born in the Bahamas after that date at least one of whose parents was a Bahamian citizen. The constitution also recognized as eligible those born outside the Bahamas whose father was (or but for death would have been) a Bahamian citizen in 1972 (and also, by almost the same token, a citizen of the United Kingdom and colonies), as well as those registered as Bahamian citizens under the British Nationality Act of 1948, as long as they were resident in the Bahamas at the end of 1972 and not citizens of another country.

For all those born after July 9, 1973, however, eligibility for citizenship was more limited or chancy. Those born in the Bahamas to non-Bahamian parents could apply to be registered as citizens within a year of their eighteenth birthday and would be successful provided they were prepared to make a declaration of intent concerning residence, take an oath of allegiance, renounce any foreign citizenship held, and—a crucial catch—were not excluded by "such exceptions as may be prescribed in the interests of national security and public policy." The vague latter restriction also applied to the wives of Bahamian citizens and to applicants for registration aged eighteen to twenty-one who were born outside the Bahamas to mothers who were Bahamian citizens. Seemingly, even for those born in the Bahamas to a parent who was a Bahamian citizen, registration as a citizen was not absolutely guaranteed but was also subject to the carefully unspecified "interests of national security or public policy."

As befitted an ostensibly liberal country, aliens who were not entitled to be registered or naturalized under their existing status were nominally allowed to apply for citizenship of the Bahamas under the 1973 Nationality Act, though in addition to the usual restrictions they had to have been resident for at least five years, pledge to make the Bahamas their permanent home, and show competence in the English language.

Affecting many more people were the consequences of the PLP's abolition of the unique Bahamian Status (Belonger) category in favor of a simpler (and more orthodox) distinction between citizenship and permanent residence. The previous status had been given to British subjects and those naturalized as such in the Bahamas after at least five years' residence or automatically through marriage to a Belonger. It conferred equal rights with Bahamian citizens in respect to permanent residence, employment, engaging in business, and even the vote, though it did not pass on as a matter of right to a Belonger's children.[2]

Belongers' rights were sustained for some years after independence, and Belongers were generally given priority in applications for citizenship, but most subsequent immigrants with similar qualifications and aims had to choose between remaining as temporary residents under work permit restrictions and applying for permanent resident status. The new status was significantly different from the old. Though it was open to spouses of Bahamians not otherwise qualifying for citizenship, permanent residence was designed mainly for persons of means who wished to "put down roots in the Bahamas by investing in property or in a business" and for retirees. Obtainable only through a cumbrous two-tiered application to the Ministry of National Security and the Immigration Board and the payment of a $5,000 fee, a certificate of permanent residence was revocable through three years' nonresidence, in the case of wives through divorce or separation, through a criminal conviction, or even as the result of any conduct "that in the opinion of the

Board" was "not in the public interest." Belongers could obtain permanent resident status for their lifetimes without paying a fee if they applied before August 1976, but they were no longer allowed to vote, and those failing to apply in time "ceased to enjoy any immigration status" whatsoever. Permanent residents, other than former Belongers, were required to obtain work permits if they wished to take up employment in the Bahamas.

The Immigration Board, indeed, set out to control the issuing of work permits with even greater rigor, with the purpose of ensuring that immigrants did not "create unfair competition for employment" and that each prospective employee would be "an asset to the Bahamas." Would-be employers had to advertise and interview locally and obtain a certificate from the Labour Exchange that no Bahamian had registered who might fill the position. Permits were for a single specified post and normally for a single year, with no guarantee of renewal, though they could be granted for longer periods for "certain key personnel on contract" such as the doctors, dentists, nurses, teachers, engineers, and hotel executives of whom there was still a shortage in the mid-1990s.[3] Such key offshore operations as banks also found it relatively easy to employ their own nationals as contract personnel, especially if they were also making efforts to hire local subordinate staff.

Work permits were not to be renewed after five years (the minimum period of residence to qualify for citizenship), except in cases of exceptional need on the part of the Bahamas or hardship on the employee's side, and permits could be endorsed with the requirement that efforts be made to train a Bahamian to fill the post. If non-Bahamians ceased employment before their permits had expired, the employers had the duty of informing the Immigration Department within a month, and the employees were required to present their permits for cancellation within seven days, on pain of stiff fines.[4]

The chief impediment to the efficient working of the citizenship, immigration, and work permit system was that, inevitably in a small and young country, it depended on unsophisticated bureaucrats and the ultimate authority of a very few overworked individuals—specifically an Immigration Board that was simply the cabinet under a different name. As one former PLP minister described the operation of the system, he never saw any evidence of corruption at the cabinet level, though it was not impossible that money changed hands at lower levels to expedite applications. Though individual decisions may have been made subjectively, more often they were simply rubber-stamped. He could not recall much discussion about policy in general and almost none about particular cases. There was certainly no consistent effort to approve or disapprove any persons on any other grounds than the technical merits of the application and the perceived needs of the Bahamas. The chief determinant was simply the limited time available. Citizenship, immigration, and work permit applications came last on any cabinet agenda and were often postponed, which chiefly accounted for the backlog of ten thousand cases that the FNM was said to have inherited in 1992 and which it announced as a matter of priority to clear.[5]

Just as skilled professionals were given preference over more menial workers and well-heeled residents welcomed over mere employees, the Bahamian government (operating through an Investment Board and Licensing Authority as well as the immigration authorities), while seeking to exclude exploiters, was relatively gentle toward genuine investors in landed property and commerce.

Uneasy juxtaposition of traditional and modern: Market Street, Nassau, looking south. On right, the Loyalist-built Balcony House (ca. 1790), and left, the Central Bank of the Bahamas (1990). Photograph by Gail Saunders.

The determination to control the acquiring of Bahamian land by non-Bahamians reached its apogee in the PLP's enactment of the Immovable Property (Acquisition by Foreign Persons Act) of 1983, which required that all acquisitions, from large tracts down to single house plots, had to obtain approval and a permit from a Foreign Investment Board, as well as being subject to duties and fees. The consequent confusion, delays, and backlog, however, allowed the opposition to charge that the law actually retarded genuine investment, while facilitating the chances of corruption through payment for preferential or expedited treatment. As a result of promises in its manifesto, the FNM consequently repealed the 1983 act in favor of the International Land Holdings Act, which came into effect in 1994. This law made a clear distinction between large and small investments and decreed that non-Bahamians could acquire houses or parcels of land of less than five acres simply by registering the transaction and paying the requisite duties and fees, as long as the acquisitions were for their own residential purposes. Such property could also be bequeathed and sold, subject only to the registration of the change of ownership and payment of the proper taxes, duties, and fees. Approval and a permit from the Investment Board was necessary only if the property was intended for renting or other business purposes or was a tract larger than five acres. These changes, it was hoped, would both encourage residential investors and free up the Investment Board to consider major applicants for Bahamian landed property, including Crown land.[6]

The largest concern of the Investment Authority and Board, however, was to strike a delicate balance between the encouragement and the control of foreigners wishing to do business in the Bahamas. The PLP avidly adopted its UBP predecessors' policy of encouraging offshore companies and banks to set up operations in the Bahamas, and this continued to the point that Nassau had a new commercial core much like Hamilton, Bermuda, or George Town, Grand Cayman, if not New York's Wall Street or London's City. The benefits were obvious: the flow of money, the fees generated for government and lawyers, the creation of local employment, and the provision of ancillary services. But the scale of the rewards, the restless aggression of international capital, and the fallibilities of human nature from which Bahamians were far from immune ensured that there remained serious dangers, most obviously the continuation of the methods of operation and the entrenchment of class relations that characterized old Bay Street, but more insidiously the plundering of Bahamian resources, the retardation of local capital, and the undermining of service industries the independent country of the Bahamas needed.

Through legislation culminating in the International Bahamian Companies Act of 1990, a primary distinction was made between those companies simply located in the Bahamas and those designed to do business in the country. Far from requiring Bahamian participation in the former (which may have been the trend of policy under the UBP), the law now forbade direct participation in offshore companies by Bahamian citizens and residents. Nor did the law specifically require Bahamian participation in companies designed to do business in the Bahamas or specifically exclude any international companies from operating in the Bahamas. Instead, such companies and operators were subject to purely pragmatic controls: a system of licenses and permits with conditions issued by the Investment Authority and approved by the Investments Board, working under policy guidelines established by the National Economic Council, chaired by the prime minister. The general lines of investment policy were frequently stated, but they changed from time to time according to the economic climate and the direction of the political wind, there were many gray areas between policy and implementation, and in probably far too many cases approval or disapproval depended on individual decisions.[7]

A few examples can illustrate the manifold problems. Many of the hundreds of banks and trust companies set up in the Bahamas were truly independent operations, but those licensed to do business with Bahamians (and thus subject to regulations about employing and training local personnel) often had offshore subsidiaries. Much the same was true for insurance and accountancy firms. There was not yet a formal Bahamian stock exchange, and though many Bahamian companies and corporations issued shares, it was not clear to what extent Bahamians could deal in shares of companies listed on foreign stock exchanges, especially when such companies had offshore affiliates in the Bahamas. In licensing foreign businesses in the Bahamas, the authorities naturally favored those for which there was insufficient local capital or expertise (for example, in the manufacture or recycling of automobile tires), but officials were often unsure what degree of local participation should be required and, given that the basic conditions were expected to change, what term should be set on the license.

Restaurants were one enterprise in which Bahamians were normally protected, but arguments were frequently made that foreign-owned gourmet and ethnic restaurants should be given special consideration because of the demands of the tourist industry and Bahamians' limited expertise. This question was further complicated because Bahamian Greeks and Chinese, long established in the restaurant business, had extensive networks in their wider ethnic communities. The great proliferation of franchise operations in the 1980s and 1990s (particularly in the fast-food sector) testified to a related and even thornier problem: to what extent did franchises represent genuine Bahamian enterprises and to what extent the tentacles of supernational corporations? A plausible case could be made that franchises aided the small local businessman, but it was notable that franchises tended to be held in multiples by local entrepreneurs, who in the nature of things were dependent on foreign-owned banks, if not directly indebted to foreign investors. Such involvements came very close to the situation referred to earlier in relation to the selling by Stafford Sands and his associates of their Nassau Markets grocery chain to the American Winn-Dixie corporation in 1968.

Neither the PLP nor its FNM successors has had the ability, perhaps the will (given the vital importance of Bahamian ownership of whatever kind), either to eradicate all the old Bay Street enterprises or entirely to scotch their methods of operation. Some of the old magnates had followed Stafford Sands's lead in selling off their businesses. But most had merely lowered their profile and compensated for their political marginalization by concentrating on business, judiciously liberalizing their hiring practices, and even expanding. The notion that a cabal of "White Knights" still dominated Bahamian business from their homes on East Bay Street or Prospect Ridge was a conspiracy theory dreamed up by Ivan Johnson, the owner-editor of the weekly tabloid *Punch*. Commentators did note, however, that most of the businesses on central Bay Street continued to be white-owned throughout the 1990s and that whites carefully held on to nearly all the freeholds of the few premises leased by blacks.

That this could happen spoke to the limits and nonrevolutionary nature of socioeconomic change in the Bahamas. Two cases in 1994, however, did show a greater degree of public awareness and concern, even if the response of the government was equivocal. In line with trends in the United States toward ever-larger and all-inclusive stores, if without direct financial connections, one Bay Street chain of general stores not previously in the drink business applied for a liquor license, and another that was already the largest lumber and hardware retailer applied to sell clothing as well. Recognizing that there were demonstrably too many liquor outlets already and that clothes retailing was traditionally in the hands of small as well as large businesses, critics were concerned both with the dangers of local firms expanding outside their traditional bounds and of unrestricted businesses overwhelming smaller enterprises on their way to virtual monopolies. Although the government clearly felt that while it was legally able to control the proliferation of liquor licenses, it was less justified in limiting the natural tendency toward diversification and economies of scale—especially if the net result was of benefit to the consumer. A similar general consideration—that only large firms could operate profitably while providing reasonable prices to the consumer and absorbing the costs of government-controlled prices on essential foodstuffs—determined the government's lenient policy toward grocery chains, one of the most traditional of Bay Street enterprises.[8]

Of potentially even greater significance to the Bahamian people were the debates and decisions during the last years of the PLP's regime and the first phase of the FNM's over the questions of the nationalization, privatization, and popular ownership of financial and service institutions. From at least 1973, the Central Bank,

Monetary Authority, and Foreign Exchange Commission were pillars of Bahamian economic independence. But in the 1980s, tentatively following the lead of other newly independent Commonwealth Caribbean countries, the government first took a majority shareholding and then bought out the Bahamian subsidiary of the Bank of Montreal, renaming it the Bank of the Bahamas and providing it with almost exclusively Bahamian management. In 1994, the government announced that the majority of the shares of the bank, which accounted for about a quarter of the local commercial banking business, would be sold to the Bahamian public (non-Bahamians were ineligible), thus combining the principles of a capitalism both localized and relatively popular.

In contrast, the FNM government not only attempted to sell off to foreign investors as many as possible of the hotels acquired (of necessity) by its predecessor and made moves to abolish the money-draining Hotels Corporation. The government was far more circumspect, however, about the public service corporations. Despite "Thatcherite" arguments that privatization and public ownership would cut government costs and increase efficiency, the future of BATELCO and the Bahamas Electricity Corporation (both at least potentially very profitable) hung in the balance in the mid-1990s. But it seemed unlikely that the persistently money-losing national airline, Bahamasair, would, or even could, be pushed in the same direction.

Even more than the other Caribbean countries that had to balance the need for a national airline against its cost (and were sometimes swayed by the mere prestige of owning a national flag-carrier), the Bahamas government was faced by the vital importance of an efficient communication system in developing the country or even holding it together. The bulk of interinsular traffic, passenger as well as freight, was still carried by ship (see Map 15). Since early colonial days the modest subsidizing of what was generically called the mail boat service was regarded as a necessity, but the prevailing system was one of free enterprise so that ships served best the most traveled and most profitable routes. Thus the decline of the poorer islands in favor of the more fortunate was scarcely slowed. Air transport revolutionized the tourist industry and hugely improved the speed of communication between islands. But its far greater technological and infrastructural costs resulted in air transport even more than shipping gravitating toward the most popular and profitable routes (see Map 16), while a national airline had both to compete with foreign carriers on external routes and to struggle to provide a comprehensive service internally. That in the face of such problems (to which were added erratic management and fluctuating government support) Bahamasair by the mid-1990s was entirely staffed and flown by Bahamians, had never had a fatal accident, and maintained as good a record of reliability and service as it did were proud achievements worthy to rank with the best traditions of the Family Island mail boats and which no sensible national government would lightly jeopardize.

A matter of parallel concern to the government, perhaps even more important because it involved the national culture as well as the control of the communications media, was the future role of the radio and TV corporation ZNS. Besides providing a government mouthpiece and many well-protected jobs, ZNS had continued its long tradition of providing local news (including weather and shipping reports and community and even family announcements) and other programs of special interest and value to Bahamians. Though it was of necessity commercialized,

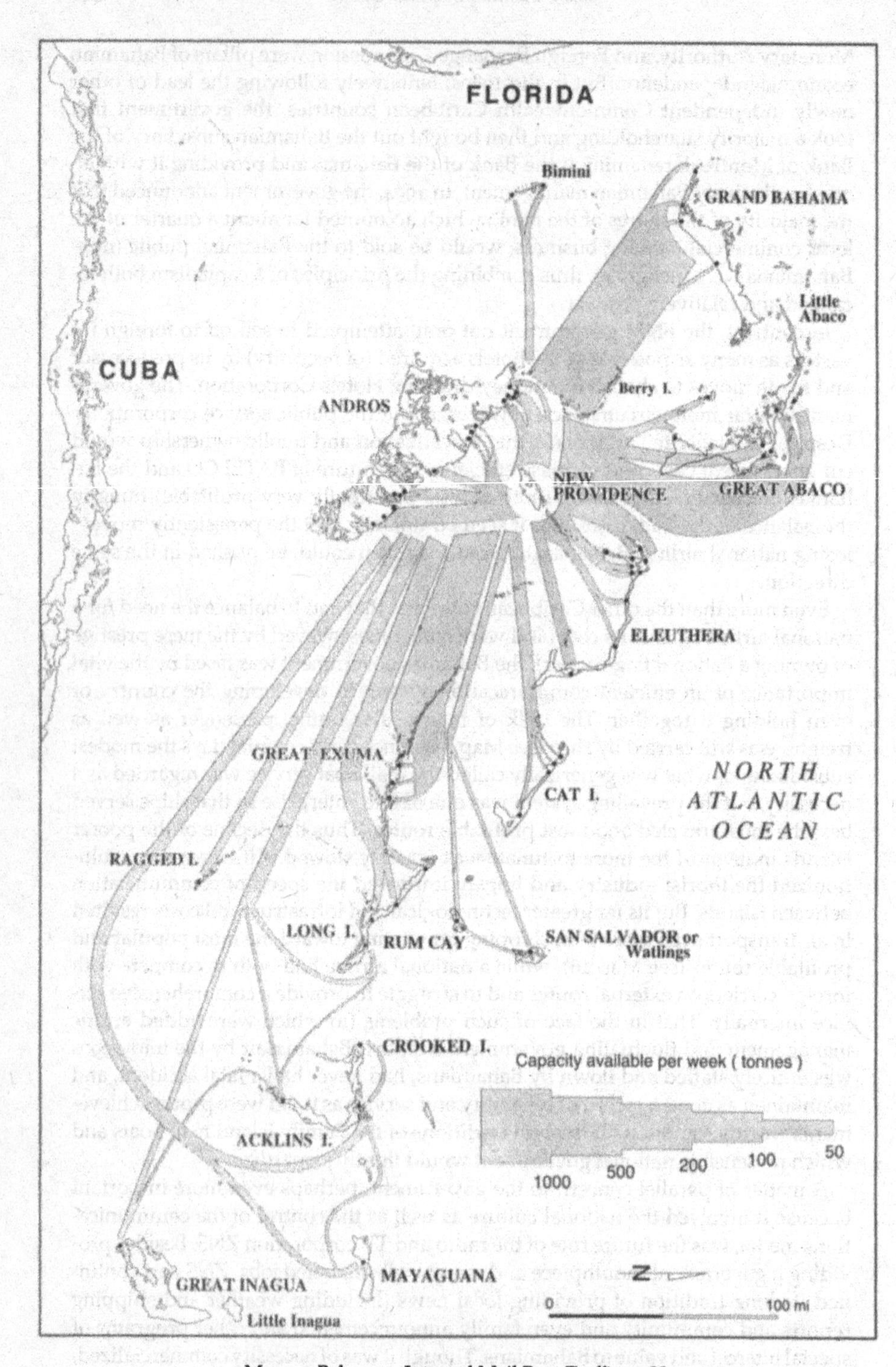

Map 15. Bahamas: Internal Mail Boat Traffic, 1988

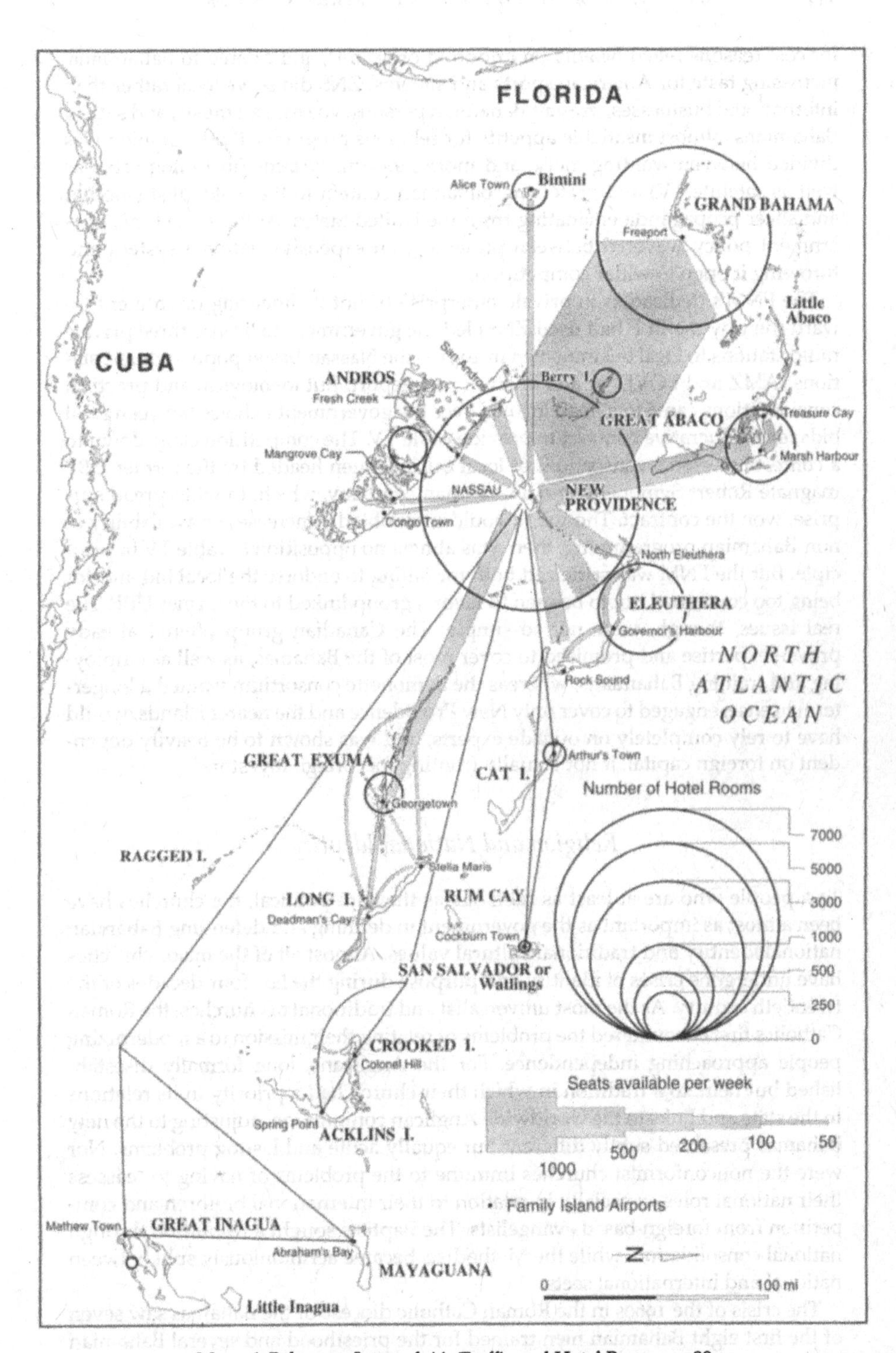
FLORIDA
CUBA
Alice Town
Bimini
GRAND BAHAMA
Freeport
Little Abaco
San Andros
ANDROS
Fresh Creek
Berry I.
GREAT ABACO
Treasure Cay
Marsh Harbour
Mangrove Cay
NASSAU
NEW PROVIDENCE
Congo Town
North Eleuthera
ELEUTHERA
Governor's Harbour
NORTH ATLANTIC OCEAN
Rock Sound
Arthur's Town
GREAT EXUMA
CAT I.
Number of Hotel Rooms
Georgetown
7000
5000
3000
1000
500
250
0
RAGGED I.
Stella Maris
LONG I.
RUM CAY
Deadman's Cay
Cockburn Town
SAN SALVADOR or Watlings
CROOKED I.
Colonel Hill
Seats available per week
Spring Point
ACKLINS I.
1000
500
200
100
50
• Family Island Airports
Mathew Town
GREAT INAGUA
Abraham's Bay
MAYAGUANA
N
0
100 mi
Little Inagua

Map 16. Bahamas: Internal Air Traffic and Hotel Rooms, 1988

for cost reasons relied heavily on imported programs, and catered to Bahamians' increasing taste for American sports and sitcoms, ZNS did serve local rather than international businesses, present Bahamian persons, voices, and music, and satisfy Bahamians' almost insatiable appetite for religious programs. Public opinion was divided between wanting more, and more modern, systems (including cable as well as satellite TV) and preferring Bahamian content to the materialist smother and sheer propaganda emanating from the United States. At the same time, government policy wavered between protecting an expensive national system and throwing it open to wider competition.

The FNM's dedication to private enterprise (if not its lingering resentment toward the way the PLP had used ZNS) led the government to license three private radio stations to local businessmen in 1993—the Nassau-based popular music stations JAMZ and LOVE '97 and another in Freeport. But ideological and practical considerations came to a head in 1994 over the government's choice between rival bids for the lucrative contract to provide cable TV. The competition came down to a contest between a consortium of local businessmen headed by the former UBP magnate Robert Symonette and a Canadian company, which, to widespread surprise, won the contract. Though it would undoubtedly increase the availability of non-Bahamian programming, there was almost no opposition to cable TV in principle. But the FNM was criticized both for failing to endorse the local bid and for being too concerned not to be seen to favor a group linked to the former UBP. The real issues, though, were not so simple. The Canadian group offered already proven expertise and promised to cover most of the Bahamas, as well as employing and training Bahamians, whereas the Symonette consortium wanted a longer-term license, engaged to cover only New Providence and the nearer islands, would have to rely completely on outside experts, and was shown to be heavily dependent on foreign capital, if not actually fronting for foreign investors.[9]

Religion and National Identity

To a people who are at least as religious as they are political, the churches have been almost as important as the government in defining and defending Bahamian national identity and traditional cultural values. Almost all of the major churches have undergone crises of identity and purpose during the last four decades of the twentieth century. As the most universalist and traditional of churches, the Roman Catholics first encountered the problems of relating their mission to a modernizing people approaching independence. For the Anglicans, long formally disestablished but heirs to a tradition in which their church had a priority in its relations to the state and links to the worldwide Anglican communion, adjusting to the new Bahamas presented subtly different but equally acute and lasting problems. Nor were the nonconformist churches immune to the problems of having to reassess their national roles, especially in relation to their international brethren and competition from foreign-based evangelists. The Baptists sought a resolution through national consolidation, while the Methodists became acrimoniously split between national and international sects.

The crisis of the 1960s in the Roman Catholic diocese of the Bahamas saw seven of the first eight Bahamian men trained for the priesthood and several Bahamian nuns give up their vocations, some of them leaving the church and getting married.

Family Island vernacular architecture. *Above*, Harbour Island. *Middle*, Spanish Wells. *Middle*, Old Bight, Cat Island. *Below*, Simms, Long Island. From Robert Douglas, *Island Heritage: Architecture of the Bahamas* (Nassau, 1992), used with permission.

This crisis was all the more bitter because of the church's proud achievements in social welfare and education, its commitment to racial harmony, and the role of some of its leading members in the formation of the PLP. As explained in 1994 by Monsignor Preston Moss (a black convert from Anglicanism who was the sole survivor of the original cohort of eight Bahamians trained to be priests at St. Augustine's School and Aquinas College in Nassau and St. John's University in Minnesota in the 1950s and 1960s), it came at a time of worldwide ferment, the important debates and changes of Vatican II (1962–65), as well as movements toward decolonization, democracy, and racial equality in many areas besides the Bahamas. It was an era of hope and idealism but also one in which the aspirations of the young tended to outrun the ideas of the older and more conservative.[10]

In the Bahamian context, the conflict stemmed broadly from the different approaches and attitudes of the well-entrenched older generation of Benedictine and Dominican missionary priests and teachers—white Americans, mainly of German extraction—and the idealistic and patriotic zeal of the black Bahamian newcomers. In a complex way, the resentment of the young novices at what they saw as the imposition of monastic rules and a calculated policy to keep them from taking over as parish priests was tied in with a wider sense, shared by many of the laity, that the ethos of the older priests was outdated and paternalistic, if not also culturally alien.

In the wake of the defection of the first wave of native trainees, the Catholic church in the Bahamas went through a phase that Monsignor Moss called "a desert experience." Significant changes occurred in the late 1960s and through the 1970s. Organizationally these included the involvement of the laity in a Diocesan Assembly, Catholic Education Board, and parochial councils; and in liturgy they went beyond Vatican II's adoption of the vernacular to the sponsoring of a Bahamian Goombay Mass, composed by Eric Cash in 1969, and even some tentative experiments with charismatic prayer. Yet, despite the gradual phasing out through retirement of the missionary old guard in favor of a second generation of Bahamian priests, the Catholic church in the Bahamas had remained essentially conservative, had never regained its original exuberant optimism, and had done no more than sustain its share of Bahamian adherents.

For Monsignor Moss and many other thinking Catholics, however, there was a profound merit in their church's conservatism. It spoke to a people to whom political independence brought new dangers and fears as well as hopes, much as did marriage to a young couple. The Catholic church in the Bahamas could not advocate the Liberation Theology, which flourished (and divided the church) in the traditionally Catholic former colonies of Latin America, because Bahamians no longer suffered from evils that called for armed struggle and in any case were an essentially nonviolent people. What the church could and did do, he believed, was to lead the way in the promotion of timeless values—the sanctity of life, respect for others (including the poorest of the poor, the Haitian immigrants), the centrality of family, and the dignity of labor—and to speak out against what it took to be the "new slavery" of modern materialism and social envy. The monsignor drove home his message by quoting a twenty-one-year old Bahamian languishing on death row in Fox Hill Prison. Asked what had brought him and his fellow prisoners to such a pass, the murderer thought deeply and answered, "Vanity." Bahamian people, he said, had become so vain and undisciplined that whenever they saw new cars and other flashy things they had to have them, and they took them, even if it cost a human life.[11]

Most of Monsignor Moss's sentiments were shared by the church in the Bahamas at large and might have been expressed by any of the leaders of the ecumenical Bahamas Christian Council, formed in 1975. Certainly they were echoed almost exactly in 1994 by Michael Eldon, the Cambridge-educated first Bahamian and first nonwhite Anglican bishop of the Bahamas. He specially praised the Catholics for no longer engaging in competitive proselytizing and suggested that they and the Anglicans had more in common than either did with the more aggressive evangelical sects based in the United States or even with their own coreligionists in the larger Caribbean.[12] The two churches had an identical range and similar number of schools and pupils (drawn in both cases as much from nonadherents as from church members), and, in part because of the Catholics' greater number of Haitians, were now almost exactly equal in membership. The problems they had faced and were facing, however, were substantially different.

Looking over his episcopate, due to end in 1995 after twenty-three years, Bishop Eldon thought that the greatest change and achievement was the "indigenization" of the Anglican ministry. In contrast to Anglican tradition, now not one of the sixty-five active priests was British. The overwhelming majority were Bahamians, with a few from the Commonwealth Caribbean and one each from Canada and the United States. The shift had produced a more permanent and stable ministry closely attuned to the national culture and should have been a source of national pride. Much of the ingrained prejudice in favor of white expatriate priests had been overcome. Perversely, though, priests who were better known and more permanently installed were more susceptible to criticism. Ironically, too, the worst disadvantages stemmed from the fact that most modern priests, unlike their mainly celibate and frugal predecessors, were married men with modern expectations about living standards. Many ministers' wives were highly qualified persons, but it was difficult to find employment for them or suitable education for the children in the more isolated postings. This not only exacerbated the general problem of an overconcentration on the more developed islands and the comparative neglect of the rest but greatly increased the cost of an adequately wide-ranging ministry.

Finance, indeed, had become the salient problem for the Bahamian Anglican church. It was not just because church members were poor, but there had never been a strong tithing tradition in the Bahamas. In early colonial days the Anglican church subsisted on government grants, supplemented by metropolitan missionary societies (particularly the Society for the Propagation of the Gospel), the support of which was all the more vital after disestablishment in 1869. The government gave aid to Anglican schools from the 1950s, but metropolitan funding abruptly ended in 1972, at the same time that Bernard Markham, the last English bishop, resigned. Bahamian Anglicans were proud to be more reliant on their own resources, but it was a continuous struggle, particularly in maintaining the schools and other social services, sustaining the outreach to their poorer parishioners, and countering the competition from the more affluent evangelical sects based in the United States. Inevitably, too, Bahamian Anglicans were drawn closer into the community of the Caribbean archdiocese, which presented its own problems, as well as rewards.

In 1994, Bishop Eldon expressed some nostalgia for the time when the Anglican bishop stood next to the governor in local protocol (a position now occupied by the rotating chairman of the Bahamas Christian Council) or when the governor-generals were almost inevitably staunch Anglicans (even the fiery politico Sir Milo Butler had been churchwarden of St. Matthew's).[13] He honored the dedicated white priests (mainly Anglo-Catholics) who extended the Anglican mission to the ordinary people long before he was born, and he greatly valued the English education that had given him a personal self-confidence so that he had not "felt threatened" by the reigning forces of race and class bigotry when he entered the ministry. But he looked to the future with hope as well as some trepidation.

In an emergent nation, the church (though still called Anglican) had loosened its English ties, while avoiding the alternative subjection to North American influences characterizing the culture at large. It had shaken off the image that, if not quite "the ruling class at prayer," it was an elite church for the aspiring brown bourgeoisie. The long conflict between "Prayer Book" and Anglo-Catholic factions was laid to rest. Spiritual and practical sustenance had come from ecumenism and from closer ties to Anglican brethren in the Commonwealth Caribbean. Yet Bahamian Anglicans still had to find their special place within both the broader church and the Bahamian national context. The recently deadlocked debates in the synod to choose Bishop Eldon's successor had been symptomatic, revealing a division between older conservatives and younger radicals over such key issues as evangelization, the mission to the poor, the role of women in the church, the value of charismatic worship, and the relevance of other features of what was currently being defined as Caribbean Theology.[14]

The nine sects of Bahamian Baptists covered a range of liturgical styles and affiliations but generally had fewer problems adjusting to Bahamian independence and modernization than the other major religious bodies. Baptists had always been closely identified with ordinary black Bahamians and had a long and proud association with political populism, and these traditions provided them with a special sense of authenticity after the coming of majority rule. Moreover, the Baptists' participatory and congregationalist traditions, along with their long history of being sociopolitical outsiders, had entrenched a strong tendency toward self-reliance. Coincidentally with self-government and independence the Bahamian Baptists moved closer together by forming a loose convention; they took an increasingly prominent role in the Bahamas Christian Council; and they reached a kind of apotheosis when a Baptist prime minister, Hubert Ingraham, allowed the Baptist Sir Clifford Darling (appointed by the Pindling administration) to continue as the fourth governor-general for two years after the FNM victory in 1992. The only dangers were comparatively mild—that success might lead to complacency and an unreflective self-confidence. Some internal critics felt that the Bahamian Baptists' novel respectability left them vulnerable to inroads from more aggressive and radical evangelizers, while Bahamian nationalists claimed that the local Baptists—who in January 1986 proudly hosted the National Baptist Convention of the United States—tended to ignore the dangers to national cultural identity implicit in their intimate historical associations with American black Baptists, dating back two centuries.[15]

The problems of national identity faced by the Bahamian Methodist church were quite different and far more severe, coming to an almost riotous climax in 1993. The Methodist church in the Bahamas was born and grew up divided, with a hard and fast separation between white and nonwhite churches.[16] This conflict eased in the mid-twentieth century, but as metropolitan missionary society influence waned (concurrently with the move toward self-government and political independence), there remained a residuum of familiar custom that gave the Bahamian Methodist church a uniqueness the majority of its members wished to preserve. Desegregation became almost complete even in the former all-white strongholds, but as a younger generation of Methodists agonized about the role of their church in the modern and independent Bahamas, a new and more disruptive division appeared between those who accepted closer ties with the larger regional Methodist community, represented by the Methodist Council for the Caribbean and the Americas (MCCA), and the majority who rejected them.[17]

The crisis originated in 1986 with the return to the Bahamas from an unfruitful stint in Jamaica of the dynamic and idealistic young minister Colin Archer. Appointed to the aptly named post of minister for caring, he preached and campaigned for changes that would revive the church's flagging mission, but entirely from within itself. At the synod for the Bahamas and Turks and Caicos Islands Methodists held at Rock Sound and Tarpum Bay, Eleuthera, in January 1991, the agenda called for attention to evangelization and the needs of education and social welfare (including consideration of the Haitian problem). But discussion was soon monopolized by the question of whether any of the necessary changes could be accomplished while the islands continued under the authority of the Caribbean-oriented MCCA.[18]

After a stormy debate in a supplementary synod called by the MCCA in March 1991, the Bahamian Methodists (along with those from the Turks and Caicos Islands) voted forty-three to twenty-three for autonomy, to come into effect on September 1, 1992. A constitution for a separate church was approved, and a steering committee set up to seek the necessary legislation. The MCCA, strongly supported by a few conservative Bahamian ministers and their congregations and by the considerable number of Jamaican and other West Indian ministers in the Bahamas, did its utmost to reverse the decision. In June 1992 it appointed a new superintendent in the Bahamas, Rev. Kenneth Huggins, but local Methodist demonstrators, under the banner of Colin Archer's Association for the Revival of Methodism (ARM), barred his entry to the official residence, Turton House, and similarly blocked other West Indian appointees. The MCCA ordered the reposting of Colin Archer to Jamaica, but he refused to go, and the steering committee made its own appointments to all the vacant ministerial posts.[19]

A bill was drafted that not only included a deed of union but granted to the new Methodist Church of the Bahamas (MCB) all existing Methodist property, including churches, schools, and money in the banks. The bill provoked heated debate in the 181st Methodist synod, held in January 1993, but received decisive majority support. An exchange of letters appeared in the press in which former prime minister Pindling said that he approved Methodist autonomy in principle but had doubts about its implementation (particularly the protection of the dissidents), and Prime Minister Ingraham somewhat pusillanimously said that the government was supporting the bill mainly because it had become an issue of law and order. Despite statements by the General Board of Ministers of the United Methodist Church deploring what they called political intervention in religious matters and desperate efforts by the MCCA to block the bill in the Supreme Court, it was passed by the House of Assembly on April 15 and by the Senate on May 17, 1993. The defeated ministers and their followers, with the support of the MCCA, then announced the establishment of separate Methodist congregations. The MCB had achieved what its most ardent supporters regarded as a heroic victory for Bahamian religious and cultural identity, but at the cost of an irreparable split in the Methodist church and an accelerated decline in the number of its adherents.[20]

The Bahamian Self and the Haitian Other: The History of Haitian Migration

A people defines itself even more in contrast to very different peoples with whom it comes in contact than by comparisons with those whom it sees as most similar or wishes to emulate. Thus, as has just been suggested, the majority of Bahamian Methodists have sought their true identity by rejecting religiocultural characteristics epitomized by West Indian pastors, while Bahamian Baptists have, less consciously, tended toward an identity historically shared with their black American coreligionists. Native Bahamians as a whole have likewise sought self-identification by assessing, consciously or not, what it is that makes them similar to, and dissimilar from, Britons, Americans, and people from the Caribbean proper. No people, however, has served more effectively as the defining other for the Bahamian self than have the Haitian migrants to and through the Bahamas, particularly since the 1950s.

The close human linkage between Haiti and the Bahama Islands has existed as long as there have been people in the archipelago, producing conflict and tensions but also bringing mutual benefits. As we showed in Volume 1, the aboriginal people of the Bahamas themselves came, more or less immediately, from the northern part (which they called Haiti) of the large island Columbus was to christen Española. Even after they had established themselves in the islands and developed their Lucayan subculture, these Taino migrants, besides sometimes coming into armed conflict with their cousins in Haiti, seem to have engaged in an important trade with them, involving the exchange of salt, dried conch, and perhaps cotton, for fashioned hardstones, pottery, and the precious alloy called *guanin*.[21]

The connection revived when both Española and the Bahama Islands became peopled by Europeans, and it included in the early years the association between the buccaneers, freebooters, and pirates of Tortuga and New Providence. Once France acquired the western half of Española from Spain (1697) and, as St. Domingue, made it the richest slave plantation colony in the world, however, an effective naval curtain was drawn between French and English settlers, and the Turks Islands and Windward Passage became bones of contention between the two chief imperial powers for most of the eighteenth century.[22]

Haiti and the Bahamas were thrown together once more by the upheaval of the French and Haitian revolutions. A phase of relations followed, which, as Sean McWeeney has argued, foreshadowed the modern situation in certain key respects. Shielded by the ideological struggle between *blancs* and nonwhite nonslaves (*affranchis*), the majority of St. Domingue plotted against their masters and burst into bloody rebellion in 1791. Many of the surviving whites and *affranchis* fled with the slaves they still controlled, and the flight became a general exodus between 1793 and 1794 once the French Jacobins declared racial equality and slave emancipation and went to war against Britain and Spain.[23]

The intended destinations for most of the enforced migrants were Cuba or the United States, but many ended up in Jamaica or the Bahamas, either because they lacked the means to move on from their first place of refuge or because they were landed at Port Royal or Nassau after being captured by British privateers. In the Bahamas, Governor Dunmore and many of the whites were concerned about the economic and political effects of the influx from the beginning. But the first response of the Assembly in September 1793 was simply to pass an act levying a tax of £30 on each "French" slave and of £100 on each *affranchi.* Restrictions on entry, strict policing, and deportations were soon ordered, however, and regulations further tightened after a plot among the francophone slaves was uncovered in 1797. The migration had almost ceased by the time the Haitians achieved their independence from France in 1804. Bahamian planters were moderately concerned about competition from the white French émigrés but, like all whites, were terrified by the prospect of the spread of a Haitian-style slave revolt. For this reason, as many as possible of the francophone whites and their slaves were located in islands distant from Nassau, out of sight and mind. At the same time, though, the whites in the colonial capital were made almost paranoid by the fear that the *affranchis* now boosting the urban middle class might not just displace them as craftsmen and petty merchants but might be infected with revolutionary French ideas.[24]

This last fear was certainly exaggerated. Most notable of the nonwhite nonslave newcomers was Stephen Dillet, landed in Nassau as a boy after being seized with his widowed mother by a British privateer in 1802. Displaying great enterprise, intelligence, and discretion, he became a successful businessman and the most active spokesman for the rights of the free coloreds in the Bahamas during the late 1820s and early 1830s. The achievement of full civil liberties for the free coloreds on the very eve of slave emancipation and Dillet's own distinguished later career as an assemblyman and civil servant, however, are most plausibly seen as a victory for hegemonic rather than more radical principles.[25]

Despite the marked tendency of modern Bahamians to disclaim any Haitian provenance or to admit descent from refugees (especially among the lighter-skinned descendants of émigrés), undoubtedly it was the great influx between 1791 and 1804 of Haitian slave owners and their slaves (who, as was common elsewhere, normally took their masters' surnames) that chiefly accounted for the prevalence of French surnames among modern Bahamians: Beneby, Bodie, Bonaby, Delevaux, Demeritte, Deveaux, Dillet, Dupuch, Duvalier, Laroda, Moncur, Moree, Poitier, Symonette. Yet the Haitian connection was far from sundered by Haitian independence and British slave emancipation. Throughout the late nineteenth and early twentieth centuries, Haitian and Bahamian mariners, mainly from the northern Haitian ports and the southern Bahamian islands, ranged from Nassau in the north to Port-au-Prince in the south, exchanging salt and dried conch (as in ancient times), fish, and some American and British manufactured goods for vegetables, fruits, livestock, and the technically contraband raw Haitian rum called taffia. They also carried on a more intimate intercourse, and there were probably as many children with Bahamian fathers in the northern Haitian ports as there were Haitian-fathered children in the southern Bahamian islands.

The islands of Tortuga and Inagua, only fifty-five miles apart, had special roles in the informal traditional linkages between Haiti and the Bahamas; the former was the most fruitful producer of peasant provisions in northern Haiti, the most active shipbuilding center, and home to the most intrepid of Haitian mariners (who retained something of the rough reputation of the Brethren of the Coast), while infertile but relatively prosperous Inagua was a good market for Haitian produce, the largest and cheapest depot for salt, and (with Long Cay) both an entrepôt for American and European manufactures and a modest source of negotiable currencies. Far closer to Haiti than Nassau, Mathew Town merchants had mercantile connections with Port-de-Paix and Cap Haitien, and as late as the 1940s some were sending their girls to be educated in convent schools in Port-au-Prince. In those simpler days, when there was comparatively little disparity of wealth or development between Haiti and the Bahamas, almost as few Haitians aimed to settle in the Bahamas as Bahamians in Haiti, while the fortunate few nonwhite Bahamians who visited Haiti as tourists came back enthused by the vitality and authenticity of Haitian popular culture and with an admiration bordering on envy for the Parisian elegance and political power of the Haitian brown elite.[26]

The situation changed in all respects from the 1950s and substantially again from the 1970s onward. As the lightly populated Bahamas began its upward curve of prosperity, achieving political change without losing stability, Haiti slid inexorably downward to become one of the poorest and most overcrowded nations on earth, oppressed by a corrupt and cynical regime. The total number of Haitians resident in the Bahamas when "Papa Doc" Duvalier came to power in Haiti in 1957 was probably no more than a thousand, but those at least temporarily living and working in the Bahamas reached ten thousand by 1962, twenty thousand by 1969, and by the time of independence was widely believed to be forty thousand—six times the total reported in the 1970 census and more than ten times the number with valid work permits. Though equaling no more than a third of Haiti's annual population increase (and only a fraction of its exports of people to the Dominican Republic, the United States, and Canada), this body of migrants represented as much as 20 percent of the people living in the Bahamas.[27]

The total number of Haitians living in the Bahamas, legally and illegally, does not seem to have increased greatly between 1973 and the mid-1990s, when the census reported twelve thousand, and forty thousand remained the most commonly quoted aggregate. But the problem the Haitians posed was greatly exacerbated by many factors: the downturn in the Bahamian economy, particularly in respect to employment; the political and economic chaos in Haiti after the flight of "Baby Doc" Duvalier in 1986; the tendency of more Haitians to remain the Bahamas rather than to move on or return; the rapid rise in the number of Haitians born in the Bahamas and the start of a second generation of the Bahamian-born; and the Haitians' increased visibility and vocality as more of their children passed through the schools and more adults became established in regular jobs, in churches, and in quasi-political organizations. The unfortunate human tendency to despise and denigrate those who are susceptible to exploitation may have affected the attitudes of the host people, if not also an inferiority complex on encountering others made more energetic and enterprising by economic desperation. Finally, and not least, tension and antagonism were increased by irrational fears, based not so much on the obvious differences of language and culture as on mutual ignorance of each other's aspirations and intentions.

The pioneer study by Dawn I. Marshall, *The Haitian Problem: Illegal Migration to the Bahamas* (published in 1979), went much of the way to explain what motivated the Haitian migrants and describe the Bahamians' responses to them, as well as to illuminate other areas of obscurity, furnish valuable statistics, and provide an admirable analytical model. Unfortunately, though, Marshall concentrated her analysis on one, or one type, of Haitian settlement (Carmichael in New Providence) and stopped short at the time of Bahamian independence (1973). The book was not followed up by further scholarly studies, despite the magnification of the "Haitian problem" over the succeeding two decades.[28]

As Marshall discovered in the late 1960s and Haitian informants have corroborated since, over 90 percent of the Haitian migrants to the Bahamas have come from northern Haiti, at least 67 percent of them being from the northwestern littoral between Môle St. Nicholas and Cap Haitien and Tortuga. Very few came from south of Gonaïves, including the teeming capital of Port-au-Prince—the areas that had provided the bulk of the migrants to Cuba, the Dominican Republic, and the rest of the Caribbean in the past and in the modern era were more inclined to target the United States and Canada directly than by way of the Bahamas. This helps to explain why internal Haitian politics were not of paramount importance to Haitian migrants to the Bahamas (at least before 1986), emphasizing that the overwhelming majority of them were economic, not political, refugees.

The North West is isolated from the rest of Haiti and divided into separate districts by mountainous terrain and poor roads. Internal trade is further hampered by the taxes levied at each departmental boundary. Though each district in the North West is the hinterland of a small coastal town, the proportion of rural peasants, some 88 percent, is higher than the Haitian average. Though traditionally self-sustaining, it is a poor area even by Haitian standards. Less than 10 percent of the land is cultivable (compared with national average of 23 percent), and although the population density is half that of Haiti as a whole, the soil is overtaxed. Deforestation and soil erosion have worsened conditions in an area already subject to frequent droughts and occasional hurricanes. In the 1960s, the North West Department had a per capita consumption of electricity a tenth that of Haiti overall and a fifth as many hospital beds. With school places for only about 18 percent of the eligible children and about 60 percent of the children in school failing to progress farther than first grade, illiteracy ran at about 90 percent.[29]

Cut off from Port-au-Prince and neglected by the Haitian government, subject to a downward spiral of poverty and even occasional starvation, the subsistence peasants of the Haitian North West naturally regarded the Bahamas as a land of opportunity from the 1950s onward. Those farmers with a small surplus found it more profitable to ship their plantains and ground provisions all the way to Nassau than to sell them in Haiti, and the ship captains soon saw illegal migrants as a valuable extra cargo. The official value of Haitian food exports to the Bahamas rose from $8,500 in 1950 to $37,000 in 1962, though tailing off sharply after 1967.[30] The Haitian provision sloops, sailing by way of Mathew Town, Inagua (where they were officially entered and cleared customs), to Potter's Cay in Nassau, brought back information about job opportunities—in Grand Bahama and Abaco as well as New Providence—at wages at least twice as high as those received by the very small minority of wage earners in Haiti. Word also filtered back of the money that young women might earn as prostitutes in the expanding Bahamian tourist industry.[31]

In response, a busy traffic in migrants soon developed, nearly all of them persons in their twenties and two-thirds of them males. Of Dawn Marshall's sample of this first generation, some 71 percent of the males reported that they had been farmers in Haiti, 11 percent sailors or fishermen, and only 8 percent involved in craft or artisanal work. Of the females, 30 percent listed their original occupation as farmers, 11 percent as seamstresses, only 2 percent as housewives, but no less than 45 percent as *commerçantes* (market women). Two-thirds of the women and 43 percent of the men had received no schooling, another 16 percent of the total no more than three years in school, and only one in eight, six years or more.[32]

In the earlier years, almost all intended to be merely temporary migrants, following the *kweyole* adage current in North West Haiti: *Nou vin Nassau, nou pa vin rété se g-in-n dola no vin chaché* ("We come to Nassau, we don't come to stay, we come only to look for dollars"). The ideal model for a young male in this phase was a rotational migration: to make enough money on a first venture to build a house; after a second to get married (on the *kweyole* principle *Se moun rich ke marié*, "One must be rich to marry"); and after a third to set up in some form of business. Certainly, within a decade, many traditional earth and thatch *cailles* had been replaced by concrete and corrugated iron "Nassau houses," and in La Môle, Port-de-Paix, St. Louis, and Le Cap were to be found small general stores owned by returnees, one of whom grandly styled his (after a notable Bay Street merchant) the Bethell Shop.[33]

The evidence of the migrants' success encouraged emulation, but as conditions in Haiti became yet more miserable—and the owners of Nassau houses and new shops found it impossible to generate rents or make retail profits—more persons were forced to migrate through sheer desperation, and fewer willingly returned. At its peak, the migration reached at least five thousand persons a year, carried in as many as 120 sailing sloops and 30 motorized vessels. Word of each planned trip was circulated by word-of-mouth—the legendary Haitian *télédiol*—but a passage required much preparation and negotiation. The fare charged for those without impeccable documentation (almost all) was never less than U.S.$200 and rose to U.S.$1,000 during a period when the average Haitian family's annual income wavered between U.S.$200 and U.S.$350. Migrants paid the captains a deposit (a quarter of the total or less), with a promise for the remainder once they had earned money in the Bahamas; they borrowed from moneylenders on a promise of repaying double within a year (with their Haitian property as security); in the most extreme cases, they sold their houses and land.

Conditions on the passage were normally bad and could be worse than in the old slave ships. Gross overcrowding was usual, supplies minimal, and safety equipment nonexistent. Vessels making a pretense of legality sometimes carried "crews" of thirty or forty, half of them women, all with purported seamen's articles. Others entered and cleared at Mathew Town while their passengers were temporarily left on a remote beach; the completely illegal majority sailed furtively and at night through some of the trickiest waters in the world. Motorized vessels could make the voyage to Nassau in three or four days, but sloops usually took two weeks and much longer if the prevailing winds failed. One informant told Dawn Marshall of a voyage that lasted thirty-five days, in which food and water ran out after twenty-two and several persons died. Vessels that properly carried only a crew of ten or less were intercepted with one hundred or more passengers, while an unknown number foundered. Oral legends told of captains (usually said by Haitian mainlanders to be Tortugans) who thought nothing of tipping sick or troublesome passengers overboard, expected the sexual favors of female passengers, and landed ignorant passengers on a desert island, telling them that they had reached New Providence, Grand Bahama, or even Florida.[34]

Haitian migrants fell into several distinct categories, and their lifestyles in the Bahamas varied greatly, partly as a consequence. Though Bahamians tended to view them as an undifferentiated mass, they exhibited very different characteristics according to family circumstances and, more subtly, to the region of the Haitian North West from which they came and with which they retained close affiliations. Family and subregional ties, indeed, were a vital feature of the close networking and information circulation that characterized the migration system—and remained a mysterious wonder to most Bahamians. General features exhibited by the Haitian migration, though, were that (as in many other areas worldwide) the will to migrate and the ingenuity of the migrants outran the ability or interest of the host people to stop them until it was too late easily to reverse the flow. Above all, it should be emphasized that the Haitians were as much drawn by the need for them as they were driven out by conditions in Haiti and that there were (if in steadily declining numbers) always Bahamians—employers, rentiers, suppliers, even immigration officers and policemen—prepared in their own self-interest to ignore the regulations, if not directly to exploit the Haitians.

Scattered among the Haitian economic refugees to the Bahamas were at least some political émigrés. Gaining a spurious encouragement from the PLP victory in 1968, small groups of anti-Duvalierists secretly began military training in Grand Bahama and Abaco, and in July 1968 Duvalier's newly appointed vice-consul for Abaco was murdered in Freeport. As a consequence, David Knox, a British official visiting from Nassau, was imprisoned in Port-au-Prince. Moves by the Bahamas government to conciliate the regime in Haiti and ensure Knox's release and the rounding up and deportation of seventy-seven "Freedom Fighters" discovered at Burrows Cay, Grand Bahama, in March 1968 drove the Haitian activists further underground and persuaded them that the burgeoning refugee communities in Miami, New York, Washington, and Montreal were far more suitable than the Bahamas for political organization.[35]

As the emigration from Haiti surged, the job market in the Bahamas became saturated, and the prospects for—and possibility of—a rotational migration declined, a large and increasing proportion of the Haitians in the Bahamas were either immediately in transit to the United States or Canada or regarded those countries as their ultimate destination. Such persons, of course, were likely to harbor very different feelings and attitudes toward the Bahamas from those who were putting down roots in the islands. The situation was complicated, however, by the reality that by the 1980s even those Haitians most firmly established in the Bahamas had close or extended family connections with communities in mainland North America, as well as back in the Haitian homeland. One inevitable result was that political awareness became more general throughout the Haitian diaspora, especially in the wake of the Duvaliers' fall and the election, exile, and return of President Jean-Bertrand Aristide (1986–94). This heightened concern fed back to the Bahamian Haitians, though the critical factors for almost all of them remained economic rather than political.

Of the majority of migrants who went to the Bahamas for work, some were drawn by word of companies authorized to employ gangs of non-Bahamians such as the forestry, sugar planting, provision farming, and general laboring operations in Abaco, Grand Bahama, Andros, and south Eleuthera. That several times the number of Haitians strictly authorized or required flocked to the labor camps (augmented in many cases by their families) served the employers' interests, competitively driving down wages while absolving the employers from any responsibility for providing services for the surplus migrants. At the same time, the ostensible legality of the employment (as well the general principle of encouraging industries) meant that the authorities rarely inspected or even visited the camps. In Grand Bahama, to which Haitians had been drawn since the development of Wallace Groves's lumbering operation in the middle 1940s, the Port Authority for long maintained that the Hawksbill Creek Agreement gave it carte blanche to employ Haitian and other migrant laborers without any government regulation whatsoever, and the rejection of this claim by the PLP in 1967 may actually have worsened conditions for the Haitians by making their employment more generally clandestine.[36]

The most scandalous effects of company employment by Haitians, however, occurred in Abaco. Large-scale farming by American operators began in the 1950s and was said to have transformed the Marsh Harbour area by 1957, thanks largely to the seasonal labor of up to a thousand Haitians. These workers were actively recruited in northwestern Haiti, though the operators did not seem to have bothered with work permits, for 90 percent of the Haitians who were reported to make up a third of the five thousand population of the Marsh Harbour district in 1963 were said to be illegal immigrants, living in crowded and unhygienic conditions.[37] The chief American farming operation was phased out in 1968. But by then large numbers of Haitians were available or had migrated specifically to work for the Owens-Illinois forestry operation and its succeeding sugar plantation. At first they shared the work with laborers from the Turks Islands, living alongside them in the camps at Lake City and Campbell Town. But the Haitians gradually squeezed out the Turks Islanders by working for lower wages. When logging moved on to Andros, some Haitians went with that operation. But a larger number stayed, and when the sugar venture petered out, most of the Haitians gravitated back toward Marsh Harbour in quest of casual labor, crowding into the sordid shanty suburbs of Pigeon Peas and the Mud.[38]

At least the Marsh Harbour Haitians had some access to schools, churches, and clinics and were sufficiently visible to concern, if not shame, the Bahamian authorities. Hidden from sight and lacking even minimal facilities were the denizens of the shantytown called simply the Camp some twenty miles to the north, attached like an abscess to the three-thousand-acre Key-Sawyer farm, the chief owner of which, until the late 1980s, was the Abaconian who was the first white member of Parliament for the PLP. Though the farm never employed more than 130 workers, the Camp was home to up to 1,000 Haitians, living in conditions scarcely better than the slums of Port-au-Prince.[39]

Greatly outnumbering the Haitian migrants who worked (more or less licitly) for companies were those employed, and to a certain extent protected, by Bahamian individuals. But the largest number of all were those with even less security: the casually employed, those looking for work, and the dependents of those working. As the Bahamian economy declined yet the number of Haitians seemed to increase in reverse correlation, the latter were the migrants who caused the most public concern. No one denied that Haitians performed an essential economic function in taking jobs that Bahamians no longer wanted. But unemployed Bahamians increasingly claimed that they were squeezed out by unfair competition, and almost no Bahamians accepted the argument of the Haitians' strongest advocates that the immigrants paid more in indirect taxes than they drained from social services. Fewer still, however, made the conclusion that the intractability of the Haitian problem could be attributed not just to the tenacity, ingenuity, and endurance of the Haitians themselves but to the fact that too many Bahamians had a vested interest in exploiting them.

Haitians Within the Workforce and Society at Large

The example of the Mason-Smiths cited at the end of the previous chapter illustrated how extensively Bahamians came to depend on Haitians for performing agricultural and gardening labor, and it suggested how, despite the special relationship that grew up between mutually reliable employers and employees, employers benefited from the ready availability of Haitians (through networks of family, kin, and clannish community), from the relatively casual or impermanent nature of the employment, and from the employers' lack of responsibility for the welfare of employees and their dependents. Most Bahamians of any substance had their "own" Haitians, on whom they were to a degree dependent but who in turn depended on them for protection, in the form of help with the authorities or documentation, as well as for wages. This delicately reciprocal relationship, though virtually institutionalized throughout New Providence and in Freeport-Lucaya, ironically perhaps, was most clearly developed in the formerly all-white communities of the Family Islands. By the 1980s, each of the Abaco cays had its small resident group of Haitian migrants, informally assigned a location for their settlement in the remotest spot; at Man-o-War Cay, adjacent to the garbage dump. The case of Spanish Wells, off northern Eleuthera, traditionally the most exclusive of all Family Island settlements and from the 1960s also the most prosperous, however, calls for closest examination.[40]

With most of the young men off crawfishing or making their fortunes in Nassau rather than engaged in farming, the Sigillians relaxed the tradition that decreed that no blacks be allowed to live among them and all leave for the mainland at nightfall. From the 1960s, Haitians began to perform all the menial tasks and were allowed to encamp among the extensive citrus groves on Russell Island, separated only by a narrow channel from Spanish Wells's main island, St. George's Cay. As the income from crawfishing (and, to a scarcely whispered degree, from drug-running) soared in the 1970s, St. George's Cay built up and grand new houses spilled over on to Russell Island, now connected by a bridge. At the same time, the number of Haitians living on Russell Island multiplied and, under cloak of the changes that saw the first black Bahamians (officials, nurses, teachers, and their families) living in Spanish Wells, they became even more boldly visible in the main settlement. By 1989 a crisis was reached when twenty-five white children were withdrawn by their parents from the public school on the grounds that they were now outnumbered by Haitian pupils, who were said to be uncleanly, carry infectious diseases, and to speak only *kweyole*.

With the connivance of the government, the crisis was resolved in a pragmatic manner that allowed the white Sigillians paternalistically to boast that they alone knew how to deal with inferiors of another race. Between 1989 and 1992, stricter checkups were made of the Haitians living on Russell Island, and those without work permits or specific employment were "persuaded" to leave the island, along with their families. Those allowed to remain were given assistance to build better houses, with electricity, water, and toilet facilities, though they were not given title and were charged rent, making them tied and dependent cottagers. In contrast, more than three hundred of the Haitians expelled, still hoping for casual wage labor, scraped a bare farming subsistence on the nearby mainland and formed the squalid shanty settlements at Blackwood and Gene's Bay. No longer under the protection of white employers, they became the targets of the wrath of the north Eleutheran blacks on whose commonage land they squatted, as well as easy marks for the police and immigration authorities.[41]

The situation in New Providence, where at least half of all Bahamian Haitians lived, was similar to that in Spanish Wells and north Eleuthera, though on a larger scale, closer to public notice, and consequently even more tension-ridden. Nassau Harbor was an obvious hub of the movement of Haitians to, from, and within the Bahamas. The boldest or best-documented of the immigrants still traveled into Nassau on the rude but picturesque Haitian sloops, a dozen or more of which might be seen anchored at any one time, after 1985 at Arawak Cay at the western end of the harbor rather than Potter's Cay in the east. The sloops often arrived in the small hours, before the immigration authorities were on duty. Invariably, though, they were met by Haitian residents, who had been alerted by lookouts at the eastern end of the harbor and by the *télédiol* (augmented by the telephone), arriving at Arawak Cay on foot or in well-worn cars. By the 1980s, Haitians also made up the majority of passengers on the Family Island mail boats, the Nassau base of which was Potter's Cay. Since mail boats were engaged only in internal traffic, their passengers were not subject to close scrutiny by the authorities, though clearly many were illegal immigrants, and some coming into Nassau had been landed directly from Haiti at the island where they had boarded the mail boat.

Most illegal immigrants to New Providence, though, were landed on the almost deserted southern shore, sometimes having to wade a mile or more through the shallows with their belongings on their heads. Even here they were sometimes met and nearly always had a clear notion of their destination within the island. Very much as Bahamian Out Islanders had traditionally come to Nassau, almost all Haitians were coming to join family members or an established group from their home district, though their living conditions were for the most part very much worse, and they were subject to exploitation by fellow immigrants as well as natives.[42]

Completing the urban drift that affected so much of the Caribbean and Latin America, not least Haiti itself, more than half of these displaced peasants wanted to live as close as possible to the available work—within the orbit of Nassau's jitney network—in the sections of Over the Hill Nassau and Fox Hill already largely forsaken by Bahamians in favor of more recent and commodious suburbs. With little hope of purchasing their own property, Haitians were forced to rent from Bahamian landlords and hope to recoup by subletting to as many of their compatriots as could be crammed in. Though most of the houses had electricity, some toilet facilities, and water nearby and were within reach of schools and the hospital, they were badly maintained by indifferent landlords and so densely packed and closely surrounded by unfriendly neighbors that there was little chance for an orderly family life or the development of a Haitian barrio culture, let alone the growing of subsistence crops close by.

The remainder of the New Providence Haitians lived a more reclusive, scattered, and isolated existence in locations up to a dozen miles from downtown Nassau. Plywood and tin shanty villages and yards sprang up in the bush adjacent to almost every modern subdivision or in undeveloped areas close enough to roads where at least some crops could be coaxed from the soil. Few Bahamians except occasional policemen ventured into the sprawling *favelas* by Seabreeze Estates, Cowpens Road, Fire Trail Road, or on the margins of Carmichael Village, but those who did retailed horror stories. Clean water was a rare commodity and sanitation primitive to nonexistent; garbage and human excrement were scattered around the settlements. The shacks that had electricity obtained it by paying a high rate for running a wire from a house connected to the mains or even (it was said) by bribing BEC employees to allow them direct access to the main line by jumper cable. Though they provided no services, the alleged owners of the land exacted rents (passed on to subtenants at exorbitant rates), on the threat of eviction or giving information to the authorities. Some casual subsistence farming was carried on, but it was a discouraging and diminishing pursuit. Though often accused of stealing from other farms, Haitian cultivators had absolutely no protection for their own crops. Cultivation was also impeded by the time taken searching for work and other necessary trips to town and by the travel time—in addition to the long working hours—if and when work was found. As in their homeland, Haitians were prodigious walkers, but those furthest from Nassau inevitably were dependent on unlicensed taxi men (Haitians as well as Bahamians), almost as much of the money earned going for transportation as to purchase food.[43]

Under such daunting urban and semirural conditions it was remarkable, from different viewpoints, both how much of their proud cultural identity the Haitians retained and the degree to which they adapted to their Bahamian environment and host culture. What remained to be seen, however, was whether Bahamian xenophobia, economic circumstances, and purely demographic factors would allow for such a large and distinct segment to be peacefully incorporated into a new national mosaic.

Many Bahamians claimed that they could identify a Haitian simply by physical appearance, an exaggeration based on the facts that many Haitians were of smaller stature, poorly dressed, and, of necessity, pedestrians. A much more marked defining characteristic was linguistic. All those born in Haiti spoke *kweyole* by choice, and some had no more than a pidgin version of English. Though Haitians born in the Bahamas acquired Bahamian English with such facility that they were rarely distinguishable by their accent, they retained *kweyole*, which continued to be spoken in the home and in Haitian contexts. Educated new Bahamians who were perfectly bilingual, such as the lawyer Eliezer Regnier (born in Haiti), claimed that though standard English was the essential medium for integration, *kweyole* was a language of great flexibility and subtlety, even beauty (and certainly superior to standard French), which Bahamians ought to recognize as potentially enriching, rather than as a cultural affront.[44]

Conditions among the uninvited underclass. a Haitian shanty yard in New Providence. Courtesy of *The Tribune*, 1995.

The same might have been said of some, but not all, of the other characteristics that distinguished the Haitian community in the Bahamas. Along with the ineluctable affinities that were respected but fading among Bahamians, to family, kin, and the place where one's forebears as well as oneself were born, the Haitians retained African-based beliefs and customs that Bahamians had come to regard as outlandish, or superstitious, or which they were outgrowing. Afro-Haitian festivals, folklore, music, and the practices and beliefs of vodun survived, though forced largely undercover and even more rapidly undergoing the same erosion process that had affected Bahamian obeah and threatened the authentic remnants of Afro-Bahamian culture. Though family incomes rarely exceeded half the Bahamian average, as *re-su*, the Haitians preserved the *a-su* system of folk savings once the norm among poor Bahamians (as with Trinidadian *su-su*, Jamaican "partner" and Barbadian "meet and turn") that had become largely supplanted by formal banking.[45]

Countering their habits of thrift, Haitians (to the scandal of the churches) were even more fervent gamblers than were Bahamians. This interest had led them virtually to take over the technically illegal but popular "numbers" game with its network of runners and gangster-type bankers, leading to some conflict with the former Bahamian operators and, it was rumored, a bribery-protection racket involving the police. Most notorious of all was the Haitians' continued addiction to their traditional cockfighting. Illicit cockpits were found in all sizable Haitian settlements, where hundreds gathered on weekends and at festivals, thousands of dollars changed hands, and—again it was rumored—the police played their own canny game by alternating the turning of a blind eye for protection payments with unannounced raids and the seizure of stake money, little if any of which was officially accounted for.

Besides such symbiotic transactions—which were most widespread in the trade in official documents—and such crossovers as the flocking of Haitians to Fort Charlotte grounds to support the team in the soccer league that was largely made up of their compatriots, it was the ingenious and resolute efforts that the Haitians made to assimilate to the dominant Bahamian culture that most impressed an outside observer. Most surprising, perhaps, was the very large proportion of Bahamian Haitians—traditionally Roman Catholic with a vodun overlay—who had become ardent adherents of evangelical fundamentalist and pentecostal churches. Eliezer Regnier attributed the phenomenon to four factors: the targeting of the Haitian community by well-funded and energetic evangelists (many of them Americans); the opportunities for participation and leadership; the greater encouragement of spiritualist worship than found in the Bahamian Catholic church; and the well-founded perception that Haitians would be more respected and accepted if they were members of churches that also had a large following among ordinary black Bahamians. There was thus, perhaps, a moral in the Bahamian joke heard in the 1990s that those Haitian pedestrians not carrying a cutlass were to be seen carrying a Bible, the Good Book being a symbol of civility, whereas the cutlass represented a potentially threatening weapon.[46]

Bahamians complained that it was impossible to get service at the Princess Margaret Hospital and other clinics because of the crush of Haitians. Yet even more evident—and more worrisome to some Bahamians—was the extent to which the Haitians seized the chances provided by the Bahamian school system to educate their children. Bahamian parents and teachers reported classes in which half, three-quarters, or even 90 percent of the pupils were Haitians—though they undermined their case by also complaining that it was becoming difficult to tell Haitian and Bahamian children apart. Without anyone admitting it, what probably gave rise to the most concern was the observation that the Haitians were among the most dedicated and successful of the pupils. It was commonly remarked, usually with disdain not approbation, that the chief reason Haitian children did well at school (and were not so truant as Bahamian children) was that their parents, even their *fathers*, escorted them to and from school, usually on foot.[47]

Apart from marriage to Bahamians or having children by them, schooling was the most effective medium of assimilation and virtually the only route to upward mobility for most Bahamian Haitians. Mixed marriages were rare, and the claim that the first purpose of Haitian immigrant women was to entrap a Bahamian man was just another ethnic slur. Without education, almost the only means of getting ahead for Haitians were by taking advantage of their fellows, as tenants in chief, subcontractors, intermediaries, agents, traders, or other types of entrepreneur or by working on the fringes of the law or beyond it, through prostitution, pimping, drug-dealing, theft, or other petty crimes. Yet by the 1980s, many Haitian children had graduated from high school, done well at the College of the Bahamas (one becoming student president), and, like Eliezer Regnier, had graduated from the University of the West Indies and other universities with professional degrees. In key respects indistinguishable from Bahamians and with ever stronger claims on Bahamian citizenship, they also represented a more generalized and potent threat. The more they became established and educated, the more the Haitian Bahamians seemed likely to move out of the ranks of the underclass and, with the energy and enterprise of the formerly dispossessed, challenge the complacent and easygoing ethos of Bahamian society, as well as its structure and balance.

As Dawn Marshall described, the Bahamian government's intermittent and somewhat ambivalent efforts to round up and deport illegal Haitians began as soon as large-scale migration was recognized, peaking first in 1963 with "Operation Clean Up" and again in 1967, in what Haitians even ten years later still referred to as the "Big Trouble." In both years more than twenty-eight hundred Haitians were repatriated. In 1967 the United Nations Refugee Organisation was sufficiently concerned to send a representative on a one-day inquiry. But this official determined that the Haitians were economic, not political, refugees. In 1968, the PLP also held ostensibly friendly, if inconclusive, discussions with the Duvalier government about resolving the problem.[48]

By 1986, however, both the magnitude and the nature of the problem had changed, and it reached a climax in the early 1990s. With the ouster of the Duvaliers in 1986 it was hoped that the tide of Haitian emigration would be reversed, but when the Duvalier regime was succeeded by political anarchy and economic collapse, the opposite occurred. The United States, faced by an internal and international issue more inflammatory than the longer-lived and larger Cuban migration, became more closely embroiled than ever before, while the Bahamas found itself painfully in the middle. Both in the last years of the PLP regime and the first FNM years, forthright immigration ministers were appointed who attempted to crack down on illegal immigrants, but such a hornet's nest was stirred up that the moves proved counterproductive and both ministers had to be transferred.

In 1986 and 1988, when the PLP minister Loftus Roker authorized sweeps to round up Haitians in New Providence, Grand Bahama, and Abaco, there was widespread public support. But there were also complaints about the inefficiency of the process and the costs of housing, feeding, and attempting to repatriate the detainees. These factors became critical, and the criticism more strident, when, after a brief period of optimism following his democratic election, President Aristide was overthrown and exiled, renewing the flow of political refugees and making repatriation almost impossible. More significant, more persons were now speaking out for the Haitians. Backed up by international human rights organizations and encouraged by worldwide press coverage, social workers and clergymen ministering to the Haitians, as well as well-established Haitians themselves, complained of the heavy-handedness of the police, defense forces, and immigration authorities, the detention of persons resident for decades and with valid work and residence papers, the splitting of families, and the housing of children as well as adults in the grossly overcrowded and unsanitary jails.[49]

When the FNM came to power, it pledged to alleviate the Haitian problem with the support of the United States but soon found itself hamstrung and enmired. The U.S. embargo dramatically worsened conditions in Haiti, increasing the numbers desperate to leave, while the naval blockade and surveillance, with Bahamian cooperation, harvested unprecedented numbers of refugees, many of whom landed in the Bahamas. To relieve pressure on the jails, a special detention center was constructed on Carmichael Road, in which those rounded up from settlements in the islands by Minister Arlington Butler's campaign were added to those taken up at sea. Some critics condemned the cost of accommodations and food, said to be superior to those most Haitians enjoyed while at large (part of a bill for interdiction, detention, and repatriation claimed in 1994 to be running at $75 million a year); those sympathetic to the Haitians spoke of the Carmichael Detention Center as like a concentration camp.[50]

Under the pretext of support for Aristide and condemnation of the Americans for dragging their feet over his reinstatement, Haitians in New Providence for the first time came out in public demonstrations, frightening Bahamians by their numbers and their unwonted anger and convincing many that they were in fact expressing a far more general dissatisfaction. This attitude was underlined by the increased boldness of statements made on the Haitians' side in the press and in a public forum held early in 1994, which broke up in disarray. Eliezer Regnier, for example, warned Bahamians that "unlike their parents, the children born to Haitians here will not turn the other cheek, they will fight back." At least two others called for more immediate action: the lawyer Fred Smith (Haitian-born, despite his name), and Mary Reckley, commonly regarded as a "pure" Bahamian, who "came out" at a public meeting with the revelation that she was born to Haitian parents. Reckley (who was thought by many Haitians to have special potency because she was rumored to be the mistress of a former immigration minister) called on all persons like herself to align themselves with the Haitians' cause, while both she and Smith urged the Haitians to stand up, march, and even be prepared to fight for their rights.[51]

To its credit, the local press reported the Haitian news and the public debates with reasonable objectivity, and the *Tribune* even introduced a weekly column of news and comment in *kweyole*, written by an employee of the Haitian consulate.[52]

But all of the local papers also published a great number of letters so consistently anti-Haitian as to indicate a virulent backlash. Some letters verged on the paranoid, lumping all Haitians together and accusing them of importing TB, cholera, malaria, and yellow fever as well as AIDS and VD, of being the main perpetrators of the prostitution, drug-dealing, theft, violent crime, gun-running, and gang warfare afflicting the Bahamas, and raising the specter that soon *kweyole* would have to be the language of instruction in the schools. More literate than most but scarcely more temperate was the broadside, taking up almost a whole page, by a Long Islander named Norris Carroll, published in the "Editor's Mailbag" of the *Nassau Guardian* on May 28, 1994.[53]

Carroll made three or four strong general points before dissolving into rhetoric and contumely. Because the flow of Haitians was practically uncontrolled and unregulated, far more migrants landed in the Bahamas than the country knew about, needed, or could handle, bringing with them diseases, guns, and narcotics that would otherwise be detected. The Haitian question had become a political football, kicked around not just between the American and Bahamian governments but between the two Bahamian political parties. Criticism by political opponents and wavering attitudes toward the United States had hampered the PLP and FNM successively so that neither had achieved success. All Bahamians should therefore unite to determine what aspects of the general Haitian problem most affected their country and solve them together. Above all, what Carroll feared was the threat to, or what he termed the theft or swamping of what he declared to be, without defining it, the distinctive Bahamian culture.

"Haitians with Bahamian citizenship are Bahamians and have all the rights I have," Carroll magnanimously acknowledged, "Haitians with work permits have all the rights such permits allow them; and I have no problem whatsoever with either of these situations." But, he added:

> It is the illegal, sneaky invader that I have every problem with. . . . It is generally accepted that there are at least forty thousand Haitians illegally in this country. . . . I seem to remember reading somewhere recently that the government claims that there are only three thousand, eight hundred work permit holders in the country. That's all of them together: English, Americans, Africans, Lebanese, Jamaicans, Haitians, Greeks. . . . So if less than three thousand Haitians are working, then what are the other thirty seven thousand doing? When Bahamians are sleeping at night, what are thirty seven thousand alien criminals doing under cover of darkness? . . . The Haitian comes silently in the darkness while the government sleeps, and while the Opposition sleeps. And people like that priest [Rev. Remi Sansariq, Roman Catholic missionary] and the Grand Bahama Human Rights Association tell us that we are guilty! Why? Because we have a natural desire to keep our society Bahamian and because we shall not allow it to become Haitianized.

Once President Aristide was reinstalled by the Americans in October 1994—an action strongly supported by the Bahamas government and the majority of Bahamians—and a greatly accelerated process of repatriation began the following year, there were signs of at least a temporary easing of the Haitian problem and a related cooling of the public debate. Even before Aristide's return, with the encouragement of the United States, the Bahamas Defence Force and police stepped up coast guard patrols and carried out roundups on land, housing those captured in an enlarged detention center at Carmichael on New Providence.[54]

Just three months after Aristide had been returned to power, on January 12, 1995, the Bahamas government signed an accord in Port-au-Prince by which the Haitian government agreed to the enforced repatriation of eight hundred illegal Haitian migrants per month over the following year. In return, the Bahamian government agreed "to continue the regularisation of Haitian nationals who have been residing continually in The Bahamas for 10 years or more and can furnish evidence to this effect" and "in accordance with its Constitution to extend the benefit of the protection of its laws and institutions to all children born in the Bahamas of Haitian parents."[55]

As the result of unprecedentedly thorough sweeps of the Haitian shanty yards, Bahamian officials were able to claim the detention and repatriation of fifty-six hundred illegal Haitians, some 75 percent of whom were males, by the end of 1995. Those Haitians detained at Carmichael were escorted under guard back to their homes and into town so they could close bank accounts and sell household goods or arrange for them to be sent back to Haiti before being shipped to Port-au-Prince, at first in the tender MV *Eastore* and then, far more quickly and efficiently, by jet planes chartered from Carnival Airlines. Once landed in the Haitian capital, the deportees (nearly all of them originally from the Region du Nord) were met by the Haitian Red Cross, which arranged buses for onward travel, handed out food and clothing to the needy, and handled the ex gratia payment of $100 donated to each deportee by the Bahamian government under the terms of the 1995 accord.

Besides those forcibly repatriated, Bahamian officials calculated that almost an equal number of illegal migrants either anticipated the roundups or were optimistic about an improvement in Haitian conditions and returned to their homeland on their own, thus more than fulfilling the Bahamian government's target of ninety-six hundred returnees within the year. Though exact figures were difficult to obtain, the worldwide airing of the Haitian question, the involvement of the United Nations and other refugee organizations, and the widespread (though by no means general) sympathy for the Haitians' plight probably made it easier for economic refugees to go on to Canada and other countries, if not to the United States, which took pressure off the Bahamas.[56]

Consequently, by the beginning of 1996, there were reports that there were far fewer Haitian children in the Bahamian schools, that the lines of Haitians at the Princess Margaret Hospital and other clinics were greatly reduced, and that many of the Haitian shanty yards, in the Family Islands as well as New Providence, were deserted. Authorities at Marsh Harbour, Abaco, bulldozed the most notorious of Haitian *favelas*, aptly nicknamed the Mud. The incidence of Haitians begging for work became a rarity, employers of casual labor complained of a shortage of workers and a rise in the wages they had to pay, and large-scale employers even petitioned for the renewal of block contract labor permits. Concurrently, angry letters about illegal Haitian migrants almost disappeared from the newspapers, to be replaced in February 1996 by complaints about the 250 illegal Cubans then held at the detention center, who, some claimed, were receiving more favorable treatment than Haitians because of their color and a greater sensitivity toward them on the part of the U.S. government.[57]

That these changes represented more than a temporary easing of the problem posed to the Bahamas by illegal Haitian migrants, however, depended mainly on a continuing improvement in economic, social, and political conditions in Haiti.

Without such an improvement, the migration would surely be renewed and once more press on the ability of the Bahamas to accommodate it. In 1995 and 1996 Bahamian authorities made real progress in reducing the backlog of Haitian applications for work permits and residency certificates. Yet there remained the more fundamental problem for the Bahamas and Bahamians of what to do with, and how to regard, those of Haitian provenance who were either determined to remain permanently in the Bahamas or who had no option but to do so—above all, those long-term residents and those born in the Bahamas whose status and rights the Bahamas government had promised to regularize and protect in the 1995 accord.

Would, could, or should such Bahamian Haitians (or Haitian Bahamians) be assimilated to become unhyphenated Bahamians? Alternatively, would, could, or should the Bahamian majority be persuaded that those of Haitian birth or stock were sufficiently akin to themselves and had valuable enough qualities to contribute to the country that they would be accepted into a multicultural national mosaic?[58] The most—perhaps the only—positive effect of the long-running debate was that it gave all those born and living in the Bahamas and those with Bahamian affiliations their best opportunity yet to resolve in their minds the question of what it meant to be a Bahamian, rather than a Haitian or anyone else. And it is to this essential question that we must finally turn.

What Makes a Bahamian? Food and Sports

Without proving that a nation is what it eats, the diet and eating habits shared by all Bahamians are certainly distinctive and can be related to sociohistorical factors. One American anthropologist, struck by the central role that food plays in social gatherings, has even categorized the Bahamas as a "food culture."[59] No christening, wedding, or wake, no festival, fete, or fair, is complete or regarded as successful without a conspicuous display and copious consumption of food and drink—imported meats, wines, and exotic delicacies are added to the traditional native fare of ground provisions, plantains, corn grits, peas and rice, fish, lobster, and the emblematic conch in its many culinary manifestations. This is true of all islands, communities, and ethnic subgroups. The common Bahamian habits of sharing food and bingeing on special occasions (and of measuring success by conspicuous food consumption) clearly derive from a harsher past of perennial near famine and occasional windfall plenty. Their survival into the present era of general prosperity and more frequent opportunities for celebration probably betokens a nostalgia for a more communitarian past and a fleeting fear that the good times may not last forever, rather than mere self-indulgence.

As an index of the changed times, the characteristic modern Bahamian, in contrast to most West Indians and especially Haitians, is certainly a larger physical specimen than his or her forebears. He or she is also fitter on the average than the even more overfed inhabitants of the United States. Although a large number of Bahamians suffer obesity and hypertension as the effects of overeating, the essential soundness of the traditional diet—the combination of fish, starches, and fruits—the generally open-air life, and greatly expanded leisure time have produced more than just a generally healthy nation but also a generation of outstanding athletes out of all proportion to the nation's size. Even if TV viewers and

The sloop *Cobra* (or *Unka Boss*) racing at the Out Island Regatta, George Town, Exuma. The boat's huge sail area is counterbalanced by the large crew out on the "pry," all of them hugely enjoying the competition. Photograph by Art Paine, used with permission.

spectators greatly outnumber participants, sports are a modern Bahamian preoccupation, if not obsession. In this the Bahamas is, of course, by no means unique in the modern world. But there is sociohistorical significance in which sports Bahamians prefer and excel in and even more in the Bahamian style of competition.

Most revealing in every respect has been the modern history of the most traditional of Bahamian sports, competitive sailing. It may be argued that sailing skill originated in the race to overhaul a prize or to evade a more powerful enemy, to slip past a blockade or customs men, to be first to a profitable wreck, or first to market. Governor Carmichael Smyth sponsored a regatta for working sailboats as early as 1831. But until modern times, sailing in the Bahamas was essentially a livelihood, and formal racing began as an elite sport, for the benefit of the more leisured locals and visiting yachtsmen. It originated at the snooty Royal Bahamian Sailing Club but in the prosperous 1920s tapped into the native skills and competitiveness of the Conchy Joe sailors who founded and made up the core membership of the rival Nassau Yacht Club. As late as the 1940s competitive sailing was merely the favored leisure activity of a few whites, some of them wealthy expatriates or tourists, but many of them Bahamians of no more than modest means, sailing locally made boats because they were inexpensive, and the most skilled (like Durward Knowles, the son of one of the two chief Nassau pilots) still making a living by the sea.[60]

The surge of prosperity after World War II gave local white yachtsmen more leisure to compete and money to invest in more sophisticated, foreign-built boats. Prized crewmen for millionaire owners of the huge yachts engaged in ocean races, such as between New York and Bermuda, Miami and Nassau, the Bahamians came into their own on the more skittish, shallow-draft two-man Star class boats (said to have been introduced into Nassau in 1941 by Alfred de Marigny). Durward Knowles, now a Nassau pilot himself, won an Olympic medal at Melbourne in 1956, the World Championship of 1960 with Sloane Farrington, and the Olympic Gold Medal at Tokyo in 1964 with Cecil Cooke.[61]

Yet ironically, the growing sophistication and fame of white Bahamian yachtsmen and the wider realization that the Bahamas provided some of the finest leisure sailing and cruising waters in the world were paralleled by the decline of the native sailboat and the numbers of Bahamians actually sailing the seas for a living. In a spirit of nostalgic patronage (that was to be echoed later among the founders of the Bahamas Historical Society and the Bahamas National Trust), a group of wealthy American yachtsmen, inspired by J. Linton Rigg, and Bay Street magnates (led by Bobby Symonette, Speaker of the House and UBP member for Exuma) founded the Out Island Squadron in 1954, with the main purpose of organizing an Out Island Regatta for working sailboats to be held each April at George Town, Exuma.

As admitted in 1994 by its eloquent oral historian, the American-born Howland Bottomley (settled in George Town and associated with every regatta since the first), the Out Island Regatta began as a picturesque spectacle and social occasion for the benefit of its Bay Street and wealthy expatriate sponsors, an exercise in noblesse oblige that was symbolized by the patronage of the British royal consort Prince Philip in 1959. There was much good humor (and the sailor prince was given a ride on one of the winning sloops) but no social mixing on shore between the white patrons and the black competitors. Success was guaranteed by the intrinsic attraction of the sport—with its authentic boats, enthusiastic and athletic crews, and rules that included the hoisting of the sails and raising the anchor as part of the race—and by its skillful promotion by Stafford Sands's Tourist Board.[62]

But what garnered respect and widespread popularity for the Out Island Regatta was the recognition that, irrespective of color, the best of the Bahamian captains—Rolly Gray of Staniel Cay, Exuma, Hezron Moxey of Ragged Island, Alfred Bain of Lisbon Creek, Andros, and several members of the Knowles clan of Deadman's Cay, Long Island—were as skillful sailors as any in the world. This was conclusively proven (at least for Bahamians) in the mid-1970s when the fisherman and mail boat captain Rolly Gray took on five world-class skippers in a six-race series in which boats were chosen by lot and rotated, and beat them all.[63]

By then, as a litmus of political and social changes, the Out Island Regatta had radically changed its style. Recognizing its national importance and political value, the PLP government adopted the regatta soon after coming to power so that by the early 1970s it had been democratized and virtually nationalized. Concurrently, and especially after the cessation of local horse racing, informal betting on sail races became one of the most active forms of Bahamian gambling. Planeloads of black Nassauvians, led by the prime minister and his entourage, came to join in the action, mingling as amicably with the visiting yachtsmen as with the competitors drawn from dozens of different Family Island settlements but inevitably dominating the social scene ashore. The regatta increased in international repute and prestige to draw up to three hundred visiting yachts each year. As much because of the shortage of accommodations ashore as for any other reason, their passengers and crew lived and socialized largely afloat, even, after 1981, holding their own George Town Cruising Regatta in the week before the main event.[64]

Now that so much money was involved and lesser regattas were being held in half a dozen other islands, spread throughout the nonhurricane months, boats were custom-built and captains and crews came close to becoming professional competitors. The native boatbuilding industry was injected with new life, but the increasing stakes meant that boats were progressively more like racing machines. This change can be illustrated by comparing the traditional Bahamian smack boats that competed in 1954—virtually unchanged for two hundred years, with their twenty-eight-foot overall length, ten-foot beam, thirty-two-foot mast and normal crew of three—with the Class A racing sloops of 1994—ostensibly with the same body dimensions and draft but, with no bowsprit, having a far sleeker length-to-beam ratio, a sixty-two-foot mast, huge sail area, and crew of fifteen.

Howland Bottomley (commodore for two decades after Bobby Symonette tactfully resigned) and the other core organizers—native Exumians as well as long-time residents—moved readily with the changing times, while fighting a valiant battle to retain the cherished authenticity of the regatta. As the years went on, their resolute idealism involved not just the maintenance of strict building and sailing regulations and the preservation of the regatta as an amicable meeting point for sailors of any country, island, class, or color but also the defense of the integrity and values of Family Island life against the perils of modernization, materialism, and the metropolitan dominance of Nassau.

In 1994, Howland Bottomley singled out several significant events or trends during his forty years of life in Exuma and involvement in the Out Island Regatta. The first made him, as senior adjudicator, the hero of the episode in which a few die-hards of the old regime made a final desperate attempt to prove that Bahamian whites were inherently superior sailors but merely succeeded in demonstrating the persistence of the tendency to deploy the power of money and to bend the rules to their own advantage. In 1979, a Bay Street liquor merchant commissioned the building, with no expenses spared, of a beautiful Class A sloop called (after the gin he was promoting) the *Tanqueray.* Under the command of the Olympic yachtsman Kenneth Albury, the sloop ran away from the field to win both the Prime Minister's Trophy and the overall championship. The following year, however, the *Tanqueray* was disqualified, not just for the use of untraditional materials and an improperly weighted keel but because it had been largely built in an American yard with the expertise of a famed American sailor-boatbuilder, who, moreover, had had the temerity to sail in the trophy race as an ostensible crewman.[65]

Not that rivalry was not still fierce and sometimes bitter; nor was competitiveness deprecated by the organizers as long as it stayed within the rules. Competition within a community was natural in persons who shared the challenges of a common element. Competition represented the positive side of the Bahamians' traditional dichotomy between independence and dependency. Besides helping to preserve, sharpen, and spread traditional boatbuilding and sailing skills, competition also encouraged pride in the different islands and settlements where the boats were built and the sailors born. Over the first forty years of the Out Island Regatta, prizewinning sloops and dinghies came from no less than forty-five settlements in seventeen different islands, under 168 different captains—many of whom had built their own boats. Reflecting their islands' subtly distinct social histories and different involvement with the sea, black fishermen and provision shippers from Exuma, former sponge fishermen from Andros, and Ragged Islanders brought up on the smuggling trade to Cuba competed from the beginning. From the third year of the regatta they were challenged by the Long Island whites from Deadman's Cay and Mangrove Bush—fiercest of all competitors, in the earliest years keeping very much to themselves and not above making racialist remarks in the heat of contest.[66]

Later, fresh competition came in from the black settlements of Cat Island, Eleuthera, Acklins, and Mayaguana, though this was nothing to the challenge represented by Nassau boats, which began in earnest with the Independence Regatta of 1973, or the first competitive entries from all-white Abaco settlements in 1981, which produced the overall winner in 1983 and 1984, Scott Weatherford's *Abaco Rage*, from Man-o-War Cay. The first entry from Freeport, the Class A sloop *Lucayan Lady*, was a third place prizewinner in the Quincentennial Races of 1992 with Nan Stuart at the helm, the first female skipper to win a prize. By this time, only Spanish Wells and Harbour Island of the traditional maritime centers remained notable standouts from the Out Island Regatta, as much because both were so taken up with commercial activity that they had no time to build sailing boats or to race, as through standoffishness or fear of losing.

The noninvolvement of two of the most independent and independently viable Family Island communities was additionally regretted by Howland Bottomley and his fellow Exumians because of the undoubted ways that the Out Island Regatta promoted the kind of self-reliance that facilitated the shift toward local government, which both the PLP and FNM governments were dickering with in the 1990s. As the third stage of the regatta's history, much more responsibility devolved upon the people of Exuma as a whole. Except for the actual participants, Exumians had hitherto been little more than passive spectators of what they regarded as an annual April shower of pennies from heaven—exhibiting, according to some critics, the negative, dependent side of the Bahamian social psyche. This attitude was reversed largely through the activities of the All Exuma Association, formed by seventeen local patriots immediately after the 1989 regatta. From expecting to be paid wages for what they did, Exumians now volunteered unpaid help and subscribed a substantial share of the escalating costs of running the regatta. The changes were symbolized by the election of one of the All Exuma Association's (AEA) leading members, Danny Strachan, as chairman and commodore of the Regatta Committee in 1993.[67]

The AEA also strongly supported the project of the local Education Resource Centre (an island affiliate of the College of the Bahamas) to help pupils of the Exuma High School build and race a traditional Class C dinghy. Under the direction of the master builder Sherwin Gray of the Ferry, Little Exuma, the seventeen-foot *Scholarship 500* was completed in time for the 1994 regatta, where it came an honorable fourteenth out of twenty-four boats competing. With the high school at Governor's Harbour, Eleuthera, already building a boat to compete in the 1995 regatta, it was hoped to initiate a separate Scholarship Class for Family Island High School pupils in 1996 or 1997.[68]

The activities of the AEA paralleled the first moves to provide a local government structure for Exuma and the other Family Islands. By 1994, local councils had been set up in some islands, including Exuma, but the devolutionary process stopped far short of the level at which local optimists considered would reverse the islands' economic and demographic decline and the gravitation toward New Providence and Grand Bahama. On the plea that there were too few qualified persons and not enough potential electors, councils were appointed rather than democratically elected, and the powers they were given were severely limited. The government's plausible argument for not moving farther and faster hinged on the very unevenness of the islands in development and wealth. The few islands that were most obviously qualified to be self-supporting because they generated more in taxes than they currently received back from government (Grand Bahama, Abaco, Eleuthera, perhaps Exuma) would be reluctant to give up their surplus, so that the government would be deprived of the income it would need to subsidize the majority of islands generating far less than they would need. Proponents of devolution (including most Exumians) claimed that this was no more than a half-truth. Government was slow to devolve, they believed, because too many politicians feared the decentralization of power and the loss of the local patronage that were at the heart of the traditional parliamentary system.[69]

Sloop sailing was officially declared the national sport of the Commonwealth of the Bahamas in 1993, but even more important for the majority of Bahamians were sports in which all Bahamians might potentially compete and which commanded a greater following in the larger world. Here the influence of the United States (and especially American television) was paramount, though emphasis was more on individual performance than team games. Of the many sports originating in Britain, cricket did not gain the hold it achieved in the British West Indies (the former subjects transforming the game and mastering the former masters by the 1950s); nor did soccer become a popular obsession, for players and spectators, as in most Latin American countries. The prolonged physical demands and team conflict of rugby football suited neither the Bahamian character nor climate, though tennis and golf proved much more compatible with both—especially when tourism multiplied the available facilities and brought them within the reach of ordinary Bahamians. Boxing, as a sport that had provided opportunities for disadvantaged blacks in tougher days, despite a few outstanding exceptions, declined with the coming of easier times.

In the late colonial period cricket was revived by the injection of skills and enthusiasm from British West Indian migrants, especially policemen (the majority from Barbados). As an extension of the complex social rivalries between Bahamians and non-Bahamians, extremely keen competition developed in Nassau in the 1960s between teams based on the local parishes and those dominated by expatriates, all but a handful of them blacks. Important league matches drew thousands of spectators to Windsor Park, Haynes Oval, and St. Bernard's Park. After this brief heyday, however, cricket faded, as the number of expatriate recruits diminished, many of the most accomplished Bahamians moved to other sports, and spectators were drawn away by TV. After the mid-1970s Bahamian cricket reverted to little more than a tourist curiosity, kept alive mainly by the same aging expatriates.[70]

Some of the outstanding local cricketers moved on to playing baseball in the United States, most notably Andre Rodgers, who played for several major league sides between 1957 and 1967. Almost as much as American football and basketball, the "national American game" attracted Bahamian aficionados after the advent of

Bahamian athletic stars of the 1980s and 1990s. *Top Left*, Shonel Ferguson, Commonwealth Games gold medalist and record-holding long jumper, 1982. *Top Right*, Bradley Cooper, Commonwealth Games gold medalist and record-holding discus thrower, 1982. *Bottom Left*, Troy Kemp, World Champion high jumper, 1995. *Bottom Right*, Pauline Davis, 1995 World Championship 400 meters silver medalist. Photographs by Derek Smith, courtesy of *Nassau Guardian*.

Bahamian sports stars of the 1980s and 1990s. *Left*, Mychal "Sweet Bells" Thompson, first pick of the NBA college draft in 1978. *Right*, Mark Knowles, world's third-ranked tennis doubles player, 1995. Photographs courtesy of *Nassau Guardian.*

TV, but it provoked nothing like the countrywide absorption found in Puerto Rico or the Dominican Republic, where baseball was almost the only way for poor youngsters to make fame and fortune and the careers of successful aspirants were followed with pride and passion by their countrymen. Much more suited to Bahamians for several reasons was basketball. Bahamians were at least as competitive as other Caribbean and Latin American peoples, and by the mid-twentieth century were, on the average, taller and more athletic. As a sport in which blacks had come to predominate, basketball was especially agreeable to the Bahamian black majority. Professional basketball, moreover, recruited largely through schools, which offered scholarships to talented youngsters, and Bahamians were attracted to a system that would provide a higher education even if it did not lead to sporting stardom.

First promoted in the Bahamas by the American Roman Catholic clergy, basketball took off with incredible rapidity from the 1950s. By the late 1970s the Bahamas was able to field a national team (drawn almost entirely from those studying at schools in the U.S. South) capable of matching or beating all nations in the hemisphere save the United States and Cuba. This promise was not sustained because of the difficulties of gathering such dispersed talents for training together, the internal discords that showed up Bahamians' reluctance both to accept the authority of a single coach and to subordinate the ego to team discipline, and, above all, the counterattractions of professional basketball—which saw two Bahamians star in the Harlem Globetrotters' circus and climaxed in the selection by the Portland Trailblazers of the 6 foot, 10 inch, 230-pound Mychal "Sweet Bells" Thompson as first in the National Basketball Association college draft in 1978.[71]

Bahamians' gift for basketball was related to skills deployed to even more effect in track and field athletics, in the development of which American schools also played a significant role. From the 1950s, a remarkable number of Bahamians reached world-class levels in athletics, though almost exclusively in events involving sprinting and jumping. Explaining this special adeptness has elicited theories more imaginative than the simple combination of physique, climate, and opportunities. Blacks, some have said, ran and jumped to escape slavery; Bahamian blacks were especially successful in doing so; jumping and sprinting skills epitomized the principle of independence in the Bahamian spirit. Even more fancifully, it has been suggested that there may be a counter symbolism in the crawling *under* a bar in the limbo "dance" that was one of the displays which Bahamian (and other West Indian) blacks put on for the amusement of white tourists. Masters of ceremonies—better jokesters than historians—retailed the legend that the limbo was such a popular diversion for the masters in slavery days that the slaves who were able to get down lowest were given special rewards, even their freedom. As we have argued earlier, simulated dependence for the sake of the advantages gained, even to the point of self-abasement, was an antithetical principle in the character of black Bahamians that only national self-confidence could finally expunge.[72]

The first Bahamian athlete to excel in the international arena was the sprinter Tommy Robinson.[73] A scholarship student at the University of Michigan, he was "Big Ten" champion at 100 yards when sent to the 1958 British Empire Games in Cardiff, Wales. Carrying the flag in the opening parade as the sole representative from the Bahamas, he captured the imagination of the British public as much by his cheery and modest demeanor as by taking the silver medal in the 100 yards final and the gold in the 220. Winning many other medals in a ten-year career and competing in four Olympics, Robinson had his finest moment when he led at the 60-meter mark in the final of the 100-meter race in the 1964 Tokyo Olympics—only to pull a hamstring and limp in last. For the ordinary black Bahamian, Tommy Robinson's great achievements were a source of pride, to set alongside the victories of the white yachtsmen. Robinson, though, always suffered from the native self-confidence of his supporters, expressed in the thought, "Well, of course Tommy's one of the best in the world; he's the best we've got."[74]

Deeply and more realistically impressed by Robinson's performances at Cardiff and by what the Bahamian told him of the untapped potential of his compatriots, the English long-jumper and Olympic decathlete Keith Parker took a teaching post at the Government High School in Nassau in 1958, moved on to work for the Education Department and Ministry of Education, and for thirty years was involved in athletics coaching throughout the Bahamas. Besides natural sprinters, he found a generation of young athletes merely lacking the technical expertise and top-flight competition to excel in jumping and throwing events as well. Within a year some of his high school athletes had achieved English national youth standards, and within three years several were challenging his own points total in local decathlons. In 1963, while studying at different universities in the United Kingdom, the future deputy leader of the PLP, Bernard Nottage, and the future director of the Bahamian Archives Gail Saunders, were British Inter-University male and female sprint champions respectively, and other Bahamian students performed well on the track while at the University of the West Indies. From then on, however, the majority of promising Bahamian athletes were on athletic scholarships in the United States. Though informal foot races had long been a local pastime, the explosion of popular interest and the new sophistication of Bahamian athletics were amusingly signified by the elevation of the esoteric triple jump into something of a craze. Enthusiastic performers became a hazard to traffic as they leaped from one backyard to another across main roads.[75]

The Bahamas won its first Olympic medal in 1992 when Frank Rutherford came third in the long jump at Barcelona, and three years later the young nation made a real impact on world athletics when, within ten minutes on August 8, 1995, Troy Kemp won the men's high jump and Pauline Davis came in second in the women's 400 meters in the World Championships at Gothenburg, Sweden. Almost exactly a year later, on the last day of the Atlanta Olympics, Chandra Sturrup, Eldece Clarke, Savatheda Fynes, and Pauline Davis were narrowly beaten by the U.S. quartet to take the silver medal in the final of the women's 4 × 100 meters relay—arguably the finest achievement by such a small nation in the history of the Olympic Games.

Yet the stellar athletic achievements of the 1990s were a natural culmination of highly impressive performances at Caribbean, Pan-American, and Commonwealth Games levels over the previous three decades. Ever individualistic, Bahamians won medals and broke event records with increasing frequency through the 1960s and 1970s, and in 1981 they defeated their longtime Jamaican rivals to win the Carifta Games as a team, with forty-three medals. An early peak of achievement was reached in the Commonwealth Games in Perth, Australia, in November 1982. With resources sufficient to send only seven athletes, the Bahamas team, coached by Keith Parker, won six medals. Shonel Ferguson (long jump) and Bradley Cooper (discus) won gold medals with Commonwealth records, and Stephen Wray equaled the record in coming second (on a count-back) in the high jump. An Australian commentator calculated that on a per capita basis the Bahamas had won 21 track and field medals per million population, with only Bermuda (11.6) otherwise topping 2 per million, and the figures for Jamaica, Australia, Canada, and England being 1.8, 1.5, 0.9 and 0.7 respectively.[76]

In 1994, Keith Parker recounted an incident of even greater national significance that occurred at Perth in 1982. An early winner, Shonel Ferguson was on the rostrum to receive her gold medal when the loudspeakers mistakenly started playing the British national anthem. Ferguson stepped down and the music stopped. She remounted the rostrum and the music restarted, but again it was "God Save the Queen." Once more Ferguson dismounted, making it politely clear that she expected to hear the Bahamian anthem. To their embarrassment, the authorities were unable to find a tape, whereupon the minuscule Bahamian delegation came forward and sang "March on Bahamaland," much to the appreciation of the packed stadium crowd.[77]

Cultural Affairs and Bahamian National Identity

Formal cultural arts—music, dance, festivals, folklore, literature, painting, crafts, architecture—are even more important than cuisine and sports in Bahamian national identity, though they depend much more on a conscious locating in their sociohistorical contexts and on a preservationism that runs the danger both of static conservatism and elitism. To have real meaning—and to remain alive—they must have contemporary and popular relevance as well as authentic and distinctive roots. As in all countries, a genuine cultural identity comprehends (if it cannot meld) both vernacular and elite forms, includes diverse as well as common elements, and concentrates on characteristics that are nationally unique. Being a small and young country set between the millstones of dominant North American and Caribbean cultures, the Bahamas is hard put to claim the distinctiveness of its folklore, crafts, and architecture, to preserve its distinctive styles of music and dance, or to develop a national literature. Only in the lively development of the national Junkanoo festival and, interestingly, in painting has the Bahamas so far attained real distinction, though the achievements in these areas point the way in other fields.

As was perhaps inevitable, until well after political independence the preservation of the Bahamian past was mainly the concern of outsiders fascinated by the islands as a kind of cultural or ecological museum threatened by modernization or of locals concerned to sustain particular myths: imaginary worlds of lost pioneer ruggedness, Loyalist values, or, in counterpoint, racist oppression and an abstract negritude no longer firmly rooted in Africa. The preservation efforts of such non-Bahamians as the folklorists Charles L. Edwards and Elsie Clews Parsons in the 1890s and early 1900s, the anthologist Samuel B. Charters of Folkways Records in the 1950s, the Trinidadian Meta Davis Cumberbatch, who pioneered a National Festival of Arts and Crafts at the Dundas Civic Centre in the early 1960s, or the Creole linguists John Holm and Alison Shilling in the 1970s should not be devalued. The initiatives of those who founded the Bahamas Historical Society and National Trust in the 1950s and, at opposite ends of the cultural spectrum, set up the Wyannie Malone Museum in Hope Town, Abaco, or Jumbey Village in Over the Hill Nassau in the 1970s were likewise valuable. Yet far more important were the indigenization, popularization, and widening conspectus of Bahamian cultural studies that began in the 1970s and accelerated in the 1980s and 1990s. Key factors or indicators in this process were the transformation of the Dundas Civic Centre (originally a school for black domestics) into an unofficial cultural headquarters, the gradual increase of Bahamian cultural content and the use of the Bahamian vernacular (after a prolonged and heated debate) in the programs of ZNS radio and TV, and the promotional activities centered on the Department of Archives and the College of the Bahamas. The symbols of this change, though not its fulfillment, were the activities associated with the Columbus Quincentennial in 1992, the creation of the nucleus of a national museum and art gallery in 1993—housed in the former slave Vendue House on Bay Street and named after Pompey, the quintessentially Bahamian slave rebel—and the prominent participation of the Bahamas in a cultural extravaganza hosted by the Smithsonian Institution in Washington in 1994.[78]

As Winston Saunders, actor, director, and playwright, longtime chairman of the Dundas Centre, and driving force behind both the Quincentennial celebrations and the Pompey Museum, wrote in his 1987 play, *I Nehemiah Remember When,*

> I live long enough, thank God, to see my own in the highest places in the land. I just know erryting goin' to be alright. We move fast in this li'l town. We progress fast. But you know when you old, you does always want it to be the way it was. But can't be. We

still young you know. . . . I was tellin' you 'bout the tings what ma cousin did bring from ma parents dem house. She say museum openin' soon and wan' dem to go in dere. . . . Here of late, every pickney gat culture on dey lips. Gat roots and culture on dey lips. I remember when you didn't hattie talk 'bout no culture in the olden days, 'cause you was who you was, and dat was dat. . . .

And what is Bahamian culture? . . . Peas and Rice . . . Boil fish . . . Conch salad . . . Junkanoo . . . The Vola . . . Fishing techniques . . . The Coral reefs . . . Women with big bongies. Sweethearting too! . . . Serasee . . . Obeah . . . Sunday funeral . . . Big Saturday wedding . . . Black people. Conchy Joe! Half red people too! And straight red people, how you mean!

Everyone is talking and they don't know that they are part of it. Living it. Creating it. Painters are interpreting it. Writers. Dancers. Performers. Directors. Composers. Architects. Conservationists. Anthropologists. Naturalists. It's the age of discovery of what it is to be Bahamian.[79]

The difficulties of recognizing an authentic Bahamian style, let alone preserving and propagating it, are well illustrated in the field of architecture. As in all colonies established where there was no native population, the colonial architecture of the Bahamas was a transplantation (at one colonial remove from the mother country), pragmatically adapted to local conditions and materials. At the poorest level, the houses were mean and impermanent; at the median level, functional wooden replicas of maritime New England style; at the most substantial, more like the planters' houses of the coastal towns of the southern American colonies, built of cut limestone and timber and employing the solidly elegant skills of the shipwright. Commercial buildings were composite extensions of the residential, with the proprietor and his family often living over the shop. The public buildings, including the churches, were modeled on those of the prerevolutionary mainland or followed an all-purpose colonial-Georgian style. In late colonial and postcolonial times the traditional stone and woodworking crafts died out, and different materials—almost never brick but eventually breezeblock, concrete, metal, and plastic—phased out the traditional buildings. The proliferation of building materials and methods and the absence of either an aesthetic consensus or strict planning regulations led to an increasing eclecticism, the invasion of Floridian influences throughout the twentieth century, and, at the upper end of the socioeconomic scale during the boom years, a trend toward tasteless ostentation.

Yet, as has been recognized by amateur and professional plantation archaeologists, the dedicated volunteers of the Preservation of Historic Buildings Committee of the Bahamas National Trust and the Department of Archives, the more sensitive local architects, and perceptive independent recorders such as Robert Douglas, local conditions and materials and the creolization process did create a distinctive Bahamian style, at least for residential and commercial buildings—and with subtle variations between Nassau and the Family Islands.[80] Bahamian traditional houses were strictly functional, with the elegance of simplicity. Usually designed and made by those who lived in them, they conformed to a narrow range of invention, using the bonelike native limestone—either square-cut or as freestone in mortar—and the native hardwoods, silver-weathering pine, and shingles. They were family-oriented units, whether isolated behind high white walls in town, clustered in villages around a harbor, or as isolated fisher-peasant homesteads. Even the "great houses" of planters or merchants were seldom ostentatious, though situated on ridge land and balconied to catch the summer breezes and to look out over fields, town, or sea. Gardens were a rarity, the ultimate sign of luxury, leisure, and privacy in an ecology with much sun, little soil, and an economy demanding unremitting toil.

These features can be treasured and preserved and used to influence the modern: no grandiose or exotic ornament save perhaps on the roof ridgeline; cut stone, wood, and shingle where possible (or at least their simulations); coigns, dormers, shutters, jalousies, verandahs; white and tropical pastel colors. This style can be adapted to modern materials and needs but departs from the Floridian by eschewing the Hispanic and falls somewhere between the stone-built pink and white preciosity of Bermuda and the gingerbread woodwork and filigrees of the true Caribbean.

Hotels and office buildings, though, are more problematic. Paid for by foreign capital and designed by foreign architects, they continue to be influenced by international concepts of what attracts and impresses modern tourists and businessmen: a sharp-edged display of concrete, steel, and glass that (to adapt Philip Larkin) "shows nothing, and is nowhere." The hotel and casino complexes on Paradise Island, Cable Beach, and at Freeport-Lucaya have no authentic Bahamian features and are virtually interchangeable with those in Florida, Hawaii, or Mexico, save for the merciful ban on neon and large billboard advertisements. The most incongruous and tasteless example of this rootless internationalism is the architectural gallimaufry of the International Shopping Bazaar in Freeport. Similarly, central Bay Street in Nassau, though busier than ever when the cruise ships are in, has lost its special waterfront character (and is tawdry rather than raffishly picturesque) with the building of parallel docks to accommodate up to eight liners at a time, the transfer of the old produce and fish markets, and banning of working sailboats. Only restrictions on height and scale and the preservation of most (but not all) of the finest of the older buildings prevent the new business heart of Nassau from swamping the traditional landmarks and reshaping the city in an entirely international image.[81]

With the crucial exception of Junkanoo (which must be considered separately), similar problems apply to the recognition, preservation, and encouragement of authentic Bahamian modes of music and dance in the face of almost overwhelming extraneous influences. As the folklorists discovered, there were strong traditions of folk music rooted in Africa and the churches that remained lively in proportion to the ethnic distance from Nassau. "Darkest Andros" remained the last bastion of extempore, contrapuntally harmonized "antems," narrative ballads, and "launching songs." Early tourism, when the Over the Hill or after-dark Bay Street nightclub rather than the hotel was the focus of tourist entertainment, moreover, gave a great impulse to Bahamian goombay, which stemmed from the same tradition. This irresistibly danceable rhythm to mildly satirical or salacious lyrics probably originated among strolling barefoot players such as Philip Brice of Fox Hill and the ukulele-playing Shorty the Serenader in the 1920s. Curiously, it was taken up (and given some respectability) by a talented member of the white elite, Charles Lofthouse, who wrote the popular "Bahama Mama" and "Goombay Pappa, Beat the Drum Again" in the 1930s. Goombay reached its peak between the 1940s and 1960s through the creative genius of such self-taught black entertainers as the banjoist

Alphonso "Blind Blake" Higgs, the pianist George Symonette, and the guitar-playing "Songbird" Eloise Lewis.[82]

The increasing number of Bahamians receiving musical training, however, were either coached in European styles by expatriate bandmasters and piano teachers (notable among them the wife of a Trinidadian doctor, Meta Cumberbatch, whose graduates performed classical music in black tie and tails on a grand piano) or came under mainland jazz and dance-band influences through spending formative years in the United States. At the popular level, prosperity brought a surfeit of music from Trinidad, Jamaica, and the United States through the radio, TV, and the successive revolutions in recording, at the same time that more Bahamians shared the entertainment provided in hotels and discos. Traditional goombay was first overlaid then swamped by calypso and steelband music, reggae, Rasta music, rhythm and blues, rock, and rap. By November 1994, "A Strong Supporter of the Bahamian Culture" could write to the editor of the *Nassau Guardian:*

> I am very closely involved with the music industry in our country and every day it depresses me more and more when I see and hear a total lack of respect and awareness for our own Bahamian sound. . . . Since the change of government, we have seen the addition of two radio stations on the FM dial. . . . [But] when 100 JAMZ came on the air, it was quite apparent what their format was. Their style was . . . designed to be predominantly foreign with a few local songs stuck in at their own convenience. . . . 100 JAMZ has even employed American DJs and their programme director is also an American. . . . The younger Bahamian DJs on this station all have an identity problem. I am almost certain they would all prefer to be Jamaicans or to live in Jamaica. If you listen to their programme called "The Thunderstorm" you would have to wonder which country you are in. . . . We cry every day about our young people forgetting their past and not knowing their culture, yet we sit down and let the most powerful medium we have to reach them do foolishness and say nothing about it.[83]

Anyone observing young Bahamians at discos and Bahamians of all ages at parties is in no doubt that Bahamians are accomplished and distinctive as well as avid dancers. But Bahamian dance as much as music in general has suffered from the confusion between high and low culture and the overwhelming influence of foreign styles. The development of dance has generally lagged behind the other performing art forms in the Bahamas. A local ballet group (the Civic Ballet) pioneered in the 1960s by dancer Hubert Farrington, brother of a white Olympic gold medal yachtsman, never developed into a national company. It fell uncomfortably into a no-man's-land between classical European and American Negro ballet techniques and did not appeal to the majority of Bahamians, who were descended from Africa. Farrington, however, encouraged Alex and Violet Zabine, dancers from Mexico, who established the New Breed Dancers, which were the inspiration for a National Dance School, established in 1976 under the Ministry of Education and Culture's Cultural Affairs Unit headed by Clement Bethel. It was not until 1992, during the preparations for the Columbian Quincentennial, that consultant Winston Saunders spearheaded the establishment of the National Dance Company, headed by Robert Bain and Shirley Hall Bass, but it had far to go before it could emulate the exuberant professionalism, prestige, and popular appeal of the Cuban Ballet Folklorico or the Jamaican and Barbadian National Dance Companies.[84]

As was demonstrated by the first anthology of Bahamian writing, produced by the College of the Bahamas in 1983, the first decade of independence had brought forward many earnest strivers but no creative geniuses, save, perhaps, in the fields of vernacular storytelling and drama.[85] This was entirely predictable, for the Bahamas had always possessed rich oral resources, but it had not had the widespread literacy of larger, richer, and older countries, nor had it enjoyed the cultural cross-fertilization that had spawned a galaxy of literary stars across the Caribbean and even brought a Nobel Prize for Literature (along with another for Economics) to St. Lucia, a country with half the population of the Bahamas. Yet, though by the 1990s the Bahamas had produced not one novelist or poet of international stature and no storytellers or playwrights of more than local fame, an examination of its aspiring writers (locally or privately printed, if published at all) nevertheless tells us much about the nature and range of Bahamian culture and brings us closer to an understanding of Bahamian identity.

Bahamians are great talkers and good listeners, particularly when the medium is Bahamian dialect. Mizpah Tertullian, citing the authority of the Guyanese populist writer Jan Carew, expressed the liberating value of the vernacular in the 1983 College of the Bahamas anthology: "For a long time I keep twisting and turning and couldn write a word down. Then all of a sudden, bam!—I bust right out. Carew say ya must express yourself in words how ya think first. For heavens sake don't be afraid to espress tings in yer own language, ya could always translate it into formal English later on. But ter tell you de truth I don't feel like translating it today. Ye think ya could forgive me this once? Brethers and sisters lemme use mer language this once, it does feel good ya know."[86]

Such an impulse produced the brilliant series of newspaper stories by Eugene Dupuch called "Smokey Joe Says" as early as 1936 and the crescendo of "Ol' Story" telling from the 1960s by Cleveland Eneas, Mizpah Tertullian, Mabel Williams (San Salvador), Kayla Lockhart Edwards, Robert Missick, Derek Burrows, Greg Lampkin, Patricia Glinton-Meicholas, and others in newspapers and on radio and tapes. It led to the folklore shows organized by Clement Bethel in the 1970s and the successful "Kanoo" produced by Kayla Lockhart Edwards at the Culture Club she organized in the 1990s. In drama, it similarly inspired and explained the popularity of the long-running soap opera "The Fergusons of Farm Road" by Jeanne Thompson put out by Radio ZNS in the 1960s and a burgeoning wealth of plays, both comic and serious, by Susan Wallace, Jeanne Thompson, James Catalyn, Telcine Turner, Sam Bootle, Percy Miller, Winston Saunders, Ian Strachan, and Nicolette Bethel, produced by the Bahama Drama Circle, the University Players, and in the repertory season at the renamed Dundas Centre of the Performing Arts from the 1970s onward.

During the same period, the connection between Bahamian musicality, the impulse toward dramatic storytelling, and the growth of national self-expression were borne out by the way that the Nassau Operatic Society, founded by Lady Arthur, the governor's wife, in 1959, and originally dominated by expatriates, was steadily Bahamianized and popularized. Key events in this process were the production of the folk opera *Sammy Swain*, written and produced by Clement Bethel (1975), and of the nationalist opera epic *Our Boys* by Winston Saunders, Philip Burrows, and Cleophas Adderley (1987), inspired by the *Flamingo* incident of 1980. Even more popular and successful, though, was the marriage of storytelling, dance, and song in the vernacular musical comedy *Dis We Tings*, conceived by Kayla Lockhart Edwards and originally scripted by Nicolette Bethel (1990).

Whether simply retelling familiar fables, poking affectionate or satirical fun, or (as was increasingly the case) making strong comments about the problems and flaws in Bahamian society, Bahamian storytellers and dramatists appealed to the Bahamian national community (the implied family of Tertullian's "brethers and sisters"), using its common and everyday language in familiar contexts and situations. As the Bahamian-born literary critic Anthony Dahl has commented, this holds true even of the work of Winston Saunders, the most sophisticated and widely performed of Bahamian playwrights, whose most ambitious and impressive 1985 play *You Can Lead a Horse to Water* (which played for six weeks at the Julian Theater in San Francisco) recasts the Oedipus legend in a Bahamian mold, with the hero reacting against a typically absent and unsatisfactory father not by ultimately supplanting him as the husband of the dominant mother but by strangling her to death.[87]

Generalizing in 1995 from the rich resources of vernacular storytelling and plays, as well as from the best of modern Bahamian poetry and from the mere five novels he rated worthy of consideration (including one of his own), Anthony Dahl stressed the centrality of the family and its problems in Bahamian literary discourse. Feelings of alienation or exile and a nostalgia for a Promised Land of an imagined past and hoped-for future are other themes which Dahl identified in modern Bahamian literature. Yet even these relate to an idealized vision of traditional family values and to the alienation that comes from bastardy, miscegenation, and the absent father as much as to the continuing need to migrate for an education and economic opportunities and the tendency to look for cultural models everywhere but in the islands. More positively, however, Dahl recognized in Bahamian literature and its authors the emergence of a new generation of self-confident women, a sense of national purpose and pride that transcended the traditional divisions and alienations produced by class and color, and a growing sophistication that allowed Bahamian writers to select their archetypes and models from the artistic world at large.[88]

Certainly, the expanding nucleus of Bahamian writers is notable alike for the inclusion of representatives from all sectors of the Bahamian population, their shared commitment, and the way that most of them combine an aspiration to literature with other forms of artistic expression. Of the thirty-one writers included in the 1983 College of the Bahamas anthology, more than half were born in Nassau (thirteen were educated at Government High School), but there were four from Long Island and single representatives from Abaco, Grand Bahama, Bimini, Eleuthera, Exuma, Ragged Island, and the Turks and Caicos Islands. The majority were blacks or browns (some expressing a somewhat conventional negritude), but seven were whites and five "Long Island whites." Half of the committee responsible for producing the volume, its introductory commentator, and more than a third of its contributors were women—evidence of the strong and growing commitment of Bahamian women to literary expression as part of their social advance in general. Most of the 1983 contributors were middle-class professionals, whose higher qualifications were almost evenly derived from the United States, UK, UWI, and Canada. Yet a surprising number were not only involved in different forms of writing but also in acting, play and film production, singing, instrumental music and painting. The black architect Patrick Rahming, for example, was described (or described himself) as "born in Nassau in 1944. He attended Government High School and later McGill University. He is a versatile artist who, as a singer, has produced albums and won an award. As an actor he is a member of the Bahama Drama Circle and has performed in several productions. He is a keen sportsman. His artistic work springs from his 'concern for the disintegration of the human community, the lack of continuity in Bahamian traditions, and political frustration.' He has been inspired by Dylan, Sparrow, Adamson, Leroi Jones, Jenks and Melvin Rahming and has published an anthology, *Reflections*."[89]

Equally versatile (and eclectically inspired) members of the artistic vanguard were Susan Wallace (born in 1931), who was described as "the proprietor of a native craft shop, a dress designer, the musical director of a choir and a writer of poems, short stories and plays," and Eddie Minnis (born in 1947), who was even better known as an artist, political cartoonist, songwriter, singer, and instrumentalist than as the poet represented in the 1983 anthology.

As the Jamaican cultural guru Rex Nettleford tactfully suggested in his Foreword to the 1983 anthology, most Bahamian poems were beginners' efforts from an unfinished nation. The impulse to expression was strong, and in a newly prosperous economy the bookstores displayed many vanity publications, doggerel effusions of trite description, and commonplace sentiments. Yet even at their most banal, the descriptions expressed an affinitive love for the Bahamian environment, the sentiments a worthy affection for the best of Bahamian traditions, a condemnation of past oppressions, and a rhetorical optimism about the Promised Land of the Bahamian future. As Nicolette Bethel, one of the most talented and self-conscious of the new wave of writers, has observed, there is a recognizable divide between poetry (as well as drama) that stems from the oral and vernacular tradition and that (perhaps less promising, if not unauthentic) which aspires to a more literary, and formally literate, form.[90] Yet in the better poems of either mode, descriptive images, history, social comment, and national consciousness meld imaginatively into each other to provide a distinctively Bahamian statement, however lacking in technical expertise. Patrick Rahming, for example, wrote in *Still and Maybe More: A Trilogy*,

> The image
> of Bain Town/Grassroots
> which sat boisterously
> drinking
> in a hundred bars named Briteley's
> or eating boiled grouper
> served by
> (perhaps) the last, fierce
> big-bubbied Nango woman
> has climbed the hill
> and descended
> and seeped under the door
> like the smell of boiling guava
> into the Houses of Parliament
> where boiled crab and dough
> is now served under glass.[91]

Rather more appositely, and in a more consciously literary style, Robert Elliot Johnson in "Back to the Root" echoed Winston Saunders's Nehemiah:

Confounded with new business;
This all my energy;
Dollars and cents, the office rent
And money for payroll bothers me.
I try for the root, the dark shoot
Snaking down to the foot of my brain
Where all I want to do remains.

It is simple to say that I am trapped,
A dancing racoon snagged by the feet,
By Commerce in an iron clamp;
It is easy to hope—no, to know—that someday
Comes the scamper of running free . . .
Free to get to the root of things,
To get to the root of me.

The surge of young poets, they say,
The flowering of art, the birth of creation;
Our minds are now blossoming, spring is the thing
As witness the birth of the nation.
The racoon in me claws at the root of things
To get at the root of me.

Stark is the picture we must outline,
Bare as the shell on the sand,
White as bleached coral, coconut hard,
Black as the back of my hand.
We must get down to the root of things,
To the root of the breadfruit tree:
Writers must get down to the root of things
To define nationality.[92]

Expressing the Bahamian Soul: Painting and Junkanoo

If the independence generation of Bahamian artists seem almost Renaissance men and women in their creative versatility and enthusiasm, the truly nascent Bahamian art is painting. Without obvious antecedents, accomplished painters suddenly emerged in the 1960s and multiplied so rapidly that by the 1990s scarcely a month went by, it seemed, without a new show displaying yet another remarkable talent. The explosion was a direct function of the booming Bahamian economy: early Bay Street patronage (notably, to his redemptive credit, by Sir Harold Christie), the sudden expansion of technical education, the presence of expatriate painter-teachers, and, above all, the novel existence of a competitive bourgeois market, which priced new canvases by popular artists high enough to enable them to live by their work. Yet it was also a product of spontaneous combustion, the sudden excited discovery of a vivid new medium of expression, of latent talents, and of the way one talent could play off, refine, and excel another.[93]

The Bahamian painting nascence was truly nationalist in that its practitioners were drawn from all sectors of the people and yet, without stylistic homogeneity, shared (even more than in Bahamian literature) common themes and inspiration. The first survey of Bahamian painting, published under the patronage of the Finance Corporation of the Bahamas in 1992, depicted more than thirty highly talented artists. Selection is invidious, but five painters stand out as representing both the range and the essence of what might (with some exaggeration) be termed the Bahamian School: the instinctive black former house painter Amos Ferguson (born in 1920), the reclusive black United States resident (and only part-time painter) Maxwell Taylor, the white Abaconian Alton Lowe and Nassauvian Brent Malone (these three born in the early 1940s), and, perhaps the precursor of an even finer second generation, the black middle-class Nassauvian Antonius Roberts (born in 1958).[94]

The work of Amos Ferguson, fittingly gathered as a permanent exhibition on the upper story of the new Pompey Museum in 1993, wonderfully illustrates the latency of painterly genius among the ordinary people. Begun as a hobby in spare time from house and sign painting, Ferguson's painting became full-time only in retirement, and he continued to use ordinary house paint and brushes on plywood and cardboard even after his fame spread and his work commanded high prices. Though he worked with awesome rapidity when the mood took him, he was probably too old and wise to be corrupted by success. Like the naive painters of Haiti (before their work became a tourist commodity and cliché-ridden) Ferguson painted what he knew and what inspired him: themes from folk life and the Bible, the intertwining of the mundane and the spiritual life. Many of his paintings display Old and New Testament characters and incidents translated into familiar Bahamian figures and locations ("Somebody is nocking at your hart door it nok like Jesus"); others show remembered folk dances and folk tales ("Mamaid halfish and half people live in jumphole . . . come out to catch the sunshine"), or the Cowhead and Pitchy-Patchy Junkanoos of his youth. Though they can be described as two-dimensional, crudely drawn, and repetitive, Ferguson's paintings are magical, combining invention with formal simplicity in a way that is as unexpected and thrilling as his colors are brilliant.[95]

Far more somber but equally pure is the vision of Maxwell Taylor. Discovered as a schoolboy and apprenticed alongside Brent Malone, Eddie Minnis, and Kendal Hanna in the branch of the Chelsea Pottery brought to Nassau by Harold Christie in 1957, Taylor even sooner than his peers outsoared the work of his English mentors, David Rawnsley, Joyce Morgan, and Eve Gossett. He was strongly influenced by black power artists when he migrated to New York for further training. Taylor's uncompromising commitment to social realism and portrayal of ordinary, poor, and oppressed Bahamians, in woodcuts, etchings, and stark canvases, though always admired by fellow artists, were ahead of his time. For years he shared the struggle to make a living with the subjects of his work, combining art with labor on construction sites. This heroic formative period bore fruit in Taylor's contributions to the exhibition "Bahamian Art Today" at Brent Malone's Matinee Gallery in 1977 and to a triumphant one-man show after his temporary return to Nassau in 1979. For many, Taylor was the undoubted star of the exhibition "Ten Artists" held in July 1983 to celebrate the tenth anniversary of Bahamian independence.[96]

At first glance, the polar opposite to the work of Maxwell Taylor is that of Alton Lowe of Green Turtle Cay, Abaco. Lowe was largely self-taught and stayed deeply and affectionately rooted in his white Abaconian milieu, having created a museum and Loyalist Sculpture Garden in his native township to celebrate the Loyalist legacy as well as to display his own paintings. His descriptively realist canvases show the seas, skies, marine activities, and, above all, the people of his native cays, the Conchy Joe mariners, their women, and children. In their way as naive as those of Amos Ferguson, many of Lowe's paintings superficially seem to have no more than a charming, chocolate-box verisimilitude. Yet a closer and longer look—at the patient ancient mariner, hand on tiller, quizzically gazing over the emerald shallow to the dark blue deep; the blond, blue-eyed young women forever scanning the horizon for a returning sail—conveys a more profound and complex mix of endurance, isolation, and poignant longing. Though blacks are as rare in Alton Lowe's work as whites are in Maxwell Taylor's, the two artists exhibit more than a complementarity: a shared sensibility to a common humanity within the contexts of a shared and common but unique history and environment.

The common elements, the Bahamianism, are far more apparent in the work of the other major artist of Conchy Joe provenance, Brent Malone. If in Lowe's work there remains a deep and almost tragic nostalgia and in Taylor's an angry rejection of poverty and oppression, that of Malone is far more optimistic and progressive. A Nassauvian whose art training was completed in England, Malone is academically more polished than Lowe (his technical skill equaled only, perhaps, by his fellow white Nassauvian Rolfe Harris and by the two brilliant daughters of Eddie Minnis) and his range far wider. Like Lowe, Malone has an admirable commitment to Bahamian history and to preservation, and he retains the Conchy Joe spirit of enterprise by being as much an art entrepreneur as a generous associate and encourager of other artists. From 1972 he lived and worked in the magnificent gingerbread mansion owned by Lady Symonette on East Bay Street called the Temple, with his studio and quarters upstairs and a gallery downstairs. There in 1982 the show "In Praise of Nature" (opened by Lady Pindling) saw seventeen artists present fifty-seven pieces in support of the Bahamas National Trust. In 1987 Malone became a shop owner near Bay Street when he took over Marlborough Antiques, the principal retailer of historic Bahamiana, adding to it an elegant modern gallery. But in 1991, at the climacteric age of fifty, he also joined with the five black artists Maxwell Taylor, the brothers Jackson and Stanley Burnside, and the younger Antonius Roberts and John Beadle to form the group called B-CAUSE (Bahamian Creative Artists Unified for Serious Expression), dedicated to the promotion of a national school of art and the creation of a Bahamian National Gallery.

Malone's brilliantly colorful work proudly, almost arrogantly, celebrates the Bahamas, its people, and their culture in a range of styles, conveying a precise realism, formal symbolism, and riotous patterning. He finds inspiration in the Bahamian ecology, its flora, fauna, seashells, and seascape, informing them with a symbolism that derives from European classicism and African legend as well as Bahamian folklore. Yet in depicting the sea and its ways he deploys a realism even more meticulous than that of Alton Lowe: the accurate minutiae of sailing ships and the precise physiognomies of the men who work them, blacks far more often than whites. Malone's fascination with, and sensitivity toward, Bahamian blacks, indeed, extends into a profound interaction with their Afro-Bahamian culture, notably in his near obsession with the Bahamian Junkanoo. Malone's identification with the Junkanoo—most memorably stated in his 1979 exhibition of fifty pieces dedicated to the festival—transcends mere reportage to signify a belief that if a minority culture (such as that of the Conchy Joes) is to contribute to that of the nation, it must participate, at the risk of becoming almost subsumed.[97]

The mark of Brent Malone's significance is that his work was almost as highly respected by his most important successor, Antonius Roberts, as that of Amos Ferguson and Maxwell Taylor—and emphatically much more than the work of Alton Lowe. Trained in Miami and Philadelphia and initially making his living as a teacher and gallery curator rather than by his painting alone, Roberts held his first major one-man show at Malone's Marlborough Gallery in October 1994. Its success seems to have saved him from the familiar artist's dilemma of choosing between what he wished to paint and what the public would pay for. Roberts somewhat disparagingly entitled his exhibition "Splash, Scrape and Scrabble," but with sales approaching $200,000 he could also feel that his decision to eschew descriptive realism for a free-flowing nonfigurative style was a gamble that had paid off. Asked who and what had most influenced him, Roberts (speaking to a non-Bahamian) emphasized three: Gauguin, Matisse, and the Bahamian Junkanoo. The first two, however, represented as much a principle as stylistic models that brilliant Europeans carried back from the "primitive" Pacific and Africa to aid in the reinterpretation of their own environment. The native environment and culture remained crucial, and these for Bahamians were enshrined in the sea, sun, and sky and in the color, movement, music, rhythm, iconography, and magic of Junkanoo. Though he was closely involved as a designer with a specific Junkanoo group significantly called Roots, Antonius Roberts (like his fellow artists in B-CAUSE) ardently attributed much more to the Junkanoo festival than a celebration of African origins; it was, he claimed, the essential soul of the Bahamian people, signifying light, color, the mixing and melding of colors, freedom, celebration itself.[98]

Despite their creative individualism, the work of Ferguson, Taylor, Lowe, Malone, and Roberts—and that of other important Bahamian artists—is linked by a celebration of Bahamian light and color; the invocation of the surrounding element of the sea and the people's responses to it; the common identity of the people themselves; their shared legacies, from Europe and elsewhere as well as Africa; and above all, the symbolic importance to them all of the syncretic, if predominantly African, Junkanoo festival, with its bloodbeat rhythm of the goombay drums. As Robert Elliot Johnson spoke for the ordinary, common Bahamian,

> There is sun in my skin;
> I do not have the graces
> Of the rich and cultivated.
> Cutlery confuses me
> And when I go to banquets
> The food don't agree with me.
> But in my brash vibrating arm
> The cowbell dances;
> And when sun meets brother in my skin
> Its fire enhances what I am:
> Bahamian.[99]

Like all such syncretic phenomena, the Bahamian Junkanoo owes its survival and vitality to its popular relevance, a combination of authentic roots and dynamic

Bloodbeat rhythm of cowbell and goombay drum. A modern Junkanoo group before New Year's dawn on Bay Street. By the 1970s, masks were becoming rare and more women were taking part. Courtesy of Bahamas Archives.

adaptability. That it became and remains the essential expression of Bahamian identity owes as much to its shaping in Bahamian social history—from slavery and its aftermath of poverty, race, and class distinctions, to great if uneven prosperity, majority rule, political independence, and national integration—as to its deep roots in Africa and Europe alike and its irresistibly somatic music of goombay drums, conch shell, cowbell, whistle, and bugle.

As has been shown by Judith Bettelheim and other folk festival specialists, Bahamian Junkanoo shared its origins and much of its early character with similar festivals throughout the former British slave colonies acquired before 1763, that is, those that were not formerly French or Spanish (whose official religion was Roman Catholic) and therefore developed the very distinct alternative tradition of Carnival.[100] From common African roots came the goombay drums and rhythm, the masks, horns, staves, and stilts, and the central figure of Pitchy-Patchy, alias John Canoe; from England (or Europe in general) the mumming tradition of masked playacting and caroling for handouts (notably influencing the "Old Bunce" variant of Junkanoo found on Green Turtle Cay, Abaco); and from the slave plantation culture, the seasonal largesse, permitted license, and satiric role reversals of the turn-of-the-year holiday.

Yet the unique features of the Bahamas and its social history, described earlier in this work, led Bahamian Junkanoo to diverge from Jamaican Jonkonnu and differ ever more from Belizean John Canoe, the John Cooners of North Carolina (defunct by 1900), or the Gombeys of Bermuda. The most important of these formative features were five in number: the absence of a prolonged and intensive plantation economy and the consequent opportunities for the black majority to sustain and develop their own traditions; the increasing concentration of the population on the metropolitan island of New Providence, which alone had the resources to develop a full-fledged festival; the spatial separation of commercial, bourgeois, white elite, and brown middle-class downtown Nassau (where Junkanoo was performed) from the predominantly poor and black Over the Hill suburbs (where Junkanoo was prepared and rehearsed); the early formalization of the parades as a legitimized, if tightly controlled, spectacle-confrontation; and finally, the revivifying influence of the intermittent immigration from 1811 to 1860—a quarter-century before until a quarter-century after slavery ended—of thousands of liberated Africans, the last of whom did not die until well into the twentieth century.

As was shown in Chapter 4, Junkanoo by the early twentieth century was a carefully regulated annual descent on Bay Street by the people of Over the Hill, a distinctly Bahamian episode of social, political, and cultural theater rather than mere folklore survival. Deprecated by the churchmen and authorities as primitive and potentially riotous, it was regarded by its massed performers as a proud assertion of cultural skills with a hint of latent power and by the white elite and visitors as a picturesque spectacle on the titillating edge of menace, magic, and mass hysteria. These contrapuntal elements guaranteed Junkanoo's continued vitality, but it was both recharged and changed by the years of prosperity, social reshuffling, and political advance.

In the late 1940s the Tourist Board adopted Junkanoo as a tourist attraction, and sponsorship money also flowed into the festival from tourist-oriented Bay Street businesses. The regulations were relaxed to allow for two Junkanoos, on Boxing Day morning (December 26) as well as the morning of January 1, though other regulations still specified the precise route that the bands could take, and a formal committee of sponsors and band leaders laid down standards of presentation. These decreed, for example, that to qualify for prizes masqueraders should indeed be masked (a rule soon largely ignored) and their costumes temporary, that is, made of papier-maché and crepe paper. Competition for sponsorship and prize money (substituted for door-to-door solicitation or, indeed, any solicitation from spectators) reduced the number of groups while increasing their size and sophistication—a trend that strengthened the identification of the chief bands with specific areas of Over the Hill Nassau. Spontaneous participation was limited in the 1960s by controls placed on "rushing" by the crowd, though a degree of spontaneity was sustained, if with some difficulty, by the continued appearance of informal "scrap gangs," which trod the difficult line between the support of the purists and the populace on the one hand and official regulations and the sheer difficulties and expense of obtaining authentic materials on the other.[101]

Commercialism and competition also contributed to other controversial developments. Bands became ever more thematic, and the range of themes stretched beyond the traditional in the search for originality. At its best this effort summoned up from history authentic Bahamian archetypes, myths, and legends or lent the dynamic of contemporary relevance to the festival; but the search for novelty also ran the risk of banality and irrelevance.[102] Bands, as in the Trinidadian Carnival, increasingly focused around a person carrying a giant representation of the chosen theme, obscuring the original personae of John Canoe–Pitchy Patchy and his traditional attendants. This trend perhaps inevitably led to the evolution of the band leader/designer/choreographer as a crucial figure, diluting the original anonymity and mystery while at the same time raising artistic creativity above traditional authenticity. The gravitation toward the model of Trinidadian Carnival was even more directly signified by the infiltration of calypso music and rhythms in the 1980s, though this was stoutly resisted by purist judges in favor of the essential Bahamian combination of goombay drums (tom-tom, tenor, mid-range, second, and bass), conch shells, cowbells, whistles, and minimal brass.[103]

The most important change in Bahamian Junkanoo after the mid-twentieth century, however, was its adoption by the government once majority rule was achieved and acceptance by the people as the quintessential expression of the new nationalistic ethos. Though transcending mere party politics, it was an occasion when political leaders, following the example of the PLP's helmsman, Lynden Pindling, made a point of "rushing" with the people whenever this was permitted. Political points were also being made with the Junkanoo motifs of the rather short-lived Jumbey Village built under PLP auspices deep in southern Nassau in the 1980s and by the FNM government's official support for the long-promoted Junkanoo Expo, set up in 1993 on Prince George's Wharf, where the tourist liners dock. Junkanoo's main focus continued to be the double-headed celebration of the old year's end and the new year's beginning, when at least fifty thousand spectators watched some thirty-five hundred participants in a dozen or more major groups. But full Junkanoos were also staged on special national occasions such as the morrow of independence and the five-hundredth anniversary of Columbus's landfall; miniature Junkanoos were presented at international cultural gatherings such as CARIFESTA; and elements of Junkanoo—goombay drums, cowbells, bugles, and costumes, if not the full regalia—appeared at lesser national events or whenever the Bahamas was entertaining international gatherings or major personalities, including, of course, the Royal Family.[104]

Junkanoo also spread more widely. It became more prevalent throughout the Family Islands, particularly in Grand Bahama, Eleuthera, and Abaco, where the predominance of Nassau-style Junkanoo seemed to threaten the continued existence of Old Bunce. Junkanoo also became established among expatriate Bahamian communities, notably in Miami and Toronto, where Junkanoo bands were to be seen at the Orange Bowl and Caribana parades respectively. Though the overwhelming majority of Junkanoo participants remained blacks (and male), the hard and fast division between black performers and white spectators gradually broke down, to the extent that the elite St. Andrew's School, with a majority of white pupils and teachers, had its own Junkanoo by the 1990s.[105] More and more whites actively participated on Bay Street, while, in tune with the greater emancipation of women, the number of female participants and spontaneous "rushers" increased each year, and by 1994 it was noticed (with approval by integrationists) that Haitians were also beginning to take part.[106]

The importance and distinctiveness of Bahamian Junkanoo were recognized and displayed in a major project sponsored by the Smithsonian Institution in Washington in the summer of 1994. This was a matter of justified pride for all Bahamians. Yet in typical Bahamian fashion the Smithsonian exercise also gave rise to considerable tensions, not so much between the personnel of the Junkanoo bands involved, whose normal fierce competitiveness was at least temporarily subsumed in a proud nationalistic display, as, in general, between traditional purists and the boldest innovators and at the sectional and personal levels between particular band leaders and between band leaders and academic theorists.[107] This volatility, overt and submerged, was, of course, absolutely consonant with characteristics displayed or immanent throughout this history of the Bahamian Islanders in the Stream. It demonstrated not just the Bahamians' love of argument coupled with a hatred of real violence but a deeper and more fundamental equivocation: a combustious, sometimes seemingly contradictory mixture, between pride and shame for the past, between the natural call of "primitive" rhythms and the restraints of "civilized" conventions, between dependence on tradition and a spirit of independence, and between what might be truly called an insular pride in family, race, color, class, island, district, or homestead and an emergent, archipelagic sense of uniqueness in diversity and interdependence.

Perhaps more symbolic of the new Bahamian nation—and of the way the Junkanoo provides an instinctual cement for the Bahamian people—was an episode that occurred in the United States in October 1993. Tennis is a minor sport but one in which Bahamians have excelled, especially since the 1970s. In the worldwide Davis Cup competition the Bahamas at first simply participated with other territories to select a representative British Caribbean team. But by the time of independence Bahamian players were winning selection more often than others, and when Davis Cup participation was divided in the late 1970s, the Bahamian team regularly beat all those from the other Commonwealth Caribbean countries. In 1993, after defeating all Caribbean and South American national teams, the Bahamas was drawn to play the mighty United States at Charlotte, North Carolina, in a Davis Cup tie for a place in the elite World Group. The Bahamas team consisted of just two players: Roger Smith, a black hailing from Grand Bahama, and Mark Knowles, a white with Conchy Joe antecedents on his father's side. Though they were beaten by the five-man U.S. squad, Smith and Knowles did their nation proud, with the memorable support of a sizable group of their fellow Bahamians, of all shades and classes, not clad in Junkanoo costume but blowing conch shells, bugles, and whistles to the insistent beat and rhythm of cowbell and goombay drum.[108]

Notes

Chapter 1

1. Michael Craton and Gail Saunders, *Islanders in the Stream: A History of the Bahamian People, Volume One: From Aboriginal Times to the End of Slavery* (Athens: University of Georgia Press, 1992), 274–81. In a masterly paper written since our first volume was published, Howard Johnson uses the Grand Jury presentments, newspaper reports, and laws to underline the already unslavelike behavior of the Nassau protoproletariat: "Slave Life and Leisure in Nassau, Bahamas, 1783–1838," paper presented at the Twenty-sixth Conference of Caribbean Historians, San German, Puerto Rico, March 1994.

2. Peter T. Dalleo, "Africans in the Caribbean: A Preliminary Assessment of Recaptives in the Bahamas, 1811–1860," *Journal of the Bahamas Historical Society* 6 (October 1984): 15–24; Howard Johnson, "The Liberated Africans, 1811–1860," in *The Bahamas in Slavery and Freedom* (Kingston, Jamaica: Ian Randle, and London: James Currey, 1991), 30–54.

3. For example, in Douglas G. Hall, *Free Jamaica, 1838–1865: An Economic History* (New Haven: Yale University Press, 1959).

4. Rebecca J. Scott, "Comparing Emancipations," *Journal of Social History* (Spring 1987): 565–83.

5. Order in Council, March 16, 1808, London, Public Record Office, P.C. 2/176, 145–58, quoted in Gail Saunders, "The Amelioration and Abolition of Slavery in the Bahamas" (B.A. thesis, University of Newcastle, 1966), 77.

6. London, Public Record Office, C.O. 23/58, 76–78; 23/59, 45–58 (hereafter C.O.).

7. *Bahama Gazette*, May 14, 1812; C.O. 23/58, 76–78; 23/61, 190; 23/62, 80.

8. C.O. 23/84, 415–20.

9. Memorial of Certain People of Nassau to Governor Cameron, 1816, C.O. 23/63, 202–3.

10. Murray to Cameron, November 16, 1816, C.O. 23/63, 361.

11. *Royal Gazette*, January 12, 1824.

12. *Settlements in New Providence* (Nassau: Department of Archives, 1982), 24–26; Poitier to Grant, May 25, 1825, C.O. 23/74, 75; Smyth to Goderich, February 5, 1832, C.O. 23/86, 39.

13. Smyth to Goderich, C.O. 23/84, 14, 173.

14. C.O. 23/89, 31.

15. *Bahama Argus*, August 31, 1831; Rigby to Smyth, August 2, 1833, C.O. 23/89, 24–25.

16. *Royal Gazette*, November 26, 1836.

17. *Settlements in New Providence*, 48, 51.

18. *Bahama Argus*, November 11, 1835, C.O. 23/94, 272.

19. Army Medical Board to Smyth, July 28, 1832, C.O. 23/83, 281.

20. C.O. 23/86, 282–88; Dalleo, "Africans in the Caribbean," 16; Saunders, "Slavery in the Bahamas," 87.

21. Balfour to Stanley, July 1833, C.O. 23/88, 248–49; C.O. 23/89, 12.

22. James Martin Wright, "History of the Bahama Islands, with a Special Study of the Abolition of Slavery in the Colony," in George Burbank Shattuck, *The Bahama Islands* (Baltimore:

Baltimore Geographical Society, 1908), 519; Dalleo, "Africans in the Caribbean," 19, citing Cockburn to Russell, February 4, 1841, C.O. 23/109.

23. Craton and Saunders, *Islanders in the Stream*, 1:291–96.

24. *Settlements in New Providence*, 28–36.

25. The population was said to consist of 160 men, 176 women, 93 boys, and 118 girls. It included 236 field laborers, 8 seamen, and 21 merchants (Colebrooke to Glenelg, December 15, 1835, C.O. 23/94, 125).

26. *Bahama Argus*, November 11, 1835, C.O. 23/94, 272.

27. *Settlements in New Providence*, 35.

28. Petition of Natives of Africa, October 1835, C.O. 23/94, 128; Colebrooke to Glenelg, April 26, 1836, C.O. 23/96, 343. See also "Rules for the Bahamas Friendly Society, 1834," C.O. 23/93, 168–69.

29. *Nassau Guardian*, August 4, 1880, May 7, 1884; *Settlements in New Providence*, 47.

30. Minutes of the Privy Council, November 28, 1838, C.O. 23/103, 171–72; Government Notice, November 1838, C.O. 23/103, 241.

31. March 12, 1836, C.O. 23/96, 244–74.

32. July 14, 1834, C.O. 23/91, 289–91; *Royal Gazette*, June 27, 1834.

33. Balfour to Spring Rice, September 13, 1834, C.O. 23/91, 380–81; *Royal Gazette*, August 6, 1834.

34. Hunter to Aberdeen, February 21, 1835, C.O. 23/93, 44.

35. Colebrooke to Donald McLean and Hector Munro, April 6, 1835, *Royal Gazette*, April 6, 1835.

36. Ibid.

37. Colebrooke to Glenelg, August 8, 1835, C.O. 23/94, 36–40; Edward Gibbon Wakefield, *A View of the Art of Colonization* (London, 1849), 328–29.

38. *Royal Gazette*, August 1, 1835.

39. August 12, 1835, C.O. 23/94, 75.

40. T. R. Winder and E. E. Hill, *Royal Gazette*, January 13, October 6, 1836.

41. C.O. 23/96, 115.

42. June 13, 1836, C.O. 23/97, 85; *Royal Gazette*, January 13, 1836.

43. Stipendiary Magistrates to Colonial Office, November 1836, C.O. 23/97, 507–12.

44. Ibid. Of the apprentices manumitted, 1,087 were praedials, 300 nonpraedials (C.O. 23/102, 111).

45. *Royal Gazette*, December 27, 1836.

46. W. L. Burn, *Emancipation and Apprenticeship in the British West Indies* (London: Cape, 1937).

47. British Sessional Papers (hereafter BSP), Commons, Accounts and Papers (1839), 35, 107, Part 1, 4 sqq.; Michael Craton, *Sinews of Empire: A Short History of British Slavery* (London: Temple Smith, and New York: Doubleday, 1974), 294–306.

48. Michael Craton, *A History of the Bahamas*, 3d ed. (Waterloo: San Salvador Press, 1986), 201.

49. Ibid., 203–5.

50. Stephen Dillet (1797–1880) had been born in Haiti of a French army officer and a free black woman, Mary Catherine Argo. He and his mother had been seized by a British privateer while en route from Haiti to Cuba in 1802 and carried to Nassau, where the mother decided to stay. Stephen, by then a fashionable tailor, was married to Charlotte Williams, a fellow free black, in 1822. A protégé of Governor Carmichael Smyth, he served in the House of Assembly for twenty-seven years, was postmaster from 1846 to 1876, and for part of that time, sometimes concurrently, inspector-general of police, assistant adjutant general, and a director of the Public Bank. Of his two legitimate sons, Thomas William became the second black Bahamian lawyer (studying at King's College and the Inns of Court in London in the 1830s and being called to the Nassau bar in 1848), sitting as a member of the House of Assembly from 1857 to 1865 and serving as Queen's advocate at Grand Turk, judge of the General Court, and acting attorney general. Joseph Eugene, the second son, apparently migrated

to Africa. Stephen Albert Dillet (1849–1930) was an illegitimate son, whose distinguished career in the Bahamian public service was made despite lacking his half-brothers' advantages and being of a considerably darker complexion. See Obituary, *Nassau Guardian*, October 9, 1880; Hartley Cecil Saunders, *The Other Bahamas* (Nassau: Bodab Press, 1991), 70–71, 92.

51. Bahamas Acts 53 Geo III, c. 8 (1812), 308–14; 2 Geo IV, c. 16 (1821), 338–43; 6 Will IV, c. 11 (1833), 54–60.

52. Shaw-Lefevre to Glenelg, February 1, 1839, BSP (1839), 35, 107, Part 1, 36.

53. Bahamas Acts 43 Geo III, c. 3 (1802), 100–106; 46 Geo III, c. 14 (1805), 141–42; 48 Geo III, c. 7 (1809), 284–89; 46 Geo III, c. 1 (1805), 58–74.

54. Bahamas Acts 57 Geo III, c. 8 (1816), 204–22; 2 Geo IV, c. 17 (1821), 404–10.

55. *Bahama Argus*, June 12, 1832.

56. Bahamas Acts 6 Will IV, c. 7 (1833), 38–43; 6 Will IV, c. 11 (1833), 54–60.

57. Bahamas Acts 2 Vic I, c. 7 (1839), 112–14; 2 Vic I, c. 16 (1839), 184–88.

58. Mathew to Stanley, March 14, 1845, C.O. 23/120, 73–74.

59. *Bahama Herald*, August 14, 1849.

60. *Bahama Herald*, November 29, 1854.

61. *Bahama Herald*, December 24, 1858.

62. Notice from Inspector's Office, March 5, 1891, *Bahama Herald*, March 8, 1851.

63. "Rules for the Government of the Prisons Within the Bahama Islands, Nassau, 1854," C.O. 23/148, 46–57.

64. *Bahamas Blue Book, 1849*, C.O. 23/135, 119.

65. *Bahamas Blue Book, 1863*, C.O. 23/176, 167.

66. Bahamas Act 20 Vic I, c. 14 (1857), 107–8.

67. Bahamas Acts 23 Vic I, c. 4 (1860), 335–43; 26 Vic I, c. 20 (1863), 149; 27 Vic I, c. 20 (1864), 201–12; 28 Vic I, c. 38 (1865), 419–20.

68. Shea to Knutsford, November 22, 1888, C.O. 23/230.

69. In 1861, when asked by the colonial secretary whether the troops of the West India Regiment could be relied on for the "suppression of sedition, tumult and turbulence," Governor Bayley replied that "in any regiment moderately well disciplined and containing natives of all the islands & of Africa, the local sentiment of a part would be lost & swamped by the military subordination of the whole body" (Bayley-Newcastle, February 11, 1861, C.O. 23/165, 19). The tendency of the troops to round on the native Bahamians and even Bahamian policemen was illustrated by a fracas that occurred in Grant's Town on August 23, 1881. A jealousy dispute between a soldier and his Bahamian sweetheart quickly degenerated into a clash between soldiers and police in which the populace was involved on the side of the police (*Nassau Guardian*, August 24, 1881).

70. C. L. Joseph, "The Strategic Importance of the British West Indies, 1882–1932," *Journal of Caribbean History* 7 (1973): 25–26. For the reorganization of 1881–91, see Howard Johnson, "Social Control and the Colonial State: The Reorganisation of the Police Force in the Bahamas, 1888–1893," *Bahamas in Slavery and Freedom*, 110–24.

71. Lees to Kimberley, July 29, 1882, C.O. 23/222, 155; Johnson, "Social Control," 111.

72. Blake to Stanley, August 8, September 19, 1885, C.O. 23/266; Louis Diston Powles, *Land of the Pink Pearl* (London, 1888), 113–14; Johnson, "Social Control," 112.

73. Shea to Knutsford, November 22, 1888; Wingfield to Kimberley, December 19, 1888, C.O. 23/230; Johnson, "Social Control," 111–13.

74. Johnson, "Social Control," 114–18.

75. Bahamas Act 54 Vic I, c. 14.

76. C.O. 23/237; Johnson, "Social Control," 118–20; Gail Saunders, "The Social History of the Bahamas, 1890–1953" (Ph.D. dissertation, University of Waterloo, 1985), 109–11. See below, Chapter 7.

77. *Royal Gazette*, January 5, 1825; *Bahama Herald*, July 19, 1851; C.O. 23/87, 47–52.

78. Smyth to Glenelg, January 1, 1833, C.O. 23/88, 8–10.

79. Craton, *History of the Bahamas*, 199–200.

80. Circular of Colonial Secretary Lord Russell, March 18, 1841, quoted in Shirley C. Gordon, ed., *A Century of West Indian Education* (London: Longmans, 1963), 38.
81. Craton, *History of the Bahamas*, 200; *Nassau Guardian*, May 19, 1844.
82. Bahamas Act 10 Vic I, c. 10.
83. C.O. 23/140, 5–9, 52–54.
84. C.O. 23/126, 364–65.
85. *Bahama Herald*, July 3, 1849.
86. *Bahama Herald*, October 9, 16, 1849.
87. Swann to Gregory, C.O. 23/143, 226–29.
88. W. J. Woodcock, *Popular Education in the Bahamas* (Nassau, 1851), C.O. 23/140, 71–80.
89. *Bahamas Blue Book, 1857*, C.O. 23/157, 53–57.
90. C.O. 23/145, 213–14.
91. Craton, *History of the Bahamas*, 200–201.
92. Colbert Williams, *The Methodist Contribution to Education in the Bahamas* (Gloucester, 1982), 61; Saunders, "Social History," 82; Craton, *History of the Bahamas*, 200.
93. *Nassau Guardian*, March 29, 1871.
94. Gregory to Grey, June 15, 1849, C.O. 23/132, 332–41.
95. Saunders, "Social History," 79–82; Cleveland Eneas, *Let the Church Roll On* (Nassau, 1983), 58–64.
96. Bahamas Government, *Report on the Census of 1891* (Nassau, 1892); Bahamas Government, *Report on the Census of 1901* (Nassau, 1902).
97. Craton, *History of the Bahamas*, 200.

Chapter 2

1. Anthony Thompson, *An Economic History of the Bahamas* (Nassau: Commonwealth Publications, 1982), 11–12.
2. Ibid., 11.
3. Ibid., 11–15.
4. *Bahamas Argus*, June 24, 1835, quoted in Howard Johnson, "The Share System in the Nineteenth and Early Twentieth Centuries," in *The Bahamas in Slavery and Freedom* (Kingston: Ian Randle, and London: James Currey, 1991), 55–68.
5. Colebrooke to Glenelg, August 8, 1835, C.O. 23/94; Johnson, "Share System," 59.
6. Nesbitt to Grey, September 7, 1847, C.O. 23/126.
7. Ibid.; Blake to Holland, March 15, 1867, C.O. 23/229; Johnson, "Share System," 59–60.
8. Bahamas Archives, O'Brien Collection; Johnson, "Share System," 60–61; Michael Craton and Gail Saunders, *Islanders in the Stream: A History of the Bahamian People, Volume One: From Aboriginal Times to the End of Slavery* (Athens: University of Georgia Press, 1992), 335–57.
9. Johnson, "Share System," 61.
10. Ibid., 62–65.
11. Smyth to Goderich, August 9, 1832, C.O. 23/87, 345–50; Michael Craton, "We Shall Not Be Moved: Pompey's Proto-Peasant Slave Revolt in Exuma Island, Bahamas, 1829–1830," *Nieuwe West-Indische Gids* 57 (Spring 1983): 31.
12. Howard Johnson, "The Credit and Truck Systems in the Nineteenth and Early Twentieth Centuries," in *The Bahamas in Slavery and Freedom*, 84–109.
13. Grant to Goderich, September 26, 1827, C.O. 23/76, cited in Johnson, "Credit and Truck Systems," 87.
14. Johnson, "Credit and Truck Systems," 86; *Royal Gazette*, June 24, July 29, 1837.
15. Johnson, "Credit and Truck Systems," 85; Smyth to Bathurst, January 25, 1832, C.O. 23/86.
16. Johnson, "Credit and Truck Systems," 85; Colebrooke to Glenelg, February 3, 1836, C.O. 23/96.
17. Johnson, "Credit and Truck Systems," 102–4.

18. Ibid., 94, citing, for example, Balfour to Spring Rice, January 15, 1835, Gregory to Grey, January 7, 1852, C.O. 23/140.

19. Johnson, "Credit and Truck Systems," citing Cockburn to Russell, April 6, 1840, C.O. 23/107.

20. Cockburn to Stanley, May 19, 1843, C.O. 23/115; Nesbitt to Grey, September 7, 1847, C.O. 23/126; Johnson, "Credit and Truck Systems," 95.

21. *The Salt Industry of the Bahamas* (Nassau: Department of Archives, 1980), 26–27; G. J. H. Northcroft, *Sketches of Summerland* (Nassau, 1900), 311 ff.

22. *Nassau Guardian*, April 27, May 8, 1889; Johnson, "Credit and Truck Systems," 83.

23. London, Lowe, Marston, Searle and Rivington, 1888.

24. Michael Craton, *A History of the Bahamas*, 3d ed. (Waterloo: San Salvador Press, 1986), 238–39.

25. Ibid., 226–27.

26. Blake to Holland, April 30, 1887, C.O. 23/229, cited in Johnson, "Credit and Truck Systems," 101.

27. Ibid., 102, referring to Bahamas Act 49 Vic I, c. 19 (1886).

28. Johnson, "Credit and Truck Systems," referring to Bahamas Act 4 Ed VII, c. 18 (1905).

29. Craton, *History of the Bahamas*, 240.

30. Ibid., 240–41.

31. Ibid., 236–38.

32. David Dilks, *Neville Chamberlain*, 2 vols. (Cambridge: Cambridge University Press, 1984), 1:54–77.

33. *The Pineapple Industry of the Bahamas* (Nassau: Department of Archives, 1977), 18–20.

34. *Nassau Guardian*, September 8, 1906, cited in Johnson, "Credit and Truck Systems," 97.

35. "Report on Long Cay, 1897," *Votes of the Bahamas House of Assembly*, March 1–August 26, 1898; Johnson, "Credit and Truck Systems," 103.

36. Johnson, "Credit and Truck Systems," 104.

37. Johnson, *The Bahamas in Slavery and Freedom*, 1–109; O. Nigel Bolland, "Systems of Domination After Slavery: The Control of Land and Labor in the British West Indies After 1838," *Comparative Studies in Society and History* 23, no. 4 (1981): 593–600. See also William A. Green, "The Perils of Comparative History: Belize and the British Sugar Colonies After Slavery," *Comparative Studies in Society and History* 26, no. 11 (1984): 114–21, and Bolland's reply, ibid., 122–30. The main part of the present chapter was published in an earlier form as Michael Craton, "White Law and Black Custom: The Evolution of Bahamian Land Tenures," in *Land and Development in the Caribbean*, ed. Jean Besson and Janet Momsen (London: Macmillan Caribbean, Warwick University Caribbean Studies, 1987), 88–114.

38. C. B. McPherson, *The Political Theory of Possessive Individualism: Hobbes to Locke* (Oxford: Oxford University Press, 1964).

39. Being, with the adjacent mainland, "yet hitherto untild, neither inhabited by ours or the subjects of any other Christian king, Prince or state But in some parts of it inhabited by certaine Barbarous men who had not any knowledge of the Divine Deitye" (*Calendar of State Papers, Colonial*, 9:70–71, quoted in Craton, *History of the Bahamas*, 50).

40. Craton, *History of the Bahamas*, 51–53, 66–69. The distinction between the two forms of quasi-feudal grant depended on the fact that Durham, being a borderland against the Scots, had almost autonomous privileges, and on the difference between ordinary socage and the freer kind found in Kent. The Palatinate of Durham was dissolved in the 1630s and the model thus became archaic. Socage in Kent related to the ancient system of *gavelkind*, almost unique to that county. See Marshall Harris, *Origin of the Land Tenure System of the United States* (Ames: Iowa State College Press, 1953), 29–39.

41. The word *gavelkind* comes from the Saxon word *gafol*, meaning rent-paying. Kentish custom allowed "soc-men" to partition, sell, and bequeath their land quite freely and to sue for it in the king's court, even against their lords. Unlike other forms of tenure, no fine was liable upon alienation. Besides, legal processes in Kent were more direct and less cumbersome than

elsewhere, conditions for widows and heirs were easier, and lands could not be escheated for felony (Harris, *Land Tenure System*, 37–38, quoting William Holdsworth, *History of English Law*, 12 vols. [London: Methuen, 1925], 3:260–61).

42. The headright system was inherent in the first instructions to the London Company of Virginia (1606), which specified that land ownership was not to be confined to shareholders and that everyone who immigrated to the colony or who brought or sent over another person was entitled to land. As the Virginia colony developed, though, a distinction emerged between the original (pre-1625) adventurers, who received land grants in fee simple, free of all feudal charges, and nonshareholders and later immigrants, who received land subject to annual quitrents (Harris, *Land Tenure System*, 194–236). For the Bermuda connection, see Craton and Saunders, *Islanders in the Stream*, 1:69–75.

43. Craton and Saunders, *Islanders in the Stream*, 1:170, 419 n. 25.

44. Ibid., 115–26; Craton, *History of the Bahamas*, 95–101, 156–57. Woodes Rogers became the first royal governor in 1718, but the colony was also administered for some time through a private company, which simply leased the right of collecting quitrents (along with other royalties) from the Lords Proprietor for twenty-one years, for a total of £2,450. One cause of much subsequent confusion was that Woodes Rogers's first land agent, Samuel Gohier, absconded to England with the initial record books.

45. Bahamas Act 3 Geo II, c. 4 (1729), Bahamas Archives, MSS Laws, Vol. 1, 1729–1831, 5–6. Where title was proved against an occupier, any person who had been on the land for two years or more was to be given a year to move and reimbursed for any improvements made, as assessed by a specially empaneled jury (Craton and Saunders, *Islanders in the Stream*, 1:136).

46. Craton and Saunders, *Islanders in the Stream*, 1:165–66, citing Bahamas Act 4 Geo III, c. 4 (1764), MSS Laws, 1:16–20.

47. Craton and Saunders, *Islanders in the Stream*, 1:164–66, 191, citing Bahamas Act 29 Geo III, c. 1 (1789), MSS Laws, 1:26–28.

48. Bahamas Act 43 Geo III, c. 1 (1802), MSS Laws, 1:97–99.

49. Bahamas Act 46 Geo III, c. 16 (1805), MSS Laws, 1:146–51.

50. Bahamas Act 9 Vic I, c. 10 (1846), MSS Laws, Vol. 2, 1832–50, 170–75.

51. Edward Gibbon Wakefield, *A View of the Art of Colonisation* (London, 1849), 328–29.

52. Patrice Williams, *A Guide to African Villages in New Providence* (Nassau: Public Record Office, 1979), 4–15, 27–28; Bahamas Archives, *Settlements in New Providence* (Nassau, 1982), 22–36, 44–52.

53. Heild to Nesbitt, June 1, 1842, C.O. 23/113, 142. See Chapter 3, note 9; Craton and Saunders, *Islanders in the Stream*, 1:335–57.

54. Nesbitt to Colonial Office, July 12, 1842, C.O. 23/113, 127–30.

55. Bahamas Act 9 Vic I, c. 10 (1846), MSS Laws, 2:170–75.

56. Craton, *History of the Bahamas*, 199; Williams, *African Villages*, 21–26; *Settlements in New Providence*, 37–43.

57. *Settlements in New Providence*, 53–56.

58. Craton and Saunders, *Islanders in the Stream*, 1:335–57.

59. Rolle to Spring Rice, August 11, 1834, C.O. 23/92, 497.

60. Craton and Saunders, *Islanders in the Stream*, 1:170. In 1840, when the Harbour Islanders petitioned for clear title in common for six thousand acres, they offered $1,000 for the land. It was said that they had worked the tract for more than a hundred years, that is, for at least forty years before Deveaux came on the scene. The Council had ordered in 1810 that these customary lands should not be sold to others but did not give specific title to the Harbour Islanders (Report of Colonial Land and Emigration Commissioners to James Stephen, July 23, 1840, C.O. 23/100).

61. Bahamas Act 59 Vic I, c. 14 (1896), *Statute Law of the Bahamas*, rev. ed. (London, 1965), 123. Lands held in common are defined as "any lands which have been granted to more than twenty people and not partitioned."

62. The existence of such documents, of course, placed the law in an impossible dilemma, a reverence for the wishes of those making formal wills and deeds conflicting with a general preference for simple lineal inheritance and transmission. Such legislative attempts to cut the Gordian knot as the 1830 Act to Amend the Law of Inheritance (3 Will IV, c. 20), being based on English conditions, were almost nugatory in the Bahamas.

63. Keith F. Otterbein, "A Comparison of the Land Tenure Systems of the Bahamas, Jamaica and Barbados: The Implication It Has for the Study of Social Systems Shifting from Bilateral to Ambilineal Descent," *International Archives of Ethnography* 50 (1964): 31–42; Otterbein, *The Andros Islanders* (Lawrence: Kansas University Press, 1967); Edith Clarke, "Land Tenure and Family in Four Communities in Jamaica," *Social and Economic Studies* 1, no. 4 (1953): 81–118; Clarke, *My Mother Who Fathered Me* (London: Allen & Unwin, 1957); Sidney M. Greenfield, "Land Tenure and Transmission in Rural Barbados," *Anthropological Quarterly* 33 (1960): 165–76. See also Raymond T. Smith, "Land Tenure in Three Negro Villages in British Guiana," *Social and Economic Studies* 4 (1955): 64–85; Michael G. Smith, "The Transmission of Land Rights in Carriacou," *Social and Economic Studies* 5 (1956): 103–38; Besson and Momsen, *Land and Development in the Caribbean*. For Bahamian tenure practices in relation to farming and family in various islands, see also Alan G. La Flamme, "Green Turtle Cay: A Bi-Racial Community in the Out Island Bahamas" (Ph.D. dissertation, University of New York, Buffalo, 1972); William B. Rogers, "The Wages of Change: An Anthropological Study of the Effects of Economic Development on Some Negro Communities in the Bahamas Out Islands" (Ph.D. dissertation, Stanford University, 1965); Joel S. Savashinsky, ed., *Strangers No More: Anthropological Studies of Cat Island, the Bahamas* (Ithaca: Ithaca College, 1978).

64. Bahamas Act to Provide Summary Remedy Against the Occupation of Land by Persons Having No Title to the Same, 4 Will IV, c. 37 (1834). In an ejection, all buildings and "improvements" were to be dismantled and all goods and chattels sold. Fifteen days' grace was given before the lawful owners could move in.

65. Bahamas Act 2 Vic I, c. 2 (1839).

66. Bahamas Act 3 Vic I, c. 3 (1840).

67. This principle, which followed English precepts, came into effect in 1847, the year after the Commutation Act. See Craton, *History of the Bahamas*, 198–99.

68. Quieting of Titles Act, 1959, *Statute Laws of the Bahamas, 1965*, 1:895–1, 906. See below, Part II.

69. *Bahamas Blue Book* 1838 (Nassau, 1838), 166–67; ibid., 1845, 132–33; ibid., 1851, 144–45; ibid., 1861, 166–67; ibid., 1871, 172–73; ibid., 1881, 184–85; *Report on the Census of the Bahama Islands, Taken on 27 June, 1891* (Nassau: *Nassau Guardian*, 1891); *Report on the Census of the Bahama Islands, Taken on April 2, 1901* (Nassau: *Nassau Guardian*, 1901).

70. Gregory to Pakington, November 10, 1852, C.O. 23/140, 188–96.

71. Gregory to Pakington, December 2, 1852, C.O. 23/140, 207–12.

72. For treatment of the Bowe case and subsequent fate of the Forest, see below, Chapter 10.

Chapter 3

1. James McQueen, *West Indian Mail Communication: In a Letter to Francis Baring Esq., M.P., Sec. to the Treasury etc. etc.* (London: B. Fellowes, 1838), 4–5.

2. The number of proposed routes was cut by half in 1843. As early as 1841 a special committee of the Royal Mail Steam Packet Company had stated that the Bahamas, especially with its lack of lighthouses and absolutely reliable maps, "presented dangers of the most formidable description" and concluded that "it would seem almost a miracle to make 112 voyages each year, through these countless rocks and shoals without the occurrence of disaster" (National Maritime Museum, Greenwich, RMS 1/1, Court of Directors' Minute Book, November 4, 1841). See also Rodney Baker and Alan Leonard, *Great Steamers White and Gold: A History of Royal Mail Ships and Services* (Southampton: Ensign Publications, 1993).

3. Michael Craton, *A History of the Bahamas*, 3d ed. (Waterloo: San Salvador Press, 1986), 212.

4. James H. Stark, *Stark's History and Guide to the Bahama Islands, Containing a Description of Everything on or About the Bahamas Islands of Which the Visitor or Resident May Desire Information. Including Their History, Inhabitants, Climate, Agriculture, Geology, Government and Resources* (Boston, 1891), 8–10.

5. Harold G. D. Gisburn, *The Postage Stamps and Postal History of the Bahamas* (London: Stanley Gibbons, 1949), 19–30.

6. Ibid., 31–48.

7. Ibid., 49–64.

8. Craton, *History of the Bahamas*, 215.

9. *Bahamas Blue Book*, 1861, 1862; C.O. 23/169, 211–12; 23/172, 266–67, 483–84; *New York Herald*, July 3, 1863.

10. *Nassau Guardian*, June 15, 1864.

11. *Bahamas Blue Book*, 1865, C.O. 23/185, 109; *Nassau Guardian*, December 12, 1868.

12. *Nassau Guardian*, October 21, November 4, 7, 1868.

13. R. Langton-Jones, *Silent Sentinels: The Story of the Imperial Lighthouse Service* (London: Muller, 1944).

14. The revised computation, however, was largely the result of changed definitions of areas of salt marsh, flats, and tidal "swash."

15. Louis Diston Powles, *Land of the Pink Pearl* (London, 1888), 183.

16. *Nassau Guardian*, February 8, 1873, May 12, 1875, September 11, 1875.

17. Powles, *Land of the Pink Pearl*, 182.

18. Stark, *Guide*, 250; Charles Ives, *The Isles of Summer; or Nassau and the Bahamas* (New Haven: Ives, 1880), 17–20.

19. Stark, *Guide*, 4–7; Craton, *History of the Bahamas*, 245–46.

20. Powles, *Land of the Pink Pearl*, 50–51.

21. Dickinson and Dowd, *A Winter Picnic* (New York, 1888), 61–62. The "devoted postmaster" referred to was probably T. N. G. Clare, who in November 1889 was tried and convicted of embezzlement of £1,200 (*Nassau Guardian*, November 2, 1889).

22. *Nassau Guardian*, August 3, 1864.

23. G. J. H. Northcroft, *Sketches of Summerland, Giving Some Account of Nassau and the Bahama Islands* (Nassau, 1900), 60. The first "velocipede" was reported in Nassau in 1869, though they were still not common in the 1890s (*Nassau Guardian*, March 3, 1869).

24. Ives, *Isles of Summer*, 146; Northcroft, *Sketches of Summerland*, 60.

25. *Bahama Argus*, October 29, 1831.

26. Ives, *Isles of Summer*, 147.

27. *Laws of the Bahamas, in Force on the 14th of March, 1842* (Nassau, 1843), 178; *Bahamas Herald*, January 29, 1855; *Nassau Guardian*, January 10, 1855.

28. *Nassau Guardian*, February 18, 1863.

29. *Nassau Guardian*, January 28, 1873.

30. Northcroft, *Sketches of Summerland*, 59.

31. Gail Saunders, "The Social History of the Bahamas, 1890–1953" (Ph.D. dissertation, University of Waterloo, 1985), 88 n. 195.

32. *Nassau Guardian*, February 23, 1870.

33. Ives, *Isles of Summer*, 120–21; Stark, *Guide*, 106–7.

34. Ives, *Isles of Summer*, 121.

35. *Bahama Herald*, June 15, July 10, 1849.

36. Powles, *Land of the Pink Pearl*, 225.

37. Ives, *Isles of Summer*, 72–73, 121–22.

38. Ibid., 73.

39. Ibid., 74.

40. Ibid., 121–22.

41. *Illustrated London News*, January 5, 1856, quoted in *Bahama Herald*, February 27, 1856.

42. *Bahama Herald*, August 6, 1856.
43. *Nassau Times*, September 8, 1880.
44. William Drysdale, *In Sunny Lands* (New York: Harper, 1884).
45. For the furor caused by Powles over the Lightbourne case in 1887, see text at note 66 below; Craton, *History of the Bahamas*, 201–3.
46. Powles, *Land of the Pink Pearl*, 120.
47. Ibid., 122–23. For the Dillets, see Chapter 1, note 50, above, and text at note 66 below.
48. The colored gentleman referred to was almost certainly James Carmichael Smith, son of a Yorkshireman and his colored Bahamian wife. Educated at Nassau Grammar School, he was postmaster in succession to Stephen Dillet Sr., MHA for the Western District (1882–96), member of the Board of Education (1885–93), and founder of the outspoken newspaper the *Freeman* (1886–89). See below, at note 63. Ironically (and to the satisfaction of his white opponents), Smith's reputation and political career were shattered in a sexual scandal some five years later. See Saunders, "Social History," 154.
49. Powles, *Land of the Pink Pearl*, 127.
50. The American Charles Ives tactfully expressed the ambiguity of the Bahamian whites' "purity" in 1880: "It is true that the blood of a portion of the 'gentry' is said to be perfectly pure, but it is difficult in some cases of mixture to accurately draw the color line, and it is wise to ignore it, and ask no questions of one's partner in the voluptuous waltz, which might result in banishing the inquisitor from high-toned society. It is at times injudicious to scrutinize closely hair that appears straight or nearly so" (*Isles of Summer*, 292). The injudicious Irish magistrate Powles typically quoted a blunter jingle: "God bless the white folks one and all, though hark ye, / I see no harm in blessing too the darky! / But which is the darky and which the white? / God bless us all! That is beyond me quite!" (*Land of the Pink Pearl*, 120–23; Saunders, "Social History," 75–76).
51. Powles, *Land of the Pink Pearl*, 131.
52. Northcroft, *Sketches of Summerland*, 62.
53. The kirk did establish the Quarry Mission School for black children in Delancey Town in 1891, perhaps as a form of compensation. The school was taken over by the Board of Education in 1925 (Saunders, "Social History," 73).
54. Edwards to Osborn, February 12, 1889, Wesleyan Methodist Missionary Society (hereafter WMMS) Letters, School of Oriental and African Studies, London, quoted ibid., 72.
55. Gostwick to Macdonald, Nassau, February 10, 1898, WMMS Letters, ibid.
56. E. T. Churton, *The Island Missionary of the Bahamas* (London, 1888); Roscow Shedden, *Ups and Downs in a West Indian Diocese* (London: A. R. Mowbray, 1927); Evelyn Shedden, *Ins and Outs of the Bahamas Islands* (Norwich: Goose and Sons, 1930).
57. As late as the 1950s, an aged black beadle at Christchurch would direct his fellow blacks to the rear, while guiding even casually visiting whites to more favored pews.
58. Gostwick to Macdonald, Nassau, June 7, 1898, WMMS Letters, quoted by Saunders, "Social History," 90.
59. *Nassau Quarterly Mission Papers, 1888–1918* 9 (September 1894): 43; 4 (September 1889): 177; 1 (March 1887): 121, ibid.
60. Craton, *History of the Bahamas*, 232; Colman J. Barry, *Upon These Rocks: Catholics in the Bahamas* (Collegeville, Minn.: St. John's Abbey Press, 1973), 103–245.
61. Saunders, "Social History," 80–83.
62. Ibid., 83–85.
63. Ibid., 83–84; Etienne Dupuch, *The Tribune Story* (London: Benn, 1967).
64. C.O. 23/102, 45. The original four were Stephen Dillet for Nassau, John P. Dean for western New Providence, Samuel Minns for Andros, and one of the two members for Exuma. In 1859, the three blacks in the Assembly were Stephen Dillet, his son Thomas W. H. Dillet, and William Edward Armbrister (the last the only nonwhite elected from 1870 to 1874). Other early nonwhite MHAs included Henry Stevenson (first elected in 1849), Thomas M.

Matthews (1867), Joseph Dupuch (1879), James C. Smith (1882), William C. Adderley (1889), Joseph W. H. Deveaux (1889), and Charles O. Anderson (1896) (Hartley Cecil Saunders, *The Other Bahamas* [Nassau: Bodab Press, 1991], 30–32, 55–56, 70–78).

65. Powles, *Land of the Pink Pearl*, 211; Stark, *Guide*, 139; Saunders, "Social History," 76.

66. Powles, *Land of the Pink Pearl*, 105–9, 307–9; Powles to Holland, July 29, 1887, C.O. 23/229, 621–30; Blake to Holland, September 12, 1887, C.O. 23/229, 448–49; Saunders, "Social History," 77.

67. Saunders, "Social History," 77; Taylor to Holland, August 19, 1887, C.O. 23/229, 427; Powles, *Land of the Pink Pearl*, 105.

68. Saunders, "Social History," 92.

69. In Nassau's small but class- and race-conscious society, Stephen Albert Dillet occupied a niche close to but significantly just below that of James C. Smith. Born out of wedlock in 1849, the dark-hued Dillet began work in the post office during the postmastership of his father but spent all his working years from 1868 to 1910 rising through the ranks in the Imperial Lighthouse Service, of which he became first mate. Literate and articulate, he wrote frequently for the local papers and edited Smith's *Freeman* for a time. In his later years he was associated with the radical *Watchman* (1903–6), associate editor of *Strombus Magazine*, and one of the most active recruiters for the Recruiting Committee in World War I. He died in 1930 (*Nassau Tribune*, November 24, 1924; Saunders, "Social History," 154 n. 235).

70. Shea to Ripon, April 29, 1893, C.O. 23/236, 256–65, cited in Saunders, "Social History," 92–93.

71. Ibid., 93.

72. Powles to Buxton, July 31, 1893, C.O. 23/238, 281–82, 395; Haynes-Smith to Chamberlain, December 21, 1896, C.O. 23/245, 170; Saunders, "Social History," 93.

73. Powles, *Land of the Pink Pearl*, 141. An advertisement for David Patton's Union Livery Stables on Bay Street in 1900 offered "Fine Rubber & Steel Tired Phaetons and American Horses . . . at all hours, day or night" to be hired by the day, week, or month at "reasonable prices." Patton, however, had stiff competition from at least three other similar establishments in town, all owned by whites, of which the grandest was the Colonial Livery Stables, "one block from the Colonial Hotel," owned by B. W. Roberts (Northcroft, *Sketches of Summerland*, 315–38).

74. Benson McDermott, "A. F. Adderley," *Bahamas Handbook and Businessman's Annual* (Nassau: Dupuch, 1980), 15–45.

75. Ives, *Isles of Summer*, 72–78; Powles, *Land of the Pink Pearl*, 164–65.

76. Powles, *Land of the Pink Pearl*, 165.

77. For the influence of Marcus Garvey on the Bahamas, see Chapter 7.

Chapter 4

1. Louis Diston Powles, *Land of the Pink Pearl* (London, 1888), 146–47.

2. Ibid., 151.

3. A map of 1752 shows Fox's Point near the present site of St. Ann's on East Bay Street, at the turning to Fox Hill village (*Settlements in New Providence* [Nassau: Department of Archives, 1982], 37).

4. Ibid., 37–43.

5. Ibid., 44–52, 22–27.

6. Powles, *Land of the Pink Pearl*, 149.

7. Ibid., 150.

8. Charles Ives, *The Isles of Summer; or Nassau and the Bahamas* (New Haven: Ives, 1880), 55.

9. *Report on the Bahamas Census*, 1891 (Nassau, 1982); Gail Saunders, "The Social History of the Bahamas, 1890–1953" (Ph.D. dissertation, University of Waterloo, 1985), 95.

10. Ives, *Isles of Summer*, 53–54; Powles, *Land of the Pink Pearl*, 151–52.

11. Bahamas Act 13 Vic I, c. 8 (1850), An Act for Establishing a Market in Grant's Town, in

the Island of New Providence, and for other purposes (March 14, 1850); *Settlements in New Providence*, 32.

12. Powles, *Land of the Pink Pearl*, 170; Wilhelmina Kemp Johnstone, *Bahamian Jottings* (Nassau: Brice, 1973), 11, 15; Interview with A. Fernandez, Gambier Village, New Providence, September 11, 1970; Saunders, "Social History," 98; Riva Berleant-Schiller and William M. Maurer, "Women's Place Is Every Place: Merging Domains and Women's Roles in Barbuda and Dominica," in *Women and Change in the Caribbean*, ed. Janet H. Momsen (London: James Currey, 1993), 76.

13. Powles, *Land of the Pink Pearl*, 142, 144–45.

14. Ibid., 167–77, quote on 169.

15. Ibid., 172–74.

16. Ibid., 170–72.

17. Ibid., 174–76.

18. Ibid., 176.

19. Ibid., 176–77.

20. Petition of Congo Society to King of the Belgians, August 1888, quoted in Philip Cash, Shirley Gordon, and Gail Saunders, eds., *Sources of Bahamian History* (London: Macmillan Caribbean, 1991), 228. It was stated that the potential party included 171 persons, though it is not clear how many of these were African-born and how many their Bahamas-born offspring.

21. The petition was signed on behalf of the Congo Society by John O'Brien (with an X), James Read, and William Higgs, whom the Baptist superintendent referred to as "perhaps the most intelligent." The most eloquent of the elderly Congoes, though, was one called Roach, who was quoted as saying, "Some say we go to that land to die—we lie in our belly 'cause we die hungry here—we must die if stay—I—if I know I die when my foot touch land I go by God's power" (Baptist Superintendent to BMS, December 6, 1888, ibid., 228–29).

22. Baptist Superintendent to Government and BMS, August 18, December 6, 1888, replies of Belgian Government, October 23, 1888, February 17, 1889, ibid., 229–30.

23. Dickinson and Dowd, *A Winter Picnic* (New York, 1888).

24. Michael Craton and Gail Saunders, *Islanders in the Stream: A History of the Bahamian People, Volume One: From Aboriginal Times to the End of Slavery* (Athens: University of Georgia Press, 1992), 329–34.

25. Gail Saunders, "Bahamian Women in Popular Culture in the Late Nineteenth and Early Twentieth Centuries," paper presented at the Twenty-seventh Annual Conference of Caribbean Historians, Georgetown, Guyana, April 1995.

26. Stanley Johannesen, "Third Generation Pentecostal Language," in *Charismatic Christianity as a Global Culture*, ed. Karla Poewe (Columbia: University of South Carolina Press, 1994).

27. Dickinson and Dowd, *A Winter Picnic*, 130–31.

28. Report of the Commission on the Working of Friendly Societies of the Colony, 1911, *Appendix to the Votes of the House of Assembly, 1911* (Nassau, 1911), 164.

29. *Nassau Guardian*, February 13, 1885.

30. Dickinson and Dowd, *A Winter Picnic*, 151–57.

31. *Nassau Quarterly Mission Papers* 11 (December 1896): 79.

32. Norman Cousins, *Albert Schweitzer's Mission: Healing and Peace* (New York: Norton, 1985), 46–56, 85–105.

33. Mrs. Leslie Higgs, *Bush Medicine in the Bahamas* (Nassau: Privately published, 1974).

34. *Nassau Quarterly Mission Papers* 31 (September 1917): 45.

35. Cleveland Eneas, *Bain Town* (Nassau: Privately published, 1976), 12.

36. Ibid., 9.

37. Dickinson and Dowd, *A Winter Picnic*, 157.

38. Charles L. Edwards, *Bahama Songs and Stories* (1895; rpt. New York: Stechert, 1942), 17.

39. Samuel B. Charters, Program notes for *Music in the Bahamas*, Folkways, No. FS3845

(1959), cited in E. Clement Bethel, "Music in the Bahamas; Its Roots, Development and Personality" (M.A. thesis, University of California, Los Angeles, 1978), 86, 93.

40. Edwards, *Bahama Songs and Stories*, 18.

41. Powles, *Land of the Pink Pearl*, 159–65.

42. Saunders, "Bahamian Women," 19.

43. John Holm and Alison Shilling, *Dictionary of Bahamian English* (Cold Spring, N.Y.: Lexic House, 1982).

44. Dickinson and Dowd, *A Winter Picnic*, 142.

45. Ibid., 142–43.

46. Powles, *Land of the Pink Pearl*, 165–67.

47. Daniel J. Crowley, "Form and Style in a Bahamian Folktale," *Caribbean Quarterly* 3 (August 1954): 218–34; Peter J. Wilson, *Crab Antics: The Social Anthropology of English-Speaking Negro Societies of the Caribbean* (New Haven: Yale University Press, 1973); Roger D. Abrahams, *The Man-of-Words in the Caribbean: Performance and the Emergence of Creole Culture* (Baltimore: Johns Hopkins University Press), 1983.

48. Crowley, "Form and Style in a Bahamian Folktale," 219.

49. Ibid., 230.

50. Edwards, *Bahama Songs and Stories*, 18–19; Holm and Shilling, *Dictionary of Bahamian English*, 79; G. J. H. Northcroft, *Sketches of Summerland* (Nassau, 1880), 71; Saunders, "Social History," 104–5.

51. Northcroft, *Sketches of Summerland*, 46.

52. *Nassau Quarterly Mission Papers* 10 (December 1895): 84.

53. Bethel, "Music in the Bahamas," 125–26.

54. Ibid., 126.

55. Powles, *Land of the Pink Pearl*, 148–49.

56. For example, Rev. E. G. Strachan to Friendly Societies, *Bahama Herald*, August 3, 1849; Rev. Robert Swann to Friendly Societies, Christchurch, *Nassau Guardian*, August 3, 1864.

57. Saunders, "Bahamian Women," 23.

58. *Accara* in its Bahamian form is made from split peas, okra, flour, pepper, and baking powder. The ingredients are made into a batter and deep fried. *Foo-foo* is a stew made with okra and, alternatively or together, fish, conch, or meat. It is eaten with cornmeal. *Moi-moi* (or *my-my*) is a highly seasoned tart made from mashed peas and flour, served in almond leaves. *Agidi* is a dessert made from grits, milk, sugar, and nutmeg (Interview with Dr. C. R. Walker, Grant's Town, July 31, 1970; Saunders, "Social History," 107).

59. *Nassau Guardian*, August 10, 1886.

60. *Nassau Guardian*, January 3, 1857.

61. E. Clement Bethel, ed. and expanded by Nicolette Bethel, *Junkanoo: Festival of the Bahamas* (London: Macmillan Caribbean, 1991); Bridget Brereton, *A History of Modern Trinidad, 1783–1962* (London: Heinemann, 1981), 133–35, 224–26.

62. *Bahama Herald*, December 30, 1854.

63. *Nassau Guardian*, December 29, 1886.

64. *Nassau Quarterly Mission Papers* 4 (March 1890): 245.

65. *Nassau Guardian*, December 24, 1890; Bethel, "Music in the Bahamas," 218.

66. C.O. 23/236, 408, 479–82; 23/237, 98–138, 179–88; Saunders, "Social History," 109–11.

67. Evidence of T. A. Thompson, Acting Chief Justice, in Shea to Ripon, July 8, 1893, C.O. 23/237, 185–86; Saunders, "Social History," 110–11.

68. Saunders, "Social History," 110–11, Shea to Ripon, July 8, 1893; evidence of S. M. Rae in Jackson to Ripon, July 20, 1893, C.O. 23/237, 98–106, 186–87.

Chapter 5

1. Francis Albury of St. George's Cay (Spanish Wells), for example, owned five slaves in 1828; see Register of Return of Slaves, 1828, 16, Bahamas Archives.

2. Report of Rev. C. C. Wakefield, *Nassau Times*, September 1874.
3. Louis Diston Powles, *Land of the Pink Pearl* (London, 1888), 69.
4. *Bahama Herald*, September 1864.
5. George Burbank Shattuck, ed., *The Bahama Islands* (Baltimore: Geographical Society, 1905), 410–14.
6. *Nassau Times*, 1875.
7. Alan G. LaFlamme, "Green Turtle Cay: A Bi-Racial Community in the Out Island Bahamas" (Ph.D. dissertation, University of New York, Buffalo, 1972); Gail Saunders, "The Social History of the Bahamas, 1890–1953" (Ph.D. dissertation, University of Waterloo, 1985), 128.
8. Matthew to Grey, April 13, 1848, C.O. 23/128, 143–46.
9. T. W. Mills, "The Study of a Small Island Community, the Bahama Islands," *American Naturalist* 21 (October 1887): 875–85.
10. Clement A. Penrose, "Sanitary Conditions in the Bahamas," in Shattuck, ed., *Bahama Islands*, 387–418.
11. Rawson Rawson, *Report on the Bahama Islands, 1854–1864* (London, 1865), 65.
12. Steve Dodge, *Abaco: The History of an Out Island and Its Cays* (Miami: Tropic Isles, 1983), 37.
13. Ibid., 39.
14. Ibid., 40, 53–55; William R. Johnson, *Bahamian Sailing Craft* (Nassau: Explorations, 1974).
15. Haynes-Smith to Chamberlain, July 7, 1896, C.O. 23/244, 107–8; Gail Saunders, "The Social History of the Bahamas, 1890–1953" (Ph.D. dissertation, University of Waterloo, 1985), 32.
16. Dodge, *Abaco*, 34–61; Haziel L. Albury, *Man-O-War My Island Home: A History of an Outer Abaco Island* (Hockessin, Del.: Holly Press, 1977), 53–63.
17. *Nassau Herald*, September 1864.
18. *Bahamas Blue Book*, 1859, C.O. 23/163, 73–74.
19. *Nassau Guardian*, May 14, October 31, 1853.
20. *Bahama Herald*, July 4, 1851; Report of Magistrate Inglis, August 25, 1851, C.O. 23/139, 51–60; *Nassau Guardian*, March 15, 1865.
21. Rawson, *Report*, 67–68.
22. *Nassau Guardian*, June 20, 1877, June 3, 1882.
23. Walter C. A. Maloney, *A Sketch of the History of Key West, Florida, 1876*, ed. Thelma Peters, Floridiana Facsimile Series (Gainesville: University of Florida Press, 1968); Jefferson B. Browne, *Key West, the Old and the New* (St. Augustine: Record Company, 1912); S. Wells, *Forgotten Legacy: Blacks in Nineteenth Century Key West* (Key West: Historic Preservation Board, 1982); R. Pierce, "From the Bahamas to Florida," *Florida Genealogist* 11 (1987): 19–24.
24. Howard Johnson, "Late Nineteenth and Early Twentieth Century Labour Migration to Florida," in *The Bahamas in Slavery and Freedom* (Kingston: Ian Randle, and London: James Currey, 1991), 163–80. See below, Part II.
25. A. H. Stuart, *World Trade in Sponges* (Washington, D.C.: U.S. Government Printing Office, Industrial Series, No. 82, 1948); Powles, *Land of the Pink Pearl*, 84–96.
26. The mission, called St. Cuthbert's, was at the western end of the central section of Bay Street, Nassau. See *Nassau Quarterly Mission Papers* 21 (June 1897); ibid., 4 (September 1890): 56; Shea to Knutsford, May 26, 1888, Duplicate Governors' Despatches, 1887–93, fol. 63, Bahamas Archives; Saunders, "Social History," 40.
27. Dodge, *Abaco*, 77; Albury, *Man-O-War*, 67–68.
28. For example, many thousands of oranges were exported from northern Eleuthera to Charleston, South Carolina, in 1849; see *Nassau Guardian*, November 24, 1849.
29. Powles, *Land of the Pink Pearl*, 227.
30. *Nassau Quarterly Mission Papers* 1 (September 1886): 45; 1 (June 1887): 147; Powles, *Land of the Pink Pearl*, 204; Saunders, "Social History," 123.
31. *Bahamas Blue Book*, 1864, C.O. 23/183, 187.
32. *Nassau Guardian*, September 26, 1853.
33. *Bahamas Herald*, January 7, 1860.

34. Powles, *Land of the Pink Pearl*, 111–12.
35. Dodge, *Abaco*, 72; Saunders, "Social History," 125.
36. *Nassau Quarterly Mission Papers* 4 (June 1889); Saunders, "Social History," 126.
37. *Nassau Times*, July 28, 1880.
38. Powles, *Land of the Pink Pearl*, 96–97, 215, 221–23.
39. Ibid., 205.
40. Shea to Ripon, April 24, 1894, No. 63, Duplicate Governor's Despatches, May 4, 1893–August 3, 1897, 133, Bahamas Archives; Saunders, "Social History," 123.
41. *Nassau Guardian*, October 15, 1873, signed "G."
42. *Nassau Guardian*, December 17, 1884, signed William Lowe Glenville.
43. Powles, *Land of the Pink Pearl*, 267–72.
44. *Nassau Guardian*, May 23, 1888, signed Aranha.
45. Powles, *Land of the Pink Pearl*, 268.
46. No less than thirty-six of the forty-five settlement names on a modern map of Long Island are family surnames. These are written, sometimes alternatively, as plain family names in the singular, as plurals, or in the possessive case with an apostrophe (for example, McKann, McKanns, McKann's). From north to south, they are Seymours, Glintons, Adderley, Millertons, Deals, O'Neills, Tatnalls, Simms, Bains, Morris's, Wemyss, Sam McKinnons, Millers, McKanns, Thompson, Pinder's, Bowers, Grays, Anderson, Buckleys, Cartwrights, Pettys, Hamiltons, Benzie, Stevens, Deans, Turnbull, Morrisville, McKenzie, Taits, Roses, Berrys, Fords, Mortimers, Gordons. The remaining settlement names are nearly all descriptive, as Burnt Ground, Salt Pond, Mangrove Bush, Scrub Hill, Cabbage Point, and the specially resonant Hard Bargain and Deadman's Cay. Dunmore (or Dunmore's) was named after the titled governor who once owned that property, and the administrative "capital," Clarence Town, was named after one of Queen Victoria's sons. Stella Maris suggests that it is the invention of a modern developer. See Map 9.
47. Powles, *Land of the Pink Pearl*, 274–83.
48. *Nassau Guardian*, March 20, April 3, 7, October 23, 1869.
49. Saunders, "Social History," 130.
50. *Nassau Quarterly Mission Papers* 10 (March 1896): 114, quoted in Saunders, "Social History," 130.
51. Keith Otterbein, *The Andros Islanders: A Study of Family Organisation in the Bahamas* (Lawrence: University of Kansas, 1966), 44, 55; LaFlamme, "Green Turtle Cay," 181–82. For an account of a black wedding ceremony at Albert Town, Long Cay, see Powles, *Land of the Pink Pearl*, 296–97. Also see *Nassau Quarterly Mission Papers* 10 (December 1895): 83; Saunders, "Social History," 130–31.
52. Joel S. Savashinsky, *Strangers No More: Anthropological Studies of Cat Island, Bahamas* (Ithaca: Ithaca College, 1978), 214.
53. Otterbein, *Andros Islanders*, 77–84.
54. In Nassau, the percentage of those married was 30.5 percent in 1891. Of those between eighteen and seventy years of age, the percentage was 54.6 (*Report on the Census, 1891* [Nassau, 1892]; Saunders, "Social History," 131–32).
55. M. G. Smith, *West Indian Family Structure* (Seattle: University of Washington Press, 1962), 247, 260; Otterbein, *Andros Islanders*, 67–84, 106; La Flamme, "Green Turtle Cay," 106; Saunders, "Social History," 131–33.
56. *Nassau Times*, September 1874.
57. *Nassau Quarterly Mission Papers* 3 (June 1888): 52.
58. Powles, *Land of the Pink Pearl*, 238.
59. Roscow Shedden, *Ups and Downs in a West Indian Diocese* (London: A. R. Mowbray, 1927), 144–45. Father F. Barrow Matthews collected a great deal of information on obeah and witchcraft from Cat Island and Andros, where he served as Anglican priest for many years (ibid., 145–50).
60. Amelia Defries, *In a Forgotten Colony, Being Some Studies in Nassau and at Grand Bahama*

During 1916 (Nassau: *Nassau Guardian*, 1916), 81–86; Albury, *Man-O-War*, 82–83; Savashinsky, *Strangers No More*, 159–69; Saunders, "Social History," 134–35.

61. Otterbein, *Andros Islanders*, 61–63. Blacks at Green Turtle Cay believed that if a menstruating woman entered the room occupied by a newborn infant, the child's umbilical cord would not heal properly (LaFlamme, "Green Turtle Cay," 172–73; Saunders, "Social History," 135).

62. Neville Chamberlain to Ida Chamberlain, Andros, December 25, 1893, Neville Chamberlain Papers, I/16/2/24, University of Birmingham Library; *Nassau Quarterly Mission Papers* 7 (December 1892): 89.

63. *Nassau Guardian*, January 1, 1897.

64. Bahamas Archives, *Junkanoo* (Nassau, 1978), 15.

65. *Nassau Quarterly Mission Papers* 3 (September 1888): 54; Charles L. Edwards, *Bahama Songs and Stories* (1895; rpt. New York, 1942), 18, 90; Saunders, "Social History," 138–39.

66. Powles, *Land of the Pink Pearl*, 207.

67. Joyce Mary Lumsden, "Robert Love and Jamaica Politics" (Ph.D. dissertation, University of the West Indies, Jamaica, 1987); Donn Selhorn, "The Bahamian Pioneer of Broadway: Bert Williams, Comic Legend," *Bahamas Handbook and Businessman's Annual, 1996* (Nassau: Dupuch, 1995); James Weldon Johnson, *Along This Way* (New York: Viking, 1933), cited in Lumsden, "Robert Love," 28–29.

68. Powles, *Land of the Pink Pearl*, 223.

69. *Nassau Guardian*, August 5, 1885.

Chapter 6

1. Colin A. Hughes, *Race and Politics in the Bahamas* (St. Lucia: University of Queensland Press, 1981); see below, Chapter 9 and 10.

2. *Report on the Census of the Bahama Islands, Taken on the 14th. April, 1901* (Nassau: *Nassau Guardian*, 1901).

3. One apparent anomaly is that while Cat Island and other islands that were sources of emigration had a superfluity of females above the Bahamian average of 115:100 because a majority of the migrants were male (Cat Island 123:100, Exuma 125:100, Long Island 121:100), the migrant-receiving islands of Andros and Inagua each had almost equal numbers of males and females (Andros 99:100, Inagua 94:100). This may indicate that whereas emigration from the Bahamas was overwhelmingly male and temporary, much if not most migration within the Bahamas occurred in family units and was more permanent.

4. In the 1911 census it was noted that widows outnumbered widowers by three to one and in 1921 (and 1931) that the disparity had risen to four to one.

5. The one positive health indicator in the 1901 census was that 30,382 persons were recorded as having been vaccinated against smallpox, up from 28,633 in 1891. Somewhat contrary to the bleak and slanted picture provided by Clement Penrose in 1905, the totals of those listed as deaf and dumb, blind, imbecile or idiot, and lunatic were 27, 135, 110, and 59 respectively, and the numbers from the allegedly inbred white settlements of Abaco and northern Eleuthera were not noticeably higher than average (*Report on the 1901 Census*, 6). See above, Chapter 5.

6. *Report on the 1901 Census*, 7.

7. The number of African-born, though, exceeded Brook's expectations. Those listed in the 1911 census totaled 68, in the 1921 census 20, and in the 1931 census 5—seventy-one years after the last liberated Africans were landed on the Bahamas. It is not known for certain when the last survivor of the Bahamian liberated Africans died, but it was probably in the mid-1930s.

8. *Report on the Census of the Bahama Islands on the 2nd April, 1911* (Nassau: *Nassau Guardian*, 1911).

9. *Report on the Census of the Bahama Islands Taken on the 24th April, 1921* (Nassau: *Nassau*

Guardian, 1921); *Report on the Census of the Bahama Islands Taken on the 26th April, 1931* (Nassau: *Nassau Guardian*, 1931).

10. See above, Table 4, and below, Table 8.

11. That is, 30,998 females to 30,721 males (*Commonwealth of the Bahamas: Statistical Abstract, 1980* [Nassau: Department of Statistics, 1980], 33). See below, Table 8.

12. The Moyne Commission, convened because of the riots in the sugar colonies between 1935 and 1938, hardly considered either the Bahamas or Bermuda, and the palliative measures initiated almost immediately in the Caribbean colonies had virtually no effect on the two relatively quiescent Atlantic colonies.

13. Both were English-born. Albert Woods, near retirement in 1943, had been appointed the first headmaster of the Government High School in 1925 (and was for some time the only teacher there). John A. Hughes, who migrated to the Bahamas in the 1930s, rose from being a district commissioner in several islands to chief Out Island commissioner during World War II. He was the father of Colin A. Hughes, author of the important study *Race Politics in the Bahamas* (1981). In August 1943, Albert Woods recommended that "at least one year before the next Census, an inquiry be made to ascertain whether the present arrangements for taking the Census, which were devised in 1911, meet the requirements of changed conditions." No changes having been made in the interim, John Hughes repeated Woods's recommendations almost verbatim in May 1954 and added that "it should be noted that Dr. R. R. Kuczynski in 'A Demographic Survey of the British Colonial Empire, Volume III, The West Indies and American Territories,' suggests the desirability of having the census forms tabulated and analyzed by a Central Office as was the case with the other West Indian colonies which took a census in 1946" (*Report on the Census of the Bahama Islands Taken on the 25th April 1943* [Nassau: *Nassau Guardian*, 1943], 18); *Report on the Census of the Bahama Islands 1953* [Nassau, 1954], 10).

14. Figures arrived at by estimating annual births as totals in 0 to 4 age bracket in each census plus 10 percent, divided by five; estimating median total populations and total nubile females in five-year segments by projections from 1953, 1943, and 1931 census totals for total population and females in cohorts from age 15 to 39.

15. An additional factor was the undoubted advantage for admission into the United States of having "white" entered under the heading "race" in passports. Bahamians who could realistically "pass" as whites often had their passports altered accordingly, whereas those who were unequivocally nonwhites had no choice but to enter "Negro." As in the United States, families were sometimes damagingly split by such calculated equivocations.

16. The large amount of data, among other things, accounts for the fact that the official reports on the censuses were progressively more delayed each decade and that data from the 1990 census had still not appeared by the end of 1994. One of the most problematic areas was also one of the most vital—the prediction of future population trends. See below, Chapter 11.

17. The Project finally ended in 1966. See below, Chapters 9 and 10.

18. The total of immigrants was made up to 26,926 by the inclusion of 3,541 persons born abroad—overwhelmingly in the United States—who were able to establish Bahamian nationality.

19. See below, Chapter 13.

20. The official excess of registered births over deaths would have produced a 1963 population total of 117,000 rather than 130,000. The increase in the number of immigrants was about 10,000 so, given that the number of deaths was likely to have been accurate, it seems that the number of births may have been undercounted by some 500 a year. The figures have been arrived at by using these assumptions and projections that give a median population between 1953 and 1970 of 120,000, of whom 19.6 percent would have been females aged fifteen to forty.

21. Michael Craton and Gail Saunders, *Islanders in the Stream: A History of the Bahamian People, Volume One: From Aboriginal Times to the End of Slavery* (Athens: University of Georgia Press, 1992), 271–76. The late slave rate of increase, of course, would have been even greater

but for the much higher rate of infant mortality then. The slave crude birthrate was as high as 44.6 per thousand between 1831 and 1834, compared with 1953–1970 rates of around 42.0 per thousand.

22. See below, Chapter 11.

23. *Economic and Social Progress in Latin America: 1989 Report* (Washington, D.C.: Inter-American Development Bank, 1980), Table B1, 463. The GDP of the Bahamas increased proportionately less rapidly than that of either Barbados or Jamaica and no faster than Trinidad between 1960 and 1970, and in the following decade, when Barbados made a small improvement and Trinidad nearly doubled, the Bahamas made a small decline. Haiti fell even lower by 1970 from its pitiful 1960 level, making a painfully small improvement by 1980, which it subsequently lost once more. In 1988, Haiti's annual per capita GNP, at U.S.$319, was lower than in 1960 and only 2.8 percent of the Bahamas's figure of U.S.$11,317.

24. Ibid.; Michael Craton, *A History of the Bahamas*, 3d ed. (Waterloo: San Salvador Press, 1986), 274; Hughes, *Race and Politics in the Bahamas*, 83.

Chapter 7

1. The *Nassau Guardian* had actually printed and published a *Bahamas Handbook* as early as 1849, which went through many editions and was a hardcover publication by 1876. Several official government publications printed at the *Guardian* before 1900 may also qualify as books. Northcroft's personal claim to priority might also have been challenged, at least by Louis Diston Powles, author of the indispensable *Land of the Pink Pearl* (London, 1888). Powles spent considerable time in the Bahamas and probably visited as many islands. Northcroft himself cited several previous books, all published abroad, and specially praised the bibliography in Rev. George Lester's *In Sunny Lands* (London, 1897). See G. J. H. Northcroft, *Sketches of Summerland* (Nassau, 1880), ix, 305–9.

2. The bank's officers were as follows: president and managing director, Hon. R. H. Sawyer; vice-president, A. T. Holmes; cashier, J. F. W. Turtle; directors, Hon. Joseph Brown, Hon. J. B. Albury M.D., J. W. Culmer, D. A. Brice, and R. N. Musgrove. For the demise of the bank in 1916 and the temporary disgrace of several of these officers, see below, text at note 72.

3. Edwin Charles Moseley (1812–85) had come to the Bahamas in 1837 and first worked on the *Bahama Argus*. After a stint as a teacher at the private King's College, he founded the *Nassau Guardian* in 1844. He edited the paper until his death forty-one years later, by which time it held a virtual monopoly of government printing and was established as the conservative voice of Bay Street. In 1887, Alfred Edwin Moseley took over the editorship from his elder brother, handing it down to his redoubtable daughter Mary Moseley (1878–1960) in 1904, who remained editor and publisher in the 1950s (Etienne Dupuch, *The Tribune Story* [London: Benn, 1967], 112–13). After the defeat of Bay Street in 1967, the *Guardian* floundered until it was taken over by PLP interests and became once more the semiofficial organ of the (now black) ruling party.

4. Most of the Cuban families that settled in Nassau, such as the Cancinos, Vargases, and De Gregorys, arrived in the 1890s. Similarly, the influx of Greeks, pioneered by the Damianos family in the late 1880s, occurred mainly in the 1890s with the arrival of spongers from the island of Kalymnos (Gail Saunders, "The Social History of the Bahamas, 1890–1953" [Ph.D. dissertation, University of Waterloo, 1985], 54, n. 138). For the Syrian pedlars in Eleuthera, see Northcroft, *Sketches of Summerland*, 218. It is likely that the Solomon family, important Bay Streeters in the twentieth century, were of Sephardic origin, but they were well-rooted in Harbour Island by the end of the nineteenth century (Benson McDermott, "Opinionated, Warm-Hearted, Autocratic, Patriotic: Kenneth Solomon Served and Ruled the Bahamas," *Bahamas Handbook and Businessman's Annual, 1983* [Nassau: Dupuch Publications, 1983]).

5. "Pages from a Veteran's Note-Book: Some Account of the Career of Mr. J. F. Coonley," *Wilson's Photographic Magazine* 44 (March 1907): 105–8. The parents of J. O. Sands moved from Rock Sound, Eleuthera, to Nassau in the 1890s so that the children would have a better

education. Sands set up shop in the premises of the Masonic Building vacated by Coonley. Sadly for one who made his living by recording the visual world, Sands's career as a photographer was ended by failing eyesight and he died almost blind. Considerably more tragic, though, was Fred Armbrister, an even more talented photographer, a near-white haunted by exclusion from white society, who died in the Nassau asylum in the 1950s (McDermott, "Opinionated," 22).

6. Northcroft himself probably fell into both of the former categories. In an ingratiating chapter titled "The Social Life of Nassau," he wrote, "With the smiling carelessness, the easy inconsequence, and the love of the spectacular which characterise the 'junior race' they live and laugh, work and play together—amusing or annoying by turns but always interesting to the unprejudiced eye and sympathetic ear" (*Sketches of Summerland*, 67). For early postcards, see Shelley Boyd Malone and Richard Campbell Roberts, *Nostalgic Nassau: Picture Postcards, 1900–1940* (Nassau: Nassau Nostalgia, 1991).

7. 3 and 4 Geo. V, c. 7, 1913, Act for Establishing Telegraphic Communications between the Colony and parts beyond the limits of the Colony; Saunders, "Social History," 185.

8. 5 and 6 Edward VII, c. 22, 1906; *Colonial Annual Reports, Bahamas, 1918–1919*, C.O. 23/286, 84; *Bahamas Almanack, 1911*, 89; Haddon-Smith to Harcourt, July 29, 1913, C.O. 23/272, 171; Allardyce to Bonar Law, August 25, 1916, C.O. 23/277, 462; Saunders, "Social History," 186–87.

9. 7 Edward VII, c. 8, 1907, Act to provide Electric Light and Electrical Energy for the City of Nassau and its Suburbs; *Nassau Guardian*, June 17, 1909; Saunders, "Social History," 187–88; *Colonial Annual Reports, Bahama Islands, 1946* (London: HMSO, 1947), 30–31.

10. *Nassau Tribune*, September 16, 1911; "Proposals for a Modern Electric Light and Power Plant," *Votes of the House of Assembly, 1920*, Appendix B, 3–5; Bahamas No. 13 of 1923, Act to Provide for the Control of the Ice House and to Regulate the Supply and Sale of Ice; Saunders, "Social History," 188–89.

11. *Nassau Tribune*, January 3, 5, 1911; 2 and 3 Geo. V, c. 8, 1912; *Strombus Magazine* 1 (February 1913): 1; Saunders, "Social History," 188.

12. Saunders, "Social History," 225, n. 88.

13. Interview with Herbert McKinney, November 8, 1975, ibid., 189–90; Malone and Roberts, *Nostalgic Nassau*, 59.

14. 7 and 8 Edward VII, c. 31, 1908, Act Regulating the Law as to Motor Cars in the Island of New Providence. The license fee for private cars, not let out for hire, was reduced to £11 a year in 1913. The fee for motorcycles was five shillings a year. See *Nassau Tribune*, January 4, 1911; *Strombus Magazine* 1 (February 1913): 1; Saunders, "Social History," 190.

15. Steve Dodge, *Abaco: The History of an Out Island and Its Cays* (Miami: Tropic Isles, 1983), 83–86; *Colonial Annual Reports, Bahamas, 1916–1917*; Saunders, "Social History," 182.

16. Out Island Commissioner's Reports, Cherokee Sound, Abaco, 1912; Wesleyan Methodist Missionary Society Papers, Foreign Field VII, 1910–11, February 1911, 167 (hereafter WMMS), School of Oriental and African Studies, London; Saunders, "Social History," 182; Dodge, *Abaco*, 84.

17. Haddon-Smith to Harcourt, January 1, 1914, C.O. 23/273, 4–7; *Nassau Tribune*, December 17, 1913; *Colonial Annual Reports, Bahamas, 1913–14*, 20; Asa Paine, General Manager, Bahamas Timber Company to Haddon-Smith, and Bernard L. Wyatt to Commandant R. H. Crawford, December 21, 1913, C.O. 23/273, 8, 9; Saunders, "Social History," 183.

18. See above, Chapter 3.

19. *Colonial Annual Reports, Bahamas, 1916–1918*, 13; Saunders, "Social History," 183; Dodge, *Abaco*, 85–87, 98–103. Also see below, Chapter 13.

20. See above, Chapter 5.

21. Bayley to Newcastle, April 25, 1860, No. 38, C.O. 23/163, quoted in Howard Johnson, "Late Nineteenth and Early Twentieth Century Labour Migration to Florida," in *The Bahamas in Slavery and Freedom* (Kingston: Ian Randle, and London: James Currey, 1991), 164; Philip Cash, Shirley Gordon, and Gail Saunders, eds., *Sources of Bahamian History* (London: Macmillan Caribbean, 1991), 245.

22. As in the mixed settlements of the Bahamas Out Islands, much of the tension stemmed from the desire of white Methodists to have segregated churches. One Methodist missionary reported to London in June 1893 that he had turned down a request from the whites in the recent synod: "Our church here and throughout the world recognises no colour lines. This stand on our part in the South, where colour feeling runs so high, bore good fruit a few years ago in Key West, in a race war. Not one of our Coloured members had any part or lot in it. We recognise in our church that colour does not indicate character. . . . We are not, however, loved and respected on this account" (Missionary, Key West to WMMS, June 9, 1893, quoted in Cash, Gordon, and Saunders, eds., *Sources of Bahamian History*, 96–97).

23. Blake to Stanley, August 8, 1885, C.O. 23/226; Johnson, "Labour Migration to Florida," 164.

24. One factor, as in Nassau, was the competitive entry of Greeks into the sponge industry, the center for which came to be Tarpon Springs on the Florida Gulf Coast, some three hundred miles to the north of Key West. Some Bahamians, both from Key West and from the Bahamas, were involved as navvies in the construction of the railroad down the Florida Keys from 1905 to 1912 (Methodist Minister, Key West to WMMS, May 8, 1907, in Cash, Gordon, and Saunders, eds., *Sources of Bahamian History*, 98).

25. Arva Moore Parks, *Miami: The Magic City* (Tulsa: Continental Heritage Press, 1981), 87–88; speech of Governor Grey-Wilson, February 5, 1907, *Votes of Legislative Council*, February 5–July 8, 1907, 8; letter from "Twist-Back," *Nassau Tribune*, January 19, 1911; Johnson, "Labour Migration to Florida," 167.

26. Johnson, "Labour Migration to Florida," 163, 171.

27. British Ambassador, Washington, to Colonial Office, April 13, 1911, in Cash, Gordon, and Saunders, eds., *Sources of Bahamian History*, 161.

28. Grey-Wilson to House of Assembly, October 1911, ibid., 257.

29. The U.S. census of 1910 reported that the black population of Miami was five thousand, of whom thirty-five hundred were British West Indians. See Johnson, "Labour Migration to Florida," 171–72; Raymond A. Mohl, "The Settlement of Blacks in South Florida," in *South Florida: The Winds of Change*, ed. Thomas D. Boswell (Miami: Association of American Geographers, 1991), 112–39.

30. Arva Moore Parks, "The History of Coconut Grove, Florida, 1821–1925" (M.A. thesis, University of Miami, 1971); Mohl, "Settlement of Blacks in South Florida," 121–24. See also L. Smith, "Coconut Grove: Bahamian Roots in Florida," *Nassau Tribune*, October 12, 1977.

31. As early as 1898 a Bahamian labor migrant had petitioned Queen Victoria from Miami, writing, "Some of our number have been lynched and others have had mock trials and [been] hanged or imprisoned unjustly—and we live in fear of mob violence from the southern white element." After Bahamians had complained of police violence in Key West and Miami in 1907, Ambassador James Bryce urged the Foreign Office to investigate but admitted to Foreign Minister Sir Edward Grey that "coloured people are not treated with much consideration. . . . Cases such as the present are unfortunately so frequent as to excite no censure in the Southern States." In 1927, when a Bahamian had been shot by a policemen after a traffic arrest, the British government demanded compensation for the victim's family. See *Nassau Tribune*, July 8, 1931; R. A. Mohl, "Shadows in the Sunshine: Race and Ethnicity in Miami," *Tequesta* 49 (1989): 63–80; Mohl, "Settlement of Blacks in South Florida," 127–28.

32. Methodist District Chairman to WMMS, July 1, 1919, and Methodist Minister for Florida to WMMS, May 26, 1921, in Cash, Gordon, and Saunders, eds., *Sources of Bahamian History*, 99. In 1921, an FBI agent reported that most of the one thousand UNIA members in Miami were Bahamians, who "bitterly resent the color line as drawn in Florida." See Mohl, "Settlement of Blacks in South Florida," 128; Robert A. Hill, ed., *The Marcus Garvey and Universal Negro Improvement Association Papers*, 9 vols. (Berkeley: University of California Press, 1983–95), 3:513–15; 4:594–95.

33. *Nassau Tribune*, August 14, 1911; Zora Neale Hurston, "The Florida Negro" (Florida Writers Project, n.d.), 12, 22; Hurston, *Dust Tracks on a Road: An Autobiography* (Philadelphia: Lippincott, 1942); Mohl, "Settlement of Blacks in South Florida," 121–22.

34. Johnson, "Labour Migration to Florida," 171.

35. Appendix to *Votes of the Legislative Council* (January 11–June 6, 1910), 86; Johnson, "Labour Migration to Florida," 174–75.

36. See below, Chapter 11.

37. Out Island Commissioners' Reports, the Bight, Cat Island, 1912, Bahamas Archives; Johnson, "Labour Migration to Florida," 175.

38. Appendix to *Votes of the Legislative Council* (February 15, 1921–January 16, 1922), 275; Johnson, "Labour Migration to Florida," 170.

39. 5 and 6 Edward VII, c. 7. At the height of the stevedoring traffic there was a small hospital at Mathew Town, Inagua, with ten beds, though in 1912 the resident medical officer asked for a transfer out of the colony halfway through his contract, complaining of conditions there, as well as his lack of chances for promotion in the Bahamas (Hart-Bennett to Harcourt, November 26, 1912, C.O. 23/270, 222; Saunders, "Social History," 191).

40. Rev. Henderson to Perkins, June 24, 1904, WMMS; Medical Report, 1914, enclosed in Hart-Bennett to Harcourt, April 7, 1915, C.O. 23/275, 211–12; Pharmacy Act, 3 and 4 George V, c. 18 (1918); Evans W. Cottman with Wyatt Blassingame, *Out Island Doctor* (London: Hodder and Stoughton, 1963).

41. The lunatic asylum in particular was referred to by Governor Grey-Wilson in 1912 as "accommodation of the poorest class of negroes." Of the eighteen cases of leprosy identified in 1911, only seven persons were accommodated in the leprosarium. One was at home elsewhere in New Providence, two each in Abaco, Acklins, and Inagua, and three in San Salvador. The Leprosy Act of 1913 attempted a greater degree of control, but as late as 1920, the Health Report noted that even those lepers admitted to the hospital "came and went as they pleased" (*Report on the Census, 1911;* Grey-Wilson to Harcourt, January 2, 1912, C.O. 23/269, 9; Leper Act, 3 and 4 Geo V, c. 19 [1913]; Grant to Milner, October 6, 1920, C.O. 23/287, 24; Saunders, "Social History," 193–94).

42. Saunders, "Social History," 192–96; Medical Department Act, 1 and 2 Geo V, c. 7 (1911); Public Health Act, No. 17 of 1914; E. Hair to English Nursing Association, January 21, 1914, C.O. 23/274, 566.

43. Quarantine regulations had actually been instituted as early as 1794 by the Act of 35 Geo III, c. 1, but they were greatly tightened in the mid-nineteenth century. As mentioned in Chapter 6, the number vaccinated by 1911 was 35,400, an increase of over 5,000 since 1901. See Grey-Wilson to Elgin, March 28, 1906, C.O. 23/261, 63–64; *Report on the Census, 1911;* Hart-Bennett to Harcourt, March 12, 1915, C.O. 23/275, 155–57; Medical Report, 1914, enclosed in Hart-Bennett to Harcourt, April 7, 1915, C.O. 23/275, 218–22; *Sanitary Regulations, Board of Health, April 11, 1872* (Nassau, 1872); Saunders, "Social History," 192–95.

44. Saunders, "Social History," 195–96.

45. Ibid. For the section of the act applying to the trades, the "infectious diseases" listed were plague, smallpox, yellow fever, cholera, diphtheria, typhoid, scarlet fever, typhus, and puerperal fever. Elsewhere, the following infectious diseases were included: scarlatina, mumps, measles, German measles, whooping cough, hydrophobia trachoma, relapsing fever, dysentery, cerebro-spinal fever, poliomyelitis, influenza, and pneumonia.

46. As shown by the lists in note 45, neither tuberculosis nor VD was specifically listed as an infectious disease in the 1914 act (nor was leprosy). As the Medical Report for 1914 made clear, however, the general rules laid down by the act meant that those suffering from tuberculosis, and probably also VD, were effectively barred from the listed trades and from school, if not also bound to be committed to medical care. Leprosy was so evident a disease that formal notification was hardly necessary, though it was presumably enforced by the separate Leprosy Act of 1913. The strict notifiability of VD, though required by law in the 1940s, has remained a touchy question right up to the present, never fully enforced, even with guaranteed confidentiality. See *Medical Report, 1912, Medical Report, 1914,* C.O. 23/271, 272, C.O. 23/275, 209–10; Saunders, "Social History," 196–98.

47. Many cases of VD had previously gone undetected. It should be remembered that clinical detection of the spirochetes of syphilis was made possible by the work of Schaudin and

Wasserman between 1905 and 1906. See Haddon-Smith to Harcourt, June 17, 1913, March 11, 1914, C.O. 23/271, 263–68, 23/273, 143–47; Allardyce to Macnaughten, July 4, 1917, C.O. 23/280, 462; *Medical Report, 1919–1920* in Grant to Milner, October 6, 1920, C.O. 23/287, 16–18; Saunders, "Social History," 196–97.

48. *Report of the Commission on Venereal Diseases* (Nassau: *Nassau Guardian*, 1918); Immoral Traffic Act, 4 Geo V, c. 13 (1914). An act was passed in 1919 (9 and 10 Geo V, c. 12) attempting to regulate dance halls. See Saunders, "Social History," 197–98.

49. *Report of the Commission on Venereal Diseases*, 13. At least twenty-eight men who volunteered for the third Bahamian contingent in 1916 did not pass the medical examination (*Nassau Guardian*, May 10, 1916).

50. Geo V, c.1, and 5 Geo V, c.2; Frank Holmes, *The Bahamas in the Great War* (Nassau: *Tribune*, 1924); Haddon-Smith to Harcourt, August 13, 1914, C.O. 23/274, 4–6; *Nassau Guardian*, August 7, 8, 1914. The Bahamas chapter of the IODE, an organization born in anglophone Canada, was founded in 1901. It flourished until long after World War II, its meeting hall being now the home of the Bahamas Historical Society (Saunders, "Social History," 198–99).

51. Saunders, "Social History," 199–200. The English official was R. H. Crawford, the two local whites G. M. Cole and D. S. Moseley, the colored S. A. Dillett, and the black L. W. Young (*Nassau Tribune*, September 22, November 24, 1914; Haddon-Smith to Harcourt, December 16, 1914, C.O. 23/274, 394–95; Holmes, *Great War*, 109).

52. *Nassau Tribune*, October 17, November 7, 1914. Mary Moseley, who owned the *Guardian* from 1907 until 1952, actually went to England to pursue war work, spearheading the Ladies' Committee of the West Indian Contingent. For this she was rewarded with the MBE after the war. Gilbert Dupuch (1891–1959) was the son of Leon Dupuch, founder of the *Tribune*, who had died earlier in 1914. Trained as a painter and printer in Montreal, Leon founded the short-lived *Strombus Magazine* and narrowly kept the *Tribune* afloat, until bought out by his younger brother Etienne. See Saunders, "Social History," 200, 231–32; Dupuch, *Tribune Story*, 23–27.

53. Etienne Dupuch, *A Salute to Friend and Foe: My Battles, Sieges and Fortunes* (Nassau: *Tribune*, 1982), 31–32.

54. Allardyce to Bonar Law, August 9, 1915, Asquith to Bonar Law, June 16, 1915, C.O. 23/276, 49–53, 408; Dupuch, *Salute to Friend and Foe*, 64; *Nassau Guardian*, August 5, 1915; Saunders, "Social History," 200–201.

55. Saunders, "Social History," 201–2, 233. Except for William Sparkman—an Englishman who had drifted into Nassau, joined a later contingent, was made sergeant, and had his head blown off at Passchendaele—these seem to have been the only whites among the 486 recruits sent to Jamaica (Dupuch, *Salute to Friend and Foe*, 59).

56. Dupuch, *Salute to Friend and Foe*, 34; *Nassau Guardian*, September 11, 1915.

57. Holmes, *Great War*, 122; *Nassau Guardian*, November 24, 1915, May 10, August 5, 1916. Later contingents sailed to Jamaica on the schooner *Zelleas*, lent by a Jamaican rum merchant settled in Nassau, Horace Myers, who was rewarded after the war with an MBE and a piece of plate donated by the Bahamas legislature (Dupuch, *Salute to Friend and Foe*, 34).

58. Hart-Bennett to Harcourt, February 23, 1915, C.O. 23/275, 117; Allardyce to Bonar Law, August 25, 1916, C.O. 23/277, 466. Warships visiting Nassau included HMSS *Essex* in October 1914, *Sydney* in May 1915, and *Berwick* in September 1916. The lighting restrictions were put into effect late in 1916 and were lifted for a time during the 1917 winter season (Holmes, *Great War*, 155–60; Saunders, "Social History," 202–4).

59. Commissioner Cleare at Crooked Island had also reported in December 1917 that "never in the history of the islands has there been such a turning to the soil as in the year 1917" (Allardyce to Long, February 5, 1918, C.O. 23/282, 83–92).

60. Allardyce to British Embassy, Washington, December 11, 1917, Allardyce to Long, January 26, 1918, C.O. 23/282, 37–38; Holmes, *Great War*, 177.

61. Allardyce to Long, January 26, February 13, 1918, C.O. 23/282, 46, 236. See also *Votes of the House of Assembly*, January 24, 1918; Hart-Bennett to Long (Confidential), January 19, 1918, C.O. 23/282, 14–15; War Contingent Act, No. 15 of 1916; Saunders, "Social History," 204.

62. Saunders, "Social History," 214–15. The Charleston facilities were expanded because of the needs of the American expeditionary force sent to Europe. A government proclamation in July 1918 allowed the Mason and Hanger company to recruit directly in the Bahamas (*Nassau Guardian*, August 21, 24, 1918; Allardyce to Long, July 31, August 24, 1918, C.O. 23/283, 124–26, 163). Father Langton, an Anglican priest, and Phillip Bailey, a Methodist minister, were sent to Charleston by the Bahamian government generally to assist the men and act as their "guide, philosopher and friend." They especially helped the men with their remittances home (*Nassau Quarterly Mission Papers, 1888–1918* 33 [December 1918]: 70).

63. Allardyce to Long (Confidential), July 2, 1917, C.O. 23/280, 192–208; Saunders, "Social History," 205–6.

64. Dupuch, *Salute to Friend and Foe*, 31–106; Dupuch, *Tribune Story.*

65. Dupuch, *Salute to Friend and Foe*, 31–72.

66. Ibid., 54–55.

67. Ibid., 778–79. Private Johnny Demeritte did not return to Nassau until December 1921. See *Nassau Guardian*, December 6, 1921; Colin A. Hughes, *Race and Politics in the Bahamas* (St. Lucia: Queensland University Press, 1981), 14.

68. Dupuch, *Salute to Friend and Foe*, 100.

69. Ibid., 99–106; Dupuch, *Tribune Story*, 101–2.

70. Dupuch, *Tribune Story*, 101–2; Dupuch, *Salute to Friend and Foe*, 185–208.

71. Allardyce to Long (Confidential), July 28, 1917, March 4, November 25, 1918, C.O. 23/280, 326–27, 23/282, 248–50, 23/283, 254; Saunders, "Social History," 212, 237 n. 304.

72. The cashier of the bank, R. W. Turtle, was charged with larceny and falsification of accounts and sentenced to seven years in jail. The directors and auditors were simply fined, in amounts from £75 to £150. W. C. B. Johnson, the current owner of the J. S. Johnson sisal, tomato, and pineapple cultivation and canning operation, was one of the principal employers of labor in New Providence. See Saunders, "Social History," 212, 237 n. 305; Benson McDermott, "L. W. Young: Formidable Force from Fox Hill," *Bahamas Handbook, 1984*, 24–28.

73. This letter, and another echoing it, drew a complaint of libel from the American consul general in Nassau, Mr. Doty. The editor of the *Guardian*, D. S. D. Mosely, took the usual editorial way out: an apology, a reminder that his paper did not necessarily endorse the opinions of its correspondents, and an announcement that the matter was now closed (*Nassau Guardian*, November 3, 7, 1917; Allardyce to Long [Confidential], October 29, 1917, C.O. 23/281, 53; Saunders, "Social History," 213).

74. Saunders, "Social History," 215–16, 282. Archdeacon Irwin, who had been ordained in Nassau, had ministered at St. Agnes in Coconut Grove, Miami, since 1915. Accused of preaching equality to Negroes, he was seized on July 17, 1921, by eight masked men, gagged, handcuffed, whipped, tarred and feathered, and dumped out of a speeding car. Threatened with death if he did not leave Miami within forty-eight hours, he refused to comply. See *Miami Herald*, July 18, 19, 1921; *Nassau Guardian*, July 21, 1921; E. D. Cronon, *Black Moses: The Story of Marcus Garvey and the Universal Negro Improvement Association* (Madison: University of Wisconsin Press, 1955), 32–33; Hill, ed., *Marcus Garvey and Universal Negro Improvement Association Papers*, 3:145, 470.

75. Minister of Florida, May 26, 1921, WMMS, quoted in Cash, Gordon, and Saunders, eds., *Sources of Bahamian History*, 99.

76. Killbridge to Brunet, Nassau, July 25, 1921, WMMS, ibid.; Saunders, "Social History," 216.

77. *Nassau Guardian*, January 14–24, April 21, 1920; Johnson, "Labour Migration to Florida," 172, 179, nn. 70, 71.

78. Saunders, "Social History," 219.

Chapter 8

1. Sir Bede Clifford, *Proconsul: Being Incidents in the Life and Career of the Honourable Sir Bede Clifford, GCMG, CB, MVO* (London: Evans Bros., 1964), 191; Phillip Cash, "Colonial Policies

and Outside Influences: A Study of Bahamian History, 1919–1947" (M.A. thesis, University of Wales, 1979). The Eighteenth Amendment to the United States Constitution, prohibiting "the manufacture, sale or transportation of intoxicating liquors within, the importation thereof into, or the exportation thereof from the United States and all territory subject to the jurisdiction thereof, for beverage purposes," was ratified in January 1919, requiring concurrent federal and state legislation to become operative within a year. The Volstead Act, passed in December 1919 to become effective at the beginning of 1920, was that legislation. The Eighteenth Amendment was repealed by the Twenty-first Amendment, coming into effect December 5, 1933.

2. *Colonial Reports, Bahamas, 1919–1920* (Nassau: Bahamas Government, 1920), 40; Gail Saunders, "The Social History of the Bahamas, 1890–1953" (Ph.D. dissertation, University of Waterloo, 1985), 242.

3. Michael Craton, *A History of the Bahamas*, 3d ed. (Waterloo: San Salvador Press, 1986), 254; *Statute Law of the Bahamas, 1929*, Vol. 2, C. 106; *Votes of the House of Assembly, 1923* (Nassau: *Nassau Guardian*, 1923), 428.

4. *The Times*, March 3, 1920.

5. *Bahamas Blue Books*, 1919–1920, 1923–1924; Cash, "Colonial Policies," 59, 140; Saunders, "Social History," 243–44; Craton, *History of the Bahamas*, 250–52.

6. Hugh McLachlan Bell, *Bahamas: Isles of June* (New York: Robert M. McBride, 1934), 190.

7. Few of the advertisers in G. J. H. Northcott's *Sketches of Summerland* (Nassau: *Guardian*, 1900) advertised liquor, and then incidentally. Yet despite the editor's disapprobation of the liquor business, nine of the advertisers in Mary Moseley's *Bahamas Handbook* (Nassau: *Guardian*, 1926) gave it as their chief stock-in-trade. Six were white Bahamians; three, recent British or American immigrants. See Craton, *History of the Bahamas*, 254; Cash, "Colonial Policies," 82.

8. Campbell to Geddes, July 22, Geddes to Curzon, August 4, 1922, F.O. 371/5699; Cordeaux to Churchill, October 21, 1921, F.O. 371/2274; Hughes to Geddes, June 26, 1922, C.O. 23/292, Misc.; Cash, "Colonial Policies," 67–72; Saunders, "Social History," 245.

9. Cordeaux to Churchill, October 3, 1921, Secret, C.O. 23/289, 212–16; Orr to Amery, September 3, 1927, Secret, C.O. 23/344; Saunders, "Social History," 245, 249. In 1926, in response to U.S. complaints about bootlegging practices and local countercomplaints about the activities of the U.S. Coast Guard within Bahamian waters, the Foreign Office held an internal inquiry, under the chairmanship of Lord Vansittart, though inconclusively. See Sir Alan C. Burns, *Colonial Civil Servant* (London: Allen & Unwin, 1949), 87.

10. Chilton to Foreign Office, May 11, 1921, F.O. 371/5699; Cash, "Colonial Policies," 61–62.

11. Hughes to Geddes, June 26, 1922, C.O. 23/292, Misc.; Chamberlain to Amery, March 24, 1927, Private, C.O. 23/344; Saunders, "Social History," 250, 293 n. 75.

12. Hughes to Geddes, June 26, 1922, C.O. 23/292, Misc.; Grant to Churchill, August 31, 1922, Confidential, C.O. 23/291, 215; Nellie Symonette to Devonshire, December 29, 1923, C.O. 23/294, Misc. Roland Symonette, who had begun his career as an ordinary seaman, used his bootlegging profits successively to buy shares in a liquor business (originally Rost and Symonette, later Robertson and Symonette), to found the Symonette Shipyard (at first on Hog Island, later on East Bay Street), to build the Rozelda (later Carlton House) Hotel (in 1929), and to develop an extensive business in real estate, construction, and road building. He was first elected to the House of Assembly in 1925 (Saunders, "Social History," 276).

13. Cordeaux to Geddes, April 2, 1923, C.O. 23/294, Misc. The directors of the British Transportation and Trading Company were all American subjects, save for Bruce K. Thompson, later a successful liquor merchant. See Frederick Van de Water, *The Real McCoy* (New York: Doubleday, 1933), 12–46; *Nassau Tribune*, December 16, 1983; Saunders, "Social History," 246–47.

14. Bell, *Bahamas*, 186; Van de Water, *Real McCoy*, 93–94; Cash, "Colonial Policies," 65.

15. *Nassau Guardian*, September 1, 19, 1921, September 14, 1922, January 13, 1923; Bell, *Bahamas*, 184–86; *Nassau Tribune*, January 22, 1925, February 10, September 11, 1926.

16. Bell, *Bahamas*, 192–93; Craton, *History of the Bahamas*, 252.

17. *Colonial Annual Report, Bahamas 1928* (Nassau: Bahamas Government, 1928); *Colonial Annual Reports, Bahama Islands, 1946* (London: HMSO, 1947), 30–32.

18. *Nassau Guardian*, September 30, 1922, May 19, 1923; *Year Book of the West Indies*, 1929, 134; Saunders, "Social History," 251.

19. Saunders, "Social History," 252. Cordeaux to Churchill, April 22, 1922, C.O. 23/290, 216–17; *Nassau Guardian*, August 20, October 8, 1921, February 3, 1923, December 29, 1926; *Nassau Tribune*, June 27, 1925, July 17, 1926; Bell, *Bahamas*, 193; *Colonial Annual Reports, Bahamas, 1928, 1931*, in C.O. 23/405, 23/454.

20. By 1928 there were 1,000 telephone subscribers in Nassau, rising to 1,150 in 1931. In the latter year, Eleuthera had sixty-five miles of telephone line, Long Island forty-five miles, and Cat Island thirty miles. See *Nassau Tribune*, June 17, 1925; Haziel L. Albury, *Man-O-War, My Island Home: A History of an Outer Abaco Island* (Hockessin, Del.: Holly Press, 1977), 89–92.

21. Saunders, "Social History," 253; Algernon Aspinall, *The Pocket Guide to the West Indies, British Guiana, British Honduras, the Bermudas, the Spanish Main, and the Panama Canal* (London: Sifton Praed, 1923), 63–64.

22. Moseley, *Bahamas Handbook*, 204–5.

23. Aspinall, *Pocket Guide*, 63; Michael Craton, "Grand-Pappy of All Pilots," in *Bahamas Handbook and Businessman's Guide, 1965–6* (Nassau: Dupuch, 1966), 57–65.

24. Saunders, "Social History," 254; Moseley, *Bahamas Handbook*, 54–57; Aspinall, *Pocket Guide*, 63.

25. According to Etienne Dupuch, Munson was so bigoted that even in New York, where elevator operators were normally blacks, he employed only whites in such jobs. Local opposition to Munson's practices was increased by his use of hotel vehicles and boats rather than privately operated boats and taxis—a perennial complaint not resolved until 1958. Under pressure, a few blacks were employed as bellboys in the New Colonial Hotel from 1925. See *Nassau Guardian*, February 3, 1923, February 21, 1925; *Nassau Tribune*, February 13, 1924, February 6, 1926, December 16, 1983; Saunders, "Social History," 269, 280–88.

26. Saunders, "Social History," 255, 329. On the license for the Bahamian Club, see Cordeaux to Churchill, Confidential, December 23, 1921, C.O. 23/289, 311–12; Burns, *Colonial Civil Servant*, 83.

27. Moseley, *Bahamas Handbook*, 224–25; Saunders, "Social History," 258.

28. Cordeaux to Darnley, Private, August 8, 1925, C.O. 23/296; Saunders, "Social History," 256–57.

29. Saunders, "Social History," 255, 257; Peter Barratt, *Grand Bahama* (Newton Abbott: David and Charles, 1972), 75–140.

30. Burns to Amery, Confidential, November 20, 1926, C.O. 23/297; Moseley, *Bahamas Handbook*, 35; Philip D. Hall, *A Study of Prominent Bahamian Businesses in the 1920s* (Nassau: College of the Bahamas, 1980); Saunders, "Social History," 258.

31. Saunders, "Social History," 258–59; *Nassau Guardian*, March 6, 1923.

32. Conveyance, June 5, 1937, between Guy Robert Brooke Baxter and the Vendor and the Baxter Estate, Clause 14.

33. *Nassau Tribune*, January 20, 1923, November 24, 1924; Saunders, "Social History," 259.

34. Saunders, "Social History," 262–63; Maj. Gen. Sir Wilfred W. O. Beveridge, *Report on the Public Health and on Medical Conditions in New Providence, Bahama Islands* (London: Waterlow, 1927), 65. Born in 1864, Beveridge served in the Royal Army Medical Corps from 1890 to 1924, retiring as a major general with a knighthood. Clearly an adherent to his own health precepts, he survived until 1962.

35. Beveridge, *Report*, 26.

36. Ibid., 45.

37. Cordeaux to Amery, April 9, 1926, C.O. 23/297, 23/383; Burns to Darnley, May 23, 1926, C.O. 23/297; *Nassau Tribune*, March 17, 1926, May 14, 1927; Bell, *Bahamas*, 188–89; Craton, *History of the Bahamas*, 264–65; Saunders, "Social History," 270–71.

38. Saunders, "Social History," 271–72; *Report of the Commission on the Prison Department*

(Nassau: *Guardian*, 1928); Burns to Amery, July 28, 1928, C.O. 23/391 File 56320; *Nassau Guardian*, July 28, 1928.

39. *Report to Inquire into the Establishment of an Industrial School, January 1923* (Nassau: *Guardian*, 1923), enclosed in Cordeaux to Thomas, March 12, 1924, C.O. 23/295; *Nassau Guardian*, September 5, 23, 1922, January 24, 1925; Saunders, "Social History," 273.

40. Saunders, "Social History," 274; *Report on Industrial School*, 18–28.

41. *Votes of House of Assembly*, February 28, 1921; *Nassau Guardian*, May 7, October 29, 1921; *Nassau Tribune*, July 22, August 22, September 29, 1925; Saunders, "Social History," 275.

42. Gail Saunders, *Bahamian Society After Emancipation* (Kingston: Ian Randle, 1994), 29–30.

43. Ruth Bowe, "Mary Moseley, 1878–1960," *Journal of the Bahamas Historical Society* 2 (October 1980): 20–21.

44. Interview with E. B. North, March 2, 1991; Saunders, *Bahamian Society*, 30–31.

45. Kim Outten, "A Brief Historical Review of Straw Work in the Bahamas," in *Aspects of Bahamian History* (Nassau: Department of Archives, 1989); *Nassau Guardian*, March 23, 1989; Saunders, *Bahamian Society*, 34–35.

46. Gail Saunders, talk to "Women '80 Exhibition," *Nassau Tribune*, July 8, 1980; Saunders, *Bahamian Society*, 32.

47. Allardyce to Grindle, Private, October 5, 1918, C.O. 23/283, 205.

48. See Rhoda Reddock, "Feminism and Feminist Thought: An Historical Overview," in *Gender in Caribbean Development*, ed. Patricia Mohamed and Catherine Shepherd (Mona: University of the West Indies, 1988), 55–66; Saunders, *Bahamian Society*, 35.

49. Taped interviews with Ivy Mackey, December 6, 1990, and Rowena Eldon, May 3, 1983, Archives of the Bahamas; Saunders, *Bahamian Society*, 36.

50. In 1920 the Miami UNIA Ladies' Division had as its president, Lily Farrington; vice president, Nettie Troublefield; secretary, Emma Rolle; assistant secretary, Olga Minus; and treasurer, Alicia Johnson. The Advisory Board consisted entirely of "men, all Bahamian negroes" (Robert A. Hill, ed., *The Marcus Garvey and Universal Negro Improvement Association Papers*, 9 vols. [Berkeley: University of California Press, 1983–95], 3:247). That Bahamian black emigrants played such an active role in Florida and the women a far more active role than in their native Bahamas not only suggests that the emigrants included some of the more socially progressive black Bahamians but also tells something of the roles, aspirations, and opportunities of black men and women (relative to each other as well as to the dominant elements in society) in the United States compared with the Bahamas at that time.

51. *Nassau Tribune*, November 14, 1925; Gail Saunders, talk to "Woman '80 Exhibition," *Nassau Tribune*, June 10, 1980; Saunders, *Bahamian Society*, 36–37.

52. "American and Canadian visitors spent their money liberally, and the few British tourists with greater care. It was a glorious playground, but a very expensive place. The tourists poured money into the colony, but the people, both white and coloured, gave a great deal of their character in exchange for it" (Burns, *Colonial Civil Servant*, 84). Leo Amery, secretary of state for the colonies, concluded that although the majority of Bahamian legislators saw the necessity to hire outsiders for the most senior posts in civil service, "this is all part of the chronic hostility which prevails in the Bahamas against imported officials, or foreigners as they are impudently called in the colony." See Cordeaux to Amery (Confidential), June 11, 1925, C.O. 23/296; Saunders, "Social History," 284–85.

53. Howard Johnson, "Safeguarding Our Traders: The Beginnings of Immigration Restrictions, 1925–33," in *The Bahamas in Slavery and Freedom* (Kingston: Ian Randle, and London: James Currey, 1991), 129; *Nassau Guardian*, December 28, 1887, March 3, 1888, October 5, 1889; Saunders, "Social History," 286.

54. Saunders, "Social History," 286; "Nassau's Incomparable Greeks," in *Bahamas Handbook and Businessman's Guide, 1970–1* (Nassau: Dupuch, 1971), 57; "The Greek Connection," *Nassau Tribune*, March 26, 1981; Johnson, "Safeguarding Our Traders," 129–30.

55. Johnson, "Safeguarding Our Traders," 129–30; Saunders, "Social History," 286.

56. Maldwyn Jones, *American Immigration* (Chicago: University of Chicago Press, 1960),

203; David Nicholls, "No Hawkers and Pedlars: Levantines in the Caribbean," *Ethnic and Racial Studies* (1981): 416; *Nassau Guardian*, May 15, 1897, May 11, 1902. An exception to the Lebanese pattern was the Armaly family, which arrived in 1905 and became involved in the sponge business. See Johnson, "Safeguarding Our Traders," 130–31; Saunders, "Social History," 286.

57. "Death of Mr. Joseph Kail Amoury," *Nassau Tribune*, February 10, 1926; *Nassau Tribune*, February 10, December 23, 1924, July 4, 1925, May 19, October 27, November 27, 1926, January 1, 12, February 2, 1927; Johnson, "Safeguarding Our Traders," 130–33, 137–38.

58. Johnson, "Safeguarding Our Traders," 133–34, 138–39; *Nassau Tribune*, February 10, 1923, June 7, 1924, November 6, 27, 1926; Saunders, "Social History," 287.

59. Saunders, "Social History," 285; *Nassau Guardian*, December 3, 15, 1897; Johnson, "Safeguarding Our Traders," 134.

60. Johnson, "Safeguarding Our Traders," 135; *Nassau Tribune*, July 25, 1925, September 1, 1926.

61. Howard Johnson, "Labour on the Move: West Indian Migration, 1922–1930," in *The Bahamas in Slavery and Freedom* (Kingston: Ian Randle, and London: James Currey, 1991), 149; *Nassau Tribune*, October 18, 1924, April 4, 1925.

62. *Nassau Guardian*, December 8, 1926; Johnson, "Safeguarding Our Traders," 126–27; Saunders, "Social History," 287.

63. Reports of meetings of the House of Assembly, *Nassau Guardian*, April 30, May 2, 1925; Johnson, "Safeguarding Our Traders," 126–27.

64. Johnson, "Safeguarding Our Traders," 127; *Nassau Guardian*, May 2, 1925; Saunders, "Social History," 287.

65. Report of meeting of House of Assembly, March 19, 1926, *Nassau Guardian*, March 20, 1926; Johnson, "Labour on the Move," 154.

66. Report of meeting of House of Assembly, August 13, 1928, *Nassau Guardian*, August 15, 1928; Johnson, "Safeguarding Our Traders," 136–37.

67. Johnson, "Safeguarding Our Traders," 141–42; Report of meeting of House of Assembly, September 4, 1928, *Nassau Guardian*, September 8, 15, 1928.

68. *Nassau Tribune*, October 2, 12, 1929; Johnson, "Labour on the Move," 158.

69. "The Alien Invasion," *Nassau Tribune*, November 15, 1930; *Nassau Guardian*, December 6, 1930, May 9, 20, 23, 1931; "An Act for the Licensing of Shops," 23 and 24 Geo V, c. 8 (1933); Johnson, "Safeguarding Our Traders," 143.

70. Total Bahamian revenue and expenditure was £455,000 and £427,000 in 1931–32. After severe budget cuts, the figures were £352,000 and £326,000 in 1932–33 and £338,000 and £310,000 in 1933–34. See *Colonial Annual Reports, Bahamas*, 1930–33; Cash, "Colonial Policies," 201–30; Saunders, "Social History," 316–20. For the sponge blight, see *The Sponge Industry* (Nassau: Archives Department, 1974), 23–28, and below, Chapter 12.

71. Orr to Passfield, January 27, 1931, C.O. 23/434; Clifford to Cunliffe-Lister, February 9, 1933, C.O. 23/449, July 31, 1934, C.O. 23/503; Saunders, "Social History," 324–26. Somewhat ingenuously, Governor Clifford told the Assembly that an income tax "would be a democratic gesture towards the poor, and narrow the gap between them and the rich or comparatively rich" (Clifford, *Proconsul*, 195–200).

72. Clifford, *Proconsul*, 194.

73. Clifford to Cunliffe-Lister, February 23, 1935, C.O. 23/507; Clifford, *Proconsul*, 196–97; Saunders, "Social History," 327–28.

74. Two of the most notable private island owners were Betty Carstairs of Whale Cay, Berry Islands, and Louis Wasey of Cat Cay. Ernest Hemingway, flamboyant frequent visitor to Bimini between 1936 and 1950, set his posthumously published novel *Islands in the Stream* there but did not own property in the Bahamas. See *Who's Who, 1935*, Vol. 2, No. 4 (London, 1935); 22; *Who's Who, 1936*, Vol. 3, No. 2 (London, 1936), 19; Saunders, "Social History," 328–29, 339–40; Clifford, *Proconsul*, 195–200.

75. For the Dundas Civil Centre, see *Nassau Tribune*, June 13, 1931. The local orchestras,

such as Leonard White's Chocolate Dandies and the even more accomplished ensemble led by Bert Cambridge (later an important moderate politician) were composed entirely of nonwhites, playing in the hotels to strictly segregated customers. Aspiring young musicians sometimes managed to obtain permission to listen to them outside the hotel windows. More like the West Indian Negro bands of slavery days than the American Negro jazz bands, the Bahamian groups of these times featured fiddles as well as wind, reed, and percussion instruments (Saunders, "Social History," 330–40).

76. If the whites rarely ventured from the nightclub balconies to dance, local nonwhites, though seated at separate tables, mingled unself-consciously on the dance floor as they did in most of the West Indies. As someone commented on seeing the prominent black lawyer Alfred F. Adderley and his wife dancing in the same space as the common drayman who commonly called him "Boss" on Bay Street, "In the day gotta tip the whip, but in the night you rub shoulders." The black nightclub owner-manager was an important social intermediary, as ambivalent as the black butler or domestic headman of slavery days. Dandified, outwardly deferential to social superiors, they were also likely to be ambitious and opportunistic, inwardly hating their social subordination and what it entailed. It is probably significant that all four of the black co-owners of the Zanzibar nightclub had later political as well as business interests. One of them was the shopkeeper-politician Milo Butler who, as Sir Milo, was to be the first governor-general in 1973 (Saunders, "Social History," 334–35).

77. E. Clement Bethel, *Junkanoo: Festival of the Bahamas*, ed. and expanded by Nicolette Bethel (London: Macmillan Caribbean, 1991); *Nassau Tribune*, December 27, 1932, December 27, 1933, December 26, 1934, January 11, December 3, 26, 1935. The most obvious changes in Junkanoo were the decline in the number of impromptu "Scrap Gangs," the imposition of a rule that everyone in the parade wear a masked costume, and the substitution of colored crepe paper for newspaper, sponge, and sacking as costume materials (Saunders, "Social History," 334–35).

78. Clifford, *Proconsul*, 190. That Clifford deserved far worse treatment than he received can be seen from his tasteless description of a meeting of those he called the "Holy Rollers," "a curious native religious sect which injected a measure of comedy into the fervour of their religious services. Hymns were sung (off key) to music-hall tunes. The pulpit consisted of a raised structure like a ship's bridge. Up and down this contraption the officiating clergyman, in white flannel trousers and co-respondent shoes, jauntily strutted, one-stepped and rolled, chanting hymns to the accompaniment of a native jazz band. Sometimes the words were as flippant as the music and would have sounded very irreverent to canonical ears. Indeed the Holy Rollers were frowned upon by the orthodox churches, who disapproved of the tone of their services" (ibid., 214–15). In fact, there was never quite the same asperity of social and political satire of Trinidadian calypso found in Bahamian goombay, probably because of the tourist entertainment element in it and the way the music crossed over social lines. One prolific goombay songwriter, Charles Lofthouse, composer of the famous "Bahama Mama," "Goombay Papa Beats the Drum Again," and "Moonlight Nights in Nassau," was a white. George Symonette was an accomplished trained musician who first performed as one of Leonard White's Chocolate Dandies. Alphonso Higgs had less formal training, but after his "discovery" in the Nassau market played in hotels for most of his career, ending up employed by the Tourist Board to greet visitors at Nassau International Airport (Saunders, "Social History," 332–33).

79. Saunders, "Social History," 340–42; Anthony Thompson, *An Economic History of the Bahamas* (Nassau, 1979), 30.

80. Louis Bleiweis, *Austin T. Levy, 1880–1951* (Cambridge, Mass.: Riverside, 1953), 48–49; Saunders, "Social History," 345–46.

81. Saunders, "Social History," 346–47; *The Salt Industry in the Bahamas* (Nassau: Archives Department, 1980), 31.

82. Peter Deveaux, "The Story of Centreville and Collins Wall," *Nassau Guardian*, October 17, 1983. The rock for "tabbying" the wall was excavated from the ridge. The northern front

of Collins's property on Shirley Street was protected by equally formidable iron railings, said to be the entire cargo of a freighter sent from England (Saunders, "Social History," 321–22).

83. Oakes also donated £15,000 to the Nassau General Hospital (ibid., 343–34); Geoffrey Bocca, *The Life and Death of Harry Oakes* (London, 1962); "Sir Harry Oakes—The Man Behind the Myth," in *Bahamas Handbook and Businessman's Guide, 1976–7* (Nassau: Dupuch, 1977), 15–29.

84. For a detailed account of race-class relations in the interwar period, see Saunders, "Social History," 352–64.

85. On R. M. Bailey, see ibid., 260–62, 298 n. 152. The nine nonwhite MHAs in 1928 were W. P. Adderley (Andros), A. J. Kemp (Exuma), Etienne Dupuch (Inagua), S. C. McPherson (New Providence, South), L. W. Young and W. G. Cash (New Providence, East), T. A. Toote (San Salvador/Rum Cay), and Thaddeus "Sankey" Toote (Cat Island). Those returned in the 1935 election were Etienne Dupuch (Inagua), Leon Dupuch (Long Island), L. W. Young (New Providence, East), and Dr. C. R. Walker (New Providence, South). S. C. McPherson had been apprenticed to R. M. Bailey as a tailor, which was also the occupation followed by A. J. Kemp (ibid., 364–66).

86. Though he himself roguishly put about the rumor that he was a communist, Brown was a man of principle. He gave up the *Herald* to J. S. Lowe when the Assembly passed the Newspaper Security Act in 1938, requiring a security bond of £100, saying that he would not be the editor of a shackled newspaper (ibid., 364–66).

87. *Nassau Tribune*, July 15, 31, September 8, 16, October 8, 11, 1935, September 30, October 5, 27, 1937; Dundas to Parkinson, Confidential, July 11, 1938, C.O. 23/653; Saunders, "Social History," 366–67.

88. Saunders, "Social History," 365–66. Christie, a shoe merchant, was elected MHA for New Providence West in 1935. Rhodriguez, a dry goods merchant, had been born and lived all his life in Nassau, save for service in World War I, but his father was Mexican-born. Though the Welsh-born John Hughes (who had migrated to the Bahamas in 1922) was appointed labor officer in 1938, according to Randol Fawkes the relevant laws dealing with labor unions in the Bahamas remained the reactionary Combination Acts of 1825 and 1859, repealed in England seventy years earlier. Neither Christie nor Rhodriguez (nor, for that matter, Hughes) had much knowledge of labor law or practical union experience. The best that could be said for them was that their hearts were usually in the right place (Randol Fawkes, *The Faith That Moved the Mountain* [Nassau: *Guardian*, 1979]), 23.

89. Gail Saunders, "The 1937 Riot in Inagua, the Bahamas," in Saunders, *Bahamian Society*, 49–69 (originally published in *Nieuwe Westindische Gids* 62 [1988]: 129–45); A. W. Erickson to Ormsby-Gore, October 25, 1937, C.O. 23/618; Dundas to Ormsby-Gore, Confidential, February 21, 1938, C.O. 23/638; Saunders, "Social History," 369–70.

90. Saunders, "Social History," 370–74; *Appendix. Votes of the House of Assembly, October 18, 1937–February 21, 1938* (Nassau: *Guardian*, 1938), 191–222; Saunders, "1937 Riot in Inagua," 55–63.

91. J. A. Hughes Report, February 23, 1938, enclosed in Dundas to Ormsby-Gore, March 18, 1938, C.O. 23/638; Saunders, "Social History" 373; Saunders, "1937 Riot in Inagua," 61–69.

92. Dundas to MacDonald, Confidential, July 11, C.O. 23/653, October 29, 1938, C.O. 23/659; Saunders, "Social History," 367.

93. Saunders, "Social History," 368; Dundas to MacDonald, Confidential, August 9, 1938, C.O. 23/653.

94. Dundas to MacDonald, Confidential, July 11, 1938, C.O. 23/653. The secret ballot was declared permanent in New Providence in 1942. Its general extension was determined in 1946 but did not come into effect until the general election of 1949.

95. Dundas, Memorandum, March 1940, C.O. 23/712, quoted in Cash, "Colonial Policies," 258.

96. E. A. McCallan, *Report on the Development of Agriculture in the Bahamas* (Nassau: *Guardian*, 1939).

97. Dundas to Lloyd, August 8, 1940, C.O. 23/678, quoted in Cash, "Colonial Policies," 266.
98. Quoted in Michael Pye, *The King Over the Water* (London: Hutchinson, 1981), 55–56.
99. Ibid., 65–67, citing C.O. 23/681.
100. Ibid.

Chapter 9

1. J. Henry Richardson, *Review of Bahamian Economic Conditions and Post-War Problems* (Nassau: *Guardian*, 1944), 94–95; A. H. Stuart, *World Trade in Sponges* (Washington, D.C.: U.S. Department of Commerce, 1948), 1–2, 56–60; Phillip Cash, "Colonial Policies and Outside Influences: A Study of Bahamian History, 1919–1947" (M.A. thesis, University of Wales, 1979), 260–62; Gail Saunders, "The Social History of the Bahamas, 1890–1953" (Ph.D. dissertation, University of Waterloo, 1985), 405–7.
2. Saunders, "Social History," 407, 419–20; Winston S. Churchill, *The Second World War*, Vol. 2: *Their Finest Hour* (London: Cassell, 1949), 354–68; Cash, "Colonial Policies," 268.
3. Saunders, "Social History," 265.
4. Michael Pye, *The King Over the Water* (London: Hutchinson, 1981); Michael Bloch, *The Duke of Windsor's War* (London, 1982), 154–57; Saunders, "Social History," 407–11.
5. Saunders, "Social History," 412–18; "War Years in Nassau," *Bahamas Handbook and Businessman's Annual, 1978–79* (Nassau: Dupuch, 1979), 69–77; *Bahamas Annual Report, 1946* (London: HMSO, 1947), 6.
6. *Bahamas Annual Report, 1946*, 7; Etienne Dupuch, *The Tribune Story* (London: Benn, 1967), 48–50; Saunders, "Social History," 412–14.
7. Quoted in Bloch, *Windsor's War*, 146–47; Saunders, "Social History," 409–11. For a detailed and judicious, if perhaps too kindly, account of Windsor's tenure, see Philip Ziegler, *King Edward VIII* (London: Collins, 1990), 367–426.
8. Though written earlier, this song was first recorded in 1951 as one of ten Bahamian calypsos issued on five 78 rpm disks by Songs of the Islands, Ltd. Aimed at the tourist market, none of these calypsos—which included "Pretty Boy," "Jones Oh Jones," and "My Name Is Morgan, but It Ain't J.P."—contained any satiric or even serious social content. See *Nassau Tribune*, July 20, 1951; Saunders, "Social History," 409; Ziegler, *Edward VIII*, 380–81.
9. Quoted in Bloch, *Windsor's War*, 128. For the Duke's own private attitudes about race and class in the Bahamas, see Ziegler, *Edward VIII*, 385–86, 423.
10. Mrs. Leslie Higgs, quoted in Pye, *King Over the Water*, 55–56; Ziegler, *Edward VIII*, 387.
11. Radio broadcasting had been initiated at the time of Governor Clifford in 1932, being organized as Station ZNS in 1937, transmitting at 640 kc/s. It was to change to 1540 kc/s (at 10,000 watts) in 1946 and become completely commercial and self-supporting in 1950. See *Bahamas Annual Report 1946*, 37; *Bahamas, 1958 and 1959* (London: HMSO, 1959), 56–57; Paul Albury, *The Story of the Bahamas* (London: Macmillan, 1975), 203. Philip Ziegler is much more generous to Windsor's activities as governor, pointing out the extent of his official correspondence and that he wrote his own speeches (*Edward VIII*, 387).
12. Rosita Forbes, *A Unicorn in the Bahamas* (London: Jenkins, 1939).
13. Rosita Forbes, *Appointment with Destiny* (London: Cassell, 1949), 108.
14. Ibid., 109.
15. Ibid., 207–10.
16. Ibid., 197, 201–4, 212.
17. Ibid., 193.
18. Sidney Poitier, *This Life* (New York: Ballantine, 1980), 1–4.
19. Ibid., 5–6.
20. Ibid., 6–7.
21. Ibid., 10. Another account of the hardships of family life in the southern Out Islands during the interwar years was given (from the point of view of a sympathetic outsider) by the

Anglican missionary Bishop Roscow Shedden, in *Ups and Downs in a West Indian Diocese* (London: A. R. Mowbray, 1927).

22. E. W. Forsyth of Andros in the *Reports of the Out Island Commissioners for 1930*, 12, quoted in Cyrus J. Sharer, "The Population Growth of the Bahama Islands" (Ph.D. dissertation, University of Michigan, 1955), 62.

23. Ibid., 63.

24. Poitier, *This Life*, 17–18.

25. Ibid., 15–36.

26. Evidence of Bert Cambridge to Russell Commission, in *Report of the Commission to Enquire into Disturbances in the Bahamas Which Took Place in June 1942* (Nassau: *Guardian*, 1942), 92; Gail Saunders, "The 1942 Riot in Nassau: A Demand for Change?" in *Bahamian Society After Emancipation* (Kingston: Ian Randle, 1993), 1–47; Saunders, "Social History," 420–23.

27. Saunders, "Social History," 424; Evidence of Bert Cambridge, Russell Commission, *Report*, 92, 199.

28. Evidence of Leonard Storr/Green, Karl Claridge, Edward Sears, and in Harold Christie, Russell Commission, *Report*, 54–67, 147–54, 182–83, 229–30, 279–83; Saunders, "1942 Riot," 5; Saunders, "Social History," 425–26.

29. Saunders, "Social History," 426–27; Evidence of John Hughes, Charles Rhodriguez, A. F. Adderley, and Bert Cambridge, Russell Commission, *Report*, 93, 145, 391–98; "Report of the Select Committee of the House of Assembly [to Enquire into the 1942 Riots]," *Votes of the House of Assembly* (Nassau: *Guardian*, 1942), 313.

30. Interview with Napoleon McPhee, November 24, 1982; Saunders, "1942 Riot," 6; Saunders, "Social History," 427; Randol Fawkes, *The Faith That Moved the Mountain* (Nassau: *Guardian*, 1979), 23. The Project was popularly associated with the Burma Road, built by the British and Americans to aid the Chinese against the Japanese, with which many Bahamians would be familiar from cinema newsreels and feature films.

31. Eric Hallinan, Bahamian attorney general from 1940 to 1944, had wide experience in politically troubled British colonies, first in Nigeria (1930–38) and, after the Bahamas, in Trinidad and Nigeria again. He was knighted in 1955. See Saunders, "1942 Riot," 6–7; Saunders, "Social History," 427–28.

32. Aubrey Bethel testified to the Russell Commission that the rampage started when an unnamed teenager threw a Coca-Cola bottle through the window of Thompson's Pharmacy. See Evidence of Aubrey Bethel, Reginald Erskine-Lindop, Stafford Sands, and Asa Pritchard in Russell Commission, *Report*, 28–53, 260–63, 350–58, 497–508; Saunders, "1942 Riot," 6–7; Saunders, "Social History," 427–28.

33. Saunders, "Social History," 428–29; *Nassau Guardian*, June 2, 1942; Evidence of Eric Hallinan, Stafford Sands, and Asa Pritchard in Russell Commission, *Report*, 350–58, 497–508, 515.

34. Fawkes, *Faith That Moved the Mountain*, 25; Evidence of Bert Cambridge, L/Cpl McDonald Goody, John Damianos, and Leonard Storr/Green in Russell Commission, *Report*, 93, 145, 182–86, 297–98. The words of Milo Butler seem to have inflamed rather than calmed the crowd, and the House of Assembly report later called him "a most unsatisfactory witness," who "attempted to obstruct the enquiries made of him by the Committee, even to the extent of refusing to answer questions" (House Report, 310). See Saunders, "1942 Riot," 8–9; Saunders, "Social History," 429–30, 440.

35. Saunders, "Social History," 431; Russell Commission, *Report*, 28–53. Lt. Col. Reginald A. Erskine-Lindop was an Englishman who had served in World War I and then in the Leeward Islands and Barbados, coming to Nassau in 1936.

36. Evidence of Percy Christie, A. F. Adderley, Richard Holbert, and Bernard Nottage in Russell Commission, *Report*, 25, 31–33, 149, 333–34; House Report, 311–15; Saunders, "1942 Riot," 8; Saunders, "Social History," 431–33. Curiously, two of the sons of Bernard Nottage, the policeman attacked by the mob, were to be ministers in the black PLP government thirty to forty years later (*Nassau Tribune*, August 2, 1955).

37. "Fifty-four Governors have preceded Your Excellency but not one ever brought a ray of

hope to the poor and oppressed. We believe that you are not just another Governor for one class of people but the Governor for all colours and classes of the people. In faith, believing, I ask on behalf of all my brothers and sisters, 'Art thou he that cometh or look we for another'" (Fawkes, *Faith That Moved the Mountain*, 31; Ziegler, *Edward VIII*, 407–9).

38. Telegram, Windsor to Stanley, June 4, Heape to Stanley, June 20, 1942, C.O. 23/731, 25, 43–44; Russell Commission, *Report*, 39–40; Saunders, "Social History," 433–34.

39. Supreme Court Criminal Minutes, April 7–July 30, April 29–August 1, 1942, Public Records Office, Nassau, S.C. 20/90–91; Magistrates Court Criminal Minutes, April 15–July 30, 1942, Public Records Office, Nassau, M.A.G. 7/104; Russell Commission, *Report*, 12, 31, 39–40; Saunders, "1942 Riot," 9; Saunders, "Social History," 434.

40. Saunders, "Social History," 442–43; Windsor to Cranbourne, December 9, 1943, C.O. 23/731. The U.S. vice-consul provided the neatest (though not necessarily most accurate) analysis: "This outbreak has been a smoldering fire for years and there is little doubt but that it is a colour question. Bay Street business houses were the first attacked and the pent-up fury of the mob wreaked its vengeance against what, in their minds, were the oppressing forces, *namely* the white Bahamians as represented by business" (Confidential report by Vice-Consul, Nassau, June 30, 1942, Records of the War Department, Washington, General and Special Staff O.P.D. 319.1 Bahamas). Besides Stafford Sands, the House committee consisted of Roland Symonette, Asa Pritchard, Frank Christie, Raymond Sawyer, Percy Christie, and T. A. Toote (*Votes of the House of Assembly, 1942–1943*, 58).

41. Russell Commission, *Report*, 51–57. The two nonpolitical members of the commission were Herbert McKinney and Herbert Brown. See Windsor to Stanley, October 6, 1942, C.O. 23/731; Saunders, "Social History," 443; Ziegler, *Edward VIII*, 409–12.

42. Act Relating to Trade Unions, March 31, 1943, No. 9 of 1943; Act for Injury Compensation, June 21, 1943, No. 25 of 1943; Closing Speech to the Legislature, September 14, 1943, *Votes of the House of Assembly, 1942–1943*, 196.

43. Executive Council Minutes, January 8, 1943; Windsor to Stanley, December 9, 1942, January 30, August 10, 1943, C.O. 23/731, 140, 23/733, 20, 23/734; Saunders, "Social History," 444.

44. Doris L. Johnson, *The Quiet Revolution in the Bahamas* (Nassau: Family Islands Press, 1972), 15–24; Fawkes, *Faith That Moved the Mountain*, 23–36; Colin A. Hughes, *Race and Politics in the Bahamas* (St. Lucia: Queensland University Press, 1981), 16–18, 212–13.

45. Duchess of Windsor to Aunt Bessie, September 26, 1942, quoted in Bloch, *Duke of Windsor's War*, 281; Executive Council Minutes, March 17, 1943, Appendix, *Votes of the House of Assembly, 1943*, 302–5; Saunders, "Social History," 445–51; Tracey L. Thompson, "Remembering the Contract: Insights Towards a Thesis," paper presented at the Twenty-fifth Conference of Association of Caribbean Historians, Mona, Jamaica, 1993; Ziegler, *Edward VIII*, 309–91, 409–12.

46. Thompson, "Remembering the Contract," 1–4; Saunders, "Social History," 445–47; Murphy to Hall, January 23, June 19, 1946, C.O. 23/814; David Greenberg, "The Contract, the Project, and Work Experiences," in *Strangers No More: Anthropological Studies of Cat Island, Bahamas*, ed. Joel Savashinsky (Ithaca: Ithaca College, 1978).

47. Richardson, *Bahamian Economic Conditions*, 26; *Colonial Annual Reports, Bahamas, 1950–1951* (London: HMSO, 1951), 7; Bahamas Administrative Reports, 1953, C.O. 23/856; Saunders, "Social History," 447.

48. Interview with Cordell Thompson, November 1990; Thompson, "Remembering the Contract," 1; Greenberg, "The Contract," 193.

49. Testimony of Samuel Miller, December 18, 1991, in Thompson, "Remembering the Contact," 8. When Miller left the Contract in 1955, the Labour Office in Nassau had $1,800 waiting for him, on top of the considerable funds he had already sent to a family member.

50. Testimony of Calvin Bethel, January 1, 1992, in Thompson, "Remembering the Contract," 8. Bethel was one of the minority of Contract workers who stayed in the United States, eventually purchasing a fifty-acre tract which he developed into a citrus grove at Vero Beach, Florida.

51. Greenberg, "The Contract," 172–201; Saunders, "Social History," 448–49.

52. Testimony of H. R. Bethel, December 1991–January 1992, in Thompson, "Remembering the Contract," 6–7.

53. Testimony of "Samuel Whately," of "Bramley," Cat Island, in Greenberg, "The Contract," 201.

54. Testimony of Samuel Miller, December 18, 1991, in Thompson, "Remembering the Contract," 7; Testimony of "Samuel Whately," in Greenberg, "The Contract," 201; Poitier, *This Life*, 40. For fights between Contract workers and black Americans, Murphy to Hall, January 23, 1946, C.O. 23/814.

55. *Colonial Annual Reports, Bahamas 1946* (London: HMSO, 1946), 5; "War Years in Nassau," 69; Saunders, "Social History," 417–18. Wenzel Granger was the son of David and Catherine Granger, who had migrated from Inagua in 1920 and operated a bakery in the Out Islanders' and coloreds' Nassau suburb of Chippenham. He became deputy commissioner of police in 1962, director of immigration in 1964, and first commandant of the police reserve in 1969.

56. *Nassau Magazine* 12 (December 1945): 9; Albury, *Story of the Bahamas*, 212; "War Years in Nassau," 68–70; Saunders, "Social History," 451.

57. Saunders, "Social History," 416–17; Interview with Rowena Eldon, May 3, 1983; Dupuch, *Tribune Story*, 90; "War Years in Nassau," 76–77; Bloch, *Windsor's War*, 283.

58. Group Captain R. N. Waite to Windsor, December 31, 1943; Windsor to Stanley, Secret, January 4, 1944, in "Colour Bar" (1944) in Unofficial File, Governor's Office, Nassau; "War Years in Nassau," 77–78; Saunders, "Social History," 452–453, 491 n. 313.

59. Alfred de Marigny, *More Devil Than Saint* (New York: Beechhurst Press, 1946); Marigny, *A Conspiracy of Crowns* (London: Bantam Press, 1990); [Eugene Dupuch], *The Murder of Sir Harry Oakes* (Nassau: *Tribune*, 1959); Geoffrey Bocca, *The Life and Death of Harry Oakes* (London: World Distributions, 1962); Marshall Houtts, *King's X* (New York: Morrow, 1972); Pye, *King Over the Water*, 213–44; Bloch, *Windsor's War*, 217–20; James Leasor, *Who Killed Sir Harry Oakes?* (London, 1983).

60. Windsor to Oliver, August 10, 1943, quoted in Bloch, *Windsor's War*, 312; Ziegler, *Edward VIII*, 412–15.

61. Windsor to Stanley, November 28, 1944, C.O. 23/770; Cash, "Colonial Policies," 280; Ziegler, *Edward VIII*, 425–26.

62. In giving examples of the high cost of living in Nassau, the *Annual Report* for 1958–59 gave the daily tariff for smaller hotels as from £2 to £8 and for the larger from £5 to £18 (inclusive), according to season. It was estimated that for a married couple with two children to live "in modest comfort" would cost from £2,800 to £3,000 a year. The same figures are quoted in the *Annual Report* for 1964–65. At that time a large loaf of bread cost 2 shillings, fresh milk 3 shillings a quart, butter 5 shillings and 6 pence a pound, and rice 5 shillings and 6 pence for five pounds. The minimum wages for unskilled men in 1959 ranged between 3s. 6d. to 4s. 4d. an hour and for women between 2s. 6d. and 2s. 9d. (with female shell and straw workers earning as little as 2 shillings an hour). Skilled male workers earned between 6s. 6d. for carpenters and 12s. 11d. for the highest-paid mechanics. These had all risen by as much as 40 percent by 1965, with male laborers making a minimum of 5s. 6d. an hour and skilled mechanics 14s. 9d. At that time U.S.$1 was worth about 8 shillings (*Annual Reports, Bahamas, 1958–59*, 7–8; *Annual Reports, Bahama Islands, 1964 and 1965*, 14, 100–101).

63. Expenditure by the Development Board rose from £557,000 in 1957 to £730,000 in 1959, £1,000,000 in 1962, and £1,493,000 in 1964, while the figures for the expenditure on the Education Department for the same years were £325,000, £484,000, £771,000, and £1,164,000 respectively (*Annual Reports, 1958–59*, 10–11, *1964–65*, 17–18).

64. *Annual Reports, Bahamas, 1946*, 34; *1958–59*, 52–54; *1964–65*, 82–85; Cash, "Colonial Policies," 343; Saunders, "Social History," 457.

65. Peter Barratt, *Grand Bahama*, 2d ed. (London: Macmillan Caribbean, 1982), 71–72; Murphy to Creech-Jones, September 30, 1949, C.O. 23/868; *The Times*, July 3, September 5, 1950; *Annual Reports, Bahamas, 1950–1951*, 7; "Failure of Butlin's 'Vacation Village' in the Bahamas, 1952–1953," C.O. 1031/976; Saunders, "Social History," 458–59.

66. *Annual Report, Bahama Islands, 1964 and 1965*, 8–9; Michael Craton, *A History of the Bahamas*, 3d ed. (Waterloo: San Salvador Press, 1986), 266–67.

67. *Annual Report, Bahama Islands, 1964 and 1965*, 7.

68. *Bahamian Review Magazine* 1 (October–November 1952): 29; Saunders, "Social History," 467–68, 498 n. 435.

69. Fawkes, *Faith That Moved the Mountain*, 50–56; *Bahamian Review* 13 (1971): 25; Saunders, "Social History," 469. The first black teller in a Bay Street bank was Pauline Allen, who had been among the first students of the Government High School to achieve a Higher School Certificate. She went on to be a branch manager for Barclays Bank, a director of the Bahamas Development Bank, and, in December 1993, managing director of the Bank of the Bahamas.

70. Bloch, *Windsor's War*, 163; Murphy to Creech-Jones, September 30, 1949, C.O. 23/868; Lord Listowel's Report on the West Indies, 1949, C.O. 23/888; Annual Medical and Sanitary Reports, 1953, Bahamas Administrative Report, 1953, C.O. 26/156; Gail Saunders, "Outstanding Women in the Bahamas," speech delivered to Women 80 conference, June 11, 1980; Saunders, "Social History," 463–65.

71. *Votes of the House of Assembly*, July 22, 1946; Report on the Bahamas in 1949 in Murphy to Creech-Jones, September 30, 1949, C.O. 23/868; *Annual Reports, Bahamas, 1950–1951*, 21; Colbert Williams, *The Methodist Contribution to Education in the Bahamas* (Gloucester: Alan Sutton, 1982), 70–71; Education Act, No. 26 of 1951; Saunders, "Social History," 465.

72. Saunders, "Social History," 528–29; Williams, *Methodist Contribution*, 103; Colman J. Barry, *Upon These Rocks: Catholics in the Bahamas* (Collegeville, Minn.: St. John's Abbey Press, 1973), 324–88.

73. Williams, *Methodist Contribution*, 108; Memorandum of Association, St. Andrew's School, November 11, 1948, Registrar's Department, Nassau; Saunders, "Social History," 466. Until the 1970s, when it was relocated near Yamacraw Beach in southeastern New Providence, St. Andrews School was fittingly housed in the Collins mansion, Centreville. Among the first nonwhite children accepted were grandchildren of Sir Milo Butler, the first Bahamian governor-general.

74. Rev. H. H. Brown, sermon at Governor's Harbour, Eleuthera, January 14, 1946; Brown to Wesleyan Methodist Missionary Society, January 29, 1946, quoted in Philip Cash, Shirley Gordon, and Gail Saunders, eds., *Sources of Bahamian History* (London: Macmillan Caribbean, 1991), 291.

75. Constitution of the Citizens' Committee, Dr. Cleveland Eneas Collection, Public Records Office, Nassau; Fawkes, *Faith That Moved the Mountain*, 44–45; *Citizens' Torch* 1 (June, September 1951); Interview with Maxwell J. Thompson, January 17, 1984; Saunders, "Social History," 466–69. Besides *No Way Out*, the government Censorship Board also banned the films *Pinky* and *Lost Boundaries* on the same grounds. A. F. Adderley, the only nonwhite member of the Censorship Board, resigned over the banning of *No Way Out*, though the film was allowed to be shown in October 1950.

76. Neville to Lyttelton, July 15, 1953, C.O. 1031/138; *Nassau Guardian*, September 29, 1953; Fawkes, *Faith That Moved the Mountain*, 45; Hughes, *Race and Politics*, 36–37.

77. Hughes, *Race and Politics*, 36–39; Johnson, *Quiet Revolution*, 29–42; Fawkes, *Faith That Moved the Mountain*, 69–88; Henry M. Taylor, *My Political Memoirs: A Political History of the Bahamas in the 20th Century* (Nassau: Privately published, 1987), 122–43; Saunders, "Social History," 472–73.

78. Taylor, *Political Memoirs*, 198–238; Hughes, *Race and Politics*, 40–41.

79. *Nassau Guardian*, September 29, October 22, November 2, 1953, February 9, 1954, April 30, May 13, 1956; *Nassau Tribune*, January 3, 24, March 1, 20, 1956; Hughes, *Race and Politics*, 40–46; Dupuch, *Tribune Story*, 27, 139; Johnson, *Quiet Revolution*, 56; Taylor, *Political Memoirs*, 198–208.

80. Hughes, *Race and Politics*, 45–46; D. Gail Saunders, "The 1956 Revolution: Breaking Down the Barriers of Racial Discrimination in the Bahamas," paper presented at the Twenty-sixth Conference of Caribbean Historians, San German, Puerto Rico, 1994.

81. Hughes, *Race and Politics*, 49–54; Johnson, *Quiet Revolution*, 33–34; Fawkes, *Faith That Moved the Mountain*, 82–88; Taylor, *Political Memoirs*, 219–24.

82. Hughes, *Race and Politics*, 54–60; Taylor, *Political Memoirs*, 225–38; D. Gail Saunders, "The 1958 General Strike in Nassau: A Landmark in Bahamian History," paper presented at the Twenty-fifth Conference of Caribbean Historians, Mona, Jamaica, 1993.

83. *Nassau Tribune*, January 14, 1958; *Nassau Guardian*, January 14, 1958; Hughes, *Race and Politics*, 62–64.

84. Hughes, *Race and Politics*, 63; *Nassau Guardian*, January 15, 1958; Johnson, *Quiet Revolution*, 35–36; Fawkes, *Faith That Moved the Mountain*, 98–126; Taylor, *Political Memoirs*, 239–40.

85. Hughes, *Race and Politics*, 63–67; Johnson, *Quiet Revolution*, 36; Fawkes, *Faith That Moved the Mountain*, 123–25.

86. Hughes, *Race and Politics*, 64–65.

87. Ibid., 65–66; Fawkes, *Faith That Moved the Mountain*, 127–67. For the ideological conflict between UBP, PLP, and Labor, see Felix Bethel and Michael Stevenson, "The State, the Crowd, and the Heroes: The Struggle for Control in the Bahamas, 1958–1968," paper presented at the Twenty-fourth Conference of Caribbean Historians, Nassau, 1992.

88. *Nassau Guardian*, January 26, 1960; *Nassau Tribune*, February 9, 1960; Hughes, *Race and Politics*, 73–74. The PLP wavered in its attitude toward the boards during 1960 and 1961, membership being one of the points of contention between Henry Taylor and Lynden Pindling (Taylor, *Political Memoirs*, 265–67).

89. Hughes, *Race and Politics*, 78. The three most important recruits to the PLP in 1960 were lawyers, the son of lawyer A. F. Adderley, Paul (later a notable PLP minister), Orville Turnquest (later to lead the opposition to the PLP government and in 1996 appointed governor-general), and Livingstone Coakley.

90. *Nassau Tribune*, June 10, 1960; Hughes, *Race and Politics*, 80–89; Johnson, *Quiet Revolution*, 36, 67; Fawkes, *Faith That Moved the Mountain*, 164–84; Taylor, *Political Memoirs*, 239–78.

91. The American journalist Peter Knaur was said to be employed by the UBP as a propagandist. See *Nassau Herald*, October 10, 1959; *Nassau Guardian*, October 16, 1959; Hughes, *Race and Politics*, 70–71.

92. *Nassau Herald*, May 23, 1959; Hughes, *Race and Politics*, 71–77.

93. *Nassau Guardian*, October 31, 1962. Milo Butler had been quoted as declaiming: "All these years these people have had their feet on our necks—now you have the chance to throw them off. Three hundred years ago our pride was ripped out of us slaves in a nasty manner. Now if a man of the other race should kick you, you should kick back, and then you will know that you have your pride back" (Hughes, *Race and Politics*, 87–88).

94. *Nassau Tribune*, November 24, 1962, quoted in Cash, Gordon, and Saunders, eds., *Sources of Bahamian History*, 291. For the 1962 election in general, see Hughes, *Race and Politics*, 89–93; Taylor, *Political Memoirs*, 305–12; Craton, *History of the Bahamas*, 274.

95. *Nassau Tribune*, November 25, 1962, quoted in Cash, Gordon, and Saunders, eds., *Sources of Bahamian History*, 291, and Hughes, *Race and Politics*, 89.

Chapter 10

1. Jack Ford, *Reminiscences of an Island Teacher: Life in the Bahamas, 1948–1963*, ed. Jack Hardy (Decatur: White Sound Press, 1992).

2. Ibid., 1–4.

3. Ibid., 4–5. For the Abaco Cays from the sailor's viewpoint, see Harry Kline, ed., *Yachtsman's Guide to the Bahamas*, 33d ed. (Miami: Tropic Isle Publications, 1983), 153–221.

4. Ford, *Island Teacher*, 5–7.

5. Ibid., 7–13, 28–32, 37–38.

6. Ibid., 44, 64–70.

7. Ibid., 14–23; Kline, ed., *Yachtsman's Guide*, 164–70.

8. Ford, *Island Teacher*, 41, 89; Haziel Albury, *Man-O-War, My Island Home: A History of an*

Out Island Abaco Island (Bridgeton, N.J.: Holly Press, 1977). Most notable of Walter Sands's former pupils was Patrick Bethel, who went from Cherokee Sound to be a pupil teacher under Jack Ford at Green Turtle Cay and was to be an early principal of the Teacher Training College in Nassau. He wrote a foreword and an afterword to Ford's memoir.

9. Ford, *Island Teacher*, 20–22; Kline, ed., *Yachtsman's Guide*, 164–70. There are two other settlements in the Bahamas called Hard Bargain, in southern Long Island and eastern San Salvador. There is also one in central Trinidad, almost certainly settled by the former slaves of Burton Williams from San Salvador, Bahamas. See Michael Craton and Gail Saunders, *Islanders in the Stream: A History of the Bahamian People, Volume One: From Aboriginal Times to the End of Slavery* (Athens: University of Georgia Press, 1992), 291–96.

10. Ford, *Island Teacher*, 91–92.

11. Patrick Bethel, "Afterword," ibid., 101.

12. Ford, *Island Teacher*, 88.

13. In 1967, each of Abaco's 1,905 registered voters voted for three candidates. The three white UBP candidates, John Bethell, Leonard Thompson, and Frank Christie, received 1,254, 1,247, and 1,176 votes respectively, and the two black PLP candidates 758 and 176. The top-scoring PLP candidate, S. C. Bootle, was returned for Cooper's Town (northern Abaco) in 1968 by 592 votes to 400 for the UBP's black nominee, in an electorate of 1,193, while a black UBP candidate prevailed at Marsh Harbour (southern Abaco) by 672 to 289, in an electorate of 1,348. See Colin A. Hughes, *Race and Politics in the Bahamas* (St. Lucia: Queensland University Press, 1981), 237.

14. Groves obtained permission to log trees as small as four inches in diameter, compared with the previous eight inches. See Peter Barratt, *Grand Bahama*, 2d ed. (London: Macmillan Caribbean, 1982), 66, 74, 140; Kline, ed., *Yachtsman's Guide*, 99. For the earlier history of the Abaco Lumber Company, see above, Chapter 7.

15. The Owens-Illinois connection, which demonstrates parallels with the exploitative operations of giant corporations in Africa, South America, and other parts of the Third World, calls for the attention of an investigative historian. Having largely stripped Abaco from its base at Snake Cay (where the company offices were housed in the dry-docked Mississippi riverboat *Robert Fulton*), Owens-Illinois transferred its attention to the virgin pinelands of Andros. In Abaco, as Bahamas Agricultural Industries, Ltd. (BAIL), it set out to grow and process sugarcane with a mobile mill, having finagled a ten-thousand-ton annual sugar quota in the preferential U.S. market, at a time when the embargo on Cuba raised world prices to an unprecedented $600 a ton. This operation failed and the company pulled out when world sugar prices tumbled. Owens-Illinois and BAIL operations in Andros followed a similar pattern, with other agricultural crops and cattle raising. See Michael Craton, *A History of the Bahamas*, 3d ed. (Waterloo: San Salvador Press, 1986), 268, 297; Steven Dodge, *Abaco: The History of an Out Island and Its Cays* (North Miami: Tropic Isle Publications, 1983), 98–104.

16. *Hawksbill Creek Agreement [Principal Agreement]* (New Providence, 1955); Hawksbill Creek, Grand Bahama [Deep Water Harbour and Industrial Area] Act, 1965; Barratt, *Grand Bahama*, 77–80, 178.

17. Barratt, *Grand Bahama*, 79–81.

18. Ibid., 82–83. Jack Hayward, besides building a villa as grand as Groves's, was active in the local amateur dramatic society, patronized the Olde-Englishe-style Pub-on-the-Mall, sponsored local cricket, and was largely responsible for the creation of Churchill Square in downtown Freeport, with its central bust monument to the Old Imperialist. Retaining his British links, he saved Lundy Island from developers and Wolverhampton Wanderers soccer club from bankruptcy and became the chief sponsor of the Women's Cricket World Cup in the 1990s.

19. *Hawksbill Creek Agreement [Supplemental Agreement]* (New Providence, 1960); Hawksbill Creek, Grand Bahama [Deep Water Harbour and Industrial Area] (Amendment of Agreement) Act, 1960; Barratt, *Grand Bahama*, 87–88, 178.

20. Barratt, *Grand Bahama*, 82, 87–88, 134–35. The Ranfurly Circus and the Bahamas Cement

Company plant were opened on the same day, March 15, 1965, in ceremonies presided over by Governor Grey, with former governors Ranfurly and Neville in attendance (ibid., 95).

21. Ibid., 92–94. The story of the Lucayan Beach treasure—coins minted in Mexico City, probably carried on a ship seized by the Dutchman Piet Heyn at Mantanzas Bay in 1628—was told by one of the divers, Jack Slack, in a book aptly entitled *Finders Losers*.

22. Barratt, *Grand Bahama*, 88, 93, 95.

23. For a somewhat hyperactive account, see Michael Craton, *Sun 'N Sixpence: A Guide to the Bahamas* (Nassau: Dupuch, 1964). Tourism peaked at around four hundred thousand in 1970, and the resident population of Freeport-Lucaya was still no more than twenty-five thousand in 1996.

24. Michael Craton, "White Law and Black Custom: The Evolution of Bahamian Land Tenures," in *Land and Development in the Caribbean*, ed. Janet Momsen and Jean Besson (London: Macmillan Caribbean, 1987), 88–114.

25. Judgement in the Case of the Petition of James Maxwell Mitchell Bowe under the Quieting of Titles Act, 1959, concerning the Forest Estate, Bahama Islands Supreme Court, Equity Division, No. 137 of 1961.

26. Bowe Judgement, April 11, 1962, 2.

27. Ibid., 3.

28. Ibid., 5.

29. Ibid., 6–7.

30. Ibid., 8–9.

31. Craton, "White Law and Black Custom," 105–6.

32. Price-Robinson Case, Bahama Islands Supreme Court, Equity Division, No. 171 of 1960, 391 of 1963, Appeal to the Privy Council, No. 40 of 1964 (Decision, 1968). A more internal case with important political ramifications was the 1963 application for Quiet Title by Cat Island Farms, owned by Harold Christie, in which twenty-five local farmers were adverse claimants. In June 1964, three women were committed to jail for twenty-one to twenty-eight days for refusing to vacate the land pending the court's decision. Milo Butler led a deputation of the farmers to Government House in protest and created a disturbance in the Assembly when he interrupted the obsequies for the recently deceased white politician Sir George Roberts with the cry: "Three Negro women have been sent to gaol and no-one cares a damn about them" (*Nassau Guardian*, June 26, 1964; Hughes, *Race and Politics*, 104).

33. Craton, *History of the Bahamas*, 268, 79–83; Paul Albury, *The Paradise Island Story* (London: Macmillan Caribbean, 1985). Huntingdon Hartford's Paradise Tennis was a doubles game played with cut-down racquets on an oversized Ping-Pong table. The final of the 1962 tournament, billed as the first World Championship of Paradise Tennis, saw tennis superstars Pancho Gonzalez and Pancho Segura pitted against two local expatriate schoolteachers, Keith Parker and Eric Howells. When Gonzalez and Segura prevailed in a surprisingly close match, they were declared world *professional* champions and their opponents consoled with the title of world amateur champions.

34. See particularly *Grand Bahama Port Authority* v. *Albert Cox of Smith's Point*, Grand Bahama, Bahama Islands Supreme Court, Equity Division, No. 170 of 1961; *A. S. Nesbitt and Daisy Cox* v. *Abaco Lumber Company etc.* (Riding Point, Grand Bahama), No. 70 of 1967; Barratt, *Grand Bahama*, 165.

35. Barratt, *Grand Bahama*, 164–65.

36. Ibid., 164.

37. As late as the 1980 census, when 33,102 persons were enumerated in Grand Bahama, 9,170 lived west of Hawksbill Creek, 7,486 between Hawksbill Creek and the central mall in Freeport, with the remaining 16,446 in the rest of Freeport-Lucaya and further east. See Barratt, *Grand Bahama*, 144–45.

38. Ibid., 48–49, 53–56, 60, 163.

39. Ibid., 144, 163–64.

40. The Hawksbill Creek, Grand Bahama (Deep Water Harbour and Industrial Area Amendment of Agreement) Act, 1965; The Freeport Bylaws Act, 1965; *Hawksbill Creek Agreement (Amendment of Agreement)* (Nassau, 1966).

41. Hughes, *Race and Politics*, 95–97.

42. The 1964 Constitution is fully described in Randol Fawkes, *The Faith That Moved the Mountain* (Nassau: *Guardian*, 1979), 204–18.

43. Hughes, *Race and Politics*, 100–103.

44. Ibid., 103–8.

45. Ibid., 99–100. Hughes tellingly quotes a July 26, 1963, letter in the *Tribune* rushing to the defense once Uncle Tom had been attacked by Lynden Pindling: "Today people of the P.L.P stripe try to debase this fine character. If a coloured person is not a tough—if he is not a ruffian—if he shows any gratitude for benefits received—if he possesses the qualities one would expect of a man born and reared in a Christian society—then he is an Uncle Tom and traitor to his race. A coloured man is expected to hate anything white—although white people fought and died for his causes—and they are still leading the battle for the full establishment of his rights in a free and democratic society."

46. *Nassau Guardian*, August 30, 1966. A correspondent predictably responded in the same paper ten days later: "Most countries teach their own histories and that of historically democratic people such as Britain and the U.S. However, the Bahamas does not have an appreciable history that can be taught alone in schools and since we are a British colony it follows that British should be the main requirement of our schools. But African history, Holy smoke man, what culture or civilization does Africa have anyway? None, unless you call ignorance, savagery and deep superstition culture" (quoted in Hughes, *Race and Politics*, 115–16).

47. Hughes, *Race and Politics*, 99.

48. Ibid., 105; *Nassau Tribune*, April 27, 1965.

49. Hughes, *Race and Politics*, 107; Doris L. Johnson, *The Quiet Revolution in the Bahamas* (Nassau: Family Islands Press, 1972), 51–53; Fawkes, *Faith That Moved the Mountain*, 233–38.

50. Johnson, *Quiet Revolution*, 53–56.

51. Ibid., 57–60, 157–66.

52. *United Nations, Committee of Twenty-Four, Proceedings, 1965*, A/600/aAdd 7, 86-111; Johnson, *Quiet Revolution*, Appendix A, 157–61.

53. Bahamas: Hearing of Petitioners (A/AC. 109/Pet.377 and Add. 1), Johnson, *Quiet Revolution*, Appendix B, 161–66.

54. Johnson, *Quiet Revolution*, 158; Hughes, *Race and Politics*, 100–101.

55. Because of the concentration on the Freeport casinos issue, many other deals made by the UBP government went unexamined. They were not likely to be exhumed later once the successor PLP government itself became involved in similar transactions. The delicate matter of the fine line between public benefit and private gain in the exploitation of Bahamian resources is considered in Part III, below.

56. Hughes, *Race and Politics*, 98–99.

57. Heartening evidence that the Bahamas enjoyed a free press was the fact that the *Wall Street Journal* article was reproduced in both the *Bahamas Observer* (October 8, 1966) and the *Tribune* (October 10, 1966). See Hughes, *Race and Politics*, 116–17; Johnson, *Quiet Revolution*, 113–16.

58. Hughes, *Race and Politics*, 119–20.

59. For the 1967 election, ibid., 119–21, 216, 230–41; Johnson, *Quiet Revolution*, 85–111; Fawkes, *Faith That Moved the Mountain*, 270–84.

60. Fawkes, *Faith That Moved the Mountain*, 280–82; Hughes, *Race and Politics*, 124; Johnson, *Quiet Revolution*, 89, 102–4.

61. Hughes, *Race and Politics*, 124–30.

62. Ibid., 128–29. The most controversial immediate measure was the voting of salaries for all parliamentarians, ranging from $10,200 a year (plus a 17.5 percent housing allowance) for

MHAs, up to $27,142 (plus $11,428 entertainment allowance) for the premier—more than the governor received. The UBP abstained from the vote on salaries and one UBP member announced that his salary would be donated to charity.

63. For the Bacon Commission, see Johnson, *Quiet Revolution*, 113–23; Hughes, *Race and Politics*, 134–35; Fawkes, *Faith That Moved the Mountain*, 266–68. The support which the PLP received from Mike McLaney came back to haunt the party and its leader in the early 1970s. A witness in a U.S. Senate inquiry alleged that he had been offered $100,000 to assassinate Pindling by McLaney and Elliott Roosevelt, who were angered by failure to obtain a casino license in return for a gift of $1 million to the PLP. Both McLaney and Roosevelt denied the allegation, and Prime Minister Pindling spoke out to put the record straight. No promise had ever been made to McLaney, who had not donated $1 million but merely provided transportation estimated to have been worth $60,000. The amount had subsequently been reimbursed by a levy on PLP parliamentary salaries. See Hughes, *Race and Politics*, 175.

64. Hughes, *Race and Politics*, 138–39.

65. For the 1968 general election, see Hughes, *Race and Politics*, 138–40, 230–41; Johnson, *Quiet Revolution*, 128. Though he was to be knighted in 1975, Randol Fawkes was virtually extinguished as a parliamentary politician in 1972 when he came third in the poll for St. Barnabas constituency (receiving 146 votes to the PLP candidate's 961 and the FNM's 159). In the same election, A. R. Braynen, still unopposed by the PLP, was to lose his seat to the FNM (by 320 votes to 249). He too retired from active politics at that time, though he was to be appointed the first Bahamian high commissioner in London after independence (1973–77).

66. For the 1969 constitutional reforms, see Johnson, *Quiet Revolution*, 130–32; Philip Cash, Shirley Gordon, and Gail Saunders, eds., *Sources of Bahamian History* (London: Macmillan Caribbean, 1991), 303–5.

67. Cash, Gordon, and Saunders, eds., *Sources of Bahamian History*, 305–6; Johnson, *Quiet Revolution*, 134.

68. Craton, *History of the Bahamas*, 281; Hughes, *Race and Politics*, 145–46. For the full development of PLP education policy, see the 1973 White Paper on Education and subsequent documents excerpted in Cash, Gordon, and Saunders, eds., *Sources of Bahamian History*, 325–29.

69. Cash, Gordon, and Saunders, eds., *Sources of Bahamian History*, 179–80.

70. Ibid., 152–53; Barratt, *Grand Bahama*, 101–2.

71. *Nassau Tribune*, July 26, 1969; Barratt, *Grand Bahama*, 102–8; Hughes, *Race and Politics*, 152–54.

72. Barratt, *Grand Bahama*, 107–8.

73. *Report of the Royal Commission Appointed on the Recommendation of the Bahamas Government to Review the Hawksbill Creek Agreement*, 2 vols. (Nassau: Bahamas Government, 1971); Barratt, *Grand Bahama*, 110–12; Hughes, *Race and Politics*, 154, 167; Craton, *History of the Bahamas*, 283–84.

74. Under fire, the prime minister was among those at pains to dissociate from Robert Vesco. Though a Disclosures Act was not passed until 1978, in September 1973 Lynden Pindling made a voluntary disclosure about his private finances. This, as Colin Hughes suggests, demonstrated no more than the possibilities for steady wealth accumulation among the more astute nonwhite emergent bourgeoisie. From savings from his legal practice of $6–$8,000 a year in the 1950s, Pindling was able to buy a site in downtown Nassau with a $200,000 mortgage from the bank subsequently acquired by Robert Vesco. This site had later been sold for $400,000, and Pindling had then bought for $450,000 a renovated new home in one of Nassau's most prestigious areas, with the help of further mortgages from two other banks, neither owned by Vesco. When the disclosure of the private wealth of parliamentarians became mandatory in 1978 there were no less than twenty-two declared millionaires in the legislature—divided equally between the PLP and opposition FNM members. Though one minister, born poor (and later discredited), almost bragged of being worth $7 million, to some popular disbelief Prime Minister Pindling was not among the declared millionaires, stating

his assets to be $976,807. See *Nassau Guardian*, September 19, 21, 1973, November 3, 1979; Hughes, *Race and Politics*, 174–75, 206–7.

75. Craton, *History of the Bahamas*, 284.

76. To sustain its claim to be both socialist and nationalist, as well as revolutionary, the Vanguard Party declared in July 1971: "We call ourselves vanguard because we are the first party in the country that will address itself to the complete reconstruction of society. We call ourself socialist because we believe that the wealth of the country belongs to the community and that there should be broader ownership of the means of production. We call ourselves nationalist because we believe that all principal institutions should be geared to suit the Bahamian people." In October 1971 it made a swingeing attack on the PLP government: "The lack of a basic and coherent political philosophy in the PLP has been a major factor in its failure to do much to correct the abuses of Bahamian society by the wealthy few, or to create genuine political and economic opportunity for the majority of the people. In effect, the PLP since taking over the Government has resorted to a more subtle process of corrupt methods and practices employed by the UBP in its days of power. There has been almost no improvement in the general lot of the people and the Government is dominated more than ever by foreign capital." See *Nassau Guardian*, July 28, 1971; *Vanguard*, October 1971; Hughes, *Race and Politics*, 186–87. Though it continued on into the 1980s, the Vanguard Party never consisted of more than a handful of zealots, unabashedly sustained by support from Cuba. In the 1977 general election, the four candidates put up by the VSNP polled a grand total of 55 votes. The VSNP's chief theoretician and polemicist, John McCartney, was eventually forced by straitened circumstances to resume his previous job as a professor of political science in the United States.

77. Hughes, *Race and Politics*, 161–62.

78. Ibid., 166–67, 187; Craton, *History of the Bahamas*, 285.

79. The courtesy campaign was launched by Prime Minister Pindling in March 1970 and was enthusiastically endorsed in Freeport-Lucaya (Barratt, *Grand Bahama*, 108). In response to a tourist complaint given front-page treatment, a correspondent to the *Guardian* wrote: "Perhaps he is part of a plan to return the Bahamas to the old days when freedom and justice, and democracy and pride was only for the whites and, as we call them, Conchy Joes. Possibly he expects to meet here conditions like some of the Southern States of America." See *Nassau Guardian*, June 13, 15, 1972; Hughes, *Race and Politics*, 168–69.

80. *Nassau Guardian*, November 26, 1971; Hughes, *Race and Politics*, 168. For the early years of the "Haitian Problem," see Dawn Marshall, *The Haitian Problem: Illegal Migration to the Bahamas* (Kingston: ISER, 1979). Also see below, Part III.

81. Hughes, *Race and Politics*, 182–83.

82. The decision to take over the casinos (which by 1973 had already contributed $29 million to government revenue and undoubtedly mitigated the tourism slump) caused the resignation of the minister for development, Carlton Francis, and a statement from the Baptist Convention that it would "find it difficult to support any government that utilizes gambling as a source of national income." See *Nassau Guardian*, January 10, 1974; Hughes, *Race and Politics*, 171–72.

83. When the personally popular white Basil Kelly retired from Crooked Island in favor of the FNM's black candidate Cyril Tynes in February 1972, he stated: "The UBP way of life is finished for ever in this country. Face facts, we are living in a black man's country and they are going to run it their way, not ours. I accept this and so should we all." See *Nassau Guardian*, February 26, 1972; Hughes, *Race and Politics*, 188.

84. Hughes, *Race and Politics*, 188. The worst incident occurred when two bombs were detonated, without serious damage and with no injuries, while Prime Minister Pindling was speaking in Marsh Harbour, Abaco. See Steve Dodge, ed., *Modern Bahamian Society* (Parkersburg, Iowa: Caribbean Books, 1989), 48–49.

85. For the 1972 general election, see Hughes, *Race and Politics*, 188–91, 230–41.

86. Dodge, "Independence and Separatism," in *Modern Bahamian Society,* 48–50.
87. According to Dodge's authoritative account, all of these overtures occurred before independence (ibid., 52–56).
88. Quoted by Leonard Thompson to Steve Dodge in private interview, ibid., 50 n. 23.
89. In Dodge's words, Pindling showed "patience and generosity regarding the role of Abaconians in the Bahamian nation" when, for instance, he told the fearlessly critical *Tribune* journalist Nicki Kelly: "I believe it will be a while before the white community will be . . . enthusiastic [about independence], however the place of Abaconians in History is somewhat different from the other white or black Bahamians. They felt that as loyalists they had a special niche and there were many of us that appreciated that, but what we didn't understand were those that tried to exploit this" (Nicki Kelly, "Foreign Press Query PM on Vesco, His Rolls Royce, and Discrimination," *Nassau Tribune,* July 9, 1973).
90. Dodge, "Independence and Separatism," 52–64. Adrian Day, the English editor of the *Abaco Independent* (under the pseudonym Childe Harold) from 1973 to 1977, was later the owner-editor of the U.S.-based *Bahamas Newsletter,* a well-informed monthly subscription journal consistently critical of the PLP regime.
91. The preliminary Green Paper published on March 8, 1972, and the White Paper published on October 18, 1972, are excerpted and fully discussed in the concluding chapter, "Symbolic Politics in a Racially [misprinted as "Radically"] Divided Society" of Hughes, *Race and Politics,* 222–24. For the diplomatic problems of transfer from colony to nation, see Godwin E. L. Friday, "Islands in the Stream: The Development of a Machinery for the Conduct of External Affairs in the Bahamas and Bahamian Foreign Policy, 1973–1985" (M.A. thesis, University of Waterloo, 1985).
92. Craton, *History of the Bahamas,* 287–88.
93. Hon. Eugene Dupuch, QC, quoted by Paul Albury, *The Story of the Bahamas* (London: Macmillan Caribbean, 1975), 283–84.
94. Craton, *History of the Bahamas,* 300.

Chapter 11

1. "Interview with Sir Lynden O. Pindling conducted by Steve Dodge, Tara Castens and Carey Weltig, Nassau, Bahamas, 23 March 1993," in *The Bahamas Index and Yearbook, 1992,* ed. Christopher Benjamin et al. (Decatur: White Sound Press, 1993), 43.
2. Quoted from Associated Press report, August 23, 1992, in Susan Love Brown, "This Is the Real Bahamas: Solidarity and Identity in Cat Island" (Ph.D. dissertation, University of California, San Diego, 1992), 283.
3. *Nassau Guardian,* February 2, 1971, quoted in Godwin L. Friday, "Islands in the Stream: The Development of a Machinery for the Conduct of External Affairs and Bahamian Foreign Policy, 1973–1985" (M.A. thesis, University of Waterloo, 1985), 20.
4. *Nassau Tribune,* August 7, 1971; Friday, "Islands in the Stream," 21.
5. Friday, "Islands in the Stream," 42–56.
6. Ibid. For a list of treaties applicable to the Bahamas in 1973, ranging from the original treaty of peace and commerce with Sweden of April 1654 to a consular convention with Romania in September 1968 and including eighty-six multilateral treaties (1856–1949) and thirty-nine agreements with the United States (1814–1963), ibid., Appendix M, 201–30.
7. Ibid., 61–63, 76–85.
8. The following is a list of the international organizations the Bahamas joined after 1969, in sequence: Caribbean Development Bank (CDB), October 18, 1969; International Monetary Fund (IMF) and International Bank for Reconstruction and Development, August 21, 1973; International Telecommunication Union, October 6, 1973; World Meteorological Organisation, December 29, 1973; World Health Organisation (WHO), Pan American Health Organisation, April 1, 1974; Universal Postal Union (UPU), March 22, 1974; Customs Co-operation Council, August 10, 1974; International Civil Aviation Organisation, June 26, 1975; Inter-

national Telecommunication Union, October 6, 1975; Food and Agriculture Organisation of the United Nations (FAO), November 7, 1975; African Caribbean Pacific Group of European Economic Community (EEC), April 1, 1976; International Labor Organisation (ILO), May 25, 1976; Inter-Governmental Maritime Consultative Organisation, July 22, 1976; World Intellectual Property Organisation, January 4, 1977; Inter-American Development Bank, December 15, 1977; Intergovernmental Oceanographic Commission, January 29, 1979; Caribbean Center for Development Administration, January 21, 1980; United Nations Educational, Scientific and Cultural Organisations (UNESCO), April 23, 1981; Organisation of American States (OAS), March 3, 1982; Caribbean Community (CARICOM), July 4, 1983.

9. These titles include the Order of the British Empire (OBE, MBE) and the British Empire Medal (BEM). The quintessence of this connection was Prime Minister Pindling's acceptance of a knighthood in 1982; he traveled to his investiture in London in a chartered jet along with family, PLP officials, and supporters.

10. Friday, "Islands in the Stream," 121–25. For the draft articles by Fiji, Indonesia, Mauritius, and the Philippines relating to archipelagic status, see UN Document A/Conf. 62/c.2/L.49, August 9, 1974, Appendix T, ibid., 275–76.

11. Friday, "Islands in the Stream," 136–38.

12. Fisheries Resources (Jurisdiction and Conservation) Act, 1977, Appendix S, ibid., 264–74.

13. Friday, "Islands in the Stream," 131–34.

14. See above, Chapter 8; *A History of the Royal Bahamas Police Force, 1840–1990* (Nassau: RBPF, 1990), 70–71.

15. *Bahamas Dateline* 3 (September 1978): 1–3. The Lobster War was said to have started in the early 1960s, but it heated up in the mid-1970s with the increased activities of Cuban-Americans and genuine confusion over Bahamian-U.S. territorial waters. See Ken Boodhoo and Joan Harnshaw, "The US-Bahamian Lobster Dispute: International Legal Perspectives," *Caribbean Studies*, March 1980, 57–58.

16. *Bahamas Dateline* 5 (May–June 1980).

17. When the Cuban fishermen's trial was held in July 1980, they were fined $95,000 and their boat and catch were ordered to be confiscated. The total indemnity paid by Cuba in December 1980 was $5.4 million (*Bahamas Dateline* 5 [July, December 1980]).

18. See, for example, "Statement on Vanguard Scholarship Programme," *Vanguard* (July 27–August 3, 1983): 1–2. This article claimed that the *Vanguard*'s acceptance of scholarships was in line with the policy of nonalignment ostensibly followed by the PLP government, pointed out that the Bahamas officially enjoyed diplomatic relations with Cuba, and showed a picture of the Cuban ambassador to the Bahamas, Raul Roa Khouri, in a friendly discussion with Governor-General Sir Gerald Cash at Government House, Nassau.

19. "'A sense of unity sweeping through the community' is how local journalist Gordon Knowles described reactions. . . . Some Bahamians said they were willing to die as martyrs in any retaliation moves against the Cubans. One group, the Bahamas-American Federation, called for the breaking of diplomatic relations with Cuba" (*Bahamas Dateline* 5 [May 1980]: 3).

20. Hanford Darville, Commissioner, Governor's Harbour, Eleuthera, to Chief Out Island Commissioner D. H. Burrows, October 15, 1956, Bahamas Archives, Colonial Secretary's Office Papers, 14210K.

21. S. A. Gomez, Commissioner, Abraham's Bay, Mayaguana, to Director of Education, Nassau, September 16, 1953, and to Chief Out Island Commissioner, March 29, 1953, ibid.

22. For example, "$20m. US Base Facilities Abandoned for 3 Years," *Nassau Tribune*, June 15, 1983. The five-hundred-acre base at Governor's Harbour operated by the United States from 1956 to 1980 was described as "totally self-sufficient in that it has its own theatre, laundry facilities, Chapel, galley, barber shop, youth centre, carpenter and tool shop, garage, snack bars, airport, docking facilities and elementary school." The first-class housing was sufficient for twenty-seven families and twelve bachelors. Between 1980, when it was given over to the Bahamian government, and 1983, the base employed seventeen persons, ten for

maintenance, five for security, and an assistant and chief superintendent, though later it was abandoned.

23. Jerome W. Lurry-Wright, *Custom and Conflict on a Bahamian Out Island* (Lanham, Md.: University Press of America, 1987).

24. *Bahamas Dateline* 3 (September 1978): 1–3; 8 (July 1983): 3; Dean W. Collinwood, *The Bahamas Between Worlds* (Decatur, Ill.: White Sound Press, 1989), 47–51.

25. *Report of the Commission of Inquiry Appointed to Inquire into the Illegal Use of the Bahamas for the Transshipment of Dangerous Drugs Destined for the United States of America, November 1983–December 1984* (Nassau: Bahamas Government, 1984), 1–10.

26. Appendix II, List of Exhibits, ACP Lawrence Major's Reports, "Illegal Activities, Andros Island," January 17, 1977; "Illegal Activities Through the Bahamas," March 12, 1979, Appendix VIII, Persons arrested, drugs seized, and locations, January 1981–June 1984, ibid., 86–97.

27. *Wall Street Journal*, January 22, 23, 1982; NBC broadcast, November 5, 1983; "A Nation for Sale," *Miami Herald* Special Report (articles dated September 23–October 10, 1983), n.d. (1983); *Report of the Commission of Inquiry*, section 18, pp. 352–60.

28. Collinwood, *Bahamas Between Worlds*, 53–54.

29. Ibid., 54–56.

30. Ibid., 57.

31. *Nassau Tribune*, November 8, 1983; Collinwood, *Bahamas Between Worlds*, 56–59.

32. *Report of the Commission of Inquiry*, 11–17.

33. Ibid.

34. Ibid., 20–25.

35. Ibid.; Michael Craton, *A History of the Bahamas*, 3d ed. (Waterloo: San Salvador Press, 1986), 302.

36. *Report of the Commission of Inquiry*, 25.

37. Ibid., 48–56.

38. Ibid., 60–65.

39. Ibid., 65–68.

40. Ibid., 221–32, 243, 256–67.

41. Ibid., chaps. 4, 11, 13, Conclusions, 402–8.

42. Ibid., chaps. 8, 9, 10.

43. Ibid., chap. 18, "Bahamas-US Relations," 351–401.

44. *A History of the Royal Bahamas Police Force, 1840–1990; Royal Bahamas Police Force Magazine* 21–27 (June 1988–June 1991).

45. *Nassau Guardian*, February 6, August 2, 1990; *Nassau Tribune*, February 14, 1990; Jeffrey Solterman and Steve Dodge, eds., *The Bahamas Index, 1990* (Decatur, Ill.: White Sound Press, 1990), 181–85; *Nassau Guardian*, August 17, September 12, 1991; Steve Dodge, Deanna Wise, and Angela De Witt, eds., *The Bahamas Index and Yearbook, 1991* (Decatur, Ill.: White Sound Press, 1991), 158–60.

46. Brown, "This Is the Real Bahamas," 250–80.

47. Perry Christie, the other sacked PLP minister who had stood successfully as an Independent, rather inopportunely returned to the PLP fold on the promise of office. In 1977, the PLP had won thirty-one of thirty-eight seats to the FNM's eleven in an expanded House, with 57 percent of the vote to 43 percent. See *Bahamas Dateline* 2 (June–August 1977), 7 (May–June 1982). For the 1987 general election, ibid., 11 (June–July 1987); *Bahamas Index and Yearbook, 1993*, 131, 135.

48. Robert Genardo, "Social and Cultural Issues, 1992," *Bahamas Index and Yearbook, 1992*, 19–20, 195–99.

49. For example, Athena Damianos, "Airport Project $24 Million Over Budget," *Nassau Tribune*, July 23, 1992; *Bahamas Index and Yearbook, 1993*, 131–55.

50. For example, Athena Damianos, "Carnival to Pull Out of Bahamas," *Nassau Tribune*,

January 16, 1992; Gladstone Thurston, "Carnival to Sell Crystal Palace," *Nassau Guardian*, January 23, 1992; Athena Damianos, "Tourist Industry Hits 21-Year Low," *Nassau Tribune*, February 4, 1992; *Bahamas Index and Yearbook, 1993*, 150–52.

51. William M. Koontz, "Some Observations on the 19 August 1992 General Elections in the Bahamas," *Bahamas Index and Yearbook*, 1993, 246.

52. Ibid., 244–48.

53. Ibid., Appendix, 251–53.

Chapter 12

1. The statistical information in this chapter is derived largely from Commonwealth of the Bahamas, Department of Statistics, Ministry of Finance, *Statistical Abstract, 1980* (Nassau: Department of Statistics, 1982); Azellah Major et al., *Some Aspects of Fertility in New Providence* (Nassau: Department of Statistics, 1981); *Report on the 1980 Census* (Nassau, 1986); Norma Abdulah, *The Bahamas and Its People: A Demographic Analysis* (St. Augustine, Trinidad: ISER and CARICOM Secretariat, n.d. [1987?]); Census Office, Department of Statistics, Nassau, *Census 1990; Preliminary Results* (Nassau, 1993); various preliminary tables, private communication, 1994.

2. In 1985, Norma Abdulah made three population projections based on the 1970 and 1989 censuses. The high variant, based on the continuation of the fertility and immigration rates of the 1970s, projected a total population of 328,469 in the year 2000 and 432,218 in 2015. Even the low variant—based on a fertility decline from 2.8 to 2.1 percent and a gradual decline in mortality and immigration—projected populations of 291,000 in 2000 and 340,000 by 2015. After the 1990 census (which showed 255,095 people, compared with Abdulah's projected range of between 252,253 and 264,043), this was revised downward by the Department of Statistics to 309,525 for 2000 and 387,531 for 2015 (Abdulah, *Bahamas and Its People*, 6–11; Census Office, Department of Statistics, "Mid-Year Population Projections, 1980–2015," personal communication, July 1994).

3. Census Office, "Mid-Year Population Projections, 1980–2015."

4. The 1990 census, taken on May 1, 1990, purported to include "all persons who on the census day had been residing in the Bahamas, regardless of their legal status, as well as students studying abroad and Bahamians serving with diplomatic corps and living abroad." It therefore included a fair proportion of illegal Haitian immigrants, though clearly far from all. The inclusion of Haitians even if "illegals" in the 1990 census may account for the disturbingly high number of "not stated" in the age statistics—no less than 19,758 out of the total of 255,095, compared to only 270 out of 209,505 in 1980. The noncounting of ages in 1990 probably most affects the middle cohorts of the age profiles, especially in New Providence and Grand Bahama. See above, Chapter 9.

5. Within New Providence itself, the population varied hugely, from the 243 per square mile (psm) of the 32.3-square-mile tract called Delaporte, and the 723 psm of the 11.5-sm of Adelaide (between them, more than half the island by area), to the 25,519 psm of the quarter square mile of St. Michael's district and the 26,152 and 28,284 psm of similar-sized Englerston and Bain Town, respectively (Census Office, *Preliminary Results*, Table 7, 16–17).

6. Abdulah, *Bahamas and Its People*, Tables 4F, 4G, 4H, 4J, 78–81.

7. A curious feature of the 1990 statistics for the southern islands was that while females constituted 58.5 percent of the population over age forty-five, this was almost offset by the predominance of males in each of the first five cohorts, constituting 54.8 percent of the population aged under twenty-five. As the result of this inexplicable anomaly, the overall ratio of males to females in the southern islands was almost exactly 100:100 compared with 100:106 in favor of females for the Bahamas overall.

8. Census Office, *Preliminary Results*, Table 5, 13.

9. Abdulah, *Bahamas and Its People*, 189–90: "Because of the definition used in the 1980

Census, data have given us fewer households, fewer small households, and many more large households, than would emerge [with a better definition. . . . Rather than limiting the concept of 'family' to conjugal family] it is suggested that blood relation be used as one of the criteria for determining a family relationship. Thus brothers and sisters living together would constitute a family. So would a grandmother and her grandchild; or two unmarried sisters, etc."

10. Ibid., 87–126, 187–88.

11. Ibid., 127–62, 188–89. Women without any education were as likely to be in common-law unions as in formal marriage (about 27 percent of the total in each). Those with elementary and university education were as likely as each other to be married (46–48 percent), but the latter were less likely to have a common-law union (3 percent compared with 9 percent). The marriage rate was generally much higher among high school graduates (27 percent), but this was clearly the product of the recent explosion of high school education. The fertility level (that is, the CEB or mean number of children ever born per thousand women aged over fifteen) of women with no education was calculated at 2,678, for those with only elementary education 2,905, with high school education 2,531, and with college or university education, 1,391 (ibid., Tables 6C, 6G, 147–48, 152).

12. Ibid., Tables 6N, 6P, 6Q, 6L, 156–60. For the 34.3 percent of mothers aged 20–24 who had had children in 1979–80, the average age at which they had their first child was 18.7 years. In August 1994, Dr. Franklin Walkine, the PLP MP for Crooked Island, told a Public Forum on Crime that teenage births in 1992 were 17.3 percent more than in 1991. The pregnancy rate in the female age range 15–19, 96 per thousand, was said to be "four to twelve times that of developed countries." More than 84 percent of children born to teenage children were born to men over 20. See Walkine, "Paper on Crime Presented at Public Forum on Crime, August 1994" (Nassau, 1994), 4.

13. Numbers of Children to Mothers in Sample, by Religious Affiliation, New Providence, 1980

Children	*0–1*	*1–2*	*3–4*	*5–6*	*7–8*	*9+*	*Un-stated*	*Total mothers*	*Approximate average*
Roman Catholic	18	68	28	14	6	2	2	138	2.90
Anglican	19	62	29	9	6	1	4	130	2.80
Baptist	26	104	42	20	12	10	1	215	3.21
Totals	63	234	99	43	24	13	7	483	2.96

Major et al., *Some Aspects of Fertility*, 9–30.

14. The actual numbers are less startling: an increase from a total of 441 and 262 males over the period 1980–83 (or 7.2 and 8.9 per thousand of the age-specific populations), to 656 and 418 males (8.0 and 10.4 per thousand of those aged twenty to forty) during 1989–91 (Tables Q4, Q9, 1990 Census, Deaths [excluding still births] by Age Group Sex, 1980–87, 1984–91, personal communication, 1994).

15. Of the 18,768 (out of 50,312) multiperson households headed by "single," divorced, separated, or widowed persons in 1990, 14,947, or 79.6 percent, were headed by females (Table 22, 1990 Census, Private Households by Sex and Marital Status of Head and Size of Household, personal communication, 1994). Of the 42 percent of New Providence households headed by women in 1992, 56.6 percent were said to have a combined income below $10,000 a year (Walkine, "Paper on Crime," 3).

16. Table 6, 1990 Census, Private Households by Type of Dwelling and Main Source of Water Supply, personal communication, July 1994.

17. Table 7, 1990 Census, Private Households by Type of Dwelling and Use of Toilet Facilities, ibid.

18. Susan Love Brown, "This Is the Real Bahamas: Solidarity and Identity in Cat Island" (Ph.D. dissertation, University of California, San Diego, 1992).

19. *Bahamas: Report for the Years 1958 and 1959* (London: HMSO, 1961), 52; *Royal Bahamas Police Force Annual Report for the Year 1984* (Nassau: RBPF, 1984). In 1984, 6,587 car accidents were reported in New Providence by the police (5,143 involving cars, 697 trucks, 272 buses, and 187 taxis), 1,456 in Grand Bahama, and 220 in the rest of the Bahamas.

20. "World Telecommunication Day Special Supplement," *Nassau Tribune*, May 17, 1994, 1–12.

21. *Bahamas Handbook and Businessman's Guide, 1986* (Nassau: Dupuch, 1986), 346.

22. Table 11, 1990 Census, Total Population by Sex, Age Group and Religion, personal communication, July 1994.

23. Department of the Census, Q9, Table 3.1, Employed Persons by Sex and Industrial Group, 1993; Table 4:1, Employed Persons by Sex and Occupational Group, 1993, ibid. The figures for "Industrial Groups" for Grand Bahama were simpler than for the Bahamas as a whole and for New Providence, being listed in only four categories. Of the 19,030 employed, 6 percent were in "Agriculture, Hunting, Forestry and Fishing," 24 percent in "Community, Social and Personal Services," and 35 percent each in "Wholesale & Retail and Hotels & Restaurants" and "Other Industries."

24. Table 14, 1990 Census, Population 15 Years and Over Not Attending School, by Sex, Age Group and Educational Attainment, ibid.

25. Dean W. Collinwood, *The Bahamas Between Worlds* (Decatur, Ill.: White Sound Press, 1989), 72–81.

26. Ibid., 76–77.

27. Dean W. Collinwood, "The Bahamas: Educational Progress and Problems; The Archer Affair," in *Latin American and Caribbean Contemporary Record*, Vol. 2, *1982–1983*, ed. Jack W. Hopkins (New York: Holmes and Meier, 1984), 663–64. See above, Chapter 10.

28. Collinwood, *Bahamas Between Worlds*, 75–89, citing Harriet P. Lefley, "Modal Personality in the Bahamas," *Journal of Cross-Cultural Psychology* 3 (June 1972); Albert Memmi, *The Colonizer and the Colonized* (Boston: Beacon Press, 1965).

29. *Nassau Guardian*, March 24, 1973, quoted in Colin A. Hughes, *Race and Politics in the Bahamas* (St. Lucia: University of Queensland Press, 1981), 179–80. In April 1992, Minister of Education Bernard Nottage admitted that Bahamian children were leaving primary school reading at kindergarten level, or seven grades below their expected level (*Nassau Tribune*, April 30, 1992).

30. E. Stubbs, "GCE 'O' Level Analysis, June 1991," Bahamas Ministry of Education and Culture Planning Unit, 1991.

31. *Bahamas General Certificate of Education, History Syllabus, 1993* (Nassau: Ministry of Education, 1990). See also *1982 Curriculum for History (Senior High), Commonwealth of the Bahamas. Grade 10, The Origins of Our People; Grade 11, Bahamian and West Indian History; Grade 12, Twentieth Century Bahamian History* (Nassau: Ministry of Education, 1982), quoted in Michael Craton, "The Historiography of the Bahamas, Turks & Caicos Islands, Cayman Islands and Belize," chap. 25 in *UNESCO General History of the Caribbean*, Vol. 6, *Historiography*, ed. Barry Higman and Jean Casimir (Paris and London: UNESCO and Macmillan, 1997).

32. Dean W. Collinwood, "Problems of Research and Training in Small Islands Without a Social Science Faculty," in *Social Sciences in Latin America and the Caribbean*, Vol. 1, *The English-Speaking Caribbean and Suriname: Social Science Needs and Priorities* (Paris: UNESCO Reports and Papers in the Social Sciences, No. 48, 1980), 27–30; Collinwood, *Bahamas Between Worlds*, 74.

33. Despite Prime Minister Lynden Pindling's affirmation of the need for a university of the Bahamas during the 1992 election campaign (*Nassau Tribune,* July 20, 1992), in the same speech, Pindling advocated raising the school leaving age and promised a national health insurance scheme.

34. *Bahamas Dateline* 9 (April 30, 1984): 1–2; *RBPF Annual Report of the Year 1984* (Nassau: RBPF, 1985).

35. *Bahamas Dateline* 9 (April 30, 1984): 1–2.

36. *Bahamas Dateline* 9 (January 21, 1985): 3.

37. *RBPF Annual Report, 1985* (Nassau: RBPF, 1986). In 1984, the Royal Bahamas Police Force (said to be 35 percent under its authorized establishment) included a commissioner, deputy commissioner, 2 assistant commissioners, 3 chief superintendents, 43 assistant superintendents, 4 chief inspectors, 74 inspectors, a staff sergeant, 139 sergeants, 183 corporals, 1,024 constables, and 51 recruits. In addition, there were 72 first and 12 second grade local constables, 26 beach wardens, 233 police reservists, and 42 civilian staff.

38. "Firearms Bill Passes in House," *Nassau Guardian,* July 28, 1994. The psychic validity of firearms to the frustrated disadvantaged, and perhaps the motivation for crimes of violence including rape, were conveyed by a convicted armed robber quoted by Franklin Walkine in August 1994. Neither Genet nor Foucault could have expressed such feelings better: "When you walk into a place with the threat of heat, nobody's going to ask question, nobody in fact is going to say a word. The joint buzzes in silent harmony, in unspoken appreciation for your authority" (Walkine, "Paper on Crime," 9–10).

39. *Bahamas Dateline* 9 (April 30, 1984): 2; *Nassau Guardian,* December 29, 1992. The new prime minister, Hubert Ingraham, announced that his government would not oppose the death penalty.

40. "Magistrate Paints Black Crime Picture," *Nassau Guardian,* August 3, 1994.

41. Ibid.

42. *Nassau Guardian,* April 27, July 2, 1992; *Nassau Tribune,* July 1, 1992.

43. *Nassau Guardian,* May 27, 28, 1992.

44. Robyn Adderley, "Police and Public Form Meaningful Relationship," *Nassau Guardian,* May 15, 1993.

45. "A Dangerous Young Element," *Nassau Guardian,* October 19, 1992; "Victims Describe Discovery Day Violence," *Nassau Tribune,* October 21, 1992.

46. "Violence Rages in Schools," "Psychologist Warns of Increase in Violence," "Nottage Admits Educational System Has Problems with School Violence," *Nassau Tribune,* January 14, 25, February 4, 1992.

47. "Rights Group Reports Intolerable Conditions at Fox Hill Prison," *Nassau Guardian,* September 2, 1992.

48. Timothy O. McCartney, *Neuroses in the Sun* (Nassau: Executive Printers, 1971), 123–31.

49. Sandra Dean-Patterson, "A Longitudinal Study of Changes in Bahamian Drinking Patterns, 1969–1977" (Ph.D. dissertation, Brandeis University, 1978).

50. McCartney, *Neuroses in the Sun,* 115–23; Dean W. Collinwood, "The Bahamas" in *Latin American and Caribbean Contemporary Record,* Vol. 4, *1984–1985,* ed. Jack W. Hopkins (New York: Holmes and Meier, 1986), 628–29.

51. "Too Many Young Men in Prison Abuse Drugs," "BASH Chairman Says Drug Addiction 'Worse Than It Has Ever Been,'" *Nassau Guardian,* January 29, 1993, November 24, 1992.

52. *Nassau Tribune,* March 6, December 1, 1992. In August 1994, Magistrate Gregory Hilton reported that "over 30 per cent of persons at Fox Hill [Prison] are either HIV positive or have Hepatitis B" (*Nassau Guardian,* August 7, 1994).

53. Lindsay Thompson, "Country Ranks High in HIV, AIDS Infections," *Nassau Guardian,* November 30, 1994.

54. Taped transcript, Senate Commission Hearing, Nassau, Tuesday, May 17, 1994.

55. McCartney, *Neuroses in the Sun,* 142–45.

56. "Doctor Explores Connection Between Alcohol and STDs," *Nassau Guardian*, January 20, 1992.

57. *Manifesto '92: Free National Movement, the Better Way* (Nassau: FNM, 1992), 2023.

58. Ibid., 21.

59. "Pindling Promises Health Care to Pay All Doctors' and Hospital Bills," *Nassau Tribune*, July 20, 1992.

60. *Manifesto '92*, 22, 25–26.

61. "Finance Crunch Scraps New Hospital," *Nassau Tribune*, December 18, 1992.

62. Taped interviews with "Delia Mason-Smith," December 13, 1983, October 10, 1994.

63. Ibid. For the question of Haitian employment, see below, Chapter 13.

Chapter 13

1. Nationality Act, No. 18 of 1973, *The Statute Law of the Bahamas, Revised Edition, 1987* (Nassau: Bahamas Government, 1987), chap. 178, 2126–39. For a summary of Bahamian citizenship requirements, see *Bahamas Handbook and Businessman's Guide* (Nassau: Dupuch, 1986), 245–47.

2. In 1980, following the D'Arcy Ryan case, when the minister responsible for immigration was threatened with imprisonment for contempt of court, the PLP government passed the enabling act for a referendum to decide whether the constitution could be changed to allow the immigration minister to overrule the courts in immigration decisions; eighteen years later the referendum had still not been held. See Michael Craton, *A History of the Bahamas*, 3d ed. (Waterloo: San Salvador Press, 1986), 294–95.

3. *Bahamas Handbook* (1986), 299.

4. Ibid., 296–98.

5. Taped interview with Hon. Sean McWeeney, former attorney general and chairman of the PLP, Nassau, October 27, 1994.

6. Immovable Property (Acquisition by Foreign Persons) Act, No. 3 of 1981 (to come into effect, November 1, 1983), *Statute Law of the Bahamas* (1987), 1761–77; International Persons Landholding Act, No. 41 of 1993 (to come into effect, January 1, 1994), *Extraordinary Official Gazette of the Bahamas* (Nassau: Bahamas Government, 1993), 1–14.

7. The Companies Act, No. 18 of 1992, repealed both the previous Companies Act and Foreign Companies Act and was distinct from the International Business Companies Act, 1989. See *General Information Relating to the Formation of Companies Incorporated Under the Companies Act 1992* and *All You Need to Know About Incorporation of an IBC in the Bahamas* (Nassau: Registrar General's Department, 1992).

8. Taped interview with Terry North, Nassau, October 24, 1994.

9. Ibid.; *Nassau Guardian* and *Tribune*, October–November 1994.

10. The first black Catholic priest in the Bahamas was the American Fr. Prosper Meyer OSB (1947–61), who initiated the mission to the Haitians. The first locally ordained Catholic priest was the white Anglican convert Fr. Arthur Chapman (Easter 1955). The first native Bahamian priest, Fr. Charles Coakley, was ordained by Bishop Leonard Hagerty on June 24, 1960. He was the first to resign in 1968, followed by six young Bahamian Benedictine priests at St. Augustine's, six Bahamian nuns, and three white American Benedictine priests. See Colman J. Barry OSB, *Upon These Rocks: Catholics in the Bahamas* (Collegeville, Minn.: St. John's Abbey Press, 1973), 498–522; taped interview with Preston Moss, Nassau, October 28, 1994.

11. Moss interview, October 28, 1994.

12. Taped interview with Rt. Rev. Michael Eldon, Nassau, November 1, 1994. For some of the early ecumenical moves between Bahamian Catholics and Anglicans, see Bishop Bernard Markham (RC), quoted in Barry, *Upon These Rocks*, 543–50.

13. The second governor-general, Sir Gerald Cash, was an Anglican, the third, Sir Henry Taylor, a Catholic convert from Anglicanism. Taylor's successor was Sir Clifford Darling, a

Baptist. His FNM successor was expected to be Sir Kendal Isaacs (an Anglican), but Isaacs's ill health led to the appointment of Sir Orville Turnquest, also an Anglican.

14. See, for example, Kortright Davis, *Emancipation Still Comin': Explorations in Caribbean Emancipatory Theology* (Maryknoll, N.Y.: Orbis, 1990).

15. Steve Dodge et al., eds., *Bahamas Index, 1986* (Decatur, Ill.: White Sound Press, 1986), 322–36.

16. Michael Craton and Gail Saunders, *Islanders in the Stream: A History of the Bahamian People, Volume One: From Aboriginal Times to the End of Slavery* (Athens: University of Georgia Press, 1992), 331–34.

17. Steve Dodge et al., eds., *Bahamas Index and Yearbook* (Decatur, Ill.: White Sound Press, 1991–93), 1991, 177–78; 1992, 183–86; 1993, 177–80; *Nassau Guardian*, November 27, 1991. Only in Spanish Wells had race issues divided the Methodists, a hard core of local whites separating to form their own congregation when they were sent a white minister who was married to a black West Indian.

18. *Nassau Guardian*, January 12, 1991.

19. *Nassau Guardian*, March 16, April 11, September 30, 1991.

20. Dodge et al., eds., *Bahamas Index and Yearbook*, 1992, 183–86; 1993, 177–80; *Nassau Guardian*, January 27, 31, June 4, 1992, January 5, February 19, March 3, 1993; *Nassau Tribune*, May 31, 1992, January 6, February 24, April 1, 15, June 30, 1993.

21. Craton and Saunders, *Islanders in the Stream*, 1:3–20.

22. Ibid., 65, 159–63.

23. Ibid., 206; C. L. R. James, *The Black Jacobins: Toussaint L'Ouverture and the San Domingo Revolution*, rev. ed. (London: Alison and Busby, 1980); David Geggus, *Slavery, War and Revolution: The British Occupation of Saint Domingue, 1793–8* (Oxford: Oxford University Press, 1981); Robin Blackburn, *The Overthrow of Colonial Slavery, 1776–1848* (London: Verso, 1988); Sean McWeeney, "The 'Haitian Problem' in the Bahamas at the Close of the Eighteenth Century," *Journal of the Bahamas Historical Society* 16 (October 1994): 2–9.

24. McWeeney, "'Haitian Problem,'" 3–8; Craton and Saunders, *Islanders in the Stream*, 1:204–12.

25. David E. Wood, "The Free People of Colour in Bahamian Society," *Journal of the Bahamas Historical Society* 12 (October 1990): 20–24. Sean McWeeney is currently working on a full-length study of Stephen Dillet and his times (taped interview with Sean McWeeney, Nassau, October 27, 1994).

26. Taped interview with Eliezer Regnier, Nassau, November 1, 1994. Other Haitian material in interviews with Leila Greene, Barbara Pierre, Howland Bottomley, Rt. Rev. Michael Eldon, Msr. Preston Moss, Nassau and Georgetown, Exuma, October 21–November 2, 1994.

27. Nothing is more tricky than determining accurate figures for Haitians in the Bahamas. The censuses, though making no distinction between legal and illegal residents, seriously undercount because most illegals avoid the census-takers. The 1943 census reported 903 West Indians (including the British West Indians); that in 1953, 557 West Indians (excluding the British West Indians); in 1963, 4,170 Haitians; 1970, 6,151; 1980, 8,000; 1990, 12,000. See Dawn L. Marshall, *The Haitian Problem: Illegal Migration to the Bahamas* (Kingston, Jamaica: ISER, 1979), 95–128, esp. Table 4:1, "Number of Haitians in the Bahamas, 1943–1973," 97.

28. Ibid., 106–17. Marshall's book generalized as well as it could. It has useful material on Abaco but very little on the other Family Islands or on the New Providence settlements other than Carmichael, where Marshall surveyed 71 households, 135 adults and 55 children.

29. Ibid., 1–60, esp. Table 1:3, Table 2:4; François Gayot, "La Pastorale face à L'évolution de la vie rurale en Haiti: Étude socio-religieuse de diocèse de Port-de-Paix" (Ph.D. dissertation, University of Strasbourg, 1971).

30. Marshall, *Haitian Problem*, 95–128, esp. Table 4:3. The largest single item imported was Barbancourt rum, beginning in 1956, and reaching $28,110 in value in 1967.

31. Ibid., 98–106, also 57–58; Regnier interview, November 1, 1994.

32. Marshall, *Haitian Problem,* Tables 2:5, 2:6, pp. 31–32.

33. Ibid., 16–18. Marshall quotes here mainly from Gayot, "La Vie rurale en Haiti."

34. Marshall, *Haitian Problem,* 55–57.

35. Ibid., 106–17. The seventy-seven Haitians were ordered "deported, but not to Haiti."

36. Agribusiness was begun near Marsh Harbour by J. B. Crockett in 1952. See ibid., 136–41, quoting Bahamas Out Island Reports, Marsh Harbour Abaco, 1957–60; Gayot, "La Vie rurale en Haiti."

37. Marshall, *Haitian Problem,* 131–36. Marshall estimated the combined population of the four Abaco camps in 1960 at 2,370, of whom probably 600 were Turks Islanders.

38. Though Key-Sawyer Farms was leased to the Gracewood Packing Company of Florida in October 1988 and a human rights group visiting the Camp in 1992 found only about three hundred people permanently living there, conditions if anything were worse than ever. See "Haitians at Abaco Farm Say They Are Treated Like Dogs," *Nassau Guardian,* October 24, 1988; *Report of Haitian Refugee Mission, October 1992* (Nassau, 1992).

39. See above, Chapter 12; interviews with Leila Greene, Nassau, December 13, 1983, October 21, 1994.

40. Athena Damianos, "Haitians Told to Leave Russell Island," *Nassau Tribune,* May 5, 1992; Clunis Devaney, "Govt to Tackle Custom of Hiring Illegal Immigrants," *Nassau Guardian,* May 2, 1993.

41. Catechist George Dorsette of the Bluff, Eleuthera, quoted in *Nassau Guardian,* May 3, 1993.

42. Regnier interview, November 1, 1994.

43. For Haitian conditions in general, see references and synopses of newspaper reports in Dodge et al., eds., *Bahamas Index and Yearbook, 1986–1993.* Also see Nassau Public Library and Bahamas Archives newspaper cuttings files, 1986–94. For conditions in New Providence, see, for example, letters from "Ashamed," headlined "Bemoans Haitians & Their Living Habits," *Nassau Tribune,* April 6, 1993; Tamara V. Capron, "Bahamians Need to Learn French or Creole," *Nassau Guardian,* April 7, 1993; Carl E. Treco, "Bahamians, Bahamians, Where Are You?" *Nassau Guardian,* June 22, 1993.

44. Regnier interview, November 1, 1994.

45. Ibid; and see above, Chapter 4.

46. Regnier interview, November 1, 1994.

47. Greene interview, October 21, 1994.

48. Marshall, *Haitian Problem,* 102–17.

49. Dodge et al., eds., *Bahamas Index,* 1986, 281–306; 1987, 231–34; 1988, 200–201; 1989, 90–193; *Bahamas Index and Yearbook,* 1990, 39–40, 189–90; 1991, 13–15, 165–67.

50. Dodge et al., eds., *Bahamas Index and Yearbook,* 1992, 23, 176–77; 1993, 16–17, 168–69. For later developments and conditions, see "Illegal Haitians a Burden, UN Assembly Told," *Nassau Guardian,* October 7, 1992; "Roundup Nets 400 Illegal Immigrants," *Nassau Guardian,* May 24, 1993; Nicki Kelly, "The Haitian Dilemma," *Nassau Tribune,* November 2, 1993; "Bahamas Pressing Haitians to Flee: Immigration Policy Includes Police Raids and Jailings," *New York Times,* January 2, 1994; "PM: Country Cannot Carry Haitian Burden," *Nassau Guardian,* May 7, 1994.

51. Regnier interview, November 1, 1994.

52. The articles, generally on a Monday, were in *kweyole,* but an English version was available at the *Tribune* office on demand, for the price of photocopying. Both were written by the very Bahamian-sounding Kelly North.

53. Norris R. Carroll, "Concerned About Haitian Problem," *Nassau Guardian,* May 28, 1994. See also Howard Hall, "Illegal Immigrants May Start Epidemic," *Nassau Tribune,* May 3, 1994; "One Fed-Up with Gang Mentality" letter "Haitians Breaking Laws, Destabilising Bahamas' Peaceful Way of Life," *Nassau Tribune,* June 24, 1994; Greg Mullings, "Haitians Killing Local Culture," *Nassau Guardian,* July 7, 1994; Dianne Penn, "Haitian Refugees & 'Boat People' a Growing Problem for Bahamas," *Nassau Tribune,* July 8, 1994. For an official reaction, see

Gladstone Thurston, "Haitians Threaten Bahamian Way of Life, Says DPM," *Nassau Guardian*, April 7, 1994; Colin Higgins, "Turnquest: Illegal Haitians Major 'Threat' to Development," *Nassau Tribune*, April 8, 1994.

54. Lindsay Thompson, "Charter Flight Takes 94 Haitian Immigrants Home," *Nassau Guardian*, April 25, 1994; Gladstone Thurston, "Commission Lauds Treatment of Haitian Refugees," "Govt. Upholds Haitian Sanctions," *Nassau Guardian*, May 30, 1994.

55. Bahamas Ministry of Foreign Affairs, Agreement signed on January 12, 1995, between the Government of the Bahamas and the Haitian Government, at Port-au-Prince, Haiti, Annex III, clauses 4–5.

56. Interview with Carlton Wright, Deputy Permanent Secretary, Bahamas Ministry of Public Safety and Immigration, February 22, 1996; Michael Craton, "Between Rock and Hard Place: The Bahamian Haitians," *Hemisfile* (La Jolla, Calif.), May–June 1996.

57. "Smaller Haitian Presence After Year of Repatriation," *Nassau Tribune*, February 19, 1996, 1, 12.

58. For an assimilationist argument, see Alfred Sears, "The Haitian Question in the Bahamas," *Journal of the Bahamas Historical Society* 16 (October 1994): 17–21.

59. Susan Love Brown, "The Is the Real Bahamas: Solidarity and Identity in Cat Island" (Ph.D. dissertation, University of California, San Diego, 1992).

60. Douglas Hanks Jr., *Driven by the Stars: The Story of Durward Knowles* (Nassau: Privately published, 1992).

61. Wendell P. Bradley, *They Live by the Wind* (New York: Knopf, 1969), 211–67.

62. Taped interviews with Howland Bottomley, Georgetown and Stocking Island, Exuma, June 26, 1983, October 25, 1994. For excellent articles on the Family Island Regatta, see Art Paine, "The Family Island Regatta: A Personal Journey," *Wooden Boat* 104 (January–February 1992): 66–81; "Boats of the Shallow Sea: Art Paine Investigates the Development of the Bahamian Racing Classes," *Boatman* 13 (April 1994): 16–25. See also Bradley, *They Live by the Wind*, 211–67.

63. Interview with Howland Bottomley, October 25, 1994.

64. In 1974 a Prime Minister's Trophy and a Governor General's Cup were instituted for the first races in the regatta, for A and B Class boats respectively. By 1993, Prime Minister Ingraham was referring to "this National Family Island Regatta," though the organizers stubbornly continued to style it the Out Island Regatta (ibid.; *George Town Bicentennial, 1793–1993: 40th Out Island Regatta Program* (Georgetown, Exuma: Regatta Committee, 1993).

65. Interview with Howland Bottomley, June 26, 1983.

66. *George Town Bicentennial*, 37–45; Bottomley interview, October 25, 1994.

67. By 1994, nearly seventy boats were competing in the regatta, of which more than two-thirds were dinghies. These, with a usual crew of four, could still be constructed for under $10,000, compared with up to $100,000 for even a "traditional" A or B Class boat, with its crew of fifteen or more. Owners were, of necessity, usually wealthy businessmen, though the winning skippers remained almost entirely working sailors, still predominantly from Exuma, Andros, Long Island, and Nassau (Bottomley interview, October 25, 1994).

68. *The Scholarship 500: A Class "C" Bahamian Racing Dinghy Built by the Students of L. N. Coakley Secondary School Under the Guidance of Captain Sherwin Gray* (Georgetown, Exuma: MOE Education Resource Centre, 1994).

69. In 1994, the FNM government passed an act to set up local government initially in Abaco, Exuma, Eleuthera, Grand Bahama, and Bimini, with the first local council elections scheduled for October 1995. At the same time, the government encouraged the Ministry of Tourism to advertise all Family Islands individually and especially to promote eco-tourism. This commitment was underlined by the creation of the Commission on the Environment, Science and Technology, with committed environmentalist Lynn Holowesko as chairperson, in 1995. See Bill for an Act to make provision for Local Government in the Commonwealth of the Bahamas, No. 75 of 1993 Session; interview with Cecil Marche and Archibald Nairn, Ministry of Local Government, Clarence Bain Building, Nassau, October 31, 1994.

70. For earlier cricket in the Bahamas, see above, Chapters 3 and 5. For West Indian cricket in general, C. L. R. James, *Beyond a Boundary* (London: Hutchinson, 1963); Michael Manley, *A History of West Indies Cricket* (London: Andre Deutsch, 1988); Hilary Beckles and Brian Stoddart, eds., *Liberation Cricket: West Indies Cricket Culture* (Kingston: Ian Randle Press, 1995).

71. *The Bahamas Ten Years After Independence, 1973–1983* (Nassau: Archives Department, 1983), 28.

72. Michael Craton, "The Ambivalencies of Independency: The Transition out of Slavery, c. 1800–1850," in *West Indies Accounts: Essays in the History of the British Caribbean and the Atlantic Economy in Honour of Richard Sheridan*, ed. Roderick A. McDonald (Barbados, Jamaica, Trinidad: UWI Press, 1996), 274–96.

73. As early as 1927, however, the Bahamian Charlie Major was said to have jumped 6′ 8½″ in a local high jump competition—then close to the world record. This stood as the Bahamian record for forty years, though by the 1980s and 1990s Stephen Wray and Troy Kemp had both cleared 7′ 7″ ("A Tribute to Charlie," *Nassau Guardian*, Special Supplement, November 18, 1986).

74. Special Supplement for Bahamas Amateur Athletic Association 30th Anniversary, 1952–82, *Nassau Guardian*, November 26, 1982, C1–4.

75. Taped interview with Keith H. Parker OBE, Nassau, October 31, 1994.

76. Colin Tatz, *Australian*, October 12, 1982, quoted in *Nassau Guardian* Special Supplement, November 26, 1982. See also *The Bahamas Ten Years After Independence*, 25–31. Debbie Ferguson's name should be added to those of the silver medalists at Atlanta; she ran in the preliminary rounds of the 4 × 100 meters relay while Chandra Sturrup was competing in the final of the 100 meters (in which she placed fourth).

77. Parker interview, October 31, 1994. The value of sporting activities in unifying the Bahamian nation was the motive for the organization of the Bahamas Games, an interinsular mini-Olympics, held biennially from 1991. The theme for the Third Bahamas Games, staged in Nassau in July 1995, was "Bridging the Islands: Building the Nation Through Sports." Hundreds of athletes took part in a wide variety of sports, and the competition was fierce. Perhaps not surprisingly, New Providence won overwhelmingly, despite the provision that an athlete could compete for any island in which he or she had roots.

78. See above, Chapter 4. Charles L. Edwards, *Bahama Songs and Stories* (Cincinnati: University of Cincinnati, 1895); Elsie Clews Parsons, *Folk Tales of Andros Island, Bahamas* (New York: American Folklore Society, 1918); Samuel B. Charters, *Music of the Bahamas* (New York: Folkways Records, 1959), FS 3844–46; Peter K. Siegel and Jody Stecher, *The Real Bahamas in Music and Song* (New York: Nonsuch Explorer Records, 1965), H 72013; John Holm and Alison Shilling, *Dictionary of Bahamian English* (New York: Lexic Press, 1980). Soon after coming to power, the FNM acknowledged the centrality of culture to Bahamian identity and signaled its intention to raise public cultural consciousness by sponsoring a Senate Select Committee on Culture, which held many sessions over the following eighteen months. See Dianne Penn, "Senate Committee into Culture Opens in Rawson Square," *Nassau Tribune*, May 13, 1993.

79. Winston V. Saunders, *I, Nehemiah Remember When* (Nassau: Privately published, 1987), 63–64, 31–34. Pickney–children; the Vola–Junkanoo; bongies–buttocks (female); serasee–strictly the orange-fruited vine *mormodica charantia* but generally any bush tea or medicine. See Patricia Glinton-Meicholas, *How to Be a True-True Bahamian: A Hilarious Look at Life in the Bahamas* (Nassau: Guanima Press, 1994). For Winston Saunders's strongly expressed views on Bahamian culture and his advocacy of a National Arts Council, see "Performing Artists Testify Before Senate Committee on Culture," *Nassau Guardian*, June 11, 1993.

80. Much pioneer work on plantation archaeology was undertaken in the 1980s and 1990s by the archives under the supervision of the Jamaican archaeologist Tony Aarons and by the amateur volunteers of the Bahamas Archeological Team (BAT). Besides its splendid work in promoting national parks and the preservation of endangered flora and fauna, the Bahamas National Trust had an active Preservation Division concerned about the Bahamian architectural heritage from about 1975. See Robert Douglas, *Island Heritage: Architecture of the*

Bahamas, the Drawings of Robert Douglas (Nassau: Darkstream Publications, 1992); Bahamas Archives, *A Selection of Historic Buildings of the Bahamas* (Nassau: Bahamas Archives, 1975); Seighbert Russell, *Nassau's Historic Buildings* (Nassau: Bahamas National Trust, 1979); Gail Saunders and Donald Cartwright, *Historic Nassau* (London: Macmillan Caribbean, 1983); D. and N. Popov, *Island Expedition: The Central and Southern Bahamas* (Miami: Graphic Media, 1988). For archaeological, architectural, conservation, and preservation issues in general, see evidence of D. Gail Saunders before Senate Select Committee on Culture, reported by Keva Lightbourne, "Archives Director Says Protective Laws Needed for Cultural Heritage," *Nassau Guardian*, June 5, 1993.

81. Philip Larkin, *High Windows* (London: Faber, 1974), 17. A particularly grievous loss was the Royal Victoria Hotel, originally hoped to be, after restoration, the Bahamian National Gallery and Museum, but demolished after a fire in 1991. In 1994, Christchurch Anglican Cathedral was also the focus of a heated debate between renovators, restorers, and preservationists. See, for example, Nicki Kelly, "Sacred and Profane," *Nassau Tribune*, October 11, 1994, 7.

82. Gail Saunders, "The Social History of the Bahamas, 1890–1953" (Ph.D. dissertation, University of Waterloo, 1985), 330–34.

83. *Nassau Guardian*, November 30, 1994. See also the outspoken critique of Bahamian music and cultural trends in general by the composer and music director Cleophas Adderley, given before the Senate Select Committee on Culture and reported in *Bahamas Journal*, June 5, 1993.

84. *Nassau Guardian*, March 15, 1986.

85. Marcella Taylor et al., eds., *Bahamian Anthology: College of the Bahamas* (London: Macmillan Caribbean, 1983). Though less impressive and suggesting even less artistic progress than had really occurred, see also *From the Shallow Seas: Bahamian Creative Writing Today* (Havana: Casa de la Americas, 1993).

86. Mizpah Tertullian, "Psychologically Speaking," in Taylor et al., eds., *Bahamian Anthology*, 27.

87. Anthony Dahl, *Literature of the Bahamas, 1724–1992: The March Towards National Identity* (New York: University Press of America, 1995), 200–201, 213; Nicolette Bethel, "National Identity and the Oral Tradition" (Ph.D. dissertation in progress, University of Cambridge, private communication, 1996).

88. Dahl, *Literature of the Bahamas*, 139–243.

89. Taylor et al., eds., *Bahamian Anthology*, 170. Rahming's list of inspirational mentors could hardly be more eclectic: a white (Jewish) popular folksinger (Dylan), a black Trinidadian calypsonian (Sparrow), an American white Marxist historian of Guyana (Adamson), a black American playwright (Leroi Jones), and two of Rahming's own cousins, fellow artists, and bar buddies (Jenks and Melvin Rahming).

90. Nicolette Bethel (currently completing a Cambridge doctoral dissertation on Bahamian literature), personal communication, August 1995.

91. Taylor et al., eds., *Bahamian Anthology*, 66–67.

92. Ibid., 72. That formal Bahamian poetry is so often labored and trite is unfortunate when ordinary Afro-Bahamians salt their discourse with proverbs and Bahamian seamen use a limited vocabulary with a felicity naturally poetic: "What we call with accuracy but no imagination a moderate breeze they call a social wind, ascribing to it affability and including in the name the ease and pleasure and relaxation of the crew at such a time—often . . . after an uncomfortably strong wind . . . the Baptist minister who owned the *Thunderbird* [from Mangrove Cay, Andros], describing how his helmsman sailed her through the storm to George Town, said 'I thought this boy would be very good. He was wonderful. He felt them. He felt those seas. He put her down like paper'—paper, calling up exactly the placing of a vessel's bulk against a big, oncoming sea, so delicately she does not pound or labor, does not stagger, but touches gently across its rolling surface." At other times, an Androsian "stagnated" a "half fathom long" iguana with a rock, and another, describing the advantage of cotton duck over coarse canvas sails: "'Light cloth feels the wind quicker' . . . concisely pointing out the

wind's way with sails, how its slightest movement billows the light sail into action, curved and full, while heavy sails hang limp, wrinkled, unsentient" (Bradley, *The Live by the Wind*, 241–42).

93. The 1970s generation of Bahamian painters in particular praised the formative influences of the U.S.-trained Bahamian Don Russell (1921–62), who set up the Academy of Fine Art in Nassau in the 1950s, the Chicago-born schoolteacher Horace Wright (1915–85), and the English expatriate David Rawnsley, director of the transplanted Chelsea Pottery, which lasted from 1957 to 1962. One remarkable feature of Bahamian painting is its tendency to run in families, such as the brothers Stanley and Jackson Burnside and their offspring and Eddie Minnis and his even more talented children, Nicolette and Shan.

94. Other Bahamian artists, of course, have their enthusiastic advocates, notably Eddie Minnis, the Burnsides, and Rolfe Harris among those born in the 1940s. Important painters of the second generation besides Antonius Roberts include John Beadle, Ricardo Knowles, and Chan Pratt. For a galloping survey, see Patricia Glinton, Charles Huggins, and Basil Smith, *Bahamian Art, 1492–1992* (Nassau: FINCO, 1992).

95. Born in Exuma in 1920, Amos Ferguson was a small farmer and carpenter before moving, when still a young man, to New Providence. His switch to painting pictures he attributed to "divine inspiration." His earliest paintings were sold to tourists at the Nassau Straw Market by his straw vendor wife, Beatrice. He was "discovered" by the New Yorker Sukie Miller, who organized a one-man show at the Wadsworth Atheneum in 1985.

96. Taylor contributed to shows organized by Brent Malone in the 1960s and had a one-man show at the Loft Gallery in 1969. But this exhibition was not a conspicuous success, and the Loft Gallery closed shortly thereafter. Kendal Hanna was an even more uncompromising artist than Taylor. His commitment to a pure negritude led to abstract arrangements in black, eventually blocking in (or blotting out) his canvases altogether. These creations did not command many sales.

97. *Brent Malone: Retrospective, 1962–1992, Central Bank Gallery, Nassau, Bahamas* (Nassau: Central Bank, 1992).

98. *Antonius Roberts* (Nassau: Privately published, 1994); Interview with Antonius Roberts, Marlborough Gallery, Bay Street, Nassau, October 31, 1994. The creative influence on young Bahamian artists of the Art Department at the College of the Bahamas, presided over by Stanley Burnside before Antonius Roberts, must not be understated.

99. Taylor et al., eds., *Bahamian Anthology*, 73. Sean McWeeney added a rider. To him an important cultural legacy to Bahamian blacks was the dichotomy between day, belonging to the workaday world and the masters, and night, which belonged to the slaves and their ancestral spirits and traditions. Junkanoo, the essential festival and celebration, belongs to the forest, the bloodbeat. It is mounted and performed in the night and fades with the dawn (McWeeney interview, October 27, 1994).

100. Michael Craton, "Decoding Pitchy-Patchy: The Roots, Branches and Essence of Junkanoo," *Slavery and Abolition*, special issue on slave leisure, 1995.

101. Ibid., 8–11; Craton and Saunders, *Islanders in the Stream*, 1:74–91, 108, 112, 140, 182, 216, 379, and above, Chapter 4; E. Clement Bethel and Nicolette Bethel, *Junkanoo: Festival of the Bahamas* (London: Macmillan Caribbean, 1991); Keith Wisdom, "Bahamian Junkanoo: An Act in a Modern Social Drama" (Ph.D. dissertation, University of Georgia, 1985); *Junkanoo: A Booklet of the Exhibition Held at the Art Gallery, Jumbey Village, 13 February–3 March, 1978* (Nassau: Archives Section, Ministry of Education and Culture, 1978). Not all sponsorship was from major tourist-oriented businesses. Some small locally targeted businesses, such as Malcolm's Garage and Mosko's department store, also supported groups in the 1960s and 1970s (Nicolette Bethel, personal communication, August 1995).

102. Among the irrelevant themes are those derived from Hollywood, Disney World, or other American reference points, those celebrating law and order (Junkanoo's historical antithesis), the tourist industry (Junkanoo's audience), or, narcissistically, Junkanoo and its stars themselves.

103. For example, see the Boxing Day 1993 Junkanoo Judges' Report by Nicolette Bethel, Bahamas Archives, 1994 Smithsonian Report File. The music was said in general to have been "fairly poor," with rhythms "boring, overused and untextured, except in one or two cases." Costuming was said to have "reached a plateau," there was too little choreography, and too much brass. Of the large groups, Fox Hill Congoes were said to be "by far the best. Their lack of brass should not hurt them at all, as they made up for that by creating the most solid sound of the parade. Their slower beat allows them to present *textured* Junkanoo music—with a bass, a tenor, a treble, *and* a lead rhythm sustained for the whole time." Of the small groups, the best was Sting: "They played a solid, consistent, interesting beat throughout the first lap. Unfortunately, by the second they had been joined by a number of lost scrappers, whose uneven play ruined the sound completely." The validity of scrap gangs in general, though, was strongly asserted.

104. Bethel and Bethel, *Junkanoo*.

105. Early exceptions to the black male predominance in Junkanoo were the involvement of the white and near-white Westerners and Arawaks, such individual performers as Paul Meeres, John "Chippie" Chipman, and "Sweet Richard" Dean from the 1940s and the organizers John Malcolm and Philip Kemp in the 1960s and 1970s. Exceptional women such as Maureen Duvalier, Sue Moss of the Westerns, and Becky Chipman (Chippie's daughter) also "rushed" before women almost disappeared from Junkanoos in the 1970s. Returning in the late 1980s under such leaders as Arlene Nash and Sandra North, women made up as much as 30 percent of groups by the mid-1990s, mostly as dancers, many as cowbellers, a few carrying costumes, but very few in the drum sections (Nicolette Bethel, personal communication, August 1995).

106. Material derived from Freeport, Green Turtle Cay, Andros, and Miami by Nicolette Bethel, Philip Burrows, and other researchers, January 1994, Bahamas Archives, 1994 Smithsonian Report File. For Haitian participation, Regnier interview, November 1, 1994.

107. Bahamas Archives, 1994 Smithsonian Report File; Interview with Anthony Morley, choreographer of "Roots" Junkanoo group, Nassau, October 27, 1994.

108. *Tennis Magazine*, December 1993, 84–88; Craton, "Decoding Pitchy-Patchy," 15.

Index